ENERGY TRADING AND INVESTING

ENERGY TRADING AND INVESTING

Second Edition

Davis W. Edwards

McGraw Hill Education

New York Chicago San Francisco Lisbon Athens London
Madrid Mexico City Milan New Delhi San Juan Seoul
Singapore Sydney Toronto

1 2 3 4 5 6 7 8 9 LCR 21 20 19 18 17 16

ISBN 9781265915872
MHID 1265915873

e-ISBN 978-1-259-83539-1
e-MHID 1-259-83539-1

This publication is designed to provide accurate and authoritative information in regard to the subject matter covered. It is sold with the understanding that neither the author nor the publisher is engaged in rendering legal, accounting, securities trading, or other professional services. If legal advice or other expert assistance is required, the services of a competent professional person should be sought.

—From a Declaration of Principles Jointly Adopted by a Committee of the American Bar Association and a Committee of Publishers and Associations

Library of Congress Cataloging-in-Publication Data

Names: Edwards, Davis W., author.
Title: Energy trading and investing : trading, risk management, and structuring deals in the energy market / Davis Edwards.
Description: Second edition. | New York : McGraw-Hill, [2017] | Earlier edition published as: Energy trading & investing.
Identifiers: LCCN 2016031689 (print) | LCCN 2016047103 (ebook) | ISBN 9781265915872 | ISBN 1265915873 | ISBN 9781259835391 Subjects: LCSH: Commodity exchanges. | Power resources.
Classification: LCC HG6046 .E39 2017 (print) | LCC HG6046 (ebook) | DDC 332.64/4—dc23
LC record available at: https://catalog.loc.gov

McGraw-Hill Education books are available at special quantity discounts to use as premiums and sales promotions or for use in corporate training programs. To contact a representative, please e-mail us at bulksales@mheducation.com.

Contents

Preface

PREFACE TO THE SECOND EDITION

In the seven years since I wrote the first edition, lots of things have changed. I've received a lot of feedback about the original edition, and there have been many dramatic changes in the energy markets. For this edition, I substantially expanded the coverage of oil markets, added more mathematical discussions, and provided clear-English descriptions on some of the less documented parts of the energy markets. I also substantially expanded the discussions on mark-to-market accounting, hedging, and risk management. I kept the same structure as the original book—broad discussions at the beginning of the book followed by separate discussions on specific aspects of the energy markets later in the book.

The energy markets have also changed. In the original book, policy makers were very concerned with the world running out of affordable energy. Less than a decade later, those concerns are much less pronounced. Concerns about global warming and carbon emissions are still present, but it is less clear how these concerns should be addressed. Despite having a string of record temperatures, few changes have been driven by legislation or international treaties. Progress has largely been made by the adoption of new technology in free markets.

The first major shift occurred with the development of technology that could be used to free fuel trapped in shale rock formations, called *hydraulic fracturing* or *fracking*. Fracking opened up a vast supply of natural gas in the United States. In 2009, when I wrote the first edition, a major concern of the energy market was that rapidly dwindling supplies of fuel would soon lead to imports from other countries. By 2016, fracking was flooding the United States with cheap natural gas. Natural gas terminals constructed to import gas in 2009 were undergoing conversion to export fuel.

This has had a domino effect across other energy markets. First, it drove down the price of electricity since fuel costs are one of the major components of electricity prices. Second, by lowering the cost of natural gas, coal became much less attractive as an electrical generation fuel. This largely achieved the goals of carbon legislation proposed between 2000 and 2010. Finally, fracking triggered a price war in the crude oil markets by raising the possibility that a very large economy (the United States) might transform from a net importer of fuel to a net exporter.

In the future, other technologies could have a similar transformative effect. For example, mobile telephones and tablets have driven down the cost of batteries and low-power video displays. Energy-efficient tablets and phones are replacing energy-hungry televisions and desktop computers at a very fast rate. These technologies are also spilling over into related areas like electric cars and LED lightbulbs. Along with better home insulation, these changes have kept consumer demand for electricity stable for nearly a decade.

It seems likely that technology changes will continue to drive changes in the energy markets for the immediate future. Across the energy industry, change is usually a mix of both good and bad news. With any market change, there will both be winners and losers. However, as an investor, rapidly changing markets provide opportunities unavailable in less turbulent periods.

As always, I am grateful for the support of my wife, Angela, and my two children, Spencer and Brianna. Writing doesn't keep regular hours, and they helped me through the process. I would also like to thank my long-time agent, John Willig, the editor of the second edition, Cheryl Ringer, and the project manager, Dipika Rungta.

Davis W. Edwards
Houston, 2016

Preface to the First Edition

The inspiration for this book came early in my energy trading career. Previously, I had traded a variety of other products. However, after the boom years in the stock markets in the 1990s and the real-estate boom in the early 2000s, energy became the hot new area around 2005. A wave of financial professionals, including me, left our previous trading desks to join the hot "new" energy market. Of course, it wasn't really a new market, but with the fall of Enron and market deregulation, trading opportunities were wide-open and expanding.

From the start, there was a huge culture clash between long-term energy traders and Wall Street traders. On Wall Street, the old intuitive traders had lost out to disciplined traders with technical backgrounds. Called *quants,* these math-savvy traders with degrees in physics, science, or engineering had taken over traditional trading desks by being more disciplined and organized. And, now, those same quants had set their eyes on invading the old-boy network of the energy markets.

In reality, it takes both an intuition and discipline to be successful. *Energy Trading and Investing* is written for every smart person who looked at a problem and said, "I could do it better than those guys," but didn't quite know where to get started. This is the book that I wished I'd had when I started trading energy. It grew out of the notes that I made then and later used to train new analysts. This book explains the energy market, how financial professionals trade energy products, and how they manage their business. It is written at the introductory level, without the use of jargon or complicated mathematics.

My philosophy on trading is that *there is no substitute for understanding what is actually going on.* Details are important. While writing this book, I had to fight back the temptation to eat up a lot of pages on interesting mathematical details to keep the discussions at a reasonable length. My major goal here is to provide a comprehensive introduction of energy trading from the first principles of exploration all the way to deal structuring. Even in a book of this size, that's a lot of material to cover. I decided to tackle this material using the divide and conquer method. *Energy Trading and Investing* is organized to introduce energy trading in several steps. The first part—the executive summary—is a microcosm of the entire book. It's the abbreviated version for people who want a nontechnical overview of the energy market without a lot of details. It's a good starting point that hits most of the key points in the book. I expand on the summary in later chapters.

The detailed sections start with a discussion of each energy product. These are products like electricity, natural gas, and oil. Next, I go into cross-disciplinary discussion. I show how chemistry, physics, and option pricing all affect energy trading. I then move on to a discussion of specialized energy topics like alternative energy investments, energy storage, and transmission. I finish with a discussion of how traders actually manage their trading through risk management techniques.

To make things easier, I begin each chapter with a summary that lets you know what to expect from the chapter. Not every chapter is important to every job, and right at the start I try to indicate why each chapter is important. Stylistically, I break up discussions every couple of paragraphs and separate beneficial, but off-topic, details into sidebars.

In a number of examples, I use financial options to model nonfinancial assets like power plants, storage facilities, and undeveloped oil wells. In the industry, this is called a *real options* approach. Because of their simplicity and relatively few parameters, I have found that options are a useful way for me to think about real-life issues. I also think it is a good way to make people comfortable with options mathematics.

That doesn't imply that options are universally superior to other approaches to solving these problems. For example, Monte Carlo simulations are also commonly used to solve the same problems. However, statistical sampling techniques, like Monte Carlo simulations, make for less intuitive descriptions of how to solve a problem.

I also include several discussions on global climate change and pollution. These issues are closely linked to the power industry and are shaping its future. Any solution to the world's energy problems will probably require consumers to use less power. However, this isn't a book about conservation. It is about meeting 100 percent of consumer demands for power in a cost affordable and ecologically sensible manner.

I owe a debt of gratitude to my wife, Angela, for her help on this book. Without her editing and assistance, this book would never have gotten off the ground. My brother, Colin, was also instrumental with his help and editing. I would also like to thank my editor at McGraw-Hill, Leah Spiro, and my agent, John Willig, for their enthusiastic support of this project. Finally, I would like to thank my long-time boss at Bear Stearns, Eli Wachtel. He took a chance to put a young guy in charge of a lot of money and a team of traders, and I am grateful for being offered that opportunity.

Davis W. Edwards
New York, 2009

1.1

An Overview of the Energy Markets

30-Second Summary

Purpose

This chapter summarizes the most important points in the book. It provides an introduction to the energy market and an overview of energy trading. It is structured identically to the entire book, and is intended as a summary of the major topics that will be discussed in detail.

Summary

The energy market is a collection of interrelated businesses focused on delivering electricity, petroleum products, and heating fuel to consumers. One set of businesses finds and develops new sources of power—drilling for new fuel reserves or developing better solar panels. Another group transports these sources of power closer to end users using pipelines or cargo ships. Some businesses generate power, like power plants, wind farms, and solar installations, and others convert raw materials into finished products. Additional businesses, like public utilities and gas stations, are responsible for actually distributing power and natural gas to consumers. The energy sector affects almost every facet of the U.S. economy.

The fragmented nature of the energy market means that most people only see a small portion of the whole market. The energy market is shaped by the details of its subindustries. Ultimately, the market revolves around drilling for fuel reserves, building power plants, and running power lines. Each of these subindustries has unique aspects that need to be understood by decision makers. However, it is also important to understand how the entire market fits together.

The major commodities in the energy market are petroleum, natural gas, and electricity. Coal, carbon emissions (greenhouse gases), nuclear power, solar power, and wind energy are also part of this dynamic market. Energy has always been a major industry, but with deregulation allowing more active trading, it has also become a major financial market. It now stands alongside stocks, bonds, and other commodity markets as an equal. With the influx of Wall Street and financial interests, there is now a large body of people involved in energy trading.

Many complex aspects of energy trading are due to the physical characteristics of energy commodities. Energy is hard to transport and store. Like other commodity markets, a portion of energy trades are settled by the physical delivery of a commodity. For example, this might require taking delivery of a million barrels of crude oil. When delivery or receipt is required as part of a trade, it is called a *physical trade*. When a trade involves only the transfer of cash—without a physical delivery—it is called a *financial trade*. Physical trading is both more complex and potentially more financially rewarding than financial trading.

Several major energy products (electricity and heat) can't be easily stored—they must be generated as they are needed. They are also expensive to transmit over long distances. Because of this, power and heat are typically generated close to the consumers that need those products. As a result, the energy market is further divided into another two pieces—a collection of small local markets concerned with today's activity (*spot markets*) and a separate market concerned with national expectations of the future (*the forward market*). Unlike the stock or bond market, the energy *spot* and *forward markets* aren't closely linked. This is because it is impossible to buy electricity at one point in time, store it, and deliver it at a later point in time.

The more markets that traders can access, the higher their potential profits. Being able to transact in a variety of different energy markets allows traders to benefit from a variety of opportunities. In most financial markets, it is very unusual to find profitable trades with no financial risk. These types of trades are called *arbitrage*. Energy markets will have many more of these opportunities, although they will often substitute operational risk, like figuring out how to take delivery of thousands of gallons of oil, for financial risk.

Another complication facing traders in the energy markets is the difficulty finding trading partners in some markets. Traders describe the ease or difficulty of finding trading partners with the term liquidity. A *liquid* market is one where it is easy to find trading partners and the cost of trading is low. An *illiquid* market is one where it is difficult to find trading partners and the cost of trading is relatively high.

Common Terms

Physical Contracts. Contracts that are settled by a physical transfer of a commodity from one owner to another.

Financial Contracts. Contracts that are settled by a transfer of cash. Financial contracts are used by investors who don't wish to take delivery of a commodity like crude oil but still want an exposure to prices.

Spot Market. A spot transaction involves a transfer of goods *on the spot*. A synonym for *spot* is *cash*, as in *cash market* or *cash transaction*.

Forward Market. A forward transaction involves a transfer of goods at some point in the future. For example, an agreement to have natural gas delivered six months in the future.

Arbitrage. *Arbitrage* means to make a risk-free profit by simultaneously buying one security and selling another. A common assumption in option pricing is that arbitrage opportunities do not exist. Or, if they do exist, they do not last for long.

Liquid Asset. A liquid asset is easy to buy or sell on short notice. A U.S. government bond is an example of a liquid asset.

Illiquid Asset. An illiquid asset is difficult to buy or sell on short notice. A nuclear power plant is an illiquid asset. It may be worth a lot, but it might be hard to find a buyer willing to give a fair price.

From a trading perspective, the spot markets are complicated. They are full of local regulations and subject to a laundry list of physical constraints. The most liquid markets are the forward financial markets. It is tempting to ignore the physical markets in favor of the easier to understand financial markets. However, this is a mistake. The financial markets contain hundreds of features that are inexplicable unless the physical markets are understood. The complexity of the physical spot markets defines energy trading. None of these issues are individually difficult to understand—but there are a lot of distinct issues to keep track of.

The major commodities in the energy market are petroleum, natural gas, and electricity. Coal, carbon emissions (greenhouse gases), nuclear power, solar power, and wind energy are also all part of this dynamic market. Energy has always been a major industry, but with deregulation allowing more active trading, it has also become a major financial market. It now stands alongside stocks, bonds, and other commodity markets as an equal. With the influx of Wall Street and financial interests, there is now a large body of people involved in energy trading.

The energy market is composed of many separate products concerned with the production and delivery of electricity and fuel to consumers. Of these, the most important energy markets are for crude oil, natural gas, and electricity. Coal, carbon emissions, refined petroleum products, and alternative energy are examples of some secondary commodities in the energy market.

Major Players

To deliver electricity and fuel to consumers, someone has to locate the fuel, get the fuel to where it needs to go, and turn the fuel into something useful. The start of the process—finding fuel—is usually performed by exploration companies. The fuel has to be extracted and prepared for transport by a drilling company. In specialized parts of the market like solar power, manufacturing solar panels replaces exploration and mining. Likewise, hydroelectricity requires a civil engineering firm to construct a dam.

Next, the fuel needs to be transported somewhere useful. Natural gas can be transported as a gas in a pressurized pipeline or it can be turned into a liquid and transported by cargo ship. If liquefied, the natural gas needs to be returned to gaseous form after transportation. Coal is transported on trucks and railroads. Oil is transported by tanker ship and liquid pipelines. Of course, not all portions of the market require transportation—the sun handles delivery of solar energy by itself.

Finally, useful products must be produced and distributed to end users. Public utilities and merchant power operators generate electricity at power plants. Then, they transmit their power to customers over a power grid maintained by a *Transmission System Operator* (TSO). Natural gas is moved out of transcontinental pipelines and into the systems of local gas utilities. Local gas utilities distribute natural gas to consumers through their own pipeline networks. Petroleum products need to be refined and transported to local residences and gas stations via pipelines and trucks.

Common Terms

Regulated Market. A regulated market is where a government appointed commission, usually called a *public utility commission* or *public service commission,* regulates a state monopoly over some aspect of the energy market.

Deregulated Market. A deregulated market is one where legislative involvement has been removed to allow for competition between market participants. Usually a substantial amount of government oversight remains in place.

The energy market is largely composed of three groups—energy companies, regulators, and traders. Energy companies typically are involved in some physical aspect of the energy industry. Oil exploration companies, power grid operators, and pipeline operators are all examples of energy companies. Regulators are government agencies that have been given oversite of some part of the energy market. Traders and financial companies make up the last part of the industry.

Each industry will have its own structure. For example, in the electrical power industry, the companies that manage the power grid, TSOs, are often run by local governments. When a TSO is unaffiliated with the local government, it is called an *Independent System Operator* (ISO). An ISO that crosses state boundaries is also commonly referred to as a *Regional Transmission Operator* (RTO). Most electricity trading occurs on power grids run by RTO/ISOs operating in deregulated markets, i.e., markets that allow free trading of electricity. Local rules vary between power grids. However, most *deregulated* power markets are still highly regulated. In this book, *TSO* is used to describe any power grid operator, and *RTO/ISO* is used to describe the operator of a power grid in a deregulated market.

Each energy market also has its own history. For example, allowing anyone to trade electricity is a relatively new concept. Prior to deregulation, only power plants owned by utilities could sell power into a power grid. After deregulation, anyone could build a power plant, produce power, and offer that power for sale. In deregulated markets, utilities have shifted away from running power plants to concentrating on operating transmission grids. Power plants started being owned by power traders and operated by specialized service companies. These changes revolutionized the power industry—they created a market for electrical power.

The last groups of market participants are the traders, investors, and marketers. Financial trading has grown up around the physical trading business. Funding exploration or building new manufacturing plants isn't cheap—it requires raising capital from investors. Local utilities need to use financial contracts to guarantee a steady supply of fuel and electricity for their customers. Power plants need to buy fuel and sell their electricity. Major industrial facilities might want to guarantee future supplies of affordable power. Financial firms might wish to speculate on the price of power. To do this, any of these parties can enter into transactions. These transactions can be done directly between two parties. This is called *bilateral* or *over-the-counter* trading. Alternately, trading can be done using an intermediary organization (often an exchange). Energy products are commonly traded on the New York Mercantile Exchange (NYMEX) and the Intercontinental Exchange (ICE).

Common Terms

Power Marketer. A power marketer is a company specializing in the buying and reselling of power.

Long an Asset. A trader is long an asset if he benefits when the price appreciates.

(*Continued*)

Short an Asset. A trader is short an asset if he benefits when the price declines.

The ramification of buying an asset in the future is often confusing. For example, a trader who agrees to buy an asset in the future at a fixed price benefits if the future price goes up. He has locked in a price already. However, a trader who agrees to buy an asset in the future without fixing the price benefits if that price declines. Then, he can buy more cheaply. To clarify the financial implications of owning an asset in the future, traders will use the terms *long* and *short* instead of *buy* or *sell* to describe their financial exposures.

Natural Gas

Natural gas is a fossil fuel used for heating and producing electricity. It is a combination of colorless, odorless gases composed primarily of methane (CH_4). It often contains substantial amounts of other hydrocarbons, like ethane (C_2H_6), propane (C_3H_8), and butane (C_4H_{10}). The composition of natural gas varies from location to location. It is often found mixed with nitrogen, carbon dioxide, and other trace gases. Natural gas is considered "dry" when it is almost pure methane, and "wet" when it has substantial quantities of the other hydrocarbons. Its central role in the energy industry is due to its role as a clean, comparatively inexpensive fuel—almost all of the electrical power generators that have been built in the United States for the past 20 years use natural gas as a fuel.

Natural gas is extracted from underground wells and transported to customers through pipelines. End users of natural gas are often called *the burner tip*. At one point, gas appliances were fitted with special dispersing heads to make natural gas suitable for lighting, cooking, and heating. Modern appliances no longer use burner tips, but the nickname has stuck.

Natural gas pipelines are located throughout the country and are capable of providing a constant supply of gas to consuming regions. Natural gas hubs are located at the interconnection between major pipelines. The most important natural gas hub, Henry Hub, is located on the U.S. Gulf Coast, about halfway between New Orleans and Houston. Henry Hub is the delivery location for the NYMEX natural gas futures contract and it is used as the benchmark for all natural gas sold throughout the United States.

Like many other energy products, the forward and spot markets for natural gas are distinct from one another. There is an extremely well defined seasonal component to forward prices. Prices in the forward market tend to mirror consumer demand—both are high in the winter and fall dramatically in the spring of every year. Spot prices don't show the same kind of predictability—spot prices are heavily influenced by supply and demand. However, despite the different behaviors, arbitrage between the two markets is impossible without a physical storage facility. It is possible to make a profit buying gas on the spot market, storing the gas, and selling it for future delivery. However, this requires an ability to make physical trades—to take delivery and store large quantities of a gas—which many market participants lack.

The natural gas industry is undergoing a major shift in how natural gas is extracted from the ground. Through a process known as *hydraulic fracturing*, or *fracking*, natural gas has become very cheap to remove from certain types of rock formations. Hydraulic fracking tends to produce a large percentage of the lighter, more valuable, hydrocarbons (like methane, propane, and naphtha) than other technologies. It is also relatively abundant—large shale deposits containing hydrocarbons are located in politically stable regions, like the United States.

Common Units

Because the composition of natural gas can vary substantially, it is commonly described in terms of its heat energy rather than a volume or weight based measurement. *Heat energy* is the amount of energy that can be obtained from burning a substance.

Btu (British Thermal Unit). A Btu is a measurement of heat energy used in the United States. Heat energy is commonly traded in millions of Btus (**MMBtus**).

Bcf (Billion Cubic Feet). A common measurement of natural gas storage facilities. There are approximately 1 million MMBtus (million Btus) in 1 bcf (billion cubic feet) of natural gas.

J (Joule). A measurement of heat energy in most of the world. Commonly energy is traded in thousands of joules (**kilojoules, kJ**) or millions of joules (**megajoules**, or **MJ**). One Btu is equal to 1054.35 Joules.

Electricity

Generating electricity is one of the major purposes of the energy market. Electricity is used to power a large variety of modern devices. Electricity is so common that it is hard to imagine life without it. Unfortunately, electricity can't be easily stored and it's very expensive to transmit over long distances. Consequently, there is no national electricity market—it's a collection of small regional markets each having unique characteristics and regulations. In each of these markets, supply and demand must constantly be matched. This results in a highly volatile spot market.

The most important physical markets are the daily power auctions held in each region. These auctions allow power producers to sell their electricity to consumers on their local power grid. Typically these auctions allow the sale of power by hourly increments on a day-ahead basis or in five-minute increments during the day that power is to be delivered. These auctions are the mechanism for setting the price of power in a region. Most speculative power trading goes on in forward markets that are separate from the daily power auctions. The forward markets are typically based on the price of delivering power at a major hub. Time horizons for forward trades range from the rest of the current month to approximately five years out.

As a general rule, on the day of delivery, the price for electricity is the same for all the participants in a local market. All producers receive the same price per megawatt and all consumers pay the same price per megawatt. This is called the *clearing price* for power. In deregulated markets, the clearing price is based upon bids submitted by power producers. These bids contain a price schedule, matching volumes of power to prices. Power plants are activated in lowest cost to highest cost order until the consumer demand is met. The clearing price of power is set by the cost of the most recently activated power plant. The cost of bringing the last unit of electricity into the market is called the *marginal price* of power, and the most recently activated plant is the *marginal* power plant. In general, the *clearing price* is set by the *marginal price* of power.

Electrical demand changes constantly. Every time a light is turned on or a computer is turned off, the load on an electrical system changes. Since electricity can't be stored, this changing demand must constantly be matched against supply. There is a huge infrastructure built to manage the real-time balancing of electricity supply and demand. Being able to estimate average demand is a critical part of both the physical and financial energy markets.

Power usage is cyclical. The demand for power varies by the season, day of week, and time of day. Daytime power is a different product from nighttime power. August power is a different product than January power. This has a big effect on the trading of power—there isn't a single electricity product. Instead there are hundreds of separate electricity products that differ based on location, month or season, and time of day.

Daytime hours (usually 7 a.m. until 11 p.m.) are called *peak* hours. Nighttime hours are called *off-peak* hours. Every region of the country uses slightly different definitions for their power products. As a result, power products are commonly described in shorthand. This abbreviation is always weekdays by hours. For example, 7×24 refers to power 7 days a week, 24 hours a day. Peak power is 5×16 or 7×16 (depending on whether weekends are included). If weekends aren't included in peak power, there will be a separate 2×16 product. Off-peak hours are typically 7×8 or an off-peak wrap that combines 2×16 and 7×8 hours.

It is also important to understand that electrical supply and demand are regional phenomena. Each area of the country has an electrical market with unique features. These differences can make trading electricity between adjacent power grids profitable. Transporting power is called *wheeling*. For example, the Pacific Northwest contains abundant hydro plants that produce extremely cheap electricity when there is sufficient water flow on local rivers. Sometimes after a major snow melt in the spring months, the price of electricity can fall to zero or negative since the dams can't be closed and every other power plant needs to be incentivized to shut down. Because this power is inexpensive, transporting it into Northern California can be profitable even though a lot of the power is lost in transport.

Common Units

Electricity is commonly described in units of *power* and *energy*. In physics, *power* is the rate at which work can be done. This is similar to a speed of a car (i.e., a car is traveling at 60 miles per hour). *Energy* is an amount of work. This is similar to the distance that a car travels (i.e., a car traveled 60 miles per hour for four hours to go 240 miles).

Megawatt (MW). A megawatt is a unit of power used to measure the electrical energy that can be produced by a power plant or carried by a transmission line.

Megawatt-Hour (MWh). A megawatt-hour is a measure of energy. It is the product of power (measured in megawatts) multiplied by some period of time (hours).

The Physics of Electricity

Electricity is a term used throughout this book to mean power obtained through the movement of charged particles, most commonly electrons, through some type of conductive material like a metal wire. A more precise term for this quantity is *electrical current*. Electricity is actually a general term that can refer to a number of different types of electromagnetic forces.

Electromagnetism is one of a couple fundamental forces that hold the universe together. For the purpose of energy trading, the most important property of electromagnetism is that magnetic fields can create electric currents in metals, and vice versa. By using this relationship, it is possible to move charged particles, like electrons, by manipulating magnetic fields. The combination of motivating force (a spinning magnet), along with a supply of electrons (found in conductive metal wires), and a closed path for them to move around (a *circuit*) is the basis for the electrical power industry.

One way to think about electricity is like water moving through a river. The amount of water that moves through the river determines how much work can be done. Unless it evaporates along the journey, the amount of water will be the same throughout the river's length even though the pressure and width of the river might change in places. In some places, the river might be wide and slow and at other places narrow and fast. In a power line, voltage and current work much the same way. The voltage of an electrical line is similar to water pressure and electrical current is similar to the size of the channel. For a fixed amount of power, voltage and current are inversely proportional. Just like water pressure will increase if the nozzle of a hose is narrowed, voltage will increase if electrical current is reduced.

Just as evaporation reduces the water in a river, friction can cause wasted energy on a transmission line. More water is lost when a river is wide and slow than when it is narrow and fast. Electricity works the same way. The amount of power lost during transmission is proportional to the length of the power line and the speed of the electrical current—high voltage/low current lines lose less power than the other way around. As a result, power grids typically convert electricity to high voltages for long-distance transmission and then lower the voltage just before it is delivered to consumers.

Another concept is that electrical power needs to flow in a loop. It needs to flow in and out of every location—it can't stop anywhere. Continuing the pipe example, water flowing through a channel can only produce work when it is flowing (like a river powering a sawmill). If the flow of electricity is ever stopped, an electromagnetic field will build up resulting in a potentially dangerous shock when it is reconnected. A related problem is a *short circuit*. Short circuits are like poking a hole in a straw and then trying to use the straw to drink.

Electrical Generation

Although there are many ways to produce electrical power, most power plants use a similar technology—electromagnets rotated by super-heated steam. *Fossil fuel plants* burn oil, natural gas, or coal to produce this steam. All of these fossil fuels produce greenhouse gases like carbon dioxide (CO_2) when they are burned. Compared to the other fuels, coal-fired generation produces two to three times the pollution of the other fuels. *Nuclear generators* use nuclear fission to turn water into steam. Nuclear fuel provides a lot of electricity per weight—a pound of highly enriched uranium is approximately equal to a million gallons of gasoline. But, enriched uranium is subject to severe shortages and is difficult to store safely once it is discarded.

A lot of modern research is exploring alternative energy sources. Geothermal power plants tap into steam released from the Earth as part of a standard steam turbine. Geothermal power is efficient, but it is extremely limited to specific geographic areas. Wind power plants use the wind to directly spin the copper wires inside a generator to create an electric current. Hydroelectric dams use falling (or flowing) water to spin the generator. Solar power facilities turn the sunlight directly into electricity.

In many power plants, superheated steam is a byproduct of producing electricity. A recent trend in power plants is to reuse this steam instead of releasing it into the atmosphere. This is called *cogeneration*. If a power plant can sell steam in addition to its power output, it becomes much cheaper to operate. As a result, the final products of a cogeneration plant are often described as both heat and electricity. Topping cycle plants produce electricity first, and then use the exhausted steam for heating. In contrast, bottoming cycle plants first produce heat for an industrial process and then use the leftover heat to power a steam generator.

The efficiency at which a plant converts fuel into electricity is called its *heat rate*. The heat rate is typically expressed as a ratio of heat input to work output (e.g., Btu/kWh or MMBtu/MWh). A lower heat rate implies a more efficient power plant.

Electrical Transmission and Distribution

Once power is generated, it needs to be brought to the customer. *Transmission* refers to the bulk transfer of power from the power plant to a substation via high voltage lines. *Distribution* refers to the transfer of power from a substation to various consumers using much lower voltages.

Power plants, transmission lines, and substations form the power grid—a set of interconnecting power lines that provide multiple ways to route power between any two locations. The redundancy of a power grid is crucial for reliability— it prevents any single line from overloading. This helps to prevent blackouts due to a single point of failure.

Most power lines are overhead lines. They are attached to tall poles suspended safely above ground level. In urban areas, electrical power lines are sometimes buried. However, burying lines makes them much less reliable and harder to maintain. Burying power lines is uncommon in suburban and rural areas.

The choice of voltage and location for power lines is a trade-off between safety, reliability, and efficiency. As part of the transmission process, power is wasted—it's converted into heat that must be dissipated on the power line. This waste can be reduced by using higher voltages. However, higher voltage lines are more dangerous than lower voltage ones. As part of delivering power to consumers, power plants use transformers to increase voltage for long distance transmission, and then decrease voltage for local distribution.

Common Terms

Transmission. Transmission is the long distance transfer of power over high voltage power lines.

Distribution. Distribution is the short distance transfer of power over low voltage power lines.

AC and DC Power

Most power is transmitted using alternating current (AC) power lines rather than direct current (DC) lines. With AC power, the voltage and current on the power line alternate directions making an oscillating wave. The terminals have no fixed positive or negative voltage. The primary advantage of AC power is that it's simpler to build an AC transmission system since the voltage can be easily scaled up or down to match a specific voltage.

Both types of currents are created by placing a conductive wire into an electromagnetic field. When this happens, the electrons are pushed away from the negative part of the field and toward the positive side of the field. If the magnetic field stays constant, all the electrons will move in the same direction.

Placing a negative charge at one end of the wire will start to accelerate the electrons close to that point away from it. The electrons closest to the point will be accelerated faster than electrons farther away. Because it is moving fastest, the last electron in line will slam into the electrons ahead of it. This creates a chain reaction as each subsequent electron is pushed into the next electron in line. This is similar to a multicar collision on a highway where a shockwave moves between cars although the cars don't move very far. Creating a shockwave at the other end of the wire will return all the electrons back to their initial state.

There are two ways of getting power through a power line. The first way to pass power through an electrical line is through the movement of electrons. This is DC power. Another way is through the shockwave caused by the collision of electrons. This wave, properly called an *electromagnetic wave*, propagates down the wire much faster than any of the individual electrons can move. This is AC power. It is possible to transfer energy through a power line using electromagnetic waves rather than the motion of individual electrons.

On a DC power line, whenever the line is used to provide power to some point, the voltage on the line will decline after that point. For a power grid serving variable consumer demand, this means that it will be very hard to predict the voltage on certain parts of the power grid. However, when they produce DC electricity, power plants do not need to worry about synchronizing themselves with other power plants.

The challenge with AC power is different. Although it is easy to change the voltage on the power line, it is necessary that every power generator oscillates their voltage at precisely the same time. Otherwise, the shockwaves from different power generators will collide and cancel out. AC power creates a synchronization problem that gets progressively more complicated with a large number of power providers.

Congestion

Given sufficient transmission capability, the price of power throughout a grid will be the same cost everywhere. It will be equal to the cost of the most recently activated generator. However, in periods of peak demand, the power lines connecting low cost generation plants to consumers may become overloaded. To relieve that overloading, power plants closer to the actual demand will need to be activated out of the usual order of cheapest to most expensive. Rather than spreading that higher cost between all members of the power grid, only those customers in the congested area will pay higher prices. Because this price only occurs for a single location, this is known as the *locational marginal price* (LMP). Most of the United States is moving toward this model of allocating costs to consumers.

To help customers manage the price risk of having purchased power at a major node and then paying a higher price for power due to congestion, a financial instrument, financial transmission rights (FTRs), can be traded. FTRs are contracts between two parties. The two parties take opposite sides of an obligation to pay or receive the difference in price between two nodes. If there is no congestion, the price at the two nodes will be the same. However, if there is congestion, one party will need to pay the other. This payment can go either way—either party can end up paying or receiving cash. Sometimes, that isn't what is desired, so these contracts can be structured as options. FTR options allow one party to pay an upfront fee (a premium) to avoid paying on the FTR at a later point. Essentially, buying an FTR option is like buying insurance against bad prices due to congestion.

Mechanics of the Physical Electricity Market

In the United States, the physical energy markets are run as daily auctions by ISOs. Usually, there are two auctions—a day-ahead auction and a real-time auction. The day-ahead auction is an hourly auction for the following day. The real-time auction occurs throughout the day whenever extra generation is required. Generators participate in the auctions by submitting offer curves (their generation levels associated with prices) and their technical constraints (startup costs, minimum up time, etc.). After collecting offers from generators, the ISO selects the winning generators in a manner that minimizes the cost to the market.

The two auctions are distinct from one another. When creating a bid, a generator needs to decide whether to attempt to sell all of its power in the day-ahead market or to reserve some capacity to sell into the real-time market. There are potentially greater profits in the real-time market, but the risk of being inactive is also higher. In most cases, the bidding strategy used by a power plant will be dictated by its physical characteristics—how quickly it is able to come online and its efficiency at converting fuel into electricity. If a generator is not selected to operate in the day-ahead market, it is still eligible to participate in the real-time market.

However, since these are physical markets, the generators participating in the real-time auction need the ability to deliver power. Because of this, usually only generators that can start up quickly or have excess capacity participate in the real-time auction. Primarily for this reason, most of the generation capacity is allocated in the day-ahead market—the real-time market is used for balancing short-term fluctuations and unexpected demand.

Oil

Oil, or *petroleum,* is a liquid fossil fuel formed when decaying plant life becomes trapped in a layer of porous rock. After millions of years, heat and pressure convert decaying plant life into hydrocarbons. Some of these hydrocarbons are gases, others are solids, and still others are liquids. *Petroleum* is the generic name for any hydrocarbon that is liquid under normal temperature and pressure conditions. Like other fossil fuels, the mixture of hydrocarbons in petroleum can vary widely. When petroleum is first extracted from the ground, it is called *crude oil*. After crude oil is distilled, there are specific names for each liquid (gasoline, heating oil, etc.). The term *petroleum* refers to crude oil and all of the products refined from it.

The liquid properties and high energy density of petroleum make it a popular fuel for vehicles. Compared to hydrocarbon gases like methane or propane, petroleum contains a lot of energy per unit of volume. For example, a tank of a hydrocarbon gas, like propane, will only fuel a backyard grill for a couple of hours. However, the same volume of gasoline will be sufficient to drive a car for several hundred miles. Additionally, compared to solid hydrocarbons like coal, liquids are much easier to move around inside an engine.

Crude Oil Markets

The trading of crude oil is dominated by the relationship between suppliers and consumers. The major consumers of crude oil are the industrialized nations in North America, Europe, and the Asian-Pacific region. The major exporting regions are less developed countries in the Middle East and South America.

From a trading perspective, crude oil is the most important petroleum product. Historically, major oil refiners have considered it less risky to be located near consuming areas in industrialized countries rather than near the producing areas. As a result, there is an active global trade in transportation of crude oil. The refiners trade for and transport crude oil over long distances. Then, it is refined near the consuming region where it is sold to customers. Although there is some international trading of refined petroleum products like gasoline and diesel, it is much smaller than the crude oil market. Typically, the prices for refined petroleum products are regional in nature—they are determined by local regulations, supply, and demand.

There are many varieties of crude oil. The three most common crude oil benchmarks are WTI and Brent contracts. WTI crude is a common benchmark for crude oil produced in the United States. Brent crude is a common benchmark for oil delivered by ship in the northern Atlantic Ocean. There are no similar liquid trading contracts for the third common benchmark, Persian Gulf crude oil, although spot prices from Oman and Dubai are commonly available.

Common Units

Barrel (bbl). In the United States, petroleum of all types is traded by volume. A barrel contains 42 U.S. gallons (in the United States) or approximately 159 liters (metric units).

Tonnes (t). In Europe, oil is typically traded by weight. A tonne (or metric ton) is a unit of mass equal to 1,000 kilograms or approximately 2,204.6 U.S. pounds.

Conversion Between Barrel and Tonne. A rough approximation is that there are 7.5 barrels in one tonne of crude oil. However, because the composition of crude oil can vary substantially, each type of crude oil will have its own conversion ratio. These ratios can range from approximately 7.2 barrels per tonne (for Persian Gulf crude) to about 7.5 barrels per tonne (for premium light crude like WTI or Brent).

Crude oils are typically described by their density and sulfur content. Low density (light) crude oils have a higher proportion of light hydrocarbons that can easily be converted into high value products like gasoline. In contrast, heavy crude oils contain a larger portion of low value products that require additional downstream processing to be valuable. The density of crude oil is fairly apparent by visual inspection—light crude oil will flow freely while heavier crude oil will be more viscous. High sulfur content is highly undesirable for crude oil. Sulfur is a major pollutant and can only be removed through expensive processing. Sweet crude oil has low sulfur content, while sour crude oil contains a much higher amount.

The most valuable types of crude oil are light, sweet crudes. Both WTI and Brent crude fall into this category. These are commonly called *premium* crude oils.

Distillation and Crack Spreads

Refined petroleum products are created by separating crude oil into various pure liquids. Crude oil contains a variety of different liquid hydrocarbons mixed together—everything from gasoline to asphalt. To create useful products, it is necessary to separate these liquids from one another. This is done through *distillation*. Since each type of liquid hydrocarbon turns into a gas at a different temperature, the most common way to separate mixed liquids is to place them into a large container and heat them. As the temperature rises, the liquids will turn into a gas one at a time. This gas can be suctioned off and then returned to liquid form in a separate container by cooling. It is often necessary to go through this process several times before a sufficiently pure end product is created.

A single barrel of crude oil is turned into a large number of separate refined products. Of these, the most valuable products are gasoline, diesel fuel, and heavy fuel oils. It is impossible to produce just one distilled product without producing the others. The process of converting crude oil into gasoline involves creating every refined petroleum product at the same time. If a refiner wants to produce more gasoline, it is also necessary to produce more of the other distillates like diesel fuel, home heating oil, and asphalt.

The process of distillation links the prices of refined petroleum products to crude oil prices. If the price of crude oil rises, all of the refined products will become more expensive. However, there is a different type of link between the prices of the refined products. If a gasoline shortage forces refiners to increase their gasoline production, the market may become glutted with the other petroleum products. As a result, there is often a negative correlation between the prices of the refined products. The relationship between crude oil and distilled products is known as the *crack spread.*

Coal

Coal is a solid hydrocarbon fuel that is readily available throughout the world. It is easy to store, and relatively inexpensive to extract from the ground compared to the amount of electrical power that it can generate. Except for the pollution that it produces, coal is in many ways the perfect fuel for generating electricity. Unfortunately, coal is a major source of carbon (CO_2) and sulfur (SO_2) emissions. The pollution that results from burning coal has made it unpopular among consumers.

Coal is traditionally a low cost way to generate electricity. However, it has the drawback of being the most polluting fossil fuel. The competing desires for cheap electricity and less pollution are at odds with one another. Global efforts to reduce carbon emissions have typically deadlocked on the issue of coal-powered generation. Most countries want to use coal-fired power plants for cost reasons and would like other countries to stop using them because of pollution concerns.

Because the price of coal is generally low, transportation makes up a much higher percentage of the delivered cost of coal than other fossil fuels. As a result, most coal is used within a couple hundred miles of where it is mined. By far the biggest application for coal is electrical generation. Electrical power plants and coal mining companies are often located close together. As a result, there are relatively few people buying or selling coal on the open market. Coal is important to electrical generation, but not a heavily traded financial product by itself.

Emissions Markets

Motivated by signs of global climate change, countries have begun taking steps to reduce global levels of carbon dioxide, sulfur dioxide, and nitrogen dioxide emissions. The two most popular ways to limit pollution are through taxes and cap and trade systems. Of the two, only the cap and trade system is a trading market.

A cap and trade system sets a limit on the amount of a substance that can be produced. Everyone producing that substance is required to have a license for their production. This has the advantage of ensuring a cap on pollution levels. When licenses are freely tradable, anyone with an ability to shift to a less polluting technology can do so and make a profit by selling their licenses. By reducing the amount of licenses over time, a free market encourages that the most economical changes be made first. The two main problems facing cap and trade systems are how to distribute licenses and how to enforce compliance.

Because emissions markets create a valuable good from nothing, there is an intense debate over how licenses should be initially distributed. There are drawbacks to every approach, whether they are public auctions, assigning rights based on historical usage, or assigning rights based on population.

Tracking carbon dioxide emissions is also complicated. Lots of activities—everything from breathing to burning fossil fuel—produces carbon dioxide. Many activities remove carbon dioxide from the air as well—everything from planting a garden to injecting carbon dioxide into an underground storage facility. It is impossible for governments to monitor, require licenses, or provide carbon credits for all of those activities. This makes enforcement of carbon markets problematic.

The emissions markets are also closely linked to the use of coal to generate electricity. Although it produces more pollution, coal historically was able to produce electricity for a fraction of the cost of any alternative fuel.

The increased popularity of natural gas fracking has largely derailed carbon legislation in the United States. It has done this by making natural gas cheaper than coal. Since the primary goal of emissions markets was to remove coal as a major electrical generation fuel, many of the objectives of this legislation have been achieved at little or no cost to consumers.

Natural Gas Liquids

Natural gas liquids (NGLs) are combustible gases heavier than methane (natural gas) but still light enough to exist in a gaseous state at standard temperature and pressure. There are five NGLs: ethane, propane, butane, iso-butane, and pentane.

Compared to natural gas, the heavier NGLs, like propane and butane, are much more easily liquefied by compression. Converted to a liquid, NGLs are approximately 270 times more compact than when they exist as a gas. Since the compression for these gases can be done under only moderate pressure, this allows these gases to be transported and stored in a liquid state. A typical use for these products is as a fuel for cooking (like a backyard grill). For this use, propane might be stored in a pressurized container that will start to evaporate (convert to a gas) when a valve is opened to release it.

NGLs are commonly found dissolved within crude oil or natural gas. They are abundantly found in shale deposits that can be developed through the use of natural gas fracking. NGLs are separated from natural gas at natural gas processing plants or from crude oil at refineries. A related term, *liquefied petroleum gas*, refers to a mixture of two of the heavier NGLs (propane and butane).

TECHNICAL PRIMER

The technical primer is a brief introduction to some of the more complicated parts of energy trading. The goal of this section is to provide a more intuitive understanding of these topics.

Pollution

The combustion of fossil fuels produces a substantial amount of greenhouse gas emissions and other pollution. There are a number of different types of pollution. The first general category of pollution is caused when impurities or small particles trapped in the fuel are released into the air when the fuel is burned. The second type of pollution is an intrinsic part of combustion—the creation of greenhouse gases. Greenhouse gases don't present a health hazard and are generally safe. However, when large quantities of greenhouse gases are released into the atmosphere, they have the potential to change the world's climate.

Carbon dioxide is an odorless, nontoxic gas that is formed by the combustion of organically derived fuels. Organic fuels are composed of long chains of carbon molecules that can be broken down by combining them with oxygen. A spark is required to kick off combustion, but afterward, it is a self-sustaining process that produces more heat than is required to start the fire. The process of combining carbon with oxygen produces carbon dioxide. It is impossible to burn carbon based fuels (which encompass nearly all fuels) without producing carbon dioxide. Large amounts of CO_2 can strengthen the greenhouse effect (Figure 1.1.1).

The Greenhouse Effect

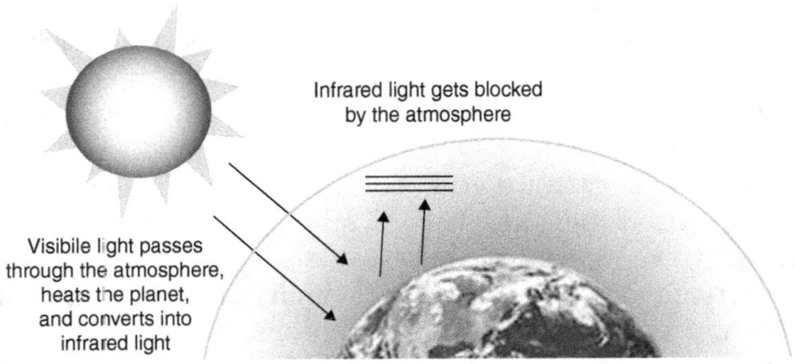

The Earth's atmosphere allows visible light to pass through and absorbs infrared light. Sunlight can pass through easily, warms the Earth, and converts into infrared light. This light is radiated away from the Earth, but much of it is absorbed by the atmosphere. This traps heat near the surface of the Earth. The greenhouse effect is vital for the survival of plants and animals, but too much carbon dioxide causes the atmosphere to absorb too much infrared energy and raises global temperatures.

Figure 1.1.1 Graphic depiction of the greenhouse effect

Nitrogen and sulfur oxides are also produced during combustion. Nitrogen is present in the atmosphere and trace amounts of sulfur are commonly trapped in fossil fuels. When these oxides combine with water, they form acid rain. Acid rain is a regional problem that can kill vegetation and wildlife. Although most rain is slightly acidic, when large amounts of acid build up in a small area, it is poisonous.

Heavy metals like mercury, lead, and plutonium are often trapped in fossil fuels and released in the combustion process. When these metals build up in the body, they don't decay. A large enough accumulation of these substances is toxic to humans and wildlife.

Fly ash and *soot* are general terms for inert particulate matter trapped in fossil fuels. Commonly, these are supersmall grains of sand or coal that were not completely burned. When suspended in the air, it is easy for these particles to get caught inside someone's lungs. This will create breathing problems and can lead to lung damage and diseases like *silicosis*.

Gas, Liquids, and Solids

All substances have two major types of properties—chemical properties and physical properties. The chemical properties of a substance determine how it combines with other substances. For example, combustion is a chemical reaction between a fuel and oxygen. Physical properties involve changes in substances that don't represent a chemical change in a substance. Water turning into steam when heated is an example of a physical phase shift. Physical phase shifts are generally reversible.

Another important physical property of materials is that if you compress a gas, it gets hot. If you want to compress it enough to make it into a liquid, you need to cool it substantially. If you don't keep it cool, it will start to expand again. The ability to shift substances between liquid and gas forms and compress gas is the key to air-conditioning and refrigeration systems.

Physical phase shifts are the reason that distillation works. Gases and liquids will separate at certain temperatures. This is helpful for distillation, but problematic for other processes. For example, the temperature in pipelines isn't constant. As a result, liquids often condense inside a pipeline when natural gas cools down. This causes a problem because these pipelines are air-tight so the liquids can't evaporate.

Statistics

Statistics is the branch of mathematics focused on organizing, analyzing, and summarizing data. A substantial amount of trading vocabulary comes from the mathematical discipline of statistics. Two of the most important terms are *volatility* and *correlation*.

Volatility is used by traders to describe the risk of holding an asset. It measures the likely dispersion of prices between two periods of time. Mathematically, it is defined as the standard deviation of continuously compounded returns. A highly volatile asset is one that commonly experiences large price changes. The term *volatility* does not describe the investment merit of a trade.

Correlation is used by traders to describe how closely two things are related. When two assets are highly correlated, their prices tend to move together. There may or may not be a causal relationship between the two assets. Correlation can result from either random chance or a shared cause for behavior.

Financial Options

An option is a contract between two people. It gives the buyer of the contract the right, but not the obligation, to buy or sell property at some future date at a fixed price. The right to buy is called a *call option*. The right to sell is called a *put option*. Options have an up-front cost, called a *premium*, which is paid when the buyer purchases the option. For the buyer, options have limited downside risk. Buyers will either lose their premium or they will make a profit.

An option is an all-or-nothing type of instrument. It is possible to buy millions of dollars of options and lose the entire investment if the options expire worthless. Buying an option contract is similar to buying insurance. Most often, the purchaser will pay a premium and have the option expire worthless. Occasionally, the option will pay off big. Even though the size of the downside is small (losing the premium) compared to the potential upside (a big profit), the odds of making a profit are stacked against the option buyer. The option seller is taking on a risk from the buyer, and needs to be compensated for taking that risk.

Two common applications for options are risk management and modeling energy investments. In the energy market, there are a lot of physical decisions that need to be made on a daily basis. Do I turn the power plant on and convert my fuel into electricity? Do I lock in a fuel supply for the winter now or should I wait a little longer? Should I invest in building a new power line between Oregon and Northern California? Option theory provides a way to quantify those decisions.

From a transaction standpoint, option trading requires both a buyer and a seller. The seller takes on the possibility of a big loss in exchange for money up front. The buyer pays a *premium* to the seller for that service. If the option pays off, the seller will need to find the cash to pay the buyer. With options, money is not magically created; it is simply transferred between the two parties. The option buyer is described as being *long the option* or being *long volatility* (since rare events will mean a big profit). The option seller is described as being *short the option* or being *short volatility* (since rare events will mean a big loss).

When the option expires, the amount of money that needs to be transferred between the buyer and seller is determined by the *payoff* of the option. Every option is assigned an *exercise* or *strike price*. This is the fixed price at which trading can occur in the future. For example, a call option involves the right to buy an asset at a fixed price. The owner of a call option benefits when an asset price rises above the strike price. This allows the owner to buy at a lower price than is otherwise available. The owner can also make an immediate profit by reselling the asset at the current price.

$$\text{Call\_Payoff} = \text{Asset\_Price} - \text{Strike\_Price}$$

if the Asset_Price > Strike_Price at expiration

A put option works similarly. A put option gives the owner of the option the right to sell an asset at a fixed price. If the asset price is greater than the fixed price, a put option is worthless. No one will willingly sell at a lower price than necessary. However, if the fixed price is higher than the asset price, the put buyer makes a profit by selling at a higher price.

$$\text{Put\_Payoff} = \text{Strike\_Price} - \text{Asset\_Price}$$

if the Strike_Price > Asset_Price at expiration

Option Valuation

Options theory has simultaneously revolutionized the financial markets and caused a huge number of financial collapses. The mathematics behind option pricing can be very complicated. However, the basic principles are straightforward. Options prices are calculated by approximating their actual behavior.

Using models to value options isn't a perfect process. Real life is more complicated than any model. As a result, option models are not a substitute for understanding what is actually going on. Very complex models usually mean that few people actually understand what is going on. As a result, simple models, even when they have flaws, are usually preferred over complex models. The more people who understand a model, the less chance it has of failing disastrously. It is often easier to address weaknesses in option models by making observation easier than it is to create more complicated models.

Option models are based on assumptions about asset prices. A standard set of assumptions define commonly traded, or *vanilla*, options. When the standard assumptions work reasonably well to describe the behavior of the underlying prices, option valuation is easy. It is possible to plug numbers into a well-known option pricing formula. In other cases, the standard assumptions don't work so well. In those cases, it is necessary to use a more complicated approach to calculating option prices.

Options that use nonstandard assumptions about prices are commonly called *exotic* options. Knowing when to use an exotic option model requires understanding what is going on in real life. Option formulas basically say that "I can be used if X, Y, and Z are true." It is up to the user of an option to determine if X, Y, and Z are true in their specific case. If not, some other formula needs to be found. There is a substantial amount of academic literature describing nonstandard option models.

While it is possible for model assumptions to change over time, option models seldom experience a catastrophic failure overnight. Usually, problems in an option model start to show up years before there is an economic impact. It is up to the people using the model to identify when things aren't working and make sure problems are fixed quickly.

Modern option trading sprung out of research by Fischer Black, Myron Scholes, and Robert Merton in the late 1960s and early 1970s. Their research combined earlier ideas of dynamic hedging, price diffusion, and put/call parity into a continuous time framework. This allowed the creation of easy to use option pricing formula. That formula, the Black Scholes formula, opened up option trading to the masses. The Black Scholes formula and related work on continuous time finance revolutionized the financial markets and won a Nobel Prize. The most widely used option models are variants of this work and are known as Black Scholes genre option models.[1]

The concept behind option pricing is counterintuitive to many. Options are priced by replicating their payout by continuously trading the underlying product. Generally, the approach that was first developed by the 1970s, *dynamic hedging*, still works well today. The general concept of dynamic hedging was that it is possible to duplicate the payoff of a stock option by constantly trading the stock and a risk-free investment (usually a government bond). This concept has been carried into the energy market.

Options are also closely associated with volatility. Since there is an asymmetric payout for holding an option, a large price move that has a 50/50 chance of going up or down helps the buyer of the option more than the seller. The potential losses of the buyer are limited, but the potential profit is not. An option buyer benefits from large price moves, and an option seller benefits from price stability.

Deltas, Gammas, and Other Greeks

When evaluating option positions, traders often need to answer questions like "Do I expect to make or lose money if the price of oil continues to rise?" or "How much money do I expect to make or lose if an unlikely event becomes more likely?" These types of questions can be answered by sensitivity analysis. This analysis estimates the sensitivity of a trading position to something else. Most commonly, traders

---

[1] The Bank of Sweden Prize in Economic Sciences in Memory of Alfred Nobel, 1997 was awarded to Robert Merton and Myron Scholes who developed, in collaboration with the late Fischer Black, a pioneering method of determining the value of stock options.

Black, F. and M. Scholes, 1973, "The Pricing of Options and Corporate Liabilities," *Journal of Political Economy*, Vol. 81, pp. 637–654.

Merton, R.C., 1973, "Theory of Rational Option Pricing," *Bell Journal of Economics and Management Science*, Vol. 4, pp. 141–183.

want to estimate the profit or loss that will occur when some benchmark goes up or down. In other cases, they will want to know how their risk will change if some type of event happens.

Many questions about risk are common enough to have acquired a well-known name, usually a letter in the Greek alphabet. These questions can be expressed as the sensitivity of one quantity to changes in another. Because they are commonly represented by Greek letters, these factors are collectively called the *Greeks*. A *Greek* is never a standalone piece of information like a price. *Greeks* are always a comparison between two assets (one of which is usually called an *asset* and the other an *underlying*). The value of the asset is sensitive to changes in the underlying.

There are five common measures of sensitivity (collectively called the *Greeks*):

1. **Delta.** The profit or loss (P&L) that occurs when the underlying changes in price.
2. **Gamma.** The change in an asset's *Delta* when the underlying changes in price.
3. **Vega.** The P&L that occurs when the volatility of the underlying changes.
4. **Theta.** The P&L that occurs from the passage of some period of time (usually one day).
5. **Rho.** The P&L that occurs when the interest rate changes.

Spread Options

A specific type of option—a *spread option*—is especially common in the energy market. Spread options are used to price a large variety of physical energy deals. With these options, the owner of the option benefits when the difference between two prices is above a certain level. This is like a normal option except with two asset prices. Alternately, this can also be thought of as an option with a variable strike price. A spread option can be constructed to look like a standard option payout in a couple of ways. One way is to set the "price" of the option equal to the spread between the two assets:

$$\text{Call\_Payoff} = (\text{Asset\_Price1} - \text{Asset\_Price2}) - \text{Strike\_Price}$$

Another way is to lump the second asset price into the "strike price":

$$\text{Call\_Payoff} = \text{Asset\_Price} - (\text{Asset\_Price2} + \text{Strike\_Price})$$

The prevalence of spread options in energy deals is a result of the way the energy market operates—there is a focus on moving energy from one location to another, storing it for sale at a later point, and converting it from one form to another. The profitability of doing these actions depends upon the spread between two prices compared to the cost of doing the conversion—the price here versus the price there compared to transportation costs, the price now versus the price later compared to storage costs, and the price of fuel versus the price of electricity compared to conversion costs.

Valuing spread options is substantially more complicated than valuing options on single assets. In the two-asset case, the correlation between the two assets is very important. The spread between the prices of two highly correlated assets will behave differently than the spread between two uncorrelated assets. In fact, the correlation between the two assets becomes the single most important factor in the option valuation. There often isn't a good way to estimate this correlation either—historical data may be misleading, and there isn't usually a liquid enough market to determine the correlations being used by other people in the market.

Because of correlation's effect on the price of spread options, and the difficulty in estimating it, correlation requires a lot of scrutiny. Managing the risk of an options portfolio requires building an infrastructure to examine correlations between products. Incorrectly estimating correlation is the single easiest way to mess up an option valuation. This estimate isn't just important when a spread option trade is initiated—it needs to be monitored over the entire life of the trade.

ELECTRICITY MODELS

Various aspects of the electricity market are complicated enough that they merit individual discussions.

This section starts by examining the supply and demand of electricity. These topics are covered in reverse order starting with an examination of consumer demand. In most regions, there is a relatively constant baseline demand for electricity. Most of the variability in demand is a result of the weather. Over very long time frames, a decade for example, economic growth and residential trends also become important.

The next section examines the electrical supply—specifically, how ISOs pick which power plants will operate each day. Power plants must submit quotes to the ISO. Power plants are continually activated and deactivated depending on the demand for electricity. The power plants willing to offer power at the lowest cost are selected before the higher cost units. However, all power plants get paid the same price for their power. Every operating power plant gets the price submitted by the *marginal* power plant—either the last one activated or the next one to be turned off (depending on whether demand is increasing or falling).

After that, several important electricity trading topics will be examined in detail—models of power plants, long distance transmission lines, and various electrical generation technologies.

Forecasting Demand for Electricity: Spatial Load Forecasting

Spatial load forecasting is the study of where and when power will be required. Since power can't be stored and must be generated on demand, it is necessary to anticipate changes in demand. In the context of this book, *load* is synonymous with *demand for electrical power*. *Load* is an electrical engineering term referring to the power consumed by a circuit or drawn from a power line. In the short term, load forecasts are used to schedule power plants for operation and maintenance. In the long run, load forecasting is used to construct new power lines, build new power plants, and build infrastructure projects.

One of the most important characteristics of a region is the minimum amount of power that has to be supplied at any given time to a power grid. This minimum level of power is called the *base load power*. It sets a threshold on the number of power plants that will be operating full time the entire year. On the other end of the extreme is predicting the maximum amount of energy that will be required at any given time (the *peak demand*). Power grids use estimates of peak demand for capacity planning to ensure sufficient power to meet any demand in a region. However, traders can use the same information to predict how often power prices will spike and when those spikes will occur.

Forecasting the Supply of Electricity: The Generation Stack

Power prices are set by nondiscriminatory auctions—every power producer is allowed to submit bids, the lowest bidders become the winners, and all winners receive the same price for their power. Usually there are two auctions. Most power grids hold an initial auction the day before delivery (a day-ahead auction), and then use real-time auctions to fill in unexpected shortfalls.

Because of the nature of the auctions, certain power plants tend to be very influential in setting the price of power. The most influential power plants are the ones on the *margin*—either the last generators selected for operation or those that just missed being selected. As the bidding strategy for power generators is often largely determined by the physical characteristics of the power plant, it is possible to group power plants into general categories. *Baseload* generation plants produce power cheaply, are expensive to shut down, and want to run continuously even when demand is at its lowest level. *Peaking* generation plants provide short bursts of power in periods of maximum demand—they are cheap to keep inactive, start up quickly, and don't need to be very efficient. *Mid-merit* generation fills the gap between the two extremes. Demand for power will determine which of these general categories is *on the margin*.

Baseload generation plants are defined by being relatively inexpensive to operate and expensive to start up or shut down. Hydro, nuclear, and coal plants fall into this category. Hydro plants don't have any fuel costs and may not be able to shut down without flooding nearby communities. Nuclear plants require the use of control rods to slow down the nuclear reaction—without cooling the nuclear reaction keeps on going at maximum capacity. The effect is that nuclear plants need to spend money (use control rods) in order to slow down. Coal plants are easier to shut down but can be expensive to restart if allowed to cool down completely. Most of these plants run full time. They try to avoid being on the margin, and may offer power at low costs in order to avoid going offline.

The other extreme, peaking generation, provides short-term electricity during periods of peak demand (typically summer afternoons). The primary consideration is that these plants need to start up quickly and be cheap to maintain. They don't need to be cheap to operate—conserving fuel is an afterthought. Many of these power plants are essentially jet engines. Fuel is pumped in and ignited; there is a minimum of moving parts and there is a lot of wasted heat energy. Many of these plants only operate a couple hundred hours a year. In order to recover costs, these plants will charge very high prices for electricity.

Mid-merit plants are somewhere between the two extremes. In many cases, these plants are older, less-efficient baseload plants that are no longer cost effective enough to run full time. In other cases, these are highly efficient natural gas plants that are easier to cycle than the baseload generators. These generators are commonly on the margin and show a lot of variability in their bidding strategies. Baseload generators are always going to bid low—they need to operate full time. Peaking generators are always going to bid high—they are extremely expensive to operate. Most of the time, mid-merit plants are going to control how power is priced in a region.

There is a fair amount of gamesmanship in setting these prices. On one hand, power plants want to get the highest price possible for their product. On the other hand, since there is a single price for power in a region, it isn't important to be the top bidder. As long as a power plant is operating, it is getting the same price as the highest bidder. There is no downside to bidding a zero price if someone else sets the price at a higher level. The marginal power plants—the ones actually setting the price—have the most complicated task. The most common strategy among mid-merit power plants is to bid some capacity at or slightly below cost and then offer progressively more capacity at higher prices.

Tolling Agreements

A *tolling agreement* is an arrangement where a power marketer (someone who trades electricity) rents a power plant. These agreements are for any length of time (often 20 or 30 years) and divide the job of running a power plant between two parties. One party maintains the power plant for a pre-established fee while the other party, the trader, makes all of the economic decisions. The trader (the power marketer in a tolling agreement) is responsible for supplying fuel to the plant and selling the resulting electricity into a competitive market. The trader takes on all of the economic risks and earns most of the profits (everything above the fixed maintenance fee).

A common approach to modeling both power plants and tolling agreements is to price them as a series of spread options. The power plant operator can produce electricity by burning fuel. The payoff is the difference between the two prices less the operating cost of the plant. In general, when the price of power is above the generator's cost of production, the generator can run profitably. Otherwise, it can shut down and receive nothing. A spread model of a power plant is called a *spark spread model*.

There are dangers to using options to approximate physical behavior—a spread option model can ignore important physical aspects of generation like the time it takes to turn on (*ramp up* or *cycle*) and variable costs (like startup and cooling that vary based on the ambient temperature). A generator might take longer to start in the winter than during the summer. An option based model may assume power plant decisions can be made instantaneously. No matter how quickly a power plant can be cycled, it is going to be slower than instantaneous decisions implied by a spark spread model. Other real-life issues—like the effect of local regulations regarding grid reliability—can also be difficult quantify.

Because spark spread option models are less constrained than actual generators, they run the risk of overestimating profitability. This over-estimation can be as high as 20 percent to 30 percent. This can result in large errors in profit estimates and value-at-risk calculations. Since the magnitude of this error depends on local characteristics, there isn't a rule of thumb that can be used as a "correction factor."

Another criticism of spark spread option models is that they are reactive—in essence, they assume that a generator simply turns on or off in response to the current price. In reality, the optimal schedule for a generator must anticipate price changes, perhaps incurring a loss in some periods in order to position the generator to capture higher expected profits later on. Again, there is no one-size-fits-all rule for this. The relative importance of this problem is different for each generator.

Finally, it is far easier to price a power plant if each decision to produce power is independent of earlier decisions. In some cases, power plants are *path dependent*—whether the power plant was operating yesterday will factor into the decision on whether it operates today. This means that the simpler models may not be appropriate. More complicated models are harder to verify, take longer to run, and are more likely to be invalidated over time. Under most circumstances, using simpler models is preferable to using complicated models. However, because simple models are not always appropriate, it is necessary to test them regularly.

Wheeling Power

Wheeling refers to the long distance transmission of power. The cost of electrical power depends on both generation and transmission costs. Minimizing the total cost for power involves balancing these two requirements. Transmission costs are lowest if electricity is produced where it is used, while generation is often much more efficient at larger power plants. Historically, there has been a trade-off between large centralized power plants and less efficient local plants. Wheeling models analyze the trade-off between generation and transaction costs.

The purpose of wheeling is to get low cost power into an area of high prices. If allowed as a free market activity, wheeling can help lower the cost of power for consumers. As a result, wheeling is one of the primary reasons why the electrical markets were deregulated. There are a number of practical applications of wheeling models. They can be used to examine construction of new high-efficiency power plants or long distance transmission lines.

High-efficiency power plants and alternative energy plants often have specific locations where they need to be located. Their lower cost of power needs to offset the cost of transmitting power from that location. For example, a cogeneration plant needs to be located adjacent to a large user of its steam output. A hydroelectric plant needs to be located on a river at a dam, and solar facilities need to be located in sunny areas.

Another application for wheeling models is analyzing transmission of power between two power grids. There are three major interconnected groups of power grids in the United States—the Eastern Interconnect (east of the Rocky Mountains), the Western Interconnect (west of the Rocky Mountains), and ERCOT (Texas). Within each of these groups, it is possible to transmit power between the constituent power grids. For example, it is possible to purchase power in the Midwest and transmit it to the Gulf Coast. Since the Midwest tends to have coal power plants on the margin, and the Gulf Coast has natural gas plants on the margin, this provides a way to profit from any divergence in the price of coal and natural gas. This behavior also looks like an option—a fixed cost is paid to rent capacity, and there is a payoff if the prices diverge.

Financially, wheeling deals are interesting because they allow traders to buy an option based on the construction costs of the equipment rather than on the financial value of the option. This is a key aspect of trading physical products—option premiums can be extremely expensive. If the construction costs are affordable, physical investments provide an alternate way to get the financial exposures at a lower cost. Of course, the trader can lock in a profit by selling off the financial option and pocketing the difference in costs as a profit.

Solar Power

Solar power is one of the most promising sources of renewable energy. There are two main types of solar power, *photovoltaic (PV) solar* power and *thermal solar* power.

PV power converts solar power into electricity. It is produced by solar panels exposed to sunlight. The type of equipment and the intensity of the sunlight directly affect the amount of power that is produced by a solar panel. Correctly estimating the amount of power that will be produced by a solar installation is critical to its successful adoption. If estimates are too conservative, solar power will be deemed uneconomical and bypassed for other technologies. If estimates are too high, there will be a power shortfall and the economic goals of an installation won't be met.

Thermal solar power uses sunlight to produce heat. In many cases, this heat can be used to produce electricity by powering steam turbines or replace electricity that would have been used to produce heat. There are many types of thermal solar installations. They can be anything from small-scale systems to heat outdoor pools to electrical generation facilities. A big advantage of solar power is that heat is relatively easy to store, and this allows these facilities to operate around the clock. Although they can only store heat during the day, they can use the stored heat any time.

Solar radiation varies throughout the year—it is affected by weather, the changing location of the sun, and the amount of daylight. The angle of the solar panel, its efficiency of handling direct and diffuse light, and surrounding environment all impact how much power is collected. To analyze solar installations, historical averages of solar radiation are used. These averages are collected by the regional or national governments, and provided for the purpose of estimating solar installations.

Wind Power

The wind is another source of renewable energy. It has been used for thousands of years as a pollution-free way to power windmills and sailboats. Since the 1970s, specialized windmills, called *wind turbines*, have been built to harness the wind as a source of electrical power. These windmills are typically grouped into wind farms and located in areas exposed to sustained high winds.

Wind is inherently unpredictable. Not only does it blow irregularly, but the amount of energy in wind is related to the cube of the wind speed. Fast gusts contain far more energy than slow steady breezes. As a result, the wind supplies irregular bursts of power. Occasionally, wind energy will provide a lot of energy. But, much of the time, it may not provide much energy at all.

Wind turbines can be expensive to install and maintain due to the constant stress that the wind places on their moving parts. When exposed to high winds for prolonged periods, a substantial amount of torque is placed on the frame of the wind turbine. This can cause the superstructure of the wind turbine to break down and deform over time. This is especially a problem when there are a number of wind turbines in close proximity. When a wind turbine is alone, the air flow around its fan blades is fairly predictable. However, when there are a large number of wind turbines together, the turbulence from the blades of the upwind units can cause chaotic air flow over the downwind units. This puts unpredictable stresses on the superstructure of wind turbines and can lead to sudden equipment failure.

The two most common reasons for consumer opposition to wind farms are the danger they present to migratory birds and aesthetic considerations. Wind turbines are often placed on major migration corridors due to the steady sustained winds in those areas. As birds fly past the wind turbines, they can be hit by the spinning blades and killed. Environmental groups are concerned that if wind power becomes common, the wild bird population will be decimated. Other protests are caused because people think that wind farms are ugly and don't want them destroying the scenic beauty of nature.

Nuclear Power

Although it is not a renewable fuel, nuclear power is an alternative to fossil fuel–based electricity generation. Nuclear power plants, like coal-fired power plants, operate by producing superheated steam to drive electrical turbines. Both coal and nuclear plants benefit by operating at extremely high temperatures. The higher the temperature that these plants can operate at, the more efficient they become. A low temperature plant might return 25 percent of its heat energy as electricity. A larger, hotter plant might return 50 to 60 percent of its heat energy as electricity.

The primary difference between nuclear and coal plants is the way that they generate heat. Nuclear power plants generate heat through nuclear fission. Nuclear fission breaks protons and neutrons free from the nucleus of the nuclear fuel. This isn't a combustion process, so no carbon dioxide is produced. However, nuclear power produces a different type of pollution—radioactive waste.

When concentrated, uranium, the fuel used in most nuclear reactors, is highly toxic. The fuel can also be very difficult to obtain. Although there is a lot of uranium in the Earth's crust, it is seldom found in large deposits. There are a limited number of areas where sufficient quantities can be found to make its extraction economically feasible. Another worry is that the refining process is often identical to the process needed to make fuel for nuclear weapons. As a result, concerns of nuclear weapon proliferation are closely linked to the construction of nuclear reactors.

Energy Storage

Electricity can be stored by converting it into another form of energy, like kinetic energy or heat, and then using that energy to generate electricity. Even though efficiency of these conversions is usually low, there are cases where it becomes economically worthwhile. For example, any time electricity can be obtained for very low cost, even inefficient storage systems are economical if they were inexpensive to build. There are a large number of ways to store energy. One of the primary ways to store electricity is to use chemical energy to store energy in a battery or to use a capacitor to store voltage directly. Other ways to store energy are through the use of pressurized gas, kinetic energy, and gravity.

Levelized Cost of Entry

To forecast power prices over a very long horizon, it is often useful to examine the price at which developers might willingly build new generation in the future. If prices rise above that point, new generation will be built and push prices lower. As a result, it is possible to estimate an upper bound for power prices that might exist over a long horizon. This can be done by dividing the cost of building the unit by its expected generation volume adjusted by the time value of money. This value is called the *levelized cost of entry* (LCOE). This analysis can be expanded by incorporating the fixed and variable cost of running a unit (fuel, maintenance, and operations overhead). This approach is commonly used to estimate prices in both capacity markets and *power purchase agreements* (PPAs). Some uses for LCOE analysis include:

- PPA
- Fundamental forecasts
- Capacity markets
- Renewable energy certificate markets

The LCOE is also a convenient way to compare the overall competitiveness of different generating technologies. It represents the cost of building and operating a generating plant over a typical life span and duty cycle. Key inputs into this type of model include an estimate of the cost needed to construct new units, called the cost of new entry (CONE). This cost is spread across the expected life of the facility using a discounted cash flow (DCF) analysis to calculate the amount of daily revenue (in units of $/MW-Day). Mathematically, the analysis is very similar to the calculation of an annuity (a fixed income product often used as an example in finance or MBA classes).

Secondary Electricity Markets

There are a variety of markets that have developed around the edges of the electrical market. Three of these markets—*ancillary services*, *capacity markets*, and PPAs—help power grids reliably deliver power to consumers. Ancillary services and capacity markets are typical features of a deregulated market. PPAs are features of a power grid operated by a regulated utility. Another market, FTRs help traders manage congestion risk.

- **Ancillary Services.** Ancillary services markets allow a power grid to pay generators to stay partially unused so that the generator can increase or decrease production to match the changing consumer demand.
- **Capacity Markets.** Capacity markets help power grids ensure that they have an ability to meet the consumer demand for electricity several years into the future. Capacity markets pay money to generators to incentivize new construction and ensure that generators don't close down too many underutilized generation units.
- **Power Purchase Agreements (PPAs).** In regulated markets, the regulated utility can ensure that it obtains a sufficient supply of renewable power by signing PPAs with third-party generators.
- **Financial Transmission Rights (FTRs).** These rights are a hedge for congestion costs. They give market participants the ability to offset the cost of transmitting power over the power grid. In most cases, they can result in both positive and negative outcomes to the owner.

NATURAL GAS MODELS

This section introduces transportation and storage models of the natural gas market. The key to understanding these models lies in understanding the physical nature of gases. Since it is a gas, transporting and storing natural gas requires different technologies than those used for solids (like coal) or liquids (like oil).

Gas isn't very dense—it contains substantially less energy per volume than either solids or liquids. Natural gas (methane) is one of the least energy dense hydrocarbon gases—it has much less energy per volume than a gas like propane. As a result, it isn't practical to use tanks to transfer natural gas for heating or industrial use. Because natural gas needs to be kept at supercold temperatures (–263°F) to remain a liquid, it is also impractical to distribute natural gas to consumers in that form.

Because of these constraints, natural gas is typically moved through the country via gas pipelines. Pipelines are a very efficient way to transport gas, but they do have some limitations. Gas needs to be continually injected into the pipeline from a well or storage facility and removed at the burner tip. The *burner tip* is a term that means a natural gas consumer. Since gas moves from areas of high pressure to areas of lower pressure, it is important that the pipeline maintains the proper ratio of pressure throughout its length. If the pressure at the burner tip were to be higher than the pressure at the well head, gas would flow back into the well.

In practical terms, this means that if a pipeline is operational, neither the injections nor removal of gas can be allowed to stop. If gas isn't added continuously at the injection point (to create a high pressure zone) and removed at the burner tip (to create a low pressure zone), gas won't flow in the proper direction, and the pipeline won't operate. This is a very important concept—for a pipeline to operate, neither injections nor removals can stop just because they are uneconomical. Gas pipelines provide a public service—sometimes they can't be turned off. If no consumer is using the gas at the burner tip, and there isn't any storage available, it might be necessary to burn off the excess gas or make otherwise uneconomical decisions.

To prevent wasting gas, a popular solution is to store it in a storage facility. Unused oil wells, salt mines, and aquifers have all been modified for storing natural gas. Typically, these have to be kept at a higher pressure than the pipeline—this allows gas to eventually flow out of the storage facility and back into the pipeline.

Natural Gas Transportation

Compressor stations are the key to transporting natural gas through pipelines. Compressor stations create suction on one side (the intake side) and high pressure on the other side (the discharge side). Gas flows by expanding. It moves from the high pressure discharge point of one station to the low pressure suction point of the next station. Choosing the right number of compression stations to ensure reliable service is a key aspect of the pipeline business.

When arranging transportation on a pipeline, there are two major levels of service—*firm* service and *interruptible* service. Firm service is offered with a guaranteed availability except when prevented by acts of *Force Majeure*.[2] Firm service is highly reliable but also highly expensive compared to interruptible service. Interruptible service is offered on a "best efforts" basis and is relatively cheap. However, it can be interrupted for any reason and may not be available at all. There

[2] ***Force Majeure*** is French for "greater force." This is a common clause in contracts that frees both parties from liability in cases of wars, natural disasters, and other extraordinary events. Typically these events are outside the control of either party, which would prevent one or both of the parties from fulfilling their obligations under the terms of the contract.

are a number of valid reasons why interruptible service might be disrupted. The most common reason is to balance the flow of gas on a pipeline. Because of the nature of gas, its movement can never be precisely controlled. Optimizing even a relatively simple pipeline can get very complicated. Although *firm* and *interruptible* are commonly used general descriptions of service levels, each pipeline company will have a slightly different definition for the types of services that are offered.

Pipelines get paid substantially more for guaranteed levels of service than for service that is likely to be interrupted. The economics of a pipeline are based on balancing the need for redundancy in the system (allowing the sale of higher margin guaranteed service) against the cost of additional compression stations and pipes.

Natural Gas Storage

After gas is transported, it may not be necessary to use it right away. Fortunately, it is possible to store natural gas for extremely long periods of time. Most natural gas is already millions of years old. Pipelines need to keep operating around the clock, but demand is more cyclical, and natural gas must either be stored or burned off. Storage facilities help to smooth out these periods of short-term supply and demand. These facilities are located on both ends of pipelines.

Demand for natural gas is highly seasonal—the highest demand comes during the winter (for heating) and during the summer (to provide electricity for air conditioning). Storage facilities allow stockpiling of gas during periods of low demand for use in higher demand periods. This storage also provides a crucial margin of safety for short-term regional changes in demand. Storage facilities differ by the quantity of gas that can be stored and how quickly it can be removed.

All storage facilities work in a similar fashion—a large volume suitable for storing natural gas is found and connected to a gas pipeline. Unless it is nearly empty, the pressure in the storage facility will be higher than the pressure of a pipeline. Gas will need to be compressed to get it into the storage facility. This compression is done by applying suction to a pipeline (similar to attaching a vacuum cleaner to it). As long as the suction is stronger than the pressure in the storage area, the gas will flow into the storage area and not back into the pipeline. When the suction is turned off, the connection between the storage facility and pipeline will need to be closed.

The speed at which gas can be extracted will depend on the pressure of the storage facility. As a result, the extractable gas is generally divided into two pieces—*base gas* (or *cushion gas*) and *working gas*. The base gas is used to create sufficient pressure to get the working gas out of the storage facility in a reasonable amount of time. Base gas is usually never removed during normal operation. Operators of a storage facility have to trade-off having a large volume of working gas that can only be removed slowly or a smaller volume of working gas that can be removed quickly. During periods of peak demand, some of the base gas can be removed from the facility and delivered as working gas. However, over the long run, since removing the gas cushion slows down the speed at which gas can be removed (because removing gas lowers the pressure of the storage facility), keeping a fixed cushion of gas is required to meet ongoing operational requirements.

This last major physical constraint on a storage facility is its maximum pressure. Higher pressure means that you can store more gas in a given volume and that you can get the gas out more quickly. However, higher pressure can also cause structural problems—more stress on the facility—and a greater possibility of gas escaping into the environment. Since there are a fairly limited number of locations suitable for the storage of natural gas, the pressure constraint is usually a function of what can be found, rather than what is desired.

For a particular area, there is a limited inventory of possible locations suitable for storing natural gas. The cheapest and most reliable storage is depleted gas reservoirs. The highest performance facilities are converted salt caverns. In areas where neither of those two is available, aquifers can be used. Aquifers are permeable layers of underground rock often containing ground water. From a performance perspective, salt caverns are far superior to the other options—they can stand up to significantly higher pressures.

Liquefied Natural Gas

Another major trend in the natural gas market is to import it from other countries. It isn't feasible to build pipelines across the ocean. Instead, natural gas is transported as a liquid. Natural gas turns into a liquid at –263° F and becomes 600 times denser than its gaseous form. Specially insulated tanker ships can be used to transport the natural gas across long distances. When the liquefied natural gas (LNG) tanker reaches a port, the LNG can be turned back into a gas by heating it. At that point, it can be placed into a pipeline for delivery to consumers.

From an environmental perspective, transporting natural gas is fairly safe. Other than being freezing cold, it is nontoxic and noncorrosive. When it is left exposed to the atmosphere, perhaps by a spill, LNG will rapidly evaporate without leaving a residue. Because of the speed at which it evaporates, natural gas also does not pose a large explosion risk. Natural gas is only explosive in concentrations between

5 and 15 percent of air. This can occur when gas is trapped in an enclosed space like a house or a storage facility. But, in any other concentrations, it will not ignite. Any time a large amount of flammable substance is in one place, there is some fire risk. However, there is much less risk with natural gas than with either oil or coal storage facilities.

There are no LNG contracts currently being traded. However, being able to transport LNG around the globe makes the natural gas market into a global market rather than a set of regional ones. For example, without LNG, the natural gas markets in Europe and the United States are completely separate. However, with the ability to transfer supply from one region to another, prices will start to converge toward a single global price.

RISK MANAGEMENT

Modern financial risk management is largely a combination of two practices—*mark-to-market accounting* and *an analysis of earnings volatility*. Supporting activities associated with risk management are an analysis of credit risks, an analysis of trading of unusual or stressed conditions, using financial transactions to reduce risk (*hedging*), and managing modeling risk.

Mark-to-Market Accounting

Mark-to-market is a type of fair-value accounting that applies to financial investments. It is the most common valuation standard used for energy transactions. Accounting policies around mark-to-market defines what is meant by a trading price. As a result, mark-to-market affects anything that uses prices as an input (like risk management and financial reporting). The primary alternative to mark-to-market accounting, *historical cost accounting*, applies to physical assets like buildings and equipment. With a few exceptions, this type of accounting values assets at their acquisition costs and this value does not change over time.

Mark-to-market is not always easy to implement for energy transactions. One cause of difficulty is a lack of potential trading partners. Sometimes there is no counterparty willing to transact a particular commodity at a specific location. In other cases, a contract might not be easily assignable to another party. For example, a PPA might obligate a utility to purchase power and various nontradable items like capacity and ancillary services from a specific electrical generation unit. If this contract specifies the generation facility, it might not be possible to sell the contract to anyone else without selling them the physical unit at the same time. This might result in a gray area where accountants would need to determine which accounting rules might apply to a particular investment.

Even so, there is a big advantage to using mark-to-market accounting—it is fairly intuitive for most assets. If an asset is purchased for $100 and the same asset starts selling for $120, under mark-to-market accounting, it will show a $20 profit. The alternative, *historical cost*, keeps assets marked to their purchase price until they are actually sold. Historical cost accounting can be misleading in the cases of long-dated assets because the value of those assets isn't regularly updated. Typically, there is little choice about which type of accounting can be applied—accounting rules will specify the type of accounting that must be used.

Mark-to-Market Accounting. Mark-to-market accounting uses recent prices quoted in the financial markets to determine the value of investments. Any contract that can be traded (futures, swaps, options) will typically be subject to mark-to-market accounting.

Historical Cost Accounting. Historical cost accounting uses the purchase price of assets to determine the value of investments. This is most commonly used for physical investments (buildings, equipment) that can't easily be traded.

On the downside, mark-to-market accounting assumes there is a liquid, fair market for price discovery. It can fail catastrophically when markets can be manipulated or are illiquid. Most of the models discussed in this book—power plants, storage facilities, and almost everything modeled as an option—are not actively traded in a liquid market. This lack of liquidity can lead to large gains and losses occurring for very little reason. For example, maybe only one trader was trying to transact on that day and had to pay a large premium to get someone to do a transaction.

From a risk management perspective, there are many issues that can be caused by mark-to-market. For example, many investment funds force a mandatory liquidation when prices drop below a certain point (this happens because a risk limit that uses price as an input is activated). In an illiquid market, it may not be possible to sell an expensive asset immediately. This can affect an investor even if they are not doing the transaction. If another trader holding an illiquid asset needs to sell (maybe they need the cash for a better opportunity), this can cause havoc in the marketplace. The other trader might end up selling an asset at low prices. This can cause a chain reaction if the price triggers risk limits at other firms. This can cause traders at those other firms to sell their investments. This will drive prices lower and cause more selling. The falling prices will force more and more traders to sell and prevent anyone from buying the cheap assets. This can trigger or exacerbate a market crash.

Finally, mixing mark-to-market instruments with historically priced instruments also creates problems. An extreme example might be a power plant that has completely locked in fuel supplies and sold its power for the next 20 years using OTC forwards. The power plant is hedged—there should be limited market risk or cash flows prior to the date of electricity delivery. However, if the power plant receives historical cost accounting and the hedges are mark-to-market, daily profits and losses in the OTC forwards will make the combination of investments look substantially riskier because the power plant does not change in value at the same time. There are special accounting rules that cover this situation called *hedge accounting rules*.

Value at Risk

Value at risk (VAR) is a risk management statistic that describes the size of an investment. It was originally developed to combine different types of investments into a single measure of size. For example, describing the combined size of a million-dollar stock investment and 15,000 crude oil futures is difficult. It isn't clear which of the two investments will result in greater earnings or losses. VAR addresses this by describing the combination of investments by something that they have in common—daily changes in value. Daily changes in value are also known as *earnings* or *profit and loss* (P&L). While risk management practices vary widely, size is one of the most important components of risk, and almost all risk management is at least partially based around a VAR methodology.

Mathematically, VAR summarizes the risk of a portfolio by predicting the size of P&L movement that will occur with some frequency. For example, it is possible to calculate an estimate of the largest P&L move that will occur approximately once a month. VAR simplifies a large distribution of possible earnings into a single point. Not everyone uses the same frequency for VAR—some people prefer points that are more likely to be accurate and can be checked commonly while others prefer numbers that are more representative of a worst-case scenario. There are two main steps to calculating a VAR number (Figure 1.1.2). First, it is necessary to construct the possible P&L movements by simulation or examination of historical data. Next, it is necessary to find the value corresponding to the desired probability of occurrence.

By picking a single point, VAR produces a simpler estimate of risk than having to use entire distribution of predicted results. VAR gives up accuracy for simplicity. In many cases, different assets can have the same VAR (Figure 1.1.3).

The methodology for calculating the percentile also can vary between firms. Some risk managers prefer to examine only losses, others prefer to look at the volatility of both profits and losses. If only losses are examined, the VAR is called a *one-sided VAR*. If both profits and losses are examined, it is called a *two-sided VAR* (Figure 1.1.4). One-sided VAR is more commonly used than two-sided VAR.

Because VAR is a single number, it has some limitations—it abstracts away the fundamental behavior of a portfolio. It also has many of the weaknesses associated with other measures of size. For example, it is better at indicating commonly observed changes. For instance, a 95 percent 1-day VAR of $1,000,000 doesn't give substantially more information about a worst-case scenario loss than knowing that it is based on a $20 million stock portfolio.

VAR often assumes that most losses follow a statistical distribution. However, future events are often difficult to describe statistically.

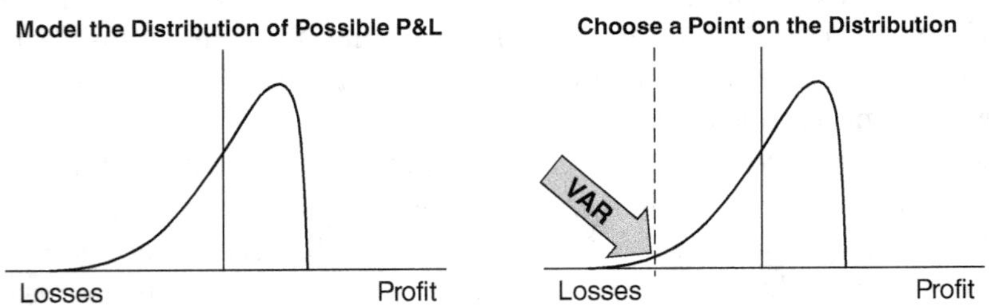

Step 1. Construct a distribution of possible P&L movements by simulation or through observation of past history.

Step 2. Find the value corresponding to the Nth percentile of the distribution. The 95th and 99th percentiles are popular choices for VAR.

Figure 1.1.2 Calculating VAR

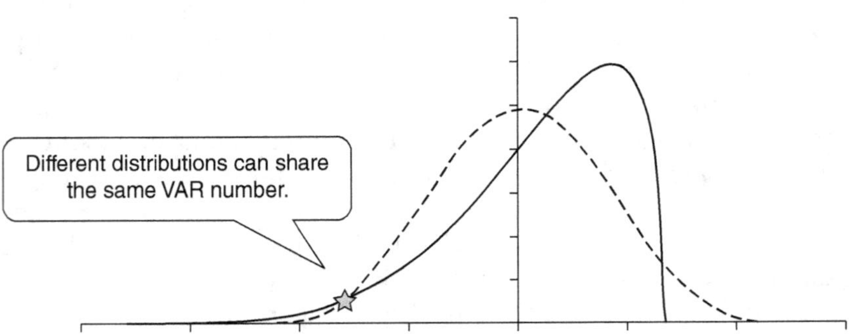

Figure 1.1.3 VARs for two assets

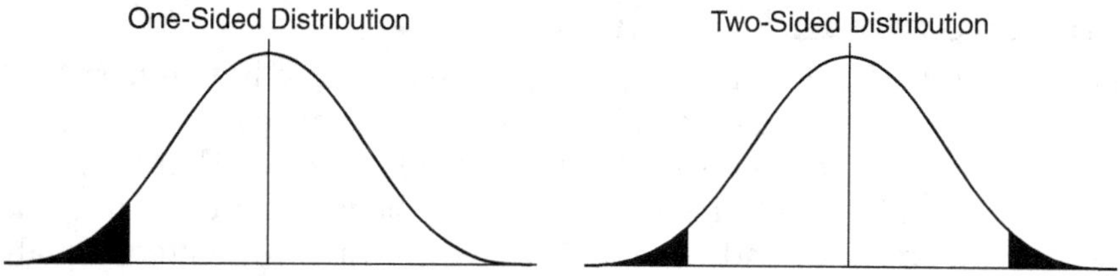

Figure 1.1.4 One-sided and two-sided VARs

For example, P&L is not usually normally distributed—there isn't always an equal chance of making and losing money. Many energy assets—particularly the ones that can be modeled by options—also have asymmetrical payoffs. For instance, a peaking power plant is going to lay idle for most of the year—it will lose money regularly whenever it is inactive. In all but the summer months, small operational charges will accumulate daily. A couple times a year—usually hot summer afternoons—the power plant will have the opportunity to make large windfall profits as it is pressed into duty (Figure 1.1.5).

With this kind of seasonal effect, it might be possible to have season-specific VAR distributions, but that isn't a general solution to the problem. A gas pipeline that is selling firm delivery will make steady profits until a problem is encountered. Then, the pipeline will hemorrhage money. There might be some seasonality to equipment failures—but the pipeline's is not going to show nearly the seasonality as a peaking power plant P&L where the price of power is determined almost exclusively by a seasonal factor—temperature.

Ultimately, VAR is an approximation; being simple means that it gets implemented and examined regularly. However, it is not going to handle all types of portfolios well. Sometimes additional analysis will be required. There are so many possible special cases that no general model will be able to address them all. This doesn't make VAR worthless, just limited. It is useful precisely because it is a simple measure.

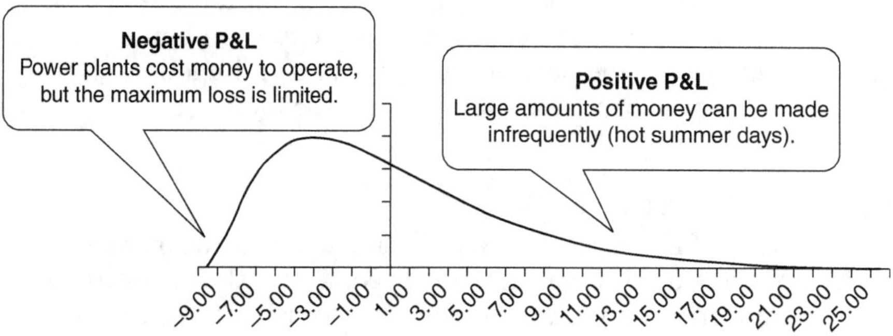

Figure 1.1.5 An investment that benefits from volatility

Counterparty and Credit Risk

The energy market is full of agreements made directly between two counterparties. Assessing the ability of counterparties to meet their contractual obligations is crucial to the energy business. There are two parts to examining credit risk—establishing the magnitude of the risk (the credit exposure) and the likelihood of the risk (the credit quality). Getting this information correct is important; firms will have hard limits on how much exposure they can have to a single counterparty. If estimates of loss are too high, business will be hurt and it won't be possible to make trades. If the estimates are too low, there is risk of a catastrophic counterparty collapse.

Credit exposure identifies how much money could be lost in the event of a default. At its simplest, calculating credit exposure can assume a complete loss on every contract. This does place an upper bound on the potential loss but also tends to overestimate its severity. A more accurate estimate must include the probability of recovering assets through a bankruptcy proceeding. Certain debts (preferred debt) have priority over other debts. It is important to understand where the contracts in question fall in the recovery order.

Credit quality is the other aspect of modeling credit risk. It attempts to describe how likely a firm is to default on its payments. This is a forward-looking measure—many energy contracts last several years. There are a number of ratings agencies that provide credit ratings. These ratings can be augmented by in-house research focusing on a couple of key counterparties. There can be several layers to this analysis—a counterparty's credit risk will depend on the credit quality of its own clients. Finally, a company is less likely to default if its large trades have moved in its favor, and more likely to default if trades have moved against it.

As a summary, credit risk can't be eliminated, but it can be mitigated through the use of collateral and managed through supervision. If controls are too strict, it will be impossible to conduct an ongoing business. The possibility of missing trading opportunities and damaging relationships because of counterparty exposure limits needs to be balanced against the need to protect against a huge loss. Neither extreme is good—a happy medium needs to be found.

Managing Model Risk

Another type of risk is *model risk*, the risk that either the methodology or assumptions used to value assets becomes invalid. Poor assumptions and incorrectly designed models cause risk management problems in every financial market. However, the complexity of energy models and their extended lifetimes, make these problems especially common in the energy markets.

The energy market is full of nonstandard instruments and models of physical assets. Many energy companies will use models to value assets with lifetimes of 20 years or longer—things like power plants, pipelines, and natural gas wells. Even if a model was sufficient when first developed, it can still fail before its lifetime is up. Assumptions made 15 years earlier are often invalidated due to regulatory changes, population shifts, and technological changes. Exacerbating this problem is the problem of employee turnover—commonly, the original developers of the models have moved to another job before problems develop. After a number of years, organizations need to take steps to ensure that someone still understands every model that is in production.

Another issue common across many energy products is that many physical trading points aren't very liquid. These trading points often need to be approximated by prices at a nearby hub. The implicit assumption is that the actual price will experience the same changes as the local hub. Sometimes, this is a good assumption. Other times, the expected relationship between the two points breaks down after a couple of years.

Another assumption that can cause problems is the correlation between two assets. The importance of spread options in energy was discussed earlier. The value of these deals is incredibly sensitive to the correlation between the two underlying assets. In these cases, the correlation can't be readily determined from an independent source; it must be estimated and reviewed regularly.

Hedging

A *hedge* is a type of trading position that is intended to lock in profits or losses associated with another investment. The contract associated with a hedge is called a *hedging instrument*, and the other investment (the one being *hedged*) is called the *hedged item*.

Hedging transfers risk from one trader to another. Traders often use hedging to protect against risks when liquidating their trading position would be undesirable, difficult, or impossible. For example, the bondholders who lent to a wind farm might require that the owners of the wind farm lock in future income by hedging as a requirement for their money. This would guarantee that the wind farm could meet its bond payment obligations. Since the wind farm will generate power that it needs to sell, the sale price could be locked in by selling forward contracts. On the downside, locking in prices would prevent the wind farm owner from benefitting if prices rose in the future.

Although it is often hidden, there is generally a cost associated with hedging. Many producers would like to fix a price for their products. This would allow them to finance projects with other people's money (e.g., bondholders), since production and locked-in prices would present a very safe cash flow. The issue is that there are only a limited number of counterparties who would have an incentive to arrange purchases. Most commodities are ultimately purchased by consumers (individuals or small companies) that don't lock in prices for more than a year or two at the most.

Hedging also presents a substantial number of risk management issues. Although a hedge is equal in size (and risk) to the original investment, it generally receives much less scrutiny. This can create its own set of risks where a company will have hundreds of people agree that the original investment is worthwhile, and then under the guise of risk management, make an equally large investment exactly opposite of the investment that everyone thought was good.

Hedging also presents specific accounting issues since it often involves both tradable and nontradable investments. The hedged item (e.g., power that a power plant might produce in the future) may not be valued the same way as the hedge (the futures). Hedge accounting rules allow the hedger to avoid mark-to-market accounting for the hedged item as long as it and the hedge pass certain tests.

Weather Derivatives

Weather derivatives are financial products whose payoff is tied to weather conditions. These derivatives are usually bilaterally negotiated between market participants who want protection from or exposure to weather events. The most common weather derivatives are based on temperature. However, derivatives can also be constructed on average rainfall, snowfall, hurricanes, or similar weather data. Typical users of weather derivatives include utilities and insurance companies.

Weather presents an unusual set of risks to energy companies because it affects both volume and prices. This makes it difficult to hedge using typical financial products. For example, an uncharacteristically cold winter might lead to natural gas companies depleting their stored natural gas because more heating is required. At the same time, natural gas prices can spike due to utilities competing to acquire dwindling reserves of fuel for their customers at progressively higher prices. The combination of price and volume risk is difficult to hedge with standard financial instruments.

Weather derivatives are similar to insurance but there are differences. First, weather derivatives tend to deal with events that happen with a reasonably high degree of probability. Second, weather derivatives tend to deal with less extreme events than insurance. For example, insurance might be purchased to protect against flood or hurricane damage (involving a very large loss that might only happen once every 100 years). Weather derivatives might be purchased to protect an airline from lost business if rainfall is 10 percent more than average (a smaller loss, but one that might happen several times over a 10-year period).

1.2

TRADING MARKETS

30-Second Summary

Purpose

This chapter introduces several financial concepts related to trading and investing. It starts off as a review of concepts mentioned in the previous chapter and then goes into a lot more detail.

Summary

The energy market is a type of commodity market that specializes in electricity, heat, and fuel products. Difficulties in storing and transporting energy products distinguish energy trading from other financial markets. In most financial markets, future prices are linked to current prices by the ability to buy a product today and store it for future delivery. However, buying and holding is difficult in the energy market. Many types of energy are difficult or expensive to store. In addition, these stored products have to compete with a steady supply of new products that are coming to market. As a result, current prices and future prices are rarely linked the same way as prices in other markets. Instead, energy markets tend to experience cyclical variations in prices.

Key Topics

- Energy trading markets are a type of commodity market that consists of both physical exchanges of cash for energy and forward markets where transactions are arranged ahead of time. Most energy trading occurs in the forward markets.
- It is impossible to substitute energy products that are not available at the same time and location. For example, electricity in New York is different than electricity in California.
- Many concepts developed for other financial markets—like dynamic hedging and risk management—have to be modified to take into account the inability to aggregate risks among energy products at different locations and delivery dates.

Trading means buying, selling, and exchanging commodities, products, and services. Not all energy markets are *trading* markets. Sometimes it is possible to buy a commodity, like gasoline at a service station, and not be able to resell it. The difference between a cash market and a trading market is that it is possible to both buy and sell in a trading market.

The most important commodities in the energy market are crude oil, natural gas, and electricity. Additional energy commodities are refined petroleum products like gasoline, alternative fuels like ethanol, pollution, weather derivatives, and carbon emissions. All of these products are related to the generation of either heat or electricity. Electricity and heat cannot be easily stored or transported. In most cases, arrangements to store or transport energy have to be made in advance. Because of this, it is difficult to trade most physical energy commodities on short notice. As a result, *energy trading* primarily consists of buying and selling agreements to deliver power at some point in the future. The *time* and *location* where the energy needs to be delivered is a key component in these agreements.

In most financial markets, the price for future delivery is closely related to the price for immediate delivery. However, in the energy market, this relationship works differently. In most financial markets, it is possible to buy the product today, hold the traded product for a while, and be able to resell the product in the future. Because of this relationship, it is feasible to react to expectations of future prices by trading for immediate delivery. Energy is different. If physical electricity is purchased the current day, it is usually necessary to use it immediately.

By itself, energy isn't intrinsically valuable. Heat to warm a house is only valuable in the right place and time. In the summer, for example, home heating isn't valuable at all. Quite the opposite is true. In hot weather, people pay money to remove heat from their homes. Likewise, if an extremely cold winter in Chicago causes natural gas prices to skyrocket, owning undeliverable gas somewhere else isn't very valuable. Only the natural gas that can actually be delivered to customers in Chicago will be worth the high prices. The spot prices in Chicago don't reflect expectations of future prices. Customers need heating immediately and can't put off their purchase until prices are cheaper in six months. Nor can all of Chicago relocate overnight to an area with more natural gas supply or warmer weather.

Supply and Demand

Traders commonly think of asset prices as being set by supply and demand. This is often a good description of commodity markets where consumers bid on a limited supply of goods. A fundamental economic concept in a free market is that prices will gravitate to a level where the supply and demand are equal.

The Law of Demand. Higher prices reduce demand.

The Law of Supply. Higher prices increase production.

(*Continued*)

Theoretically, the intersection of supply and demand determines the fair price for an asset. However, in practice, supply and demand don't always respond to price changes. The degree that supply and demand react to changes in price is called *elasticity*. In many cases, supply and demand are constant regardless of how much the price changes. When this happens, there is a disruption in prices. In an inelastic market, prices skyrocket when demand exceeds supply. Prices crash when supply exceeds demand. Both events occur fairly commonly in the energy market.

In the energy market, there is a substantial lag between high prices and increased supply. Increasing energy supplies usually involves making long-term capital investments like the construction of a new well, refinery, or power plant. These investments are not typically made in response to a short-term change in price. These assets will only be built if a permanent change in price is expected, and even then might take a substantial amount of time to construct.

Another problem is caused by consumers being unable to substitute one type of energy demand for another. They cannot relocate where they live, modify their car to run on an alternative fuel, or do without heating in the winter. To a large extent, energy consumers are a captive audience.

Spot and Forward Markets

The *spot market* is a market where commodities are delivered immediately. Given the complexity of delivering some energy commodities, this means sometime between the next five seconds and next month. Spot transactions are usually consumers purchasing small quantities of a commodity for immediate use. The *forward market* is a financial market where delivery is scheduled at some agreed upon point in the future. Typically, forward markets schedule deliveries at least a month ahead of time.

Spot Market

The spot market, also called the *cash market*, is the market for instantaneous delivery of a commodity. The spot market gets its name because the transaction is done *on the spot*. This is the market with which ordinary people are most familiar. Trades in the spot market involve the physical transfer of an agreed on quantity of a standardized product for a specific price. Buying a meal at a fast-food restaurant is an example of a spot market transaction—the buyer gets immediate delivery of a standardized product for a set price. Another example of a spot transaction occurs when a light switch is turned on. The owner of the light switch buys electricity and immediately takes delivery of the product. Trading in the electricity spot market is restricted to people who can either deliver or use power immediately.

The spot market for energy is complicated by the fact that producers don't know what the actual energy demand will be ahead of time. Consumers can turn on electrical devices and set the thermostats whenever they want. It is left to the local electric utility to cope with meeting that demand. When someone turns on a light switch, power needs to be immediately provided. It isn't possible to substitute another type of power either—when a homeowner in New York turns on a light, the power company has to provide power in New York. Providing power somewhere nearby, like New Jersey or Connecticut, won't meet the New York demand.

Because of the inability to transfer energy products without preparation, there are a large number of local spot markets. Each spot market can have its own rules and regulations. The prices in each spot market are determined by local supply and demand. As a result, since supply has to be arranged ahead of time, spot prices can be extremely volatile. It is easy for an unexpected change in demand to lead to either a shortage or glut in local supplies.

For related reasons, high spot prices in one area don't necessarily mean that nearby prices will also be high. It is very possible that one region can have a surplus of power and another region a shortage when real-time transfers between the two markets are impossible. For example, if a power plant in California unexpectedly needs to go offline, prices there will spike upward as inefficient, expensive backup generators are turned on. A nearby power market, like Oregon, might not see any price change—that market might still have a sufficient supply of power to meet local demand.

The high price volatility in the local spot markets and the lack of correlation between adjoining regions tends to disappear in the forward market. While there is still time to arrange transfers of power or line up fuel supplies, prices tend to be based on macroeconomics. For example, if a power plant outage is expected in six months, there is probably time to arrange more cost-effective backup generation rather than relying on units that can be brought up to speed immediately.

Local regulation is another feature of the spot markets. Every municipality can have specific rules governing the physical delivery of power within their boundaries. Some markets might have prices set by government legislation while other markets might be open to competitive prices. Spot markets subject to heavy government regulation are called *regulated markets*. Most regulated markets are controlled by a government-sponsored monopoly that is overseen by a government commission; there is relatively little trading in these markets. Markets with competitive pricing systems are called *deregulated markets*. Deregulated markets were largely designed to encourage trading.

Forward Markets

Forward trading markets allow buyers and sellers to agree on transactions ahead of time. For physical contracts, this gives both sides sufficient time to prepare for delivery or receipt of a physical commodity. For example, a trader might agree to deliver 500 MMBtus of natural gas at Henry Hub three months in the future at a price of $8.12 per MMBtu.

Trades in the forward market are generally specified by several factors:

- **Underlying Instrument.** The commodity being traded, usually with a description of minimum quality standards that must be met. Often, this is just called the *underlying*.
- **Quantity.** The amount of the commodity that must be delivered.
- **Delivery Price.** The price per unit due at delivery.
- **Delivery Date.** The date at which the underlying instrument will be delivered.
- **Delivery Location.** The location at which the underlying instrument will be delivered.

From an economic perspective, allowing buyers and sellers to negotiate trades ahead of time reduces the volatility of energy prices. Energy is hard to store and transport. Giving large producers and consumers the opportunity to line up trading partners ahead of time reduces the uncertainty caused by short-term imbalances between supply and demand.

Trading, meaning the buying and reselling of assets, occurs almost exclusively in the forward market. The exceptions to this are cases where a trader has the ability to immediately deliver the physical asset or where he can buy a physical asset and relocate or store it.

The Spot Market Has Higher Volatility

Nearby futures contracts are more volatile than contracts with several months to expiration. This is because distant forward prices are primarily influenced by seasonal expectations while spot prices are determined by much more volatile short-term variations in supply and demand (Figure 1.2.1).

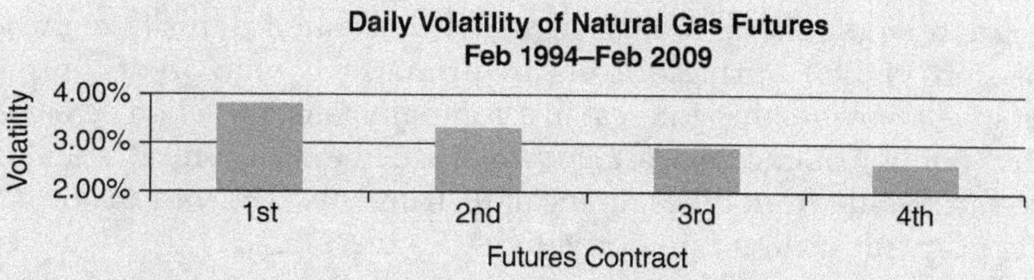

Figure 1.2.1 A diagram showing how volatility decreases with time. The ordinal numbers indicate months to expiration. The 1st contract is one month from expiration; the 2nd is two months away, and so on.

Physical and Financial Settlement

Not everyone has the desire or capability to taking physical delivery. Historically, less than 1 percent of futures contracts go to physical delivery. The remainder of the contracts are liquidated prior to being exercised.

For example, if a trucking company wants to reduce its exposure to diesel fuel prices, it might buy crude oil contracts since the price of diesel fuel is correlated to the price of crude oil. That way, if the oil/diesel relationship continues to hold and the price of diesel fuel rises, the trucking company will offset its increased fuel costs with a profit on its investment. Of course, if the price of fuel falls, the savings to the trucking company would be largely eaten up by losses in the forward contracts. Essentially, the trucking company is attempting to lock in fuel costs. However, regardless of what happens to prices, the trucking company doesn't want to take receipt of a lot of crude oil. It only wants the financial exposure.

When energy contracts are closed out in cash prior to delivery, this is called a *financial settlement*. When the trade is closed out by physically transferring a commodity, it is called a *physical delivery*. When a contract is closed out, the two counterparties to the trade essentially enter into a new trade that offsets the original trade. With a financial settlement of a trade, the two counterparties settle the difference in prices in cash.

FINANCIAL INSTRUMENTS

Trading is largely focused around the buying and selling of special types of contracts, called *financial instruments* or *securities*. The three main types of financial instruments are real assets, financial assets, and derivatives. *Real assets* include physical commodities (like crude oil, electricity, and gold) as well as legislatively created rights (like carbon emissions rights). *Financial assets* are primarily composed of contracts that give an ownership interest in a company (stocks), a lien on a company (bonds), or currencies. *Derivatives* are financial contracts that derive their value from other financial instruments. The vast majority of all energy transactions are derivatives (Figure 1.2.2).

To be a financial instrument, assets need to be tradable. *Tradable* means that an asset can be legally assigned to someone else for a cash payment. It also means that it is possible to both buy and sell the financial instrument without giving up a substantial amount of the asset's value. For example, it is generally possible to buy a cheeseburger (a standardized commodity) anywhere in the world. However, it may not be legal to resell the cheeseburger if selling food requires a license. Additionally, a typical benchmark for "giving up substantial value" is 10 percent of the value of the asset. Avoiding a 10% loss might not be possible in the cheeseburger resale market.

For an asset to be tradable, it also needs to be interchangeable with other assets of the same type. Otherwise, there will typically be some subjective value assigned to the asset. For example, a unique piece of framed art might be sellable. However, the value of the art and the time frame needed to arrange a sale would depend on the unique characteristics of the art. When assets are interchangeable with other assets of the same type, they are said to be *fungible*. In the example, the framed art is a nonfungible asset because it is not interchangeable with other art. Some other examples of nonfungible assets are property and intellectual property such as patents.

Category	Financial Instruments	Created by
Real Assets	Physical commodities Real estate Emissions rights Patents	Mining, oil drilling, farming Builders Governments Inventors
Financial Assets	Stocks Bonds Currencies	Incorporation of a company Borrowing Governments
Derivatives	Futures Forwards Swaps Options	Trading Trading Trading Trading

Figure 1.2.2 Types of financial instruments

Additionally, it is necessary to consider how much time will be needed to convert the asset into cash or vice versa. This is called the *liquidity* of the asset. A *liquid market* allows an asset to be easily converted into cash, or a liability to be removed by paying cash, without a significant loss of money. Typically, liquid markets have low transaction costs and low volatility, and it is easy to execute a trade at a favorable price. An *illiquid market* does not allow easy trading. Typically, an illiquid market requires the trader to spend a substantial amount of time finding a trading partner or to take an unfavorable price.

Common Terms

To be tradable, assets must have certain features like assignability, liquidity, and fungibility.

Assignability. Assignability means that an asset or liability can legally be transferred to another person.

Liquidity. Liquidity describes the ability to convert an asset or liability into cash (or vice versa) in a reasonable amount of time without incurring too much cost. Typically, a liquid market means that it is possible to make a round-trip transaction (both buying and selling) during a single business day and not suffer a loss of more than 10 percent of the item's value.

Fungibility. Fungibility describes the ability of an asset to be interchanged with similar assets.

Real Assets

Real assets are properties that have value due to their substance or physical attributes. In the energy markets, many real assets are *tangible*—they can be touched and manipulated. For example, oil, land, drilling equipment, refineries, power lines, and power generation facilities are tangible real assets. There are some real assets that don't have physical form. These are less commonly found in energy markets and are called *intangible assets*. Some examples of intangible real assets are patents, advertising trademarks, and works of art.

Real assets are traded in spot markets. Due to the complexity in storing and transporting physical products, the trading market for real assets is limited. Real asset transactions tend to be one-directional—a buyer will purchase from a seller to use the asset, not to resell the asset. Most commodity trading is actually done in the derivatives markets discussed below.

Financial Assets

Financial assets represent ownership of real assets or cash flows created by real assets. The primary difference between financial assets and real assets is that financial assets are created by issuers. The two most common types of financial assets are stocks and bonds. These are important markets, but not the focus of this book.

- **Stocks.** A stock is a financial instrument that provides an ownership share in a company.
- **Bonds.** A bond is a debt investment (a loan to a company) that the company has to be repay after a fixed amount of time along with any accrued interest.

Derivatives

In the energy market, the most commonly traded type of financial instruments is a *derivative*. A derivative is a financial contract whose value is based on the value of some other asset. Some common types of derivatives are futures, forwards, swaps, and option contracts. For example, a contract to buy crude oil in the future is a derivative since it is a contract whose value is based on a real asset. If a crude oil contract is traded, only the contract and its associated obligations are transferred—the crude oil does not change hands at that time. The crude oil is only delivered when the contract is exercised.

The value of a derivative is the price where someone is willing to transfer a piece of paper (a contract) to someone else. In other words, trading markets are largely composed of people transferring obligations to do things in the future rather than transferring physical commodities.

From a terminology perspective, the asset that determines that value of the derivative is called an *underlying asset*. Commonly, this underlying asset is a real asset like crude oil or electricity. However, derivatives can also be based on other derivatives. For example, it is possible to buy an option on a forward contract.

Derivatives are defined by accounting guidance and have several important features:

- The underlying asset in a derivative transaction needs to be liquid and tradable.
- A derivative is created by an agreement between the buyer and seller. This agreement forms a legally binding contract and the price of the derivative is the money that would need to be paid or received to transfer the contract to another person.

- A derivative will not create wealth. It will only transfer wealth between buyer and seller or vice versa (this is called a *payoff*). Because of this, derivatives need both a buyer and a seller.
- Derivatives have a limited life span. At some point, the derivative will expire. Usually this triggers the transfer of wealth or physical assets between the buyer and seller.
- The amount of wealth transferred, and the direction of the transfer, will usually depend on something that hasn't occurred at the time that the derivative was created. The derivative contract will state the rules for determining this quantity.

First, to be considered a derivative, the underlying asset in a contract has to be tradable. The accounting term that means tradable is *readily convertible to cash* (RCC). This means that it must be possible to both buy and sell the asset in a reasonable amount of time without losing more than 10 percent of the value in transaction costs.

A second feature of derivatives is that they are created by trading. This means that two parties (usually a buyer and a seller) are required to create a derivative. To create a derivative, the buyer and seller sign a written contract agreeing to transfer money between themselves. The profit made by one has to be paid by the other. A written contract between the two defines all of the terms of their agreement. Also, in some cases, the terms *buyer* and *seller* don't really describe the relationship between the two traders. If that happens, the two traders are typically referred to as "Party A" and "Party B." Either way, the obligations of the traders are fully described in the contract.

The price of a derivative is the cost to transfer the contract to another person. If the contract benefits the holder, then it is an asset and the owner would expect to get paid. If the contract does not benefit the holder, then it is a liability and the owner would have to pay someone to be free of the contract. Derivatives can fluctuate between being assets and liabilities. Quite often, derivatives are initially created at zero value.

Another feature of derivatives is that they have a limited life span. When a buyer and seller agree to the contract, they have to determine when they will need to fulfill their obligations to one another. The date that the obligations are finalized is called the *expiration date* or *expiry*. Shortly after that date, the buyer and seller will *settle* their obligations by paying cash or physically transferring the underlying commodity.

Finally, derivatives require some way to determine the relative obligations of the buyer and seller. This will be contractually agreed to in the contract in terms of fixed quantity of the underlying asset, known as the *notional* quantity, and price of the underlying.

TRADES AND POSITIONS

The process of completing a transaction is called *executing a trade*. After a trader executes a trade, the trader has a *position* in the commodity. A *trade* is a transaction; a *position* is the net exposure that results from one or more trades. For example, if a trader makes three transactions to buy crude oil, and one transaction to sell, the combination of all of those trades is known as a position. Positions are described by the terms *long* and *short*. When the trader benefits from a rise in the price of the commodity, he is said to have a long position. If the trader will benefit from a fall in the price of a commodity, he is said to have a short position.

Since trading typically involves the purchase and sale of contracts rather than physical commodity, different terms are used to distinguish between the trade and the result of the trade. For example, a trader might acquire a contract that requires the trader to sell something at a fixed price. If that sales price is above the prevailing market price, the contract would be an asset and would cost money to acquire. Conversely, if the sales price is below market, the contract would be a liability, and a trader would be paid money to acquire it.

A *long position* benefits from an increase in prices. For example, if a gasoline/crude oil spread is defined as the price of gasoline minus the price of oil, a long spread will benefit from a rise in gasoline prices or a fall in oil prices. In other words, the trader is long when he benefits from the spread growing larger. Long positions are commonly associated with owning an asset or agreeing to buy at a fixed price in the future.

A *short position* will benefit from a decrease in the value of the underlying. For example, a trader will be short crude oil if he has agreed to sell it to someone at a fixed price. The selling price is set, and the cheaper that the trader can obtain a supply, the greater the profit. As a result, the trader benefits from a fall in the price of crude oil. A short position is commonly associated with agreeing to sell a commodity at a fixed price in the future.

A trader can *liquidate* or *close out* a transaction by entering into an *offsetting* trade. Closing out a contract means to have no further risk or responsibility. In other words, closing out a trade means converting all positions to a liquid asset (cash).

A *flat position* is a combination of trades that is not affected by price movements. Quite commonly, it is impossible to close out a contract. For example, if the trade was a direct contractual agreement between two parties, both parties need to agree to dissolve the agreement. If a trader negotiated contracts to buy natural gas directly from one party and sold it to another, the trader is not necessarily free of his contractual obligations. The trader would still need to arrange receipt of the commodity from the first party and delivery to the second.

Finally, trades require both a buyer and a seller. These are called the *parties* to the transaction. From the perspective of each trader, the *counterparty* is the other trader involved in the transaction.

Long and Short Rather Than Buy and Sell

Traders tend to use the terms *long* and *short* to describe their positions since the terms *buying* and *selling* can refer to either the action of selling the contract or the action required by the contract. For example, it is possible to buy a contract that allows one to sell at an advantageous price.

- A **long position** always benefits from a rise in prices. Long positions are always indicated by a positive sign.
- A **short position** always benefits from a fall in prices. Short positions are always indicated by a negative sign.
- A **flat position** does not benefit from either rising or falling prices.

Always convert trades into LONG and SHORT positions. Don't rely on being able to mentally sort out buy and sell terminology as an indication of trading exposures.

BILATERAL, OVER THE COUNTER, AND EXCHANGE TRADING

There are two ways for energy products to be traded. It is possible for trades to be made directly between two parties or through an intermediary called an *exchange*. When trades are made directly between two counterparties, they are called *bilateral* or *over the counter* (OTC) transactions. When trades are made through an exchange, they are called *exchange-traded* transactions.

Bilateral and OTC Trades

Bilateral trades are direct contractual agreements between two parties. These trades involve signing a contract, or extending an existing contract, each and every time a trade is made. Like any other contract that two people might sign, traders depend on the creditworthiness and reliability of the other party. If one party goes bankrupt, there usually is no immediate recourse except to attend bankruptcy proceedings.

It can also be difficult to get out of a contractual agreement since both sides need to agree to modifications to the contract. An OTC trade is a type of bilateral agreement between a professional trading organization and a counterparty. The terms *bilateral* and *OTC* trading are largely interchangeable.

To simplify trading and contract negotiations, most bilateral agreements are based on a standard agreement produced by the International Swaps and Derivatives Association (ISDA). The most important feature of ISDA agreements is that all agreements between two parties made under an ISDA agreement form a single contract. This is important in bankruptcy cases because the credit risk under ISDA contracts is limited to the net amount of all contracts. For example, SolidGoldPower Inc. might have an agreement with Unreliable Corp. to receive 10 million MMBtus of natural gas and deliver 1 million MW/hours of power. If Unreliable Corporation went bankrupt and the trades were not combined into a single contract, Unreliable Corporation's liabilities (its delivery of natural gas to SolidGoldPower Inc.) would be frozen by the bankruptcy court, but SolidGoldPower Inc. would still be required to deliver power to Unreliable Corporation. This would be disastrous to SolidGoldPower Inc. It would need to find another supplier of natural gas, pay the costs to arrange last-minute delivery, and then give all of its electrical output to Unreliable Corporation. When the contracts are netted, Unreliable Corporation is required to deliver the natural gas if it wants to receive the electricity because it can't selectively freeze line items in a contract.

Companies with weaker credit will often need to offer collateral or insure their credit quality in order to convince others to trade with them. *Collateral* is money pledged as security. *Credit-default swaps* (CDSs) provide insurance against contractual defaults. A CDS allows a party with poor credit quality to buy insurance from someone with better credit quality. Essentially, this swaps the credit quality of the poor credit risk for someone with higher credit risk. It is important to note that CDS trades do not completely eliminate credit risk. There is still the possibility that neither the CDS buyer nor the issuer of the CDS will be able to meet their obligations.

Some of the major downsides of OTC agreements are the credit risk, contractual paperwork, and difficulty in initiating and liquidating trades.

Exchanges

Because of the difficulties associated with direct contracts, the number of people who can enter into OTC trades is often very limited. To make the markets more accessible to a wider audience, trading is often done on an exchange. Exchanges act as an intermediary where both sides of a trade agree to a transaction, but instead of transacting with one another, they enter into agreements with the exchange. This eliminates the counterparty risk associated with directly trading with a counterparty and makes it easier to buy and sell contracts.

For example, if a small hedge fund, GetRichNow Partners, wants to purchase a financial electricity contract in the OTC market, it would need to sign an ISDA agreement with all of its potential trading partners before entering into any trades. It would be an overwhelming job to sign agreements with every other small hedge fund on the speculation that someday a trade might occur. This would make it very difficult for the hedge fund to carry on its business of trading quickly.

With an exchange, much of that paperwork can be eliminated. Everyone who wants to trade can sign a single agreement with the exchange. This also allows traders to monitor the credit risk of a single counterparty, the exchange, for potential risk exposures. Even better, since exchanges are required to have solid financial backing for their commitments and can protect themselves by requiring that every trader submits a good-faith deposit, called *margin*, they are generally a very safe counterparty.

Exchanges make it much easier to enter and exit trades and allow anonymous trading. Entering and exiting a trade doesn't leave any residual credit risk to other people. Additionally, since all trades are made with the exchange, it isn't necessary to know the financial details of other traders or have them know your details. It is even possible to transact anonymously using a broker. The trades will be reported with the broker's ID rather than the trader. Only the broker will know who initiated the trade.

The primary limitation on exchanges is that they can't offer a lot of choices for contracts. To appeal to a large audience, contracts have to be standardized. Typically, there will only be a couple of contracts on each commodity. For example, all NYMEX natural gas contracts specify delivery at the Henry Hub in south-central Louisiana. This means that while there is a large liquid market for the Henry Hub contract, arranging for delivery in New York City isn't so easy.

In practice, traders tend to use exchange-traded contracts as much as possible. For things they can't do on an exchange, they will then try to arrange OTC trades.

Finally, it is important to note that while the exchange is the counterparty for every transaction, it is just matching up buyers and sellers. The exchange is only taking on the credit risk of each trade and not acting as a principal. The exchange protects itself by requiring traders to deposit good-faith deposits called *margin*. As a result, there will always be an equal number of buyers and sellers for each exchange-traded contract. Margin is described later in the chapter.

TYPES OF FINANCIAL INSTRUMENTS

Cash Transactions, Futures, Swaps, and Forwards

The four most common types of energy trades are *cash transactions*, *futures*, *swaps*, and *forwards*. Cash (or spot) transactions are an exchange of a physical commodity for cash in the spot market. Futures, swaps, and forwards are all contracts to buy an asset at a future date at a pre-arranged price. Futures are traded on an exchange. Swaps are financially settled contracts traded over the counter. Forwards are physically settled contracts traded over the counter. These contracts are similar, but have different names because of the substantial differences between OTC and exchange-traded markets.

- **Cash Transactions (Spot Transactions).** A cash, or spot, transaction is an exchange of cash for immediate delivery of a commodity. The definition of *immediate* varies by commodity—with oil it might mean within the current month while with natural gas it might be within the day.
- **Futures.** A future is a standardized commodity contract traded on an exchange. Futures will typically require traders to post a good-faith deposit, called *margin*, to transact. Futures will also result in physical delivery of a commodity if the contract is held until the expiration date.
- **Commodity Swaps.** A commodity swap is a futures or forward contract where the payment is settled in cash rather than physical delivery. In other financial markets, like the bond market, the term *swap* may refer to very different products, but in the energy markets swaps are financially settled contracts.
- **Forwards.** A forward is similar to a futures contract except that it is negotiated directly between two traders rather than being transacted on an exchange. Theoretically, because they are individually negotiated, forwards can be more customized than futures. In practice, forwards are nearly as standardized. Like futures contracts, forwards involve physical delivery.

Futures, forwards, and commodity swaps all have many features in common. They are all financial contracts between two parties to buy or sell a specific amount of a commodity for a fixed price (the *strike price*) at some point in the future (the *expiration date*). Other than a refundable good-faith deposit (called *margin*), these contracts don't cost any money up front.

Features of Futures, Forwards, and Commodity Swaps

Futures, forwards, and swaps have common features to define the asset being traded and other information relevant to trading.

- **Underlying Asset.** All futures, forwards, and swaps are based on some underlying asset. For example, a forward might be based on crude oil.
- **Strike Price.** The price that will be paid in the future to take delivery of the commodity. Alternately, the price at which the deal was struck.
- **Notional Quantity.** Quantity describes the amount of the underlying commodity that needs to be delivered upon expiration of the contract.
- **Currency.** The contract will specify which currency must be used by the buyer to pay the seller.
- **Grade (Quality).** The quality of the commodity will be specified. For example, crude oil will specify an acceptable Sulphur content and density.
- **Location.** The delivery location and the acceptable manner of delivery will be specified in the futures contract.
- **Expiration Date.** The expiration date is the last date at which the obligations imposed by the contract can be transferred to another party.

Futures

Futures are highly standardized contracts traded on an exchange. They have a limited number of product grades, delivery locations, and delivery times. The commodity must be delivered at the time specified by the exchange, in the location specified by the exchange, and at the quality level (grade) specified by the exchange. The possible permutations of these factors are very limited. Additionally, when futures settle, the counterparty for the delivery will be chosen by a *clearinghouse*. Exchange rules will determine how the buyers and sellers are matched up.

When transacting on an exchange, traders can submit instructions indicating their willingness to buy and sell. The exchange will then consolidate all of these orders into a trading book. Whenever there is an overlap between the prices where someone is willing to buy and the

Figure 1.2.3 An exchange

prices where someone else is willing to sell, a transaction will occur. Throughout this process, the buyer and seller don't know the identity of one another. After the transaction, the exchange will serve as the counterparty for each trader (Figure 1.2.3).

By acting as an intermediary, the exchange takes on the obligation for the trade should one of the traders not fulfill their obligations. To minimize this risk, exchanges will require that every trader post a certain amount of collateral, called an *initial margin*, on the trade date. *Margin* is a good-faith deposit required by the exchange to ensure that traders meet their obligations. It is not a down payment nor is it representative of the trader's position in the actual commodity. Margin is insurance for the exchange in case a trader can't meet their obligations. The initial margin will usually be large enough to cover a large one-day movement in the price of a commodity (typically 5 to 10 percent of the price).

After the transaction, there will be daily adjustments to the good-faith deposit based on the daily change in price of a commodity. Essentially, the daily adjustment will transfer money between traders. Every day, traders on the unprofitable trade will need to deposit more money into their margin accounts. That money will be paid into the accounts of the traders on the profitable side of the trade. Those traders can then remove the money and spend it. The exchange's clearinghouse is responsible for handling all the debits or credits applied to each account.

Individual traders will commonly not transact directly with an exchange. Instead, they will authorize a broker to transact on their behalf. In this case, the exchange will charge the broker margin. Brokers will typically pass those costs along to their clients. As a result, even though clearing margins charged by an exchange are distinct from customer margins charged by brokers, they serve much the same purpose.

Common Terms

Initial Margin. Initial margin is the amount of money needed to establish a futures position. Money in a margin account in excess of the initial margin required for open positions can be withdrawn from the account or used to open new positions. This excess money is called *excess equity* although it is not technically an equity (ownership) position.

Daily Margin. On a daily basis, the exchange will settle all future positions, marking the position to market prices. Essentially, this is similar to closing out the trade and reopening it at a new strike price. The net proceeds will be credited or debited to each margin account.

Margin Call. If the daily margining has resulted in excess money in a margin account, it can be withdrawn. If the amount of money in the margin account has fallen too low, more money will need to be deposited. A *margin call* will alert the trader that additional money needs to be deposited into the account.

For example, let's say a trader buys a futures contract for a 10,000 MMBtus of Natural Gas for December delivery priced at $6.35. The total value of the contract is $63,500 with an initial margin set by the exchange of $6,750. The trader will have to deposit that initial margin into a *margin account*. When the trader closes his position, he will get that deposit back. The next day, the price of oil falls by $0.15, giving the trader a loss of $1,500. That means the trader will have to deposit an additional $1,500 ($0.15 loss × 10,000 units) into his account. That $1,500 will be transferred into the margin account of some trader holding the other side of the position. The trader will not get back the daily margin when the account is closed. If instead of falling, the market raised $0.25, the trader would have received $2,500.

Every day, futures are assigned a price, called a *settlement price* or *closing price*, that determines whether the commodity moved up or down in price. This price is the same for both buyers and sellers. It determines whether each trader will pay or receive money through the process of daily margining. Every time the official settlement price of an asset changes, there will need to be a transfer of money. Essentially, the trades are closed and reopened every day.

Because of daily margining, a future contract is characterized by a series of small payments throughout the life of the contract. Every day, a little bit of money is transferred between the buyers and sellers of the contract. In contrast, OTC forwards typically don't require money to change hands until the day of delivery. At that point, if the trade is financially settled, forwards will involve a single large transfer of money. If the forward trade is physically settled, it will involve an exchange of money for a physical product.

From the standpoint of an exchange, daily margining limits the exchange's exposure to counterparty risk. Since the mark-to-market price should give a fair indication of where trading occurs, the exchange only needs to cover the risk of holding an asset for a single day.

For example, if a trader fails to make a daily margin call, the exchange can take ownership of that futures contract and the initial margin supporting that contract. It will then liquidate the contract and keep the initial margin. As long as the initial margin covers the one-day loss the exchange is taking on the deal, the exchange will make a profit from the liquidation.

Since the risk taken on by the exchange is proportional to the daily price moves, initial margins will be higher on more volatile commodities. Generally, the initial margin will be slightly larger than the biggest one-day move expected in a commodity. It can also be based on the perceived creditworthiness of traders. Small traders, or those without strong credit, might be asked to submit a larger good-faith deposit than large traders or those with strong credit.

From a trading perspective, futures are typically used as industry benchmarks. As a result, many futures are liquidated prior to delivery. This allows them to have the benefits of trading without the hassle of physical delivery. Alternately, traders can negotiate their own delivery terms with other traders. If they do this, they will need to submit a contract called an *exchange for principal* (EFP) to the exchange. This exchange will then allow the traders to pair with one another for delivery.

Key Concepts

Futures. Futures are standardized contracts that allow traders to transact for future delivery. They are typically margined and cash settled on a daily basis until the final delivery date.

- **Anonymous Trading.** Futures allow anonymous trading since the exchange acts as an intermediary between buyer and seller.
- **No Credit Risk.** Futures are margined. As a result, there is minimal or no credit risk associated with futures.
- **Daily Margining.** The daily settlement process can create cash flows throughout the life of the contract. This is generally a negative. If money has to be paid, the trader will be responsible for coming up with the money prior to delivery. If money is received, then it will have to be invested somewhere.
- **Liquidation Prior to Delivery.** Most futures are liquidated prior to physical delivery.

Exchange for Physical. EFPs allow traders to negotiate an exchange of physical commodity for a futures contract. This provides traders an alternative to settling the futures at the exchange delivery point. It also allows them to deliver a slightly different product. After negotiating an

EFP in the OTC market, the completed contract can be delivered to the exchange.

- **Delivery Location**. The parties to an EFP must agree on a delivery location and delivery process.
- **Price Differential**. The parties to an EFP must also agree on whether a price adjustment needs to be made to account for differences between the futures delivery location and the physical delivery location.

Exchange for Physical

An EFP is a transaction where one trader will give another trader futures contracts in exchange for physical gas or crude oil. One of the traders (the one who wants to buy the commodity) will need a long futures position. The other trader (the one who wants to sell the commodity) will need a short futures position. The trader with the long position will give his long position to the trader with the short position, cancelling out both positions. The trader with the short position will then deliver the physical commodity to the trader with the long position in exchange for a mutually agreed upon payment.

Using an EFP allows traders to use futures to transact at a location (like New York) that is different than the futures settlement location. The process for settling futures with an EFP is:

1. The trader who wants to purchase the physical commodity will transfer futures (valued at the latest settlement price on the exchange) to the trader who wants to sell the physical commodity. This will cancel out the futures positions of both traders.
2. The trader who wants to purchase the physical commodity will receive the agreed upon physical commodity at an agreed upon location.
3. The trader who wants to purchase the physical commodity will pay the seller for the physical commodity. This price is typically quoted in two parts—the settlement price for the futures and a differential (a *basis price*) to the futures price.

From a trading perspective, EFPs are negotiated bilaterally but executed on an exchange. Some common points that have to be negotiated are the location of the delivery, the price adjustment that needs to be made, and whether the commodity being delivered will vary from the standard for the futures contract.

Exchange for Principal Transaction

An EFP transaction allows traders using futures to customize the commodity being delivered to their needs. These trades are negotiated off the exchange—traders have to find a willing counterparty on their own. Then, the transaction can be cleared on the exchange. Some commonly found features in an EFP confirmation are:

- **Commodity.** The commodity description on the trade confirmation will describe the physical commodity being transferred. This will be negotiated as part of the EFP if there are any differences between the physical commodity that will be delivered and the commodity underlying the futures contract.
- **Index Price.** The index price is the settlement price of the futures contract.
- **Differential (Basis Price).** The difference in value between the price of the futures and the value of the physical commodity. This differential could be a positive adjustment, a negative adjustment, or no adjustment to the price. This is negotiated as part of the EFP.
- **Invoice Price.** The invoice price is the sum of the index price and the basis price. This is the amount of money that the buyer will need to pay the seller upon receipt of the physical commodity.
- **Delivery Point.** The delivery point describes the location where the physical commodity will be transferred from the seller to the buyer. This is negotiated as part of the EFP.
- **Volume.** The volume will describe the quantity of physical commodity that will be transferred. This might be described as either total volume or volume per day (if delivery takes place over more than one day). This might also be described in terms of how many futures are involved in the transaction.
- **Delivery Date.** The delivery date will describe when the physical commodity will be transferred from the seller to the buyer. This might be a single date or a period of time. For example, natural gas might be transferred over a month with an equal volume transferred every day.

Forwards and Swaps

Forwards are trading contracts negotiated directly between two traders (i.e., a bilateral or OTC transaction). A *swap* is a general term for any agreement between two parties that obligates them to exchange something in the future. The term *swap* can be used to describe many different types of financial transactions. In the energy market, *swap* is most commonly used to describe a forward trade that settles in cash rather than by delivery of a physical commodity.

Like futures, forwards and commodity swaps allow traders to arrange a transaction at a specific time and place in the future for a contractually identified price. The major difference is that forwards and swaps are bilaterally negotiated rather than being cleared on an exchange. Negotiating a contract directly has both advantages and disadvantages. The biggest disadvantage is that both parties are at risk that their counterparty won't deliver on its obligation.

Key Concepts

Forwards. Forwards are physically settled contracts similar to futures except that they are bilaterally negotiated instead of exchange cleared.

Commodity Swap. A commodity swap is a contract very similar to a forward except that it is financially settled rather than physically settled. In other financial markets, the term *swap* can refer to a variety of other contracts.

Some key features of forwards and commodity swaps include:

- **Private Contracts.** Since forwards and swaps are negotiated with a specific counterparty, an offsetting transaction must be made with the original counterparty to exit the transaction.
- **Credit Risk.** All bilateral contracts, which include swaps and forwards, require the other trader (the counterparty) to meet their obligations.
- **Settlement at Delivery.** Forwards and swaps are typically traded at zero value by setting the strike price equal to the prevailing price at the time of delivery. Usually, there is no cash flow prior to delivery.
- **Margin.** Either, or both, traders can agree to post margin. If this is done, it is typically negotiated prior to trading in a master agreement that determines the rules followed by subsequent transactions.
- **Delivery Will Commonly Take Place.** Forwards will typically go through to physical delivery rather than being liquidated early. If the traders didn't want the physical commodity delivered, they would negotiate a commodity swap instead of a forward.

In theory, forwards and swaps can be highly customized and give the traders the ability to negotiate customized contracts for unique or illiquid products. In practice, most forwards are highly standardized with terms and conditions similar to futures contracts. They are traded under standard contractual terms like the ones specified in the ISDA's master agreement. A key term in this master agreement is a *master netting clause*. This clause specifies that all of the transactions between two parties will form a single contract. This prevents a bankruptcy court from enforcing some transactions and not others in event of a bankruptcy.

Trade Confirm:

Trader A agrees to purchase from Trader B

Trader A:	Allen
Trader B:	Barbara
Quantity:	65,000
Commodity:	Grade A quality widget fuel
Location:	Barge in NY Harbor
Strike Price:	$95/gallon
Trade Date:	June 1, 2016
Delivery Date:	December 1, 2016

Figure 1.2.4 Trade confirm

When forwards or commodity swaps are transacted, the transaction typically becomes an addendum to the master agreement and is documented as a short-form transaction (Figure 1.2.4). Occasionally, when two traders have never transacted with one another, all of the terms and conditions may be spelled out in the contract to create a long-form transaction. Short-form transactions are much more common than long-form transactions.

One of the major drawbacks to forward trades is the counterparty credit risk that comes from direct agreement between a buyer and a seller. To minimize credit risk, traders who are involved in forward trading may require margin or other guarantees (like evidence of a guaranteed line of credit from a bank) from the other trader in order to make a transaction. Another way to limit credit risk with forwards is to use an exchange-based OTC clearing service. With this type of service, the trading partners arrange the trade themselves and then record the trade with the exchange. The exchange becomes the counterparty to each trader, essentially converting the forward into a future (Figure 1.2.5).

Options

An option is another type of derivative contract. It gives the buyer of the contract the right, but not the obligation, to buy or sell something at some future date at a fixed price. The right to buy is called a *call*

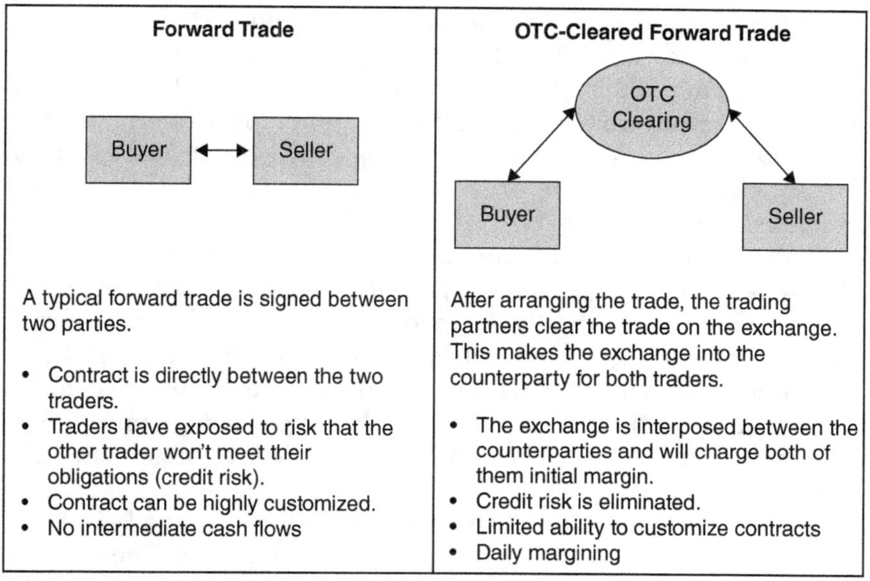

Figure 1.2.5 OTC clearing

option. The right to sell is called a *put option*. Options have an up-front cost, called a *premium*, which is paid when the buyer purchases the option. For the buyer, options have limited downside risk. Buyers will either lose their premium or they will make a profit.

In many ways, options are similar to futures, forwards, and swaps. However, unlike those instruments, the buyer of an option does not have to exercise his or her right to buy or sell. Options provide a way to ensure a worst-case price of an asset in exchange for an up-front premium. This premium can be very expensive. As a rule of thumb, buying options frequently loses money but occasionally makes a big profit. Selling options gives the opposite payout—a steady stream of small profits interrupted by occasional large losses.

TIME VALUE OF MONEY

Money in hand is almost always worth more than a promise of money in the future. For example, after winning the lottery, given the option of receiving payment of $10 million today or receiving the same amount of money 10 years in the future, most people would rather get paid today. Even if both payments were absolutely guaranteed, the ability to invest the money and spend the money today makes it a better alternative.

It would be a much tougher decision to choose between taking $10 million today and $25 million in 10 years. Then, it would be necessary to compare the size of the later payment against the expected investment return from investing the $10 million. The lottery winner's expected return from his investments is called his *individual rate of return* (IRR). The consensus of every market participant's IRRs is called an *interest rate.*

Interest rates are a measure of the time value of money and quantify the relationship between the *present value* of money (the value of cash received today) and the *future value* of money (the value of cash received sometime in the future). For example, a 10 percent annual interest rate implies that the market consensus is that $100 in cash today is equivalent to $110 a year from now. Alternately, at the same interest rate, the present value of $100 a year from now is approximately $91 today.

A separate complication to interest rates is the likelihood of getting paid. As a result, there are many interest rates available. The primary difference between interest rates is who is responsible for paying the money in the future. The more likely the debtor is to meet his or her obligations, the lower the interest rate. An example of a very low risk investment might be U.S. Treasury bonds or the London Interbank Offered Rate (LIBOR). U.S. Treasury rates describe the interest rate that the U.S. government pays to borrow money. Another popular benchmark for interest rates is LIBOR, the rate at which major banks can borrow from one another (Figure 1.2.6).

Regardless of which interest rates are used, they all have several features in common. The first is that the rate varies depending on when the cash is expected. In general, the further off the expected payment, the less valuable it is in today's dollars. This isn't usually a linear process either. For example, the interest rate for receiving payment two years from now is usually not twice the interest rate received for a one-year delay (Figure 1.2.7).

Interest rates, the shape of the interest rate curve, and the relative importance of credit quality all change over time. For example, a sharply sloping interest rate curve will typically occur when investors want their money immediately. If current investment opportunities are considered especially promising, having money today would allow investors to benefit from those opportunities. As a result, a very steep yield curve generally indicates a very positive outlook for the economy. In contrast, a flat yield curve generally indicates a negative outlook on the economy—investors are more willing to wait for their money if they don't have any good investing opportunities (Figure 1.2.8).

FEDERAL RESERVE statistical release

H.15 (519) SELECTED INTEREST RATES For use at 2:30 p.m. Eastern Time

Yields in percent per annum May 23, 2016

Instruments	2016 May 16	2016 May 17	2016 May 18	2016 May 19	2016 May 20	Week Ending May 20	Week Ending May 13	2016 Apr
Federal funds (effective)[1 2 3]	0.37	0.37	0.37	0.37	0.37	0.37	0.37	0.37
Commercial Paper[3 4 5 6]								
Nonfinancial								
1-month	0.34	0.36	0.33	0.36	0.36	0.35	0.34	0.35
2-month	0.41	0.44	0.38	0.40	0.42	0.41	0.41	0.39
3-month	0.49	0.52	0.47	0.50	0.49	0.49	0.48	0.48
Financial								
1-month	n.a.	0.28	0.39	0.42	n.a.	0.36	0.37	0.41
2-month	0.44	0.39	0.40	n.a.	n.a.	0.41	0.46	0.47
3-month	0.54	0.55	0.47	0.56	0.60	0.54	0.54	0.55
Eurodollar deposits (London)[3 7]								
1-month	0.48	0.48	0.48	0.48	0.48	0.48	0.48	0.48
3-month	0.65	0.65	0.65	0.65	0.65	0.65	0.65	0.65
6-month	0.93	0.93	0.93	0.93	0.93	0.93	0.93	0.93
Bank prime loan[2 3 8]	3.50	3.50	3.50	3.50	3.50	3.50	3.50	3.50
Discount window primary credit[2 9]	1.00	1.00	1.00	1.00	1.00	1.00	1.00	1.00
U.S. government securities								
Treasury bills (secondary market)[3 4]								
4-week	0.20	0.25	0.25	0.24	0.25	0.24	0.24	0.19
3-month	0.28	0.28	0.30	0.30	0.32	0.30	0.26	0.23
6-month	0.38	0.39	0.42	0.42	0.45	0.41	0.36	0.37
1-year	0.54	0.55	0.60	0.61	0.64	0.59	0.51	0.54
Treasury constant maturities								
Nominal[10]								
1-month	0.21	0.25	0.25	0.25	0.26	0.24	0.24	0.19
3-month	0.28	0.28	0.30	0.31	0.33	0.30	0.26	0.23
6-month	0.38	0.40	0.43	0.43	0.46	0.42	0.37	0.37
1-year	0.57	0.58	0.63	0.64	0.67	0.62	0.53	0.56
2-year	0.79	0.82	0.90	0.89	0.89	0.86	0.74	0.77
3-year	0.94	0.97	1.08	1.06	1.05	1.02	0.89	0.92
5-year	1.26	1.29	1.41	1.38	1.38	1.34	1.21	1.26
7-year	1.55	1.57	1.69	1.67	1.65	1.63	1.52	1.57
10-year	1.75	1.76	1.87	1.85	1.85	1.82	1.75	1.81
20-year	2.18	2.18	2.27	2.24	2.24	2.22	2.17	2.21
30-year	2.59	2.59	2.67	2.64	2.63	2.62	2.59	2.62
Inflation indexed[11]								
5-year	-0.27	-0.27	-0.13	-0.13	-0.13	-0.19	-0.31	-0.22
7-year	-0.08	-0.08	0.04	0.06	0.05	-0.00	-0.13	-0.03
10-year	0.15	0.15	0.26	0.29	0.29	0.23	0.15	0.19
20-year	0.59	0.57	0.70	0.69	0.70	0.65	0.58	0.60
30-year	0.82	0.80	0.88	0.88	0.89	0.85	0.83	0.86
Inflation-indexed long-term average[12]	0.62	0.61	0.70	0.71	0.71	0.67	0.63	0.67
Interest rate swaps[13]								
1-year	0.77	0.79	0.82	0.86	0.87	0.82	0.75	0.77
2-year	0.91	0.92	0.97	1.02	1.03	0.97	0.87	0.90
3-year	1.01	1.03	1.09	1.14	1.15	1.08	0.97	1.01
4-year	1.11	1.12	1.19	1.24	1.25	1.18	1.07	1.12
5-year	1.21	1.21	1.29	1.33	1.34	1.27	1.17	1.22
7-year	1.39	1.39	1.47	1.50	1.51	1.45	1.37	1.43
10-year	1.61	1.61	1.68	1.70	1.71	1.66	1.60	1.67
30-year	2.11	2.10	2.16	2.15	2.16	2.13	2.11	2.16
Corporate bonds								
Moody's seasoned								
Aaa[14]	3.62	3.61	3.71	3.66	3.67	3.65	3.63	3.62
Baa	4.65	4.65	4.74	4.70	4.71	4.69	4.64	4.79
State & local bonds[15]				3.26		3.26	3.32	3.30
Conventional mortgages[16]				3.58		3.58	3.57	3.61

See overleaf for footnotes.

n.a. Not available.

Figure 1.2.6 Federal Reserve Board H15 report

Likewise, it is possible for every interest rate to move up or down together. When all interest rates move together, it is called a *parallel shift* (Figure 1.2.9). Parallel shifts can occur because of concerns about credit quality or because a government is trying to inject money into or remove money from the economy. This generally indicates a large change in economic conditions.

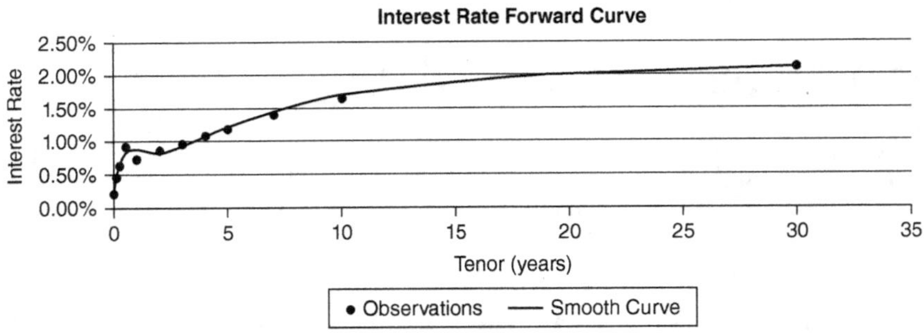

Figure 1.2.7 Interest rate curve

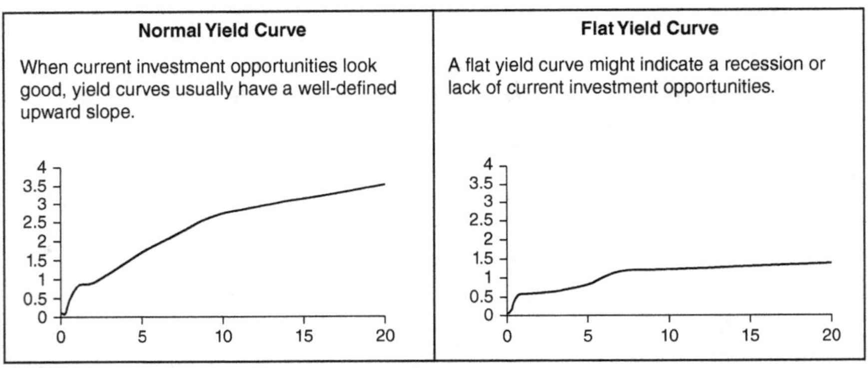

Figure 1.2.8 Normal and flat yield curves

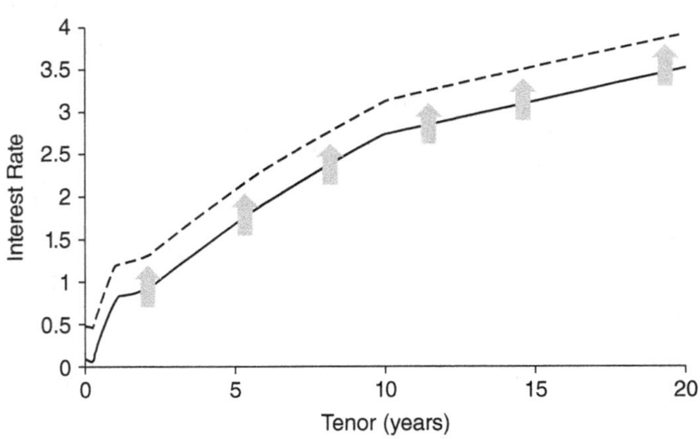

Figure 1.2.9 Parallel shift

Because they change over time, interest rates affect the value of cash flows that will be received in the future. For example, at a 10 percent annual interest rate, the present value of $1,000 received in five years is $621. Through the bond markets, it is possible to sell that $1,000 in exchange for cash. However, if interest rates drop to 5 percent, the present value of the $1,000 payment rises to $784.[1] For a trading company that routinely swaps its forward cash flows for money today, or vice versa, a change in interest rates represents an actual gain or loss in cash.

This is important to energy trading since most energy trades occur in the future. Interest rates have a big impact on the profitability of future cash flows. Going back to the previous section that discussed differences between futures and forwards, consider when these two instruments receive payments. A forward agreement has a single large cash flow that will occur at the end of the contract. In comparison, a futures trade will have small cash flows every day until maturity. The single large payment a long time in the future will be much more affected by interest rates than smaller payments occurring soon.

For small amounts of money, this effect might be small enough to ignore. For larger amounts of money, this can become a major source of risk. For example, a power company enters into a long-term contract to sell 500 megawatts of power an hour to an industrial facility between the hours of 7 a.m. and 11 p.m., five days a week, for 20 years. This is the output from just one fairly large power plant. If the price for a megawatt of power averages $75, that is a $3.1 billion exposure.

UNIQUE FEATURES OF THE ENERGY MARKET

Negative Prices

The established dogma in most trading markets is that prices can never be zero or negative. This isn't the case in the energy market. While zero or negative prices aren't especially common, they do occur. This can wreak havoc on many financial calculations. For example, in the stock market, a trader might remark that "the market is up 3 percent today." However, for an asset with a negative price, dividing by the previous price will give an undefined or misleading result if prices are zero or negative.[2]

---

[1] A future payment is essentially a bond. Bonds are more valuable when interest rates are low than when interest rates are high. Bond prices and interest rates move in opposite directions. The financial market that trades interest rates is called the Bond Market or the Fixed Income market.

[2] Negative prices break risk management systems. Finding the problems can take a long time and be extremely confusing if no one understands what happens with negative prices. Most people have a hard time grasping that a trading portfolio can be up 10 percent, lose a million dollars, and that the computer program calculating those numbers can be working as intended. In short, negative prices cause problems.

For example, if too much voltage is placed over a power line without any electricity being used, the power lines will melt. To incentivize power producers to decrease their power production, power grid operators sometimes make prices negative. Because of the costs associated with restarting power plants, many power plant operators would rather give power away for free than shut down their operations. Unfortunately, that preference can't be allowed to destroy a transmission grid, and that means that power producers need extra motivation sometimes. The common way to incentivize producers to shut down is to charge them for every megawatt of power that they produce. In periods of negative prices, consumers can actually get paid for turning on all their lights.

Cyclical Markets

As mentioned earlier, in markets where commodities are rarely created, are storable, and never get destroyed, forward prices are based on the cost of buying the commodity in the spot market and holding on to it. Particularly if the commodity produces a benefit from being stored, like stocks that produce dividends, forward prices will always be higher than spot prices.

In contrast, energy prices are based on an intersection of supply and demand. Storing energy costs money, and the value of storing it decreases the more easily energy can be produced in the future. Combined with the fact that energy is destroyed when it is used, the fundamental relationship between spot and forward prices in the energy market is vastly different than financial markets where a "buy and hold" strategy is viable.

Energy prices tend to be dominated by short-term supply and demand issues. For example, a natural gas refiner might not be able to cost-effectively shut down his plant for the weekend and restart on Monday. If the industrial steel plant that uses the natural gas doesn't operate on the weekend, there will be a surplus of gas on the weekends. Unless someone else can use it, or there is enough storage available, the price of natural gas on the weekend will be very low. The refiner will take whatever he can get paid rather than destroy the gas that is being produced. It doesn't matter whether the world will run low on natural gas in 20 years. Today's price is set by today's supply and demand considerations.

As a result, because prices are related to supply and demand, the future prices of many energy products tend to look cyclical (Figure 1.2.10).

Buy and Hold Markets

In markets where a buy and hold arbitrage is possible, futures prices tend to slope upward from the spot price and the spot price incorporates expectations of future price moves.

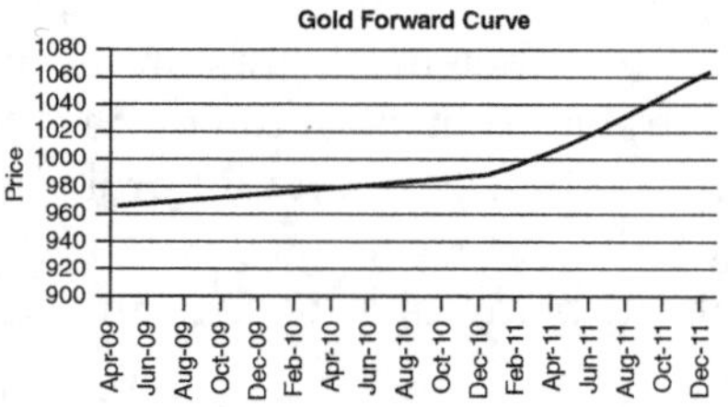

A steadily ascending forward price is typical of a buy and hold market.

Cyclical Markets

In many energy markets, it is not possible to store commodities easily. As a result, forward prices tend to be cyclical. In the natural gas graph, prices are high in the winter and are low in the spring, summer, and fall of each year.

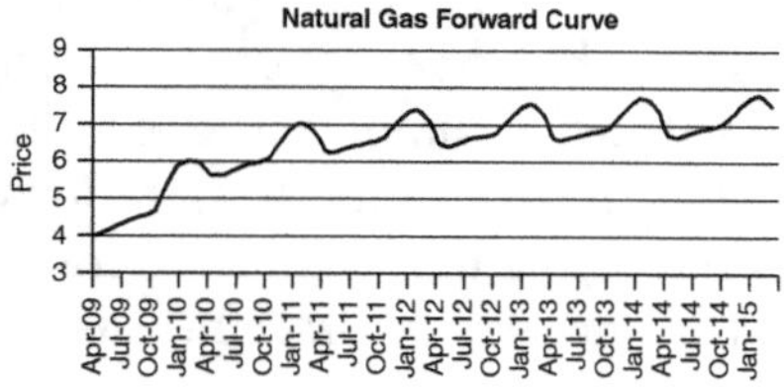

A cyclical, bumpy forward price curve is typical of energy commodities.

Figure 1.2.10 Cyclical markets

Illiquidity

In *liquid* markets, it is easy for buyers and sellers to meet one another. It is also relatively easy to convert a financial instrument or commodity into cash. As a general rule, it is a mistake to assume that energy markets will be liquid. One reason for illiquidity is the prevalence in directly negotiated contracts. Even exchange-traded contracts can become illiquid more than a couple years into the future. For example, the NYMEX WTI Crude Oil contract is one of the most liquid contracts in the world. Most of the volume is observed in the first three delivery months and it trails off quickly after that (Figure 1.2.11).

Another reason is the importance of time and location to energy products. If an owner of an industrial facility in Alaska wants to lock

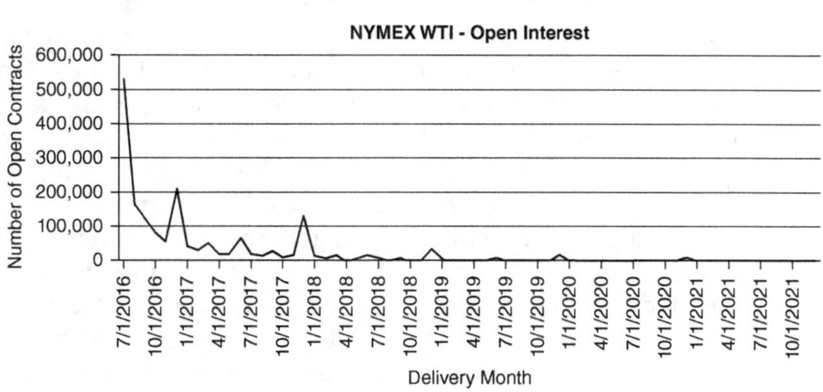

Figure 1.2.11 NYMEX WTI open interest

in power prices, there are a limited number of parties that can actually deliver power to that location. There are no exchange-traded contracts that settle nearby, so it will be necessary to find someone willing to make a bilateral transaction. For example, an electrical marketer might trade with the industrial facility for a large enough expected profit. However, if that marketer wanted out of the position, there wouldn't be anyone left to transact with. Other marketers are going to be afraid of making trades with the first marketer—if the trade is so good, why would the first trader want out of it? And, it will probably be impossible to unwind the trade with the industrial facility—the industrial facility is probably happy about being able to lock in their power prices.

Finally, another issue related to liquidity is that energy market participants tend to react as a group. For example, it is not unusual for all petroleum refiners or all power plant owners to come to approximately the same conclusions about the direction of the market at the same time. This creates a problem for trading since a liquid trading market requires both buyers and sellers, preferably in equal numbers. If everyone makes the same decision at the same time, there isn't any trading.

Price Transparency

Compounding the problem of illiquid markets is the problem that accurate pricing information commonly does not exist. Unless trades are made on an exchange, energy trades are private contracts between two parties. Neither party is under an obligation to make those prices public. Quite often, energy traders consider pricing information to be competitively sensitive and actively discourage price dissemination.

A number of companies provide estimates of OTC pricing. These estimates are not actual prices, rather they are indicative prices that indicate where trades might be made. The data for these estimates come from surveys. Historically, traders would often be caught providing misleading data on prices in an attempt to influence trading. The Federal Energy Regulatory Commission (FERC), the government agency that regulates energy trading, has since cracked down on the practice. However, if trading hasn't occurred in a region recently, estimating the likely cost of executing a trade can still be extremely difficult. If the trade is initiated by a motivated buyer, the price may be a lot higher than expected. Similarly, if a seller is highly motivated to complete a transaction in a particular region, prices may be a lot lower than previously estimated.

Outright and Spread Trades

An *outright* position in a commodity is a bet that it will go up or down in price. For example, an outright position in electricity is a bet that electricity prices are going to rise in the future relative to current expectations of future prices.

Spread trades are an alternative way of making energy trades. *Spread trades* involve a simultaneous purchase and sale of related products as with buying natural gas and selling electrical power, or agreeing to buy natural gas in Louisiana and to sell in New York. In the first case, buying gas and selling power allows the trader to benefit if the price of electricity rises faster than the price of fuel used for power generation. In the second case, the trader will benefit if the regional price of natural gas in New York, a major consuming region, rises relative to the price of natural gas in a producing region. In both cases, the trader is relatively insulated from the actual direction of energy prices. This allows the trader to concentrate on the relationship between the two prices rather than the price of energy as a whole.

Compared to other markets, a very high proportion of energy trades are spread trades. The combined volatility of a simultaneous purchase and sale of related commodities is typically much lower than the volatility of an outright position. Since margin costs are proportional to the risk of holding a position, spread trades (trading two instruments simultaneously) can actually be cheaper than owning an outright position. Offsetting trades in one financial instrument with trades in a related financial instrument is called *hedging*. Because of the popularity of spread trading, the most common spreads have specific names.

Spark spreads are the difference between the price of electricity and the price of natural gas. They approximate the profit that natural-gas-fired power plants make by burning natural gas to produce electricity. Natural gas plants determine the price of electricity in many regions.

Dark spreads are the difference between the price of electricity and the price of coal without considering emissions costs. Coal-based power plants set the price of power in some regions, and dark spreads are commonly used in conjunction with the trading of carbon dioxide emissions. Dark spreads approximate the profit from operating a coal-fired power plant.

Crack spreads are the difference between the prices of refined petroleum products (usually gasoline and heating oil) and crude oil. Most commonly, crack spreads are a three-commodity spread. Crack spreads approximate the profitability of a crude oil refinery.

Frac spreads are the difference between the prices of propane and natural gas. Natural gas wells are the primary source of propane. This spread approximates the profit from removing propane from a stream of natural gas.

Hedging

Hedging is a financial term that refers to reducing risk by taking a position that offsets the risk of an existing position. Hedging is often done when liquidating the original position is impossible or not desired. For example, if a trader has a long position through an OTC transaction, it is difficult to get out of that contract. He might hedge that position by the opposite position in an exchange-traded instrument.

In most cases, hedging is used to lock in profits or eliminate risk on an untradeable position. For example, a natural gas trader might agree to supply natural gas to a power plant in Florida for the next 10 years at a fixed price. Given the length of the contract, the natural gas marketer faces a huge risk from a rise in natural gas prices. The marketer is selling the gas at a fixed price but still must obtain the gas. If gas prices rise, the marketer could quickly find himself selling natural gas at a loss. The marketer doesn't want to get rid of the position, but neither does he want to be exposed to large price moves until he can line up a firm supply of gas. To reduce the risk of a rising commodity cost, the trader might decide to hedge that risk with natural gas futures. Since the futures don't deliver the gas to the right place, he can't use the futures to actually supply the gas. However, since most natural gas delivery locations are highly correlated in the futures market, he can use the futures to protect himself against a rise in natural gas prices.

Basis

Because spread trades are so common in the energy market, terminology related to spread trading has a different meaning than in other financial markets. In any financial market, the term *basis* refers to a spread between two prices. However, in most financial markets, *basis* refers to the difference in price between the cash price of a commodity (the spot price) and some forward price.

But, since the energy market doesn't have stable relationships between forward prices and spot prices, the term *basis* does not refer to a time effect. For example, in the energy market, the expected difference between the three-month forward price and the spot price will vary by season. Energy tends to be expensive in the summer and winter. It is inexpensive in the spring and fall. As a result, the rolling spot/forward relationship is just as cyclical as the prices.

Basis

In the natural gas market, *basis* refers to the difference in price between two physical trading locations. There is only one liquid trading location for natural gas—the Henry Hub (the NYMEX settlement location). Basis swaps allow users to use NYMEX futures and then exchange the Henry Hub price for the price at a different physical location.

Instead, in the energy market, the location of power is important. As a result, in the energy markets, particularly natural gas trading, the term *basis* refers to the difference between two locations. Since there is only a single delivery point for futures, the most common use for the term *basis* is to describe the difference in price of a specific location from the price at the futures delivery location.

Common Terms

Actual. A term that refers to a physical commodity. This term differentiates the actual commodity from financial contracts on that commodity. Since most energy trading occurs in the forward market, it is usually necessary to specify when the physical commodity is being traded. For example, "I bought 10,000 barrels of oil actuals; they are sitting on a tanker ship offshore Houston, Texas."

Cash Market. A market where cash is exchanged for the immediate delivery of a commodity. The terms *physical market*, *cash market*, and *spot market* are generally synonymous.

Counterparty Credit Risk. The financial risk due to uncertainty about a trading partner's ability to meet their financial obligations. Credit risk varies with the profitability of trades. As a trade becomes more profitable, the harder it becomes for the other party to meet that obligation. Similarly, there is very little credit risk with an unprofitable contract (you will always have to pay someone, even if your counterparty goes bankrupt).

Credit Default Swap (CDS). A credit default swap allows a party with poor credit quality to buy "credit insurance." CDS trades swap the credit quality of the credit risk for someone with better credit. CDS trades do not eliminate credit risk—there is still the possibility that the issuer of the CDS will not be able to meet their obligations.

Deregulated Market. This term refers to elimination of a government-created monopoly in order to introduce competition into a spot market. It most commonly refers to the break-up of government power generation monopolies in order to introduce competitive power markets.

(*Continued*)

Energy Information Agency (EIA). The branch of the U.S. government that produces official energy statistics.

Exchange. An exchange is any organization that maintains a marketplace where securities or commodities are traded. Securities traded on exchanges tend to be highly standardized. Exchanges act as the counterparty for all traders. They require that traders post margin as a good-faith deposit.

Federal Energy Regulatory Commission (FERC). The branch of the U.S. government responsible for regulating the interstate trading of energy products.

Financial Market. A market trading financial products like futures or forwards. Financial markets are different from markets where a physical commodity is exchanged for cash.

Forward. Forwards are OTC-traded contracts for the delivery of a product at a future date. These contracts are typically not margined and involve no cash flows prior to the delivery date. Most commonly, these are direct agreements between two parties and governed by the ISDA master agreement.

Forward Market. A market where the exchange of goods or services is arranged for a later date. Most energy trading is done in the forward market.

Fungible. A common financial term meaning a good or commodity that can be freely substituted for another unit of the same commodity. For example, a share of IBM stock is a fungible contract—any share of common stock can be exchanged for any other share of IBM common stock. A megawatt of power is not a fungible quantity—it is impossible to substitute a megawatt of power in New York for a megawatt of power in Los Angeles. However, a megawatt of power in New York Zone A delivered at 11 a.m. on Friday, December 5, 2008, is a fungible commodity.

Future. Futures are exchange-traded contracts for the delivery of a product at a future date. Typically, these contracts are freely tradable and require mark-to-market profits and losses be settled every day through margin payments.

Hedge. Offsetting positions that reduce the risk of the combined portfolio. Hedging is the act of making trades that offset the risk of current positions.

ISDA. The International Swap and Derivatives Association is an international trade association consisting of most major institutions that participate in privately negotiated derivatives contracts.

ISDA Agreement. A standard set of clauses included in almost all OTC contracts. Every contract using ISDA clauses refers to the ISDA master agreement. Changes to the ISDA master agreement affect all contracts that include ISDA clauses allowing these clauses to meet changing regulatory environments without causing the agreements to be renegotiated. The most important clause in the master agreement is the netting of positions provision. This substantially reduces the counterparty risk of privately negotiated derivatives deals.

Liquidity. A financial instrument is *liquid* if it can be easily exchanged for money or other financial products. A product is *illiquid* if it cannot be easily exchanged for cash or other financial products.

Long. A trading position where the trader benefits from an increase in the price of the position. Commonly, a long position involves *owning* an asset or commodity.

Margin. In the energy markets, the *initial margin* on a contract is a good-faith deposit of money that needs to be put down to enter into a deal. It is returned after the trade settles. *Daily margin* is a daily cash settlement of the change in price of the contract. The initial margin to enter a trade can vary depending on the trader, but everyone will pay (or receive) the same daily margin settlement depending on what side of the trade they are on.

Mark-to-Market (MTM). The process of assigning a price to a financial instrument or contract based on recent trades in similar instruments or contracts.

Natural Hedge. Positions that have not been taken on for the purpose of reducing risk but still have that effect. For example, a transportation contract to move natural gas from one location to another is naturally hedged against natural gas prices. The owner of the transportation contract is short natural gas at the source (he benefits from buying cheaply) and long natural gas at the destination (he benefits from selling at a high price). The combination of those two positions is a *natural hedge* against a change in natural gas prices since both the source and destination are likely to move up and down together.

Notional Value. The face value of a contract. For example, the notional value of an agreement to sell 1,000 barrels of oil at $80 is $80,000. The notional value of a contract does not generally change over the life of the contract, and may or may not have any relationship to either the trading profits or risk of a contract.

OTC. The over the counter market is the market for privately negotiated deals without the use of an exchange as an intermediary. OTC trades involve a high degree of credit risk but can be highly customized to meet specific trading requirements.

Physical Market. A market where cash is exchanged for the immediate delivery of a commodity. *Physical market*, *cash market*, and *spot market* are generally synonymous.

(*Continued*)

Position. The net amount of goods or services owned by an investor. Positions are described as *long* when the owner benefits from a rise in prices, and *short* when the owner benefits from a drop in prices.

Regulated Market. A term that describes a physical spot market dominated by a government monopoly. Regulated markets are still fairly common in local electrical markets.

Security. A fungible contract representing some financial value. This is a catch-all term describing almost any type of tradable contract, like a future, exchange-traded option. In contrast, OTC contracts are usually not considered securities because they can't be sold or exchanged without modifying the original agreement.

Short. A trading position is described as short when the trader benefits from a decline in the price of the position. Commonly, a short position involves *owing* someone an asset or commodity.

Spot Market. A market where cash is exchanged for the immediate delivery of a commodity. *Physical market, cash market,* and *spot market* are generally synonymous.

Trade. A trade is an exchange of goods or services.

1.3

Exploration and Production

30-Second Summary

Purpose

This chapter introduces conventional (fossil) fuels and how they are produced. It also discusses the relationship between solid, liquid, and gaseous fuels.

Summary

Fuels developed from organic sources, account for more than 90 percent of the world's energy. These fuels are composed of molecules containing hydrogen and carbon. As a result, they are often referred to by the name *hydrocarbons*. When organic fuels are obtained by extracting fuel located underground that has developed naturally over millions of years, these types of fuel are called *conventional fuel* or *fossil fuel*. These terms are used to differentiate organic fuels that are produced from newly grown crops which are called *biofuels*.

In their natural form, fossil fuels are a mixture of many different substances located underground. These mixtures have to be brought to the surface where they can be separated into substances like methane, gasoline, tar, and coal. Finding these resources and removing them from the ground is a complex job that is a major component of the energy industry.

Key Topics

- A large portion of the world's energy is produced from fossil fuel sources.
- Fossil fuels have to be located and then extracted from the ground before they can be used.
- Fossil fuels typically exist as a mixture that needs to be separated before it can be sold to consumers.

More than 90 percent of the world's energy is supplied by fossil and biofuels. These fuels are composed of molecules containing hydrogen and carbon and often are referred to by the name *hydrocarbons*. When combusted (combined with oxygen to produce a flame), these molecules produce heat that can be used to power engines or electrical generators. When obtained by exploration and production of existing resources, these types of fuel are called *conventional fuel* or *fossil fuel*.

Before they can be used, fossil fuels must first be found (exploration) and then brought to the surface (production). These are complex jobs that often require a company with a specific technical expertise (an exploration and production company) to work with the owner of the fuel (the mineral rights owner).

- **Exploration**. Fossil fuel exploration involves getting licenses to search for new resources, searching for fossil fuel resources, and then negotiating contracts with the owners of the mineral rights to extract the fuel from the ground.
- **Production**. Production involves extracting the fuel from the ground. This is typically done through drilling (for oil and gas) or mining (for coal).

After production, the fuels need to be separated from one another (in a process called *refining*) before they can be sold to consumers. There are a variety of hydrocarbon fuels, largely distinguished by the length of carbon chains in each molecule.

Hydrocarbon Fuels

The term *fuel* describes a wide variety of substances that can produce heat or power through a chemical or nuclear reaction. The most abundant type of fuel, called *conventional fuel*, is composed of hydrocarbons that produce energy when burned. This type of fuel is most commonly formed when decaying plant life has become trapped underground. The process of converting dead plants to fuel can take millions of years. Because of that, another term for conventional fuel produced from trapped, decayed plant life is *fossil fuel*. It is also possible to create fuels from recently grown plants; this fuel is called a *biofuel*.

In fuel molecules, carbon will form long chains, and the length of the carbon chain will determine the properties of the fuel (Figure 1.3.1). The typical notation to describe the length of a carbon chain is a capital C (the chemical symbol for Carbon) followed by a subscript that indicates the length of the chain. For example, C_5 indicates a hydrocarbon molecule with five carbon atoms. The shortest molecules, called *natural gases*, exist as gases at standard temperature and pressure. The mid-length molecules exist as liquids and are called *petroleum*. The longest chains are solids and are called *coal*.

To a large extent, even after processing, all fuels exist as a mixture of different hydrocarbons. Gasoline, for example, will predominantly contain hydrocarbon chains in the C_7 to C_{11} range. However, gasoline will also contain a portion of molecules on both ends of that range (C_5, C_6, C_{12}, C_{13}, and so on). The amount of gasoline composed of those

Name(s)	Typical Length of Carbon Chains	Description
Methane (Natural Gas)	C_1	Methane, also called natural gas, exists as a gas at room temperature. It is extensively used for home heating and electricity production.
Ethane	C_2	Ethane is a gas at room temperature. It is the first of the natural gas liquids, and has relatively few uses compared to other fuels.
Propane	C_3	Propane is gas at room temperature. It is considered a natural gas liquid. It is commonly used as a cooking fuel.
Butane, Iso-Butane	C_4	Butane is a gas at room temperature that will turn into a liquid under slight pressure. It is another natural gas liquid and is often used as a fuel for lighters.
Pentanes+, Naphtha	C_5 to C_7	Light, easily vaporized liquids that are often used as solvents. For example, naphtha is often used as dry cleaning fluid and paint thinner.
Gasoline	C_7 to C_{11}	Gasoline is a liquid fuel that is easily vaporized. The primary use for gasoline is as an automotive fuel.
Kerosene	C_{12} to C_{15}	Kerosene is a medium weight fuel commonly used for jet fuel.
Diesel, Heating Oil	C_{12} to C_{20}	Diesel (also called heating oil) is an automotive fuel that is heavier and less volatile than gasoline. In some areas, it is used as a fuel for home heating.
Heavy Fuel Oil	C_8 to C_{50}	Heavy fuel oil is less separated fuel commonly used as a fuel for seaborne shipping.
Lubricating Oils, Grease	C_{13} to C_{40}	Lubrication oils and grease are a mix of hydrocarbons. Each producer will produce a variety of lubrication oils that can range from liquid oil to semi-solid grease.
Paraffin Wax, Tar, Asphalt	C_{20} to C_{50}	Tar, asphalt, and wax are solids that are easily deformed when heated. A common use for these products is to make roads.
Coal	C_{50}+	Coal is a solid fuel that is most commonly burned to produce electricity.

Figure 1.3.1 Hydrocarbon fuels

lighter or heavier elements can vary substantially. Because of that, different countries, states, and even processing locations within states, may describe the carbon-chain makeup of each fuel slightly differently.

Exploration and Production Agreements

Because a high percentage of the Earth's energy is provided by fossil fuels, a major focus of the energy industry is in the exploration and production of fossil fuel resources. This requires identifying the location of potential resources and extracting them from the ground. It also requires working with the owners of the fuel to secure the rights to obtain fuel from wherever it is located.

Energy companies often will lease the property where fuel is located. They will remove the fuel from the ground and compensate both the party who owns the property and whoever owns the mineral rights to the fuel underneath the land. Land and mineral rights owners will typically get paid *royalties*, a percentage of the profit obtained by the production company.

The typical owners of the land and mineral rights will vary by location. For example, in the United States, the rights to fossil fuel resources located under the surface are often owned by private individuals. However, in most other countries, these resources are owned by the government. Regardless of who owns the land, exploration companies must typically get licenses before exploring for new resources. Then, once the resources have been identified, exploration companies will need other licenses to develop the resources for production.

The Landman

Landman is a term that refers to the men and women who negotiate titles and leases on the behalf of oil and gas exploration companies. For example, if an energy company is interested in developing a particular part of a country, it might assign a landman to identify and contact land owners to see who might be interested in selling their mineral rights. If they are interested, the landman would then also negotiate any necessary contracts.

Energy exploration and production can be extremely profitable. However, it is also a highly risky activity. First, finding and extracting fossil fuels from the ground is technically complex. Even when everything is going well, mechanical problems can cause problems. Unfortunately, things often do not go well. Sometimes exploration companies will take on a lease only to be unable to identify any fuel reserves. In other cases, energy companies can identify reserves but find the reserves uneconomic to extract. Finally, even if the reserves are originally profitable to extract, changing energy prices in the future can continue to impact profits. Exploration companies can find a reservoir of underground fuel and think it is profitable to extract, only to find that after they have drilled wells that prices have fallen.

Because of the uncertainty involved in energy exploration, there are a variety of contracts that can be used to limit the risk of various parties. The use of these contracts will depend on the interest and ability of the participants to take on the risk of developing fossil fuel reserves and the task of selling the fuel after it is extracted from the ground.

Some of the more common types of contracts are:

- **Tax and Royalty.** In a tax and royalty contract, the exploration company (the developer) will give the owner of the oil and gas rights an up-front licensing fee and a percentage of the gross profits. Because of this, the exploration company takes on all of the risk of developing the fuel resources although both parties are at risk of declining energy prices. Even so, the mineral rights owner will never have to pay money out of pocket—they are limited to lower profits. A typical contract in the United States will give the owner one-eighth of the gross profits.
- **Production Sharing.** In a production sharing contract, the exploration company gives the owner a percentage of the fossil fuels that are produced. The owner must then arrange to sell or use the fuel. This takes knowledge and the ability to handle physical energy transactions. However, because the landowner is taking on more risk, this can give him or her higher profits than tax and royalty contracts.
- **Service Contract.** With a service contract, the developer acts as a contractor and is paid a fee to produce oil and gas. The developer does not take ownership of the crude oil. Since most of the costs are paid by the owner of the mineral rights, this involves relatively little risk for the exploration and production company. This provides the highest risk, and greatest potential profit, to the owner of the land and mineral rights.

Traditional Wells

The traditional way of extracting gaseous and liquid hydrocarbon fuels from the ground is to drill a deep hole straight into the ground. If fossil fuels are located in the ground, temperature and pressure will force the fuel to the surface. There are three mechanisms that cause oil and gas to migrate to the surface—overpressure, heat, and buoyancy. Overpressure occurs when long chain hydrocarbons decay into shorter chain hydrocarbons. Since smaller hydrocarbons are less dense than larger hydrocarbons, they take up more space per unit of volume; this causes an increase in pressure. Second, oil and gas (and almost all other liquids and gases) expand when they get hot. This is important since temperatures deep in the Earth are higher than at the surface. Higher temperatures deep underground force hydrocarbons to the surface. Finally, buoyancy pushes oil and gas to the surface since hydrocarbons are less dense than most underground material like rock, decaying plant matter, or water.

Three Mechanisms Force Hydrocarbons to the Surface

The three mechanisms that force hydrocarbon fuel to the surface are:

- **Overpressure.** When plant matter decays, it breaks into shorter, less densely packed hydrocarbons. This increases the pressure in that area forcing hydrocarbons to migrate.
- **Heat.** Hydrocarbons also expand when they get hot. Even when this doesn't break the hydrocarbons into smaller, less dense chains, the increase in temperature further increases the pressure. Since deeper underground is hotter than the surface, this forces hydrocarbons upward.
- **Buoyancy.** Petroleum and natural gas are less dense than stone, water, or most everything else that is located underground. This creates a natural buoyancy.

Certain rock formations, like an impermeable layer of rock above a layer of decaying plant life, will cause a reservoir of petroleum or natural gas to form. Without this kind of barrier, the fuel would leak to the surface and eventually disperse. This gives geologists a target—they can search for specific types of rock formations. Currently, this is done by using seismic waves to create three-dimensional underground maps. Once promising areas are identified, test wells can be drilled to determine if they actually contain fuel.

Wells are created by drilling a hole into the Earth. This hole is typically between six inches and three feet in diameter (12 centimeters to 1 meter) and created by slowly lowering a drill bit into the ground. The drill bit is typically suspended by a hollow metal tube, called a *drill string*, which transfers both torque (rotational energy) and drilling fluid to the drill bit. *Drilling fluid* is a mixture of clay, water, and other chemicals used to keep the drill cool, remove bits of broken rock (*cuttings*), and maintain the proper pressure underground.

After the hole is drilled, steel pipes slightly smaller than the borehole are placed inside. The space between the pipe and the surrounding rock is then filled with cement. These pipes provide structural stability to the well and separate different underground pressure zones from each other. To maintain stability of the pipe under more increasingly stressful conditions, progressively smaller casings (and drill bits) are used. Modern oil wells may have as many as five levels of progressively smaller diameter pipes. This process is repeated several times until the rock layer containing the fuel is reached. At that point, a *perforating gun* is lowered into the well to punch holes through the steel casing and cement. This will allow petroleum or gas to flow into the well and come to the surface.

When operating the well, the driller depends on the pressure of the well to bring the fuel to the surface. Typically, wells produce most quickly when they are first produced; production declines over time. The well will eventually run dry when the pressure underground is not sufficient to bring additional fuel to the surface. Underground pressure can be augmented by pumping or introduction of various additives that increase underground pressure. Even so, traditional drilling works best for relatively low density crude oil or natural gas that can flow easily (Figure 1.3.2).

Gas and Oil Wells

The technology to produce both natural gas and oil wells is the same. All wells generally produce a mixture of both gas and oil, with the exact mixture varying from well to well. However, sometimes wells are described as gas wells or oil wells. The naming convention largely depends on whether the well produces more gas than oil or vice versa.

To determine whether a well produces more gas than oil, the gas to oil ratio for the well is calculated. This ratio is commonly described as the ratio of natural gas (commonly in cubic feet, ft^3) produced relative to the amount of crude oil (usually in barrels, BBL) produced over some period of time. A common dividing line used to separate gas and oil wells is 100,000 ft^3/BBL.

- **Oil Well.** Gas–oil ratio less than 100,000 ft^3/BBL
- **Gas Well.** Gas–oil ratio greater than 100,000 ft^3/BBL

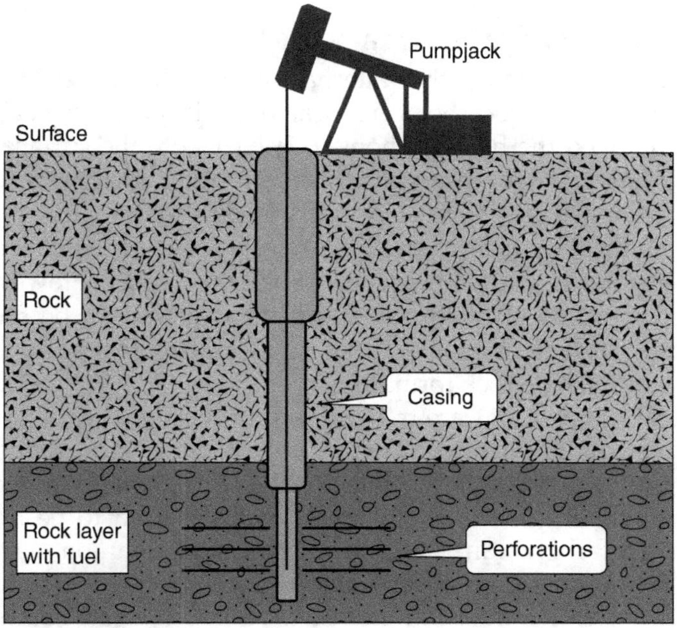

Figure 1.3.2 Traditional drilling

Oil Sands (Heavy Oil)

A limitation of traditional wells is that the petroleum or gas located in the well needs to flow to the surface. This limits the effectiveness of traditional drilling to the lighter fuels—the ones with relatively short carbon chains. Heavy fuels need to be produced differently. For example, heavy crude is extremely viscous and ranges from the consistency of molasses to a solid at room temperature. If heavy crude deposits are located close to the surface, heavy crude can be strip mined. This is similar to coal mining. Otherwise, high temperature steam can be injected underground to melt the heavy oil into a liquid that is suitable for extraction.

Because it injects high temperature steam underground, producing heavy oil requires immense amounts of energy and water. It uses more resources and is generally more destructive to the environment than traditional drilling. Heavy oil also requires more processing than lighter crude oil to convert it into gasoline or diesel fuel. This makes heavy petroleum less desirable than traditional sources of fuel.

On the other hand, heavy oil resources are much more abundant than traditional oil resources. There are about twice as many heavy oil reserves in the world as light oil reserves. Additionally, many of these reserves are located near the surface in politically stable regions. Unlike light crude resources that are difficult to locate, the primary limiting factors to developing heavy oil deposits are typically access to water (for steam) and environmental considerations.

Shale Gas (Hydraulic Fracking)

Hydraulic fracking is another alternative to traditional drilling. In a traditional well, hydrocarbons are located in a layer of permeable rock that has allowed the hydrocarbons to rise close to the surface. Traditional drilling looks for reservoirs that are formed when the migration of hydrocarbons to the surface is interrupted by an impermeable layer of rock. By drilling through the impermeable layer, the hydrocarbons can be removed from the lower level of permeable rock. However, that isn't the only type of rock in which hydrocarbons can be found. In some cases, organic matter may become trapped inside the cavities within impermeable rock formations.

When hydrocarbons are trapped within rock cavities, they can be freed if the rock is fractured. This will allow the hydrocarbons to migrate to the surface similar to traditional drilling. The difference from traditional drilling is that the rock formations need to be fractured before hydrocarbons can be removed. The most common way to create fractures in rock is to inject water or similar hydraulic fluid into a rock formation. This fluid can then be used to propagate compression waves caused by explosions deep into the formation. This process is known as *hydraulic fracturing*, or *fracking*. It has been proven as a very cost-effective way to recover hydrocarbons from shale rock formations.

Hydraulic fracking is a quickly growing technology. It tends to produce a large percentage of the lighter, more valuable, hydrocarbons (like methane, propane, and naphtha) than other technologies. It is also relatively abundant. Large shale deposits containing hydrocarbons are located in politically stable regions, like the United States. Finally, it is relatively low cost. The cost to extract hydrocarbons from shale formations is cost-competitive with the cost of extracting traditional petroleum from low cost producers in the Middle East.

Environmentally, hydraulic fracking provides a mixture of benefits and drawbacks. The biggest environmental benefit from fracking has been a reduction in carbon emissions and other air pollution from electricity generation. This has largely occurred because natural gas is much less polluting than coal. Cheap natural gas has displaced coal as the cheapest generation fuel for much of the United States. This is a primary cause for a 12 percent decrease in U.S. carbon emissions between 2005 and 2015 (Figure 1.3.3).

From a negative environmental perspective, various types of pollution—from sulfur to heavy metals—can be trapped in shale formations along with hydrocarbons. Hydraulic fracking can release that pollution. As a result, it is necessary to treat the water used by fracking to remove this pollution before it can contaminate drinking water.

Shale Oil (Shale Rock Processing)

Another way to extract hydrocarbons from shale is to use traditional mining techniques prior to crushing the rock in a processing plant.

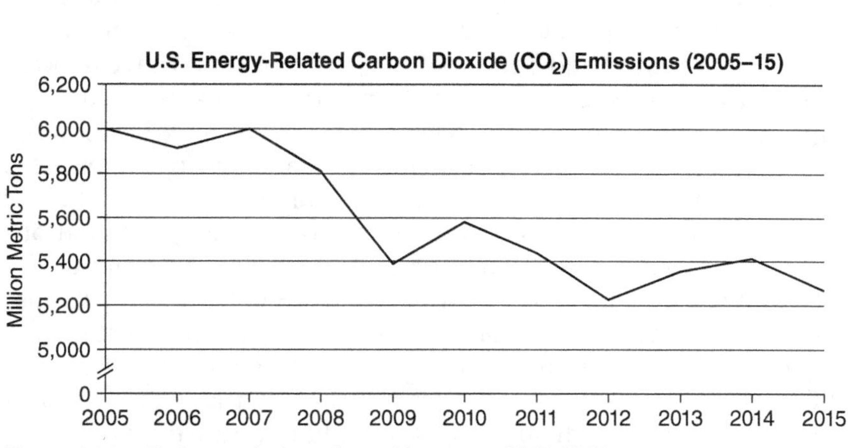

Figure 1.3.3 Carbon emissions down 12 percent, 2005–2015

The technology to crush shale and extract hydrocarbons has existed for more than 200 years. However, it is rarely economically viable—there are more cost-effective ways to get fuel. This process differs from fracking in that shale oil processing removes the shale from the ground prior to processing.

Deepwater Drilling

Oil can often be found underneath the ocean. When this drilling occurs in water more than 500 feet (150 meters) deep, it is called *deepwater drilling*. The depth of the water provides a number of difficult challenges. Pressure increases by approximately one atmosphere every 10 meters. At 500 feet (150 meters) deep, the pressure is almost 16 times water pressure at sea level—a pressure that humans cannot survive without specialized equipment. Some projects have much higher pressure still. The deepest projects are around 10,000 feet (2,900 meters) deep—about three times the world record for the deepest dive by a human.

The lack of human operators in deep sea environments places an increased burden on remote monitoring. For example, just changing a light bulb becomes a difficult task if it has to be done remotely using a robotic drone. Other problems that can face deepwater drilling are hurricanes, shifting sediments on the sea floor, swirling currents that shift the drill string, and unpredictable pressures (some higher, some lower) in the sediment layers beneath the sea floor.

In addition to making problems more difficult to fix, high pressure also increases the risk of problems. Steel pipes, electronic components, and other drilling equipment are all vulnerable to high pressure conditions. For example, gas bubbling out of crude oil is more likely to occur when drilling in deep water. This is largely due to the pressure difference between the top and bottom of the pipe. If a bend or weak point in the pipe allows the gas to collect, the resulting pressure can destroy a pipe. In addition, longer pipes have more surface area where a weak spot can occur. This problem is further exacerbated when shorter pipes need to be welded together to form a longer pipe.

In summary, there is a large amount of oil that can be found offshore. However, the combination of more problems, a greater severity of problems, and the difficulty fixing those problems means that deepwater drilling is substantially more complicated and substantially more expensive than traditional drilling. The amount of deepwater drilling activity is very sensitive to oil prices and is often seen as a leading indicator for industry sentiment around future prices.

Oil and Gas Reserves

No one knows how much hydrocarbon fuel actually exists on the planet. Even on the scale of an individual well, the actual amount of crude oil trapped underground is generally not known until a well is fully exhausted. Even after they are exhausted, wells will often still contain sizable quantities of hydrocarbons. However, the pressure just isn't high enough to bring it to the surface. As a result, crude oil reserves (the oil that is economical to remove from a location) are typically described in terms of the probability of the oil being extracted rather than as a total amount present.

The quantity of hydrocarbon fuel that is located somewhere is often described by the terms *proven*, *probable*, and *possible* reserves.

- **Proven Reserves.** Proven reserves are generally defined as having a 90 percent certainty of being produced with current technology and under current economic and political conditions.
- **Probable Reserves.** Probable reserves are generally defined as having a 50 to 90 percent probability of being produced with current technology and under current economic and political conditions.
- **Possible Reserves.** Possible reserves are generally defined as having a 10 to 50 percent probability of being produced with current technology and under current economic and political conditions.
- **Resources.** The term *oil and gas resources* refers to the total volume of fuel present in a gas or oil field irrespective of whether that fuel is economical to remove or whether the technology to remove the fuel currently exists. Any attempt to estimate hydrocarbon resources is largely a guess.

An important qualification on fuel reserves is that the fuel can be produced with existing technology under current economic and political conditions. In other words, the quantity of reserves will change based on the price of crude oil and natural gas. Higher prices make additional reserves profitable to extract. This will increase the number of oil and gas reserves. Lower prices will decrease available reserves.

The description of crude oil reserves can also be described probabilistically. For example, P90 refers to a 90 to 100 percent chance of recovery—a nearly certain amount over a number of wells. P50 refers to a 50 to 100 percent chance of recovery—on average, over a number of wells you would expect to recover this amount. P10 refers to a 10 to 100 percent chance of recovery—an unlikely, but still possible, quantity of hydrocarbons.

Another complication when describing the quantity of fuel in a location is that some different fuels have different compositions.

Some fuels, like methane and propane, exist as gas. For the purpose of calculating reserves, fossil fuels are typically represented as a single number called the *barrel of oil equivalent* (BOE) or *tonne of oil equivalent* (TOE). Other hydrocarbon fuels, like natural gas, need to be converted into these units.

Barrel of Oil Equivalent (BOE) Conversions

Fossil fuel reserves are commonly described in BOE units.

- 1 billion barrels of oil equivalents, 1 billion BOE, is abbreviated 1 BBOE.
- 1 BOE is approximately equal to 5.8 million Btus of natural gas.
- 1 BOE is approximately equal to 5,800 cubic feet of natural gas.
- 1 TOE is approximately equal to 6.84 BOEs.
- 1 TOE is approximately equal to 41,865 MJs.

2.1

NATURAL GAS

30-Second Summary

Purpose

This chapter introduces natural gas trading.

Summary

The natural gas market is one of the largest, most established energy markets. Natural gas is an important fuel for home heating and electricity generation. It is an abundant, clean-burning fuel that exists as a gas at room temperature. Natural gas is a mixture of hydrocarbon gases, the most abundant of which is methane. Because it is a gas, natural gas has to be contained in pressurized storage and distributed through pipelines. Once those pipelines are constructed, the transportation costs of natural gas are small compared to other fuels.

Key Topics

- As a gas, natural gas is difficult to transport and store.
- There is a large infrastructure of pipelines built to transport gas around the North American and European markets. The installed base of consumers linked to these pipelines is largely a captive audience because of the cost that it would take to replace this system with other fuels.
- Natural gas prices are often quoted as a spread relative to an index. In North America, that spread is relative to the price at Henry Hub, a major pipeline interconnection on the Gulf Coast.
- Natural gas spot prices are heavily influenced by weather.
- Natural gas futures prices are cyclical.
- Natural gas future prices are not linked to spot prices and carrying costs in the same way the future prices for stocks, bonds, and gold are linked to their spot prices.

Natural gas plays a central role in the energy industry. It is cleaner burning than coal and less expensive than petroleum. In the late twentieth century, the low cost of natural gas made it a very popular fuel for household heating. As a result of the infrastructure built during that time, natural gas has cemented its role as a primary residential fuel.

In addition, the limited carbon emissions, operational flexibility, and efficiency provided by natural gas make it a popular fuel for power generation. Almost all of the fossil-fuel-based power plants built in the United States since 1990 can burn natural gas. Consequently, there is a strong link between electricity prices and natural gas prices.

Natural gas was once thought of as an extremely cheap alternative fuel, but this is no longer the case. Long gone are the days when natural gas was burned off as an unwanted waste product of oil drilling. Historically, a prolonged period of low natural gas prices in the 1970s and 1980s led to a construction boom in natural gas infrastructure. Increased consumer demand eventually caused an increase in prices, but the infrastructure still remains. For most municipalities, it would be prohibitively expensive to replace this infrastructure to support another fuel. This makes North America highly dependent upon natural gas for both heating and electricity.

From a physical perspective, natural gas is a nonrenewable fossil fuel used to provide heat and generate electricity. It is a combination of colorless, odorless gases found underground. Natural gas is primarily composed of methane (CH_4) but often contains substantial amounts of other hydrocarbons, like ethane (C_2H_6), propane (C_3H_8), and butane (C_4H_{10}). Natural gas is considered "dry" when it is almost pure methane, and "wet" when it contains substantial quantities of the other hydrocarbons. It is also common to find natural gas mixed with other nonhydrocarbon gases like nitrogen and carbon dioxide. Because the composition of natural gas varies so widely, it is commonly traded in units of heat energy like British Thermal Units (Btus) or Joules rather than in units of volume (like cubic feet). It is important to know the relationship between energy content and volume for dry gas.

- There are approximately 1,000 Btus per cubic foot of dry natural gas.
- There are approximately 1 million MMBtus (million Btus) in 1 Bcf (billion cubic feet) of natural gas.
- For consumers, natural gas is typically sold in *therms*. A *therm* is 100,000 Btus or one-tenth of an MMBtu.

Natural gas is most commonly transported through pipelines. Some of these pipelines are transcontinental in length while others span a single town. Transcontinental pipelines move natural gas from producing regions to consuming regions. Local pipelines deliver gas to consumers in a limited geographical area. Pipelines are used because the primary component of natural gas, methane, contains a relatively low amount of energy per volume. Longer chain hydrocarbons like propane or butane contain enough heat energy that it is practical to transport them in pressurized metal containers. However, since methane requires a much larger storage container to hold the same amount of heat energy, and since it is impractical to use very large pressurized containers, natural gas is instead transported by pipeline.

Natural gas can also be transported in liquid form. To turn natural gas into a liquid, it must be supercooled to −263°F. This process is called liquefaction. However, since most consumers lack the specialized equipment to handle supercold liquid gas, natural gas is almost always returned to gaseous form before it is delivered to customers through the local distribution pipelines. The biggest advantage of liquefaction is that liquids are much denser than gases. Because of this, they will contain substantially more heat energy per unit of volume. Transporting natural gas as a liquid avoids the logistical problem of keeping the gas stored in an extremely large high pressure container for an extended period. Liquefied natural gas is used primarily for long-distance transportation of natural gas over oceans where building a pipeline is impractical. Sometimes it is also used for storage.

Comparing Gasoline to Natural Gas

One gallon of gasoline contains 124,000 Btus, and takes up about 0.13 cubic feet of space. For the same amount of energy, 100 cubic feet of storage would be required to store natural gas at standard atmospheric pressure. It is possible to compress natural gas to higher pressures. For example, a typical air tank used for scuba diving stores air at 200 to 300 times atmospheric pressure. However, at 250 times atmospheric pressure, natural gas requires three times the storage space of gasoline as well as a very heavy pressurized cylinder. As supercooled liquid, natural gas contains about two-thirds the energy stored in the same volume of gasoline.

Major Market Participants

There are a wide range of businesses associated with extracting natural gas from the ground and delivering it to customers. Exploration companies search for natural gas reserves underground. Drilling companies extract the natural gas from the ground and transport it to a processing facility. At the processing plant, impurities are removed from the raw natural gas as it is separated into its component hydrocarbon gases. Then, the dry natural gas (methane) needs to be transported to customers. Natural gas is transported by interstate pipelines or tanker ship. After it arrives in the consuming region, it must be stored until a consumer is ready to take delivery of the natural gas. Finally, when the customer turns on his or her gas, it needs to be delivered by a natural gas distribution pipeline.

Most of the companies on the physical side of the natural gas business specialize in one or two of these areas. Each area of natural gas production is relatively complicated, and it is hard to be equally good at every job. Moreover, the skills necessary for running physical businesses are very different than the skills used for speculating on financial commodities. The job of trading of natural gas is left to natural gas marketers.

Natural gas marketers buy and sell natural gas. They are speculators and investors who want exposure to the trading markets. Often these are Wall Street firms or spin-offs from integrated energy companies. Occasionally, they are branches of a service company. Trading does not show the steadily increasing, safe profits desired by the stockholders of a service-based organization. Because of this, many natural gas services companies no longer maintain large trading desks. They don't want to run the risk that an otherwise strong company will be destroyed by a couple of bad trades.

There are no hard rules preventing the physical businesses from being gas marketers. Many marketers started out associated with a physical company, and most physical companies still maintain a trading desk after they leave the marketing business. For example, physical companies often need to execute trades to eliminate the price risk of holding raw materials. Even the most conservative firms will occasionally make some speculative trades. Because of their expertize in a specific area, a specialist company can often recognize investment opportunities before other market participants. However, as a general rule, the goal of most physical natural gas companies is to make their profits in a hard-to-enter market niche and leave the speculation to other people.

There is a lot of specialized knowledge required to be a gas marketer. Marketers handle much of the paperwork that ties the various parts of the energy industry together. In the natural gas world, marketers do this by arranging for storage and transportation of natural gas. They have to handle the relationships, legal agreements, and processing necessary for trading with a variety of different businesses in multiple markets. Typically, this requires an extensive operations and legal teams. Marketers also need to have contractual agreements with everyone they trade with and continually monitor their creditworthiness. Because having a large number of industry contacts is a business necessity for marketers, they tend to have a wider focus than the physical companies. Marketers typically trade a wide variety of commodities like electricity, coal, oil, and emissions credits.

The Physical Natural Gas Business

- **Exploration.** Companies actively involved in the search for new sources of natural gas.
- **Drilling.** Companies focused on extracting natural gas from underground reservoirs and moving the gas to processing plants.
- **Processing.** Companies focused on converting raw natural gas into a standardized commodity—nearly pure methane gas called dry natural gas.
- **Interstate Pipeline Transportation.** Companies focused on maintaining interstate pipelines connecting producing areas (or liquefied natural gas [LNG] shipping terminals) to consuming regions.
- **LNG Transportation.** Companies focused on transporting natural gas across oceans in tanker ships. Usually, the natural gas is cooled to −260°F and turned into a liquid.
- **Storage.** Companies focused on maintaining large underground facilities to store natural gas.
- **Distribution.** Companies focused on taking natural gas from a transportation company or storage facility and delivering it to consumers.

Exploration and Extraction

Natural gas is commonly found dissolved in oil fields, coal beds, and underground rock formations. It is produced from decaying organic materials located in areas where the gases can't disperse. In nature, this commonly happens when organic material is caught between layers of impermeable rock. In nature, natural gas deposits can be millions of years old. However, natural gas can also be created by decomposing organic materials like the plants and animal wastes found in modern garbage dumps.

When organic material decomposes, methane is a common byproduct. Most of the time, this methane disperses into the atmosphere. However, when an impermeable material prevents the gas from dispersing, it can become trapped underground and later extracted. Most commonly, when gas is trapped underground, it is not located in a large open cave. Instead, gas is forced into small holes in the rock, and disperses in the rock layer surrounding the decaying material (Figure 2.1.1).

If the rock layer trapping the methane has the right physical properties, it is possible to remove the gas by drilling through the impermeable layer of rock. Typically, exploration companies look for a permeable layer of rock located underneath an impermeable layer

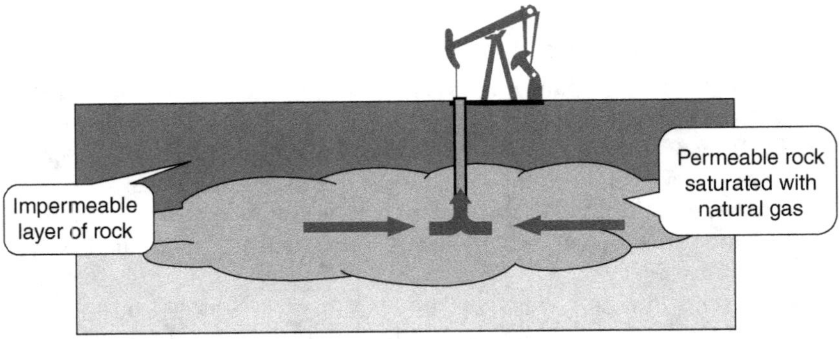

Figure 2.1.1 Formation of natural gas

of rock. In order to extract the natural gas from where it is trapped, the methane has to be able to flow toward the well (Figure 2.1.2).

Porous, permeable rock is the best type of rock for storing natural gas. This type of rock has lots of small, connected holes that allow a substantial amount of gas to be removed. The pores are small holes in the rock. It is necessary for rock formations to contain enough storage space to have an economically significant amount of gas in one area. It is also necessary for the pores in the rock to be connected to each other. Otherwise, the gas can't flow between the holes in the rock, and only the gas near the exit pipe will be removed. The physical characteristics of the rock forming a gas reservoir have a direct impact on the speed with which natural gas can be recovered from the ground.

In addition, the performance of natural gas wells is determined by the pressure of the gas in the well. Gases move from areas of high pressure to areas of low pressure. In conjunction with the natural tendency of a gas to rise, placing a vacuum at the mouth of a reservoir will pull the gas upward. The speed of this upward movement depends on the pressure of the gas in the reservoir. When it is first removed, the gas is at its highest pressure and will move quickly upward. As gas exits the reservoir, the pressure will decrease, and it will exit more slowly. Eventually, there will no longer be an economically significant amount of gas leaving the reservoir and the well will be closed. This process

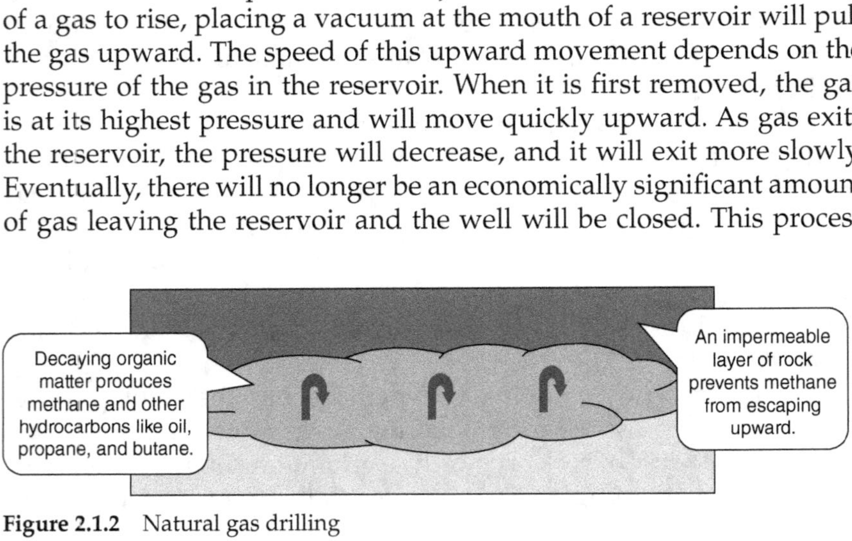

Figure 2.1.2 Natural gas drilling

can be sped up by injecting water into the well. Since methane doesn't dissolve in water, this will increase the pressure of any remaining gas.

Porosity and Permeability

In the energy industry, rock is typically defined by its porosity and its permeability. The performance of natural gas wells and storage facilities is closely related to their geology (Figure 2.1.3).

Porosity

In layman's terms, porosity refers to the number of holes in a rock. Usually, this is given as a ratio of empty space in a rock as a percentage of its total volume. Most rock will have some holes, but the size, variety, and type can vary widely between different types of rock.

Permeability

Permeability refers to the amount of interconnection between pores. Usually, this is measured by how easily a liquid can pass through a porous structure. It is possible for a porous material to be impermeable. For example, a foam coffee cup is a good insulator because it has a high porosity (heat doesn't travel through the air trapped in the pores) and low permeability (so the liquid won't leak out of the cup).

Figure 2.1.3 Porous and permeable rock formations

Hydraulic fracturing (fracking) is a way to remove natural gas from porous, impermeable rock formations. Porous, impermeable rock can be made permeable by creating microfractures throughout a rock formation. The most common way to create fractures in rock is to inject water or similar hydraulic fluid into a rock formation and create compression waves using controlled explosions. This allows the natural gas to be removed using conventional drilling techniques.

Processing

Because natural gas is not pure methane when it comes out of the ground, it is necessary to bring it up to a consistent standard quality.

All of the particulate matter and liquid water in the gas have to be removed to prevent damage to pipelines and consumer equipment. Trace pollutants like hydrogen sulfide and mercury have to be removed. The gas needs to meet a standard for energy per unit volume. For example, in North America, the heat energy of natural gas sold to consumers needs to be in the range of 1,035 Btu ± 5 percent per cubic foot at standard temperature and pressure.

Larger hydrocarbons, like propane and butane, turn into liquids at a warmer temperature than smaller hydrocarbons like methane. As a result, they need to be removed from the natural gas to prevent liquid from building up in a pipeline. Engineers utilize the different dew points of hydrocarbons to separate combined gases. The primary way of separating a combined gas into individual gases is to progressively cool the combined gas until it reaches a temperature where the larger chain molecules turn into liquids. At that temperature, the smaller molecules remain a gas, and the liquids can be siphoned off to leave only the simpler hydrocarbon gases. This process can be repeated a number of times to remove multiple hydrocarbons.

Pipeline Transportation

Natural gas is most commonly transported through pipelines. As mentioned before, the main problem with transporting natural gas is its low energy density. Methane is the simplest hydrocarbon gas and contains less energy per volume than more complex hydrocarbon gases like propane or butane. Pipelines avoid this problem by providing a continuous feed of gas to customers and operating at moderate pressures.

Interstate pipelines make a profit transporting natural gas for customers. These companies straddle the line between public utilities and for-profit businesses. Pipeline services range from guaranteed delivery of gas, the most expensive option, to various degrees of nonguaranteed service. Customers pay different rates depending on their desired level of service. Because pipelines serve an important role as a public utility, the interstate pipeline business is highly regulated and overseen by the *Federal Energy Regulatory Commission* (FERC). Some of the regulations include limits on new construction, limits on the rates that can be charged, and rules to ensure nondiscriminatory access.

Pipelines are often connected to one another. A natural gas *hub* is the location where two or more pipelines connect. A *citygate* is a special type of hub where interstate pipelines connect to local distribution networks. Most natural gas trading occurs at either hubs or citygates. The most important natural gas hub in North America, Henry Hub, is located on the U.S. Gulf Coast about halfway between New Orleans and Houston. Henry Hub is the delivery location for the New York Mercantile Exchange (NYMEX) natural gas futures contract and is used as the benchmark for natural gas sold throughout the United States. The Henry Hub price plays a major role in the energy market—similar to the role played by the S&P 500 Index for U.S. stocks. But, unlike those other indexes, the benchmark for natural gas is not an average—it is actually the price of gas at a single location.

Henry Hub Futures Contract

The single most important contract for valuing natural gas prices is the natural gas futures contract traded on the NYMEX. The underlying commodity is natural gas delivered at the Henry Hub. The Henry Hub is located near the Louisiana Gulf Coast at the interconnection of 13 pipelines. Most natural gas forward prices—and most electricity ones too—are heavily based on this contract.

In addition to being an important hub that connects 13 major natural gas pipelines, the Henry Hub is the trading location for NYMEX natural gas futures. It serves as the single most important pricing index in the energy market (Figure 2.1.4).

Transportation Contracts

Contracts for natural gas transportation can be *firm* or *interruptible*. A firm contract guarantees that the necessary pipeline capacity will be

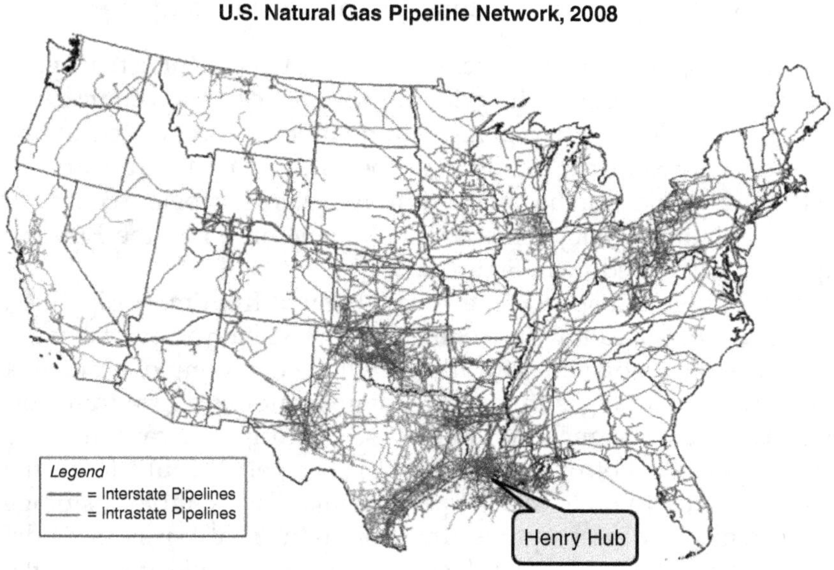

Figure 2.1.4 Natural gas pipeline map

available to transport the natural gas. An interruptible contract will allow transportation whenever customers with firm transportation contracts are not using their full capacity. There are a wide variety of terms used in transportation contracts.

- **Reservation Charge.** The reservation charge is a fixed monthly charge paid to the pipeline company to reserve transportation capacity.
- **Commodity Charge.** A commodity charge is the variable cost for transportation. This charge is usually quoted per unit of gas to be transported.
- **Annual Cost Adjustment (ACA) Charges.** The ACA is a small charge that adjusts transportation costs for inflation.
- **Gas Research Institute (GRI) Charges**. For U.S. pipelines, the GRI charge is a small fixed charge used to fund a nonprofit industry group, the Gas Research Institute.
- **Fuel Usage.** Fuel usage describes the amount of natural gas lost in transportation. This lost gas is commonly used as payment in kind to provide power to the compressors responsible for moving the gas.
- **Receipt Adder.** A receipt adder is a fixed price adjustment used to determine the price at the receipt point relative to the price of a nearby benchmark.
- **Delivery Adder.** A delivery adder is a fixed price adjustment used to determine the price at the delivery point relative to the price of a nearby benchmark.
- **Volume.** The quantity of natural gas that can be transported.

Firm transportation agreements are a way to guarantee that space is available on a pipeline. The price of firm transportation contracts is publicly available for any pipeline that qualifies as a regulated utility. The price charged by the pipeline will be listed in a public document, called a *tariff*, which can be obtained from either the pipeline company or the regulating agency. This will look something like the Pipeline Map and Tariff Schedule in Figure 2.1.5.

Interruptible transport can also be obtained from most pipelines. This type of contract allows use of the pipeline whenever space is available at a price negotiated with the pipeline. For example, a pipeline might have a natural gas fired electrical generator as a firm transportation customer. The generator might use their pipeline capacity only during especially hot or cold periods. The pipeline could resell the unused capacity to other market participants. For example, a storage facility might buy interruptible transportation. That business model might be to buy gas to fill their facility when few people are using the pipeline and sell gas out of their facility when usage is high.

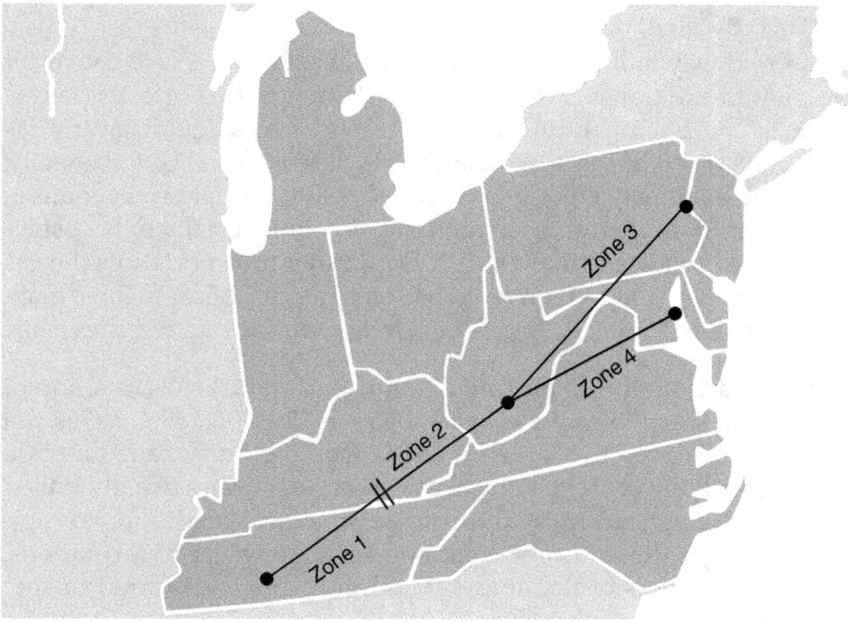

From Zone	To Zone	Reservation Charge ($/MMBtu)	Commodity Charge ($/MMBtu)	Fuel % Winter	Fuel % Summer
1	2	$0.13	$0.0150	0.21%	0.24%
1	3	$0.27	$0.0350	0.21%	0.24%
1	4	$0.22	$0.0250	0.21%	0.24%
2	3	$0.14	$0.0200	0.21%	0.24%
2	4	S0.09	$0.0250	0.21%	0.24%

Notes:
All charges are per MMBtu per day

Figure 2.1.5 Pipeline map and tariff schedule

Transportation costs are commonly quoted by the cost to move gas from one zone to another zone. However, not all pipelines are separated into zones. Some pipelines are considered a single zone and there is a fixed cost, called a *postage stamp rate*, to transport natural gas anywhere on that pipeline.

- **Zone Rates.** Areas of pipeline are commonly divided into zones. The pipeline tariff for these pipelines would list the cost to transfer gas between zones.
- **Postage Stamp Rates.** Some pipelines have a single zone. In that case, a postage stamp rate is the cost to transport gas anywhere on the pipeline.

Liquefied Natural Gas

The second way to move large quantities of natural gas is to convert it into a liquid and transport it on a ship. To liquefy natural gas, it is necessary to lower its temperature to –263°F (–160°C). As a liquid, natural gas takes only 1/610 of the space that it occupies as a gas. Unfortunately, due to the extremely cold temperatures, heavy insulation is required. The insulation needed to keep natural gas cold is usually only cost effective on a large scale (like a tanker ship). After transportation, the gas will need to be heated to convert it back into a gas. There are three main steps in the LNG process: *liquefaction*, *transportation*, and *regasification*.

- **Liquefaction and Exporting.** To transport natural gas as a liquid, it is necessary to cool the natural gas to –263°F (–160°C). This is a multistage process where sequential cooling units, called a *train*, progressively cool the natural gas. These plants are usually linked to producing regions by short-range pipelines. In addition to cooling the gas, this process separates out the heavier hydrocarbons. After the gas is cooled into a liquid, it is then transferred to specially designed tanker ships.
- **Transportation.** Once the LNG is loaded aboard ship, it is transported to an intermediate destination called a regasification facility. LNG transportation ships have to be specifically designed to handle extremely cold liquids and keep them well insulated. However, even in the best insulated ships, some liquid methane will convert back into a gas and be lost in transportation. Larger scale transports, faster travel time, and cryogenic cooling systems to refreeze the boiled-off gas can reduce these losses.
- **Regasification and Importing.** After transportation, natural gas is heated to return it to gaseous form and processed to meet local pipeline standards. Then, the gas is ready to be injected into a pipeline to travel to its final destination.

Basis Prices

The terminology for natural gas trading is different than other financial markets. When natural gas prices are quoted by a trader, the quote is usually in relation to the Henry Hub price. This is called a *basis price*. For example, if the price at the Henry Hub is \$3.52 and the price for physical gas at Waha Hub (a trading location in west Texas) is \$3.70, the basis price for Waha gas would be \$0.18. The term *price* can refer to either the basis price or the actual price depending on context. For example, if you asked a natural gas trader for the price of gas, he or she would probably assume that you mean the basis price, and quote

$0.18. If you asked a utility operator for the price of gas, he or she would assume that you mean the actual price of $3.70. Regardless of the way the price is quoted, the cost to the consumer is the same.

This pricing terminology is a result of how natural gas is traded. Most commonly, natural gas is traded using futures that are priced at the Henry Hub price. The *basis price* that is quoted by traders is similar to a transportation price to get gas from the Henry Hub to another area. The *index price* of natural gas is the price at the Henry Hub. The actual price of natural gas, the *all-in price,* is the combination of the index price and the basis price.

Common Terms

Actual. An adjective that refers to the actual physical commodity that is delivered at the completion of a contract. It can also be used as a noun, for example, "I traded natural gas actuals at Chicago City Gate."

All-in Price. The price of physical natural gas at a specific location.

Basis Price. The spread between the actual price and the index price at a specific location.

Index Price. In the United States, the price at the Henry Hub is the primary index for natural gas prices.

Basis Positions

An *actual position* means being exposed to the outright price of gas in some location. For example, a trader who owns the gas physically located somewhere is exposed to the actual price. Sometimes, this is called an *all-in position.*

A *basis position* means an exposure to a basis price rather than an outright price. Since the basis price is a spread, a basis position is an exposure to two locations—the basis location and the index location. For example, the Waha basis price is the difference between the actual price at Waha Hub minus the index price. Similarly, a long basis position at Waha Hub is like physically owning gas at Waha Hub and being obligated to deliver gas at the Henry Hub (the index location).

Actual Prices Versus Basis Prices

To trade natural gas, traders usually enter into two trades: a futures trade at the Henry Hub, and a basis swap to exchange the price at Henry Hub for some other location. Trading at the Henry Hub is very liquid—large

(*Continued*)

volumes can be executed quickly with minimal transaction costs. In general, it is much harder to find counterparties to trade at other locations.

The market is structured this way to help traders find trading partners. Natural gas futures (the Henry Hub contracts) are standardized contracts available over an exchange. These contracts eliminate concerns with counterparty credit risk and allow trades to be netted together. Traders get the bulk of their trading quickly done at the Henry Hub, and finish off trading when a suitable counterparty is found at a specific location.

How a Pipeline Operates

Pipelines transfer gas by creating an area of high pressure at one end of the pipe and an area of low pressure at the other end of the pipe. For long pipelines, intermediate compressor stations will act like fans to push air through the pipeline. These create low and high pressure zones to keep the gas moving (Figure 2.1.6).

Storage

The operational requirements of pipelines make storing natural gas necessary. Pipelines can't stop operating. For a pipeline to operate, gas has to be continuously added to one end and removed from the other. Interstate pipelines can be thousands of miles long, and if stopped,

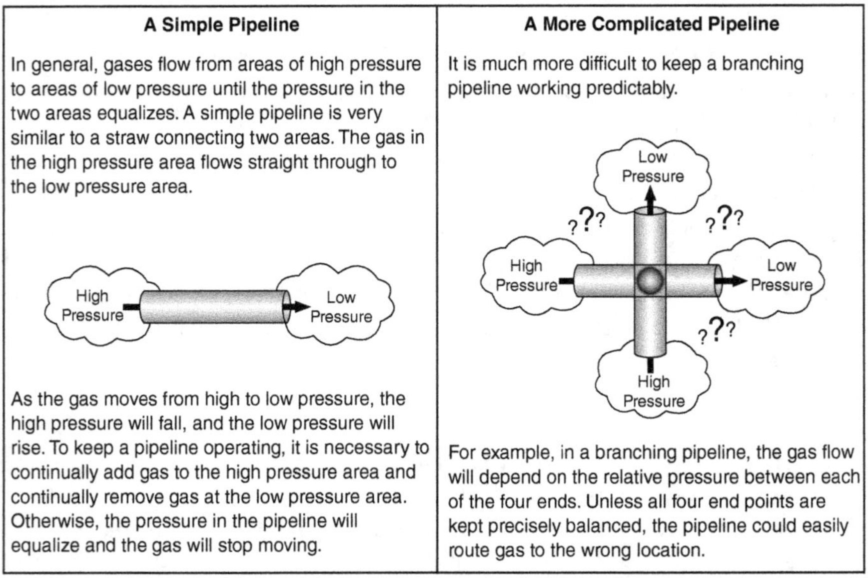

Figure 2.1.6 Pipeline structure

might take several days to resume operating at full capacity. As a result, it is impossible for most pipelines to shut down completely. Consumer demand is less constant. Consumers don't need a steady supply of natural gas around the clock. As a result, it is often necessary to store natural gas at both ends of a pipeline. This provides a cushion to balance the required continuous flow of the pipeline with refinery outputs and variable consumer demand. Natural gas is stored at the start of a pipeline to prevent interruptions at gas refineries from disrupting the pipeline. Gas is stored at the end of a pipeline to help match up the continually flowing pipeline to consumer demand.

As mentioned earlier, in gaseous form, natural gas isn't very energy dense—it takes a very large reservoir to store a significant quantity of heating energy. In general, it isn't practical to build a large enough storage container above ground. As a result, in gaseous form, natural gas is typically stored in underground reservoirs. If natural gas is stored above ground, it is usually liquefied and stored in an insulated container rather than as a pressurized gas.

There are a limited number of sites around North America that can be used to store natural gas (Figure 2.1.7). Natural gas storage requires large reservoirs located in the right area. Storage reservoirs are most commonly located close to refineries, at hubs that connect major pipelines, or close to where the gas will ultimately be used. Another consideration is that the size of the reservoir needs to be large enough to make it cost-effective to hook it up to a pipeline. Pipelines get harder

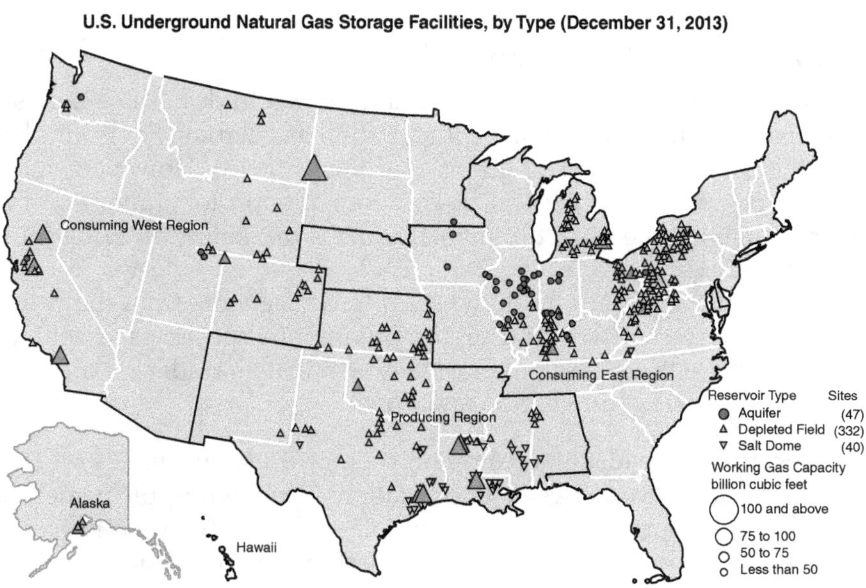

Figure 2.1.7 Natural gas storage facilities

to coordinate when they have lots of connections. Additionally, much of the cost of storing natural gas is due to the equipment to pump gas into the storage facility. This same equipment is required for both large and small facilities, and small facilities lack the volume for a reasonable economy of scale. As a result, there are only about 400 natural gas storage facilities around the country.

Distribution

Most customers don't receive gas directly from the interstate pipelines. Typically, gas is delivered to consumers by a local distribution company. These distribution companies maintain an extensive network of small pipes throughout each regional distribution area. These local delivery networks are substantially different from the interstate pipelines. Local distribution networks have to maintain connections to every home and business regardless of the economic profitability of each connection.

As a result, local distribution networks are very expensive to maintain. Local delivery charges account for a large portion of the retail price of natural gas. On utility bills, the cost that most customers pay for their natural gas will be a combination of the citygate price (the price of the gas delivered to the local utility from an interstate pipeline) and a local delivery charge. Commonly, these delivery charges make up about half the total retail cost of natural gas.

Trading and Marketing

There are several common types of natural gas trades. The simplest trade is a directional bet on the entire natural gas market. For example, that the market is going to go up or down in price. However, since natural gas prices are cyclical, it is more common for traders to try to speculate on one aspect of the natural gas market by entering into spread trades.

A *spread trade* is any trade where a trader benefits from the price difference between two securities by buying one security and selling another. These trades are popular; they eliminate a trader's exposure to the entire market moving up and down.

- **Location Spreads.** One common type of trade speculates on the price difference between two locations. Depending on demand, natural gas prices can be substantially different between two different locations. Natural gas transportation is not instantaneous, and storage is often limited. In periods of peak demand, some areas will have a greater demand for gas than can be supplied through the pipeline or storage facilities. The price of gas in those regions will rise until more supply can be brought in. In other cases, a period of moderate weather might decrease demand, creating a supply glut, and cause prices to plummet.

- **Heat Rates.** Another common trade is to speculate on the relationship between natural gas prices and electricity prices. In general, the price of electricity closely mirrors natural gas prices. Using a power plant, it is possible to turn natural gas into electricity. This keeps natural gas and electrical prices linked together most of the time. However, since two very different mechanisms are used to determine the prices of power and natural gas, they don't move together all of the time and it is possible for a trader to benefit from that volatility.
- **Time Spreads.** Spread trades can exist between two time periods as well. This type of spread trade speculates on the price difference between periods of high and low demand. For example, it might be possible to speculate on a colder than normal winter by betting that gas prices will be high. The trader might buy winter gas and sell spring gas to eliminate directional exposure to the entire market.
- **Swing Trades.** A similar type of trade relies on the physical ability of the trader to store natural gas over short periods. Pipelines must operate around the clock. However, demand for gas varies considerably even over short time periods like a week. For example, a lot of gas is used on Monday mornings to restart industrial facilities and reheat offices after the weekend. Comparatively less gas is used late at night on Saturday because there is no industrial demand and houses are less heated after people are asleep. As a result, it is often possible to pick up inexpensive natural gas when demand is low and resell it when demand is high. This requires the ability to store the natural gas.

Spot and Forward Markets

Like many other energy products, the forward and spot markets for natural gas are distinct from one another. Spot markets involve buying gas for immediate delivery. Forward markets involve buying gas for delivery sometime in the future. These markets are separate because gas production, transportation, and storage have to be arranged ahead of time.

If there is a shortage in natural gas expected in a couple of weeks, it is usually possible to increase production and bring in more supply.

However, if there were a shortage today, there is no real way to get more supply immediately. It is difficult to move a large quantity of gas into or out of storage quickly or transfer in supplies from nearby areas on short notice. In the forward markets, prices are determined by macroeconomic issues—the expected average relationship of supply and demand in the future. In the spot market, prices are based on the supply that is on hand *right now* and consumer demand *right now*. As a result, the spot markets are substantially more volatile than the forward markets.

In markets where spot and forward commodity markets are linked, usually there is a constant amount of the commodity, and it isn't consumed when it is used. The spot and forward markets for those products are linked by the ability to buy the commodity in the spot market and store it for future delivery. Since the commodity is never used up (like a gold bar or a stock certificate), those assets aren't affected by short-term fluctuations in supply and demand. Natural gas does not work the same way. A continuous supply of new natural gas is constantly required, consumer demand changes constantly, and it is difficult to store and transport.

Long-term buy-and-hold strategies are of limited use in natural gas trading. Gas has no intrinsic value by itself—it is the products created by burning natural gas that are valuable (heat or electricity). Moreover, gas in storage is no easier to deliver than gas newly extracted from the ground unless the storage is located near a consuming area. In fact, the most common storage facilities are actually previously emptied gas wells. As a result, buy-and-hold strategies are essentially the purchase of undeveloped gas reserves. Traders use storage facilities to balance supply and demand for periods less than a year. For example, traders might buy gas in the summer to sell during the next winter, but they aren't going to buy gas and hold it for several years as a long-term investment.

That doesn't mean there isn't a spot/forward relationship in forward natural gas prices. However, this relationship is more complicated and less reliable than in other markets.

Swing Swaps and Options

In addition to standard derivatives like futures, forwards, and options that deliver over an entire month, the natural gas market has derivatives with daily delivery called *swing swaps* and *swing options*. These trades are often used by utilities to manage volumetric risk—the risk that the consumers served by the utility will use more gas than expected. For example, a utility that can't pass through higher costs to consumers might wish to protect itself from the risk of a winter cold front that causes consumers to use more gas than expected.

- **Swing Swap.** These swaps will exchange a fixed price determined at the start of the delivery month for the daily spot price reported by some pricing service.
- **Swing Options.** These options will give the buyer the right to purchase some quantity of gas at a price determined at the start of the delivery month (usually by referencing a publication like the Platts Inside FERC[1], or IFERC, survey) at any time during the delivery month. These options typically have a limit on how many times gas can be purchased.

Swing swaps and options differ from standard swaps and options because the fixed price is determined at the start of the delivery month rather than negotiated during the transaction. The most common type of price used in these contracts is the prevailing price reported by various surveys at the start of the delivery month. The Platts Inside FERC survey is the most well-known survey of this type. However, a variety of market data providers provide bidweek reports that have comparable information.

Bidweek

In the week prior to the end of each month, natural gas traders will report prices where they have agreed to deliver gas over the following month at a fixed price. This week is called the *bidweek.* The average price of those transactions is reported in surveys like the Platts IFERC survey or various indexes published by other survey firms. The exact methodology that each survey firm will use to set their prices will vary slightly but can generally be found documented online.

Forward Prices

Looking at the forward market, prices are determined by seasonal expectations of supply and demand rather than on the current spot price and storage costs. Seasonal expectations of supply and demand are generally the same every year. Consequently, prices in the forward market tend to mirror consumer demand—both are high in the winter and fall dramatically in the spring of every year (Figure 2.1.8).

[1] FERC is the U.S. Federal Energy Regulatory Commission.

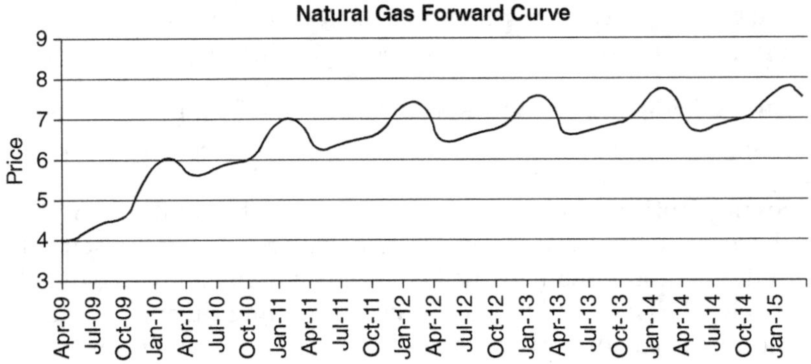

Figure 2.1.8 Natural gas forward curve

Natural gas forward prices are highly cyclical without the smooth upward slope in prices observed with storable commodities. Compared to other markets where forward prices are determined by interest rates and storage costs, this is a very different relationship.

Price Certainty

The price of natural gas becomes less certain close to delivery (Figure 2.1.9) than further away. This is very different than most other markets. This is because short-term disruptions to natural gas supplies have a big effect on prices. However, unless prices change for a lasting fundamental reason, large price movements in the spot market do not have a large effect on future prices. Forward prices tend to revert to prices based on typical consumer demand and expected supplies (Figure 2.1.9). Prices are more volatile in the spot price than in the forward markets.

Spot Prices

Spot prices do not show the same seasonality as future prices. While forward prices have a very regular, seasonal trend, spot prices are all

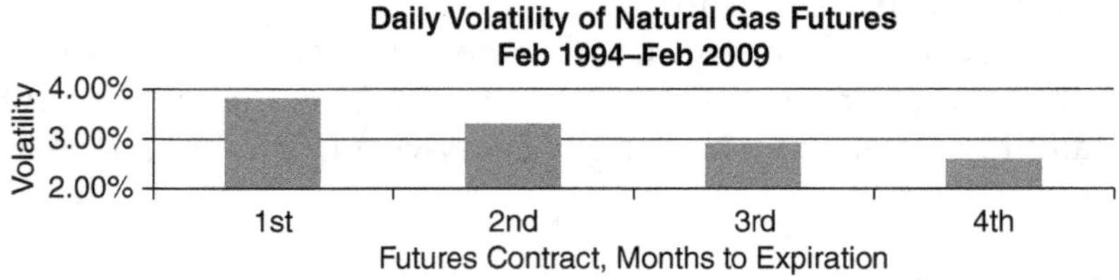

Figure 2.1.9 Volatility of nearby natural gas futures contracts

over the place. This is because spot prices are based on short-term supply and demand issues. Looking at spot prices, they are very different from the highly predictable prices in the forward market (Figure 2.1.10).

Part of the reason for this difference is complexity of storing or transporting natural gas on short notice. Natural gas in one location can't just be exchanged for natural gas in a different location—it has to be physically moved there. If there isn't enough time to arrange the transportation, there is no longer any linkage between the source and destination locations. Natural gas that needs to be delivered at a specific time has a similar issue. Natural gas requires specialized facilities to store it. If someone doesn't have access to a storage facility, and most market participants do not, they can't buy the commodity early for delivery at a later date. The typical natural gas customer is forced to buy natural gas either in the forward market or on the spot market on the day the gas will be used. They can't buy a supply of gas when it is cheap on the spot market and store it until it is needed.

There are two major effects of this. First, spot volatility tends to be higher than forward volatility. This effect was illustrated in the discussion of future prices. Second, the spot correlation between two different locations works differently than forward correlations. In the forward market, when it is still possible to arrange gas to be moved from one location to another, most natural gas prices are highly correlated. If they weren't very similar, it would be possible to shift gas between locations for an easy profit. The only constraints to this trade would be the cost of transporting and storing the natural gas.

In the spot market, none of that is possible. Just as more supply is prevented from coming in, demand is prevented from leaving. There is no way for consumers to shift demand from one area to another easily. For example, it isn't possible for most homeowners to move to another state for a week if they like the prices better there.

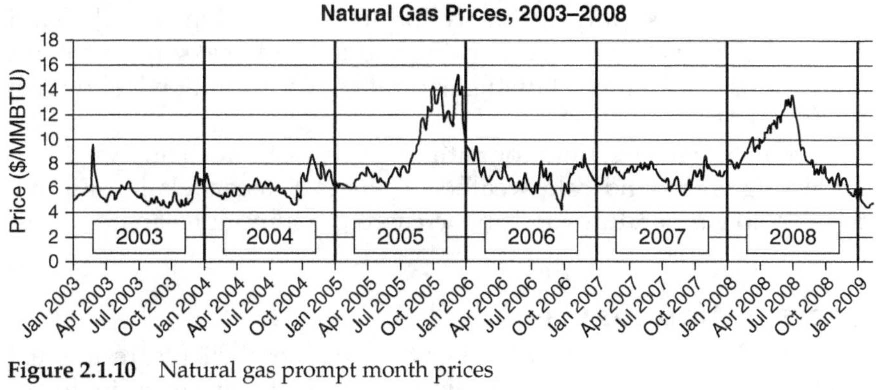

Figure 2.1.10 Natural gas prompt month prices

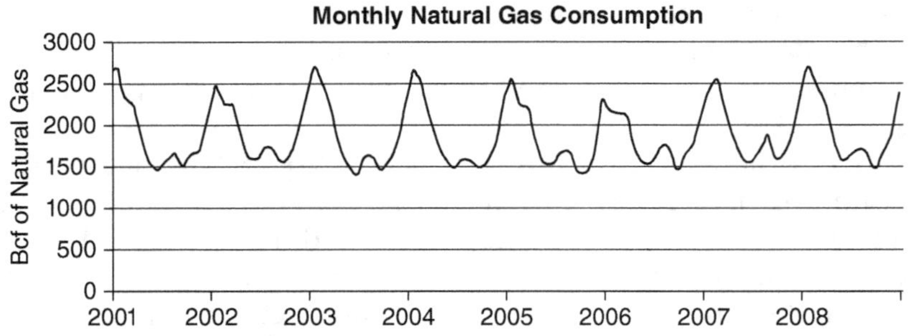

Figure 2.1.11 Seasonal natural gas consumption

Prices, Supply, and Demand

When very long time frames are considered, the assumption that natural gas prices are a function of supply and demand is misleading. For exploration and development purposes, the supply of natural gas depends on its price. Higher natural gas prices make the extraction of natural gas from difficult to reach reserves more economical. It also makes exploration a better investment. In other words, in the long run, supply depends on prices and demand rather than the other way around.

As a result, predictions about future prices are mostly a function of expected demand for natural gas. Exploration companies maintain predictions on what it will cost to deliver that supply, and factor in a set profit. Higher demand leads to higher prices, and those higher prices make it economical to open up new supplies of natural gas.

Demand and Weather

On a national basis, the single largest factor affecting demand for natural gas is temperature. During the winter, natural gas is used for heating. In the summer, natural gas is used to fuel electrical generators that are used to supply electricity for air conditioning. The demand for natural gas is lowest in the spring and fall and peaks in the coldest winter months. A graph showing natural gas consumption is shown in Figure 2.1.11.

Predicting the demand for natural gas is very much an exercise in predicting warm and cold weather. There is a linear relationship between cold temperatures and an increased consumption of natural gas.

Users of Natural Gas

The three largest users of natural gas are industrial clients, residential clients, and power plants. Of the three, the use of natural gas in power plants to produce electricity has risen the most quickly. Most of the power plants built since 1990 depend on natural-gas-fired generators.

- **Industrial.** Industrial clients commonly use natural gas as a source of heat. Natural gas ignites quickly, and turning off a natural gas furnace doesn't waste any fuel. A natural gas furnace goes out as soon as the supply of fuel is stopped. In comparison, a coal furnace will continue to burn for a while until the coal in the furnace is fully used. This can result in a lot of wasted fuel if it is necessary to start and restart the furnace multiple times. Manufacturing of metal or glass, cooking, dehumidification, and waste incineration are all examples of industrial uses of natural gas.
- **Residential.** About half the homes in North America use natural gas for heating. The largest residential use of natural gas is home heating (primarily in the winter). There are a variety of other residential uses for natural gas since it is common for natural gas fueled homes to have several natural gas appliances. Kitchen ranges, hot water heaters, clothes dryers, and outdoor grills are all commonly found throughout the country.
- **Electrical Generation.** Natural-gas-fired power plants are the fastest growing users of natural gas. Natural gas power plants produce less greenhouse gas emissions than coal or oil based plants. Some natural gas power plants operate year round; others are more seasonal. The seasonal power plants usually turn off in the winter when the price of natural gas is at its peak.

Common Terms

All-in Price. The price of natural gas at a specific location. The all-in price is equal to the price at the benchmark location plus the basis price.

Basis Price. The difference in price between a specific location and the price at the benchmark location. In the United States, this is the difference between the price at a specific location and the Henry Hub. Basis costs are a function of transportation costs and storage capability between two areas.

Burner Tip. An end-user of natural gas.

Citygate. The location at which the municipal distribution system takes possession of natural gas for distribution to retail customers.

Dry Natural Gas. Natural gas that is almost pure methane.

Hub. An interconnection between two or more natural gas pipelines.

Wet Natural Gas. Natural gas that contains substantial amounts of hydrocarbons other than methane, or natural gas that contains substantial impurities.

Western Gas Markets

The western U.S. is separated from the rest of the country by the Rocky Mountains. (Figures 2.1.12 and 2.1.13).

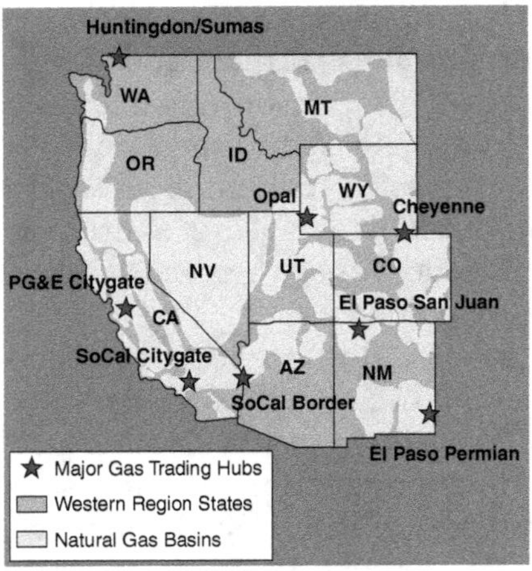

Figure 2.1.12 Major trading locations. Map courtesy of FERC.

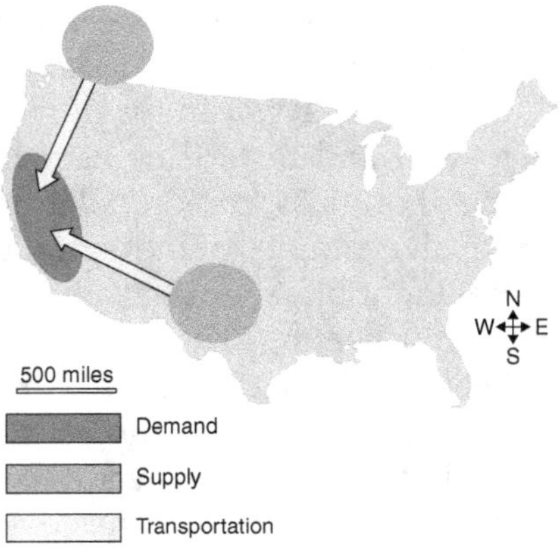

Figure 2.1.13 Supply and demand

- Electrical generators throughout the entire area depend on natural gas as a primary fuel. The southern part of the West Coast has very hot summers, and natural gas is especially in demand during those periods to provide electricity for air conditioning. The major competing power source is hydroelectric power from the Pacific Northwest. As a result, precipitation and snowmelt can have a large effect on regional natural gas prices during peak demand periods. Most of the region has mild winters.
- In the western United States, the geography is dominated by the Rocky Mountains. The West Coast (Washington, Oregon, and California) and parts of Arizona are heavily populated. However, most of the region has a sparse population. California is the biggest user of natural gas, and trading commonly revolves around imports to the California market. These imports come from Canada and the Desert Southwest.
- Storage capacity is extremely limited. This can lead to sharp price movements during periods of peak demand.
- Western basis prices are not highly correlated with NYMEX Futures (Henry Hub) since the region does not directly import natural gas from the Gulf Coast where Henry Hub is located.
- There is a substantial amount of gas produced east of the Rocky Mountains in Wyoming, Utah, and Colorado. However, most of this gas flows to the Midwest rather than to the population centers on the West Coast.

Midwestern Gas Markets

The Midwestern U.S. is an industrialized region with cold winters. (Figures 2.1.14 and 2.1.15).

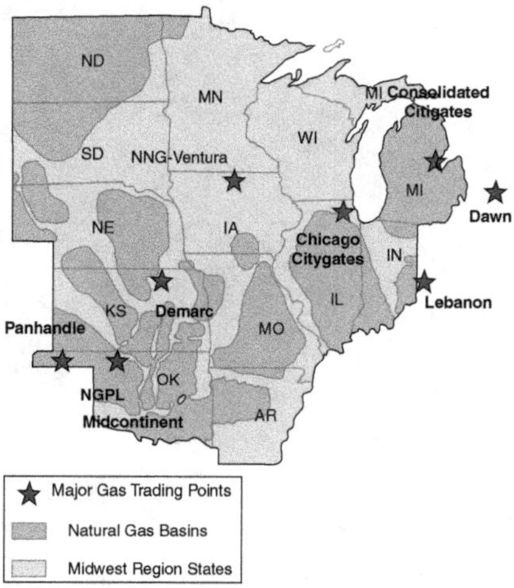

Figure 2.1.14 Major trading locations. Map courtesy of FERC

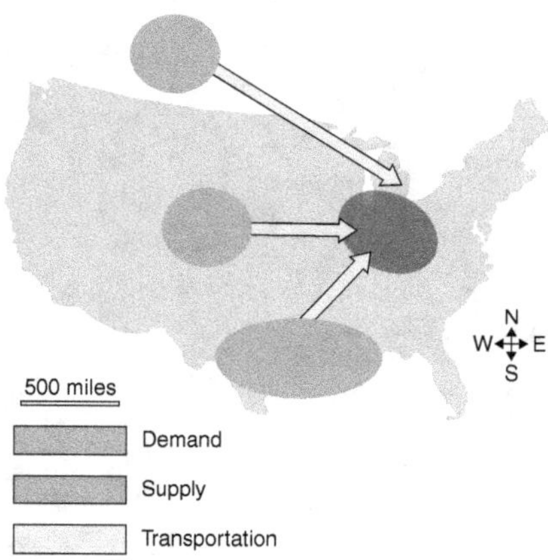

Figure 2.1.15 Supply and demand

- The Midwest is a major consuming region during winter months. Cold winters characterize the entire Midwestern Region and there is a strong seasonal demand for natural gas in the winter to provide residential heating.
- This region does not use natural gas as a primary fuel for electrical power plants. Coal is the primary fuel for power in the Midwestern United States. There is comparatively little demand for natural gas in the summer months.
- Numerous storage facilities and extensive local distribution networks are located in the region. Many of these areas have government-mandated obligations to meet residential demand during winter months. For example, to ensure consumers have access to fuel, governments might force gas in storage facilities to be delivered to residential customers rather than saving it for a commercial use.
- Large pipelines connect the Midwest to all of the major supply basins in North America. Supplies from Canada and the Rocky Mountains supply the bulk of the Midwest's natural gas requirements. However, some gas also comes from the Gulf Coast Region when it is available.
- Basis prices in the Midwest are somewhat correlated with NYMEX futures (Henry Hub). The region imports gas from the Gulf Coast, but also has access to other gas supplies.

Eastern Gas Region

The mid-Atlantic to northern part of the U.S. East Coast is a heavily populated region. The northernmost area (New England) has very cold winters and limited storage capacity. (Figures 2.1.16 and 2.1.17).

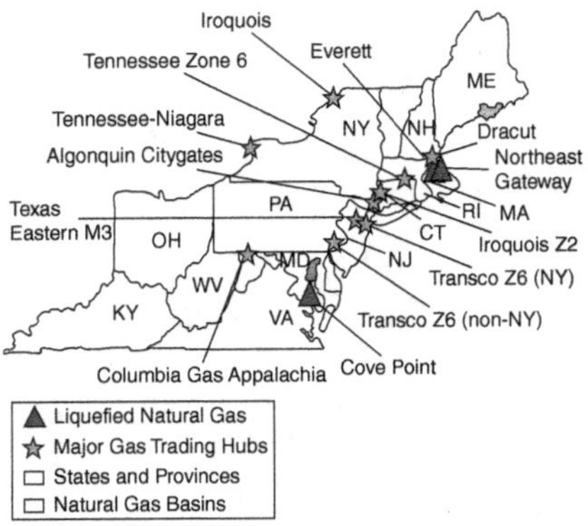

Figure 2.1.16 Major trading locations. Map courtesy of FERC

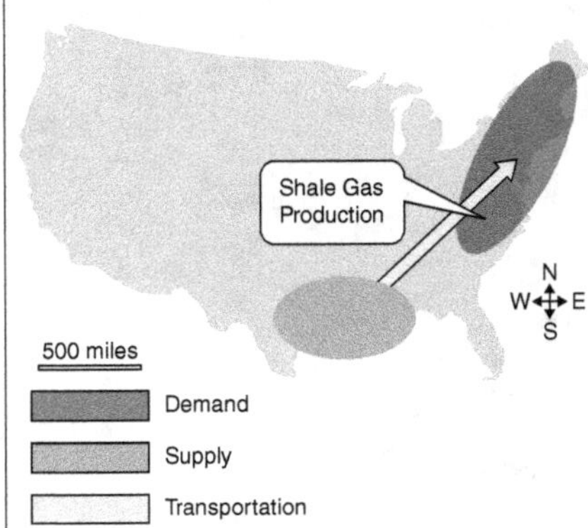

Figure 2.1.17 Supply and demand

- On the East Coast, natural gas is used extensively for both residential heating and electrical generation. As a result, there is a year-round demand for natural gas in this region.
- There is a limited amount of storage available in the region. Combined with the high seasonal demand for both heating and electricity in the winter, basis prices (prices relative to the supply regions) are often the highest in the country.
- Large shale gas deposits in the Appalachian Region (West Virginia/Pennsylvania border) are providing a large influx of natural gas into the region causing a dramatic reduction in prices during all but the coldest months.
- The East Coast is a heavy importer of natural gas from the Gulf Coast Region.

Texas and Gulf Coast

The Texas/Gulf Coast region is a major producer of natural gas. This region has mild winters and hot summers. (Figures 2.1.18 and 2.1.19).

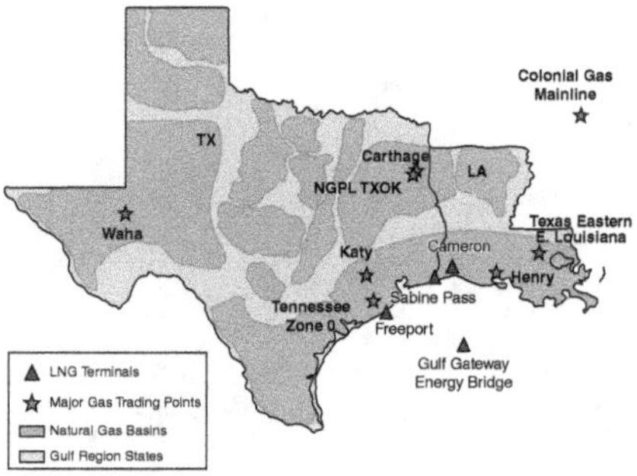

Figure 2.1.18 Major trading locations. Map courtesy of FERC

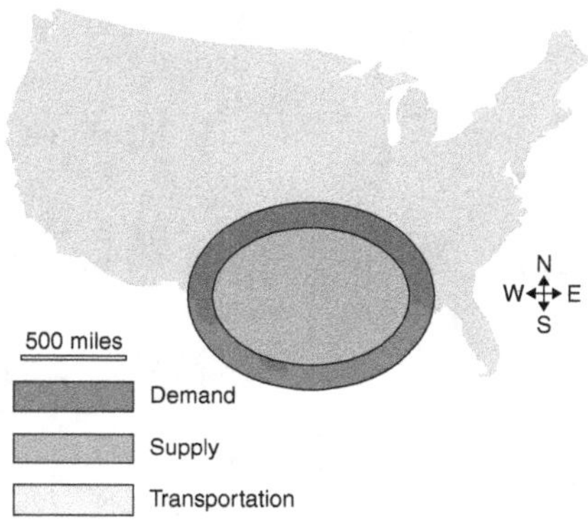

Figure 2.1.19 Supply and demand

- The Texas/Gulf Coast Region is a net exporter of natural gas. It is the most important natural-gas-producing region in North America. Most of the exports flow to the East Coast and industrialized Midwest.
- Abundant local supplies have made the region heavily dependent upon natural gas as a fuel for electricity generation.
- The region has mild winters and there is a limited seasonal demand for natural gas during winter months for heating.
- There is a substantial amount of storage in the region. Most of this region's storage helps exporting pipelines balance supplies of natural gas leaving processing plants to the demand for imports from other areas of the country.
- The basis prices in the region are highly correlated to NYMEX future prices. The settlement location for NYMEX futures, Henry Hub, is located in western Louisiana.

Southeast

The southeastern U.S. is a rural agricultural region with mild winters and hot summers. (Figures 2.1.20 and 2.1.21).

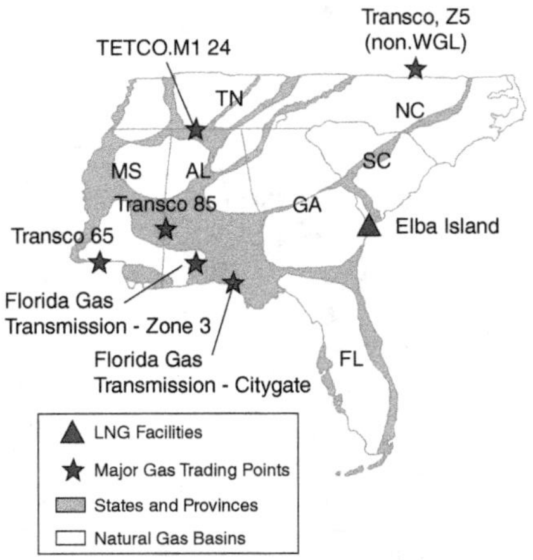

Figure 2.1.20 Major trading locations. Map courtesy of FERC

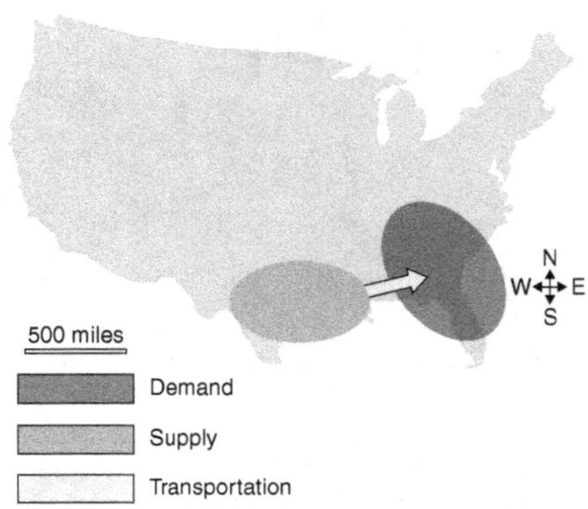

Figure 2.1.21 Supply and demand

- Natural gas is primarily used to provide electricity in the southeastern United States. The demand for electricity peaks during summer months as the hot summers create a high demand for air conditioning.
- Mild winters limit the need for seasonal residential heating.
- The southeastern region has very limited storage capacity.
- LNG terminals are being constructed to export natural gas and provide storage facilities. There is a major LNG terminal at Elba Island.

2.2

ELECTRICITY

30-Second Summary

Purpose

This chapter introduces electricity trading.

Summary

The electrical trading market is unique among trading markets because its final product is a steady supply of electricity. Electricity can't be easily stored. It must be continually generated and transmitted to customers. This makes electricity substantially different from commodities where it is possible to follow a buy and hold strategy. Understanding the physical constraints of power generation is essential to understanding the electricity trading market.

Key Topics

- Electricity pricing and trading
- Causes of electrical demand
- Generation
- Heat rates and spark spreads
- Transmission and distribution
- The major regional power markets

The generation and transmission of electricity is one of the primary reasons for the existence of an energy market. Electricity is used to power a large variety of modern devices. Industrial equipment, computers, and air conditioners are just a few examples of modern conveniences powered by electricity. Electricity is so common that it is hard to imagine life without it. Unfortunately, electricity can't be easily stored, and it's very expensive to transmit over long distances. Consequently, there is no unified national electricity market—it's a collection of small regional markets, each having unique characteristics and regulations. In each market, supply and demand must constantly be matched resulting in highly volatile prices.

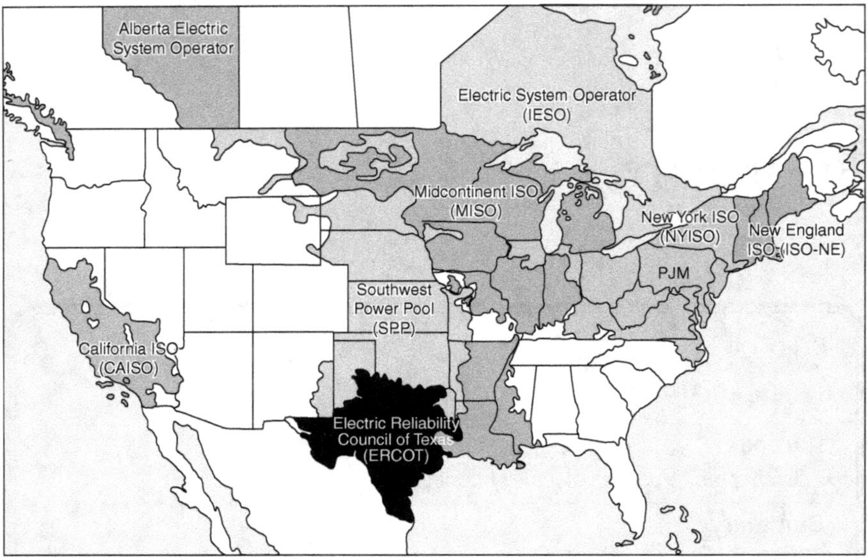

Figure 2.2.1 Map of RTO/ISO operators

Each regional market is coordinated by its own *Transmission Service Operator* (TSO). Some TSOs are government-sponsored monopolies, and others are *Independent Service Operators* (ISOs) or *Regional Transmission Organizations* (RTOs). Both ISOs and RTOs maintain the power grid in areas where the government-sponsored monopoly has been disbanded. ISOs are limited to doing service in a single state and are exempt from federal jurisdiction. RTOs do business across several states and fall under federal jurisdiction. Many RTOs began as ISOs in a single state. Later, they became RTOs when they expanded across state boundaries. Commonly, these RTOs still keep ISO as part of their name. A map showing the major deregulated markets is shown in Figure 2.2.1.

A *regulated market* is a service area where a government-sponsored monopoly coordinates the power grid. This monopoly controls all aspects of the power grid. For example, it will own generation facilities, power lines, the trucks needed to maintain the power lines, and so on. Typically, a government-appointed commission, usually called a *public utility commission* or *public service commission*, regulates this monopoly. In annual hearings, called *rate cases*, the public utility commission will approve the utility to spend money on behalf of consumers served by the utility. The utility will earn a profit as a percentage of how much money is spent.

A *deregulated market* is a service area where an RTO/ISO rather than a government-sponsored monopoly coordinates generation and transmission. In these areas, anyone can own a power plant and connect it to the transmission grid to sell power. All of the participants in a deregulated market are guaranteed equal access to transmission lines and economic innovation is encouraged. As a general rule, deregulated markets use economic incentives to effect changes, while regulated markets use legislative mandates. Most energy trading occurs in deregulated markets.

The most important characteristics of a deregulated market are daily power auctions. These *nondiscriminatory auctions* set the price of power for a transmission grid. Power producers submit the price at which they are willing to supply power and are activated in order from the lowest to highest bid. These are called *nondiscriminatory auctions* because all winning bidders get paid the same price regardless of their bids. The price of power for every producer and every wholesale consumer is set to a single price called the *clearing price*, or alternately, the *wholesale price*. Smaller customers pay a slightly higher price for their power—the *retail price* for power.

In deregulated markets, power plants are activated in order of their bids (lowest to highest) until the consumer demand is completely met. The last power plant activated sets the *clearing price* of power for the entire transmission area. Some common terminology in these auctions describes the importance of the last activated power provider. The cost of bringing the last unit of electricity into the market is called the *marginal price* of power, and the most recently activated plant is the *marginal producer*. Therefore, in deregulated markets, the *clearing price* is set by the *marginal price* of power.

Usually, there are two types of auctions coordinated by RTOs/ISOs. A *day-ahead* auction sets the price of power for the following day in one-hour increments. Usually this auction is completed in the early afternoon on the day before delivery. This allows power producers time to arrange fuel and operating schedules for the delivery day. The actual demand for power isn't known when the day-ahead auction occurs. Instead, this auction is based on a prediction of next day's required load.

The second auction is a *real-time* auction that is run continuously throughout the actual delivery day. This auction balances the actual demand against the predictions made the previous day. It is typically bid in five-minute increments. If a power plant is not chosen to operate in the day-ahead auction, it can still participate in the real-time auction. However, the real-time auctions require power plants to turn on and off quickly, and not every power plant has this capability.

Only power plants participate in the daily auctions. However, the auction mechanism is important to every market participant since it determines the price of power in each region.

Market Participants

The work of getting electricity to consumers is often broken into four components (Figure 2.2.2). The first is *generation*, the work of creating electricity. The second is long-distance transportation, called *transmission*. The third is *distribution*, which involves getting the power the last mile from the local substation to the consumer. The fourth and final step is *retail sales*, which involves billing and customer service. In regulated markets with monopoly utility, the utility is typically responsible for all four jobs. In deregulated markets, it is common for these responsibilities to be split between multiple entities.

- **Generation.** Generation refers to power plants that generate electricity.
- **Transmission.** Transmission is the long-distance transportation of power, typically done at high voltages.
- **Distribution.** Distribution is the short-distance transportation of power. This is typically done at low voltages and operates at a neighborhood level, connecting every building to the grid.
- **Retail Sales.** Retail sales involve customer service and billing. In deregulated markets, the retail sales company is typically responsible for contracting with generators to ensure sufficient capacity is available to serve their customer base.

Generators produce electrical power and place it onto the transmission system. This is done using a transformer to convert the output of the generation unit into high-voltage AC power. Then, the power is transmitted long distances over high-voltage lines. Once the high-voltage power is close to consumers, its voltage is lowered at a substation so that it can travel over residential power lines. Finally, low-voltage lines will distribute electricity to consumers.

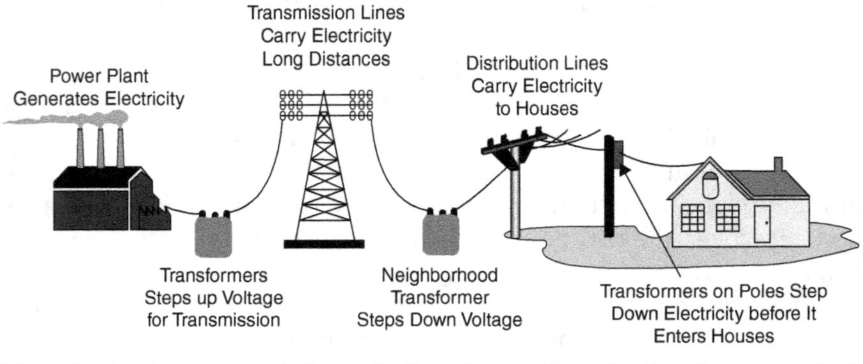

Figure 2.2.2 The power grid. (*Source:* National Energy Education Development Project)

In deregulated markets, each role in the power grid is typically handled by a different company.

- **Merchant Generator.** A generator who sells power to another company (usually a load serving entity).
- **Investor Owned Utility.** In deregulated markets, the infrastructure of the transmission system is typically owned by a single utility. This utility will not own generation and is commonly called a "wires" company.
- **Load Serving Entity (LSE).** A load serving entity is a company that provides electric service to either end-users or wholesale customers. In deregulated markets, LSEs are typically intermediaries between the power grid operator, the generators, and consumers.
- **Provider of Last Resort (POLR).** In states providing retail competition, the POLR is the load serving entity that is obligated to sell power to consumers if they don't choose a supplier or their chosen supplier goes out of business.

In regulated markets, all four jobs are commonly performed by a state-sponsored monopoly utility:

- **Integrated Utility.** In a regulated market, an integrated utility is typically a regulated monopoly that owns generation, transmission, and distribution assets.
- **Municipally Owned Utility (Muni).** A muni is a publicly owned utility owned by a local government.
- **Co-operative (Co-op).** A co-op is a not-for-profit utility commonly found in rural communities where it is unprofitable for traditional utilities to operate.
- **Federally Owned Utility.** A federally owned utility is a government entity, commonly involving hydroelectric generation, which has authority to buy, sell, and distribute power.

Electrical Trading Markets

The *forward power market* is where the bulk of speculative trading occurs. This market is open to anyone with sufficient money to meet trading requirements. The forward market depends on the prices set by the daily auctions, but they are very different markets. The daily auctions are open only to power providers with the ability to generate power and place it on the transmission grid. In contrast, the forward market is much more accessible. The forward market doesn't require any ability to generate power at all—it is possible to trade both *physical contracts* (requiring delivery of power) and *financial contracts* (which settle in cash). To distinguish the two markets, the daily power auctions are sometimes called the *spot power market*.

The forward markets trade large blocks of power at a limited number of locations around the country. This is a critical difference between the daily auctions and the forward markets. It is possible to *buy spot power* in arbitrarily small sizes for immediate use anywhere in the country. However, it is only possible to *trade* it in monthly blocks at about 30 locations. The most important of these locations are shown on the map in Figure 2.2.3. The forward markets limit the number of trading locations so that a sufficient number of buyers and sellers are forced to be active in each contract.

Trading power in large units at a limited number of locations makes it easier to standardize contracts and find trading partners. This is a necessary compromise for a liquid trading market. However, it also presents a major problem—the tradable locations represent extended geographic areas. They may not reflect the exact price of power everywhere in the surrounding area. Getting an exact price at a specific location commonly requires additional trades that may or may not be possible. As a result, power is often traded in two pieces—standardized forward trades made at major hubs to get the desired regional exposure approximately correct, and then smaller fine-tuning trades to lock in an exact price.

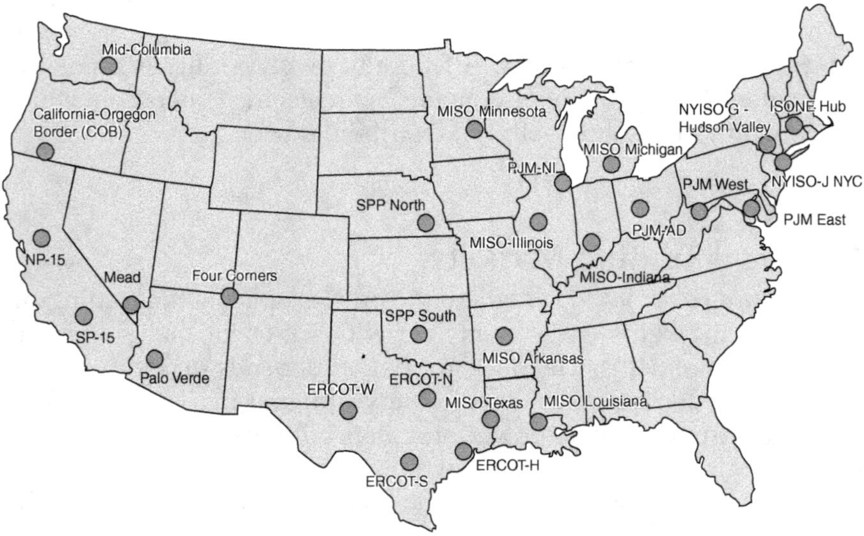

Figure 2.2.3 Major electricity trading hubs

Daily Power Auctions

In the daily auction market, the assumption that all power providers are equally able to deliver power isn't always true. In periods of heavy demand, power lines can become overloaded and may require electricity to be routed around the congestion. The primary way of rerouting power is to activate power plants closer to the areas of high demand. Because low-cost generators are normally activated first, turning on a generator closer to the demand means that a high-cost plant is being activated *out-of-merit order.* If that price was allowed to set the clearing price of power for the whole grid, there would be a jump in everyone's costs for the sake of a small minority of customers. In most deregulated power grids, rather than having the entire grid pay the higher price, it is paid only by the affected parties. Because this price only occurs for a single location, this is known as a *Locational Marginal Price* (LMP).

Aligning power prices with the actual cost of delivering power was one of the major reasons that energy markets have deregulated. The alternative to deregulated markets, having prices legislated by local governments, actually interferes with matching prices to costs. If prices are always going to match costs, there is no need for legislation—the market is deregulated. Legislation involves adding loopholes and exceptions to a general rule. Under the *Standard Market Design* (SMD) recommended by the FERC[1], the costs of line congestion are paid by the affected parties rather than being shared across every user of a power grid. Congestion costs aren't just paid by consumers, power producers pay them too. There is a charge for routing power into a high-load area over congested power lines, and a credit for producing power that bypasses the congestion. Most of the United States is moving toward this model of allocating costs.

Another part of the SMD is a penalty for remote generation. Historically, generators were paid for the quantity of power that was placed on the grid at their generation site. But, if a generator was a long distance from the demand, *line losses* on the intervening transmission could substantially decrease the amount of power that was actually delivered to customers. Under an LMP methodology, power producers only get paid for deliverable power—not on the gross power placed onto a power grid.

These two changes have had a huge effect on the business of selling power. In addition to fuel costs and efficiency, location has become a major factor in determining the profitability of a power plant. The power grids have become much more reliable. There is

---

[1] The Federal Energy Regulatory Commission (FERC) is the government agency that oversees the power grids in the United States.

an economic disincentive to build power plants that can't actually deliver power to customers, and an incentive to put up power lines that relieve congestion.

Implementing the FERC's SMD requires assigning different prices to different locations on a power grid. In most regions, this price (the LMP) consists of three parts—a clearing price, a congestion charge, and a line loss charge. The *clearing price* for power is the same everywhere on a power grid, but the *congestion* and *line loss* charges are specific to each location.

Under the SMD, there are several types of locations for which prices are calculated: *nodes*, *zones*, and *hubs*. Node prices correspond directly to the price of power at a specific piece of physical hardware. Commonly this is an interface, called an electrical bus, where power enters or leaves the transmission grid. Generators get paid the nodal price of the electrical bus where they deliver power into the transmission grid. Zone prices are the average of all nodal prices within a limited geographical area. Usually, electrical buyers pay the zone price for the power they receive. Zone prices are used for customers since they require less detailed metering equipment. A hub price is an average of selected nodal prices across several zones. The hub price serves as the benchmark price for a power grid. Hub prices are used extensively in the forward market for trading. In most ISO/RTO regions, the clearing price for power and the hub price are synonymous.

Closely linked to the concept of LMPs is a financial instrument called a Financial Transmission Right (FTR). These instruments help customers manage the price risk of having purchased or sold power at a major hub and then being forced to pay a different price when they deliver or receive power at a specific node. FTRs are tradable contracts made between two parties. These parties take opposite sides of an obligation to pay or receive the difference in price between two nodes. If there is no congestion, the price at the two nodes will be the same. However, if there is congestion, one party will need to pay the other. This payment can go either way—either party can end up paying or receiving cash. Sometimes, that isn't what is desired, so these contracts can be structured as options. FTR options allow one party to pay an up-front fee (a premium) to avoid paying on congestion charges. Essentially, buying an FTR option is like buying insurance against higher prices due to congestion.

Regulated Markets

Not all power grids are deregulated. Many power grids are operated by a monopoly utility that is regulated by a government commission. This commission is usually called a *public utility commission* or a *public service commission* and determines consumer electricity prices that can be charged by the utility. These prices allow the utility to earn a return on any money that is prudently spent on meeting consumer requirements.

In regulated markets, integrated utilities (utilities that own both transmission and generation) typically have the sole responsibility to supply power to consumers. Because of that, there is usually little or no wholesale market for electricity within the utility's service area. When trading does occur, it will occur at points where power can be imported or exported from the service area. These nodes typically have names like Into-Southern Company or Into-Dominion.

Regulated utilities are compensated for operating a power grid by being approved to charge a certain fee to consumers. This fee is determined so that the utility earns a fixed return on a regulatory value called a *rate base*. The fees and information about the rate base can be found online in a document called a *tariff*, which is the pricing structure a retailer charges a customer for energy consumption.

A rate base consists of the investments the utility has made into assets like generation, transmission, and distribution infrastructure (Figure 2.2.4). Rates are set in meetings, called *rate cases*, held between the utility commission and the utility. During these meetings, the utility commission authorizes a percentage rate that the utility is allowed to make on its investments and approves any new investments (additions to the rate base) that will occur before the next meeting.

Because of this mechanism, the primary way for a utility to increase its profit is to spend additional money on behalf of its consumer base. The more power that consumers use, the more assets that the utility gets to build, and the greater the profit for the utility's shareholders.

Authorized Return on Rate Base = (Rate Base) * (Authorized Percentage Rate of Return)

Rate Base =
Net Plant in Service
+ Plant in service
− Accumulated depreciation

Additions to rate base
+ Construction work in progress
+ Plant held for future use
+ Fuel inventories
+ Material and supplies
+ Inventories and prepayments
+ Regulatory assets
+ Cash working capital

Other Adjustments
− Deferred income taxes
− Accumulated deferred investment tax credit (ITC)
− Customer deposits
− Regulatory liabilities
− Other reserves

Figure 2.2.4 Rate base calculations

Regulated utilities don't benefit from finding cheaper ways to do things. As a result, regulated utilities tend to be much more focused on customer satisfaction and reliability than they are on reducing costs to consumers or encouraging conservation.

Public Utility Commission/Public Service Commission

Public Utility Commissions are typically staffed by political appointees called *commissioners*. Like any appointee, they may have limited engineering or energy market knowledge. Commissioners often have to balance short-term considerations that might be popular with voters, like cutting consumer prices, against long-term considerations, like making infrastructure investments needed to ensure a stable power supply in the future.

A regulated utility doesn't need to own all of the generating assets within their service area. Some types of generation require specialty knowledge to build or operate. Regulated utilities can outsource the construction and management of these generation facilities to third parties through power purchase agreements (PPAs) or to compensate the generation owner based on the avoided cost of the utility.

- **Power Purchase Agreement (PPA).** A PPA is a legal contract where the utility agrees to buy power from a generator at a fixed cost. This agreement will typically pay the generation owner a fixed price for any production for a predetermined number of years. PPAs are typically linked to the physical facility and, if the facility is sold to a new owner, the PPA will transfer along with the physical unit. Most commonly, regulated utilities sign PPAs to incentivize the construction of specialized technology like solar, wind, or geothermal electrical generation. Since PPAs are typically signed when a unit is first constructed, prices are usually proportional to the cost to construct the generation unit.
- **Avoided Cost.** Regulated utilities may be required to purchase power from third-party generators that meet certain requirements. Typically, when a utility is required to purchase power from a third party, it will need to pay the generator the cost that it would have paid to generate the power itself (the *avoided cost* of the utility).

Electrical Demand

Because of the way power auctions work, where power plants are activated until the expected demand is fully met, predicting customer demand for power before it occurs is a critical part of power trading. The actual demand for power changes constantly. Every time a light is turned on or a computer is turned off, the load on the power grid changes. Since electricity can't be stored, this changing demand must constantly be matched against supply. There is a huge infrastructure (including the day-ahead and real-time auctions) built to balance the supply of electricity against this consumer demand. However, these auctions can't just be reactive—they need to ensure there are enough power plants active or on standby to meet upcoming demands for power. Building excess capacity into a system is one way to approach this problem, but keeping too many plants on standby costs a lot of money. Making accurate estimates of the future load on the power grid is a key factor in ensuring affordable power.

Load forecasting is also important for power plant operators. Power plants often need several weeks to line up fuel supplies for extended periods of activity. They need to know when to schedule maintenance, and when it makes sense to run continuously versus stopping and restarting. In a competitive market, accurately predicting consumer demand is essential to a power plant's profitability.

Fortunately, the demand for power is fairly predictable. It varies by the season, day of week, and time of day in a cyclic manner. In each region, each part of the year has a typical demand profile that is relatively consistent under a wide variety of circumstances. However, the load profile for every part of the country is different.

During cold weather, where daily high temperatures are below 60°F, there are two distinct periods of peak demand. The first occurs in the morning when people wake up for work. Homes and offices need to be heated around 6 a.m. The second occurs in the evening when people arrive home from work. Figure 2.2.5 shows the typical demand for electricity in cold weather for a variety of high temperatures. The lines indicate the percent of daily power used each hour. The dashed line indicates the coldest days; the solid line indicates the warmest. Although more power will be used during colder weather, the time

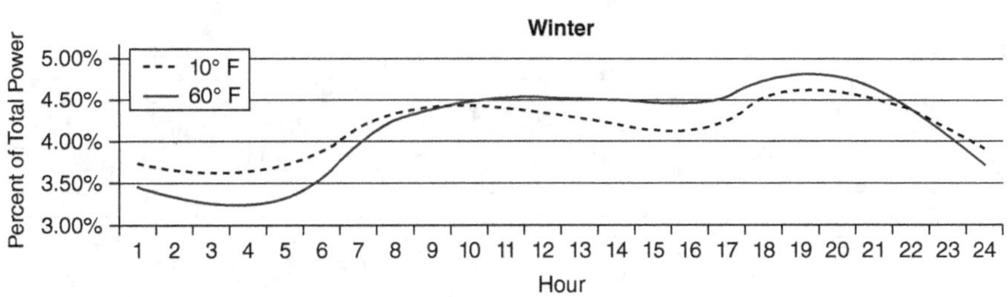

Figure 2.2.5 Hourly demand during cold weather

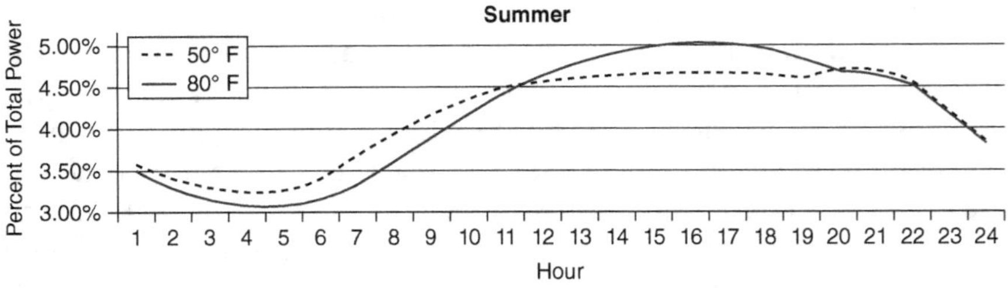

Figure 2.2.6 Hourly demand during warm weather

that people use heating is fairly constant. Colder weather will generally lead to higher overnight power usage and more sharply defined peaks at the beginning and end of the day.

While having a different profile than cold weather, the demand for power in hot weather is also fairly consistent. On hot days, demand builds all day, peaking in the mid-afternoon when air conditioning is working most heavily. This peak is most pronounced on the hottest days (the solid line on Figure 2.2.6), but much less pronounced during more comfortable temperatures (the dashed line).

Seasonality, Weather, and the Demand for Power

The relationship between temperature and demand doesn't just affect when power is used during the day—it has a major effect on the total amount of power being used too. Substantially more power is required in the summer and winter months than in the more temperate spring and fall months (Figure 2.2.7).

The distinctive peaks in the summer and winter have given a name to periods of lower demand—the fall and spring are called the *shoulder* months. Even during shoulder months, there is a *baseline* level of power required every day. Most industries keep fairly standard working hours that don't change substantially throughout the year. As a result,

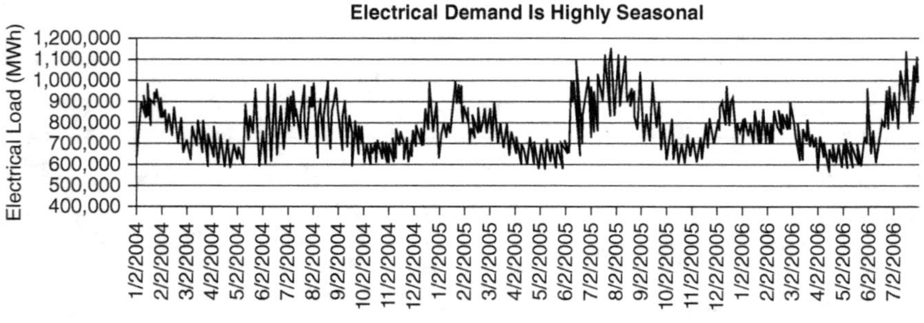

Figure 2.2.7 Seasonal demand for power

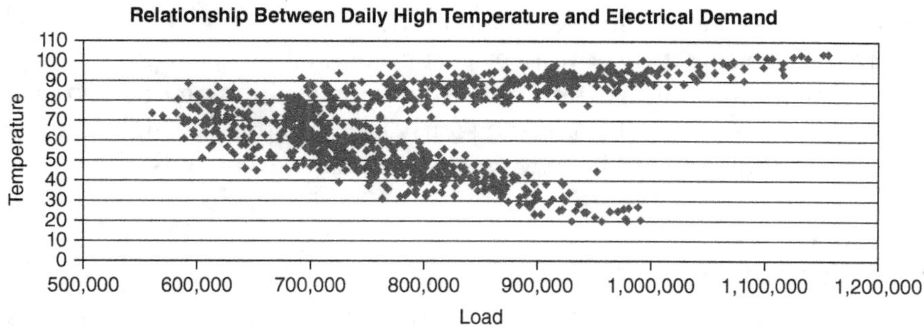

Figure 2.2.8 Relationship between electrical demand and temperature

the biggest variable demand for electricity comes from heating or cooling requirements. There is a clear correlation between temperature and electrical demand (demand is also called *load*). Since different parts of the country have different climates, there is a substantial variation in average seasonal load between regions.

The relationship between temperature and electrical demand can be seen in Figure 2.2.8. Temperature is located on the left axis. As temperatures become uncomfortable (moving above or below 65°F or 18°C), the demand for power increases (shown on the bottom axis). The points on the right side of the graph are when the peak demand occurred within the mid-Atlantic region in the years 2004 to 2006. These peaks correspond to the warmest and coldest days.

The cyclical nature of electrical power affects how it is traded. Power is normally traded for an entire month based on the time of day. Forward contracts are commonly broken up into day and night power by month. For example, it is possible to find trading contracts for August daytime power with delivery at Cinergy Hub, or January nighttime power for delivery in Southern California. However, there isn't a single commodity called *electricity* that is consistent throughout the year. Instead, there are hundreds of separately traded electricity products that differ based on location, month or season, and time of day.

Daytime hours (usually 7 a.m. until 11 p.m.) are called *peak* hours. Nighttime hours are called *off-peak* hours. Every region of the country uses slightly different definitions for their power products. As a result, power products are commonly described in shorthand. This abbreviation is *weekdays by hours*. For example, 7×24 refers to power 7 days a week, 24 hours a day. *Peak* power is 5×16 or 7×16 (depending on if weekend days are included). If weekends aren't included in *peak* power, there will be a separate 2×16 product. *Nighttime off-peak* hours are typically 7×8—they start at 11 p.m. the day before and run until 7 a.m.

Finally, technology has a big effect on electrical demand. For example, air conditioning changed the entire dynamic of the power market.

Many of the economic studies made in the late 1960s and 1970s regarding energy efficiency are now incorrect because of the increased popularity of air conditioning. With the advent of air conditioning, the demand for summer power went from being fairly low to extremely high. Predictions on typical demand have to keep up with these changes.

Generation

There are lots of ways to produce electrical power. Most power plants use a similar technology—generators driven by superheated steam.

Fossil fuel plants can burn oil, natural gas, or coal to produce this steam. All of these fossil fuels produce greenhouse gases like carbon dioxide (CO_2) when they are burned. The amount of pollution depends on the efficiency of the power plant. More efficient plants use less fuel, thereby producing less pollution, per megawatt of generated power. Of all fossil fuels, coal fired generation is the most polluting—it produces two to three times the pollution of the other fuels.

Nuclear generators use nuclear fission to turn water into steam. Nuclear fuel provides a lot of electricity per weight—a pound of highly enriched uranium is approximately equal to a million gallons of gasoline. But, like fossil fuels, enriched uranium is subject to severe shortages and presents environmental problems. It is also difficult to store safely once discarded.

A third relatively common form of power generation is *hydroelectricity*. Instead of using steam, hydroelectric dams use flowing water to drive a turbine directly. In most cases, dams are built across a river, trapping the water on one side to form a lake. Water is allowed to flow through holes in the dam into the river, which is usually located several hundred feet below the lake level. As water flows through the dam, the falling water spins a water-based turbine to generate electricity. Depending on the amount of water flowing in the river and capacity of the lake, it may not be possible to turn off the flow of water without flooding nearby communities.

For energy trading, the most influential power plants are fossil fuel plants. Fossil fuel plants are marginal producers of power in most areas. As such, in any market that sets the *clearing price* of electricity to the *marginal price* of power, fossil fuel plants have a disproportionate impact on the price of electricity. Perhaps the most common description of a fossil fuel power plant relates to its efficiency in converting fuel into electricity. This efficiency is called a *heat rate*. A *heat rate* is typically expressed as a ratio of heat input to work output (for example, Btu/kWh or MMBtu/MWh). A lower heat rate indicates a more efficient power plant.

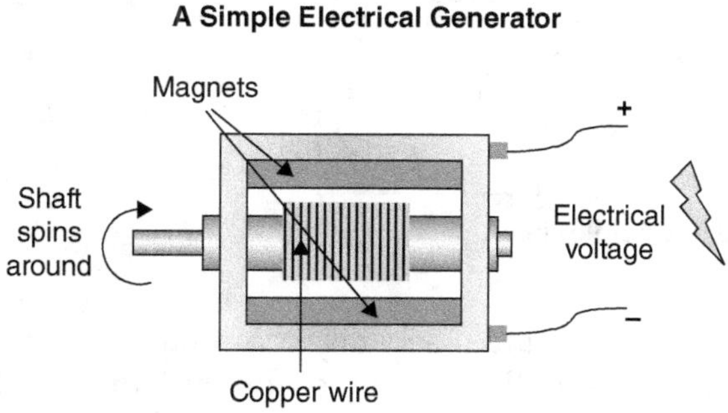

Figure 2.2.9 A simple electrical generator

Generators

Electricity is usually generated by manipulating the relationship between magnetic fields and electricity. Electricity and magnetism are two parts of the same force (electromagnetism). Spinning a wire in a magnetic field creates a current in the wire. Magnetic fields generate electrical currents, and vice versa.

The easiest way to generate electricity is to rotate a coiled wire inside a pair of magnets (Figure 2.2.9). As the wire spins, it will start to build up a magnetic charge that can be removed in the form of electricity. By continuing to spin the coiled wire, a steady supply of electricity can be removed through a circuit. This force works both ways—electric generators and electric motors use identical technology. Applying a voltage to the positive and negative terminals of a generator will cause the shaft containing the wires to spin.

When wires connect a voltage source to an electrical load, it is called a *circuit*. The definition of an *electrical circuit* is any closed loop of wire that contains a voltage source, often a generator or a battery, and a load (an electrical device of some kind). A *load* is anything that uses electricity—a common example is a light bulb, but any device powered by electricity can be described by the term. In circuit diagrams, these terms are often abbreviated. Voltage is commonly abbreviated v, current abbreviated i, and resistance (*load*) abbreviated R.

Voltage is a measure of the potential energy in an electromagnetic field. When a wire connects two points with different voltages, electrons will start flowing through the wire. They will move from the low-voltage area to the high-voltage area, eventually causing the voltage to equalize.[2] In the case of a battery, when the voltage equalizes, the battery is dead and would need to be replaced or recharged.

[2] Since electrons are negatively charged particles, they move in the opposite direction of a positive current.

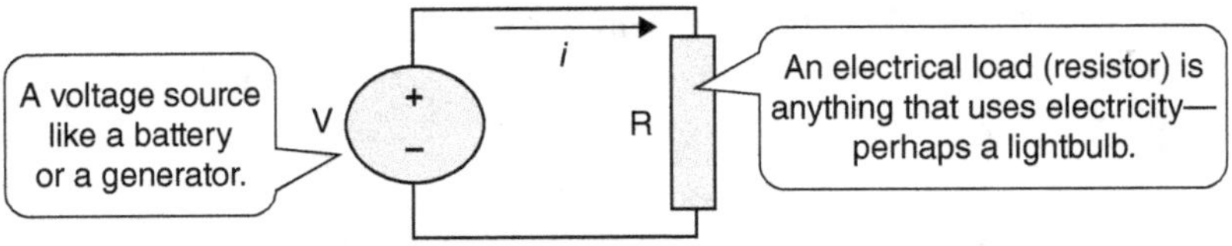

Figure 2.2.10 A simple circuit

However, if the voltage is being continually created through a generator, the current will continue to flow indefinitely. The speed at which the current (*i*) flows through the wire depends on the voltage and load. The more work that the electrons need to do on their way through the wire, the slower they travel. This is a very important relationship, because if the current moves too fast, the wire will heat up and possibly melt.

The relationship between voltage, current, and resistance can be described by the formula $v = iR$ (Ohm's Law). Voltage equals the current multiplied by the resistance. An electrical circuit is any closed wire containing a voltage source (v) and a load (R). A simple circuit diagram showing each of the fundamental pieces of a circuit can be seen in Figure 2.2.10.

The key concept is that voltage, current, and load on a system are all interrelated. This is true of the simplest circuit and the largest power grid. If the current on any transmission wire gets too fast, it will start to heat up the wire. When it gets hot enough, the wire will melt. The only way to prevent transmission wires from melting is to match the level of production (the voltage) and the demand for electrical power (the load). Since a power grid can't directly control the amount of power that consumers are using, it needs to alter the amount of power being produced. There needs to be a proper balance between generation and demand. Generating too little power will cause *brownouts*, and generating too much power will melt the transmission lines and cause a *blackout*.

Steam Turbine Plants

About 80 percent of the world's power is generated through the use of steam turbines. Steam-turbine-based power plants vary widely in efficiency and complexity. Simpler turbines are less efficient, but are cheaper to build and have lower operating costs. More complex turbines are more efficient, but they are also more expensive to maintain.

Regardless of complexity, all steam turbines operate in a similar manner (Figure 2.2.11). Superheated steam is created by heating

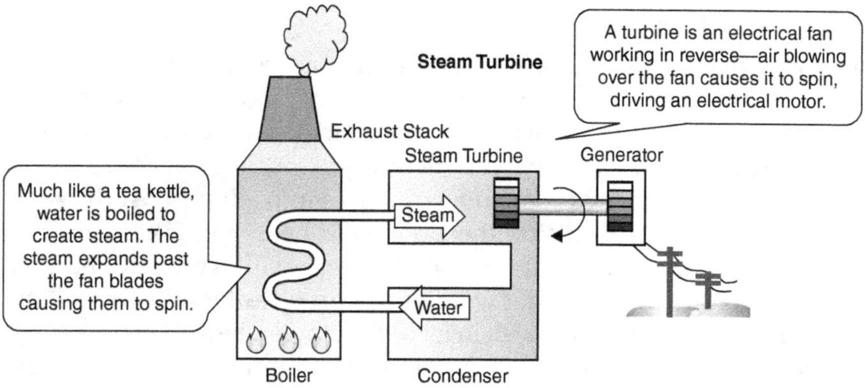

Figure 2.2.11 A steam turbine

water in a *boiler*. When the water turns into steam, it expands, moving past a turbine (which is essentially a big fan), causing the turbine to spin. The turbine is attached to a generator causing it to spin as well. Spinning the generator causes electrical power to be generated. After moving past the turbine, the steam enters a cool metal chamber (the *condenser*). As the steam touches the cool sides of the condenser, it turns back into water and is then sent back into the boiler to begin the process again. The faster the steam turbine spins, the more electrical power is produced.

A steam turbine is essentially an electrical fan operating in reverse. Instead of an electrical motor spinning a fan, a steam turbine operates by having air spin the fan. This drives the "motor" in reverse and produces electricity. From an engineering perspective, the key issue is how to push the fan blades (to spin the turbine). In a steam turbine, this problem is solved by using steam that is coming out of a boiler. The boiler acts like a tea kettle—when water starts to boil, steam exits the boiler at high speed, spinning the turbine along the way.

It takes less energy to boil already hot water than it takes to boil cold water. If the condenser cools the steam to a point just slightly below its boiling point, it is still very hot. When this hot water re-enters the boiler, only a small amount of additional heat will be required to convert it back into steam. The most fuel-consuming part of operating a steam turbine is heating up the system when it starts up. After the water is heated up, keeping the steam turbine continually operating is a very efficient way to produce more electricity. As a result, it is often worthwhile for power plant operators to keep their plant operational, and take a loss in low demand periods, in order to avoid the costs associated with a cold start.

Cogeneration

To condense the gas back into a liquid, it is necessary to cool it down slightly. The area where this cooling occurs is called the *condenser*. Fairly commonly, the condenser is a large metal container submerged in cold water. As the steam from the turbine touches the cold sides of the condenser, it cools down and condenses into a liquid. At the same time, the cold water outside the condenser heats up. If this goes on long enough, the water outside the container will eventually become hot. Most of the time, this hot water is discarded—it is allowed to flow into a local river or evaporates in a cooling tower. However, if this hot water is used for some purpose, the useful output of a plant is now increased—the plant will produce both electricity and hot water. This is the definition of a *cogeneration* plant.

Cogeneration doesn't work for all power plants. The first problem is that there is often no need for superheated hot water in an area. Selling superheated water requires a buyer that wants to purchase it. A second problem is that even if someone wants to use the hot water, the water needs to be transported from the power plant to the location where it will be used. In most cases, this requires the purchaser to build a facility adjacent to the power plant or to build a pipeline connecting the two. Third, cogeneration places increased operational restrictions on the power plant. If an industrial facility needs superheated water to operate, it will want a stable supply. For the power plant, this is bad. A power plant won't want to be obligated to produce hot water in periods where it is unprofitable to produce power.

The benefit of cogeneration is that it provides an additional income source for power plants. It doesn't make the electrical generation part of the plant any more efficient. But, since it provides more income for the same fuel use, it can be thought of as lowering the cost of fuel. When cogeneration is a result of using waste heat produced from a condenser, it is called *topping cycle cogeneration*. It is also possible to reduce fuel costs by eliminating or reducing the need for a boiler. If heat from an industrial process provides heat to the boiler, the fuel necessary to run the plant can be reduced or eliminated. This type of cogeneration is called *bottoming cycle cogeneration*.

Gas Turbine

The other major technology for producing power is a *gas turbine* (Figure 2.2.12). Gas turbines skip the step of producing steam by creating superheated gas directly through combustion. A mixture of natural gas and air is ignited in an explosive reaction that sends superheated gas past a turbine. This is very similar to the operation of a jet engine.

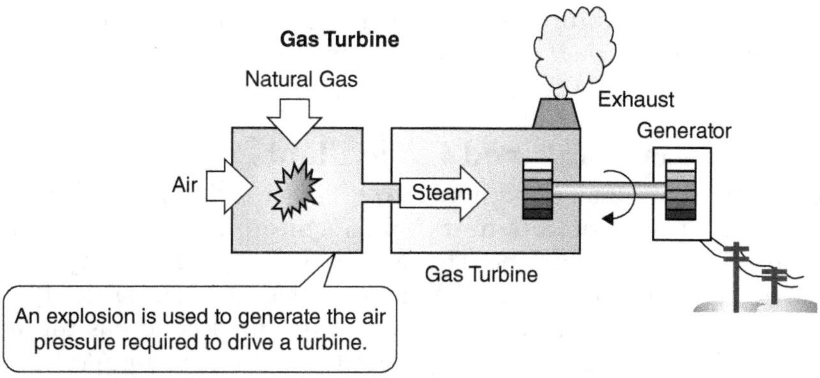

Figure 2.2.12 A gas turbine

The linkage between the spinning turbine and electrical generator works the same way as a steam turbine.

Since the waste gas can't be reused in a gas turbine, it is less efficient than a steam turbine. However, gas turbines are much simpler to build and maintain. Also, there is no lengthy process required to heat up the water into steam, so gas turbines can start producing power at peak efficiency as soon as they are turned on. As a result, gas turbines

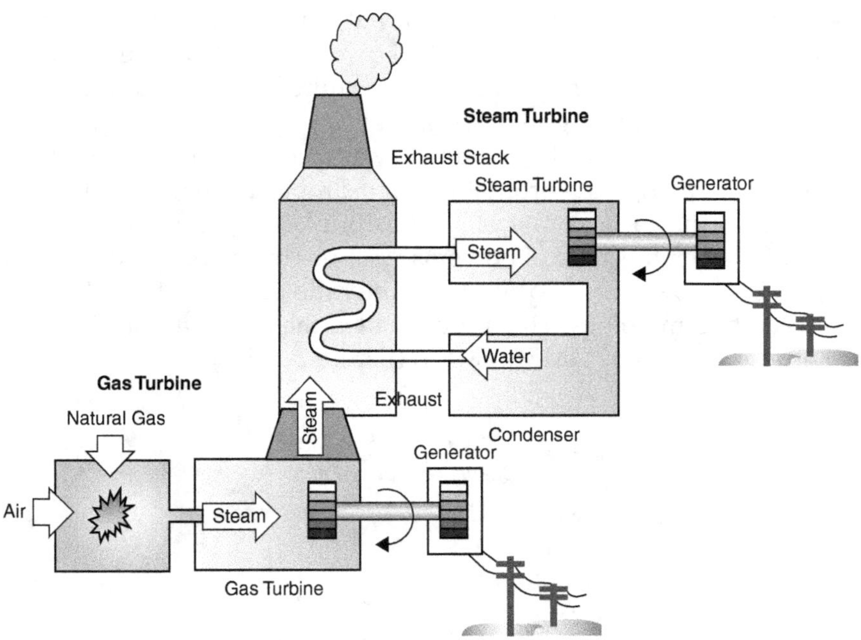

Figure 2.2.13 A combined cycle power plant

are commonly used for power plants that need to turn on quickly or that need to adjust their power output regularly.

Natural Gas Combined Cycle Plants

In the same way that a bottoming cycle cogeneration plant uses heat from an industrial process in its boiler, a steam turbine can use the exhaust heat of a gas turbine. The primary waste product of a gas turbine is superheated gas. This gas is extremely hot, but since it isn't expanding anymore, it can't be used to power a second gas turbine. However, it is perfect for heating water to produce steam. A *combined cycle* power plant is a gas turbine whose exhaust gases power a steam turbine. Combined cycle plants are more complicated than either a gas or a steam turbine plant, but they are also more efficient since there is less wasted heat (Figure 2.2.13).

The steam turbine portion of a combined cycle plant operates like a normal steam turbine and its waste product, hot water, can be reused as well. When used to cogenerate heat, a natural gas combined cycle plant is a highly efficient power plant that produces a minimal amount of pollution for each megawatt of power.

Heat Rates

As mentioned previously, the efficiency at which a plant converts fuel into electricity is called its *heat rate*. Lower heat rates imply a more efficient power plant since less fuel is required to produce the same amount of electricity (Figure 2.2.14).

The heat rate of a plant is an easy way of determining when a power plant can operate profitably. For example, if a natural-gas-fired power plant has a heat rate of 8.5 MMBtu/MWh, it can sell power profitably when the price of power is 8.5 times the price of natural gas. Since this comparison is so common, the ratio of power to fuel prices has its own terminology. That ratio is called the *market implied heat rate* and is also in units of MMBtu/MWh (Figure 2.2.15).

$$\text{Heat Rate} = \frac{\text{Quantity of Fuel Used}}{\text{Quantity of Power Produced}}$$

Figure 2.2.14 Heat rate formula

$$\text{Market Implied Heat Rate} = \frac{\text{Power Price}}{\text{Fuel Price}}$$

Figure 2.2.15 Market implied heat rate formula

*Spark Spread = Price of Electricity – (Price of Gas * Heat Rate)*

Figure 2.2.16 Spark spread formula

As a rule of thumb, power plants commonly have heat rates between 7 and 14 MMBtu/MWh. Power plants closer to the 7 MMBtu/MWh level are extremely efficient natural-gas combined cycle power plants. Heat rates close to 10 MMBtu/MWh are typical of steam turbines of all types (natural gas, coal, or nuclear). Modern gas turbines also commonly have heat rates around 10 MMBtu/MWh. Higher heat rate units are typically older units or small units intended for backup generation. Sometimes heat rates are expressed in Btu/KWh units. It is possible to convert between MMBtu/MWh units and Btu/kWh units by multiplying by 1,000. In these units, typical natural gas plants have heat rates between 7,000 and 10,000 Btu/kWh.

Spark Spreads

The heat rate of a power plant provides a way to estimate profitability. This estimate is called a *spark spread*. The spark spread is the theoretical profit that a natural gas generator can make from buying fuel and selling power at current market prices. This profit estimate does not include any charges for operating costs (Figure 2.2.16).

When multiple spark spreads are discussed, it is necessary to specify the heat rate and pricing location. Figure 2.2.17 is an example display that a trader might use to examine spark spreads and heat.

Heat Rates and Spark Spreads				
Peak Power	Location	PJM-W	SP-15	ERCOT-SC
	Price	90	75	101
Nat. Gas	Location	TET-M3	SoCal	HSC
	Price	9.51	9.34	9.21
Market Implied Heat Rate		9.46	8.03	10.07
Heat Rate (MMBtu/MWh)		Spark Spreads		
6		32.94	18.96	45.74
7		23.43	9.62	36.53
8		13.92	0.28	27.32
9		4.41	−9.06	18.11
10		−5.1	−18.4	8.9
11		−14.61	−27.74	−0.31
12		−24.12	−37.08	−9.52

Prices at a variety of trading locations

Implied Heat Rates are calculated by dividing power prices by fuel prices.

Spark Spreads estimate the profitability of various efficiencies of power plants.

Figure 2.2.17 Relationship between heat rates and spark spreads

The market implied heat rate indicates which power plant efficiencies are currently profitable in each region, while the bottom of the chart estimates the gross profitability of power plants in each region by heat rates.

If products other than natural gas are examined, different terms are used to describe the profitability spread. Dark spread refers to a coal-based generation plant. When emissions credits are included in the profitability estimates, the name of the spread typically has the word *clean* or *green* in the front (as in a *clean spark spread*).

Transmission and Distribution

Once power is generated, it needs to be brought to the customer. A higher voltage makes it easier to transfer power over long distances but it is also more dangerous. As part of the generation process, power plants use several different types of power lines—high-voltage lines are used for long-distance transmission and lower-voltage lines are used for residential distribution. *Transformers* and *substations* step the voltage up or down between different types of power lines. *Transmission* refers to the bulk transfer of power from the power plant to a substation via high-voltage lines. *Distribution* refers to the transfer of power from a substation to various consumers using much lower voltage lines.

Power plants, transmission lines, and substations form the *power grid*—a set of interconnecting power lines that provide multiple ways to route power between any two locations. The redundancy of a power grid is crucial for reliability. It prevents any single line from overloading. This helps to prevent blackouts due to a single point of failure. Most power lines are overhead lines—they are attached to tall poles suspended safely above ground level. In urban areas, electrical power lines are sometimes buried. However, buried power lines are less reliable and harder to maintain. Burying power lines is uncommon in suburban and rural areas.

The choice of voltage and location for power lines is a trade-off between safety, reliability, and efficiency. As part of the transmission process, power is wasted—it's converted into heat that must be dissipated on the power line. This waste is proportional to the current—the higher the current on a line, the greater the losses become. This waste can be reduced by using higher voltages (effectively reducing the current). However, higher voltage lines are more dangerous than lower voltage ones and can't be used in many areas.

Power is almost always transmitted over three power lines. The power on all three lines oscillates, but the sine curves are offset from one another (Figure 2.2.18). When power on the three lines is combined,

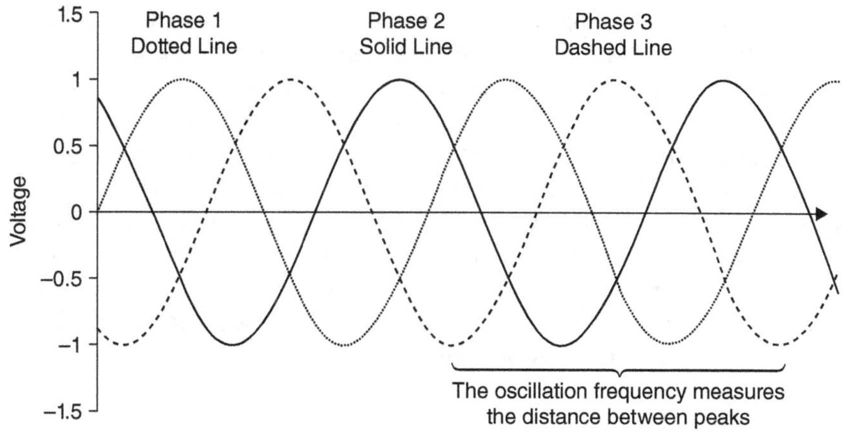

Figure 2.2.18 Three phases of AC power

the net current and voltage equal zero. This is a very important property for transmitting power. In a circuit, the net current at every point needs to be zero. Current can't just disappear. It has to be cancelled, move somewhere else, or turn into something else like heat. In most circuits, this is achieved by having the same amount of current enter and leave every point.

Using three-phase power means that electricity doesn't need to flow in a circle around the entire power grid. Instead, it can be run into a dead end and cancelled out. This addresses the problem of ensuring every point in a circuit has zero net current. If power had to flow out of each location, a single break (like a light switch turning off) would shut down the entire power grid. Three-phase power allows a transmission grid to avoid being a chain of serial circuits like Christmas tree lights, which don't work if any of the bulbs are burned out.

In a three-phase power system, power on all three lines oscillates with the same frequency, but the starting points of the waves are different.

Because it is necessary for three-phase power to cancel, it is crucial that all of the voltages in an AC network have the same oscillation frequency. Keeping the power grid operating requires every power plant to synchronize the oscillation frequency on each of its power lines with the outputs from other power plants. If two power plants are producing power with different frequencies or starting points, the line voltages will interfere with one another—sometimes canceling, sometimes adding, but never doing anything useful. If the current isn't cancelled out at every point, it doesn't just stand still. It will move somewhere else (causing short circuits or shocks) or turn into heat (melting power lines and causing fires). This will wreak havoc on a power grid.

Synchronizing power plants is a major responsibility for each TSO and a major obstacle between integrating adjoining power grids.

Almost all transmission lines use a three-phase system for transmitting power. Looking at transmission towers, this mean that most will contain a multiple of three wires. Since smaller wires help reduce the electromagnetic fields around power lines, it is fairly common for six power lines to transmit power (two groups of three lines). When multiple small wires are used to transmit three-phase power, this is called *bundling*. It helps prevent the air around power lines from picking up an electrical charge (called *ionization* or *corona*) that sometimes affects very large transmission wires.

Regional Markets

There are three major integrated power grids in the United States: the Eastern Interconnect (East of the Rocky Mountains), the Western Interconnect (west of the Rocky Mountains), and ERCOT (Texas) (Figure 2.2.19). Inside each interconnection, all of the transmission lines are synchronized. This allows power to be transported across long distances within those interconnections. However, differences in population, industry, and weather still make electrical prices a regional

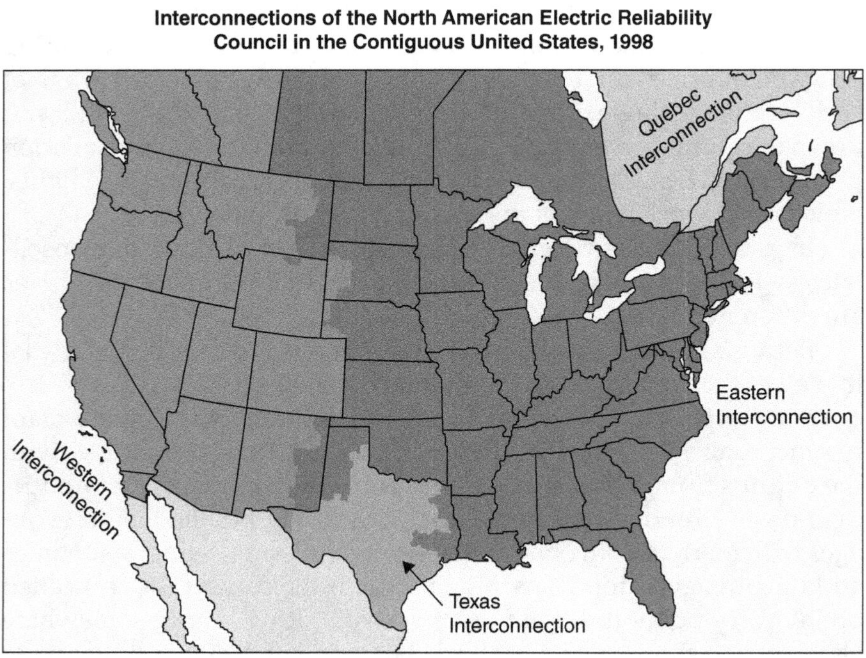

Figure 2.2.19 North American power interconnections
(*Source:* U.S. Energy Information Administration)

phenomenon. Because of this, long-distance transmission of power (called *wheeling*) between fundamentally different markets is the source of a large number of trading opportunities. Wheeling power can be expensive since there are large losses when power is transmitted over long distances. Wheeling is economically profitable if power can be obtained cheaply enough and sent to a high-price region.

Texas Interconnection

The Texas Interconnect is the smallest interconnection in the United States and is located entirely within the state of Texas. Unlike the other interconnects that cover wide geographic areas, the power in this area is coordinated by a single ISO, the Electric Reliability Council of Texas (ERCOT). There are a number of direct current (DC) power lines connecting the Texas power grid to the Eastern Interconnect and the Mexican power grids. However, those lines have limited capacity.

Western Interconnection

There are seven major trading locations in the western United States (Figure 2.2.20). The Rocky Mountains dominate the regional geography of the area. The Western Interconnect is a long line of regional grids stretching from the Pacific Northwest into the Desert Southwest, with California in the middle. Much of the trading in the Western Interconnect revolves around the flow of power into or out of the highly populated areas of California. The Pacific Northwest (MIDC) and Colorado River (Mead) near Las Vegas are major sources of hydroelectric power. During peak usage periods, power flows toward California.

The amount of available hydroelectrical power and the weather differences between regions determine how power moves around the Western Interconnect. Hydroelectric power supplies about 70 percent of the power supply in Washington and Oregon. Because it is so prevalent, small changes in water flow can result in substantial changes to regional power supplies. In the spring, when the snow melts, more power is produced in the Pacific Northwest than can be used locally, and it needs to be transmitted to an area of higher demand (usually Northern California).

California has an extremely dense population. In the summer, it often imports power from both the Pacific Northwest and the Desert Southwest to meet peak demand. However, in the fall, when temperatures in California are mild but temperatures in Las Vegas and Phoenix are still extremely hot, power can be exported from California into the desert areas. This direction of flow can change at any time based on the relative temperatures of the two regions.

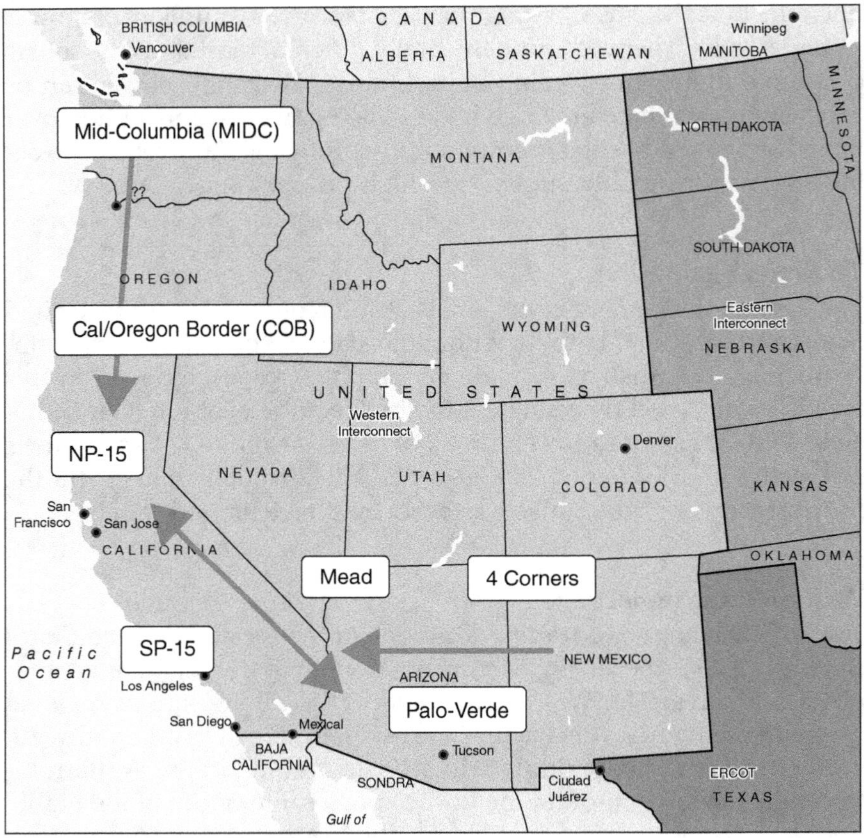

Figure 2.2.20 Western Interconnect

Since the marginal producers of power in California are usually natural-gas-fired plants, a steady supply of natural gas is required. The southern part of the region receives natural gas from the Rocky Mountains and West Texas. The northern part receives natural gas from western Canada. When the price of fuel in the two areas diverges, regional power prices can also be affected.

Eastern Interconnect

Unlike the Western Interconnection, the eastern half of the United States is less dominated by geography. It is a combination of RTO/ISOs and regulated entities forming an interconnected grid (Figure 2.2.21). The Eastern Interconnect is composed of both RTO/ISOs and regulated utilities.

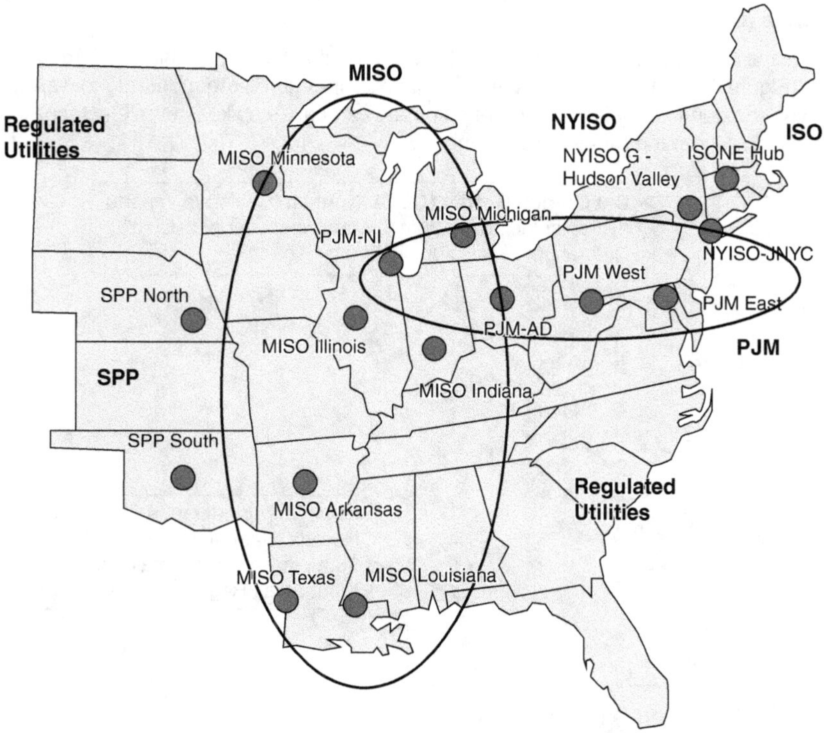

Figure 2.2.21 Eastern Interconnect

Two of the largest RTO/ISOs are in the Eastern Interconnection regions. PJM (originally named the Pennsylvania, New Jersey, and Maryland Interconnection) and Midcontinent ISO (MISO) are the two largest RTO/ISOs in North America. Other RTO/ISOs in the region include the Southwest Power Pool (SPP), New York ISO (NYISO), and ISO New England (ISO-NE). The two most liquid trading locations in the Eastern Interconnect are MISO-Indiana Hub (previously known as Cin-Hub or Cinergy Hub) and PJM Western Hub (PJM-W).

A variety of fuels and different regional weather patterns provide many trading opportunities in the Eastern Interconnect. Some of the most important trades are between regions using coal-fired plants and those using natural-gas-fired plants. Other trades are weather related. The southern part of the Eastern Interconnection has an extended summer while having mild winters. The northern part has cold winters and a shorter summer air conditioning season.

California (CAISO)

California is a heavily populated state that is divided into two major zones, NP-15 and SP-15 (Figure 2.2.22). Most of the year, the daily temperatures are moderate to warm. However, the dense population and hot summers can cause spikes in the electrical loads due to a demand for air conditioning.

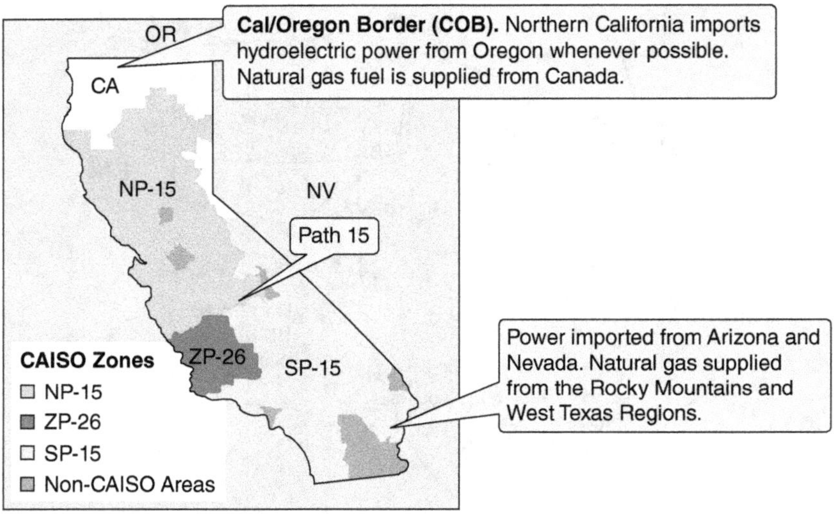

Figure 2.2.22 California power market
(*Source*: Map courtesy of FERC)

The major transmission lines are called paths. One of these transmission lines, Path 15, bisects the state into two approximately equal parts and has given its name to the two major zones, NP-15 and SP-15.

NP-15 (North Path 15) covers the northern part of the state (San Francisco Bay area) north of Path 15. When rainfall or melting snow allows, this region imports low-cost hydroelectricity from the Columbia River basin in Oregon. For the remainder of the year, natural gas plants set the price of power in NP-15. The plants are supplied primarily from western Canada.

SP-15 (South Path 15) is the pricing zone for most of southern California. It is south of Path 15. This zone is a major importer of power from Arizona (natural gas and solar power) and Nevada (hydropower from the Colorado River). Natural-gas-fired plants in the south are fed from supplies in the Rocky Mountain and West Texas regions.

ZP-26 is a large, but less important, pricing zone that has a relatively low population and excess generation capacity. It connects to both NP-15 and SP-15 zones.

Desert Southwest

The Desert Southwest has moderate winter temperatures and prolonged hot summers. Much of the year, the area has a surplus of generation capacity and is a major exporter of power to Southern California. Natural gas is the most common marginal fuel due to the abundant natural gas reserves, but coal and hydropower are also relatively common. This area also receives a great deal of sunlight, making it an attractive location for solar power (Figure 2.2.23).

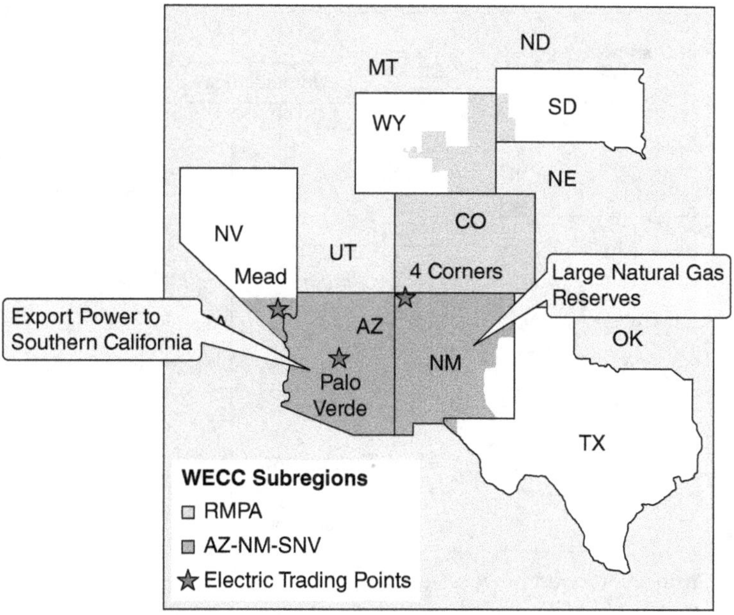

Figure 2.2.23 Desert Southwest power market
(*Source:* Map courtesy of FERC)

There are three major hubs for electricity trading in the area—Palo Verde, Mead, and Four Corners. Major power generation facilities are located near each hub.

Palo Verde is located at a major nuclear power plant and switching yard about 45 miles west of Phoenix, Arizona. Many high-power lines to California are located at this switching yard. Palo Verde is also the benchmark for most power delivered to the northern states in this region, such as Colorado and Wyoming.

Mead is located on the outskirts of Las Vegas. Lake Mead is the artificial lake formed when the Hoover Dam was built on the Colorado River. Hoover Dam is a major source of hydroelectric power and the primary delivery point for power in southern Nevada.

Four Corners is located in northwestern New Mexico at the interconnection of several major transmission lines.

Pacific Northwest

In most years, the Pacific Northwest sells surplus power into California and the Southwest. About two-thirds of all the electricity in the Pacific Northwest region comes from hydroelectric production. As a result, the quantity of surplus power depends heavily on precipitation. Water flow in this region directly affects the price of power in California (Figure 2.2.24).

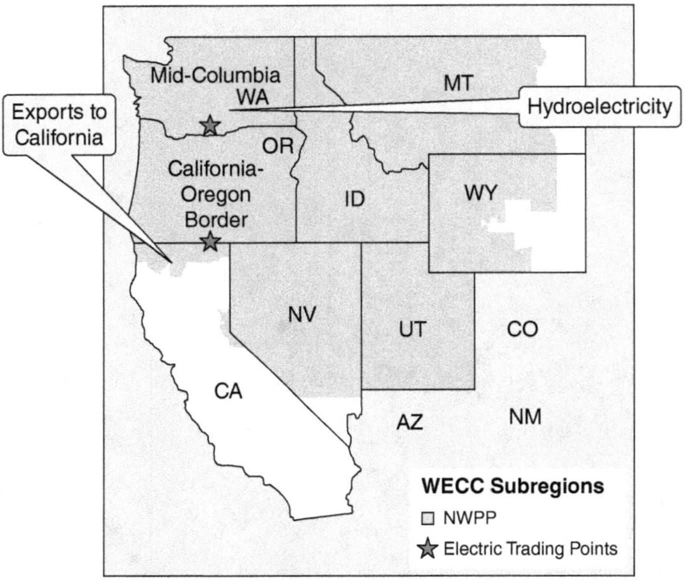

Figure 2.2.24 Pacific Northwest power market
(*Source:* Map courtesy of FERC)

Melting snow from the Cascade Mountain range, which runs through central Washington and Oregon, is a major source of river water. To the west of the mountains are several major population centers—Seattle, Washington and Portland, Oregon. The climate in these regions is fairly temperate all year. To the east of the mountains is the start of the Northern Plains states. This area is characterized by cold winters and hot summers.

Mid-Columbia (MIDC) is a delivery hub for a number of hydroelectric plants on the Columbia River.

Cal-Oregon Border (COB) is a major switching station in southern Oregon adjacent to the California border that interconnects several major transmission lines.

Mid-Atlantic (PJM ISO)

The mid-Atlantic region contains many large population centers, like Washington D.C., Baltimore, and Philadelphia, on the Eastern seaboard. This area formed one of the first independent power grids, the PJM ISO (Figure 2.2.25). This ISO was named after its constituent states (Pennsylvania, New Jersey, and Maryland). PJM has since expanded to include West Virginia, Delaware, large parts of Ohio, parts of northern Illinois, and Virginia. It is one of the largest and most liquid electricity markets. Within PJM, there are a number of active trading hubs.

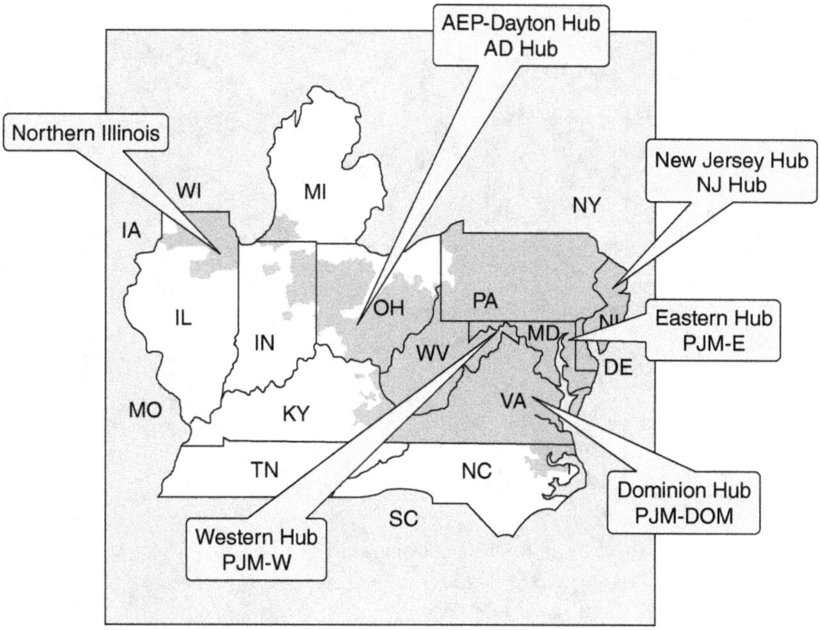

Figure 2.2.25 Mid-Atlantic power market
(*Source:* Map courtesy of FERC)

Geographically, the PJM service area is very diverse. Large reserves of coal native to Pennsylvania and West Virginia serve as the marginal fuel for the western part of the PJM service area. Power on the East Coast and Virginia is commonly determined by gas-fired power plants. The climate in the northern half of the region ranges from cold winters to hot summers. The climate in the southern half of the region is warmer—mild winters and extended hot summers.

A large number of power plants in the less populated areas of the PJM service area export power into the more populated regions. As a result, there are often congested power lines between these areas.

Midcontinent (MISO)

The Midcontinent ISO (MISO, previously called the Midwest ISO) coordinates power for much of the central United States (Figure 2.2.26). The northeastern part of this region is heavily industrialized, while the southern and northwestern sections are more rural. There are several major trading locations in the region. Of these, Indiana Hub (previously known as Cin-Hub) is the most influential.

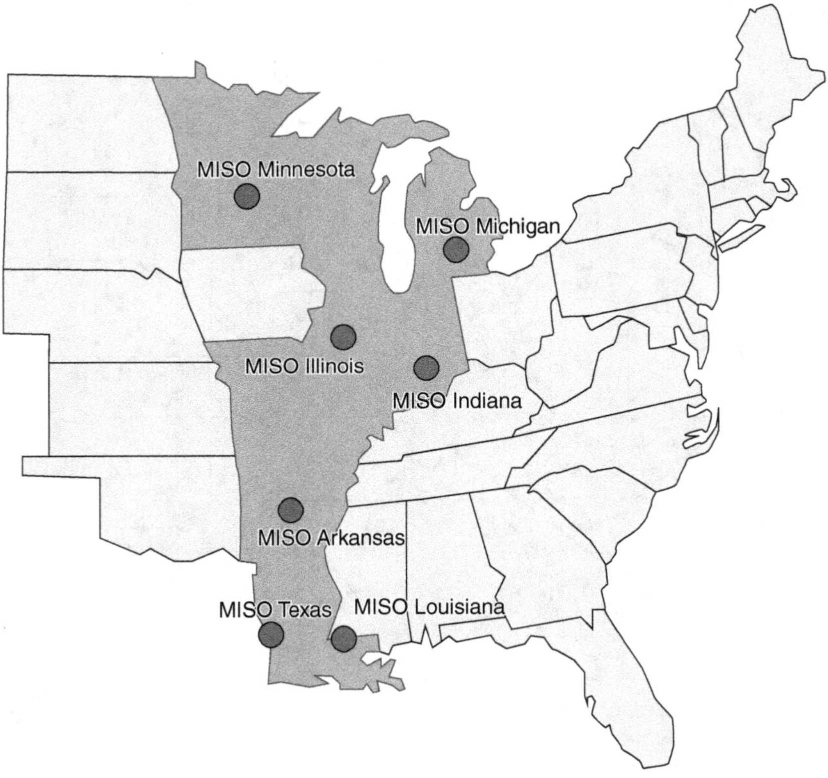

Figure 2.2.26 Midcontinent power market

From a climate perspective, the middle of the United States has cold winters and hot summers. The cold weather usually starts in December but can arrive in early November and usually lasts through April. The summer months—July and August—are hot and humid, but the weather cools off quickly in September. The southern part of MISO has mild winters and hot summers.

Many of the power plants in the northern part of this region, including a large number of marginal producers, are coal powered. As a result, coal prices commonly determine the price of power in the Midwest even in high demand periods. The southern part of the MISO territory is heavily dependent upon natural gas.

Because of the cool shoulder months (the spring and fall) in the Midwest, power is often wheeled to southern states where hot weather is more common. Some hydroelectric power is available from the Great Lakes and Tennessee Valley areas. Depending on the time of year, power might be imported from either of these two regions.

New York (NYISO)

The New York power grid is self-contained in the state of New York (Figure 2.2.27). The southeastern part of this region contains one the most heavily concentrated areas of demand for electricity in the country—New York City and Long Island. The region is characterized by the flow of low-cost power from the northern and western sections of the state into the high demand regions surrounding New York City.

Most of the New York metropolitan area is located on islands. As a result, there is limited ability to transfer power to those areas from other parts of the region and there is a high reliance on inefficient generators during periods of peak demand. This has made the New York City area one of the most expensive power markets in the country. In order to assure reliable service, power plants in the New York metropolitan area are subject to much stricter rules and regulatory requirements than are common in other regions.

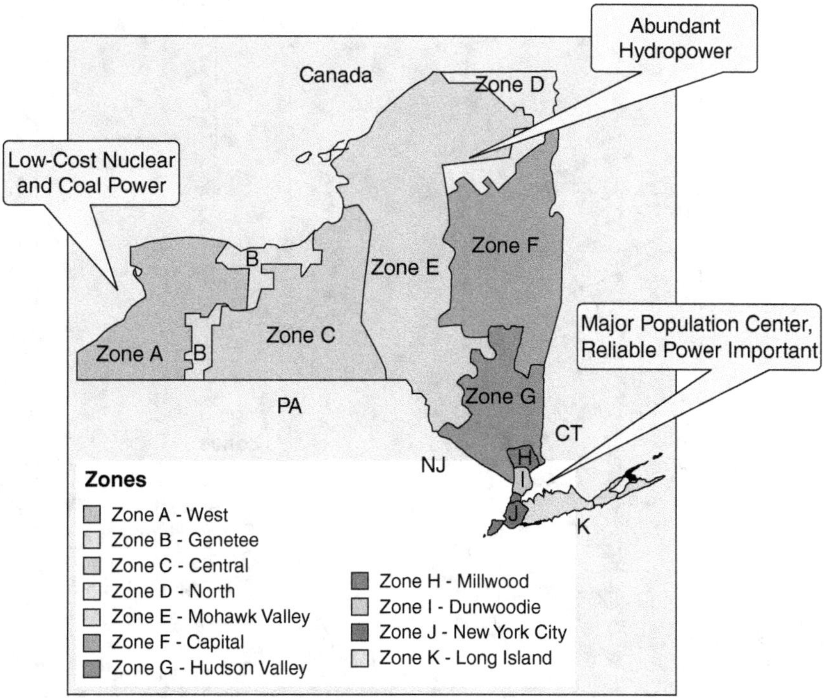

Figure 2.2.27 New York electrical market
(*Source:* Map courtesy of FERC)

New England (ISO-NE)

There is only a single trading hub in the New England region. The prices at this hub are based on selected nodes around the Boston, Massachusetts area (Figure 2.2.28).

New England has to import fuel for almost all of its power generation requirements. The marginal fuel for the region is natural gas. The bulk of this supply comes from the U.S. Gulf Coast and eastern Canada. There are efforts to augment this supply by constructing liquefied natural gas (LNG) Terminals in Massachusetts. This would help the region to augment their natural gas supplies.

Most of the population in New England is in the southern part of the region—Connecticut and the area around Boston. In comparison, the northern part of the region is relatively unpopulated.

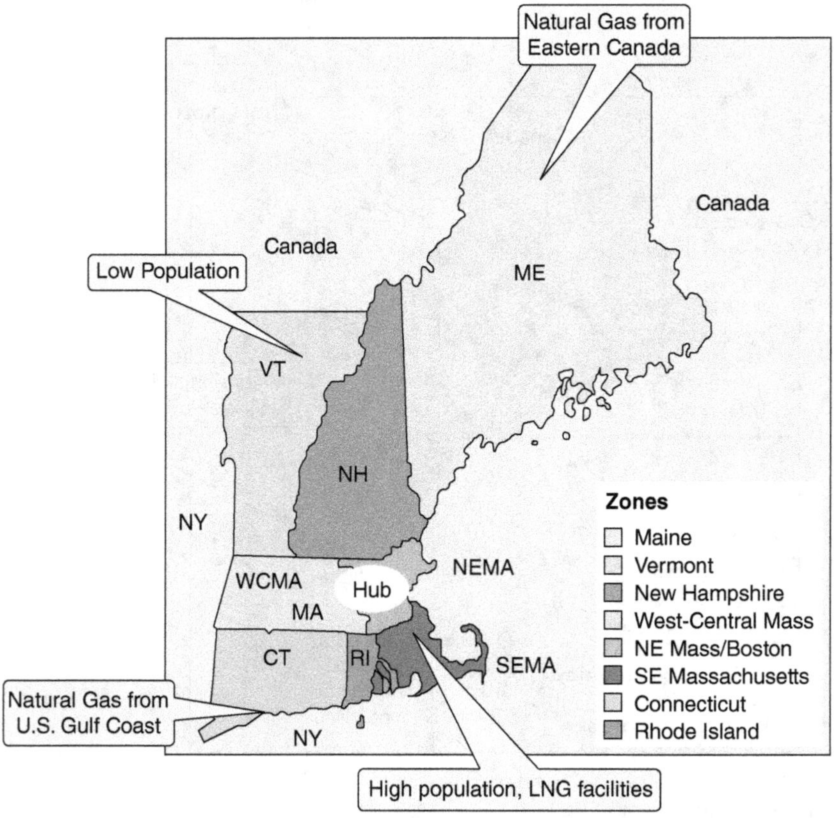

Figure 2.2.28 New England power markets
(*Source:* Map courtesy of FERC)

Texas (ERCOT)

ERCOT is the ISO that provides power to Texas; it is divided into five primary regions (Figure 2.2.29). Most of the region's population is located in the northeastern part of the state. ERCOT North contains the greater Dallas/Fort Worth area, and ERCOT Houston contains the Houston metro area.

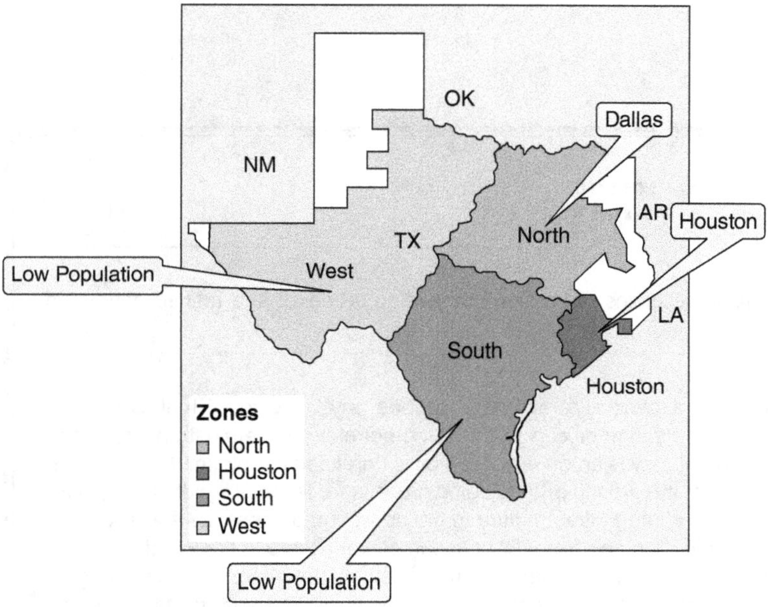

Figure 2.2.29 Texas electrical market (*Source:* Map courtesy of FERC)

Due to abundant local supplies, the marginal fuel for the area is usually natural gas. The climate is characterized by mild winters and prolonged hot summers. Currently, most of the generation is located in the north and Houston zones—close to the greatest areas of consumer demand. However, substantial solar and wind-based generation is being built in the western part of the state. This complicates congestion planning in Texas since it requires transmitting constantly changing quantities of power from the western zone into the more populated zones.

2.3

OIL

30-Second Summary

Purpose

This chapter explains the market for trading crude oil and refined petroleum products.

Summary

Petroleum is a general term that describes any liquid fossil fuel. Crude oil, gasoline, and heating oil can all be called petroleum. The most important petroleum commodity is crude oil. Crude oil is unrefined petroleum that has been removed from the ground prior to being processed. There is a global market for crude oil and a large infrastructure to transport and process it. As a result, the price of crude oil is approximately the same everywhere in the world.

There are smaller, regional markets for refined petroleum products like gasoline and heating oil. For a variety of reasons, including worker safety and the perceived stability of governments near production regions, refineries are usually located in industrialized countries near the market for their refined products. Refined petroleum products are usually not transported long distances after refining. As a result, the price of refined petroleum products is very regional in nature and local areas have their own supply and demand.

Key Topics

- Crude oil is the single most traded product in the world as measured by both volume and value.
- International petroleum trading is focused on crude oil rather than refined products.
- There are regional markets for refined petroleum products, like gasoline. The prices for these products vary substantially throughout the world, and each region's prices are set by local supply-and-demand considerations.

Oil, or *petroleum*, is a liquid fossil fuel formed when decaying plant life becomes trapped in a layer of porous rock. After millions of years, heat and pressure convert decaying plant life into hydrocarbons. Some of these hydrocarbons are gases, others are solids, and still others are liquids. *Petroleum* is the generic name for any hydrocarbon that is liquid under normal temperature and pressure conditions.[1] Like other fossil fuels, the mixture of hydrocarbons in petroleum can vary widely. When petroleum is first extracted from the ground, it is called *crude oil.*

It can be dangerous to burn crude oil directly since the lighter portions of it can form explosive vapors and the heavier portions may not flow easily or ignite smoothly. As a result, crude oil is usually separated into components that are more uniform in composition. This separation is done in a refinery through the process of distillation. After crude oil is distilled, there are specific names for each liquid that is produced (gasoline, heating oil, etc.). The term *petroleum* refers to crude oil and all of the products refined from it.

The liquid properties and high energy density of petroleum make it a popular fuel for vehicles. Compared to hydrocarbon gases like methane or propane, petroleum contains a lot of energy per unit of volume. For example, a tank of a hydrocarbon gas, like propane, will only fuel a backyard grill for a couple of hours. However, the same volume of gasoline will be sufficient to drive a car for several hundred miles. Additionally, compared to solid hydrocarbons like coal, liquids are much easier to move around inside an engine.

Crude oil is the single most traded commodity in the world. As a result, the global importance of oil is far greater than its impact on just the energy industry. Because of the global high profile of crude oil trading, the oil industry is subject to a very high level of international scrutiny. It is often viewed as a benchmark for the energy sector, and can have a disproportionate impact on electricity and heating costs.

Petroleum

Petroleum is a catchall term that can describe any hydrocarbon fuel that is a liquid at room temperature. Petroleum can mean crude oil, gasoline, heating oil, or jet fuel.

Crude Oil Market Participants

The trading of crude oil is dominated by the relationship between the suppliers and consumers. The largest importers of crude oil are the industrialized nations of North America, Europe, and the Asia-Pacific region.

---

[1] Literally, *petroleum* means "rock oil" in Latin. It comes from the words *petra*, meaning "rock," and *oleum*, meaning "oil." Petroleum, coal, and natural gas are all hydrocarbon fossil fuels. They differ in that at room temperature, petroleum is a liquid, coal is a solid, and natural gas is a gas.

The major net exporters are less developed countries in the Middle East and South America. Transportation and storage costs are the primary determinant of where supplies originate and where they end up. All things being equal, oil is transported to the nearest market first. If that market is sufficiently supplied with oil, then the next closest market is chosen.

International politics and environmental regulations also affect the flow of petroleum. Sometimes, countries will refuse to buy or sell oil to one another. For example, in 1973, OPEC[2] countries refused to sell oil to Western Europe, America, and Japan because of their support for Israel. Another example of oil not going to the nearest market is due to environmental regulations. The United States requires that gasoline and diesel contain very low quantities of sulfur. Sulfur is a major pollutant and source of acid rain. Compared to countries that don't have those restrictions, low sulfur crude oil is more valuable in the United States. This makes it worthwhile to ship low sulfur oil long distances to get to that market.

There are five major types of participants in the petroleum market—producers, refiners, marketers, governments, and consumers.

Producers. Oil is produced around the world. About half the world's supply of crude oil is located in the Middle East. Since the region has a relatively low population and a low demand for oil, it is the single largest exporting region. There are many other oil-producing regions worldwide. Several industrialized countries, like the United States, are major oil producers. However, industrialized countries tend to be net importers of oil due their high domestic demand.

Refiners. Refiners convert crude oil into finished products. These facilities are most commonly located near the consumer markets. The net profit of a refiner is proportional to the region's *crack spread*—the profit from buying a barrel of oil, splitting it into its components, and selling the components. Refiners typically try to eliminate their exposure to petroleum prices.

Marketers. Marketers buy petroleum products with an intention of reselling those products. These organizations can be anything from a hedge fund to a gas station operator. Typically, marketers will try to buy finished products and resell the same product at a higher price.

Governments. Outside the United States, most country governments will own the mineral rights to petroleum. In addition,

---

[2] **Organization of Petroleum Exporting Countries** (OPEC)—A major crude oil cartel consisting of the governments of 12 countries: Algeria, Angola, Ecuador, Iran, Iraq, Kuwait, Libya, Nigeria, Qatar, Saudi Arabia, the United Arab Emirates, and Venezuela.

governments can pass rules around trading, create consumer protection standards, use crude oil as a political tool, and can seize, or *nationalize*, the assets of producers and refiners.

Consumers. The end-users of petroleum products are consumers. Consumers run the range from industrial manufacturers to private individuals filling up their cars with gasoline.

Common Units

Barrel (bbl). In the United States, petroleum of all types is traded by volume. A barrel contains 42 U.S. gallons (in the United States) or approximately 159 liters (metric units).

Tonnes (t). In Europe, oil is typically traded by weight. A tonne (or metric ton) is a unit of mass equal to 1,000 kilograms or approximately 2,204.6 U.S. pounds.

Conversion Between Barrel and Tonne. A rough approximation is that there are 7.5 barrels in one tonne of crude oil. However, because the composition of crude oil can vary substantially, each type of crude oil will have its own conversion ratio. These can range from approximately 7.2 barrels per tonne (for Persian Gulf crude) to about 7.5 barrels per tonne (for premium light crude like WTI or Brent).

Descriptions of Crude Oil

Crude oils are typically described by their *density* and *sulfur content*.

Density is usually measured by American Petroleum Institute (API) gravity. Low density (*light*) crude oils have a higher proportion of light hydrocarbons that can be recovered through simple distillation. In contrast, *heavy* crude oils contain a larger portion of low value products that require additional downstream processing to be valuable. The density of crude oil is fairly apparent by visual inspection—light crude oil will flow freely while heavier crude oil will be much more viscous.

High *sulfur content* is highly undesirable for crude oil. Sulfur is a major pollutant and can only be removed through expensive processing. *Sweet* crude oil has a low sulfur content, while *sour* crude oil contains a much larger amount of sulfur.

Exploration and Drilling

Oil, like other fossil fuels, is formed when decaying organic material is trapped underground. Commonly, liquid and gas hydrocarbons are

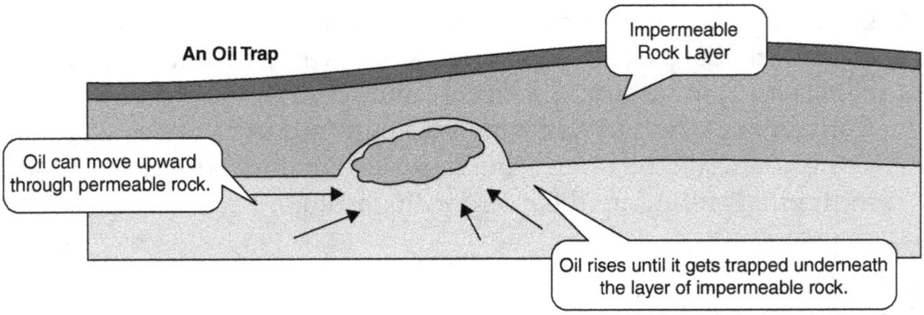

Figure 2.3.1 An oil trap

found in the same area. Both liquid and gas hydrocarbons (petroleum and natural gas) are lighter than rock and will naturally migrate upward unless that movement is prevented by a layer of impermeable rock. This combination of an impermeable layer of rock overtop a permeable layer of rock is called a *trap* (Figure 2.3.1). Oil exploration involves looking for traps in areas likely to contain oil or gas.

The most common way to search for oil traps is to use *seismology*. Seismology is the study of how energy waves, like sound waves or earthquakes pass through the Earth's surface. Different types of rock transmit energy at different speeds. Engineers can determine the type of rock layers in an area by creating sound waves and sending them into the Earth. Some of the sound will echo back toward the engineers. The timing of how quickly the sound returns and its strength will give a good indication of the type of rock layers and their relative depths. However, seismology is not an exact science. Even if seismologists know that a liquid is trapped, they might still need to dig a well to determine the exact nature of the liquid.

Common Terms

Associated Gas. Associated gas is natural gas produced from the same well as oil.

Permeability. Permeability is a measure of how easily liquid and gas pass through rock. In practical terms, the amount of connections between the pores (open spaces) within a rock. A porous rock may be impermeable if none of the pores are connected.

Porosity. Porosity is a ratio of the volume of empty space in a rock to the total volume of the rock. A highly porous rock has a lot of open space.

Trap. A trap is an impermeable layer of rock located above a porous, permeable layer of rock.

Crude Oil

Crude oil is the single most traded commodity in the world. Because of this, crude oil trading is highly influential and crude oil is viewed as a benchmark for the entire energy market. Despite having no real connection to many other energy commodities, crude oil prices often have a large impact on other energy markets.

There are many different types of crude oil. To distinguish types, crude oil will often be referred to as *sweet* or *sour*. These terms describe the percentage of a major pollutant, sulfur. During combustion, sulfur combines with oxygen to form sulfur oxides. In the presence of water (another byproduct of combustion), sulfur oxides form sulfuric acid. Crude oil with less than 0.5 percent sulfur is considered "sweet." Crude oil with a sulfur content of more than 0.5 percent is typically classified as "sour."

The terms *light* and *heavy* are also used to describe the density of crude oil. In general, less dense products like jet fuel and gasoline are more valuable than heavier products like heavy fuel oil and asphalt. As a result, crude oils that contain a higher proportion of lighter components will be more valuable than heavier crude oils. Density for petroleum products is classified by its *API gravity*. Higher API gravities are associated with less dense liquids. Liquids with an API gravity higher than 10 degrees will float on water, while liquids with an API gravity less than 10 degrees will sink. *Light crude* generally has an API gravity of 38 degrees or more. *Heavy crude* has an API gravity of 22 degrees or less. Crude with API gravity between 22 and 38 degrees is generally referred to as *medium crude*. Crude oils with an API gravity above 45 degrees are referred to as *condensate*. In general, light crudes are more valuable than heavier crudes or condensate (Figure 2.3.2).

API Gravity	Name	Relative Value
<10	Bitumen	Low Value
10–22	Heavy Crude	Medium Value
22–38	Medium Crude	High Value
38–45	Light Crude	Highest Value
>45	Condensates	High Value

Figure 2.3.2 American Petroleum Institute gravity

API Gravity	U.S. Pounds per Gallon	BBL/MT
8	8.4573	6.2066
9	8.3971	6.2511
10	8.3378	6.2955
15	8.0532	6.5180
20	7.7875	6.7405
25	7.5386	6.9629
30	7.3053	7.1854
35	7.0859	7.4078
40	6.8793	7.6303
45	6.6844	7.8527
50	6.5003	8.0752
55	6.3260	8.2977
58	6.2259	8.4311

Figure 2.3.3 Crude oil conversion factors

To an energy investor, the density of crude oil is important because in some parts of the world, like Europe, crude oil is typically traded by weight (metric tons, abbreviated *MT* or *tonnes*). In other parts of the world, like the United States, crude oil is traded by volume (barrels, abbreviated *BBL*). The denser a substance, the smaller the volume required for a given amount of weight. This means that conversion between units becomes an obstacle to investors (Figure 2.3.3).

Crude Oil Concepts

Crude oil is traded in either barrels (in the United States) or metric tonnes (Europe and Asia). Some common conversions:

- There are 42 gallons in each barrel of oil.
- There are approximately 7.5 barrels of light crude per metric tonne.
- The abbreviation for barrels is BBL.
- The abbreviation of metric tonnes is MT.

Transportation

Petroleum is typically transported as crude oil until it is close to its final destination. Only after it arrives close to the final location is the crude oil separated into its components. This business model is the result of several factors. The first factor is that refineries can cost billions of dollars to build and have expected life spans of more than 50 years. Because of that, a refinery will outlive almost any single oil field. The second factor is that oil fields are often located in remote areas of the world. A refinery needs a highly trained workforce, and it is much easier to find that workforce near major cities. A third factor is that refineries located near their customers can optimize their output to meet local demands and comply with local regulations. Finally, refineries also tend to be located where the safety of both workers and investors can be ensured. Placing a multibillion dollar investment in a safe location where it is unlikely to be damaged by violence or nationalized by an unfriendly government is an important consideration for a long-term investment.

After it is produced, crude oil will typically be transported through a pipeline to a port facility. Once it is at the port, it will be loaded onto a transport ship that will carry the crude oil to a refinery for processing. Larger ships are more cost effective at transporting crude oil. However, there are often physical constraints like the water depth at docking facilities or the width and depth of various canals (like the Suez Canal or the Panama Canal) that constrain the maximum size of ships. As a result, there are a variety of different crude oil transport ships (Figure 2.3.4).

Refining

Refined petroleum products are created by separating crude oil into various components. This process starts with simple distillation,

Capacity Millions Bbl	Length	Beam	Draft	Description
	Coastal Tanker			
0.3	205 m	29 m	16 m	Less than 50,000 dwt, mainly used for transportation of refined products (gasoline, gasoil).
	Panamax (LR1)			
0.5	230 m	32 m	13 m	Between 60,000 to 80,000 dwt. This is the maximum size vessel that can traverse the Panama Canal prior to its 2014 expansion. Panamax vessels travel about 15 knots.
	Aframax (LR2)			
0.7	245 m	42 m	14 m	Between 80,000 to 120,000 dwt. (typically 80,000 dwt). AFRA = American Freight Rate Association.
	Suezmax			
1.0	285 m	45 m	16.5 m	Tankers between 125,000 and 180,000 dwt and capable of traversing the Suez Canal without offloading any cargo. Average speed of 15 knots.
	VLCC			
2.0	350 m	55 m	22 m	Very Large Crude Carrier. 150,000 to 300,000 dwt. Can be accommodated by the expanded dimensions of the Suez Canal. Flexibility to use many terminals since many can accommodate their draft.
	ULCC			
3.3	415 m	63 m	30 m	Ultra Large Crude Carrier. 300,000 dwt to 550,000 dwt. Used for long-haul crude oil routes from Persian Gulf to Europe or East Asia (around South Africa or through Strait of Malacca). Because of their immense size, ULCC ships require custom built terminals.

Figure 2.3.4 Types of crude oil cargo vessels

where crude oil is separated into fractions by boiling it at progressively higher temperatures. Since each component of crude oil will boil at a slightly different temperature, slowly increasing the temperature of crude oil will cause products to progressively boil off. These gases are then trapped and cooled to bring them back into liquid form.

After the initial separation of products, many refiners continue to process the heavier fractions to increase their value. In general, lighter petroleum products, like gasoline and jet fuel, are more valuable than the heavier products, like asphalt. By splitting the heavier products (cracking them) into simpler products, their value is increased. Post-distillation processing (called downstream processing) also removes sulfur from the oil and is used to increase the octane of gasoline. Downstream processing can substantially alter the output of a refinery. For example, simple distillation might produce 20 percent of its output as gasoline. However, downstream processing can increase that percentage to around 50 percent. By cracking heavier products into less dense products, downstream processing typically converts a 42-gallon barrel of crude oil into approximately 45 gallons of finished products.

It is impossible to produce just one distilled product, like gasoline, without producing the others. The process of converting crude oil into gasoline involves creating every refined petroleum product at the same time. For example, if a refinery increases its output in response to higher gasoline prices, it runs the risk of glutting the market with its other refined products. The typical mix of refined products in a barrel of crude oil is shown in Figure 2.3.5.

However, the actual products from a barrel of crude oil can vary substantially. Every barrel of crude oil contains a different mix of raw materials. Crude oil that converts into a high proportion of

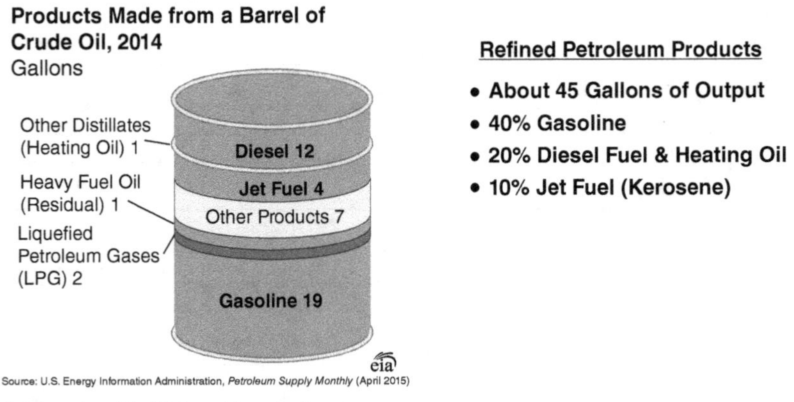

Picture courtesy of the US Energy Information Agency.

Figure 2.3.5 Approximate mix of products from a 42-gallon (U.S.) barrel of crude oil

lighter products through simple distillation is called a *premium crude*. Premium crude oils are more expensive than lower quality crude oil. Other common terms for crude oil describe its viscosity and sulfur content. *Light sweet crude oil* pours easily and contains relatively low sulfur. *Heavy sour crude* has a thick, syrupy consistency and contains high levels of sulfur.

The process of distillation links the prices of refined petroleum products to crude oil prices. If the price of crude oil rises, all of the refined products will become more expensive. However, there is a different type of link between the prices of the refined products. If a gasoline shortage forces refiners to increase their gasoline production, the market will become flooded with other petroleum products. As a result, there is often a negative correlation between the prices of the refined products. The relationship between crude oil and distilled products is known as the *crack spread*.

Is There a Shortage of Refineries in the World?

There haven't been any new refineries built in the United States since 1976. There will likely be only a limited number of new refineries constructed in the future. They are extremely expensive to construct, and it might take a new refinery 15 or 20 years to pay back its construction costs. Building a new refinery is an investment in a very long-term asset. They have to be built in expectation of market conditions 20 to 40 years in the future.

Historically, global oil production was expected to peak around 2010 and start decreasing in subsequent years. At the time, it was thought that the world was running out of crude oil. Expecting a diminished supply of raw materials, it didn't make a lot of sense for refineries to increase capacity. Ultimately, the prediction of peak oil proved overly pessimistic due to the discovery of large shale gas deposits and improvements in exploration techniques. However, those innovations created another set of problems for refiners in the form of low prices.

The number of offshore drilling rigs is also on the decline for similar reasons. Building a drilling rig is a long-term investment. Like refineries, a drilling rig may require many years to earn a profit on that investment. This is risky because offshore oil wells face competition from shale gas fracking, electric cars, and similar technological innovations.

Fractional Distillation

Crude oil is refined (separated into its component pieces) by fractional distillation. It is placed into a large vertical container, called a

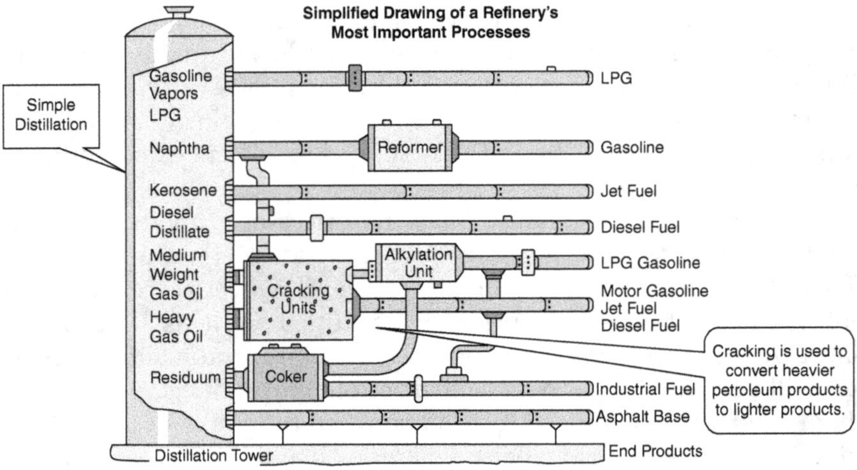

Figure 2.3.6 A distillation tower
(Source: U.S. Energy Information Agency)

distillation tower, and heated (Figure 2.3.6). The lightest elements, with lowest boiling points, rise to the top while the heavier fractions settle at the bottom. By selectively siphoning off the lighter fractions, crude oil is separated into pieces.

After crude oil is separated into its components by distillation, many of the heavier liquids are further processed by subjecting them to high temperatures and pressures. This process, called *cracking*, breaks the heavier liquids into lower density liquids.

Comparing Crude Oil to Refined Petroleum

While there is active trading in both crude oil and refined petroleum products like gasoline, the markets are very different from one another. Crude oil has a global market and is transported around the world. It is approximately the same product and price wherever it is being traded. For example, if the price of oil is higher in New York than Paris, tanker ships will be diverted from France and start heading to New York. The refineries in the northeastern United States and northern Europe can each accept crude oil intended for the other location.

Refined petroleum products, like gasoline, are typically regional markets. Prices and product formulations vary substantially between regions. Historically, it has been considered very risky to locate refineries outside the industrialized countries. As a result, finished products are refined close to their final destination. There is a limited international infrastructure for transporting finished petroleum products in bulk. There is some international trade in these products, but the volume of trading is much lower than for crude oil. Local environmental regulations further fragment the market for refined products. For example, gasoline used in North America is required to use a different formulation than gasoline used in Europe. This is true even on a national level. For example, gasoline in California might use a different formulation than gasoline in New York.

Gasoline

Gasoline is the primary fuel used to power automobiles and light trucks around the world. In 2007, it accounted for 44 percent of all petroleum consumption. In the United States, about two-thirds of the cost of gasoline is related to the cost of acquiring crude oil and refining it. Taxes, distribution, and marketing fees make up approximately one-third of the remaining cost (Figure 2.3.7). The demand for gasoline increases during periods of good weather. Demand starts to rise during the spring and peaks in the late summer.

The primary method for distributing gasoline is through pipelines. Pipelines transfer gasoline from refineries to terminals near consuming areas. At the local terminals, gasoline is mixed with additives, like ethanol, to meet local government regulations. Then, the gasoline is transported by tanker truck to local gas stations where it is sold to consumers. In the United States, gasoline is differentiated by its *octane* level and *formulation*. Along with local taxes, these factors account for most of the regional variation of gasoline prices. Other factors influencing the retail price of gasoline can include transportation costs and the marketing plan of the individual gas station owners.

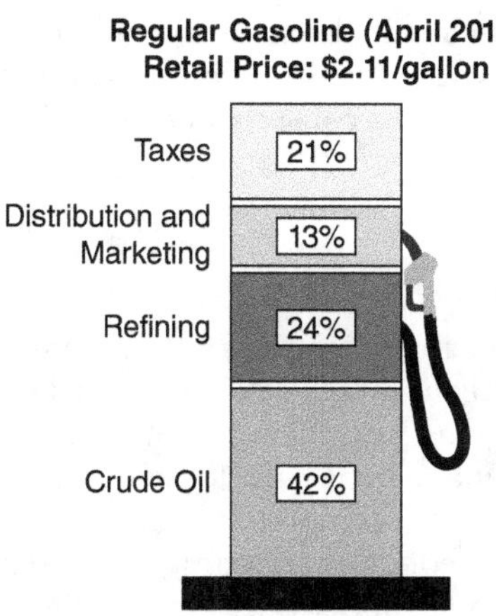

Figure 2.3.7 The price of gasoline
(*Source:* U.S. Energy Information Agency)

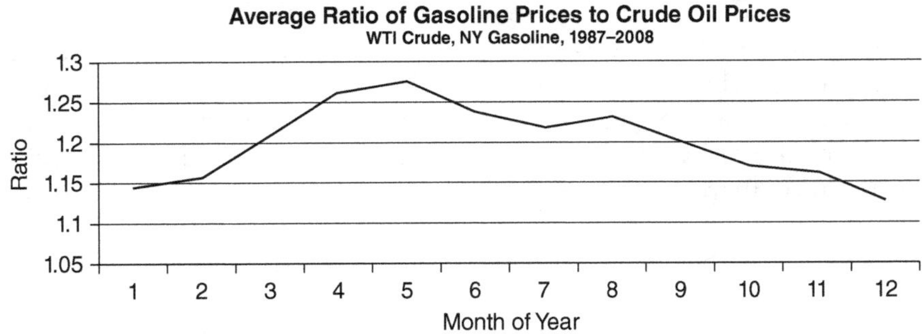

Figure 2.3.8 The ratio of gasoline prices to crude oil prices

Octane is a measure of how much gasoline resists ignition. When gasoline resists ignition, less power is delivered to the power train of the car. Instead, it will be wasted as heat. Octane is not a measure of the energy in a tank of gasoline. For example, ethanol has a higher octane than gasoline (it is easier to ignite), but contains less energy. Adding ethanol to gasoline increases the octane of gasoline, but still decreases the total miles per gallon of the car using that gasoline.

The formulation of fuel refers to the various additives that are required or prohibited. For example, a state might mandate that all gasoline sold between March and October contains 10 percent ethanol. Sometimes additives are prohibited. For example, lead was once used as an antiknock agent in gasoline in the United States. Antiknock agents are used to increase the octane rating of gasoline. However, the lead pollution from automobile exhaust became a major health hazard and its use was later banned. Sulfur is another example of a regulated pollutant.

Gasoline prices fluctuate throughout the year based on crude oil prices, consumer demand, and formulation (Figure 2.3.8). As a general rule, gas prices tend to increase rapidly in the early spring and summer. Prices stabilize in the later summer and decline in the coldest winter months. Gasoline prices tend to be very volatile because there is a limited amount of supply that can be generated from refineries and consumers can't substitute other fuels for gasoline.

Octane Ratings

Higher octane ratings mean that engines can operate more efficiently. In this case, "efficiently" means that less heat is wasted when fuel is ignited to produce power. Engines have to be optimized for a specific octane level of fuel—using higher octane fuel does not automatically make an engine more efficient. Under normal combustion, fuel is pumped into an engine cylinder and ignited. The expanding gas that results from igniting the fuel will push the cylinder outward to drive a crankshaft. This provides the mechanical power in a car.

In an engine, there are multiple cylinders that all need to work in concert with one another. The fuel in each cylinder will ideally ignite in a process that drives the piston outward in smooth motion. When the pistons on the other side of the engine ignite, the original piston will move back to its starting position. If the fuel in all of the linked cylinders does not ignite at the same time, a number of problems can occur. If one piston is still expanding when it should be falling, it will decrease the power that is being created by the engine (Figure 2.3.9).

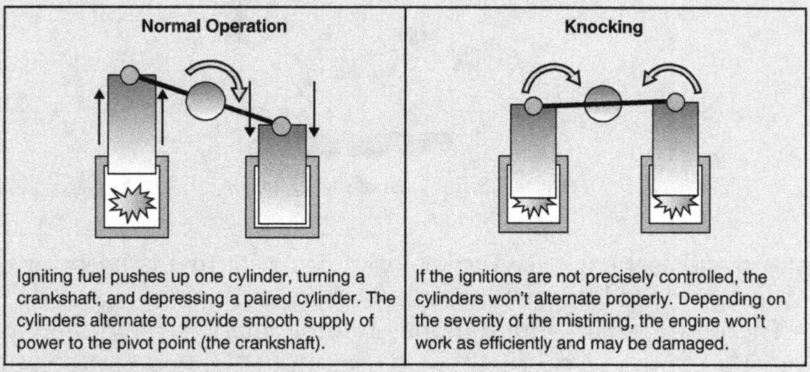

Figure 2.3.9 Engine knocking

Higher octane fuel ignites in a more predictable manner. Higher octane gas has less uncertainty about the timing of its ignition. There have been a number of fuel additives used over the years to prevent the problem of unpredictable fuel ignition. For a long time, lead was the most popular choice; currently high octane fuels like ethanol are used. Some common terms for the problem of cylinder mistiming are *knocking*, *pinging*, or *pinking*.

Diesel Fuel (Heating Oil)

Heating oil and diesel fuel are variations of the same product, a distillate of petroleum called *No. 2 fuel oil*. Of the two, diesel fuel typically has stricter requirements for a minimum pentane rating (similar to octane ratings on gasoline) and lower sulfur content. Otherwise, both chemically and in the financial markets, the two products are nearly identical and used interchangeably. Like gasoline, a large portion of the consumer price of diesel comes from taxes, distribution, and marketing expenses (Figure 2.3.10).

About 80 percent of No. 2 fuel oil is used as diesel fuel. The remainder is used for residential and commercial heating. Nearly all large trucks, buses, trains, farm equipment, and large boats in the United

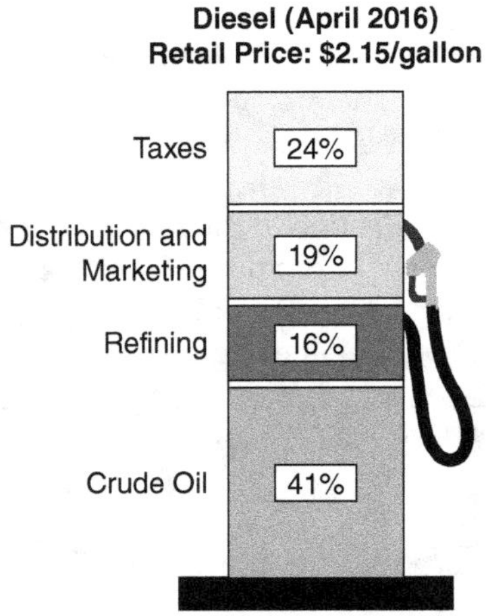

Figure 2.3.10 Cost of diesel fuel

States use diesel engines. The majority of diesel fuel is used for on-highway vehicles like semitrucks and tractor trailers.

There is a small international trading market for diesel fuel. Almost all of the diesel fuel that is used in the United States is produced domestically, with the surplus being shipped to other countries. Like most petroleum products, it is much more common for the raw materials (crude oil) to be traded internationally than the finished product.

When used as heating oil, the largest use for No. 2 fuel oil is for residential heating during winter months. In the United States, almost all of the houses that use oil heat are located in the northeastern portion of the country. As a result, heating oil prices are strongly influenced by winter temperatures in Mid-Atlantic and New England areas. Prices are lowest in summer months and spike during the winter (Figure 2.3.11). Households often try to reduce their oil costs by filling up their storage tanks during summer months when prices are low.

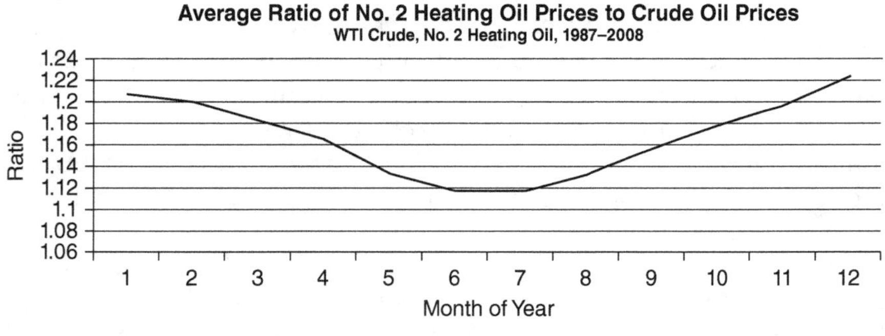

Figure 2.3.11 Ratio of diesel to crude oil prices

However, since most households lack sufficient storage capacity to go an entire winter without refilling their supply, there is continued demand for heating oil throughout winter months. Most households will need to refill their heating oil four or five times a winter.

Oil Futures

Crude oil futures are the most traded contracts in the world. The two dominant international benchmarks for crude oil are the New York Mercantile Exchange West Texas Intermediate Crude (NYMEX WTI) and Intercontinental Exchange's Brent Crude (ICE Brent) futures contracts. WTI generally represents the price for crude oil delivered in the southern United States. Brent represents the price of seaborne crude in the Atlantic Ocean. Both of these are crude oil that contains a high quantity of lighter petroleum components good for making gasoline, with low quantities of sulfur and other pollutants.

Common Terms

Futures Contract. A futures contract is an agreement traded on an organized exchange to buy or sell assets at a fixed price, with both delivery and payment occurring at some point in the future.

Spot Contract. A spot market contract is an agreement directly between two people to buy or sell assets for immediate or short-term delivery, in theory, exchanging cash and commodity on the spot. In practice, spot market delivery typically means within the next four weeks.

Physical Transaction. A physical transaction is an exchange of commodity for cash.

Financial Transaction. A financial transaction is cash settled. The commodity is not physically delivered. Instead, one party to the transaction will pay the other party in the transaction.

Each exchange will have a number of futures contracts associated with each commodity. These contracts differ based on their delivery date, with each contract delivering on a different date. The futures contract will often be described like "WTI December 2017" or abbreviated like CLZ7. In abbreviated form, the initial two characters are the abbreviation for the contract, the second to last character represents the month of delivery, and the final digit represents the year of delivery (Figure 2.3.12).

Each futures contract has a limited life span. This life span starts when the exchange allows trading and ends when the contract expires. Expiration occurs at a published date sometime before the delivery

Symbol	Month
F	January
G	February
H	March
J	April
K	May
M	June
N	July
Q	August
U	September
V	October
X	November
Z	December

Figure 2.3.12 Futures month abbreviations

period. For example, a WTI contract might specify that futures shall cease trading on the third business day prior to the 25th calendar day of the month prior to delivery. This gives holders of futures contracts a chance to schedule their deliveries prior to the start of the delivery month.

Physical Trading

Because crude oil futures are so heavily traded, most physical crude oil transactions are based on the price of crude oil futures. This is different than how most other markets operate. For most other commodities, physical transactions determine a spot price—the amount of cash required to take possession of the commodity on the spot. That spot price then determines the price for future delivery. In the crude markets, just the opposite occurs, physical transactions are usually determined by prices observed in the crude oil futures.

A spot market contract is an agreement directly between two people, also known as a *bilateral agreement*, to buy or sell assets for immediate or short-term delivery. In theory, this exchanges cash and the commodity on the spot. In practice, spot market delivery for crude oil means sometime within the next four weeks.

In theory, the terms and conditions for physical crude oil trades can be customized for each transaction. In practice, the vast majority of spot trades follow standardized terms. This allows traders to avoid having the legal department individually negotiate contracts. Standard parts of these contracts include a definition of the volumes to be delivered each month, the delivery location, the approximate composition of the product (sometimes called the *product grade*), credit terms, payment terms, and some way to determine a fair price. Sometimes, the price will be fixed. In other cases, the price will be variable. The reason for using a variable price is to link transactions to the heavily traded futures market. That market is hard to manipulate and easy to hedge. Variable pricing normally includes the following:

- **Index Price**. A common index price is the next-to-deliver crude oil contract. This is also called the *prompt contract*.
- **Grade Differential**. The grade differential is a premium or discount to index depending on the type of crude grade. The term *basis* is sometimes used instead of *differential*.
- **Location Differential**. This is a premium or discount based on the cost to transport oil to the delivery location. For example, this might represent a pipeline and or trucking fee. The term *basis* is sometimes used instead of *differential*.
- **Other Differential**. Other differential may be a premium or discount based on negotiations.

The index price is typically specified using one of several formulas. One way to do this is to base the physical contract on a specific future. However, many crude oil contracts don't expire at month end. As a result, a common approach is to use a *calendar month average*, or CMA, price.

A calendar month average price is based on the average price of the *next to expire*, or *prompt*, futures contract over a month. For example, if a January futures contract expires two-thirds of the way through December, the calendar month average price for December is based on the January contract for the first two-thirds of the month and then the February contract for the last one-third of the month.

Posting Plus (P-Plus)

Posting Plus (P-Plus) is a localized version of the CMA approach for WTI or West Texas Sour (WTS) crude purchases delivered to Cushing, OK (the NYMEX WTI delivery point). In theory, the "plus" represents the price to transport crude from the wellhead to the futures delivery point. In practice, wellhead to delivery point prices are fairly consistent, and P-Plus contracts work similarly to CMA contracts. The difference is that the price posted by a major oil producer is used as the index price instead of NYMEX WTI futures.

Crack Spreads

Cracking refers to the process of separating out and transforming the components of crude oil into commercially saleable products. A *crack spread* is the difference between the price of finished petroleum products and the price of crude oil. Since most refined petroleum products are not exported internationally, crack spreads will vary substantially throughout the world. Each region will have its own crack spread set by the supply-and-demand considerations of its local market for finished petroleum products.

The crack spread is the wholesale price of refined petroleum products less the cost of raw materials. It is approximately equal to the profit that a refiner will earn by converting crude oil into refined petroleum products. If the spread between finished products and crude oil is too narrow to produce a refining profit, refiners will cut back on production until the prices of the finished products rise.

A typical trade in a crack spread would be to "buy" a future crack spread that is too small for refiners to make a profit and benefit when refiners cut back on production and prices rise. Buying a crack spread means the trader benefits from a rise in finished petroleum products and a fall in crude oil prices. Because the price in all of these products tends to move up and down together, a crack spread has limited exposure to the price of crude oil. Another variation of a petroleum spread trade might allow traders to speculate on the relationship between gasoline and heating oil.

Each region has a typical grade of crude oil that is used as a benchmark. In North America, West Texas Intermediate Crude (WTI Crude) is most common. In Europe, Brent Crude is used. For a crack trader, the different types of crude oil don't just mean the prices vary slightly. Different crude oils vary in composition. Premium crude oils, like WTI Crude or Nigerian Bonny Light, will produce a higher percentage of the lightest

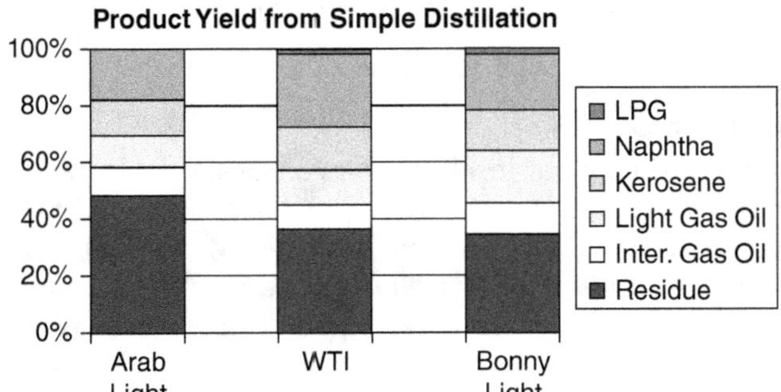

Figure 2.3.13 Yields from simple distillation
(*Source:* Courtesy of U.S. Energy Information Agency)

gasoline-like products through distillation compared to less desirable crude oils. As a result, refiners have to optimize the mix of crude oil entering the refinery to produce the most profitable mix of refined products desired in their region. The typical mix of products produced by simple distillation of several crude oils is shown in Figure 2.3.13.

Refiners are natural traders of crack spreads. Crack spreads are a primary tool for refiners to hedge their output. Refiners face a substantial price risk between the time they buy crude oil and the time when they can sell their finished products. In most cases, refiners attempt to lock in their profits by agreeing to a sales price of their most important products ahead of time. They do this by trading financial contracts in crude oil, gasoline, and diesel/heating oil. Crack spreads also allow major users of refined products to lock in spreads without taking on a large exposure to crude oil prices.

Since the major oil products are all widely traded on exchanges, almost anyone can make crack trades. There is a very active market in crack trades. The most common spread trades are based on crude oil, gasoline [Reformulated Blendstock for Oxygen Blending (RBOB)], and diesel fuel (heating oil). The ratio between these three products defines the crack trade. Usually this ratio is abbreviated X:Y:Z, where *X* is the number of crude oil contracts, *Y* is the number of gasoline contracts, and *Z* is the number of diesel fuel contracts. The most common ratio is 3:2:1, but 2:1:1 and 5:3:2 ratios are also fairly common (Figure 2.3.14).

Refiners benefit when refined products appreciate in price relative to crude oil. In other words, they are *long* the crack spread. Refiners can eliminate this exposure by selling a crack spread. Selling a crack spread (alternately, going *short* the crack spread) means the trader will benefit when the price of crude oil rises or the price of refined products declines.

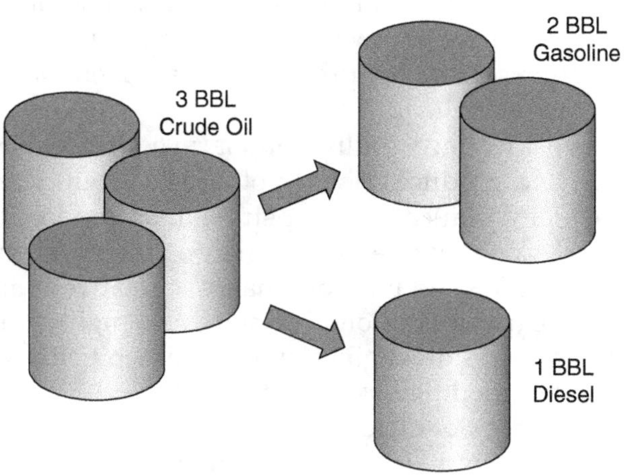

Figure 2.3.14 A 3-2-1 crack spread

Exchange Traded Spreads

Sometimes crack spreads are their own financial instrument. It is also possible to enter into a crack spread by trading futures in each of the underlying petroleum commodities. Every time a trader makes a futures trade on an exchange, the trader is required to post margin to ensure that he or she has enough money to meet his or her financial responsibilities. The amount of margin required is directly proportional to the risk of the trade. Entering into a crack spread by trading individual commodities can result in a substantial amount of capital being locked up in margin accounts. However, the combination of trades in a crack trade is much less risky than holding an outright position in any of the underlying commodities. As a result, less money is required up front to trade the spread as a single unit.

Exchanges commonly offer crack spread trading alongside markets for the underlying commodities. As a result, it is fairly common to talk about a "crack spread" as its own traded instrument. Moreover, it is often possible to buy "crack spread options" and "crack spread futures" on an exchange. The behavior of these contracts is identical to creating a crack spread through individual products. However, margin requirements are lower and all of the futures are traded simultaneously.

Ethanol

Ethanol is an alternative to petroleum fuels that can be produced by fermenting and distilling almost any starch-containing crop. It is a clear colorless liquid that is chemically identical to the alcohol found in intoxicating beverages. Ethanol intended as fuel is *denatured* to make it unsuitable for drinking because alcohol intended for human consumption is subject to a lot of government regulations. Ethanol is fairly easy to manufacture from common crops like corn or sugarcane. Ethanol is a renewable fuel source that produces fewer greenhouse emissions than fossil fuel.

On the downside, since fertilizer and farm equipment both require petroleum fuel and produce a lot of pollution, it is unclear if ethanol production actually reduces either petroleum demand or pollution. Ethanol also does not have the same energy density as gasoline. Because of this, the transportation of ethanol is relatively more expensive than gasoline transportation. Ethanol is also highly corrosive and absorbs water. As a result, engines and gasoline pipelines have to be specifically built or modified to handle ethanol.

Another drawback of ethanol is that it produces higher amounts of some types of ground level pollution than gasoline. For example, ethanol produces twice the ozone of a similar gasoline engine. Another criticism of ethanol is that it raises food prices. Ethanol is produced from crops that would otherwise be used as food. Given the limited amount of cropland in the world, using crops to produce ethanol means less food is available for a growing population.

Compared to gasoline, ethanol is an inferior fuel by most comparisons. The popularity of ethanol is a result of the expectation that the world will be running out of easily obtainable petroleum in the near future. Ethanol can be produced today in larger amounts than other alternative fuels, and much of the existing infrastructure for gasoline can be retrofitted to accept ethanol.

Starch is converted to ethanol through the process of *fermentation*. This is essentially the same process used to produce most alcoholic drinks. First, the raw materials are *milled* by grinding them into a fine powder called *meal*. Then, liquid is added to the meal to produce a slurry that is heated. Heating helps the meal dissolve into a liquid solution and kills any bacteria that might be present. Then, the mixture is cooled and enzymes are added to turn the starch into simpler sugars. After that, yeast is added into the mix. This yeast converts the sugars into alcohol and carbon dioxide. Finally, the alcohol is separated from any solids or liquids that may have formed during the fermentation process by distillation.

The Corn Crush

Because the raw materials for ethanol are food crops that must be grown every year, there can be substantial differences between the price of ethanol and its raw materials. Government regulations specify that ethanol be mixed into gasoline at a fixed ratio. Unless ethanol is more expensive than gasoline, the price of ethanol is determined by the value of the displaced gasoline. In comparison, the raw materials that are used to produce ethanol are affected by weather, crop conditions, and competing demands for corn as a food crop.

Just like a crack spread, it is possible to speculate on the relationship between ethanol and raw material prices. For example, if ethanol is highly expensive and corn is cheap, distillers can start buying up corn for conversion into ethanol. This will result in higher food prices and lower ethanol prices.

In the United States, the most common raw material for ethanol is corn. Corn represents about two-thirds the cost of producing a gallon of ethanol. The major byproducts of the conversion are distiller's dried grains and carbon dioxide pollution. Although distiller's dried grains have potential to be used as a feed crop for livestock or as the raw materials for biodiesel, they are currently extremely cheap and not

(*Continued*)

a major source of profit for an ethanol distiller. Since it takes about a bushel of corn to produce 2.6 gallons of ethanol, the spread between these two prices is often called a *crush spread* (Figure 2.3.15).

$$\text{Corn Crush Spread} = \text{Cost of Ethanol}\left(\frac{\$}{\text{gallon}}\right) * \frac{2.6\ \text{gallons}}{\text{bushel}} - \text{Cost of Corn}\left(\frac{\$}{\text{bushel}}\right)$$

Figure 2.3.15 The corn crush spread

Ethanol can be created from a variety of raw materials (corn, sugarcane, and petroleum are all relatively common). Most traded contracts will accept any variety of ethanol as long as it meets delivery grade requirements. In the future, it might be necessary to first calculate the cheapest-to-deliver raw material prior to entering into a crush trade. Alternatively, the crush spread calculation might change if a market for distiller's grains develops.

Biodiesel

Like ethanol, biodiesel is an alternative fuel that is receiving a lot of research attention.

Biodiesel is an alternative fuel for diesel engines created by removing glycerin from vegetable oils. Although biodiesel does not contain any petroleum, most diesel engines can use biodiesel without modification. Commonly, biodiesel is blended with petroleum diesel and the mixture is denoted "Bxx" where *xx* represents the percentage of biodiesel in the blend. For example B20 is 20 percent biodiesel.

There are some substantial advantages to using biodiesel. It is biodegradable, renewable, and generally produces lower emissions than standard diesel fuel. It is also nontoxic and, since it has a higher flashpoint than conventional diesel, is safer to transport and store.

On the downside, engines fueled by biodiesel have about a 10 percent reduction in fuel economy and power compared to burning diesel fuel. Biodiesel is also a stronger solvent than traditional diesel fuel. Very high percentages of biodiesel might require special engines. However, the biggest limitation of biodiesel is its cost. Currently, it can only be produced in limited amounts and is substantially more expensive than regular diesel fuel.

- **B2–B5.** B2 refers to a 2 percent biodiesel/98 percent diesel blend by volume. Similarly, B5 refers to a 5 percent biodiesel/95 percent diesel blend. Low-percentage biodiesel blends like B2 through B5 are popular fuels in the trucking industry because biodiesel has excellent lubricating properties. As a result, these blends can improve engine performance and lengthen an engine's life span.

- **B100.** B100 is pure biodiesel. Pure biodiesel is a solvent that can loosen and dissolve sediments in storage tanks. It may also cause rubber and other components to fail in older vehicles.
- **B99.9.** B99.9 is biodiesel that has been blended with a small amount of diesel. Mixtures like this are done to take advantage of tax credits that some jurisdictions give to the blenders. Since B99.9 has already been blended, the blender would be paid the credit. As a result, buyers would not get the tax credit, and B99.9 would trade at a discount to B100.

Renewable Identification Numbers

In many countries, governments have passed renewable fuel standards to increase the amount of biofuels in the country. To track compliance with these programs, a biofuel like ethanol and biodiesel might be assigned an identification number when it is created. In many countries, these identification numbers, called renewable identification numbers (RINs), can be traded independently of the actual fuel. This allows the parties that are required to meet renewable fuel standards, typically oil refineries, the ability to purchase RINs to meet their compliance requirements.

RIN Price Spikes

RIN prices can spike when the government rules require that refiners use a specific quantity of biofuel rather than requiring that a certain percentage of biofuel is mixed into conventional fuel. For example, in an economic slowdown, the economy might use less fuel as a whole. This will cause refiners to sell less fuel. Auto manufacturers will typically only rate car engines to work with a certain percentage of biofuel. If the refiners are already mixing that percent of biofuel into their fuel, they are faced with the problem of how to use more biofuel. In that situation, refiners might try to purchase RINs to meet their requirements to use more biofuel.

Common Terms

Brent Crude. Brent crude is a light, sweet crude oil that serves as an international pricing benchmark. It is a premium crude oil from the North Sea.

Feedstock. Crude oil of any type that enters a refinery is called feedstock.

(Continued)

Fuel Oils. Fuel oils are the liquid fuels heavier than gasoline. Typically, fuel oils are classified into six categories with the lower numbered oils flowing more easily than the higher numbered oils. The two most common categories of fuel oil are No. 2 fuel oil (diesel) and heavy oil (No. 4 to No. 6 fuel oil).

Heating Oil (No. 2 Fuel Oil). Heating oil is essentially diesel fuel. It is the second largest fraction of a barrel of crude oil after gasoline. Most types of crude oil will produce about half as much heating oil as gasoline when refined.

Heavy Oil (No. 4/5/6 Fuel Oil). Heavy oil, also known as Bunker fuel, is a term for the heaviest fuel oils. Typically, these fuels must be heated to turn them into liquids before they can be used. This is a delicate process, and as a result, these fuels are only commonly used aboard large ships or in power plants. Because of its limited uses, heavy oil is typically cheaper than gasoline or diesel fuel.

Kerosene (No. 1 Fuel Oil). Kerosene is the lightest grade of fuel oil. In a distillation stack, it falls between gasoline and diesel fuel. It is uncommon to see kerosene traded in the futures market.

RBOB Gasoline. RBOB is a grade of gasoline suitable for mixing with ethanol or other gasoline additives. RBOB is gasoline before it has been mixed with additives.

WTI Crude. West Texas Intermediate Oil is a premium crude oil that provides a high proportion of valuable light petroleum products through simple distillation. It is a light, sweet crude oil and the most common benchmark for U.S. crude oil prices.

2.4

COAL

30-Second Summary

Purpose

This chapter introduces coal trading.

Summary

Coal is a solid hydrocarbon fuel that is readily available throughout the world. It is easy to store, and relatively inexpensive to produce relative to the amount of electrical power that it can generate. In many ways, it is the perfect fuel. Unfortunately, it is a major source of carbon (CO_2) and sulfur (SO_2) emissions. The pollution that results from burning coal has made it unpopular among consumers.

Coal is one of the least expensive ways to generate electricity. However, it has the drawback of being the most polluting fossil fuel. The competing desires for cheap electricity and less pollution are at odds with one another. Global efforts to reduce carbon emissions have typically deadlocked on the issue of coal-powered generation. Most countries want to use coal-fired power plants for cost reasons and would like other countries to stop using them because of pollution concerns.

Because the price of coal is generally low, transportation makes up a much higher percentage of the delivered cost of coal than other fossil fuels. As a result, most coal is used within a couple hundred miles of where it is mined. By far the biggest application for coal is electrical generation. Electrical power plants and coal mining companies are often located close together. As a result, there are relatively few people buying or selling coal on the open market. Coal is not a heavily traded financial product.

Key Topics

- Coal is closely linked with electrical power generation. Coal is a popular fuel for electrical generation and 90 percent of coal production is used to generate electrical power.
- Coal-fired electrical generators are a major source of pollution. Coal produces more pollution than any other type of fossil fuel, and this has made coal politically unpopular.
- In the financial markets, coal is much less important than other fossil fuels. Coal is primarily used to provide energy for electrical power generation.

(Continued)

- Coal-based power plants have a large economy of scale. Big centralized coal-fired plants are cheaper to operate than small plants. The current nature of the power grid—centralized generation and extensive transmission lines—is in large part due to this economy of scale.
- Cheap natural gas produced by natural gas fracking is a major challenge to coal producers.

Coal is a major fuel used to generate electricity. About half of the electrical power in North America is generated from coal plants. While there are a number of industrial uses for coal, like making steel or providing raw materials for plastics, these applications are much smaller markets for coal than electrical power generation. Over 90 percent of the coal used in North America is used for generating electricity. Globally, coal generation accounts for over half of the world's electrical generation capacity.

As a solid fuel, coal has different operating constraints than either oil or natural gas. For example, it is much harder to use a solid fuel in an engine. Something has to physically move the coal into the fire box—it isn't like gasoline that can use a suction pump. Coal fires are also harder to start up and shut down than oil or natural gas fires. Natural gas or oil engines can be turned off by cutting the fuel supply. This isn't the case with coal—any coal that is currently being burned will continue to burn for a while even after the engine is shut down.

One reason that coal is much cheaper than either petroleum or natural gas is because its potential uses are more limited. It is easier to make an internal combustion engine that runs off a liquid than a solid. Another reason is that coal mining is generally less complicated than either oil or natural gas drilling. Many coal mining problems can be addressed by applying additional brute force. For example, if more coal is needed, either new technology or longer working hours can be used to address the problem.

The major drawback of coal is the amount of pollution created when it is burned. Coal is the single largest source of air pollution in the world. Some of this is because coal is so commonly used, but another part of the problem is that megawatt for megawatt, coal produces more pollution than either oil or natural gas. As a result of this pollution, the coal markets are closely associated with market-based approaches limiting global climate change.

On a physical level, *coal* is a term that can describe almost any solid hydrocarbon. The actual composition of coal, everything from the heat energy that it contains to the amount of pollution that it releases when it is burned, varies substantially. In general, coal is a black or brownish black sedimentary rock that is removed from the ground by mining. Various types of coal are classified by the amount of heat energy they can produce as well as the amount of pollutants they contain.

Compared to other fossil fuels, coal is fairly easy to store and transport. It can be stacked into a pile and won't evaporate or leak out of the bottom of a rail car. The most common method of transporting coal is by train. It is also fairly common for coal to be transported on barges and trucks. Since coal is typically traveling from mines to power plants, there isn't a large consumer distribution system.

Even though coal transportation isn't particularly difficult, it can be expensive. Since coal is cheap, even moderate transportation costs can make up a substantial portion of the retail cost of coal. As a result, it is common for coal-fired power plants to be located near coal mines. In other cases, unique technologies are built to transport coal cheaply. For example, coal pipelines can be built to link power plants to a continuous supply of coal from a distant mining location. To pass it through the pipeline, the coal might be crushed and mixed with water to form a *slurry* or compressed to form a solid *log*.

Coal Pipelines

Although coal is a relatively cheap fuel, it is fairly heavy. The cost of transporting coal can make up a substantial portion of its final cost. As a result, having access to a cost-effective transport network is an important factor in determining the economics of a coal-based power plant. Perhaps the easiest solution is to locate the power plants close to a mining region. However, that may be impossible due to the need to transmit power to some service area.

If there is a very long distance between the source and destination, coal pipelines can be an attractive alternative to rail cars or barges. There are two main technologies used to transport coal through pipelines. Slurry pipelines crush the coal into small pieces and mix the pieces in a liquid solution. Alternately, the coal can be compressed into logs that are suspended in water.

There are a number of serious environmental considerations with coal pipelines. One problem is that they use a tremendous amount of water. Coal slurry pipelines use a 1:1 ratio of coal to water and make the water very difficult to clean after it is used. Since a large coal-fired power plant might burn 1,000 tons of coal a day, the amount of water involved can be significant over the course of a year. This is particularly true if the pipeline is located in a region with limited water supplies.

(*Continued*)

For example, the 273-mile coal slurry pipeline supplying the Mojave Generating Station in Laughlin, Nevada, was using a billion gallons of water a year prior to being shut down by complaints from local Indian tribes.

To address the concerns of water usage, new pipeline technologies are being researched. For example, compressing the coal into a log allows three or four tons of coal to be transported for each ton of water used. These pipelines also leave the water cleaner than slurry pipelines.

A second problem with pipeline transportation is that the coal needs to be dried out prior to being used. The most effective way to dry the coal is to burn some of it. However, that has the side effect of further increasing carbon emissions and raising transportation costs.

There is a limited international market for coal. The primary reason is that coal power plants are generally built close to an abundant local supply. Because transportation costs account for a substantial percentage of its final price, imported coal is typically much more expensive than local coal. As a result, it is usually uneconomical to transport coal over long distances.

Partially as a result of this, coal prices are much less volatile than the prices of other fossil fuels. The major consumers of coal are power plants that operate continuously throughout the year. They sign long-term supply contracts with nearby coal mines. It is fairly straight forward for power plants to stockpile supplies, and difficult for them to resell unused coal because there are few counterparties interested in coal trading. Power plants spend a lot of time optimizing their transportation from their local suppliers to minimize that aspect of their costs. Consequently, it is difficult for them to switch over to a different supplier on short notice.

The major influences on the price of coal are the price of other fossil fuels and environmental legislation. Prolonged periods of high oil and natural gas prices can make coal relatively more attractive for generating electricity. When prices for other fuels rise, coal power plants become comparatively more economical. This ultimately leads to an increased use of coal and higher coal prices. However, even when it goes up in price, coal generally stays much less expensive than oil and natural gas.

Market-based approaches to reducing carbon emissions and pollution also have a major effect on the price of coal. Because coal is heavily used and very polluting, it is the primary target of these regulations. These approaches seek to make it less economically viable to use coal as a primary fuel. Coal is heavily used as a fuel for producing electricity because it is cheaper than the alternatives. So, to reduce coal usage, most environmental initiatives operate by making coal-based generation more expensive.

Types of Coal

Because the chemical makeup of coal can vary substantially, it is usually classified based on how much carbon it contains and how much heat energy it can produce. The four main types of coal used for fuel are *lignite, sub-bituminous, bituminous,* and *anthracite*. Other varieties of coal exist, but they are generally not used as fuel. For example, graphite and diamonds are almost 100 percent carbon, and technically can be considered coal, but are neither easily ignited nor efficient to use as a fuel.

There is a trade-off between ease of ignition and energy content of coal. Low-quality fuel is easy to ignite but does not contain as much energy as higher quality coal. Higher-quality coals are harder to ignite but contain substantially more energy. Extremely high-quality coal, like graphite or diamonds, potentially contains a tremendous amount of heat energy. However, extremely high-quality coal is nearly impossible to ignite under normal circumstances. Coal also varies by the type of pollution that it contains.

- **Lignite.** Also called *brown coal* or more colloquially as *burnable earth,* lignite contains the lowest energy content of any other fuel coal. It contains about 30 percent carbon and has a very high moisture content. As a result, it is often soft and crumbly. Its low energy density means that it is inefficient to transport over long distances, so it is almost never traded internationally. Unless stored carefully, it is subject to spontaneous combustion. The only commercial use of lignite is for power generation by nearby power plants. Compared to black coal, lignite contains an especially high proportion of pollutants, and its use is a politically charged topic. The only reason to use lignite is to provide a low-cost source of electricity.
- **Sub-Bituminous.** The properties of sub-bituminous coal fall between lignite and bituminous coal. Sub-bituminous coal has a higher carbon content than lignite, about 40 percent, and contains more heat energy. Typically it also contains less moisture than lignite. As a result, it is slightly more efficient to transport over long distances, but there is still a relatively small international trade in this grade of coal. A little less than half the coal produced in North America is sub-bituminous. Sub-bituminous coal is used almost exclusively as a fuel for electrical power generation.

- **Bituminous.** Bituminous coal has been subjected to high temperature and pressures. It is about 70 percent carbon. It is the most abundant type of coal found in North America and contains between two to three times the heat energy of lignite. There is an active international trade in bituminous coal, and it is used for both power generation and as a source for industrial raw materials. Bituminous coal is usually black, but it can also be dark brown. It commonly has striations of bright and dark material visible in the coal. About half the coal used in North America is bituminous coal.
- **Anthracite.** The highest grade of fuel coal is anthracite. Anthracite contains about 95 percent carbon and typically has a hard glossy black surface. Anthracite ignites with difficulty but produces a steady flame once lit. Anthracite has low moisture content and produces relatively little pollution. It contains approximately the same heat energy as bituminous coal. Anthracite coal is much less common than bituminous coal, and its high price makes it uneconomical to use in power plants.

Sulfur Content of Coal

The second primary classification of coal is by its sulfur content. When sulfur is burned, the sulfur oxides that are released into the atmosphere combine with water to form sulfuric acid. Along with carbonic acid and nitric acid, sulfuric acid is one of the main components of acid rain. However, the danger from sulfuric acid is not limited to rain. Almost any liquid runoff from a coal mining facility or coal-burning power plant will be somewhat acidic. Over time, this tends to kill nearby plants and wildlife. Power plants that use high sulfur coals generally have higher maintenance costs than ones that use low sulfur coal.

Sulfur oxide emissions are an example of a localized pollution problem. When sulfuric acid is present in small quantities, it is not harmful to plant or animal life. However, when it is allowed to build up over time, it can reach a critical mass where species start dying off. As a result, the areas directly surrounding coal mining and coal power plants, downwind of the plants, or downstream from the plants, are at the highest risk. Farther away, the magnitude of the problem becomes less severe. Acid raid isn't dangerous in small concentrations.

When coal contains sulfur, the sulfur usually comes in one of two forms. Most commonly, sulfur is found combined with iron to form pyrite crystals that are scattered throughout a coal vein. Pyrite is a yellow crystal sometimes called *fool's gold*. Alternately, sulfur can also be found chemically combined with the carbon in coal, named *organic sulfur*.

Pyrite can be removed prior to burning the coal, but organic carbon requires installation of scrubbers on the exhaust stacks of power plants.

Pyrite is heavier than coal and the majority of it can be removed by crushing the coal and submerging the combination of coal and pyrite in water. Coal will float to the top of the water, and the pyrite will sink. This process is called *coal washing*. This is a relatively simple process. However, it can have a high cost since the coal needs to be dehydrated prior to being burned. In some cases, there may only be a nominal incremental cost to washing the coal. For example, washing may have a low incremental cost if the coal is already being crushed, mixed with water, and transported in a slurry pipeline.

Removing organic sulfur from coal is substantially more complicated. It requires installing scrubbers on the exhaust stacks of coal-fired power plants. This process is known as *flue gas desulfurization* (FGD). A coal scrubber uses lime or limestone to remove sulfur dioxide emissions. Lime is a base that combines with acid to form a neutral product. The lime is mixed with water to form a mist that is sprayed across the top of the smokestack. When sulfur oxide gas rises out of a smokestack, it combines with the mist to form a solid byproduct called gypsum. Lime scrubbers can remove between 90 and 97 percent of the sulfur being emitted from a power plant.

Gypsum scrubbers can be very expensive to install and maintain. Since a solid byproduct is being formed, it is necessary to build ledges or shelves inside a smokestack to catch the falling residue. It is also necessary to clean out the residue on a regular basis. Generally, this means that the power plant needs to go offline throughout the year for maintenance.

Coal and the Power Grid

In addition to pollution, coal power plants play an important role in another major problem facing the energy markets—the reliability of the transmission grid. Coal power plants benefit from economies of scale. The bigger the plant, the less fuel is required to produce the same amount of electricity. However, large centralized power plants require elaborate long-distance transmission systems. Coal-fired generators are not the only power plants that benefit from a substantial economy of scale (nuclear power has a similar issue), but, historically, they have been the primary power plants used in the electrical industry.

When electric power was first being introduced, the two major advocates were Thomas Edison and George Westinghouse. Thomas Edison advocated using direct current (DC) power to transfer electricity from the generator to the consumer. The major problem with Edison's DC power was that the voltage on the power lines dropped as it traveled farther away from the generator. There is no efficient way to step voltage up or down in a DC transmission system. This means that small local generators would need to be built close to the end-users.

In contrast, George Westinghouse advocated using an alternating current (AC) system invented by Nikola Tesla. With the Westinghouse system, transformers could be used to step-up or step-down the voltage multiple times. This enabled a single large power plant to supply power to a wide area. It also enabled a single power plant to support different types of customers. For example, high-voltage power could be supplied to industrial sites, and lower-voltage power supplied to residential consumers. The greater efficiency of large generation plants tipped the scale toward AC power. As a result, AC power has become a universal standard for electricity transmission.

For most of the twentieth century, behemoth power plants were built a long way from consumers. Extensive transmission networks had to be constructed to transmit power from these outlying generation plants to get that power to customers. Unfortunately, there is a trade-off between the cost of generating power and the cost of transmitting it. North America is now experiencing problems with the complexity of its transmission grid.

When transmission systems are simple, they are relatively inexpensive and reliable. However, when they get complicated, they get progressively more expensive and less reliable. In the first 50 years after electricity was introduced, electrical generation faced a different set of problems than it does today. Historically, electrical power was used primarily for lighting and urban population density was lower. As a result, transmission systems were relatively simple. Over time, as more electrical appliances were introduced and the population increased, the transmission systems became more complicated. This has made the transmission grid more expensive and less reliable.

Coal Mining

There are two main methods of mining coal—surface mining and underground mining. Both types of mining create environmental problems. Of the two, surface mining is simpler and requires fewer miners. However, the highest-quality coal is usually located deep underground.

- **Surface Mining.** Also called *strip mining,* surface mining is the easiest way to mine coal when the coal deposits are located close to Earth's surface. The first step in the process is to remove the topsoil and rock on top of the coal. The groundcover and topsoil can usually be removed through fairly standard earth-moving equipment like bulldozers. The rock layer is more difficult to remove. It must first be cracked through the use of explosives, and then shoveled out or excavated. In general, strip mining uses equipment that is fairly similar to standard excavation equipment, built on an unbelievably large scale. The primary economic factors affecting surface mining are the amount of coal available and the amount of earth that needs to be removed.

In most cases, after an area is strip-mined, it is contoured. Then, the topsoil is replaced and the area replanted with groundcover. Historically, strip mining gained a bad reputation for blighting the environment. This is much less of a concern currently when mining companies are required to restore the land that was used for mining. Surface mining is common in the Midwestern and Western United States.

- **Underground Mining.** When the coal is too far underground to be removed by surface mining, tunnels need to be dug into the ground. Miners create a series of underground rooms to work in. Modern mining makes use of continuous mining machines that move up and down large faces of coal (approximately 50 feet in length). Although underground mining is now a highly mechanized process, it remains fairly dangerous. Because material is being physically removed from the ground, coal mines constantly face the danger of a collapse. Whether a mine collapses purposefully (to prevent a problem later) or accidently, the land on top of it will be destroyed and need to be restored. In the United States, most underground mining occurs in the Appalachian Mountain range east of the Mississippi River.

Coal Trading

Coal can be traded on both exchanges and in the over the counter (OTC) marketplace. Because of the close relationship between coal mining companies and electrical power generators, the coal market works a bit differently than other energy markets.

The only type of coal available for trading by individual investors is high-grade coal that it might be worthwhile transporting over a long distance. It really isn't possible to speculate on the relationship between different grades of coal. Most of the time, low-grade coal is never transported far—it is always used near where it is mined. Additionally, there isn't an active financial market to trade the location

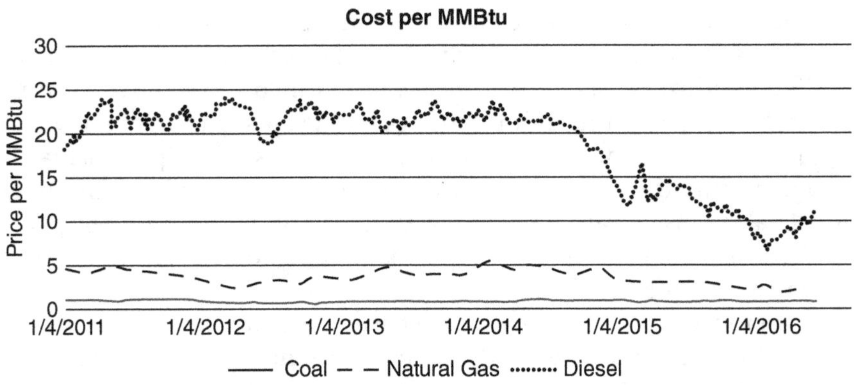

Jan 2011 Approximate Cost		**May 2016 Approximate Cost**	
Coal	$0.50/MMBtu	Coal	$0.50/MMBtu
Natural Gas	$5.00/MMBtu	Natural Gas	$2.00/MMBtu
Diesel	$20.00/MMBtu	Diesel	$10.00/MMBtu

Figure 2.4.1 A comparison of fuel prices

of coal. Unlike natural gas where transportation trades are common, there are limited opportunities to make coal transportation trades. In general, no one wants to transport coal over long distances so there isn't a lot of trading.

Another limitation on coal trading is the weak relationship between electricity prices and coal prices. The primary use for coal is electrical generation. However, except in limited cases, the prices of electricity and coal are not correlated. Electrical power prices are usually determined by the most expensive fuel in a region rather than the cheapest. The only traders that can actually benefit from the spread between coal and electricity prices are the investors that own coal-fired power plants.

Historically, coal prices are much less volatile than other energy commodities on a price per energy basis. Coal, being relatively easy to store, does not have a strong seasonal price trend. Additionally, coal prices tend to be substantially lower than both natural gas and diesel prices (Figure 2.4.1).

Common Terms

Coal prices have their own pricing terminology. There is a distinction between the price that an individual investor will pay for coal (on an exchange) and the price that a large consumer of coal pays for coal.

Spot Price. The spot price and forward prices are typically set by exchange-based trading. The spot price is the price of a cash transaction at the futures delivery point.

Captive Price. The captive price is the price for coal when it is transferred between two branches of the same company or between two affiliated companies. Because of the close relationship between coal mining and electrical power production, it is not unusual for coal mining companies and coal-fired electrical generation companies to be affiliated. It is impossible for an unaffiliated person to get coal at this price.

Open Market Price. The open market price is the price of coal sold on the open market. It is the prevailing prices for coal traded between large unaffiliated producers and consumers of coal.

Delivered Price. The delivered price of coal is the actual cost paid by a consumer of coal after transportation costs are included.

Location of Coal Deposits

Worldwide coal reserves are concentrated in the Northern Hemisphere. In particular, the United States and Siberia have vast coal deposits. There is a relative lack of coal in Western Europe, South America, and Africa (Figure 2.4.2).

Compared to other energy commodities, the global market for coal is relatively small. About 80 percent of the coal produced worldwide is used close to where it is mined. The cost of transporting coal as a percentage of its total cost effectively divides coal trading into two regions—an Atlantic market and a Pacific market. In the Atlantic, coal is imported into the United Kingdom, Germany, and Spain. In the Pacific market, coal is imported into Japan, Korea, and parts of China. About two-thirds of the international coal trading occurs in the Pacific.

Energy Independence Versus Pollution

For many large countries, energy independence and pollution are conflicting goals of an energy policy. Coal deposits are abundant in the United States, China, and India. In comparison, those countries have small reserves of petroleum and natural gas. Even though coal remains a highly polluting fuel, its low cost and local availability make it an extremely attractive fuel from the standpoints of cost and political stability.

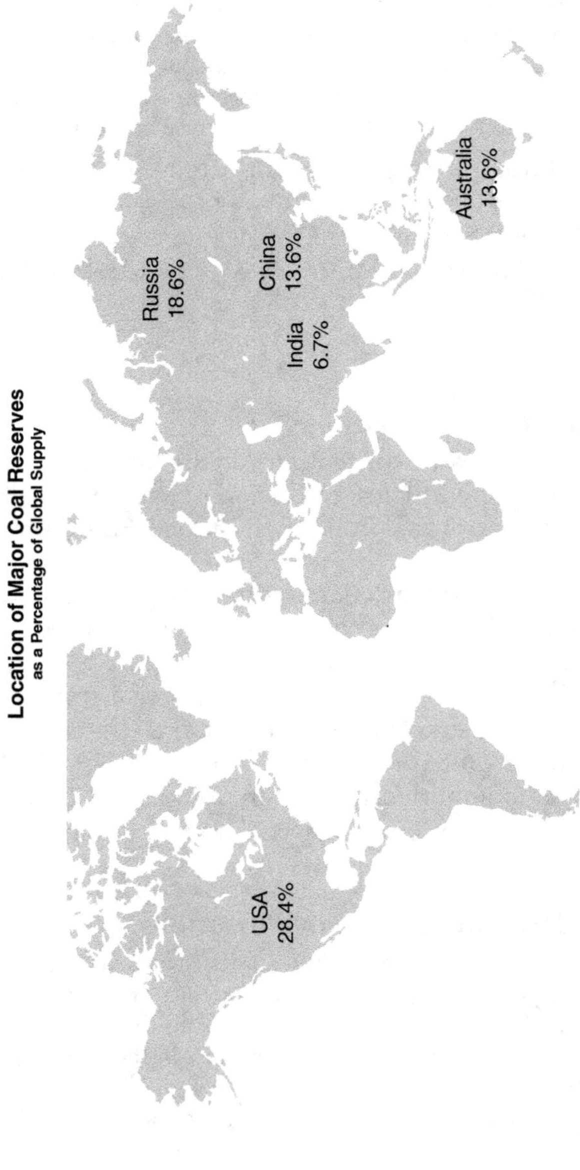

Figure 2.4.2 Locations of coal reserves

Coal-Producing Region
Appalachian Mountains
The Appalachian Mountains are a major source of high-quality coal and produce about a third of North America's total output. These mountains are located in the eastern part of the United States (Figure 2.4.3). The region is characterized by large underground mines that produce high-quality bituminous coal and anthracite. West Virginia and Pennsylvania are the largest coal-producing states in the region and have a long history of coal mining. Unlike western strip mines, which are open to the sky, mines in this region are dug deep into the Appalachian Mountains, forming extensive cave complexes.

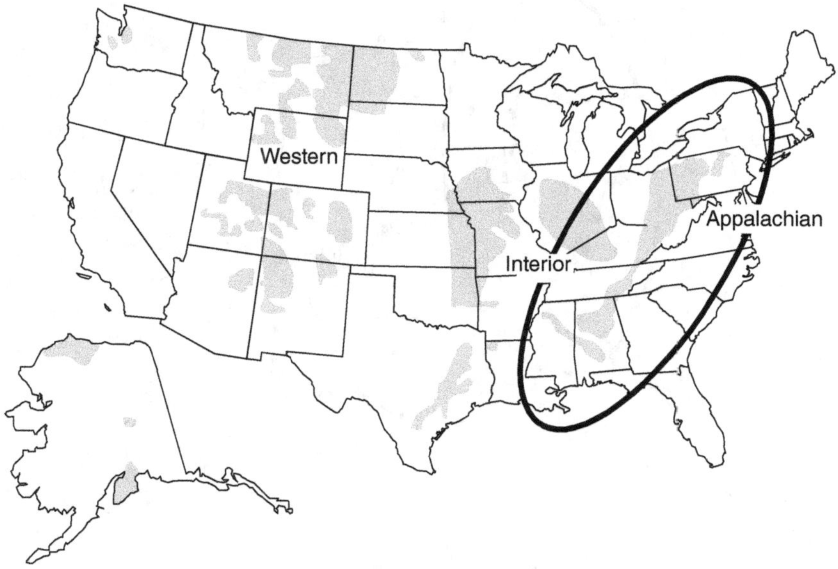

Figure 2.4.3 Appalachian coal reserves
(*Source:* U.S. Energy Information Administration)

Coal-Producing Region

Wyoming

The western United States is the single largest coal-producing region in the country. This region, centered in Wyoming (Figure 2.4.4), is characterized by extremely large surface mines. In this area, very thick bands of coal, sometimes 40 or 50 feet deep, lie close to the surface. These mines produce low sulfur, low ash sub-bituminous coal that is used to provide fuel for power plants throughout the central United States. Some of the largest surface mines in the world are located in this area. This region accounts for about half the coal produced in the United States.

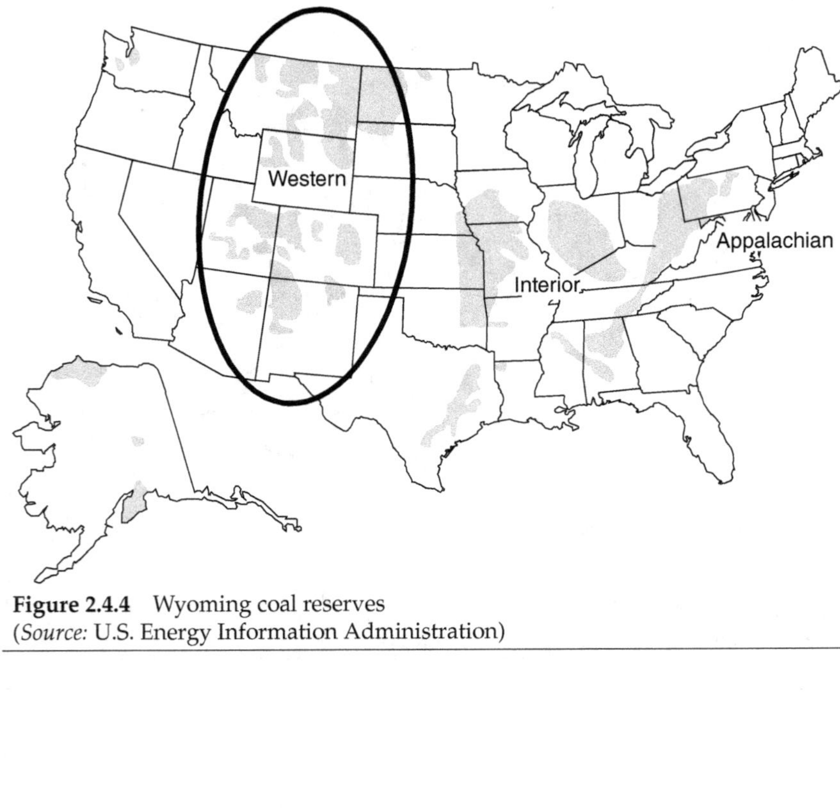

Figure 2.4.4 Wyoming coal reserves
(*Source:* U.S. Energy Information Administration)

2.5

EMISSIONS MARKETS

30-Second Summary

Purpose

Government initiatives to reduce the risk of global climate change have had a profound impact on the energy market. This chapter introduces the emissions trading markets that governments are using to achieve their environmental goals.

Summary

Motivated by signs of global climate change, countries have begun taking steps to reduce global levels of carbon dioxide, sulfur dioxide, and nitrogen dioxide emissions. The two most popular ways to limit pollution are through *taxes* and *cap and trade* systems. Of the two, only the *cap and trade* system is a trading market.

A cap and trade system sets a limit on the amount of a substance that can be produced. Everyone producing that substance is required to have a license for their production. This has the advantage of ensuring a cap on pollution levels. When licenses are freely tradable, anyone with an ability to shift to a less polluting technology can do so and make a profit by selling their licenses. By reducing the amount of licenses over time, a free market encourages the most economical changes be made first. The two main problems facing cap and trade systems are how to distribute licenses and how to enforce compliance.

The emissions markets are closely linked to the use of coal to generate electricity. Although it produces more pollution, coal historically was able to produce electricity for a fraction of the cost of any alternative fuel. However, the increased popularity of natural gas fracking has substantially lowered the cost of natural gas. This has allowed natural gas generation to displace many coal generators and has largely achieved the goals of carbon legislation without legislation being passed.

Key Topics

- Attempts to reduce pollution, particularly nontoxic greenhouse gases, are controversial because they increase the energy prices.
- Market-based approaches to reducing emissions are popular since they allow the free market to minimize the cost of reducing emissions. It is believed these systems will have a greater chance of getting fully adopted because they keep costs to a minimum.
- The most common type of emissions market is a *cap and trade* system. In this type of system, a limited number of pollution credits are issued. Anyone who pollutes is required to turn in a pollution credit.

The possibility of global climatic change, sometimes called *global warming*, has forced most countries to adopt policies that limit the creation of greenhouse gases and other pollutants. This is complicated by the fact that reducing these emissions makes electricity more expensive. Coal is the lowest cost and most polluting fuel. Completely eliminating coal from the generation stack will cause a large increase in the price of electricity. The goal of the emissions markets is to keep that cost to a manageable level. It is crucial that consumer prices be prevented from jumping to 5 or 10 times today's prices. A price jump of that magnitude would almost certainly send the economy spiraling into a depression and eliminate the possibility of future reforms.

Having someone else pay the cost of more expensive electricity is not a feasible solution. It is the primary reason that international discussions on reducing greenhouse emissions have deadlocked. Ignoring the flowery political speech, the ultimate issue is that reducing carbon emissions will be very expensive. Neither consumers in industrialized countries nor consumers in developing ones can afford to pay electrical and heating costs that are 10 times higher than their current bills.

Emissions markets offer the promise of finding the lowest cost way to lower greenhouse gas emissions. They provide a reasonable approach to what would otherwise be an intractable problem. In a practical sense, affordable power is synonymous with coal power. Coal is easy to mine and there are plentiful reserves of coal in the United States, the former Soviet Union, China, and India. Coal has such a price advantage over alternative fuels that it is hard to develop a scenario where coal power isn't being used to keep power prices affordable.

The increased popularity of natural gas fracking has largely derailed carbon legislation in the United States. It has done this by making highly efficient natural gas generation cheap enough to displace many less efficient coal generation units. Since the primary goal of emissions markets was to remove coal as a major electrical generation fuel, many of the objectives of this legislation have been achieved at little or no cost to consumers.

Why Is Global Warming Dangerous?

The primary concern about greenhouse gases is that climate change will destroy the arable land needed to provide food for a growing world population. Crops require a balance of sunlight and rain, and almost any disruption in that balance is harmful. If a regional climate changes, the local plant and animal life in that region will probably die out. Even if the climate in some other region changes so that it could support those organisms, there is no easy way to move the inhabitants from one area to the other.

History

Global climate change became a hot topic around 1990. Scientists noticed that temperatures were slowly increasing over time in many areas (Figure 2.5.1). Concerns over global warming spawned a series of international discussions on greenhouse gas emissions hosted by the United Nations (UN). The goal of these international discussions was to create a set of binding international treaties that limited emissions of greenhouse gases to 1990 levels. The UN coordinated many of the discussions since it is ineffective for a single country to cut emissions if other countries don't slow down their output at the same time. Ultimately, these discussions were derailed by disagreements over who had the responsibility for paying the cost for reducing greenhouse emissions.

For example, Europe has a high proportion of relatively efficient power plants. The European Union (EU) advocated taxing countries with highly polluting power plants and paying the proceeds to countries with efficient power plants.

Another plan was put forward by Russia and the other states of the former Soviet Union. Russia advocated capping emissions rights at the historical level of 1990. Of course, by the time of these discussions in the mid-1990s, Russia had suffered an economic collapse following the dissolution of the Soviet Union. Its emissions during the mid-1990s were 30 percent below its emissions in 1990—leaving it plenty of spare capacity to resell to other countries.

The role of developing nations in reducing carbon emissions is also problematic. China and India are first and fourth largest emitters of carbon dioxide in the world, respectively. Moreover, both countries are rapidly building coal-based power plants, and increasing the amount

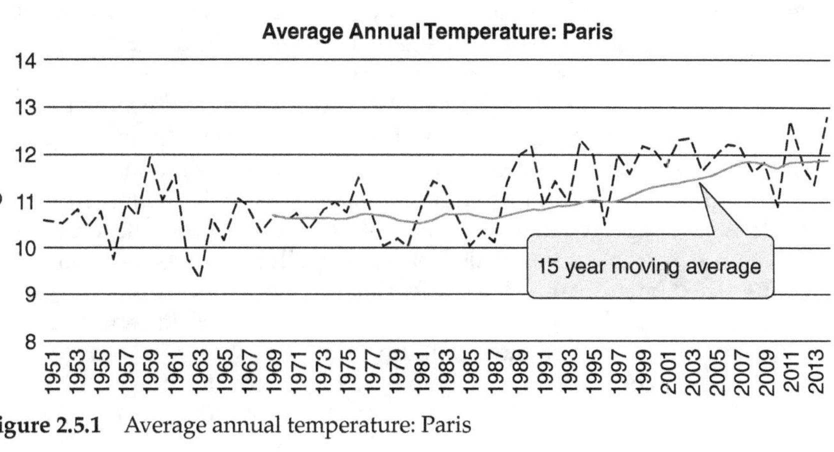

Figure 2.5.1 Average annual temperature: Paris

of pollution they produce. However, with their vast populations, these countries advocate allocating emissions targets per capita. This would allow both countries to continue to build highly polluting coal power plants while still maintaining surplus emissions rights to sell to other countries.

On the other side of the argument were the industrialized countries. The United States, EU, Russia, and Japan agreed to cut emissions to 5 percent below 1990 levels. However, these cuts—which would involve a substantial expenditure of cash—would still be insufficient to halt global climate change if developing countries continued to build highly polluting coal-based power plants. Ultimately, the UN committee was unable to reach an international compromise. Even so, a lot of countries have voluntarily agreed to follow most of the UN's suggestions. However, because of the lack of a global compromise solution, carbon emission schemes have been implemented unevenly around the world.

The Kyoto Protocol

In 1997 the Kyoto Protocol became the first global agreement to limit the production of greenhouse gases. The core of the Kyoto agreement is the creation of a *cap and trade* system that imposes both international and national limits for greenhouse gas emissions. It was approved, in principle, by almost every country in the world. However, the agreement in principle did not turn into a binding agreement.

Determining the right level for the national allocations for emissions rights became a highly political process. The core disagreement is whether the United States should be forced to replace its coal-based power plants to allow the rest of the world to construct their own coal-based generation. On one side is the argument that carbon limits should be set per person, on the other is the argument that the world shouldn't be constructing highly polluting technologies regardless of the current carbon output per person of each region. Ultimately, the disagreement is over who pays for more expensive power.

The two countries that produce the most pollution are China and the United States. China is rapidly building coal-based power plants and will soon overtake the United States as the largest carbon producer in the world. China, with its large population, would benefit if carbon limits were set per person. Population-based caps would allow China to continue its rapid construction of highly polluting coal-based power plants. The United States did not feel that it should be responsible for removing less polluting power plants so that China could replace that carbon output with even more polluting plants.

The issue comes down to who pays a higher cost for power.

Reducing Carbon Emissions

There are two popular mechanisms for encouraging the development of environmentally friendly emissions technologies—taxes and trading. The first approach, a *carbon tax,* is a tax that needs to be paid whenever carbon dioxide, or other greenhouse gas, is produced. The second approach is a trading scheme that caps the amount of emissions and requires possession of a freely tradable permit that is consumed whenever pollution is created. In practice, the two policies often coexist and are not mutually exclusive.

Carbon taxes are a price-based approach that makes more polluting technologies less attractive. Taxes are a highly effective way of making highly polluting technology more expensive and cleaner technology less expensive. This is achieved by taking money received in taxes and using it to subsidize the cost of less polluting technology. Within a single country, taxes are relatively simple to implement. Most countries already have a mechanism in place to apply taxes to many activities.

In a **cap and trade** system, the total amount of emissions is fixed (capped), and the right to create pollution becomes a tradable commodity. This allows companies to make their own economic decisions about how to lower their individual costs. Because the only transactions are generally exchanges of goods (cash for permits) between private companies, trading can easily cross country borders and span multiple currencies. Trading provides the best way to minimize everyone's cost of complying with environmental goals.

Cap and trade adds a variable surcharge to energy costs that fluctuates based on supply and demand. In comparison, a carbon tax adds a fixed cost. Another difference is that in a cap and trade system, the government is usually revenue neutral—it doesn't make a profit from the emissions system. Taxation usually involves a direct cash payment to a government. Any taxation system involving multiple governments is substantially complicated by the need to determine which government receives revenue.

Public Goods and Common Land

Emissions are hardly the first time that humanity has had to deal with the problem of sharing a cost among a large group of people. Humanity has been dealing with this type of problem for hundreds of years and economists have developed their own terminology to discuss this issue.

The term *public goods* is used by political economists to describe something that benefits everyone regardless of who pays the cost. National

(Continued)

defense is the classic example—it is impossible to defend the borders of a country without protecting everyone in the country. As long as the costs are paid by someone, everyone gets the same benefit. The term applied to people who take benefits without contributing any money is *free riders*.

One way to look at the reduction of greenhouse emissions is as a public good. There will be a cost associated with the change, but once it is made, everyone will benefit. Typically, these types of problems have been addressed by taxes—everyone is required to pay something to the public coffers. The major problem with this approach is that much of the world doesn't make heavy use of electricity nor does it have money to pay the costs of lowering emissions.

Another way to look at the problem of emissions is to think of carbon emissions rights as a limited commodity. There are a limited number of emissions rights, and when used, an emissions right gives the owner the right to low-cost electricity. Political economists refer to this subset of public goods problems as *common lands* problems. The name comes from shared lands often found in England, Scotland, and Wales prior to the seventeenth century. When thought about this way, the emissions problem becomes more of a problem of distributing low-cost electricity permits.

Emissions Trading Markets

The emissions trading markets, of which there are a number worldwide, are all based on *cap and trade* systems. The rationale behind trading emissions rights is that it doesn't matter where cuts are made—as long as emissions are reduced, everyone is better off. This allows the trading market to dynamically reallocate savings in response to changing interest rates, foreign exchange rates, and similar economic stimuli.

Cap and trade systems create property (emissions rights) where no property previously existed. These rights are a license to pollute, or alternately, the right to use affordable (coal) power. There is no way of allocating these rights that makes everyone happy. Ultimately, someone—perhaps lots of people—will have to pay a higher cost for their power.

In theory, cap and trade systems have a couple of advantages over taxes to reduce carbon emissions. By capping the maximum amount of carbon emissions, the total amount of pollution is well known. Cap and trade systems also give businesses maximum flexibility in determining how to meet government requirements. These producers can either install more environmentally friendly technology or they can buy emissions credits. Because it can be done globally, there is no danger of companies relocating factories from high-tax to low-tax regions.

Another advantage to cap and trade systems is that they are broadly applicable across countries and different types of greenhouse gases. Because no government needs to be involved as an intermediary, cross-border transactions are relatively straightforward. For example, a trading market would allow cuts to be paid for in one country using one currency, and the benefits received in another country with a separate currency. Additionally, unlike a taxation system that would need to be constantly adjusted by a legislature, a trading system can adjust itself to changing economic situations.

Distributing Rights

Because no one naturally owns emissions rights, there is the problem of determining who is allowed to produce carbon emissions. Often this problem boils down to which people have access to the low-cost electricity provided by coal-fired power plants. The tempting solution is to say that everyone pays the same amount for power is at odds with the concept of the trading market. The primary benefit of the trading market is to find the greenhouse gas emissions that can be eliminated most easily and to compensate those people for cutting their emissions.

Another complication is that consumers need to be protected during the whole process. The largest source of greenhouse emissions is power generation. Governments can't allow power generators to go out of business. When a power plant goes bankrupt, the government can't allow the municipality served by that power plant to go without power. The government would need to step in and assume the obligations of the power plant operator. In the end, it is the residential consumer who would be left paying the high cost of complying with environmental regulations.

Emissions Credits

There are two ways to get emissions rights in most cap and trade systems. The first is to receive the right from the administrator of the cap and trade system. Usually these rights are allocated or auctioned off. The other way is to create something that offsets carbon emissions in some manner. This might be through creating a carbon sink (like planting a forest), capturing carbon dioxide emissions and storing them underground (carbon sequestration), or by creating a nonpolluting source of electricity (building a hydroelectric plant or solar power installation).

The ability to creatively reduce carbon dioxide is a key advantage of a cap and trade system. Essentially, this allows countries to keep using coal power until alternative sources of power can be developed. In many cases, carbon capture doesn't have to be done close to home either. Particularly under cap and trade systems conforming to the Kyoto Protocol, it is possible to offset carbon emissions anywhere around the world. This ensures that the lowest cost alternative can be found.

Carbon Sequestration

Carbon dioxide is a necessary byproduct of almost all combustion. The process of forming carbon dioxide is what creates heat when fuel is burned. Long chains of carbon are completely broken up, forming single carbon molecules that combine with oxygen. As a result, as long as we use hydrocarbon fuels, it is impossible to stop the creation of carbon dioxide.

It is possible to capture carbon dioxide exiting from fossil fuel power plants. This carbon dioxide then needs to be stored somewhere like a depleted natural gas well or water reservoir. This is called *carbon sequestration*. Carbon storage facilities are very similar to natural gas storage facilities except that they store carbon dioxide instead of methane.

Another way of reducing carbon emissions is to use plants or bacteria. Plants use carbon dioxide to form wood, bark, and leaves. However, plants usually require the use of fossil fuels for fertilization and harvesting. Bacteria can also be used to absorb carbon dioxide. The advantage of using bacteria is that a very dense colony of bacteria can be located in a small area and it doesn't require a lot of petroleum products to maintain.

Limitations to Cap and Trade Systems

In practice, while cap and trade markets sound good, they face several implementation problems. Tracking all carbon dioxide emissions is impossible, and even if it were possible, it would be far too complicated to trade. For example, animals naturally produce carbon dioxide when they breathe. They produce even more than normal when they exercise. It isn't possible to have a cap and trade system that applies to something like jogging. As a result, emissions trading markets must pick and choose the carbon dioxide sources that they want to restrict. Most carbon trading is focused on reducing carbon dioxide resulting from the combustion of fossil fuels.

However, emissions credits can be created from almost any source. This means that cap and trade systems run the risk of funny accounting when emissions credits are granted for offsetting carbon emissions. For example, if a region is capping power plant emissions but not car emissions, it might seem to make sense to shut down a local commuter railroad that is powered from the local power plant to encourage more driving. After all, this would reduce the "emissions" at the power plant. However, in reality, since cars are also a major source of pollution, this would actually increase the amount of carbon emissions in the area.

A related limitation on carbon trading is that it can force companies into making investments in carbon mitigation systems that would normally be considered poor ideas. For example, if a power producer wants to protect its customers, it needs to minimize the risk that speculators corner the market on emissions rights. The primary way to eliminate this risk is to be able to create emissions credits on demand. Essentially, companies that utilize carbon credits need to ensure that they have a way to "manufacture" carbon credits in the event of a spike in prices.

The chance of speculators trying to corner the market is high—it is just about the only way for speculators to make a profit trading emissions credits. However, since emissions credits can be manufactured by carbon offsets, the easiest way to protect against speculators is to keep a couple of carbon offset ideas on the side. While the economic value of these ideas might be really bad, it just has to be better than being held hostage by speculators.

Carbon Taxes

Although they commonly coexist, carbon taxes are generally considered the primary alternative to cap and trade systems. Taxation adds a surcharge to energy costs and relies on high costs to incentivize adoption of new technologies. Most countries have implemented domestic energy taxes. However, an international tax remains unlikely due to concerns over who gets the money. As a general rule, countries favor tax schemes that levy taxes on other countries and benefit themselves.

Compared to a cap and trade system, there are some big advantages to taxes. They can be applied universally to a wide variety of things and require minimal administration. For example, adding a surcharge to the price of gasoline is much easier than checking if someone owns enough gas credits to be allowed to purchase gasoline. Taxes are simple. Taxes can also be used to promote domestic carbon reductions. This is accomplished through reinvesting tax money into local projects. With carbon trading, cash is commonly transferred away from local consumers to a carbon sink in some other jurisdiction. With taxes, the money can stay in the local economy.

On a domestic level, the biggest problem with taxation is that energy consumers are a captive audience. Energy companies pass along taxes directly to consumers. As a result, the only group that is being financially affected by the taxes is consumers. The power companies, who have the ability to adopt less polluting technology, don't have a lot of motivation to improve their technology under a taxation system.

Trading Carbon Emissions

It is possible for carbon emission trading to achieve its goal of reducing global climate change without ever becoming a major financial market. Speculators don't have a clear role in the emissions markets. In most markets, having a large number of people willing to transact limits volatility and keeps transaction costs low. However, in the emissions markets, it seems unlikely that speculation will limit volatility or keep costs low.

Over time, the general economic thought is that a rising population and demand for power will force the price of emissions rights upward. However, no one—particularly the government—benefits from higher carbon emissions prices. The only downside to low prices is that companies might not have any incentive to invest in environmentally conscious technology. As long as environmental targets are met, governments prefer low prices. Governments also have some excellent tools to stabilize prices—they can both issue new rights and determine how easy it is to create carbon credits through offsetting.

If carbon prices are too high, the cost gets paid by consumers (voters) and the economy. Governments have a civic obligation to keep their local power grids operating and their economies moving forward. As a result, along with a great ability to manipulate emissions market prices, governments have an incentive to keep emissions prices at the right level. Governments want prices high enough to spur changes, but low enough that the economy and their citizens are not negatively affected. Governments don't want speculators cornering the emissions markets and making a windfall profit at the expense of consumers.

Carbon Equivalents and Other Pollutants

Although this chapter concentrates on the carbon dioxide trading, there are other emissions markets. These markets are substantially similar to the carbon market, and share much of the terminology and trading limitations. The biggest difference is that most types of pollution only affect a limited area. As a result, most emissions markets are regional (covering a couple of countries) rather than global in nature.

- **Carbon Equivalents.** There are a number of greenhouse gases other than carbon dioxide. Methane, nitrous oxide, and ozone are examples of other greenhouse gases. These are usually converted into "carbon dioxide equivalents" and traded as part of the carbon market.
- **SOX.** Sulfur oxide (SOX) is a source of acid rain. Acid rain is a regional problem that is commonly addressed through emissions markets. These markets are separate from the carbon emissions markets and typically organized by region.
- **NOX.** Nitrogen oxide (NOX) markets are closely associated with the sulfur markets. Like SOXs, NOX emissions are associated with acid rain.

2.6

Natural Gas Liquids

30-Second Summary

Purpose

This chapter introduces natural gas liquids—a series of hydrocarbons heavier than methane but still a gas at room temperature.

Summary

Natural gas liquids (NGLs) are combustible gases heavier than methane (natural gas) but still light enough to exist in a gaseous state at standard temperature and pressure. There are five natural gas liquids—ethane (C2), propane (C3), butane (C4), iso-butane (IC4), and pentane (C5). They are found comingled with oil and natural gas when it is removed from the ground.

Key Topics

- NGLs is the term used to describe hydrocarbons heavier than methane but lighter than naphtha and gasoline.
- NGLs exist as gas at standard temperature and pressure but can be converted into liquid form much more easily than methane.
- Shale gas fracking produces petroleum and gas that contains a high proportion of NGLs.

NGLs are combustible gases heavier than methane (natural gas) but still light enough to exist in a gaseous state at standard temperature and pressure. There are five natural gas liquids—ethane, propane, butane, iso-butane, and pentane. Pentanes are often found mixed with slightly heavier hydrocarbons and referred to by the names *pentanes plus* or *natural gasoline* (Figure 2.6.1).

Compared to natural gas, the heavier NGLs, like propane and butane, are much more easily liquefied by compression. Converted to a liquid, NGLs are approximately 270 times more compact than they exist as a gas. Since this compression for these gases can be done under only moderate pressure, this allows these gases to be transported and

NGL Attribute Summary				
Natural Gas Liquid	**Chemical Formula**	**Applications**	**End-Use Products**	**Primary Sectors**
Ethane	C_2H_5 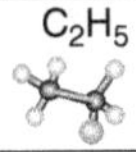	Ethylene for plastics production; petrochemical feedstock	Plastic bags, plastics; anti-freeze; detergent	Industrial
Propane	C_3H_8 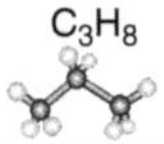	Residential and commercial heating; cooking fuel; petrochemical feedstock	Home heating; small stoves and barbeques; LPG	Industrial, Residential, Commercial
Butane	C_4H_{10} 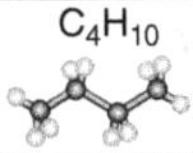	Petrochemical feedstock blending with propane or gasoline	Synthetic rubber for tires; LPG; lighter fuel	Industrial, Transportation
Isobutane	C_4H_{10} 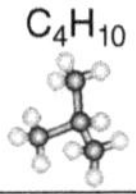	Refinery feedstock; petrochemical feedstock	Alkylate for gasoline; aerosols; refrigerant	Industrial
Pentane	C_5H_{12} 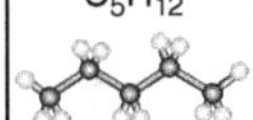	Natural gasoline; blowing agent for polystyrene foam	Gasoline; polystyrene; solvent	Transportation
Pentanes Plus*	Mix of C_5H_{12} and heavier	Blending with vehicle fuel; exported for bitumen production in oil sands	Gasoline; ethanol blends; oil sands production	Transportation

C indicates carbon, H indicates hydrogen; Ethane contains two carbon atoms and six hydrogen atoms
*Pentanes plus is also known as "natural gasoline." Contains pentane and heavier hydrocarbons.

Figure 2.6.1 Natural gas liquids

stored in a liquid state. A typical use for these products is as a fuel for cooking (like a backyard grill). For this use, propane might be stored in a pressurized container that will start to evaporate (converts to a gas) when a valve is opened to release it.

NGLs are commonly found dissolved within crude oil or natural gas. They are abundantly found in shale deposits that can be developed through the use of natural gas fracking. They are separated from natural gas at natural-gas-processing plants or from crude oil at refineries. A related term, *liquefied petroleum gas* (LPG), refers to a mixture of two of the heavier NGLs (propane and butane).

C1 Natural Gas Versus C5+ Natural Gasoline

Natural gas and natural gasoline are very different substances. Natural gas (C1) is composed of methane, the lightest hydrocarbon gas, while natural gasoline (C5+) is composed of heavier hydrocarbons and is very similar to low-octane petroleum called *naphtha*.

Hydrocarbon Gas Liquids

NGLs fall into the broader category of hydrocarbon gas liquids (HGLs). There are two main types of HGLs—NGLs that are more properly called *alkanes* (or *paraffins*) and a second set of products called *alkenes* (or *olefins*). Alkenes/olefins are commonly used as a feedstock in the petrochemical industry to make products like plastics, artificial rubber, paints, and solvents.

Chemically, alkanes and alkenes differ slightly. Alkanes have single covalent bonds joining the carbon atoms. Alkenes have one or more double bonds between carbon atoms. As a result, for the same number of carbon atoms alkenes will have fewer hydrogen atoms (Figure 2.6.2). From a trading perspective, there isn't a lot to know about refinery feedstock except to know that they exist. There isn't a major trading market for refinery feedstocks for alkenes.

Propane

Propane is primarily used as a heating and vehicular fuel. In a residential setting, propane is often used for heating and cooking where natural gas isn't available. For example, it is commonly used for drying clothes, fueling barbecue grills, and powering backup electrical generators. Propane is also often used to power farm and industrial equipment like power forklifts, electric welders, and tractors. A secondary use for propane is as a feedstock for the petrochemical industry. It is used, along with ethane and naphtha, in petrochemical crackers to produce ethylene, propylene, and other olefins.

Ethane

Ethane is mainly used to produce ethylene, a feedstock to make plastics. Because demand for ethane is almost entirely in the petrochemical sector, and because this product is difficult to transport by any mode other than in dedicated pipelines, there is a very limited trading market for ethane.

Alkanes (paraffins)	Alkenes (olefin)
Ethane (C_2H_6)	Ethylene (C_2H_4)
Propane (C_3H_8)	Propylene (C_3H_6)
Butanes (C_4H_{10})	Butylene and isobutylene (C_4H_8)

Figure 2.6.2 Alkanes and alkenes

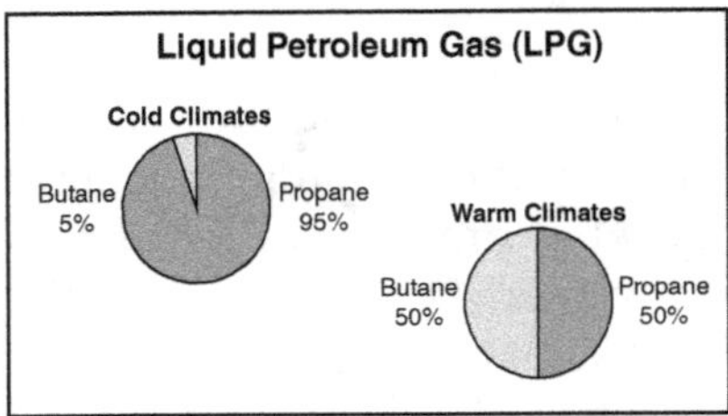

Liquid Petroleum Gas (LPG) is a mixture of propane and butane. The ratio of propane to butane will vary substantially between different regions. For example, in colder climates, LPG is often primarily composed of propane. However, in warmer climates it will be a mix of the two gases.

Figure 2.6.3 Liquid petroleum gas

Because the market for ethane is so limited, many NGL processors choose not to separate it out from methane. As a result, ethane is often left in the natural gas that enters the interstate natural gas pipeline system.

Butanes

Most butane is actually blended with either propane or gasoline. When mixed with propane, it is often called *liquid petroleum gas* (see Figure 2.6.3). Isobutane is primarily used to increase the octane of gasoline. It is less common than normal butane. As a result, it is slightly more valuable and normal butane is often converted into isobutane.

Natural Gasoline (Pentanes+)

Natural gasoline is similar to a low octane gasoline called *naphtha*. It is commonly blended into gasoline. In the United States, natural gasoline is also commonly added to fuel ethanol to make the ethanol undrinkable. About half of U.S. natural gasoline production is exported to Canada where it is used as reduce the viscosity of heavy crude oil. Mixed with heavy crude, it is called diluted bitumen or dilbit. This allows heavy crude oil to be more easily transported in pipelines and rail cars.

NGL Trading

The majority of NGL trades occur at market hubs connected to a critical mass of pipelines and refiners. The two largest hubs for NGL trading are Mont Belvieu, Texas, and Conway, Kansas. Mont Belvieu is a suburb of Houston, Texas, while Conway is located in central Kansas (Figure 2.6.4). NGLs are traded both physically (transferred from seller to buyer) and financially (via derivative transactions where the parties settle up in cash against an index price).

When traded, NGLs can be transacted at a variety of different purities. The two main grades of purities are *pipeline grade* and *fractionation*

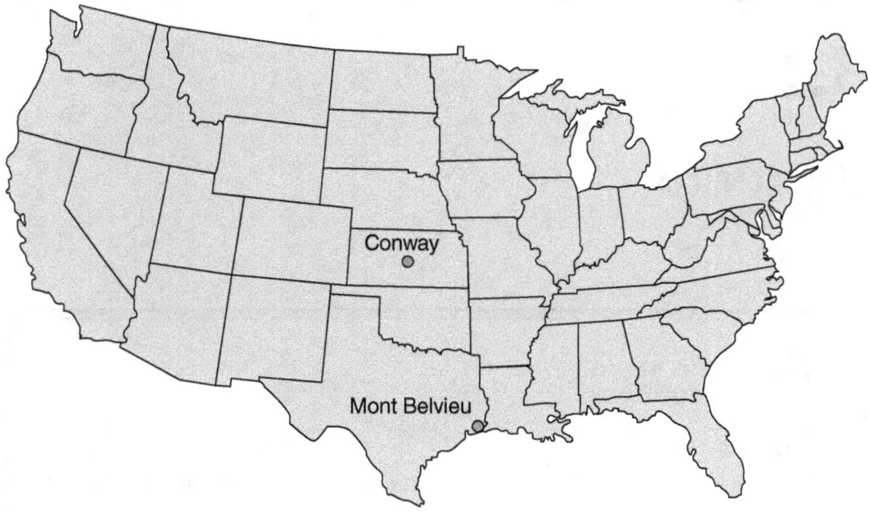

Figure 2.6.4 NGL trading hubs

grade. Generally, fractionation grade NGLs are slightly more expensive than the more purified products. That is because the less-purified products generally contain more heavy hydrocarbons. The market for these products is concentrated around the U.S. Gulf Coast where pipelines connect many refineries.

Pipeline grade has to conform to the quality standards specified by pipeline companies in the "General Terms and Conditions (GTC)" section of their tariffs. These quality standards vary from pipeline to pipeline and depend on the design of the pipeline, interconnecting pipelines, and intended consumer of the product. Some common clauses include:

- Btu content.
- A minimum dew point temperature level below which any vaporized gas liquid in the mix will tend to condense at pipeline pressure.
- Limits on pollutants and nonfuel gas.
- Limits on particulate solids and liquids that could be detrimental to the pipeline or its ancillary operating equipment.

These standards are necessary to prevent damage to a pipeline. Heavier hydrocarbons are more likely to condense into liquids. Once that happens, NGLs can be difficult to remove from a pipeline. Since pipelines are airtight, liquids will not evaporate once trapped. Also, since the NGLs are often solvents, they are corrosive. As a result, condensed NGLs in a pipeline can easily cause damage.

3.1

POLLUTION

30-Second Summary

Purpose

This chapter is an introduction to pollution caused by the combustion of fossil fuels.

Summary

There are a number of different types of pollution. The first general category of pollution is caused when impurities or small particles trapped in the fuel are released into the air when the fuel is burned. The second type of pollution is an intrinsic part of combustion—the creation of greenhouse gases. Greenhouse gases don't present a health hazard and are generally safe. However, when large quantities of greenhouse gases are released into the atmosphere, they have the potential to change the world's climate.

Key Topics

- Some types of pollution can be prevented by using fuel that contains fewer impurities.
- Other types of pollution, like carbon dioxide, are an unavoidable part of combustion.

The burning of fossil fuels (combustion) produces a variety of unwanted byproducts that are collectively termed *pollution.* Some types of pollution are poisonous to humans, while other types have the potential to harm the world around us. Combustion is an *oxidation* process. Carbon-based fuels are combined with oxygen to produce heat. Some types of pollution result from the release of particles trapped inside the fuel as it burns. Other types of pollution are a result of the chemical reaction that produces heat.

The pollutants that form a health risk are usually caused by impurities trapped within fuel. Some of these impurities are supersmall particles of sand or rock called *fly ash.* These rocks are not poisonous, but their small size means that it is easy to breath into lungs. Similar to ash, some other impurities, like sulfur and nitrogen, aren't poisonous. However, these substances can form acid rain when in the presence of water. Still other impurities are directly harmful. These include heavy metals, like mercury and lead, which are toxic to humans. Any amount of metals released into the air presents a health hazard.

In addition, every fossil fuel produces some unavoidable byproducts during combustion. Combustion of any hydrocarbon fuel (which covers almost all fuels) will produce water (H_2O) and carbon dioxide (CO_2). It is the creation of these products that produces energy. It is not possible to create energy without producing these byproducts. Neither byproduct poses an immediate health threat—these are the same byproducts caused by breathing and vigorous exercise.

There is no single approach that works equally well for every type of pollution. For example, the carbon dioxide emissions from any single power plant aren't particularly important. Carbon dioxide is a nontoxic gas that makes up a large portion of the atmosphere around us. Plants rely on carbon dioxide to grow. However, the aggregate carbon emissions from every power plant can be significant enough to affect the Earth's climate. Greenhouse gases are a global problem.

Acid rain is another type of pollution that becomes important in aggregate. A little bit of acid rain isn't dangerous. Water is commonly slightly acidic. However, while water evaporates, most acids do not. Given enough time, sufficient acid can accumulate in a single area that it starts to present a health threat to wildlife and plants. Acid rain is generally a regional problem. It declines in intensity the farther it goes from its source. Like greenhouse gases, acid rain is a cumulative problem. The output from a single plant may not be particularly dangerous. But, when combined with the output from several plants, the cumulative sum of the acid rain might be extremely harmful.

Combustion is an oxidation process. Fuels are combined with oxygen to produce heat. That heat can then be used for a variety of useful work—everything from powering an electrical turbine to powering the motor in a car. There are five main types of pollution produced by power plants—carbon dioxide, nitrogen oxides, sulfur oxides, heavy metals, and fly ash/soot. The first three are a result of the oxidation process that produces power. The remaining two are generally due to particles trapped inside the fuel.

Major Types of Pollution

- **Carbon Dioxide.** Chemical formula CO_2, carbon dioxide is one of the principle byproducts of combustion. It is impossible to burn any

(*Continued*)

plant-based fuels without producing CO_2. It is a nontoxic, odorless gas that naturally exists in the atmosphere. Large amounts of CO_2 can increase the strength of the greenhouse effect.

- **Carbon Monoxide.** Chemical formula CO, carbon monoxide is a product of incomplete combustion (a fire where there was insufficient oxygen to create CO_2). Carbon monoxide is a poisonous gas since it is highly reactive. When breathed in by a human, it will bind tightly to hemoglobin and prevent normal breathing. In the presence of nitrogen oxides or sulfur oxides, it will form acid rain.
- **Nitrogen Oxides.** Most commonly nitrogen dioxide, NO_2, but can be any combination of nitrogen and oxygen. These compounds are commonly abbreviated NOx (sounds like the word *knocks*). Nitrogen oxides are one of the major causes of acid rain.
- **Sulfur Oxides.** Most commonly sulfur dioxide, SO_2, but can be any combination of sulfur and oxygen. These compounds are commonly abbreviated SOx (sounds like the word *socks*). Sulfur oxides are one of the major components of acid rain.
- **Heavy Metals.** Mercury, lead, and plutonium are all highly toxic metals that accumulate in living organisms. When these metals build up in the body, they don't decay, so getting rid of them is difficult. These metals are often trapped in fossil fuels and released in the combustion process.
- **Fly Ash/Soot.** General terms for inert particulate matter trapped in fossil fuels. Commonly, these are supersmall grains of sand or coal that was not completely burned. When suspended in the air, it is easy for these particles to get caught inside someone's lungs. This will create breathing problems, and can lead to lung damage and diseases like silicosis.

Combustion Pollution

The first three types of pollution (carbon dioxide, nitrogen oxides, and sulfur oxides) are byproducts of *combustion*. Combustion, also called *burning*, is an oxidation process where some type of chemical bond (which will vary by the product being burned) is broken and replaced with an oxygen bond. Replacing almost any type of chemical bond with an oxygen bond is an exothermic reaction that releases heat. For example, when coal is burned, carbon-carbon bonds are broken and replaced with carbon-oxygen bonds. The source of the fire's heat is the breaking and the creation of chemical bonds. Carbon dioxide is an unavoidable part of combustion.

Different fuels have different types of bonds that can be broken to provide energy. For example, the primary component of natural gas, methane, has the chemical formula CH_4. There are four

During combustion, 1 Methane (CH_4) + 2 Oxygen (O_2) is converted into 1 Carbon Dioxide (CO_2) + 2 Water (H_2O) by breaking the C–H bonds and the O=O bonds and replacing them with C=O bonds and O–H bonds.

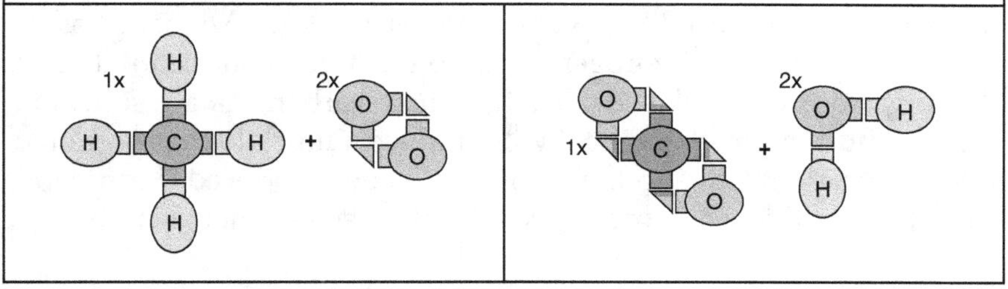

Figure 3.1.1 Combustion

carbon-hydrogen bonds that can be broken to create energy. When methane combines with oxygen, it will produce a chemical reaction that creates heat, carbon dioxide, and water (Figure 3.1.1).

When methane is burned the carbon-hydrogen bonds are broken, and the carbon and hydrogen combine with oxygen to produce heat. To be combustible, a substance needs some bonds that can be replaced with oxygen bonds. For example, it is impossible to burn water in oxygen. The chemical formula for water is H_2O—there are two hydrogen-oxygen bonds in a water molecule. There is no net energy gain that results from breaking one hydrogen-oxygen bond to create another. Therefore, water is not combustible in oxygen regardless of its temperature.

Most types of combustion require some heat, like a spark, to get started. For example, for methane to combust, something must provide the energy to break the first carbon-hydrogen bond and the first oxygen-oxygen bond so that the methane and oxygen can combine. Upon combining, heat will be produced. If the heat that is produced is sufficient to cause additional chemical bonds to break, the reaction will be self-sustaining until there is nothing left to burn.

Carbon Oxides

The most common byproducts of burning hydrocarbon fuels are carbon oxides (either carbon dioxide or carbon monoxide) and hydrogen oxides (primarily water). Since water is not considered a pollutant, the primary concern is the production of carbon oxides. Carbon dioxide is a colorless, odorless, nontoxic gas that wouldn't be considered a pollutant except for concerns over its effect on the global climate. In contrast, carbon monoxide is highly toxic. Carbon monoxide is formed when there is an insufficient amount of oxygen available for complete combustion. Power plants try to completely eliminate carbon monoxide emissions.

However, it is impossible to eliminate carbon dioxide creation when combusting fossil fuels. Any type of carbon-based fuel will produce carbon dioxide when burned. The relative quantities of carbon dioxide and water that are produced by combustion vary by fuel. Methane has the highest proportion of hydrogen to carbon (a four to one ratio). Longer chain hydrocarbons, like coal, contain more carbon. As a result, compared to burning methane, coal will produce a much higher portion of carbon dioxide relative to the amount of water produced. Restrictions on carbon dioxide emissions are commonly seen as a global issue.

Nitrogen Oxides

Nitrogen is a colorless, odorless gas that makes up 78 percent of Earth's atmosphere. Sufficiently high temperatures will force atmospheric nitrogen to combine with oxygen. Since most combustion uses air to provide oxygen, nitrogen will also be present. It is possible for either nitrogen oxide (NO) or nitrogen dioxide (NO_2) to form. This has led to the generic term NO_x to refer to any nitrogen oxide. In sunlight, nitrogen oxides will often break apart and cause ozone to form (O_3). Ozone is a major source of smog and can cause shortness of breath, chest pain, asthma, and coughing attacks. It is also a source of acid rain. NO_x pollution is generally a localized problem addressed on a regional level.

Sulfur Oxides

Fossil fuels often contain sulfur distributed throughout the fuel. When this sulfur is burned, it creates sulfur dioxide (SO_2). The generic abbreviation for a sulfur oxide is SO_x. In the presence of a catalyst, like nitrogen dioxide (NO_2), sulfur dioxide converts into sulfuric acid, a major component of acid rain. A little bit of acid rain generally isn't dangerous, but it can build up over time. When enough acidity builds up, the plants and animals exposed to the acid will die. Like NO_x emissions, SO_x emissions are usually addressed on a regional level.

Particulate Pollution

Heavy Metals

Coal-burning power plants are one of the main sources of atmospheric heavy metal pollution. For coal-fired power plants, the most dangerous of these pollutants is mercury. In many regions, coal-fired power plants can account for 90 percent of the mercury released into the atmosphere. Mercury is a powerful neurotoxin that has been associated with a host of medical problems ranging from autism and sensory impairments to death. While the magnitude of the public health risk due to mercury emissions can vary dramatically between regions, it is such a powerful toxin that cap and trade solutions are impractical. Unlike greenhouse emissions and acid rain restrictions, any level of mercury emissions is dangerous. Lead and plutonium are examples of other heavy metals that can be released through combustion.

Fly Ash/Soot

A large number of small particles can be released by combustion or formed as a result of SO_x and NO_x emissions. These particles are a major cause of breathing problems and can lead to heart attacks and strokes. Some of these particles are so small that they can easily be breathed into the lungs and enter blood vessels. Once in the body, they can cause substantial damage to the respiratory system. Children, people with asthma, and the elderly are the most at risk. Particulate pollution also reduces visibility and is a major cause of urban haze.

CO_2 Emissions and Fuel Type

Longer chain hydrocarbons that are primarily of carbon-carbon bonds, like coal, produce more CO_2 emissions than natural gas because they contain more carbon. At two extremes, comparing natural gas and coal, the difference in chemical structure is obvious. Natural gas is composed of small, self-contained molecules while coal is composed of large sheets of carbon atoms (Figure 3.1.2).

Natural Gas (Methane, CH_4)	**Coal (C_x)**
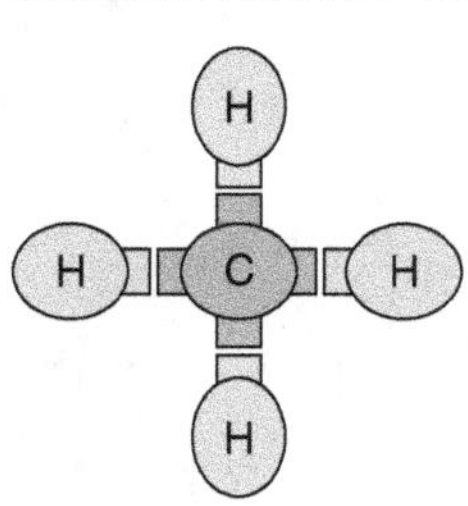	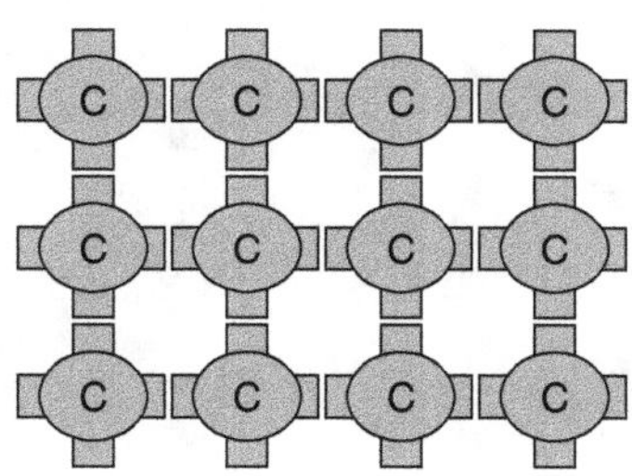
Methane has four hydrogen-carbon bonds with no carbon-carbon bonds. Combusting methane will produce one CO_2 for every two H_2O molecules. A substantial portion of the combustion byproducts are not greenhouse gas emissions.	*Coal is primarily composed of carbon with very little hydrogen and occasionally trapped sulfur. When combusted, coal will produce CO_2 as a waste product with any trapped sulfur converted to SO_2.*

Figure 3.1.2 Natural gas and coal

Toxic Pollution

After it is produced, there are only a couple of options for dealing with toxic chemicals. The first option is to combine the toxin with something that makes the substance nontoxic. Another approach is to dilute the toxic substance until it is no longer a major health risk. A third approach is to concentrate the toxin into something that is extremely deadly and then try to store it. If it can be done, the first approach is always the best approach. For example, sulfur dioxide (an acid) can be combined with lime (a base) to produce a harmless substance (gypsum). At that point, even if placed in a landfill, the toxic substance isn't a major health risk.

If it isn't possible to make the pollution safe, it's necessary to choose between two bad alternatives. For example, nuclear waste can't be made nonradioactive. Diluting a toxic substance means spreading out—basically polluting everything a little bit. The alternative isn't a lot better—to concentrate the toxin and attempt to store it somewhere it can't escape. A leak of a concentrated toxin is usually catastrophic.

3.2

Physical Properties

30-Second Summary

Purpose

This chapter introduces the science behind physical state changes and gives examples on how energy trading is affected by chemistry and physics.

Summary

Some materials transition between solid, liquid, and gas phases when heated. This is called a *phase change*, and it is a reversible process. Other materials undergo a *chemical reaction* when heated. A chemical reaction, like cooking or being burnt, is not reversible. The energy industry uses the ability of substances to shift between solid, liquid, and gas phases for a variety of jobs.

One important task that is made possible by phase shifts is the separation of specific gases and liquids out of mixtures. Refining of petroleum products and distillation of ethanol are both examples of separation processes based on this science.

Another important physical property of materials is that if you compress a gas, it gets hot. If you want to compress it enough to make it into a liquid, you need to cool it substantially. If you don't keep it cool, it will start to expand again. The ability to shift substances between liquid and gas forms and compress gas is the key to air conditioning and refrigeration systems.

Finally, pipelines are affected by phase shifts. In gas pipelines, liquids can condense and are extremely difficult to remove. In oil pipelines, bubbles can form and damage the pipes. The temperature in pipelines isn't constant, so engineers have to design pipelines to handle both gases and liquids.

Key Topics

- Every substance has a unique melting and boiling point that can be used to separate out mixed substances. The primary method of separating substances is called *distillation*. This process requires a tremendous amount of energy due to the heating and cooling that is required.
- Refrigeration and cooling systems are based on the ability to transfer materials between gas and liquid phases. Like distillation, cooling requires a lot of energy.

(Continued)

- Gases are much more complicated than either liquids or solids. They have to be contained or else they will evaporate. In addition, the pressure, volume, and temperature of a gas are all interrelated and this makes certain operations much more difficult.

All substances have two major types of properties—*chemical properties* and *physical properties*. The chemical properties of a substance determine how it combines with other substances. For example, combustion is a chemical reaction between a fuel and oxygen. Physical properties involve changes in substances that don't represent a chemical change in a substance. In general, the major difference between chemical and physical changes is that physical changes are reversible.

The physical state of a substance, called its *phase*, describes whether it is a gas, liquid, or solid. This state has a big effect on energy trading. The physical phase of fuel determines how it must be transported and what type of engine has to be built to burn that fuel. Controlled state changes, like the ones that occur in distillation or air conditioning systems, are the key to many processes in the energy markets. Uncontrolled state changes, like condensation, can be very destructive.

The reason that state changes are important is that solids, liquids, and gases each have different physical properties. Solids and liquids generally stay put—you can place either in a cup and they won't immediately disappear. This isn't the case with gas—any time a gas isn't contained, it immediately dissipates. Also, when gas is compressed, it gets hot and radiates heat into the environment. When gas is allowed to expand, it cools down and absorbs heat. For example, gas will need to be cooled substantially if you try to compress it enough to turn it into a liquid. Even then, if liquefied gas isn't kept cool and prevented from absorbing heat, it will start to expand again.

States of Matter and Separation

Energy products typically need to be purified prior to being used. This usually means separating out one piece of a raw material from everything else. Examples of separation processes are extracting gasoline from crude oil or removing ethanol from an ethanol/water mixture.

There are three primary states of matter under normal conditions—solid, liquid, and gas.[1] As temperature of a solid material is increased, it does one of two things. Usually, it will transition sequentially from a solid to a liquid to a gas, or it will undergo a chemical transformation. Exactly what happens will depend on the substance being heated. A common example of physical state transformation is ice being melted to form water, and then further heated to turn into steam. An example of a chemical reaction is cooking a piece of meat. A state change can be reversed (water can be frozen to form ice), but a chemical reaction is generally a one-way transition (once one's dinner is burnt, cooling it down won't help).

The ability to transition certain substances between liquid, solid, and gas states plays an important role in energy trading. There are discrete temperatures at which a substance will transition from one phase to another. The two most important temperatures are the *boiling point* (where liquid/gas transitions occur) and the *melting point* (where solid/liquid transitions occur). By heating or cooling a mixture of certain substances, it is possible to separate them by carefully controlling the temperature. Each substance has a unique boiling point and melting point that aren't shared with other substances. Because these points are unique, when a mixture is slowly heated, substances will melt off or vaporize one at a time.

In practice, it is fairly common for most mixtures to undergo both chemical reactions and physical state changes in response to changes in temperature. It is also possible under some conditions for substances to convert directly from solids into gases.

- **Solid.** In a solid state of matter, the molecules of a substance are closely packed and hold fixed positions relative to one another. As a result, the volume of a solid is constant unless altered through application of sufficient physical force. Application of sufficient physical force to deform a solid substance will result in a permanent deformation.
- **Liquid.** A liquid is a fluid where molecules are loosely arranged. A liquid is characterized by a distinct boundary at its edges that will hold molecules into the main mass of the substance. This surface tension is not sufficiently strong to prevent liquids from freely deforming in shape, but it will hold the bulk of the liquid in place.

[1] Under nonstandard conditions, there are a number of other states of matter that are not being included in this discussion. These can run from Bose-Einstein condensates, which exist in the center of black holes, to plastic crystals like glass, to superheated ionized gases called plasma. While these states are all important under some conditions, they are all much less common than the primary three phases.

Liquids conform to the shape of the container in which they are stored but are not permanently deformed. When a liquid is moved to a new container, it will change to conform to that shape. The volume of a liquid is determined by its temperature and pressure.
- **Gas.** In a gas, molecules are almost completely independent. As a result, gases are much less concentrated and have a much lower density than either liquids or solids. Like a liquid, the volume of gas is determined by temperature and pressure. It is relatively easy to heat or cool gas by compressing it or allowing it to expand.

Distillation

Distillation is the process of heating a liquid mixture until it starts to boil and then capturing and cooling the resulting gas. It is a common method of separating liquids and identifying unknown hydrocarbon liquids. Distillation is a physical process that does not rely on chemical reactions. Instead, it takes advantage of each substance having a unique boiling point to separate mixtures.

There are two major pieces in distillation units—a boiler and a condenser. The boiler is a container used to heat up the mixture to the boiling point of one of the liquids. At the proper temperature (the desired boiling point), one (and only one) of the liquids will turn into a gas and rise into the tubing to exit the boiler. At that point that gas (now a purified substance) is cooled in the condenser to be turned back into a liquid.

When a liquid reaches its boiling point, it will stay at that temperature until it is fully converted into a new state of matter. For example, if water is boiled, as long as the water vapor can escape, the liquid will stay at a constant temperature. Continuing to heat boiling water won't make the water hotter; it will just cause a faster liquid-to-gas conversion. Distillation is important because this is the primary method for separating a mixture of fuels into pure products.

Distillation Requires a Tremendous Amount of Energy for Heating and Cooling

The major drawback of distillation is the energy requirements. Consider how many cars are on your street. Each one of those cars has a 15- or 20-gallon tank of gasoline. Try to estimate how much fuel is required by the cars on a single street, and the energy required to bring that much liquid to a boil. Then consider the number of cars worldwide and the amount of fuel that those cars require. The amount of fuel required for all of those cars is immense. And, every bit of that fuel went through a distillation process. Every drop of gasoline and ethanol in use had to be heated up to its boiling point and then cooled down again (Figure 3.2.1).

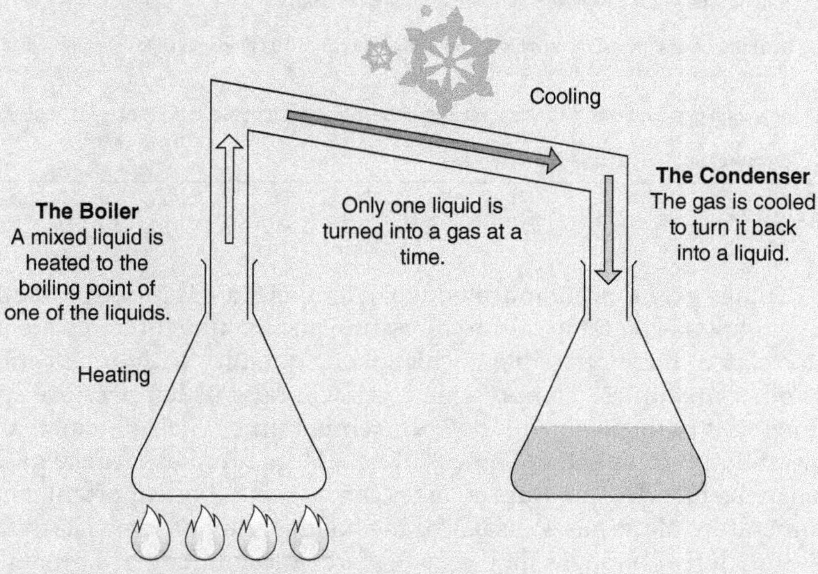

Figure 3.2.1 A simple distillation unit

Physics of Gas

Another place that science affects trading is in the natural gas markets. Unlike solids or liquids, which have relatively constant volumes, the volume occupied by a gas can change dramatically in response to outside conditions. These changes in volume affect both the pressure and temperature of the gas. This can be very important since temperature could cause the fuel to change between gas and liquid states, spark a chemical reaction, or separate from some substance with which it is mixed.

Unless constrained, gases will expand to fill whatever is containing them. Gas spreads from areas of high pressure into areas of low pressure and will continue to move until the pressure is equalized. The primary way of moving gases is to create a pressure difference between two areas. Both a straw and a gas pipeline work by this phenomenon. For example, it is possible to create a vacuum by sucking on one side of a straw. Gas will move into and through the straw to balance out the pressure. The higher the difference in pressure, the faster the gas will move through the straw.

Ideal Gas Law: PV = nRT

Where

P	**Pressure.** The force that the gas exerts on the wall of the vessel holding the gas.
V	**Volume.** The space contained by the vessel holding the gas.
n	**Quantity of gas** (measured in moles). The quantity of gas will be proportional to its energy content (that is usually measured in MMBtus).
R	**Universal gas constant.** A constant value introduced to convert between different types of units.
T	**Temperature.** The temperature of the gas.

Figure 3.2.2 The ideal gas law

Things get more complicated when temperature is introduced into the equation. The temperature, pressure, and volume of a gas are all interrelated. It is impossible to change one quantity without affecting the other quantities. Compressing a gas will raise its temperature and allowing it to disperse will lower its temperature. Fuels like methane are rarely pure methane. There will be a large number of trace gases also in the mix. Temperature changes can be especially important if the temperature of the gas cools below the boiling point of some gas in the mixture. If that happens, liquids will start to accumulate in a pipeline.

At a layman's level, the relationship between temperature, pressure, and volume of a gas can be approximately described by the *ideal gas law* (Figure 3.2.2). This law applies to gases where collisions between molecules are perfectly elastic, and is a reasonable approximation of the most important relationships described in the chapter. For example, if temperature rises (the right side of the equation gets bigger) and volume is held constant, the pressure needs to increase (because the law is an equality, if the right side of the equation gets larger, the left side needs to get larger too).

Common Relationships

- When gas in a contained area gets hotter, its pressure increases. When gas in a contained area gets cooler, its pressure decreases.
- When gas is cooled, more of it can fit into the same volume of space keeping constant pressure.

Gas Pipelines

Gas is often moved through pipelines through the use of compressors (Figure 3.2.3). These compressors operate like a fan—they create

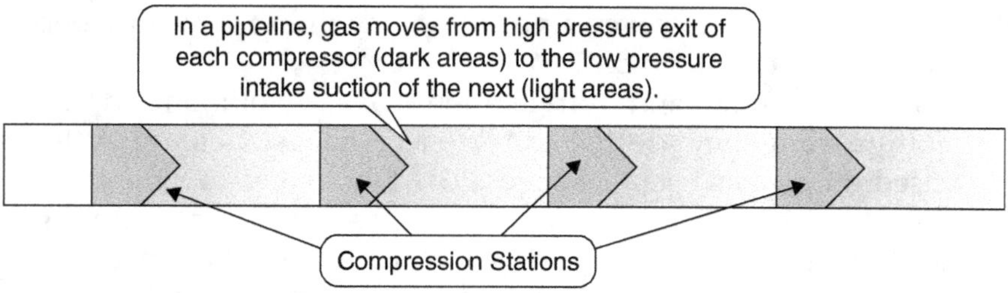

Figure 3.2.3 Compressor stations

a vacuum on one side and a high pressure area on the other. Since compressors affect the pressure of the gas, they will also affect its temperature. A pipeline is a long chain of compressors linked by pipes and provides perfect conditions for corrosion.

When a gas moves between pipe segments, it passes through a compressor unit that alters the pressure of the gas. As a result of the increase in pressure caused by the compressor, the temperature of the gas will increase. If any part of the gas is chemically reactive, corrosion becomes more likely. When gas moves away from the high pressure area toward the next compressor, it will start to cool. This might cause some of the gas to condense into a liquid. This causes issues because pipes are air-tight and the gas won't evaporate. Unless it is removed, a substantial amount of liquid might eventually build up in the pipe (Figure 3.2.4).

Air Conditioning and Refrigeration

One of the major consumer uses of energy is to maintain comfortable living and working environments. Heating techniques have existed for

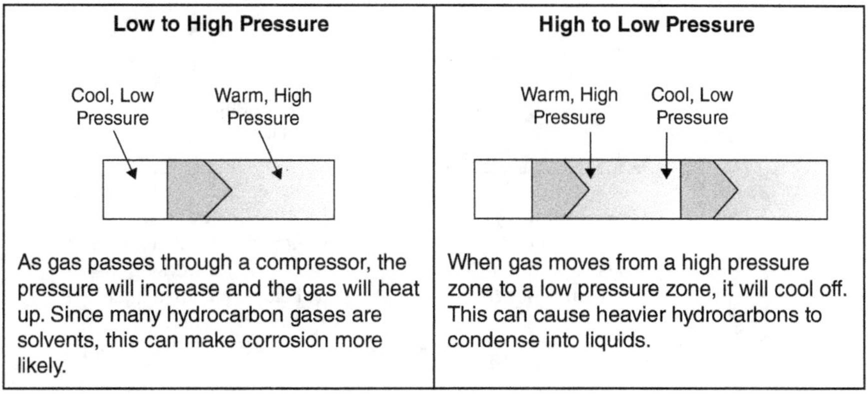

Figure 3.2.4 A simple pipeline

thousands of years. However, air conditioning didn't come into popular use until the twentieth century.

Air conditioning and refrigeration have revolutionized modern culture—but they are incredible energy hogs. Cooling systems are based on physical state changes. The key to any cooling system, whether it is a household air conditioner or an industrial natural gas liquefaction facility, is finding a chemical that can easily transition between liquid and gas phases. This chemical (the *working fluid*) is turned into a gas to cool it down (so it can absorb heat from something) and then compressed (to heat it up) so that it can radiate the heat somewhere else.

As pressure increases, the temperature of a gas increases. When pressure drops, the temperature of a gas will decrease. The core of an air conditioner is a mechanical device that compresses the fluid before it goes outside (to raise its temperature) and decreases the pressure of fluid when it comes inside (to lower its temperature).

There are three main parts to a cooling unit—a *compressor*, a *condenser*, and an *evaporator*. The compressor and condenser are typically located outside and the evaporator inside. The working fluid circulates between these three units (Figure 3.2.5).

Stage 1: Compressor. When gas leaves the interior of the house, it is pulled into a compressor. The compressor takes the warm gas from inside the house and compresses it to make it into a very hot gas.

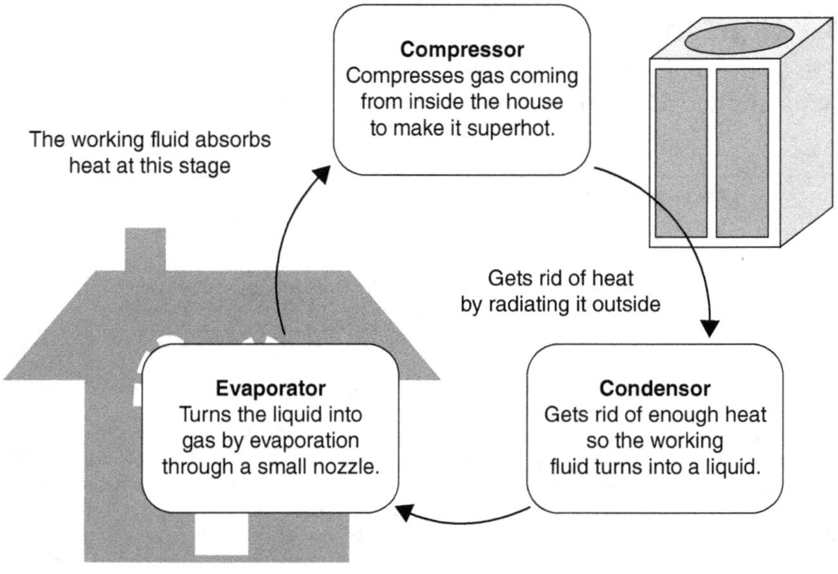

Figure 3.2.5 The air conditioning cycle

Compressing the working fluid increases its temperature substantially. When the superhot fluid is exposed to outside air, it will cool down by radiating heat into the environment.

Stage 2: Condenser. The mechanism that actually radiates heat into the environment is called the condenser. The condenser is a set of metal fins that radiate heat into the outside environment. Typically, a fan forces outside air over the fins, cooling the working fluid. When the working fluid cools down enough, it turns into a liquid and is sent inside the house.

Stage 3: Evaporator. The liquid that is sent inside is still fairly warm—it's at least as warm as the outside air temperature. It will need to be further cooled if it is to absorb heat from inside the building. To do this, the working liquid is forced through a narrow hole into a low pressure container called an *evaporator*. Liquids boil more easily at low pressures. As the liquid converts into a low pressure gas, it absorbs heat. The working liquid, now a cold gas, is then free to absorb heat from the interior environment. After warming up, the working liquid is sucked into the compressor to start the cycle again.

3.3

STATISTICS

30-Second Summary

Purpose

This chapter introduces some of the mathematical vocabulary that is used by traders to communicate numeric results between one another. A substantial amount of trading vocabulary comes from the mathematical discipline of statistics. Statistics is the branch of mathematics focused on organizing, analyzing, and summarizing data.

Summary

Statistics is a tool that traders use to describe things to other traders. Traders spend a lot of time analyzing prices, and it is necessary to convey those results unambiguously to other people. Statistical terms like *volatility* and *correlation* have a specific meaning that isn't open to personal interpretation. Every trader needs to understand those terms.

- **Volatility** is used by traders to describe the risk of holding an asset. The definition of volatility is typically based on standard deviation of continuously compounded returns. It measures the likely dispersion of prices between two periods of time. A highly volatile asset is one that commonly experiences large price changes. The term *volatility* does not describe the investment merit of a trade.
- **Correlation** is used by traders to describe how closely two things are related. When two assets are highly correlated, their prices tend to move together. There may or may not be a causal relationship between the two assets. Correlation can result from either random chance or a shared cause for behavior.

Statistics can also be used to solve difficult math problems through the use of simulation. This is called *Monte Carlo analysis* and is one of the primary ways to value complicated investments.

Key Topics

- Volatility is heavily used by traders as a measure for risk.
- Risk/reward relationships (Sharpe or Information Ratios) are commonly used to compare the merits of multiple investments.

(Continued)

- Correlation is used to describe how closely two price series are related. This is a key variable in many option pricing models used in the energy world.
- Monte Carlo Analysis involves the use of statistics to solve mathematical problems that are difficult to solve using Algebra or Calculus.

Statistics is a tool that traders use to describe things to other traders. Traders spend a lot of time analyzing prices, and it is necessary to convey those results unambiguously to other people. Statistical terms like *volatility* and *correlation* have specific meanings that aren't open to personal interpretation. Every trader needs to understand those terms.

There are three main goals of statistical analysis: *summarizing* time-series data, determining the *confidence* that the summary is accurate, and *identifying relationships* between phenomena. It is important to understand the difference between statistics, facts, and wishful thinking. Statistics aren't facts. At best, they are a simplified description of something that may or may not be true. As a result, statistics come with an error bound—a description of how likely the statistic is to be a fact.

Too much data is incomprehensible. To understand data, it is often necessary to organize it and determine whether it is important or unimportant. Sometimes this is often called *data reduction;* in other cases, it is called *summarizing* the data. In either case, it is common for some of the data to be eliminated, so that something important can be seen in the remaining data.

Data reduction is not perfect. It is as easy to eliminate important data and to summarize the unimportant data as vice versa. By judiciously removing parts of the data, it is possible to come to almost any conclusion—all this requires is eliminating the right (or wrong) data. Statistics is not a substitute for understanding what is going on. It is a tool to clearly summarize data for other people—and it is just as easy to summarize bad data as good.[1]

Because it is so easy to come to the wrong conclusion, a second focus in statistics is to attempt to estimate the probability that a conclusion is wrong. Commonly, this involves the estimate of the *margin of error* or the development of a *confidence interval.* Like summarization, estimating the likelihood of being wrong is not a perfect process.

[1] Numbers don't make wrong data more accurate—a fact that is well known in popular culture, but still confuses people on a daily basis. A famous quote on statistics was written in the autobiography of Mark Twain, where he quotes Benjamin Disraeli as saying, "There are three kinds of lies: lies, damned lies, and statistics."

However, taking the effort to estimate the reliability of a conclusion is a good habit for traders. It's one of several things that make statistical analysis more reliable than pulling numbers out of a hat.

Finally, statistics are used to precisely describe relationships between things—how much two things are alike or different. For example, a vague description of a relationship might be "the two prices act alike most of the time." A more precise estimate is "the two prices are 40 percent correlated." In this case, statistics is used to eliminate ambiguity and vagueness.

It is possible to misuse comparisons. Being overly precise with unnecessary data is both confusing and misleading. Even if a correlation exists, that does not imply that a cause/effect relationship also exists. For example, there is a superstition in the stock market that the National Football League (NFL) team that wins the Super Bowl determines whether the market will go up or down in the following year. Historically, the market has risen fairly commonly when a National Football Conference (NFC) team beats an American Football Conference (AFC) team. However, that doesn't mean there is a cause/effect relationship between the two events.

Common Notations

Statistics has its own terminology that is commonly used as shorthand. The most common notation for indicating an average is to place a bar over the top of some name. For example, $\bar{x}$ (with a line over it) represents the mean (arithmetic average) of the x distribution. Another convention is for the letter n to represent the number of elements in a distribution (Figure 3.3.1).

$\bar{x}$	A bar over a letter indicates the average of a series of numbers. The letter is the name of the series (in this case, the series is named x).
x_n	A subscript indicates a member of a series. For example, x_n indicates the nth member of the x series.
x	The lowercase letter n is a reserved letter that refers to a number. For example, n might represent the number of observations in series x. It is also common for n to receive a subscript. For example, if there are two series (named x and y), n_x would be the number of observations in series x, and n_y would be the number of observations in series y.
$\sum_{i=1}^{n} x_i$	The capital Greek letter sigma represents a sum. In this example shown, this is a sum of the first 10 elements of the x series. Below the sigma is the starting point of the sum (i = 1) and the number above the Sigma indicates the ending point of the series. The subscript on the x indicates that the letter i refers to different values of x.

Figure 3.3.1 Common notation

So, if x represents some series of numbers (1, 2, 5, 8, 10, 12, 15, 20), then subscripted values of x refer to the individual components of the series: $x_1 = 1$, $x_2 = 2$, $x_3 = 5$, . . . $x_8 = 20$. There are eight elements in this series, so $n_x = 8$. The formula to calculate the average of this series can be shown in the same notation (Figure 3.3.2). For example, the formula for the average of x, is the sum of all values of x (between values 1 to n), divided by the number of samples (n).

$$\bar{x} = \frac{\sum_{i=1}^{n} x_i}{n}$$

Figure 3.3.2 Formula for mean

In this case, there is only one series, so the n has not been subscripted. Had there been more than one series being described, it would be necessary to weigh the disadvantage of even more confusing notion (subscripting n as n_x) against the need for greater precision.

Sampling

The simplest use of statistics is to organize and describe some type of data. For example, there might be 100 gas stations in the area, each selling gasoline at a different price. However, learning anything useful about those prices will be difficult unless they are organized into some type of summary. An example of a way to summarize data is a histogram (Figure 3.3.3). This kind of chart organizes data into buckets showing the number of samples (gas stations in this example) that match each bucket.

When a large amount of data is analyzed, histograms are commonly fitted by a well understood mathematical function and represented as a smooth line. This makes it easier to use mathematics to analyze the data. The two types of charts most commonly used to summarize

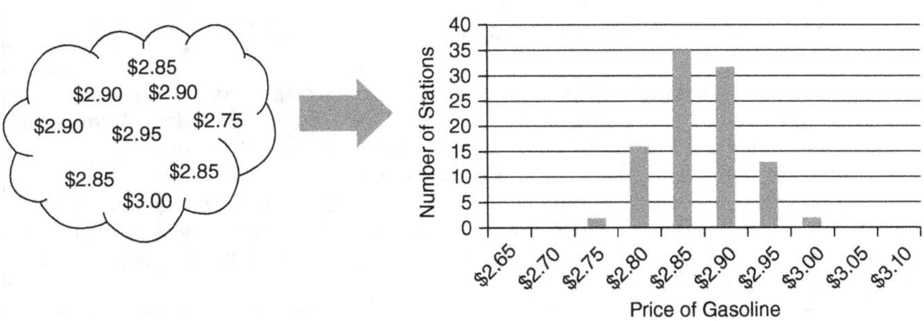

Figure 3.3.3 Organizing data into a histogram

statistical data are *frequency distributions* and *cumulative distributions* (Figure 3.3.4). Both charts allow the calculation of the probability that a random draw will be between two points in a distribution. These charts are different ways to look at the same data.

In a frequency distribution, the area under the curve represents 100 percent of the possible values. The likelihood that a random selection will be within a range of values can be found by finding that area underneath the curve between those two points. Frequency distributions are basically smoothed-out versions of histograms.

A cumulative distribution function is an alternate way of looking at the same data. For every point on the X axis (gasoline prices in the initial example), it shows the percentage of samples (gas stations) that have prices equal to or lower than that price. The benefit of a cumulative distribution function is that it is possible to find the probability that samples will be within a range found through subtraction. For example, it is possible to find the percentage of gas stations with gas prices between \$2.95 and \$3.00 by subtraction. The cumulative number of gas stations with prices less than \$2.95 can be subtracted from the cumulative number of gas stations with prices less than \$3. Although they are not quite as intuitive, the cumulative distributions are generally easier to use because of this subtraction property. As a result, most spreadsheet statistical functions use cumulative distributions.

Frequency Distribution	Cumulative Distribution

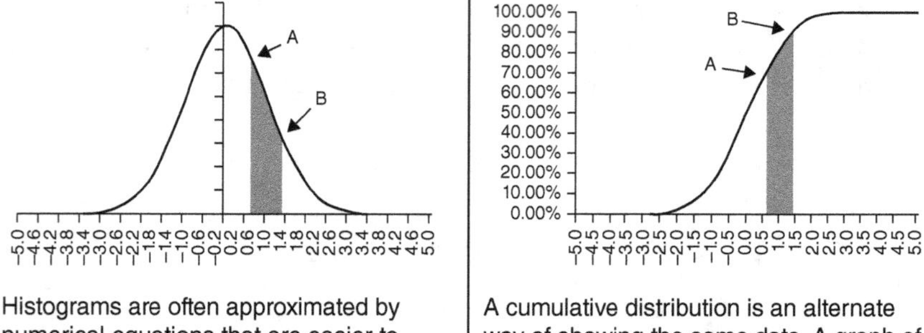

Histograms are often approximated by numerical equations that are easier to manipulate. The equations can be graphed as a curve where the total area under the curve represents 100 percent of possible values. The shaded area represents the relative frequency of values that are between points A and B.	A cumulative distribution is an alternate way of showing the same data. A graph of this function shows the cumulative frequency of values less than a certain value. The amount of samples between the two points can be found by subtracting the value at point A from the value at point B.

Figure 3.3.4 Frequency and cumulative distributions

Calculus and Statistics

Calculus examines properties of lines and this makes it well suited for examining statistical distributions. Calculus makes it easy to find the area under a line (Figure 3.3.5). This process is called *integration*. For example, it is often necessary to find the area underneath a probability curve. The area underneath a frequency distribution represents the probability of a random draw from the distribution coming from that part of the curve. For example, in the chart below, there is approximately a 22.8 percent chance that number will be between 0.5 and 1.4.

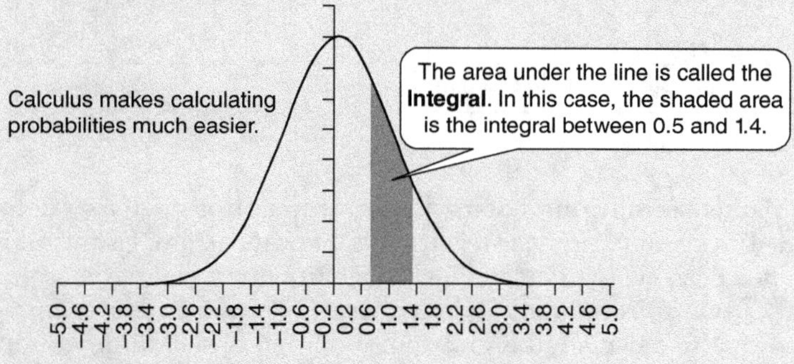

Figure 3.3.5 Area under a curve

To explain integration, it is easiest to start with a simple example. Using a histogram, it is possible to manually approximate the number of samples between two points (Figure 3.3.6). The height of each bar in a histogram indicates the number of samples in that bucket. Counting the number of samples in those buckets and dividing by the total number of samples provides an estimate of the probability that a sample would come from that area.

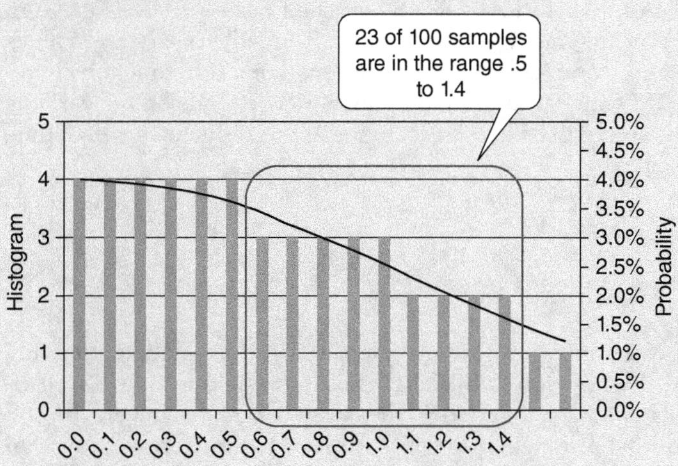

Figure 3.3.6 Comparison of a histogram to a frequency distribution

(Continued)

Integration of a line works the same way. The only difference is that the height of the line is defined by an equation, and a large number of buckets is chosen. The more buckets used for a histogram, the more precise the estimates become (Figure 3.3.7).

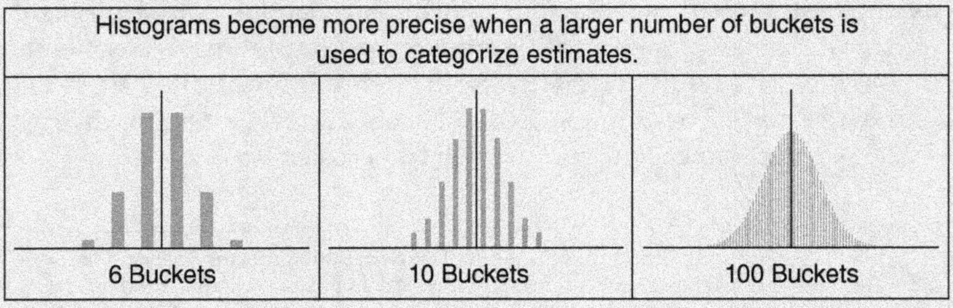

Figure 3.3.7 Histograms

Mathematically, the notation for integration is pretty straightforward. The symbol, sigma (S), is used to indicate a sum. Using summation, it is possible to calculate the probability that a sample chosen randomly from a histogram will be between two points. For example, it is possible to calculate the probability that an observation would fall between .5 and 1.4 (Figure 3.3.8).

$$Probability = \sum_{.5}^{1.4} Samples$$

Figure 3.3.8 Discrete probability

Calculus is a study of what happens when the number of buckets approaches infinity. In that case, a similar notion is used (Figure 3.3.9). An integral sign (which looks like a stretched out *S*) replaces the sum sign (S), but means much the same thing. The table of discrete values (which we called samples) is replaced by a mathematical function abbreviated *S(x)*. This can be read that the function S depends on the variable *x*. Finally, the sum will be in relation to the *X* axis (which we will denote by the symbol *dx*).

$$Probability = \int_{.5}^{1.4} S(x)dx$$

Figure 3.3.9 Continuous probability

Even if you don't know how to solve a calculus equation, knowing how to read the notation will often make it possible to find a spreadsheet formula or add-in that will do the math for you. However, you still need to know what function to call and what parameters the function requires.

Mode, Median, and Mean

One of the best ways to describe either a frequency distribution or a histogram is by its central tendency. In other words, what values of the distribution can be expected to come up most commonly? The three standard measures of central tendency are *mode, median,* and *mean.*

The mode of a distribution is the value that occurs most frequently. For example, a distribution might contain the numbers 1, 1, 1, 3, 5, 8, and 12. The number 1 comes up three times—more frequently than any other number. Therefore, the number 1 is the *mode* of the distribution. In practice, *mode* is not used very often because it is difficult to calculate. It requires searching the entire distribution for the value that comes up most frequently. Another reason that *mode* is not often used is that there can be more than one *mode* for a distribution. For example, heads and tails are equally likely on a fair coin flip. As a result, both heads and tails are *modes.*

The median of a distribution is its midpoint. It is the value that separates the highest 50 percent of samples from the bottom 50 percent. For example, in a distribution of 7 numbers, 1, 3, 5, 7, 14, 20, and 25, the middle of the distribution is 7. There are three numbers below 7 and three numbers higher. In the case of an even number of samples, the *median* is halfway between the two middle numbers. For example, if a new value of 30 was added to the distribution, the *median* would become 10.5—the value halfway between 7 and 14. In a practical sense, the big problem with using a *median* is that it requires sorting the sequence. Even on a fast computer, sorting a very large set of samples can take a while.

The mean (arithmetic mean) is the final and most important measure of central tendency. It represents the expected value of a random variable (like the typical gasoline price in one's neighborhood). The mean is the average value of all the samples. The biggest benefit of the *arithmetic mean* is that it is very easy to calculate. It can be calculated by adding up each value and dividing by the number of values.

Even though mean, median, and mode all describe a central tendency, these values do not always behave the same way. There are many different types of distributions (Figure 3.3.10). The mean of each series is indicated by a black vertical line. The white and gray shaded pieces show the bottom and top halves of each distribution. Finally, the mode is always located at the peaks of the distributions.

Variation and Volatility

In most cases, just knowing the average behavior of some data isn't sufficient information. It is also necessary to know how much variation

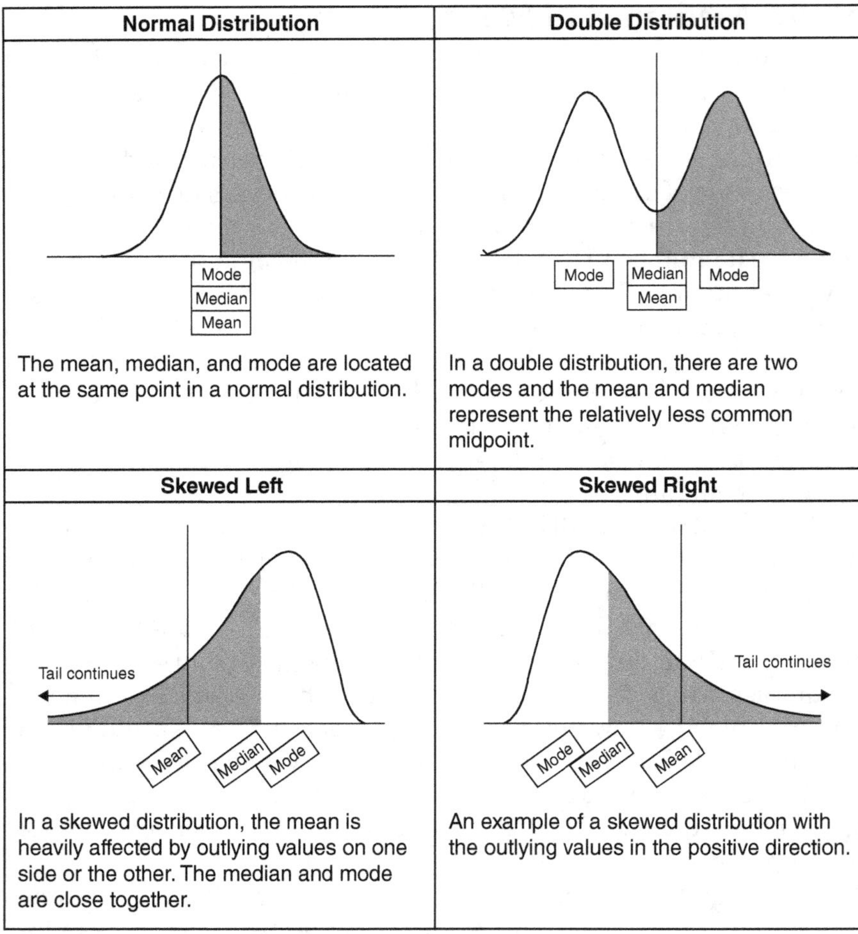

Figure 3.3.10 Variety of distributions

there is in the sample data. For example, it is possible for two sets of data to have the same average behavior and still look very different from one another (Figure 3.3.11). Even though two distributions may both be

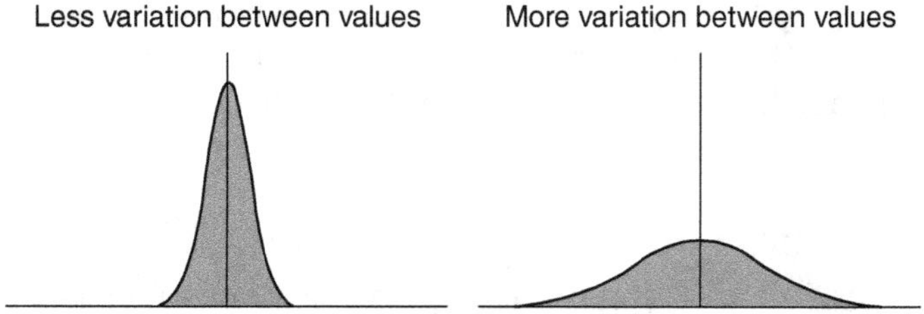

Figure 3.3.11 Distributions with different volatility

shaped like bell curves and have the same central tendency, one of them might have a much wider range of values than the other.

For energy trading, variation is often a very important piece of information. For example, suppose you are analyzing two different investments. Both have an expected payoff of $10 million. However, there is a significant difference between a relatively certain payoff (less variation in value) and one that has a huge range of outcomes (more variation in values). It's the type of information that an investor—or your boss—will definitely want to know.

In trading, the term *volatility* is used to refer to the standard deviation of a series. However, this number is fairly complicated to calculate, so two other measures of dispersion will be examined first—mean absolute deviation and variance.

The mean absolute deviation is the average distance between a set of sample points and the mean of a distribution. Since distance is always a positive number, this means that the average distance is the average of the absolute difference between each point and the mean of a series divided by the number of samples. In the formula for mean average deviation (Figure 3.3.12), x is the value of the number and n is the number of samples.

This would be an excellent measure of variance except for one problem—absolute value is difficult to incorporate into calculus equations. Calculus is the key to making statistics problems easier to solve. It's a bit more work to solve an equation the first time through with calculus, but afterward, anyone can plug in values to get the right result. Most people aren't going to actually solve the calculus themselves—they are going to use a pre-built spreadsheet function or math library that someone else has written. As a result, it will be necessary to use a measure of variance that can be used in those functions.

Fortunately, there is another way to ensure that a number isn't negative—it is possible to multiply a number by itself. This is called taking the square of a number. Applied to a variance formula, squaring the distance between the mean and each value will calculate the mean squared deviation of a number. This quantity is also called *variance*. In mathematical formulas, variance is typically abbreviated σ^2 and is called "sigma squared" (Figure 3.3.13).

$$\textit{Mean Average Deviation} = \frac{\sum |x_i - \bar{x}|}{n}$$

Figure 3.3.12 Mean average deviation

$$\textit{Variance (of an entire population)} = \sigma^2 = \frac{\sum (x - \bar{x})^2}{n}$$

Figure 3.3.13 Variance

$$\textit{Standard Deviation} = \sigma = \sqrt{\sigma^2} = \sqrt{\frac{\sum(x-\bar{x})^2}{n}}$$

Figure 3.3.14 Standard deviation

Taking the square root of the variance gives an answer in the same units as the original series. For price series, the units of variance are dollars-squared. These units are less understandable than having a result in dollars. Because the square root of variance is the most common measure of deviation, it is usually called the *standard deviation* (see Figure 3.3.14). It is typically denoted by the lowercase Greek letter sigma (σ). In scientific and engineering applications, it is called the *root mean square* (RMS). In financial applications, this value is known as volatility of a set of data.

Volatility is a key concept in trading. It is commonplace to hear traders discussing market volatility. For example, it is common to overhear someone saying, "The market was volatile today," or "The volatility in the market has doubled in the last month." Although the general intuition is that prices have moved around a lot recently, *volatility* actually refers to the root mean squared deviation of recent returns.

Estimating Variance and Standard Deviation from Sampled Data

In many cases, it is impossible to include every possible value of a distribution in a variance or standard deviation calculation. This causes a problem because estimating the volatility of an entire set of data from a set of sample data consistently *underestimates* the actual volatility and variance. This error can be corrected by modifying the formulas for variance and volatility slightly; dividing by $n - 1$ instead of by n (Figures 3.3.15 and 3.3.16).

$$\textit{Variance (of a sample)} = \frac{\sum(x-\bar{x})^2}{n-1}$$

Figure 3.3.15 Variance of a sample

$$\textit{Standard Deviation (of a Sample)} = \sqrt{\frac{\sum(x-\bar{x})^2}{n-1}}$$

Figure 3.3.16 Standard deviation of a sample

In most cases, this doesn't make much of a difference. For example, if $n = 1{,}001$, there isn't a lot of difference between dividing a number by 1,000 and dividing that same number by 1,001. However, for a small number of samples, this can be an important correction.

Exponentially Weighted Volatility

In the financial markets, one common way to estimate the volatility of an asset is to use a rolling window of time. For example, a risk manager might estimate the volatility of spot petroleum by examining daily price changes for the past year or two. This is most commonly done by examining the daily return. The daily return can be calculated by taking the natural log of the current price divided by the previous price (e.g., return = $\ln(\text{price}_t/\text{price}_{t-1})$).

In this calculation, one new value joins the distribution each day and another leaves. If a large outlier leaves the calculation, it is possible the volatility can fall dramatically overnight (Figure 3.3.17). For example, on June 11, 1986, there was a 9.21 percent one-day jump in the price of crude oil. Using seven days of historical data to estimate volatility, the June 19 calculation includes the large price move, however, the following day, June 20, does not. This causes the June 20 estimate of volatility to fall dramatically from the day before. The seven-day estimate of volatility fell from 3.5 percent to 2.1 percent because the largest variation in the data set dropped out of the sample.

To a trader or risk manager, this is important. The value of many financial instruments, like options, is extremely sensitive to volatility estimates. Many of these volatilities are estimated based on historical prices. If that largest outlier leaves the sample set, volatility estimates can drop dramatically even though recent prices haven't changed at all. Of course, the real probability of large price moves is unlikely to have changed substantially. This can make for an awkward conversation to explain why an option portfolio just made or lost millions of dollars in the absence of a major market move.

Date	WTI Crude Price	Return
Jun 06, 1986	12.73	−3.63%
Jun 09, 1986	12.61	−0.94%
Jun 10, 1986	12.38	−1.82%
Jun 11, 1986	13.52	9.21%
Jun 12, 1986	13.69	1.26%
Jun 13, 1986	13.83	1.02%
Jun 16, 1986	13.65	−1.30%
Jun 17, 1986	13.65	0.00%
Jun 18, 1986	13.62	−0.22%
Jun 19, 1986	13.73	0.81%
Jun 20, 1986	14.44	5.17%
Jun 23, 1986	14.05	−2.70%
Jun 24, 1986	13.98	−0.50%

Seven-day Rolling Volatility

Volatility, Jun 10–18, 1986: **3.7%**

Volatility, Jun 11–19, 1986: **3.5%**

Volatility, Jun 12–20, 1986: **2.1%**

Figure 3.3.17 Rolling volatility

A common modification to volatility calculations is to apply a weighting scheme that causes the recent observations to influence the estimate more than older observations. This is similar to a typical calculation for variance and standard deviation with the addition of another variable in the formula. This complicates the calculation, but eliminates the problem of large values dropping out of the calculation. As large values get further away, they have a progressively smaller impact on the calculation.

Exponentially weighted returns use a decay factor, commonly called *lambda* (λ) that progressively decreases the weight of each sample as the samples go further back in time. For example, the current day's observation receives a 100 percent weighting. Today is indicated mathematically by a variable time, *t*, being equal to zero. Previous samples get progressively less weight in the volatility calculation (Figure 3.3.18).

The addition of a weighting factor that depends on time alters the volatility calculation (Figure 3.3.19). In addition to complicating the formula, an exponential weighting places much more emphasis on recent events. Immediately when a very large daily change enters the data set, the volatility estimate will change. As time passes, that value will have less and less effect and will slowly drop out of the calculation.

Exponential weighting effectively limits the number of samples used in the equation. Eventually the weights will get so small that the value has a negligible effect on the volatility calculation. This is called *exponential decay*. For example, when lambda equals 0.94, observations older than 75 days are weighted less than 1 percent of more recent

Exponential Weighting Factor

An exponential weighting factor is typically defined by the formula:

$$p_t = \lambda^t$$

Where

t **Time.** For example, t=0 is today and t=1 is yesterday.

λ **Exponential Decay Constant.** The Greek symbol lamba is a constant chosen by the modeler. Typical range of values for lamba are between .94 and .99.

p_t **Weighting at Time *t*.** For example, if λ = .94, then

$p_0 = (.94)^0 = 1.000$

$p_1 = (.94)^1 = 0.9400$

$p_2 = (.94)^2 = 0.8836$

Figure 3.3.18 Exponential weighting factor

Exponential Weighted Volatility

An exponential weighting factor is typically defined by the formula:

$$\sigma = \sqrt{\frac{\sum p_t (x_t - \mu)^2}{\sum p_t}}$$

Where

- t **Time.** For example, t=0 is today and t=1 is yesterday.
- x_t **Observation at Time *t*.** Usually a change in price or a percent change in price like logarithmic return.
- p_t **Weighting at Time *t*.**
- μ **Mean observation.** Calculated by the formula:

$$\mu = \frac{\sum p_t x_t}{\sum p_t}$$

Figure 3.3.19 Exponentially weighted volatility

observations. At a lambda equals 0.96, this occurs after 113 days, and at lambda equals 0.98, it occurs after 228 days (Figure 3.3.20).

Risk/Reward Measures

When traders analyze trading opportunities, neither the average return nor the volatility of an investment indicates whether it was a good investment without the other factor. A more useful measurement

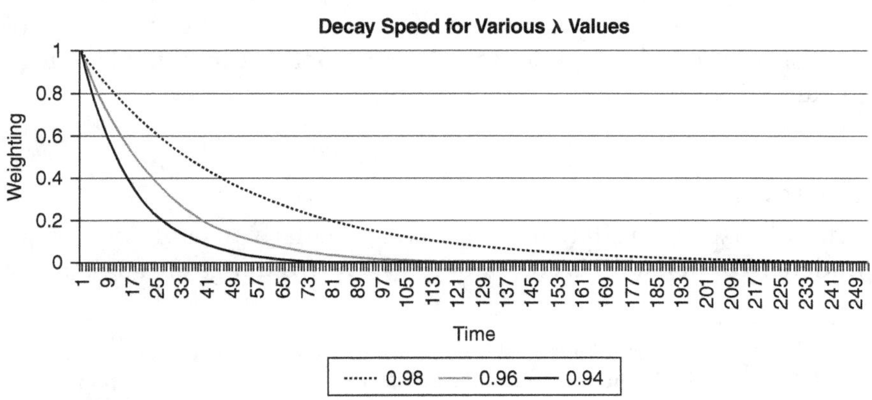

Figure 3.3.20 Exponential decay

$$\textit{Information Ratio} = \frac{\textit{Average Return}}{\textit{Volatility of Returns}}$$

Figure 3.3.21 Information Ratio

of investment performance is reward-to-risk measure. In this type of measure, the average return is divided by the standard deviation of returns. Commonly, this is known as a *Sharpe Ratio* or an *Information Ratio*[2] (Figure 3.3.21). Both of these ratios work the same way. The average return of the investment (net of some benchmark) is divided by the variability of the return (net of some benchmark). Higher ratios are considered superior investments to lower ratios.

Like any model, risk/reward ratios have to be used carefully. These measures are not predictions of the future. Typically, these ratios use historical data and they rely on that data to be representative of actual performance. If market conditions change, or if accounting sleight of hand is being used to smooth out earnings, these measures will fail to work properly. Also, these measures only work correctly when returns are positive. When returns are negative, higher volatility leads to better (less negative) ratios.

Finally, it is misleading to look at an investment opportunity without considering its effect on the entire portfolio. Unless the returns for different strategies are perfectly correlated, a combination of strategies will always have a lower volatility than any single strategy. For example, consider two strategies. One strategy always makes $1 when the price of natural gas rises, and loses $0.98 when the market falls. Another strategy always makes $1 when the price of natural gas falls, and loses $0.99 when the market rises. The long strategy (the one that makes money when the market rises) is the better strategy if the market is equally likely to rise and fall. However, the combination of both strategies is far superior to either one alone. A combined strategy makes a risk-free profit!

Correlation

Another aspect of statistics that is particularly useful for energy traders to understand is correlation. When two things are statistically

---

[2] A Sharpe Ratio subtracts out the risk-free rate of return from the average return. An Information Ratio subtracts out some industry benchmark. The distinction is important to investment managers who benchmark their returns against an index. However, for everyone else, the most important thing is to ensure that a consistent measure is used across a business and either a Sharpe Ratio or an Information Ratio will work equally well.

correlated, they have a direct linear relationship. For example, natural gas prices in New York and New Jersey are usually correlated. When prices in one area are high, prices in the other area are also likely to be high.

Often, it is possible to see the relationship between two numbers by plotting two price series on a graph. For example, it might be useful to understand if the price of peak electricity in an area is correlated to the price of natural gas. Even though this won't indicate the exact relationship between the two prices, it is a good way to see if there is a relationship. Another way of looking at the data is to use a scatter diagram to compare prices (Figure 3.3.22). Two different ways of looking at the data are shown in the graphs. The top graph shows daily prices for each commodity; the bottom graph is a scatter graph that matches natural gas prices to peak electricity prices of the same day.

Correlation assumes that there is a linear (straight-line) relationship between two data series. It's fairly obvious from both graphs that the prices of the two assets acted similarly throughout this entire period. A straight line can be drawn through the scatter diagram and

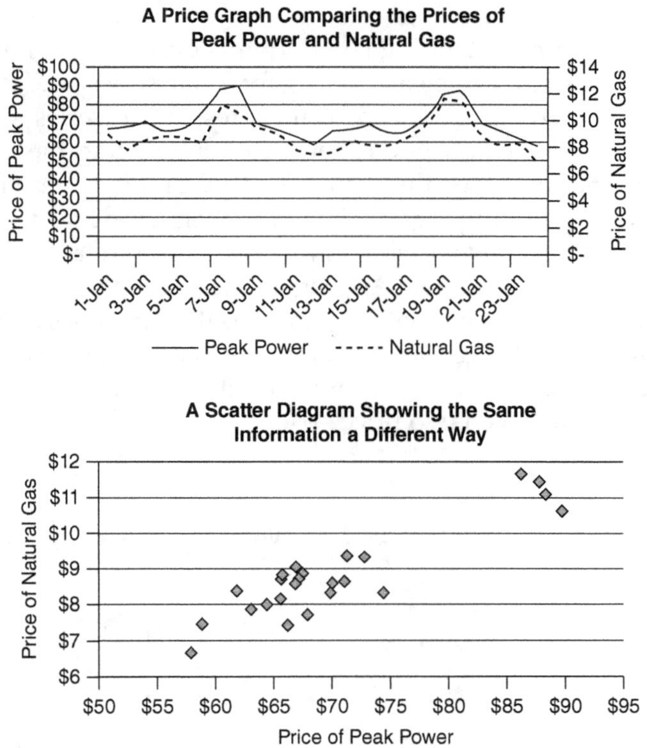

Figure 3.3.22 Different ways of looking at data

capture the primary relationship between electricity prices and natural gas prices. However, it would still be helpful to be able to define a single number that can summarize the strength of this relationship. Ideally, this would work the same way that the average and standard deviation describe a single set of data.

The most common way to measure the relationship between two sets of data is to use the correlation coefficient, abbreviated *r*. The correlation coefficient produces a number between –1 and +1 that indicates the strength of the relationship between the two data series. A correlation coefficient equal to +1 means that the series behaves identically in all situations. A correlation coefficient of –1 means that prices are inversely proportional to one another (when one price rises, the other price falls). A correlation coefficient of zero indicates no relationship between the two values (Figure 3.3.23).

Using the example of correlated prices, a positive correlation indicates that the prices move up and down together. A negative correlation indicates the prices tend to move in the opposite direction—when one rises, the other falls. No correlation means that prices tend to move up and down randomly—sometimes rising together and sometimes rising at opposite times. Correlation is calculated by a mathematical formula (Figure 3.3.24).

The key to understanding correlation is examining numbers that are far away from the mean. Prices for each series are multiplied together after having the mean of their respective series subtracted out. If either the x or y value is zero after subtracting the mean value, it will cancel out the other value. Multiplication by zero is always zero. However, multiplying two large numbers produces a very large number. As a result, what matters in a correlation relationship is the behavior of outlying results. As long as the outlying values of x (the values far from the mean) match up to the outlying values of y, the two series will show a strong relationship. Particularly in the case of energy prices that are very volatile, a couple of outlier prices often determine the correlation between two price series.

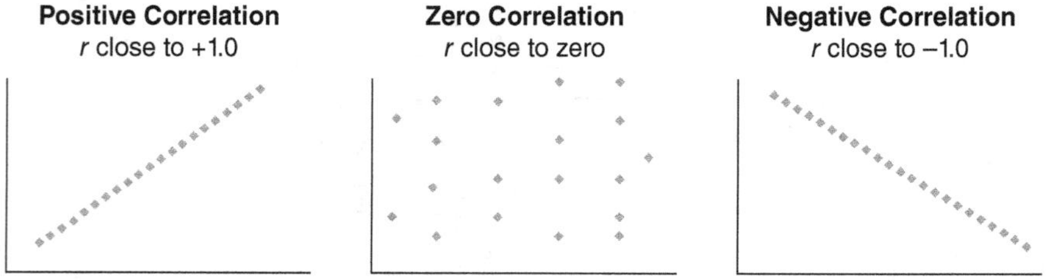

Figure 3.3.23 Types of correlation

Correlation Coefficient (r)

$$r = \frac{\sum(x - \bar{x})(y - \bar{y})}{(n - 1)\sigma_x\sigma_y}$$

Where

x	The first set of data.
$\bar{x}$	The average price of the first data set.
σ_x	The standard deviation of the first data set.
y	The second set of data.
$\bar{y}$	The average price of the second data set.
σ_y	The standard deviation of the second data set.
n	The number of samples (the first and second data sets need the same number of values).

Figure 3.3.24 Correlation coefficient

Correlated Does Not Mean a Good Hedge!

One of the most dangerous traps that an energy trader can fall into is to trust statistics without actually looking at the underlying data. For example, because energy prices are cyclical, it is common for all energy prices to be highly correlated. That doesn't necessarily mean that those prices are trending in the same direction. A graphical example of this is shown in Figure 3.3.25—the two series are highly correlated with $r = 0.5$, but they are going in opposite directions!

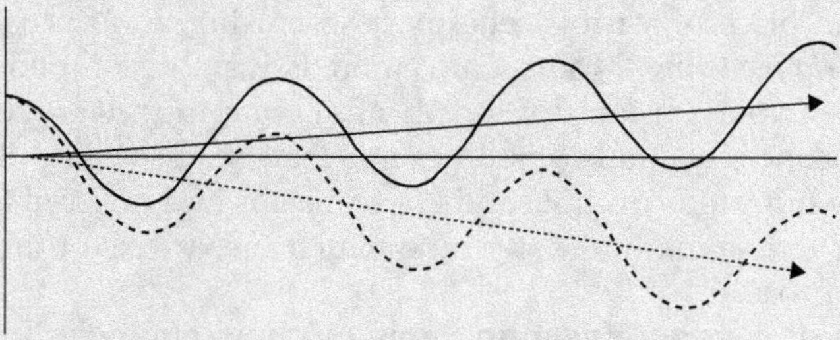

Figure 3.3.25 Correlated series trending apart

A practical example might be a steel producer that is a major user of electricity. The year is 1990, and the steel producer is located in the PJM-East service area halfway between Washington, D.C., and Baltimore. For protection against a rise in electricity prices, the steel producer wants to buy electricity futures. However, exchange-traded futures are not available for PJM-East. The closest futures trading location is PJM-West. This service area is located to the west of Washington, D.C., near the intersection of western Maryland, West Virginia, and Pennsylvania.

(*Continued*)

The steel producer checks that PJM-East and PJM-West prices are highly correlated, finds they are, and buys $500 million of PJM-West power forwards; $20 million of forwards per year for the next 25 years.

Going forward 10 years, the population in the Baltimore-Washington area has boomed. New housing developments and increased commercial activity are straining the power grid. As a result, power prices in PJM-East are soaring. However, the population to the west of Washington, D.C., has not experienced the same growth in population. Instead, power prices in PJM-West have declined. The price of power in the two regions has remained highly correlated since the weather in both areas is nearly identical. Power prices reach their peaks on the same days (hot summer days in August) and are low on the same days. However, the price of power in PJM-East has gone up in price, while the power in PJM-West has declined in value.

The steel producer, relying on estimates of correlation, never noticed that the prices were diverging for almost 10 years. Because the prices in the two areas generally moved up and down at the same time, the futures effectively limited the day-to-day volatility. Since correlations remained high, no one thought to actually look at the underlying data. As a result, by the time the problem was identified, the steel producer faced a huge loss on the hedge!

Monte Carlo Testing

A common application of statistics is to develop valuation models to determine the price of various energy assets using an approach called *Monte Carlo modeling*. Monte Carlo models were developed in the middle of the twentieth century shortly after computers were first developed. The concept is that sometimes it is faster to use computer time to calculate hundreds of thousands of scenarios and observe the results than it is to use math to determine which scenario is optimal for a specific purpose.

For example, it is very difficult to figure out how often it is possible to win the one-player card game, solitaire, with a standard 52-card deck. It is relatively easy to prove that some games are possible to win and others impossible. However, because there are so many permutations of cards, it is extremely difficult to find the probability equation that will give an exact answer as to what percent of games are winnable.

Another approach to solving this problem is to play enough games of solitaire. This is called *simulation* and is the basis for Monte Carlo analysis. If enough games were played, a computer could easily keep track of how many games were won and lost. This analysis is fairly easy to extend. For example, if one wanted to define several strategies for playing the game, it would be possible to identify which strategy was most effective by keeping track of how often that strategy won.

There is no single approach to Monte Carlo methods. Each simulation has to be individually modeled. For example, it would be necessary to program to play solitaire before you could use Monte Carlo to figure out what percentage of solitaire games could be run. However, here are several common steps that most Monte Carlo simulations have in common:

1. Develop random inputs.
2. Generate the simulation defined by the random inputs.
3. Calculate the result of the simulation.
4. Aggregate results after running the simulation multiple times.

Develop Random Inputs

Monte Carlo simulations are driven by random inputs. For example, when playing solitaire, it is necessary to shuffle the deck of cards and choose a playing card for each game. This is sometimes as much an art as a science.

Generate the Simulation

After inputs are calculated, it is necessary to implement the simulation. This is typically a deterministic process based on the random inputs.

Calculate Results

Once a simulation is completed, the results of the simulation need to be determined. In the solitaire example, this would involve determining if the game was won or lost.

Aggregate Results

Finally, the last step of a Monte Carlo simulation is to run through the process a large number of times and to aggregate results. Commonly, Monte Carlo analysis involves 10,000 or more simulations.

3.4

FINANCIAL OPTIONS

30-Second Summary

Purpose

This chapter provides a nonmathematical introduction to financial options with a mathematical discussion on option pricing in the next chapter. Options are important for two reasons. First, they are important financial instruments. They are used in a variety of trading strategies and behave differently than other types of investments. Second, options are commonly used to model energy investments where a decision is required.

Summary

An option is a contract between two people. It gives the buyer of the contract the right, but not the obligation, to buy or sell property at some future date at a fixed price. The property that may be bought or sold as a result of the option is called the *underlying asset*, or more commonly, the *underlying*. The right to buy is called a *call* option. The right to sell is called a *put* option. Options have an up-front cost, called a *premium*, which is paid when the buyer purchases the option. For the buyer, options have limited downside risk. Buyers will either lose their premium or they will make a profit. The seller of the option contract also called the option *writer*.

Key Topics

- Options are a contract between two individuals where the buyer pays the writer of the option money up front for the possibility of a bigger payoff sometime in the future.
- Options represent a decision where the buyer of the option has the ability to decide whether or not to take some action based on economic reasons.
- In many ways, options are similar to insurance. For example, it is rarely profitable to purchase them purely for speculative reasons. Additionally, they offer the promise of a big payoff with limited downside.

Option is a financial term that describes a common feature of many contracts. This feature gives one person in the contract the ability to make some kind of decision in the future, usually to buy or sell something at a fixed price. Being able to place a dollar value on the ability to make future decisions is a cornerstone of modern investing. Option contracts work by having one person pay another for the right to take some action in the future. The money paid by the buyer to the option writer when the contract is signed is called the *premium*. The decision to take action is an *exercise*. It is usually obvious when an option should be exercised. The difficult decision is determining how much to pay for the option in the first place. For example, if an option buyer purchased the right to buy gasoline in the future for $4.00/gallon, he would only exercise that right when prices were above $4.00. Otherwise, he would be wasting his money. The value of the option depends on the probability that prices will be above $4.00.

Options are important because it is possible to represent many types of investment decisions this way. For example, a combination oil well and refinery might be able to produce gasoline at $4.00/gallon. Owning this installation would give the owner the option to "buy" gasoline at $4.00/gallon for immediate resale. By comparing the cost of building and operating the installation to the economic value of the option, it is possible to determine whether this would be a good investment.

Financial option contracts, as opposed to approximations of physical investments, are an all-or-nothing investment. It is possible to buy a million dollars' worth of options and lose everything. This is like buying insurance. Most often, the purchaser will pay a premium and have the contract expire worthless. Occasionally, the contract will pay off big when an unusual event occurs. Even though the size of the downside is small (losing the premium) compared to the potential upside (a huge profit), the odds of making a profit are stacked against the buyer. Similar to buying insurance, buying options is generally unprofitable. It only makes sense as part of a broader strategy. The option writer is taking on a risk from the buyer and needs to be compensated for taking that risk.

Two common applications for options are risk management and modeling energy investments. In the energy market, there are a lot of physical decisions that need to be made on a daily basis. Do I turn the power plant on and convert my fuel into electricity? Do I lock in a fuel supply for the winter now or should I wait a little longer? Should I invest in building a new power line between Oregon and Northern California? Option theory provides a way to quantify those decisions.

From a transaction standpoint, option trading requires both a buyer and a seller. The seller (the *option writer*) takes on the possibility of a big loss in exchange for money up front. The buyer pays a *premium* to the writer for that service. If the option pays off, the writer will need to find the cash to pay the buyer. With options, money is not magically

Call Option	Put Option
Call Payoff = Max (Asset Price – Strike Price, 0)	*Put Payoff = Max (Strike Price – Asset Price, 0)*
Call options give the right to buy an asset at the strike price at a point in the future (the expiration date).	Put options give the right to sell an asset at the strike price at some point in the future (the expiration date).

Option Payoffs	
Call_Payoff = Asset_Price – Strike_Price	if *the Asset_Price > Strike_Price at expiration*
Put_Payoff = Strike_Price – Asset_Price	if *the Strike_Price > Asset_Price at expiration*

Figure 3.4.1 Option payoffs

created; it is simply transferred between the two parties. The option buyer is described as being *long the option* or being *long volatility* (since rare events will mean a big profit). The option writer is described as being *short the option* or being *short volatility* (since rare events will mean a big loss).

The amount of money that needs to be transferred between the buyer and seller is determined by the *payoff* of the option. Every option is assigned an *exercise* or *strike price*. This is the fixed price at which trading can occur in the future. For example, a call option involves the right to buy the underlying asset at a fixed price. The owner of a call option benefits when the price of the underlying asset rises above the strike price. This allows the owner to buy at a lower price than is otherwise available. The owner can also make an immediate profit by reselling the asset at the current price.

A put option works similarly. A put option gives the owner of the option the right to sell the underlying asset at a fixed price. If the market price of the underlying is greater than the fixed price, a put option is worthless. No one will willingly sell at a lower price than necessary. However, if the fixed price is higher than the market price, the put buyer makes a profit by selling at a higher price (Figure 3.4.1).

Intrinsic and Extrinsic Value

Option contracts exist for a period of time. During that time, the value of the option will change regularly. The *intrinsic value* is the money that could be obtained by exercising the option immediately—forgoing the chance at more money. The *extrinsic value* of an option is the value of the option that comes from holding on to it longer.

For example, consider a $1 lottery ticket that pays the winner $1 million and gives the owner an ability to flip a coin for more money. If the ticket holder wins the coin toss after winning the first million, he gets another $2 million. However, if he loses, he gives up the initial $1 million. After winning the first million, the lottery ticket is no longer riskless. The owner has the option of taking a million dollars and walking away. This is now the *intrinsic value* of the option. The owner of the ticket no longer has a dollar at stake—he has a million dollars at stake! The higher the intrinsic value of the option the more risk is involved.

Continuing this example, a savvy trader might realize that a 50/50 chance of making $3 million compared to losing $1 million is a profitable investment. If losing a million dollars wasn't a hardship (maybe a multibillionaire was playing the game), it would make good economic sense to take the coin toss every time it was offered. The extrinsic value of the option is the value of not exercising the option. In this case, the extrinsic value would be approximately $500,000—a 50 percent chance of making $3 million while only having $1 million at risk.

Calculating Extrinsic Value

The coin flip in the example is really a 50/50 chance of making $3 million or going home with no money. There is an option to walk away with $1 million. The coin flip represents a 50 percent chance of winning $3 million, giving the lottery ticket an expected value of $1.5 million. Since exercising the option immediately would give $1 million risk free, the value of taking the extra coin flip (the extrinsic value) is the value of the entire lottery ticket ($1.5 million) less the intrinsic value ($1 million).

Not wanting to risk losing a million dollars, and being a savvy trader, the owner of the winning lottery ticket might decide to sell the lottery ticket instead of exercising his option to take the risk-free million dollars. For example, the owner of the lottery ticket might decide to offer it for sale for $1.4 million. After all, a 50/50 chance at $3 million for $1.4 million is still a profitable investment. In this way, the owner of the option could get most of the benefit from the coin flip without actually exposing himself or herself to the risk of losing the million dollars.

The initial cost of the lottery ticket determines whether playing the lottery was a good or bad investment. For example, a free ticket would be a great investment. However, high up-front costs can easily transform options, and lottery tickets, into poor investments. The potential for a big payoff at low risk does not make a good investment by itself.

If the up-front costs are too high, both lottery tickets and options become risk-free ways to lose money!

Early Exercise

With some options, it is possible to exercise the option early. This will lock in some of the profits (the intrinsic value) but give up any possibility of any additional profits (the extrinsic value). Rather than giving up the additional profits, it is usually more profitable to sell the option. As a general rule, options are never exercised early. If the option buyer wants out of the position, the option will be sold rather than liquidated.

There are exceptions to this general rule, but they are fairly rare. Sometimes, owning the underlying gives a benefit that isn't accrued to the option owner. For example, a stock might pay a dividend that will reduce the value of the stock and make a call option less valuable. The owner of the stock will receive the dividend to offset the loss in stock price, but the option owner will not. If the dividend is large, it may be worthwhile to exercise the stock and give up the extrinsic value of the option.

In energy trading, options are typically written on futures or forward contracts rather than directly on the underlying commodity. This is because an actual transfer of a commodity takes time to set up ahead of time. For example, an option to buy electricity will almost always be an option to buy a forward contract rather than physical electricity. This eliminates the complication of being forced to deliver a commodity on short notice. It isn't possible to buy a call option on October off-peak power (cheap power) and exercise it early to get daytime power in August (expensive power). If the call option is exercised early, the buyer would get an October off-peak forward contract. This tends to eliminate the value of exercising energy options prior to the expiration date.

Typical Payoff from Trading Options

If options are priced fairly, with both buyers and sellers breaking even over the long run, a strategy of buying options loses money most of the time. This is because buying an option will occasionally return a big profit. To counterbalance that big profit, there needs to be a series of small, frequent losses. Selling options will have exactly the opposite payoff. Selling options will return steady small profits, and occasionally have a large loss (Figure 3.4.2).

Bid/Ask Spreads

Options, like other financial products, typically have a bid/ask spread. The price at which market makers sell to buyers (the ask price)

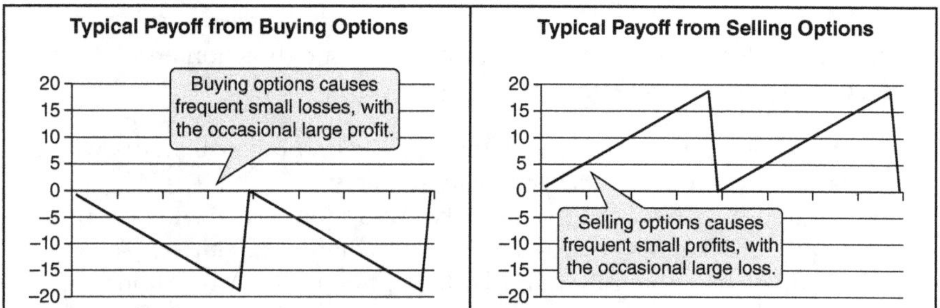

A strategy of buying options will frequently lose small amounts of money, and occasionally make a large profit. A graph of the profit will often show slow losses and occasional large profits.

Selling options will provide steady, consistent profits with an occasional large loss. The profit line will slowly increase with the occasional drop in prices.

Figure 3.4.2 Typical payoffs

is higher than the price where they are willing to buy options (the bid price). Relative to the size of the premium, most options have a very wide spread between their bid and ask prices. Somewhere between the two prices will be the fair price for the option.

The bid/ask spread is generally proportional to the amount of trading that is done in a particular option contract. If buyers and sellers can easily be matched up, allowing the market maker to make a low-risk profit, spreads will be very tight. However, if the market maker won't be able to get out of the trade easily, and thinks that he might need to hold on to the option until expiration, there will be a very large spread. For example, in an illiquid option with a "fair value" of $6, it might not be uncommon to see a $2 bid price and a $10 ask price.

Becoming an option market maker isn't particularly hard—it mostly requires enough capital to cover losses. The downside of being an option market maker is that they are always trading against informed investors. Because of the sizes of bid/ask spreads, buying and selling options in most speculative trading strategies is a losing proposition.

Volatility

Volatility is the tendency of the market to see a large price move. Market volatility goes in cycles—sometimes the financial markets are quiet and very little is going on, and other times prices can change rapidly. Because of the way that options pay out, option buyers and writers are very exposed to the market volatility cycle. For an option buyer, options

(Continued)

offer unlimited benefits if the prices move in one direction and limited losses if the prices move the other way.

- An option buyer is long volatility. An option buyer benefits when large price movements become more likely.
- An option writer is short volatility. An option writer will benefit in a quiet market or if prices stay exactly where they started. The premium is the only profit made by the option writer. An option writer won't make any more money if the option finishes very far out of the money rather than just out of the money. However, the option writer has a great deal to lose if prices move in the wrong direction.

Why Traders Use Options

Most commonly, traders buy options as insurance. Although options may not make good speculative investments, they are a very cost-effective way to buy insurance. Having an open market ensures competitive pricing. Nothing forces traders to transact at other people's bid and ask prices. Every trader, assuming they have assets to meet their obligations, can sell options too.

In some cases, options can be a good way to get into trades that would otherwise be too risky. A good rule of thumb is that no single decision should ever be so risky that it risks shutting down the trading desk. If a trading desk is close to its risk limit, and strongly believes in a trade, options can be a good way to take on more exposure without taking on a large risk.

Another reason that options are important is their use in investing. Many investment decisions can be modeled as financial options. For example, building a power plant gives the operator the option of burning fuel to produce electricity. The power plant operator will probably make the decision to produce electricity whenever it is profitable. As a result, options are commonly a good way to analyze any investment that involves a decision.

In the energy market, most options are written on forward or futures contracts. For example, when an option based on a forward contract is exercised early, it is the forward that gets delivered—not the physical commodity. Even if the option writer has to deliver a physical commodity at some point, the physical commodity won't be delivered until the expiration of the forward contract.

Basing options on forwards and futures contracts reduces the benefit from early exercise. An option that can be exercised at any time is called an *American option*. An option that can only be exercised at expiration of the option is called a *European option*. In most cases, whether an option is an American or European option isn't a big deal. It is almost always more profitable to resell the option rather than to exercise it early.

A Zero Sum Game!

One reason options are often unprofitable to trade is that they are a zero sum game. The only way to make money trading options is for someone else to lose money. Options involve a direct payment from one market participant to another. As a result, an option trader has to be smarter, or luckier, than the people with whom he or she is trading. Trading tends to be a Darwinian business—traders who lose money consistently get pushed out of their jobs—leaving only smart, lucky people still in the business of trading.

Other markets do not behave the same way. For example, in the stock market, everyone can make money at the same time. This happens because companies become more valuable as the economy expands. There is a natural tendency for the fundamental value of stocks to appreciate over time. But, even more than that, stock trading is not a zero sum game because of how profits on stock trading are calculated.

The price of everyone's stock is set by the last traded price. Every share of a particular stock is priced at the same level. If any owner of stock sells at a price higher than the previous sale, everyone makes money. For example, if there are a million shares of a stock, and one person sells the stock at a price $10 higher than the previous trade, $10 million of wealth is created. Each of those million shares has gone up in value by $10. No one had to lose money on that sale either—the seller got out of his or her position at a higher price, the buyer exchanged cash for stock, and the other owners all saw a profit without being required to do anything.

Of course, when the stock market crashes, everyone can lose money at the same time too. The different investment styles don't mean that one market is better than another market, but it is a very different dynamic.

Payoff Diagrams

Traders often represent the risks of an option position by a payoff diagram. These diagrams show the final profitability of the option with respect to the price of the underlying instrument.

For example, an option might give the buyer the right to buy a natural gas futures contract for $100. At expiration, if the futures contract is worth more than $100, the option buyer will exercise the option. Even if the option buyer doesn't plan to personally use the contract, he or she can purchase the futures contract and resell it at a profit. If the futures contract is worth $300, buying at $100 and reselling at $300, gives a payoff of $200. However, if the futures price at expiration is $50, the option is worthless. There is no good reason for the option buyer to pay $100, when the same product can be obtained for $50.

The payoff of a forward contract looks like a straight line (Figure 3.4.3). The value of the future contract varies directly with the price of the underlying product. For example, if a trader agrees to a contract to buy 100 MMBtus of natural gas at $8, that buyer loses money when prices are less than $8 and makes money when prices are above $8.

Options are agreements that allow the buyer to make a transaction at a specific price in the future but don't require the option buyer to make a transaction. If a call option expires with the price of the underlying product above the strike price, the option is valuable. Otherwise, the call buyer will choose not to exercise the option. As a result, the payoff for an option looks like half the payoff of a forward (Figure 3.4.4). When the price of the underlying product is above the strike price, the option is profitable (it is *in the money*). When it is below the strike price, the option expires worthless (*out of the money*).

The payoff of an option is further complicated because options aren't free—it costs money to buy an option. This shifts the payoff for

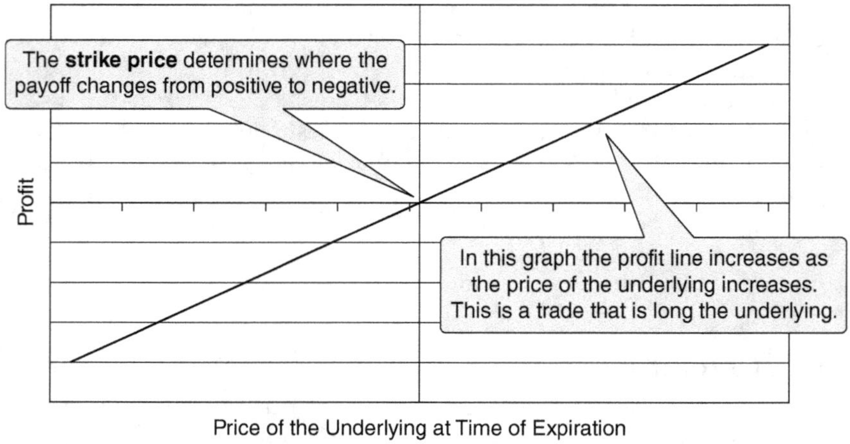

Figure 3.4.3 The payoff of a forward contract

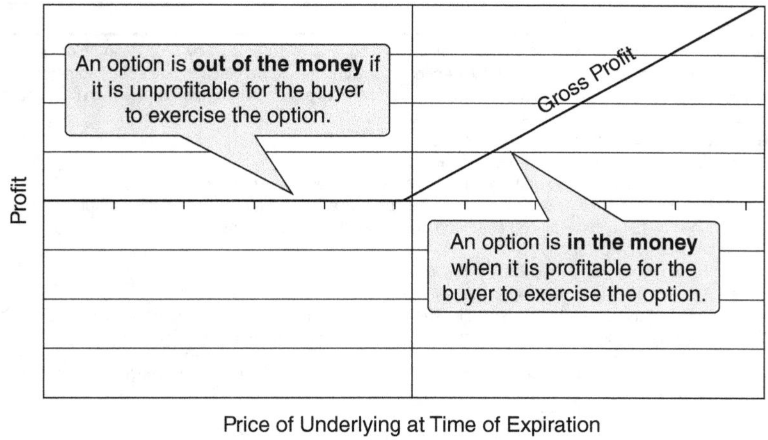

Figure 3.4.4 The payoff of a call option

the option (Figure 3.4.5). When an option expires out of the money, the option writer makes a profit. When an option expires in the money, the gross profit has to exceed the cost of purchasing the option before the buyer makes a net profit. For example, if a trader purchases an option to buy something at $100, and the option costs $20, the buyer will only make a net profit when the price of the underlying product is above $120. The breakeven price is the strike price plus the premium. The net profit is a combination of the final payoff and the premium that the option buyer needed to pay to buy the option initially. Additional details on forwards can be found in Figure 3.4.6, call options in Figure 3.4.7, and put options in Figure 3.4.8.

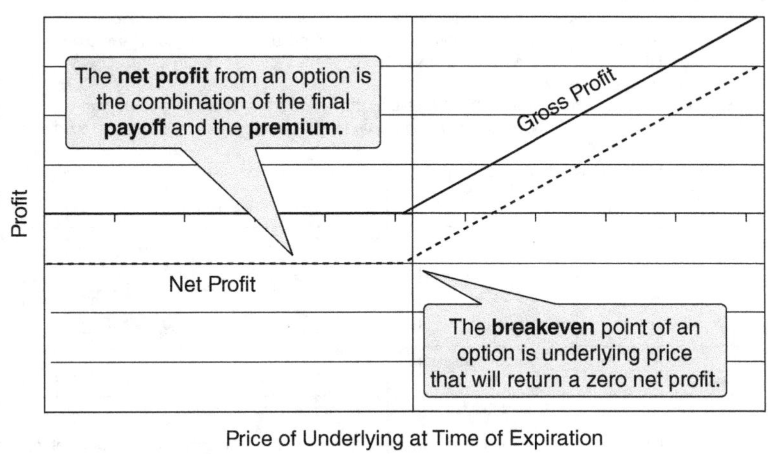

Figure 3.4.5 The payoff of a call with a premium

Forwards

Since calls and puts are options to buy or sell something, it is useful to start by considering binding contracts to buy or sell some product. Like options, forwards are agreements to buy or sell something at a pre-arranged price in the future. Unlike options, forwards are binding agreements – both sides have committed themselves to a transaction at a future date.

The Buyer of a forward will:

- Pay no money when the trade is entered.
- Agree to purchase the underlying at the strike price on the expiration date.
- Benefit if the price of the asset rises. The buyer of a forward has a long position in the asset since he benefits by buying at a price lower than the prevailing market price.

The Seller of a forward will:

- Pay no money when the trade is entered.
- Agree to sell the underlying at the strike price on the expiration date.
- Benefit if the price of the asset falls. The seller of a forward has a short position in the asset since he benefits by selling at a price higher than the prevailing market price.

Long a Forward

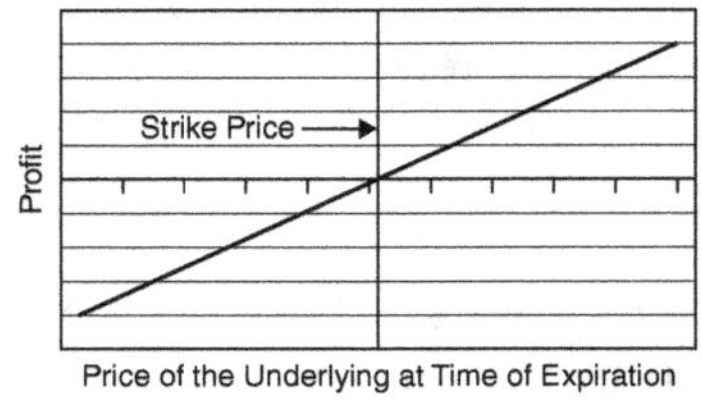

The purchaser of a forward contract enters a binding contract to purchase the underlying at a fixed price. The higher the price rises, the better this deal becomes, because the purchase is at a fixed price.

Short a Forward

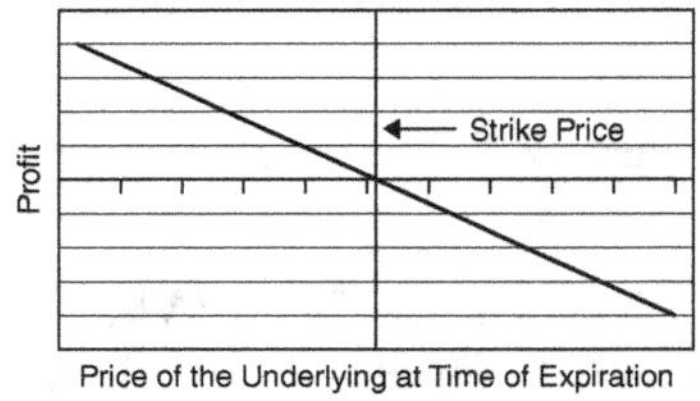

The writer of a forward contract agrees to sell the underlying to the contract purchaser at a specific price (the strike price). A forward seller will profit when the price of the underlying falls since he is selling at a high price relative to the spot price.

Figure 3.4.6 Forward contracts

Call Options

A call option is a contract between two parties that gives the option buyer the right, but not the obligation, to purchase some product (the *underlying*) at a specific price (the *strike price*) for some length of time (ending at the *expiration date*).

The Buyer of a call will:

- Pay a non-refundable premium to the writer of the option when entering the trade.
- Have the right to purchase the underlying at the strike price when the option is exercised.
- Benefit if the price of the underlying rises. (The buyer has a long position in the underlying.)

The Seller (Writer) of a call will:

- Receive a premium for writing the call, paid by the option buyer at the time of the trade.
- Be required to sell the buyer of the option the underlying at the strike price if the option is exercised.
- Benefit if the price of the underlying falls. (The seller has a short position in the underlying.)

Long a Call

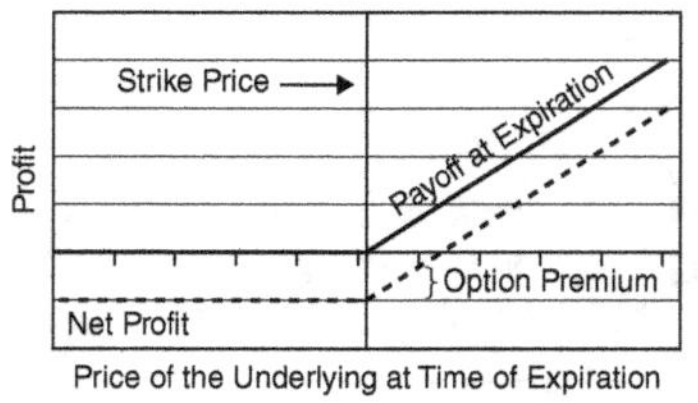

The owner of a call profits when the price of the underlying rises. The owner of the call benefits by being able to buy at a fixed price and sell high.

Short a Call

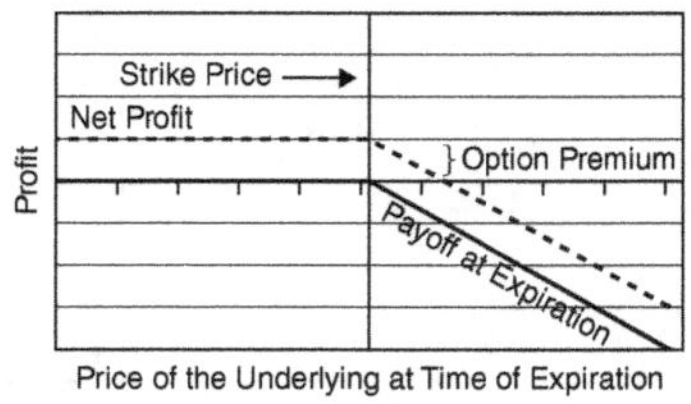

The writer of a call profits when the price of the underlying stays constant or falls. The writer of a call benefits if the option is not exercised.

Figure 3.4.7 Call options

Put Options

A put option is a contract between two parties that gives the option buyer the right, but not the obligation, to sell some product (the *underlying*) at a specific price (the *strike price*) for some length of time (ending at the *expiration date*).

The Buyer of a put will:

- Pay a non-refundable premium to the writer of the option when entering the trade.
- Have the right to sell the underlying to the seller at the strike price when the option is exercised.
- Benefit if the price of the underlying falls. (The buyer has a short position in the underlying.)

The Seller (Writer) of a put will:

- Receive a premium for writing the call, paid by the option buyer at the time of the trade.
- Be required to buy the underlying from the option buyer at the strike price if the option is exercised.
- Benefit if the price of the underlying rises. (The seller has a long position in the underlying.)

Long a Put

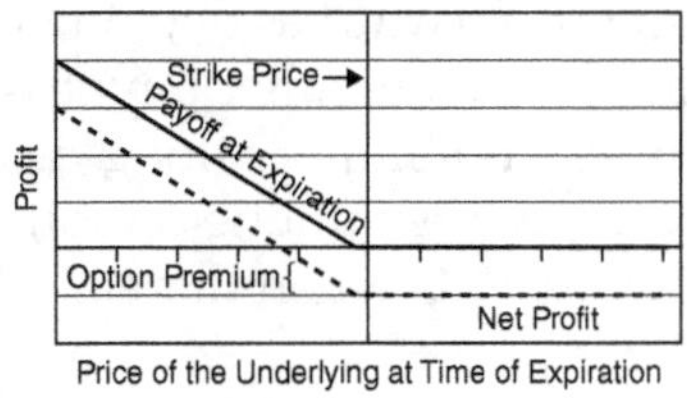

The owner of a put option benefits when the price of the underlying falls. The owner benefits by being able to buy cheaply and sell at a fixed price.

Short a Put

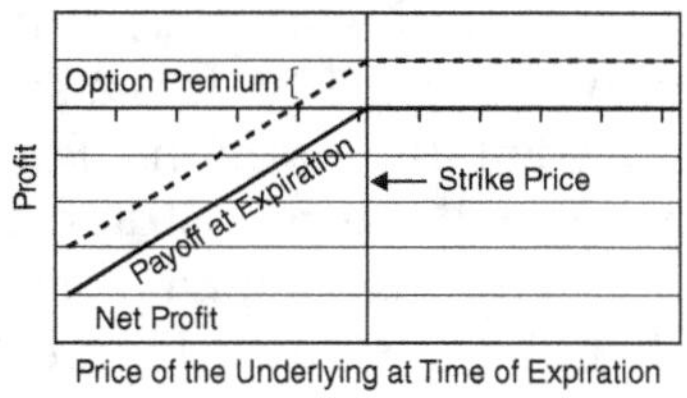

The seller of a put option profits when the price of the underlying stays constant or rises. The seller of the put benefits when the option is not exercised.

Figure 3.4.8 Put options

Put/Call Parity

It is possible to combine the payoffs from multiple option transactions (Figure 3.4.9). This is the basis of many types of option trades. The most important combination of payoffs is the combination of put and call options to form forwards. The ability to combine calls and puts to form a forward forces a link between these two products. For example, by simultaneously buying a call and selling a put, a trader can replicate the payoff from owning a forward.

The prices of the call and put have to be identical (within the limits of a bid ask spread, at any rate). Otherwise it would be possible to reverse engineer an option payoff and make an arbitrage profit. This would be done by buying one type of option and synthetically creating an identical payoff to liquidate the position. Replicating the payoff

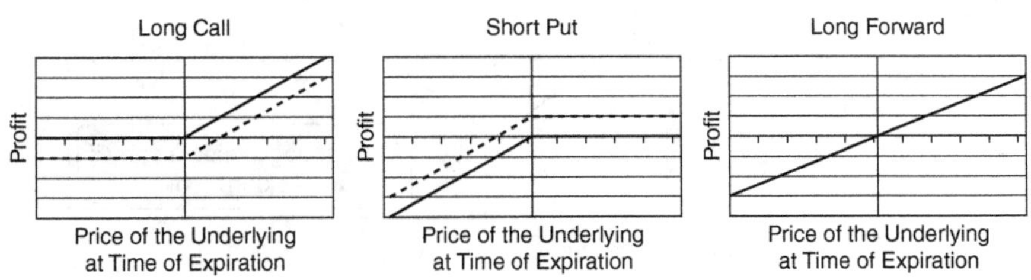

Figure 3.4.9 A synthetic forward

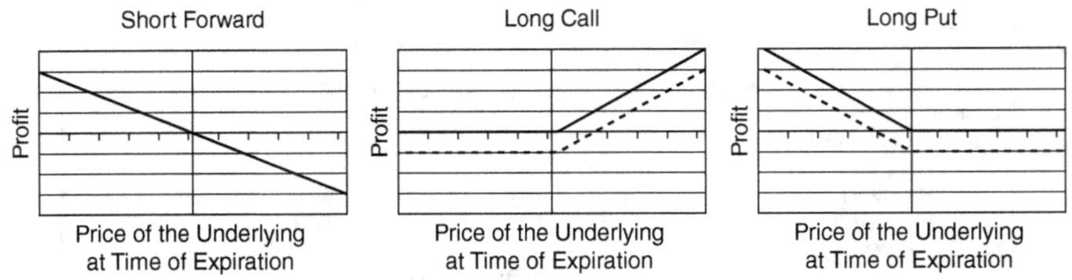

Figure 3.4.10 A synthetic put

from an option by using other options is called a synthetic option. An example of creating a long put from a short forward and a long call is shown in Figure 3.4.10. It is also possible to create other payoff structures by combining options. For example, combining a long call and a long put will create a straddle. This type of synthetic option loses money when prices remain constant but benefits when there is a large move in either direction (Figure 3.4.11).

Key Facts: Put/Call Parity and Synthetic Options

The ability to synthetically create calls and puts has several major implications:

- Combined properly, puts and calls can be used interchangeably in a trading portfolio.
- The premium for puts and calls of the same underlying, strike, and expiration has to be identical.
- The implied volatility (a quantity explained in the next chapter) of puts and calls based on the same underlying, strike price, and expiration date has to be identical.

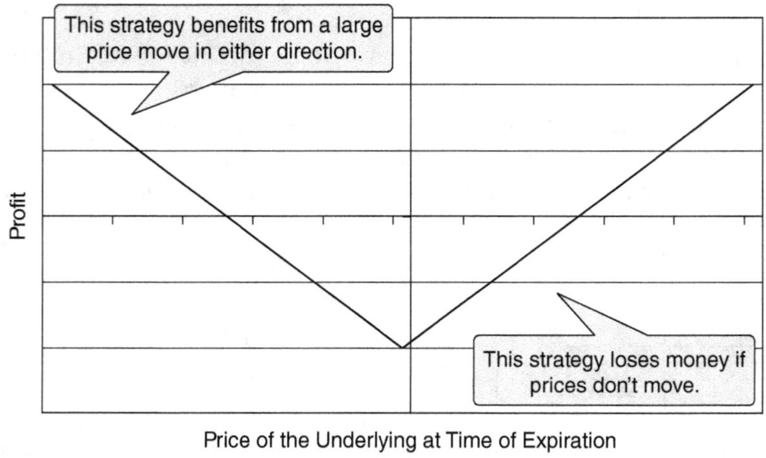

Figure 3.4.11 The payoff of a long option straddle

Common Terms

American Option. The term *American* applied to an option means an option that can be exercised at any time.

Asian Option. An *Asian* option is an *average price option*. At expiration, the value of an Asian option depends on an average of the underlying's price over some period of time. Typically, Asian options cannot be exercised early. For example, an Asian option might pay the difference between a strike price and the average cost of peak power over a month.

At the Money. An option where the strike price of the option equals the current price of the underlying.

Derivative. In its most general form, a derivative is any financial contract whose value is derived from the price of something else. In practice, a derivative usually refers to an option.

European Option. The term *European* applied to an option means that the option can only be exercised at the expiration. A European option cannot be exercised early.

Extrinsic Value. The time value of the option. This can be found by subtracting the intrinsic value of the option from the current price of the option.

In the Money. An option with a positive intrinsic value. An option that would be profitable to exercise immediately.

Intrinsic Value. The amount of money that the option buyer would receive if the option was immediately exercised.

Out of the Money. An option with zero intrinsic value. Alternately, an option that is worthless if exercised at the current time.

Premium. The money paid by the purchaser of an option to the seller of an option.

Straddle. A straddle is type of synthetic option created by buying a put and a call option with the same underlying, strike price and expiration date.

Strike Price. The exercise price of an option contract. Alternately, the price where the call buyer can purchase the underlying asset or the put buyer can sell the underlying asset.

Synthetic Option. The process of duplicating the payoff of an option by using a combination of other options and forwards.

Underlying. An asset that is used to determine the price of a derivative. It is possible for the underlying to be a derivative of some type (like a forward or a future), and for options to have more than one underlying (spread options).

3.5

Option Pricing

30-Second Summary

Purpose

This chapter introduces the mathematics behind option pricing.

Summary

Option prices are calculated through the use of models. The most commonly used option pricing models are variants of the Black Scholes option pricing formula, called *Black Scholes genre* models. Options that can be priced with these models are known as *vanilla options*. Options that use more complicated models are commonly called *exotic* options.

Mathematically, option models replicate the possible option payoffs through a strategy of trading the underlying asset and a risk-free investment in a process called *dynamic hedging*. It is important to know how option models work in order to select the appropriate model to use under various circumstances. However, in most cases, it is not necessary to actually recreate a model. It is possible to price options by choosing an appropriate model and finding the input data required by that model.

Options are closely associated with the volatility of the underlying asset's price. Since there is an asymmetric payout for holding an option, a large price move that has a 50/50 chance of going up or down helps the buyer of the option more than the seller. The potential losses of the buyer are limited, but the potential profit is not. An option buyer benefits from large price moves, and an option seller benefits from price stability.

Key Topics

- Option pricing can be used to solve problems that can't be solved in other ways.
- All option models involve assumptions about how underlying prices move. Attention needs to be paid to these assumptions to ensure they are reasonable.
- A good option model has to balance an ability to be understood against more realistic assumptions of how prices actually behave.

Options act like insurance contracts in many ways. However, they are priced very differently. Insurance is priced based on statistical tables of future probabilities. These probabilities typically don't change very quickly, and insurance writers can spend years spotting changes in trends. Option writing doesn't work in the same way. Options are based on the behavior of an underlying contract whose behavior can, and often will, change dramatically over short periods of time. Using statistical probabilities based on historical observations to price options is a sure-fire way to lose money.

Historical prices are not accurate predictions of the future. Even the most skilled financial professionals cannot accurately predict the future of the financial markets with any degree of certainty. The option pricing revolution began when traders began working on strategies to replicate option payoffs through frequent trades in the underlying product. This process, called *dynamic hedging*, required modeling the behavior of asset prices.

There is a tradeoff between using complicated models and simple models. A highly complex model will result in only a few people actually understanding the model. Simple models, even when they have flaws, are more accessible to a broader audience. The more people that understand a model, the less chance it has of failing disastrously. It is often easier to address weaknesses in option models by making observation easier than it is to create more complicated models. As a result, option models are not a substitute for understanding what is actually going on.

Option models are based on assumptions about asset prices. There are a standard set of assumptions that define Black Scholes genre models. Options that can be priced with a variant of these formulas are typically called *vanilla* options. When the standard assumptions work reasonably well to describe the behavior of the underlying prices, option valuation is easy. It is possible to plug numbers into a formula and get the same results as a Ph.D. mathematician. In other cases, the standard assumptions don't work so well. In those cases, it is necessary to use a more complicated approach to calculating option prices.

Options that use nonstandard assumptions about prices are commonly called *exotic* options. Knowing when to use an exotic option model requires understanding what is going on in real life. Option formulas basically say, "I can be used if X, Y, and Z are true." It is up to the user of an option to determine if X, Y, and Z are true in their specific case. If not, some other formula needs to be found. There is a substantial amount of academic literature describing nonstandard option models.

Option writing is the limiting factor in the option market. There is no shortage of option buyers in the market looking for a deal—after all, there is no downside to owning an option other than the cost. The difficulty is finding someone to take on the risk of selling (writing) options. The goal of option pricing, and the definition of a fair option price, is a price that fully compensates an option writer for the risk they are taking on.

History of Option Pricing

Commodity options have been traded in European financial markets for several thousand years. However, it wasn't until the start of the twentieth century that a pair of insights started to revolutionize option trading and financial analysis.

The first major breakthrough in the mathematics of option pricing occurred in 1900 when Louis Bachelier published a book, *Théorie de la spéculation,* as part of his doctoral thesis. This book discussed the use of Brownian motion to evaluate the movement of stocks. Brownian motion is a diffusion process where a moving particle (or price) diverges from its starting point in a random walk. This provided the theoretical framework for modeling price movements even when the exact probabilities of future prices couldn't be predicted.

Modern option trading sprung out of research by Fischer Black, Myron Scholes, and Robert Merton in the late 1960s and early 1970s. Their research combined earlier ideas of dynamic hedging, price diffusion, and put/call parity into a continuous time framework. This allowed the creation of an easy-to-use option pricing formula. That formula, the Black Scholes formula, opened up option trading to the masses and was the second major option pricing breakthrough. The Black Scholes formula and related work on continuous time finance revolutionized the financial markets and won a Nobel Prize.[1]

Arbitrage-Free Pricing

Arbitrage means to make a risk-free profit by simultaneously buying one security and selling another. A common assumption in option pricing is that arbitrage opportunities do not exist. Or, if they do exist, alert traders will quickly take advantage of the opportunity and force prices back into an arbitrage-free situation.

[1] Myron Scholes and Robert Merton won the Nobel Prize in 1997. Fischer Black had died in 1995, but the Swedish Academy strongly indicated that he would have been a co-winner had he still been alive. While these gentlemen were not the only contributors to option pricing theory, their work opened up the options markets to general investors.

The term *arbitrage-free pricing* refers to the concept that if two assets are worth the same amount of money throughout their lives and at expiration, then their prices should be identical at all times too. Otherwise, it would be possible to buy one asset, sell the other, and make a risk-free profit. This is an assumption because traders are always free to transact at any price they choose. However, as long as someone takes advantage of the opportunity to make a quick profit, there isn't a real difference between the *strong form* of the assumption that no arbitrage ever exists, and the *weak form* of the assumption that arbitrage opportunities don't last very long.

A major component of Black, Scholes, and Merton's research was the realization that the value of an option can be described as a percentage of the price of the underlying. For example, if a call option has a strike price of zero, it has to be worth exactly the same price as the underlying. It doesn't matter what the future probability of prices looks like—the option will always be in the money. As a result, the option premium has to be equal to the price of the underlying or else it would be possible to arbitrage the option and the underlying. On the other extreme, if the strike price for that option is so high that it would never be met, the option premium has to be zero. Since the option will never be exercised, the option is worthless!

Delta hedging is the term that describes how the value of an option changes relative to the changes in the price of the underlying. If the value of a call option with a zero strike price is exactly equal to the price of the underlying, it is said to have a *hedge ratio* of one—the payoff of one option can be exactly duplicated by holding one unit of the underlying. Higher strike prices mean the option is less valuable. If the strike price is so high that the option will never be executed, the hedge ratio is equal to zero. The option is worthless, and the payoff of the option can be duplicated by holding nothing.

Most option pricing takes place between these two extremes, where the hedge ratio is greater than zero and less than one. For example, an option that has a strike price close to today's forward price might have a hedge ratio of 0.5. The term *delta* is used synonymously with *hedge ratio*.

Common Terms

Arbitrage. Arbitrage is the simultaneous buying and selling of two different assets to make a risk-free profit. In option pricing, the value of

(*Continued*)

an option is determined by the cost of replicating the option with other assets. The process of setting the value of an option equal to the value of the replicating assets is called *arbitrage-free pricing*.

Brownian Motion (Wiener Process). The terms *Brownian motion* and *Wiener process* describe a mathematical process developed simultaneously in two unrelated branches of science to describe random motion. In botany, it was developed by Robert Brown and in physics, Norbert Wiener. This process describes the boundaries of a *random walk* taken with very small steps.

Martingale. A martingale is a special type of random number sequence (also known as the *stochastic process*) where the best estimate of the future is the current value. For example, flipping coins is a martingale process. Assuming a fair coin flip, the best estimate of the number of heads that will come up at the end of a process minus the number of tails is the current number. Flipping a coin is a 50/50 chance—heads are no more likely than tails to come up in the future. For example, if a coin has been flipped 50 times and heads has come up 30 times (tails 20 times), the most likely outcome after 100 flips is that there will still be 10 more heads than tails.

Random Walk. In finance, a random walk usually refers to a one-dimensional process where prices spread out from a starting point as a function of a single variable (time). The binomial tree model used in this chapter is an example of a one-dimensional random walk. Advanced option models sometimes use more complicated random walks based on two or three dimensions.

Stochastic Process. A term that can mean either a sequence of random numbers and/or a process for generating random numbers. The words *sequence of random numbers* can generally replace the term *stochastic process* in any sentence. *Stochastic process* is a general term since there are many different types of random number sequences. For example, flipping a coin and rolling a pair of dice are two examples of stochastic processes (they are two ways of creating a sequence of random numbers).

Replicating Portfolios

Modern option theory involves replicating the payoff of an option by holding some amount of the underlying security. Adopting this approach fundamentally shifted how the financial market approached options. It became less necessary to accurately predict future prices. From the point of view of an option seller, this is a big deal. Option sellers don't have the ability to pick and choose what they trade. They have to be willing to trade whatever product the buyer is looking to purchase. Consistently predicting the future is a nearly impossible task if you have to predict the price of every asset at every time horizon.

There are two steps to most option pricing models. The first is predicting statistical distribution of likely movements in the underlying price. The second step is determining how to replicate the option under those probability conditions.

Models of Future Prices

It is often easier to predict a distribution of likely future prices than it is to predict a single price. For example, a probabilistic description of prices might be that 60 percent of the time, tomorrow's price will be within 20 cents of today's price, 20 percent of the time the price will move between 20 and 70 cents, and that 20 percent of the time, the price will move more than 70 cents. This type of estimate is much more likely to be accurate than a directional estimate like, "the price of oil will rise tomorrow."

Most models start with the assumption that today's price for a contract is the best consensus estimate of tomorrow's price for the same contract. A risk-free profit argument is the most common justification for this assumption. For example, if the price of a natural gas future was priced at $10 today and a trader knew that it would be $20 the next day, he or she could buy the contract today and resell it tomorrow. At that point, the contract could be sold for a risk-free profit.

This assumption that today's price is the best estimate of tomorrow's price leads to the conclusion that the returns (percent changes to the current price) are distributed around today's price. In the energy market, this is a reasonable assumption to make about futures and forward contracts. For example, if the price for natural gas delivered in August is currently $10, tomorrow's price for the same natural gas contract won't change dramatically. This isn't the case for physical energy commodities. Physical energy commodities have cyclical prices that change on a daily basis due to predictable factors like weather and consumer demand.

A second common assumption is that volatility of returns will stay constant over the life of the option. For example, the magnitude of returns will be the same a week from now as they are tomorrow. Combining these two assumptions makes it relatively easy to construct a model of likely future underlying prices. The simplest model of future prices is a *binomial tree* (Figure 3.5.1). A binomial tree assumes that the underlying prices can rise or fall a certain percent every day. That percent

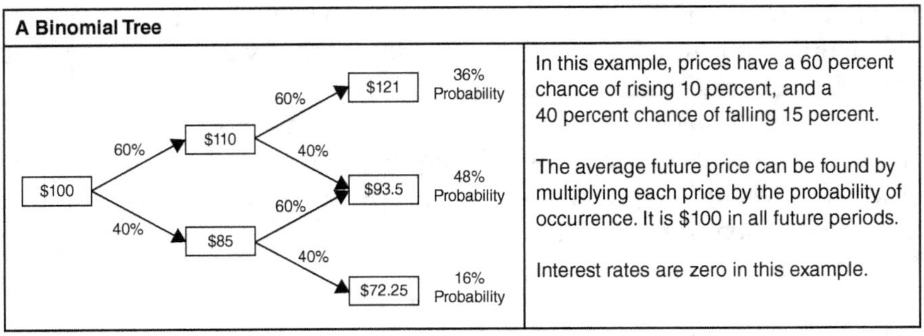

Figure 3.5.1 A binomial tree

stays constant over the life of the option. Prices start at today's price and slowly diverge from it over time.

In a binomial tree model, the price of the underlying changes over time. In the first period, the example starts at $100, and will go to either $110 or $85 in the next period. Although downside moves may be bigger than upside moves, there is a higher probability that prices will rise. As a result, the average expected price in periods 2 and 3 is still $100.

When described in mathematical literature, mathematical models are usually described by variables (Figure 3.5.2). For example, the probability that the price rises might be denoted by p and the probability that prices fall is denoted as $(1 - p)$. The amount that prices raise might be abbreviated u, and the amount that prices fall might be abbreviated v. The price of the underlying is $S_{x,}$ with the subscript

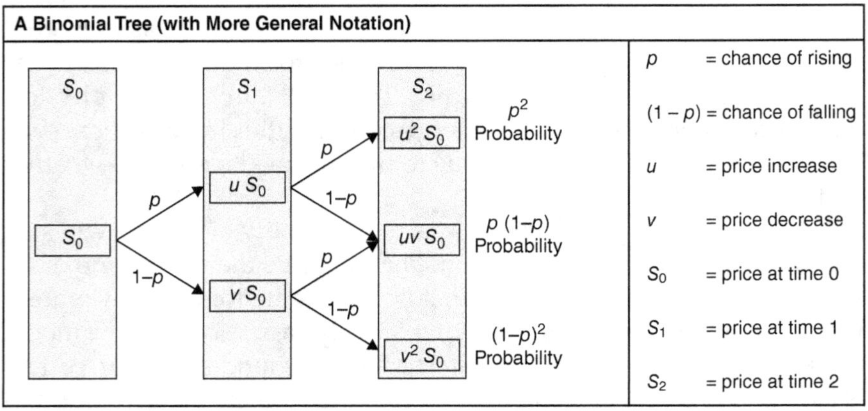

Figure 3.5.2 A binomial tree with mathematical notation

indicating it's a price at a specific period. Also, the first period will usually be period 0, the second period 1, and so on.[2]

Lognormal Versus Normal Price Distributions

Standard pricing models assume that returns, rather than prices, are normally distributed. In other words, if one were to graph all of the possible returns for an underlying, the returns would form a normal distribution (a bell curve). Mathematically, when returns are normally distributed, the logarithm of prices is normally distributed. As a result, prices are said to have a lognormal distribution.

There is one big advantage in assuming returns rather than prices are normally distributed. Assuming normally distributed returns, prices will never become negative. This is because the price movements will get smaller as the price gets closer to zero. Assuming that returns are normally distributed implies that prices can hit zero but go no lower. However, there is no upper limit to their price movement. This comes closer to describing the behavior of many asset prices than a normal distribution (Figure 3.5.3).

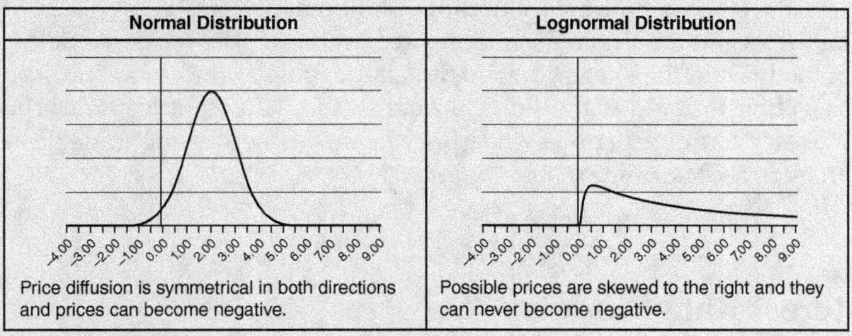

Figure 3.5.3 Normal and lognormal distributions

Returns also provide an easy way to compare price movements across different assets. For example, it is easier to compare natural gas to electricity returns rather than prices. The downside of returns is that they become undefined if the starting price ever hits zero, or if prices become negative. This isn't always a safe assumption in energy trading because electricity prices can become negative. However, this is usually the least of the problems with these distributions.

[2]Prices must either rise or fall in this model. The probability of prices rising plus the probability of prices falling must equal 100 percent. As a result, the probability that prices fall is equal to the probability that prices don't rise. If the probability that prices rise is p, the probability that prices don't rise is $100\% - p$ ($1.0 - p$ in decimal form).

The Fat Tail Problem

A major problem with the lognormal approximation of prices is that prices don't always pay attention to how statistical predictions indicate how they should behave. Large price moves in both directions are much more common than statistical models predict. For example, a statistical model would predict the chance of a stock price hitting zero as astronomically small. However, there are dozens of examples a year where stock prices hit zero because companies go bankrupt.

Stocks get taken over and go bankrupt, hurricanes destroy things, and power lines fall down. These events can have huge effects on prices, and the amount of price movement may or may not be predictable with statistical models. As a result, out-of-the-money options, the options whose values will be most affected by major price moves, typically are priced with a higher volatility than at-the-money options. The likelihood that price moves will be more than predicted by a lognormal distribution is often called a *fat tail* problem by traders.

Another problem with option pricing is that it assumes that the underlying can be traded continuously. The core assumption is that there will never be a time when trading is impossible. This can be a very dangerous assumption since trades require both a buyer and a seller. Sometimes in the energy market, it is impossible to find someone who is willing to trade at the same location where you want to trade. The industry term for periods when prices jump without being tradable at an intermediate point is *jump diffusion*.

Interest Rate Models

A model of interest rates can be calculated using the same binomial framework that was used for prices. With constant interest rates, this graph isn't terribly interesting, but will be used later on to figure out correct value for the option premium (Figure 3.5.4). In this example, with a 5 percent interest rate between periods, a dollar at Time_t is always worth 1.05 at Time_{t+1}.

Arbitrage-Free Pricing

The key insight to option pricing is that it is possible to combine underlying and bond prices to replicate an option payout if there is a way to compare their payoffs under likely future conditions. It isn't necessary to predict actual future prices. It is sufficient to predict a likely distribution of possibilities as in a binomial tree model. Then, the underlying prices and risk-free return can be compared to the payoff of a call option in the same circumstances. The combination of underlying and

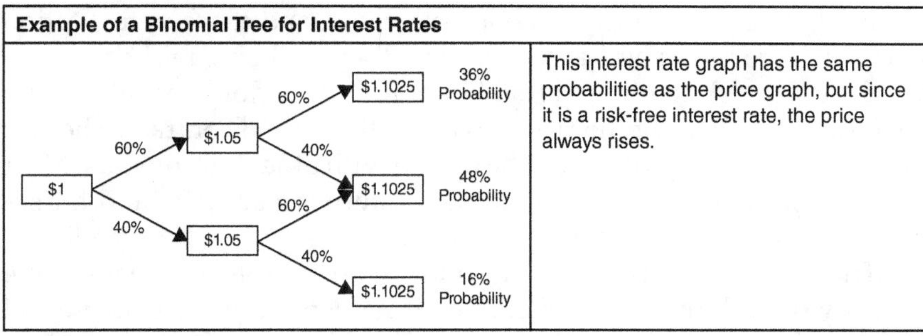

Figure 3.5.4 Binomial tree for interest rates

interest rate payoffs will be used to replicate the payoff of the option (Figure 3.5.5). Figure 3.5.5 uses the values from the earlier examples.

The temptation is to say the value of the option is $6 because it has a 60 percent chance of paying $10. However, the option seller is taking on more risk than the option buyer. If the prediction of prices is wrong, the option seller has more money at stake. As a result, a $6 price benefits the buyer more than the seller. The chance for the option seller to take a huge loss doesn't really show up on two-period binomial models.

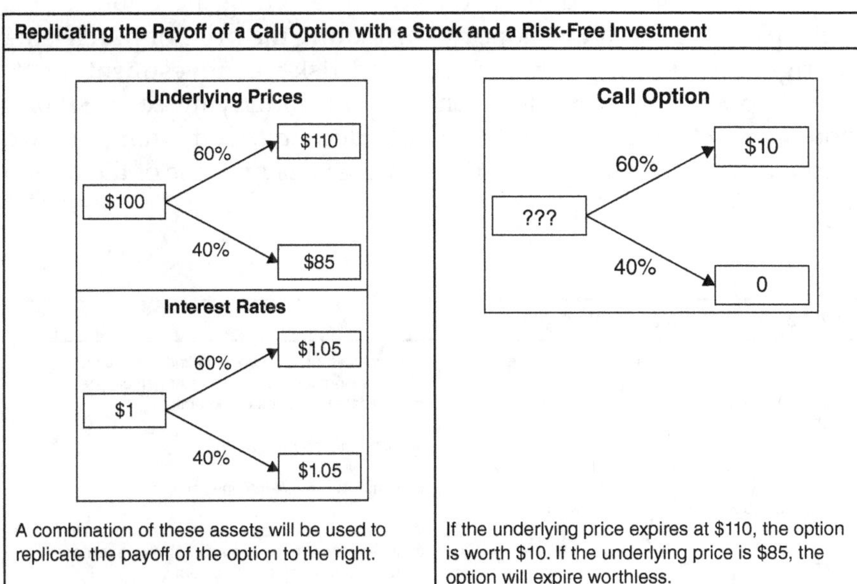

Figure 3.5.5 Replication of a call option

Predicting future prices is both subjective and inaccurate. Option sellers need to have some assurance that they are being fairly compensated for the risk that they are taking on. This is done by calculating the cost of eliminating the risk of writing the option contract. The risk can be removed by replicating the option with other instruments. Most commonly, these instruments are the underlying security and a risk-free investment like a government bond.

The general structure of the trade would be to purchase some quantity of underlying and risk-free investment at the starting period and use those profits to offset losses from the option (Figure 3.5.6). The underlying and risk-free investment positions will be liquidated at the expiration of the option. There are two unknowns (the quantity of the underlying, and the quantity of the risk-free investment) and two equations (the payoff of the option in positive and negative cases). The goal is to buy a certain quantity of the underlying and risk-free investment at Time zero that will duplicate the option payoff at Time 1.

To solve this equation it is necessary to eliminate one of the variables from the equation. This can be done by adding the two equations. The easiest variable to eliminate will be B (the units of risk-free investment) since its payoff is the same in every ending scenario. Eliminating B can be done by subtracting the first equation from the second (Figure 3.5.7).

Plugging this value for A into either equation allows us to finish solving the problem by calculating a value for B (Figure 3.5.8).

The value of the option is the cost of entering the trades at the initial period. This can be done by calculating the price of purchasing the right amount of the underlying and risk-free investment at the starting point. For example, if one unit of underlying costs \$100, it would cost \$40 to purchase .4 unit of underlying. Combining the two numbers (\$40 – \$32.38) gives a \$7.62 cost as the fair value of the option (Figure 3.5.9).

Setting up the Arbitrage Relationship	
These two equations are used to show some combination of the stock and risk-free investment duplicating the payoff of the call option under each of the two scenarios. **\$110 A + \$1.05 B = \$10** (positive scenario) **\$85 A + \$1.05 B = \$0** (negative scenario)	The purpose of this work is to find if some quantity of underlying and risk-free investment can be used to duplicate the payoff of the option. **A** = units of underlying **B** = units of the risk-free investment We want to find values for A and B that meet the constraint that the combination of investments matches the payoff of the option.

Figure 3.5.6 An arbitrage relationship

Solving for the Quantity of Underlying	
$25A = $10 **A = 2/5 or .4**	Calculated by subtracting the negative scenario equation from the positive scenario equation dividing both sides by $25.

Figure 3.5.7 Solve for underlying

Solving for the Quantity of the Risk-Free Investment	
$85 (2/5) + $1.05 B = 0	Although either scenario can be chosen to solve for B, the negative scenario is chosen here.
$34 + $1.05 B = 0	Simplifying. $85 * (2/5) = $34.
$1.05 B = −$34	Simplifying. Subtracting $34 from both sides.
B = −$34 / $1.05	Simplifying. Dividing $1.05 from both sides.
B = −32.38	Simplifying. $34/$1.05 = 32.38.

Figure 3.5.8 Solving for investment

Fair Value of Option
Fair Value = $7.62

Figure 3.5.9 Fair value of option

Extending Arbitrage Pricing over Longer Periods

It isn't necessary to stop an option calculation after just one period. It's much more common to have options valued over a large number of periods. First, a pricing tree for the underlying needs to be created for multiple periods. Then, option prices need to be calculated for the period closest to the expiration date of the option. Once those values are known, it is possible to walk backward until the price of the option on the current day is found.

Multiple period models work by calculating option prices from the expiration date backward. The calculation for earlier periods is determined by duplicating the option value of previously calculated periods (Figure 3.5.10).

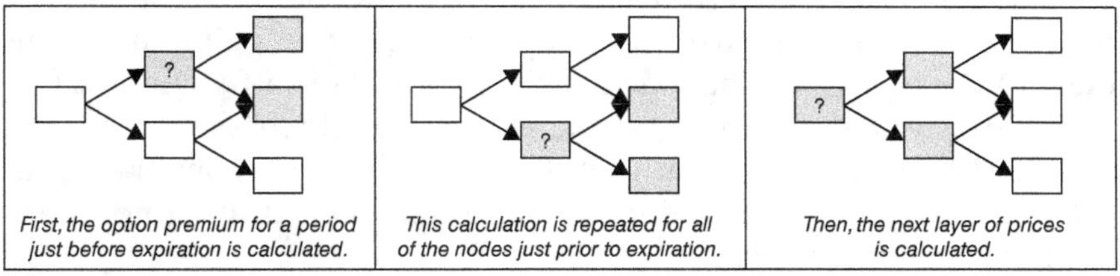

Figure 3.5.10 A multiperiod binary tree

The Benefits of Large Binary Trees

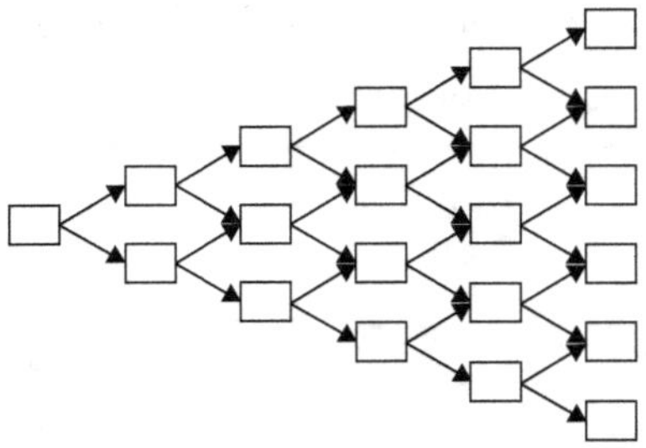

Larger trees allow for a finer level of detail. As the number of periods in an option valuation increases, the larger number of possible outcomes provides a more realistic distribution of future prices. For example, a model with only two ending conditions isn't as comprehensive as one that allows for a wide range of outcomes.

Figure 3.5.11 The benefits of large binary trees

The period size can be chosen arbitrarily small. For example, a binary tree might choose a day between pricing periods. However, it could just as easily try to replicate option prices on an hour or minute basis. The practical intuition behind smaller time periods is that trading could be done more often than once a day. In general, daily or weekly steps are usually sufficient to construct a robust binary tree (Figure 3.5.11).

The Black Scholes Formula

If taken to its logical conclusion, the ultimate extension of a binomial tree will have infinitely small time periods. At that point, it's no longer possible to algebraically solve the equations. It is necessary to use calculus. In some ways, this is a very helpful step because it allows for the creation of a formula for valuing options rather than an iterative procedure. Instead of having to iterate through each node on a binary tree, it is possible to create an equation that can be solved by plugging numbers into a formula. When this approach was first developed, it was a particularly innovative piece of work. This approach, known as the Black Scholes formula, provided an easy way to calculate the price of European style stock options and won a Nobel Prize for its creators—Fisher Black, Myron Scholes, and Robert Merton.

The Black Scholes formula is a closed form solution. That means that it has a unique answer that can be found by plugging in parameters to the equation. The Black Scholes formula is a function of five variables—underlying price, strike price, volatility, risk-free interest rate, and time to expiration. With these five numbers, anyone could calculate the price of an option. This formula opened up option trading to the general investor.

Open and Closed Form Solutions

The Black Scholes formula is so commonly used because it is a closed form solution. It is a formula that takes five variables and returns an answer. It isn't necessary to understand how the formula works to get an answer. The user of the formula just needs to supply the parameters.

Closed Form Solution

A closed form solution is a formula where a couple of variables can be substituted into the equation to find the correct answer. After it has been developed, using a closed form solution is a very fast way to calculate an option price. The downside of closed form solutions is that they are highly complicated. Quite often, insight into what is actually going on gets lost in the complexity of the mathematics.

Open Form Solution

An open form solution is a formula that must be iteratively solved by a computer. Finding an option with a binomial tree is an example of an iterative solution. The number of steps to solve an open form solution depends on the number of periods in the model. Eventually, the option model will converge on the correct answer as more periods are chosen. The calculation of open form solutions can be very time intensive.

The advantage of open form solutions is that they are simpler to describe and depend on fewer assumptions than closed form solutions. Compared to a closed form solution, using an open form solution is much less a leap of faith. Although, looking at open form solutions require some understanding of mathematics, it's an understanding that most people obtain at the high school or undergraduate level. In comparison, the mathematics behind closed form solutions can be difficult to understand even by a professional with a Ph.D. in advanced mathematics.

The Black Scholes formula can be used to value the majority of commonly traded options. However, to come up with a single equation, several assumptions about prices are made by this formula. These assumptions are generally reasonable for most of the options in the energy market that are based upon futures or forwards rather than the underlying commodity. The assumptions:

1. The price of the underlying follows a random process where the best estimate of future prices is the current price (a Martingale process).

2. It is possible to buy and sell the underlying without paying large transaction costs or taxes.
3. There is continuous trading in the underlying, and there are no price jumps. A price jump is when the price jumps between two prices without being tradable at an intermediate point.
4. It is possible to borrow and lend at the same risk-free interest rate and that the interest rate remains constant over the life of the option.
5. There is no benefit or penalty from holding the underlying—it doesn't pay dividends or cost money to store.
6. There are no arbitrage opportunities, since any such opportunities are so short-lived that it is difficult to take advantage of them.

The Black Scholes formula will be inaccurate or wrong if any of those assumptions are not met and not every option can be approximated by the Black Scholes assumptions. However, if the underlying is described by those assumptions, the Black Scholes formula makes it straightforward to calculate the value of an option. Options that use different assumptions will need to be priced differently (usually using a variant of the binary tree approach that was introduced originally).

Black Scholes Genre Option Models

There are a variety of models built on the original Black Scholes formula. Collectively, these are called Black Scholes genre option models and are the most common types of formulas used to value options. Mathematically, these formulas are nearly identical; the primary difference between these models is how the option value gets converted from the value at expiration into the value on the valuation date. To illustrate this relationship, a "generalized" form of the Black Scholes equation is explained in this section.

The Black Scholes model is based on a number of assumptions about how financial markets operate. Black Scholes models assume:

1. **Arbitrage-Free Markets.** Black Scholes formulas assume that traders try to maximize their personal profits and don't allow arbitrage opportunities (riskless opportunities to make a profit) to persist.
2. **Frictionless, Continuous Markets.** This assumption of frictionless, continuous markets assumes that it is possible to buy and sell any amount of the underlying at any time without transaction costs.
3. **Risk-Free Rates.** It is possible to borrow and lend money at a risk-free interest rate.

4. **Lognormally Distributed Price Movements.** Prices are lognormally distributed and described by geometric Brownian motion.
5. **Constant Volatility.** The Black Scholes genre option formulas assume that volatility is constant across the life of the option contract.

The first Black Scholes model was intended to price stock options. In this model, the underlying assumption was that the stock is traded at its present value and that stock prices would follow a random walk–style diffusion process as time passed. In other words, stock prices start at the spot price and, on the average, drift upward over time at the risk-free rate. Later formulas modified these assumptions slightly so that the initial formula could apply to additional types of options.

The Black Scholes genre option formula most heavily used in the energy markets is the Black 76 formula. In a Black 76 formula, prices start at the present value of the forward price associated with the expiration date of the option. Since these options are typically based on forwards, there is no benefit to early exercise. As a result, standard Black Scholes assumptions can be used by modifying the starting price of the underlying asset.

Black Scholes Genre Option Models

1. **Black Scholes (Stocks).** In the traditional Black Scholes model, the option is based on common stock—an instrument that is traded at its present value. The stock price does not get present valued—it starts at its present value (a "spot price") and drifts upward over time at the risk-free rate.
2. **Merton (Stocks with Continuous Dividend Yield).** The Merton model is a variation of the Black Scholes model for assets that pay dividends to shareholders. Dividends reduce the value of the option because the option owner does not own the right to dividends until the option is exercised.
3. **Black 76 (Commodity Futures).** The Black 76 model is for an option where the underlying commodity is traded based on a future price rather than a spot price. Instead of dealing with a spot price that drifts upward at the risk-free rate, this model deals with a forward price that needs to be present valued.
4. **Asay (Exchange Traded Futures).** The Asay model is used to price options on futures. This is similar to the Black 76 model except that there is no need to present value prices because of daily margining.
5. **Garman-Kohlhagen (Foreign Exchange [FX] Futures).** The Garman-Kohlhagen model is used to value FX options. In the Garman-Kohlhagen model, each currency in the currency pair is discounted based on its own interest rate.

Generalized Black Scholes	
$C = Fe^{(b-r)T} N(d_1) - Xe^{-rT} N(d_2)$	*Value of a Call Option*
$P = Xe^{-rT} N(-d_2) - Fe^{(b-r)T} N(-d_1)$	*Value of a Put Option*
$d_1 = \dfrac{\ln\left(\frac{F}{X}\right) + \left(b + \frac{\sigma^2}{2}\right)T}{\sigma\sqrt{T}}$	*Intermediate Calculation*
$d_2 = d_1 - \sigma\sqrt{T}$	*Intermediate Calculation*

Figure 3.5.12 Generalized Black Scholes formula

The generalized Black Scholes formula is shown in Figure 3.5.12. While these formulas may look complicated at first glance, most of the terms can be found as part of an options contract or are prices readily available in the market. The only term that is difficult to calculate is the implied volatility (σ). Implied volatility is typically calculated using prices of other options that have recently been traded. Implied volatility is discussed in greater detail later in the chapter.

The *cost of carry* term, *b*, differentiates the various Black Scholes genre formulas from one another (Figure 3.5.13). *The cost of carry* is a term that comes from the bond market and refers to the cost of "carrying," or holding, a position. Those payments are made to the owner of the underlying and not the owner of the option. As a result, they reduce the value of the option.

Figure 3.5.14 shows generalized inputs.

For energy options, almost all of the parameters can be found in either the option contract or quoted in the market. The primary

Generalized Black Scholes Cost of Carry		
Model	*Underlying*	*Cost of Carry Formula*
Black Scholes	Non-dividend-paying common stocks	$b = r$
Merton	Continuous dividend paying common stock & stock indices	$b = r - q$
Black (1976)	Forwards and Commodity Swaps	$b = 0$
Asay	Exchange Traded Futures (Daily Margining)	$b = 0, r = 0$
Garman and Kohlhagen	Foreign Exchange	$b = r - r_f$

Figure 3.5.13 Generalized Black Scholes cost of carry

Generalized Black Scholes Inputs	
Symbol	*Meaning*
F	**Underlying Price.** The price of the underlying asset on the valuation date t_0.
X	**Strike Price.** The strike, or exercise, price of the option.
T	**Time to Expiration.** The time to expiration in years. This can be calculated by comparing the time between the expiration date and the valuation date. $T = (t_1 - t_0)/365$
t_0	**Valuation Date.** The date on which the option is being valued. For example, it might be today's date if the option was being valued today.
t_1	**Expiration Date.** The date on which the option must be exercised.
σ	**Volatility.** The volatility of the underlying security. This factor usually cannot be directly observed in the market. It is most often calculated by looking at the prices for recent option transactions and back-solving a Black Scholes–style equation to find the volatility that would result in the observed price.
q	**Continuous Yield.** Used in the Merton model, this is the continuous yield of the underlying security. Option holders are typically not paid dividends or other payments until they exercise the option. As a result, this factor decreases the value of an option.
r	**Risk-Free Rate.** This is expected return on a risk-free investment. This is commonly approximated by the yield on a low-risk government bond or the rate that large banks borrow between themselves (LIBOR). The rate depends on tenor of the cash flow. For example, a 10-year risk-free bond is likely to have a different rate than a 20-year risk-free bond.
r_f	**Foreign Risk-Free Rate.** Used in the Garman Kohlhagen model, this is the risk-free rate of the foreign currency. Each currency will have a risk-free rate.
$N(x)$	**Cumulative Normal Distribution Function.** This is a common mathematical formula describing the probability of some event within a standard normal distribution. A standard normal distribution is a normal distribution with mean = 0 and standard deviation = 1. This is the cumulative version of the function. $N(x) = \frac{1}{\sqrt{2\pi}} \int_{-\infty}^{x} e^{\left(\frac{x^2}{2}\right)} dx$ Spreadsheets will usually have this as part of their standard spreadsheet library. For example, Excel will use *Norm.S. Dist (x, true)* to find N(x).

Figure 3.5.14 Generalized Black Scholes inputs

exception to this rule is the implied volatility term. The primary way to calculate implied volatility is to solve for the implied volatility (σ) by inverting the Black Scholes function. Numerical solutions based on guessing an implied volatility term, solving the Black Scholes equation, and comparing the result to traded price is the primary way of calculating the implied volatility. A succession of guesses is used to progressively get closer to the actual market implied volatility.

Asian Options

An Asian option is an option whose payoff is calculated using the average price of the underlying over some period of time. For this reason, Asian options are also called *average price options*. The reason that traders use Asian options is that averaging a settlement price over a period of time reduces the effect of manipulation or unusual price movements on the expiration date. As a result, Asian options are commonly used to make certain options, like crude oil options, less risky to trade.

An Asian option works because the average of a set of random numbers (prices in this case) will have a lower dispersion (a lower volatility) than the dispersion that might be observed on any single day. As a result, compared to a comparable European option, the implied volatility used to price Asian options will be lower. This makes these options safer for the seller and less expensive for the buyer than standard options.

From a mathematical perspective, valuing an Asian option is complicated by the fact that the average of a set of lognormal distributions is not itself lognormally distributed. However, a reasonably good approximation of the correct answer can still be obtained.

Outside the delivery month, Asian options can be valued with a modified Black 76 formula by adjusting the implied volatility (Figure 3.5.15). Within the delivery month, it is necessary to calculate the expected dispersion of prices given the fact that some portion of the prices are already observed. This will cause a rapid decline in the expected volatility during the delivery month.

Along with the standard Black Scholes inputs that were previously described, Asian options use the following inputs (Figure 3.5.16).

Implied Volatility

A major advantage of arbitrage-free pricing is that most of the parameters necessary to calculate the price of an option can be observed. Interest rates, underlying prices, expiration dates, and strike prices

Asian Option Volatility	
$\sigma_{Asian} = \sqrt{\dfrac{\ln(M)}{T}}$	*Asian Option Volatility*
$M = \dfrac{2e^{\sigma^2 T} - 2e^{\sigma^2 T}[1 + \sigma(T - \tau)]}{\sigma^4 (T - \tau)^2}$	*Intermediate Calculation*

Figure 3.5.15 Asian option volatility

Asian Option Inputs	
Symbol	*Meaning*
T	**Time to Expiration.** The time to expiration in years. This can be calculated by comparing the time between the expiration date and the valuation date. $T = (t_1 - t_0)/365$
τ	**Time to Start of Averaging Period.** The time to expiration in years. This can be calculated by comparing the time between the start of averaging date and the valuation date. $\tau = (t_2 - t_0)/365$
t_0	**Valuation Date.** The date on which the option is being valued. For example, it might be today's date if the option was being valued today.
t_1	**Expiration Date.** The date on which the option must be exercised.
t_0	**Start of Averaging Date.** The date on which the averaging period begins.

Figure 3.5.16 Asian option inputs

can either be observed or estimated without too much effort. The only parameter that can't be directly observed is the volatility of the underlying prices.

Because it can't be observed, volatility plays a critical role in option models. All of the other factors in an option model are based on publicly available prices. That means all corrections to the model can be thought of as adjustments to volatility. For example, the assumption that prices are lognormally distributed isn't completely accurate. The options most affected by the lognormal assumptions being inaccurate are those with high or low strike prices or options with very long maturities. To account for that greater risk, these options can be priced with different volatility assumptions than those used for at-the-money options.

If the volatility for out-of-the-money options is increased, graphing implied volatility against strike prices will show a *volatility smile* (Figure 3.5.17). This can be observed in the market by calculating the volatility that is implied by reported option trades. *Implied volatility* is the value calculated by backing out the volatility from the Black Scholes equation. This is done by finding the latest market price for an option, plugging in the observable parameters, and then choosing implied volatilities until the right price is obtained.

Greeks

When evaluating option positions, traders often need to answer questions like "Do I expect to make or lose money if the price of oil continues to rise?" or "How much money do I expect to make or lose if an

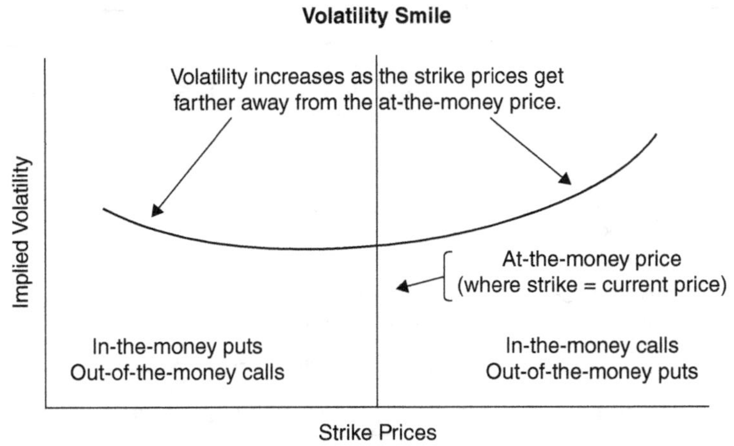

Figure 3.5.17 The volatility smile

unlikely event becomes more likely?" These types of questions can be answered by *sensitivity analysis*. This analysis estimates the sensitivity of a trading position to something else. Most commonly, traders want to estimate the profit or loss that will occur if some benchmark goes up or down. In other cases, they will want to know how their risk will change if some type of event happens.

Many questions about risk are common enough to have acquired a well-known name, usually a letter in the Greek alphabet. These questions can all be expressed as the sensitivity of one quantity to changes in another. Because they are commonly represented by Greek letters, these factors are collectively called the *Greeks*. A *Greek* is never a standalone piece of information like a price. *Greeks* are always a comparison between two assets (one of which is usually called an *asset* and the other an *underlying*). The value of the *asset* is sensitive to changes in the *underlying*.

There are five common measures of sensitivity (collectively called the *Greeks*):

1. **Delta.** The profit or loss, or P&L, that occurs when the underlying asset changes in price.
2. **Gamma.** The change in an asset's *delta* when the underlying changes in price.
3. **Vega**. The P&L that occurs when the volatility of the underlying changes.
4. **Theta**. The P&L that occurs from the passage of some period of time (usually one day).
5. **Rho.** The P&L that occurs when the interest rate changes.

Velocity (Delta)

Delta is the most commonly used Greek. It relates the change in value of a portfolio (the profit or loss) to the movement in some kind of benchmark. For example, a portfolio of stocks might be related to the movement of the S&P 500 index, or the change in an option's value related to the change in price of its underlying.

Mathematically, delta is the first derivative of price relative to some underlying. A good way to think about delta (or any other first derivative) is thinking about a car trip (Figure 3.5.18). The distance traveled by the car, the velocity of the car, and the acceleration of the car are all related. By comparing the distance away from home at different times, it is possible to determine the average speed the car had to travel between observations. The velocity of the car is the first derivative of distance relative to time. For example, if a car traveled 60 miles (a distance) in one hour (the underlying), it had to average 60 miles per hour (velocity).

Acceleration (Gamma)

The second *Greek*, gamma, is often more important than delta. *Gamma* is the Greek most closely scrutinized by risk managers. It isn't as directly informative as delta. However, it indicates a more crucial piece of information—what will happen to a portfolio when the market goes crazy and the underlying changes substantially in price. Gamma indicates the exposure of a portfolio to changes in price—whether a portfolio will get more or less risky when the market really starts to move.

	Driving a Car	***Trading Energy***
Value	**Distance (Miles)** Miles away from home	**Price** Value of the asset
First Derivative Change in the value per change in some other value	**Velocity** Velocity (speed) is the change in distance per unit of some other value (time). For example, velocity might be measured in miles per hour.	**Delta** Delta is the change in value relative to a change in the price of the underlying. For example, the option will become more valuable if the stock price goes up in value.
Second Derivative Change in the First Derivative per change in some other value.	**Acceleration** Change in velocity per unit time. It is in units of distance per time squared. For example, acceleration might be described, "the car can accelerate from *zero to 60 in 5 seconds.*"	**Gamma** Gamma is the amount that the delta changes per change in the underlying.

Figure 3.5.18 Velocity and acceleration

Using an example of a car, it's useful to know that a car is going 20 miles an hour in a residential street when it passes a radar gun. That's a very important piece of information. However, it's equally important to know if that car is accelerating rapidly. For example, even though it's going 20 miles per hour at the time of the observation, if the car is accelerating fast enough to go from 0 to 120 miles per hour in 12 seconds (maybe it's a race car), the driver is still driving in an unsafe manner.

Changes in Volatility (Vega)

Vega is the term used to represent the sensitivity of a portfolio to the change in some type of volatility. This is mostly important to a portfolio containing a lot of options. Anyone who is familiar with the Greek alphabet will recognize that vega isn't actually a Greek letter. It's a star in the constellation Lyra. However, since there aren't any Greek letters that start with *v*, the term *vega* was co-opted into the financial alphabet.

Options (and financial assets modeled as options) are often extremely sensitive to volatility. Option pricing is usually based on the concept that prices diffuse outward from a starting point. Small changes in this dispersion pattern will have a big effect on the value of an option. Since there is no downside to holding an option, an increased chance of a windfall profit makes volatility extremely valuable to an option buyer. For an option seller, just the opposite will occur. As a result, an option buyer is often described as long volatility (benefiting if volatility rises). An option seller will be short volatility (benefiting if volatility declines).

The Passage of Time (Theta)

Theta is another Greek that is primarily important to portfolios that contain option trades. Certain assets, like options, become less valuable with time. The intrinsic value of an option is the value of the option if it is exercised immediately. The rest of the option value depends on the time remaining before the option expires. If there is a long time before expiration, the option is more valuable than if it is almost at expiration. Theta measures the change in the value of an asset over time.

The time value of an option depends on its profitability. For example, if an option is out of the money, a long time horizon will give it more opportunities to become valuable. This is very helpful for an option buyer. On the other hand, if an option is already very profitable, the time value of the option is less pronounced. At least for a while, volatility will hurt the option holder almost as much as it helps.

All things being equal, option sellers will make a profit for every day that passes since it becomes less likely that they will be required to pay an even larger amount of money. Option buyers will have the opposite problem. They will *bleed* a small amount of money every day, and will need to make money from the underlying instrument changing in price or by volatility increasing.

Interest Rates (Rho)

Rho measures the sensitivity of the value of an asset to interest rates. This is primarily important to financial instruments that are very sensitive to interest rates, like bonds. While this quantity is usually less important for energy products than bonds, energy trading often requires tying up a large amount of capital for an extended period. This means that it is necessary to compare the relative return of energy investment to alternate investments (like risk-free government bonds). An investment returning 10 percent annually is worth a lot more when the risk-free rate of return is 2 percent than when the risk-free rate is at 20 percent.

3.6

SPREAD OPTIONS

30-Second Summary

Purpose

This chapter illustrates some of the problems that complicate option pricing in the real world. The previous chapter described how relatively simple, well-behaved options are priced. This chapter expands that discussion by adding in various complications. Although this chapter focuses on spread options, similar issues commonly complicate other types of exotic options.

Summary

A specific type of option—a *spread option*—is especially common in the energy market. Spread options are used to price a large variety of physical energy deals. With these options, the owner of the option benefits when the difference between two prices is above a certain level. This is like a normal option except with two asset prices. Spread options cannot be exactly priced with standard option pricing formulas, but they can be closely approximated.

Key Topics

- Spread options are exotic options. An exotic option is any option that can't be constructed out of simpler put and call options.
- Kirk's approximation is a commonly used way to modify a Black Scholes formula to value a spread option.

A specific type of option—a *spread option*—is especially common in the energy market. Spread options are used to price a large variety of physical energy deals. With these options, the owner of the option benefits when the difference between two prices is above a certain level. This is like a normal option except with two asset prices. Alternately, this is like an option with a variable strike price. A spread option has a payoff similar to a standard option except that it has more than one underlying asset (Figure 3.6.1).

The prevalence of spread options in energy deals is a result of the way the energy market operates—there is a focus on moving energy from one location to another, storing it for sale at a later point, and

Spread Option Call Payoff
A spread option has more than one underlying asset.
Call Payoff = (Finished Price – Raw Material Price) – (Conversion Cost)

Figure 3.6.1 Spread option call payoff

converting it from one form to another. The profitability of doing these actions depends upon the spread between two prices compared to the cost of doing the conversion—the price here versus the price there compared to transportation costs, the price now versus the price later compared to storage costs, and the price of fuel versus the price of electricity compared to conversion costs.

Any option that can't be replicated with standard put or call options is considered an *exotic* option. In contrast, the more typical put and call options are considered *vanilla* options. One primary difference between an exotic option, like a spread option, and less complicated options is the assumptions used to model their prices. Exotic options formulas typically include more variables than standard option formulas and sometimes those variables might not work exactly the same way.

In the case of spread options, there are typically two underlying assets—a final product and an initial product. Typically, the prices between these two assets are correlated, and this relationship determines the value of these options. There often isn't a good way to estimate this correlation either—historical data may be misleading, and there isn't usually a liquid enough market to determine the correlations being used by other people in the market.

Because of correlation's effect on the price of spread options, and the difficulty in estimating it, correlation requires a lot of scrutiny. Managing the risk of a spread options portfolio requires building an infrastructure to examine correlations between products. Incorrectly estimating correlation is the single easiest way to mess up this type of option valuation. Moreover, correlation isn't just important when a spread option trade is initiated—it needs to be monitored over the entire life of the trade.

Common Terms

Exotic Option. Any option that doesn't meet the assumptions of the Black Scholes model.

Vanilla Option. A normal, plain option with no special features. Vanilla options can usually be priced using the Black Scholes formula. For example, an option on an asset whose prices can be modeled by a lognormal distribution.

Modeling a Spread

There is a fundamental difference between spreads and the prices of individual assets. The most common approximation of asset prices (never dropping below zero, but being able to increase much more) doesn't describe a spread very well. Although that assumption works for something like a commodity where prices are almost never zero or negative, it doesn't work for a spread between two prices. Spreads between two prices can be zero or negative fairly often. Other standard measures, like the concept of a percent return, don't work either. It is impossible to calculate a percent return on something that starts at a zero price—the calculation would result in a division by zero error.

There are substantial differences between the statistical distribution commonly used to model spreads, a normal distribution, and the one used to model asset prices, a lognormal distribution (Figure 3.6.2). To get around this issue, many spread option models are the ratio of the two prices. The ratio looks a bit more like a lognormal distribution. For example, it tends not to be negative.

Another fundamental assumption in a model is how the spread is likely to behave in the future. For example, a coin flip has a 50-50 chance of coming up heads no matter what has occurred in the past. Not all distributions work in the same way. Some series have a distinct trend, and others tend to come back to a central trend (Figure 3.6.3).

Spreads might fall into either category. Any time there is a conversion relationship possible between the two assets, the spread will often oscillate around the cost of conversion. For example, a crack spread relates the price of crude oil to something made out of crude oil (like gasoline). The spread between the prices of crude oil and gasoline are linked by the ability to convert crude oil into gasoline. These prices

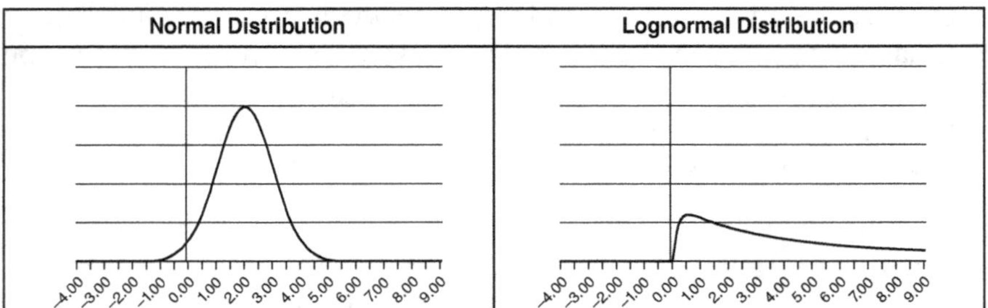

Normal Distribution:

- Commonly used to model the spread between two different asset prices.
- Depending on the assets involved, price spreads are commonly zero or negative.

Lognormal Distribution:

- Commonly used to model asset prices.
- A lognormal distribution would be a poor choice to approximate the typical behavior of a spread!
- This is a reasonable model for an asset whose price never becomes zero or negative.

Figure 3.6.2 Normal and lognormal distributions

Martingale	Mean-Reverting Sequence
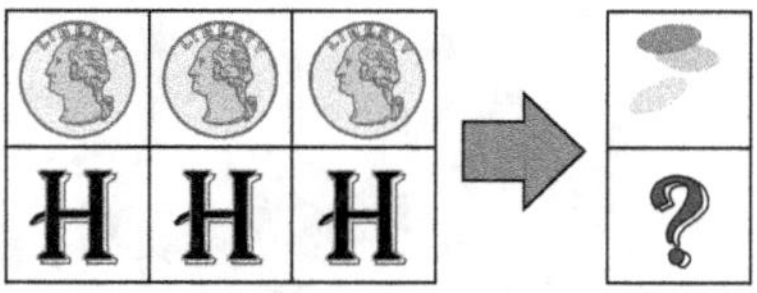	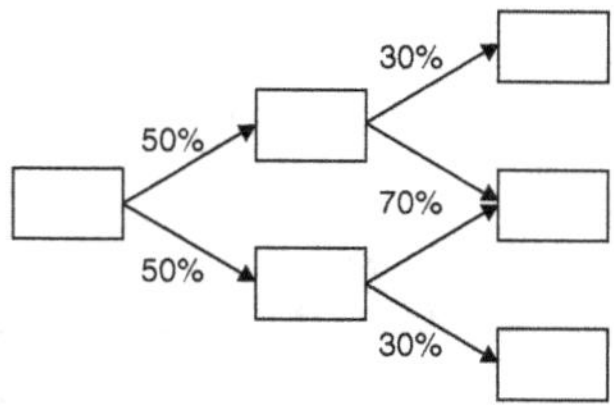
Regardless of history, a fair coin flip has a 50-50 chance of coming up heads. • A Martingale is a random sequence where each period is independent of earlier periods. • For example, a fair coin flip always has a 50-50 chance of coming up heads. It does not matter how many times heads comes up previously.	Not all random sequences ignore history. • A mean reverting sequence is more likely to return to some equilibrium than it is to move away. • The relative prices of raw materials and finished products are common examples of mean reverting sequences. • The probability distribution of the random process changes based on previous path!

Figure 3.6.3 Mean reverting or Martingale

might be driven apart temporarily by short-term supply and demand issues. However, over the long run, competition between refineries is going to bring prices together again.

Prices and Correlation Estimates

Another major complication in spread options is determining the actual relationship between two assets by looking at market data. Estimating the correlation between asset prices can be especially difficult in the energy markets. One reason is that prices are often not available. Another reason is that when prices are available, they are often spot prices, which are more volatile (and less correlated) than forward prices.

When asset prices are volatile, the spread is more likely to be wide. However, when two assets are highly correlated, they behave almost like the same asset. As a result, highly correlated assets have a narrow spread (Figure 3.6.4).

This is a big deal because dispersion has a direct impact on option profitability. An option buyer will benefit from a wide range of possible spreads because an unusual spread will never result in a loss. In reverse, an option seller would benefit from a tight dispersion of possible spreads since outlying results hurt them—they will never make more than the premium, but their losses are unbounded. If either side estimates the correlation between the assets incorrectly, they will consistently lose money to someone who does a better job estimating correlations.

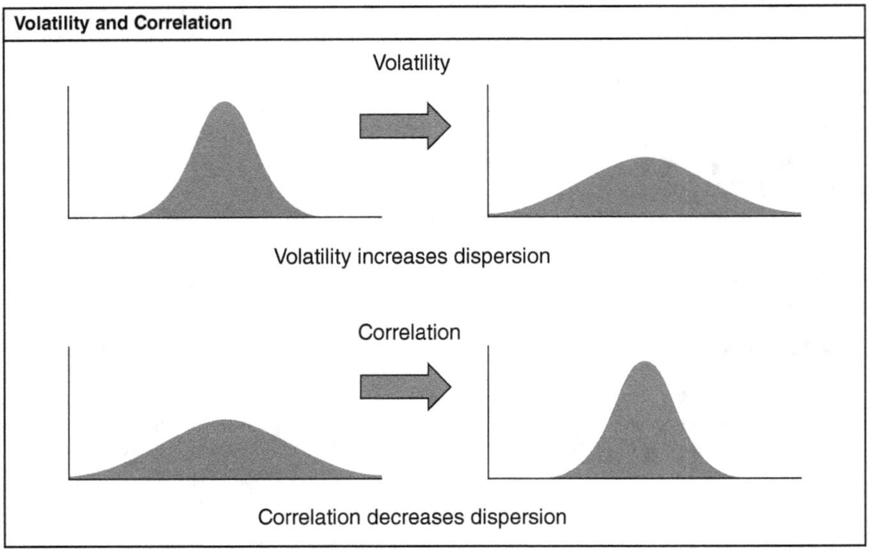

Figure 3.6.4 Volatility and correlation

What Does an Actual Spread Look Like?

Modeling spreads is not just a mathematical exercise. Behind the models, options pricing ultimately needs to capture some type of actual behavior. It is often less important to understand the mathematics behind an option model than it is to understand the approximations of the real world that are being incorporated into a model.

Spread options are a great example of the importance of looking at data. One type of spread is a spark spread—the difference between the price of electricity and a fuel, natural gas. It is possible to burn natural gas to produce electricity. This is how power plants make a profit. A power plant essentially has an option to burn fuel and produce electricity.

The operational efficiency of power plants can be approximated by comparing the price of electricity to the price of fuel in the region. For example, in one area of the Mid-Atlantic powergrid, PJM-West, during the period January 2000 to June 2002, on average, it took 9.5 MMBtus of natural gas to equal the cost of 1 megawatt hour of electricity.

Looking at the price of natural gas and peak electrical power (Figure 3.6.5), the two prices are obviously correlated. The spread in prices (assuming the typical conversion of 9.5 MMBtus gas per megawatt hour of power), oscillates around zero. Sometimes the spread is positive, other times it is negative. Graphs of spot prices and the spark spread can be seen in Figure 3.6.5.

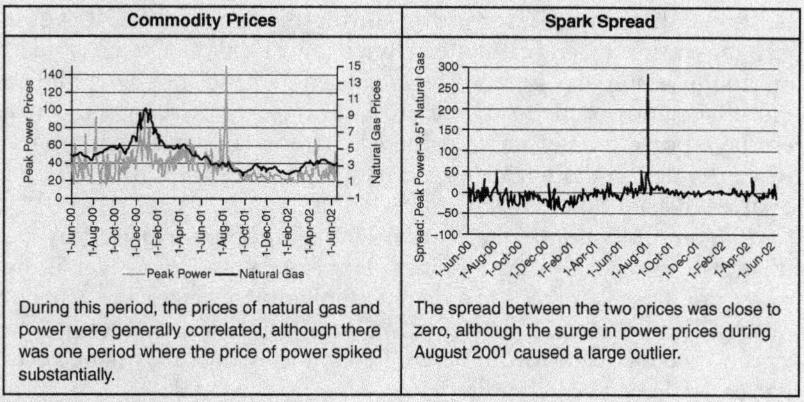

Figure 3.6.5 Historical prices

From a distribution standpoint, although there was a major outlier in prices during August 2001, the spread is clearly distributed around zero. The price of power in August 2001 was much higher than would be predicted by the cost of fuel alone. This isn't especially surprising, since power prices often spike in the summer. As a result, it is probably a mistake to assume that the outlier is being caused by bad data. Graphing the frequency of each spread price, a normal distribution (shown overlaid in Figure 3.6.6) seems like a reasonable approximation of reality except for the huge outlier.

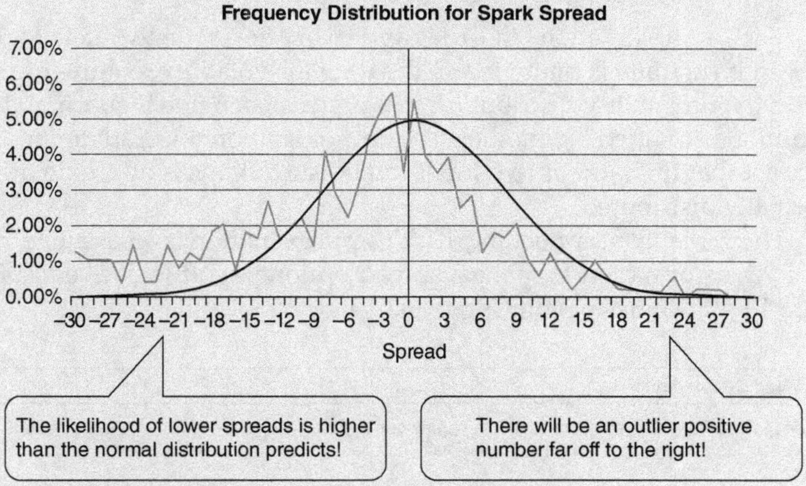

Figure 3.6.6 Modeling the distribution of a spread

Another issue that is clouding the predictive ability of this distribution is that the demand for power changes throughout the course of

(Continued)

the year. A low demand for power during the spring and fall causes only the most efficient generators to run and keeps the spark spread low. In the winter and summer, an increased demand for power allows less efficient power plants to operate and drives up prices. On the hottest days, power prices can spike if the least efficient power plants have to be activated. A more realistic estimate of prices would incorporate a separate distribution for each season.

If more outliers like the August 2001 outlier are expected in the future, the value of owning a power plant is increased. However, if the power grid has taken steps to eliminate similar price spikes, the value of owning a power plant will be reduced. As a result, even if there were a good way to model historical prices, that model may or may not be useful as a prediction of the future.

Kirk's Approximation

One way to value spread options is to modify a Black Scholes equation using an approach called *Kirk's approximation.* Although this is only an approximate solution, this approach typically gives reasonably accurate results. Instead of modeling spreads, the key behind Kirk's approximation model is to examine the ratio between the prices of two assets. This removes the problem with negative prices in a spread and generally makes the math work more easily.

The "approximation" in Kirk's approximation actually refers to the way that volatility is estimated. Estimating the volatility requires examining the probability distribution that occurs when one lognormal distribution is divided by another. The approximation takes advantage of the fact that the ratio of two lognormal distributions is approximately normally distributed.

The initial concept behind Kirk's approximation is to use an algebraic transformation to make a spread option payoff look like a standard Black Scholes payoff (Figure 3.6.7).

Spread Option Payoff

The most commonly used description of a spread option payoff is shown on the left (the first max[] on each line). On the right side, the second max[] has been algebraically manipulated.

$$C \quad = \max[F_1 - F_2 - X, 0] \quad = \max\left[\frac{F_1}{F_2 + X} - 1, 0\right](F_2 + X)$$

$$P \quad = \max[X - (F_1 - F_2), 0] \quad = \max\left[1 - \frac{F_1}{F_2 + X}, 0\right](F_2 + X)$$

Figure 3.6.7 Spread option payoff

Comparison Between Black 76 and Kirk's Approximation		
	Black 76 Model	**Kirk's Approximation**
Payoffs	C = Max(F – X, 0)	C =(F_2 + X) Max(F – 1, 0) Where $F = \frac{F_1}{F_2 + X}$
Call Option Formula	$c = [e^{-rt}\{F\,N(d_1) - N(d_2)\}]$	$c = (F_2 + X)[e^{-rt}\{F\,N(d_1) - N(d_2)\}]$

Figure 3.6.8 Comparison of Black 76 to Kirk's approximation

Modifying the formula to work as a ratio allows this payoff to be shoe-horned into a Black Scholes framework. Looking at the valuation formula, the primary difference between the Kirk's approximation formula and the standard Black 76 formula is that the spread option gets multiplied by (F_2 + X) and the F has changed from the distribution of future prices to the distribution of the ratio of F_1 over $F_2 + X$ (Figure 3.6.8).

The key complexity is determining the appropriate volatility that needs to be used in the equation. The "approximation" that defines Kirk's approximation is the assumption that the ratio of two lognormal distributions is normally distributed. That assumption makes it possible to estimate the volatility needed for the modified Black Scholes–style equation (Figure 3.6.9). These formulas use the standard Black Scholes inputs (Figure 3.6.10). These formulas also use standard mathematical functions (Figure 3.6.11).

Spread Option Call Formula	
$c = (F_2 + X)[e^{-rt}\{F\,N(d_1) - N(d_2)\}]$	*Value of a Spread Option*
$d_1 = \dfrac{\ln(F) + \left(\frac{\sigma^2}{2}\right)T}{\sigma\sqrt{T}}$	*Intermediate Calculation*
$d_2 = d1 - \sigma\sqrt{T}$	*Intermediate Calculation*
$\sigma = \sqrt{\sigma_1^2 + \left[\sigma_2 \frac{F_2}{(F_2 + X)}\right]^2 - 2\rho\sigma_1\sigma_2 \frac{F_2}{(F_2 + X)}}$	*Kirk's approximation of volatility*

Figure 3.6.9 Spread option call formula

Option Pricing Abbreviations	
Symbol	*Meaning*
F	**Forward Price or Forward Price Ratio.** In a standard Black Scholes formula, this is the price of the underlying asset. In a spread option, this is a ratio of the two prices where $F = F_1/(F_2 + X)$
F_1	**Forward Price of Asset 1.** This is the price of the finished product.
F_2	**Forward Price of Asset 2.** This is the price of the raw material.
X	**Strike Price.** This is the cost of converting the raw material into the finished product.
σ_1	**Volatility of Asset 1.** The forward volatility of the finished product.
σ_2	**Volatility of Asset 2.** The forward volatility of the raw material.
p	**Correlation.** Correlation between the prices of Asset 1 and Asset 2.
r	**Risk-Free Rate.** The continuously compounded risk-free rate of return. Because this needs to be in the same units as the time to maturity, by convention this represents an annual return.
T	**Time to Expiration.** The time to expiration of the option in years. In spreadsheets, this is typically calculated as a function of the valuation date and the expiration date where: $T = (t_1 - t_0)/365$.
t_0	**Valuation Date.** The as/of date on which the option is valued. This will change over time.
t_1	**Expiration Date.** The date on which the option must be exercised. This is set in the option contract and will not change over time.

Figure 3.6.10 Option pricing abbreviations

Standard Mathematical Functions	
$N()$	The *standard normal density function* is a prebuilt function in most spreadsheet programs and math libraries. It can also be calculated manually. $$N(z) = \frac{1}{\sqrt{2\pi}} e^{-\frac{z^2}{2}}$$
e^x	The e in the *standard exponent function*, "e raised to the power x" is a constant and approximately equal to 2.71828182845904.

Figure 3.6.11 Standard mathematical functions

Estimating Implied Correlation

Unlike a more typical Black 76 formula, which has only one unknown parameter (implied volatility), a spread option will have three unknown parameters. It will have two implied volatility terms and an implied correlation term. While it's easy to get sidetracked about what each of those values might mean under different contexts, in an option valuation the sole purpose of these parameters is to define the volatility of the ratio of the two assets in the future.

To understand what a ratio in the future might look like, both ratios and spreads can be historically observed—all it takes is historical pricing data. For example, examining a natural gas transportation spread, it is possible to look at the ratio of prices between natural gas prices at Florida Gas Pipeline Zone 3 (near Pensacola on the western part of the Florida Panhandle) and Florida City Gates (in central Florida near Orlando, Florida). It is possible to find the normal distribution that best fits historical observations using a spreadsheet (Figure 3.6.12).

Assuming that futures spreads look like historically observed spreads, it is possible to calculate the volatility of the normal distributions that best fit the historical data. Then, it is possible to find the Black Scholes implied volatility that defines that best fit distribution. Mathematically, this is relatively easy to calculate since a normal distribution is defined by a single variable, dispersion, and the dispersion in the random walk model used by Black Scholes scales in a predictable manner (with the square root of time).

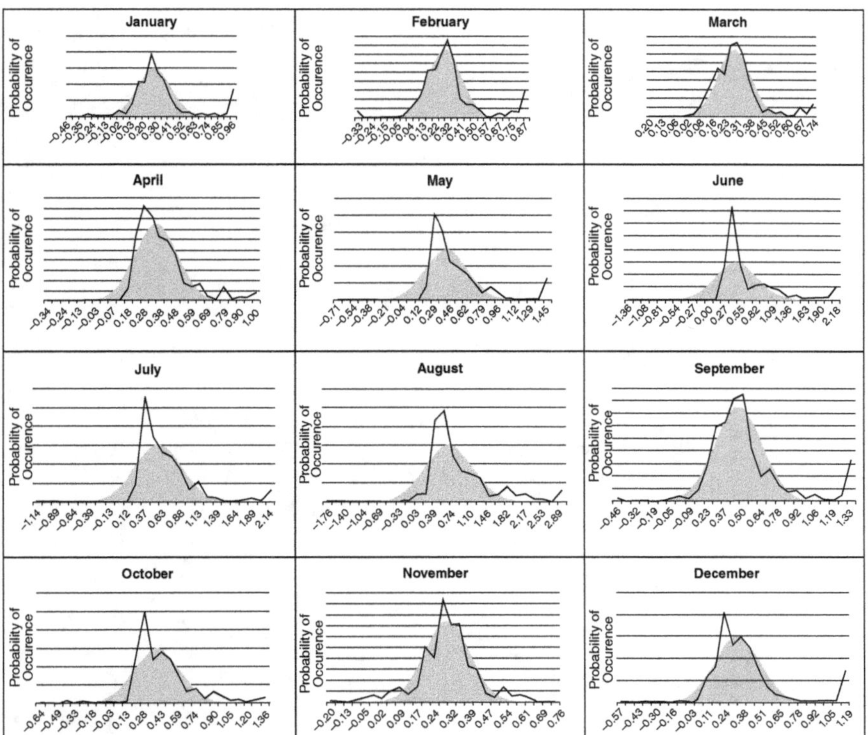

Figure 3.6.12 Historically observed spreads

Rearrangement of Kirk's Approximation

$$\rho = \frac{\sigma_1^2 + \left[\sigma_2 \frac{F_2}{(F_2 + X)}\right]^2 - {\sigma_{\text{final}}}^2}{2\sigma_1\sigma_2 \frac{F_2}{(F_2 + X)}}$$

Figure 3.6.13 Kirk's approximation, rearranged

This provides a way to examine correlation under normal conditions. One way to get around that problem is to use other markets to estimate two of the variables (like the asset volatilities) and solve for the remaining variable (the correlation) that results in the desired future distribution. Kirk's approximation equation can be rearranged to solve for the implied correlation (Figure 3.6.13).

Solving for the implied correlation this way, it is fairly common to observe negative correlations in the short term rise to a level above 90 percent after a couple of months.

4.1

Spatial Load Forecasting

30-Second Summary

Purpose

This chapter introduces the major concepts behind load forecasting. Load forecasting is a prediction of electrical demand within a specific geographical region for a specific period of time. Load forecasts are important to power traders since the demand for electricity has a significant effect on power prices.

Summary

Spatial load forecasting is the study of *where* and *when* power will be required. Since power generally can't be stored and must be generated on demand, it is necessary for power grids to anticipate changes in demand. The term *spatial* means "related to a specific region or space." Spatial load forecasting, therefore, is forecasting electrical loads for a limited geographic region. In the context of energy trading, *load* is synonymous with *demand for electrical power*. *Load* is an electrical engineering term referring to the power consumed by a circuit or drawn from a power line.

In the short term, load forecasts are used to schedule power plants for operation and maintenance. In the long run, load forecasting is used to evaluate the need for new power lines, power plants, and other infrastructure projects.

Key Topics

- Each load forecast has to be made for a specific area. Each region will have its own idiosyncrasies caused by weather, type of consumers, and geography of the region.
- Each region has a minimum level of demand that must be met at all times. This is called the *base load* of the region. The base load will typically be supplied by baseload generation units.
- Each region will have an expected maximum level of demand called the *peak load*. This level of demand will require almost all of the generation units in a region to be operating.
- Most regions will keep several generation units to act as a safety margin. These units might never be expected to operate under normal conditions.
- Even within the same region, the demand for power will vary day to day. Most of this variation can be explained by calendar effects (like day of week, or hour of day) and weather (primarily temperature).

Power grid operators (Regional Transmission operators [RTOs], Independent System Operators [ISOs], and utility companies) never know exactly how much power that they will need to supply before they need to supply it. Power grids have to estimate consumer demand. This is because consumers don't need to schedule spot electricity purchases—they just turn on electrical appliances whenever they want. Consumers independently decide how much power they use by turning on and off their appliances. There is no schedule of these decisions ahead of time. The goal of the power grid is to supply the power to consumers where and when they need it. As a result, the power grid operator needs to predict consumer demand ahead of time.

Spatial load forecasting is the study of *where* and *when* power will be required. Since power can't be easily stored, it must be generated on demand. As a result, it is necessary to anticipate changes in demand. In the context of this book, *load* is synonymous with *demand for electrical power*. Load is an electrical engineering term referring to the power consumed by a circuit or drawn from a power line. In the short term, load forecasts are used to schedule power plants for operation and maintenance. In the long run, load forecasting is used to construct new power lines, build new power plants, and build infrastructure projects.

For power grids, the goal of spatial load forecasting is to estimate both the expected and maximum amount of power that will be used by each portion of the power grid. This is necessary so that sufficient power plants can be prepared to meet any contingency. Typically power grids will have a number of power plants standing ready to turn on at any given time. Power grids need to ensure that these power plants can actually deliver electricity to the place it is needed. As a result, both the amount of power required and the location of where the power will be required are important.

For traders, load forecasts are important because the demand for power is a primary determinant of power prices. Being able to predict future prices is a key aspect to trading.

Expected or Worst-Case Scenario?

One of the key considerations for a forecasting model is determining how the model will be used. For example, a utility might want to predict the heaviest load that might be seen on a particular day for a capacity planning project. This will allow the utility to line up sufficient standby generation in order to supply power to consumers on days of peak demand. In contrast, a trader might want to predict the load that is most likely to occur on a given day as part of a trading strategy.

Although all forecasting models share many similarities, there is no single forecasting model that is perfect for everyone. The only real rule in modeling is to think about what is going on and use some common sense about how to achieve the modeling goal.

Forecasting

The key to short-term load forecasting is developing an understanding for the reasons why people use electricity. Some types of electrical usage are relatively constant. For example, an office might keep a 9 a.m. to 5 p.m. schedule. The lights might get turned on just before 9 a.m., and turned off just after 5 p.m. This is a calendar type of effect. Every weekday the same pattern will occur. In other cases, demand might vary according to environmental factors. That same office building might keep a constant indoor temperature—using electricity for air conditioning on hot days and heating on cold days. In that case, electrical demand will be based on temperature.

Not all consumers behave the same way. The central business district of a major city might have a very different electrical demand profile than a residential suburb. For example, in a suburban home, people will wake up, turn on the lights, and get ready for work. Upon leaving for work, they will turn off the lights in their houses, and drive to their offices where they turn on the lights. The office building and home have very different power requirements. However, both types of demand can be modeled by looking at historical behavior.

Location is also a major factor in forecast models. Consumers in central Florida are going to use electricity very differently than the same type of consumer in the Mid-Atlantic coastline. This is because the climate in the two regions is very different. In February, a household in central Florida might have breakfast with the windows open drinking orange juice while a household in Philadelphia huddles around a space heater drinking coffee. Some of the most important factors in a load forecast are type of consumer, location, weather, and calendar effects.

Consumer Type and Location

Load forecasts are made for limited geographical areas. The size of these areas can run from neighborhoods all the way up to multi-state regions. The boundaries of a geographical area define what types of consumers are present and the general climate of the region. This is the *spatial* component of spatial load forecasting.

In general, most regions are defined as such because they are connected to the same part of a power grid. It would be helpful if the region contained the same mix of consumers and similar climate throughout, but that is usually a secondary consideration. It's helpful if the entire region shares the same calendar for daylight savings changes, holidays, and so on.

Regardless of how a power grid is broken into pieces, each geographic area will contain a specific mix of industrial, commercial, and residential consumers. Commonly these consumers will have a relatively stable energy profile. Exceptionally large consumers of power (like an aluminum manufacturer) might need to arrange for most of their power ahead of time. However, smaller customers will typically be grouped together and treated like a single group for forecasting purposes. The most common division of electrical customers is into residential, commercial, and industrial categories.

- **Residential.** Residential consumers are households. Typically, households use most of their energy before or after the working day. As a rough approximation, these customers will use power between 6 a.m. and 9 a.m. and between 6 p.m. and 11 p.m. Some residential consumers will use power all day (leaving the lights on, or the air conditioner running). However, most households will reduce electrical usage during the working day. Residences include both apartment buildings and suburban homes.
- **Commercial.** Commercial customers are offices or retail establishments. Most commonly, these businesses operate on a standard schedule and have moderate power demands. Some commercial uses of electricity are running desktop computers or air conditioning an office building.
- **Industrial.** Industrial customers manufacture products. There can be substantial variation among these customers, and they may or may not have a stable demand for electricity throughout the year. Very large industrial customers will typically need to arrange for a steady supply of power from a power provider. This will lower the cost of power for the industrial customer and make the power grid's job much easier.

Base Load Power

One of the most important characteristics of a region is a measurement of the minimum amount of power that has to be supplied at any given time to a power grid. This minimum level of power is called *base load power*. The demand for base load power determines the number

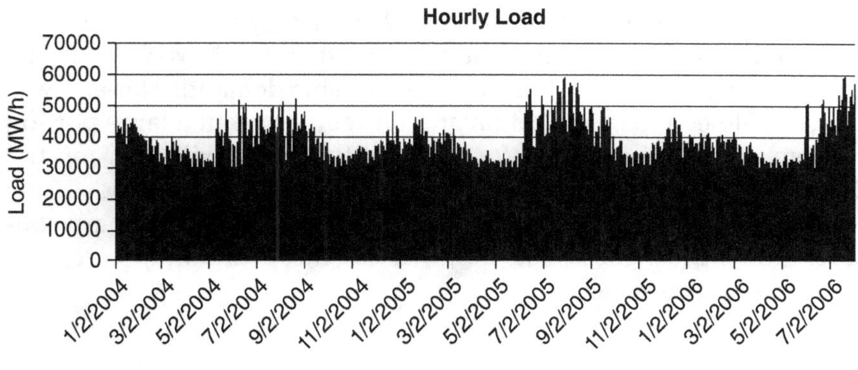

Figure 4.1.1 Hourly load

of power plants that have to run full time. Predictably, these are called *base load power plants*.

A good way to get a feeling for the power requirements in a specific region is to take a look at the historical demand. Shown in Figure 4.1.1 is the historical demand for part of the Mid-Atlantic power grid, PJM-West, between January 2004 and August 2006.

On a quick visual inspection, even though there is a substantial variation in power requirements, the demand in the region never falls below 20,000 megawatts per hour (MWh). Doing a little bit of spreadsheet manipulation, it's possible to see the percentage of time that the regional load was above certain load levels. The load was always above 20,000 MWh. It was above 30,000 MWh about half the time. The peak loads on the system were around 60,000 MWh (Figure 4.1.2).

For example, 90 percent of the time, the load on the system was less than 40,000 MWh. As a rough approximation, the region needs about 20,000 MWh of base load power capacity. To be cost effective, this demand needs to be provided by highly efficient low cost units

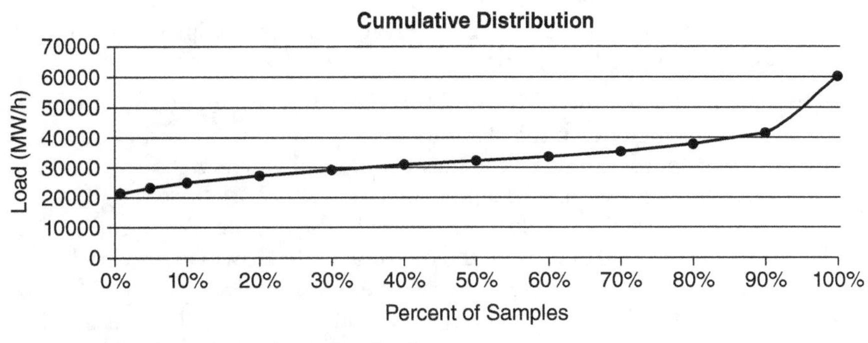

Figure 4.1.2 Cumulative load distribution

that can take advantage of the fact that they will be able to work around the clock. The region will need another 20,000 MWh of capacity that it will use to meet most of the variable demand. These power plants will need to be cycled on and off regularly, but a large portion of them will be in use fairly often. Finally, the region will need another 20,000 MWh of capacity to meet short-term spikes in demand. These units will operate less than 10 percent of the year, so the primary consideration with them is that they will be cheap to build, store, and turn on when necessary.

Temperature

Once a general understanding of a power grid is obtained, it's time to start looking at how the demand for power changes throughout the year. Both the climate of the region and the type of consumers in the region affect how the demand for power varies throughout the year.

The temperature of a region has a profound effect on energy demand. One of the most popular uses of energy is to provide heating and air conditioning. In the winter, as temperatures fall, more electricity is used for heating. In the summer, just the opposite happens—the demand for power rises when temperatures rise (Figure 4.1.3).

The relationship between demand for electrical power and load highlights the importance of short-term temperature forecasts to the electrical power industry. Temperature accounts for a very large portion of the day-to-day variation in the demand for electricity.

Common Terms

To improve the accuracy of temperature-based load predictions, it is common for energy traders to adjust temperatures for humidity and wind chill effects. These are common enough modifications that they have received their own acronyms: THI for humidity adjustments and WCI for wind chill adjustments.

Temperature Heat Index (THI). One way to improve a temperature estimate is to include humidity into the calculation. Humidity raises the apparent temperature and makes people feel warmer. Additionally, humidity slows down how quickly a region will cool off overnight. In desert areas where there is little moisture in the air, the overnight temperature falls dramatically from the daytime high. However, in very humid regions, like the U.S. Gulf Coast, the overnight temperature falls only slightly—if the daytime high temperature is 95°F, the overnight low temperature might be as high as 90°F.

From a comfort standpoint, there is a huge difference between high and low humidity. Many people don't mind high temperatures in the day as long as it is reasonably comfortable at night when they go to sleep. However, if nighttime temperatures are uncomfortable, a lot more people will use air conditioners. Once people turn an air conditioner on, they will often keep it running during the day so their house doesn't warm up. There is often higher than expected power demand during extremely humid weather because people who normally don't use air conditioners turn them on, and leave them operating.

Wind Chill Index (WCI). Much like humidity increases apparent temperatures, high wind chills can lower the apparent temperature. Anything (like a house) that is exposed to a strong wind will cool off more quickly than it would in stagnant air. When buildings cool off more quickly than usual, more heat is required to maintain them at constant temperatures.

January	August

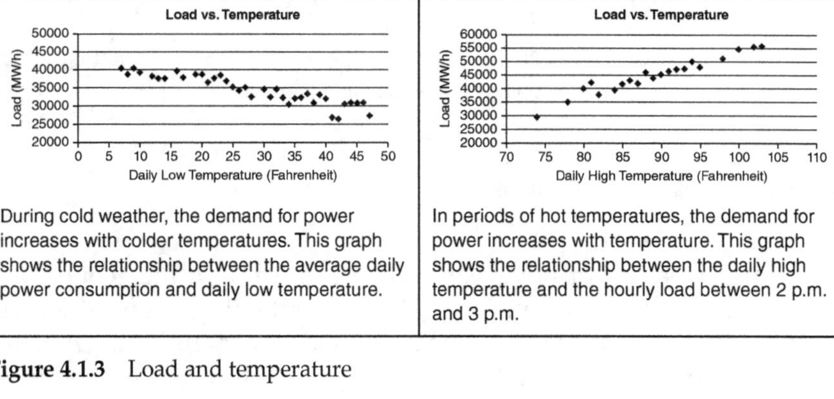

During cold weather, the demand for power increases with colder temperatures. This graph shows the relationship between the average daily power consumption and daily low temperature.	In periods of hot temperatures, the demand for power increases with temperature. This graph shows the relationship between the daily high temperature and the hourly load between 2 p.m. and 3 p.m.

Figure 4.1.3 Load and temperature

Month

Looking at average hourly load by month of the year, the effect of temperature can clearly be seen (Figure 4.1.4). The demand for power is higher in months with either extremely hot or cold weather. PJM-W is located west of Washington, D.C., and has hot summers and cold winters. Peak power demand occurs in the summer and winter months. Power demands are much lower during the spring and fall of each year.

A next step is to examine how people use power differently in different months. For example, in the Mid-Atlantic region during May, temperatures are generally fairly pleasant. There may be a couple of hot days, but generally the weather is mild. As a result, even on hot days, most people leave their air conditioners off. They wait until

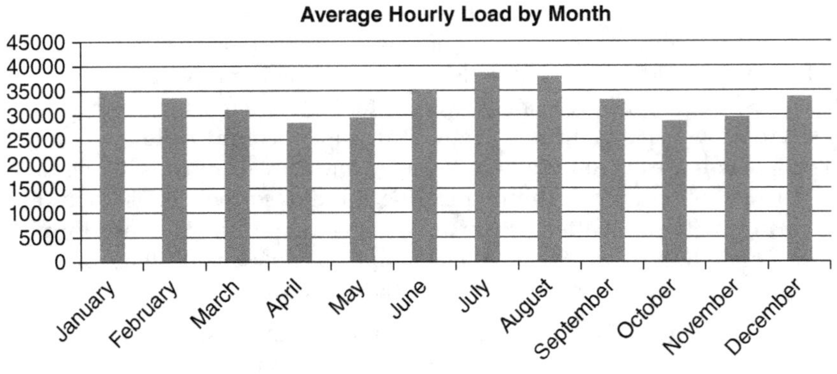

Figure 4.1.4 Average hourly load by month

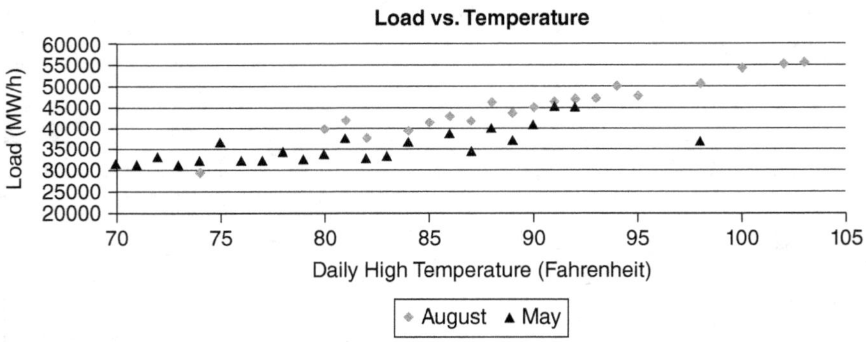

Figure 4.1.5 Load vs. temperature

a prolonged period of hot weather before turning on air conditioners for the summer. However, by August, unrelenting hot weather has convinced many people to run their air conditioners full time. As a result, for the same daily high temperature, the PJM-W region uses more power in August than it does in May (Figure 4.1.5).

Forecasts

For the United States, the primary source of hourly weather forecasts is the National Oceanic and Atmospheric Administration's (NOAA) National Weather Service (NWS). The NWS produces both short-term hourly forecasts and longer-term forecasts. These forecasts cover both temperature and relative humidity around the country (Figure 4.1.6). These forecasts can be examined at the NWS website (forecast.weather.gov).

The NWS also predicts whether regional temperatures will be above or below average in monthly and quarterly blocks (Figure 4.1.7).

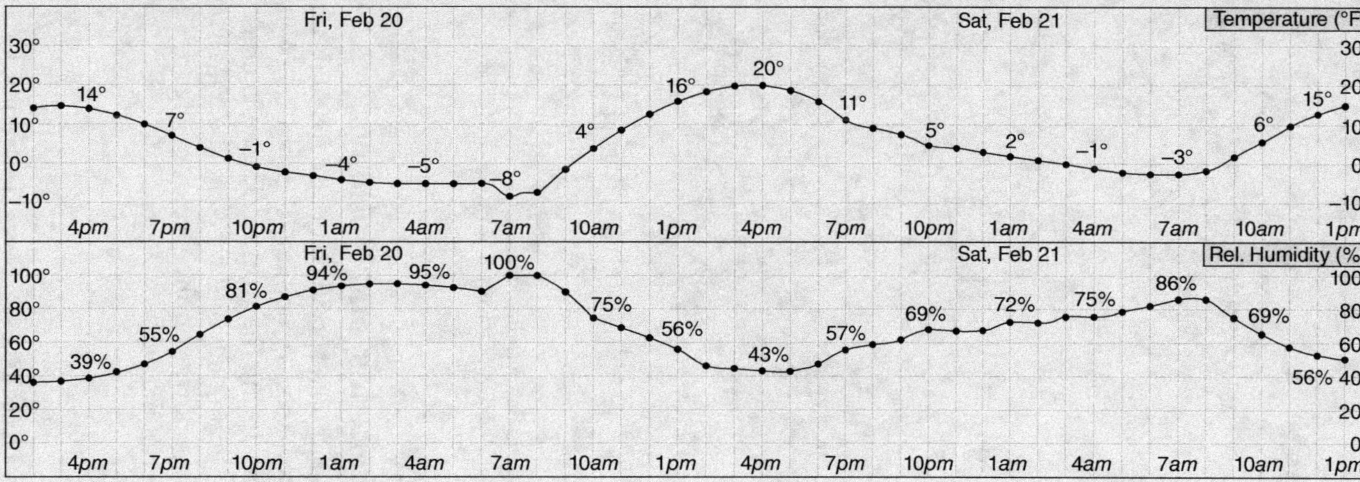

Figure 4.1.6 Hourly predictions
(*Source:* U.S. National Weather Service)

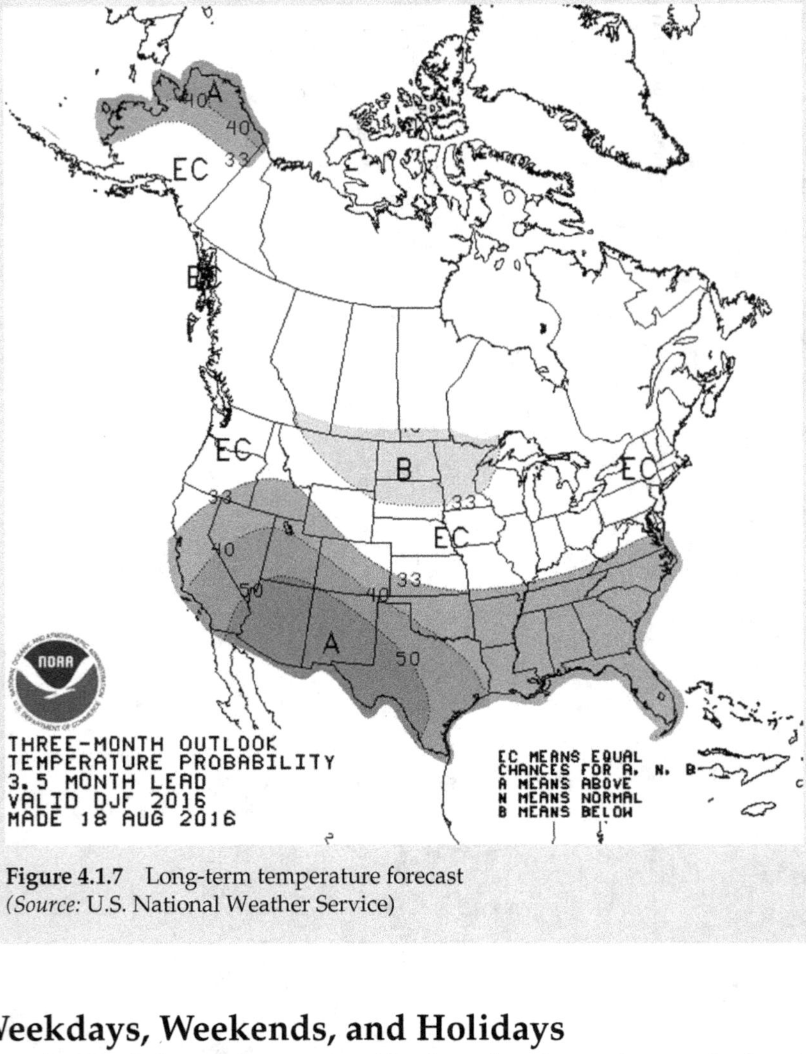

Figure 4.1.7 Long-term temperature forecast
(Source: U.S. National Weather Service)

Weekdays, Weekends, and Holidays

The electrical demand on a specific day also depends on whether the day is a weekday, weekend, or holiday (Figure 4.1.8). Not surprisingly, more power is used during the workweek than is used on weekends and holidays. For example, consumers in the PJM-West area used about 10 percent less power on the weekend. Figure 4.1.8 shows the average load by day of the week.

Hour of Day

Finally, consumers typically use power differently at different times of the day depending on a variety of factors. For example, during the

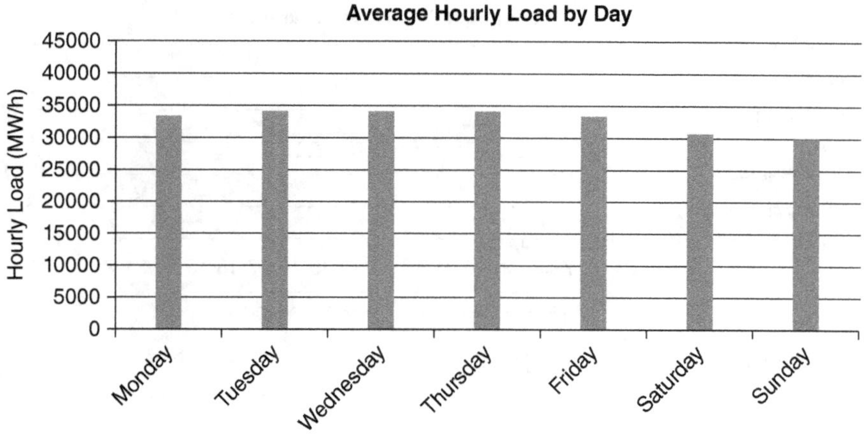

Figure 4.1.8 Average load by day of week

summer, more air conditioning is required during the hottest part of the day (early afternoon) than will be required early in the morning (Figure 4.1.9). As a result, in the summer, residential consumers will use more power in the afternoon. Similarly, during cold weather, consumers will typically turn on the heat when they are at home awake, and turn down the thermostat while they are working or sleeping. During the winter, demand can be expected to be highest early in the morning when people wake up, and in the early evening when they arrive home from work.

The August graph shows a comparison of weekday and weekend power requirements. Overnight power usage is pretty constant for both weekdays and weekends. However, substantially less power is used during the hottest part of the day on weekends. There is no need to air condition the office if no one is there!

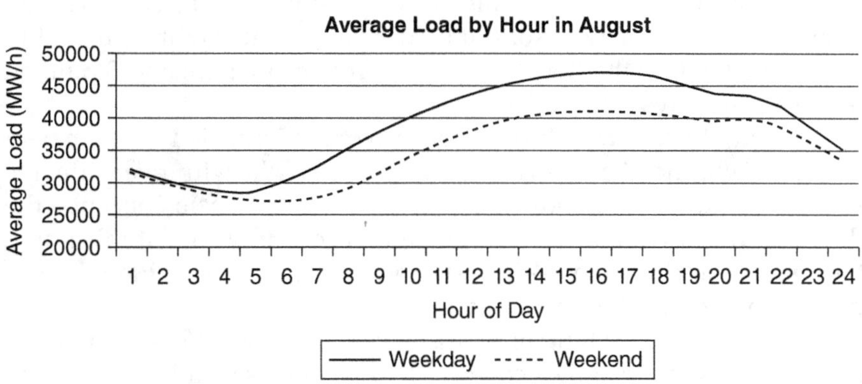

Figure 4.1.9 Hourly loads in August

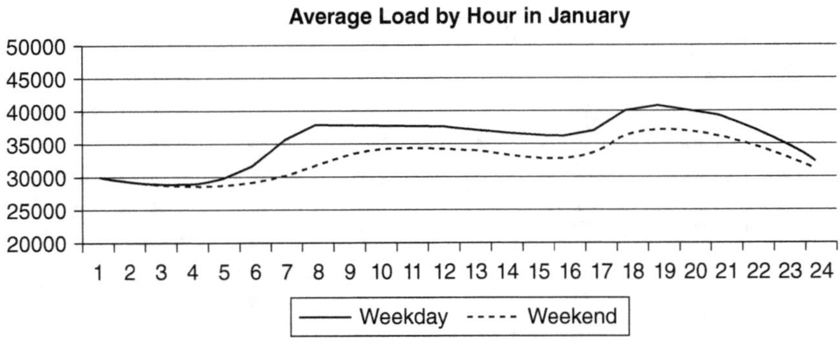

Figure 4.1.10 Hourly loads in January

The average power use in the winter is different than during hot weather (Figure 4.1.10). During the winter, the Mid-Atlantic region starts using electricity fairly early in the morning (when people start waking up) and spikes again toward the end of the day (when people arrive home from work). Notice how the power use on the weekend differs from the weekday. On the weekend, electricity doesn't start getting used until later in the day—the morning peak is around 10 a.m. rather than the 7 a.m. weekday peak. Perhaps people are sleeping later on the weekend?

Creating a Model

Creating a model from observations is not magic. The best starting point for any model is to look at historical load information. Building some graphs and looking at what is actually going on is an excellent starting point. After that, the next step is to develop a preliminary model. In general, a first model should not try to explain too much. After a simple model is completely understood, it can be expanded to account for other types of data. For example, it might be useful to model the load on the PJM-West region between 2 p.m. and 3 p.m. on August weekdays (Figure 4.1.11).

This model says that the base load power at 2 p.m. is approximately 32,850 MWh and that power increases 750 MWh with every degree the temperature rises above 72°F. It captures the basic concept—the demand for power goes up with temperature. However, at this point, the model isn't complete—it is still necessary to determine where it does a poor job explaining demand.

Before doing anything else, it is necessary to see when this model gives a bad estimate of the actual load. This process is called *error analysis*. When a scientist is working on a new theory, the scientist will create

Load Forecast Model

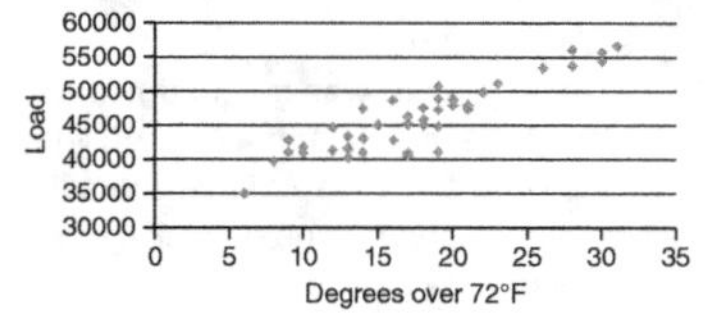

Step 1: Look at the Data
The first step is to look at the data that is being modeled. The left axis shows the hourly load between 2 p.m. and 3 p.m. The bottom axis shows the temperature as degrees above an arbitrarily chosen comfortable temperature of 72°F.

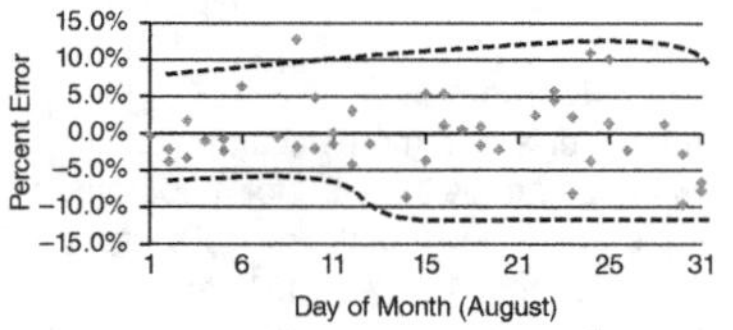

Step 2: Create a Linear Model
Since there is a relatively clear relationship, linear regression can be used to create a linear approximation of the observations. Using a spreadsheet, this can be done by adding a trend line to approximate a scatter diagram.

Figure 4.1.11 Load forecast model

a hypothesis and then try to disprove it. Modeling works much the same way. A modeler creates an initial model and sees where it doesn't work well. The model can then be modified, hopefully making it more accurate. This process continues until the modeler is comfortable with the model.

Error analysis will compare the model's predictions against actual data. The difference between the actual load observations and the model's predictions is called the *error of the model*. To analyze the error, it will be examined several ways. In this case, three possible reasons for modeling errors will be examined. Initially, the data will be compared to the same data that was used to create the model. This is called an *in-sample* test (Figure 4.1.12). Later, the model might be compared to data not used to create the model. That is called an *out-of-sample* test.

The purpose of error analysis is to explain why the model might not work perfectly all the time. Therefore, it is necessary to think of reasons why the model might not work and test them. One possible reason for errors might be that consumers use power differently in late August compared to early August. For example, we know power is used differently in May than it is in August. This effect might be visible throughout a month too.

Alternately, the model might be biased against high or low temperatures. The linear estimate of load has been fit to a large number of samples. It's reasonable to think that some part of that sample is consistently misestimated. For example, the efficiency of air conditioners might go down when it is extremely hot outside. If that's true, air conditioners will need to do more cooling and require more energy to do that cooling on hot days.

Error Analysis

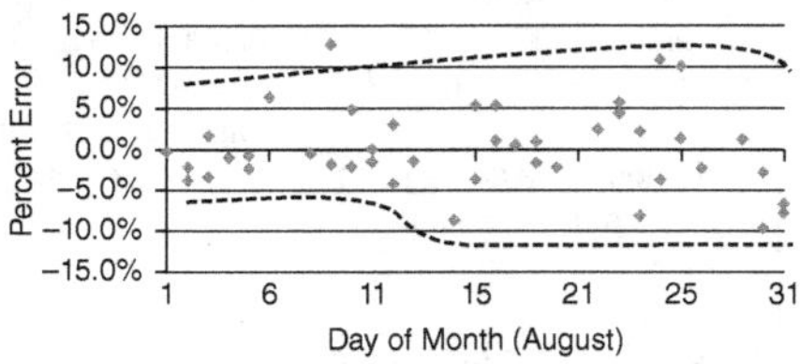

Step 3: Day of Month
The percentage error was graphed relative to the day of the month, and a dashed line shows the location of most of the errors. The errors don't seem to be especially biased toward one part of the month compared to any other part.

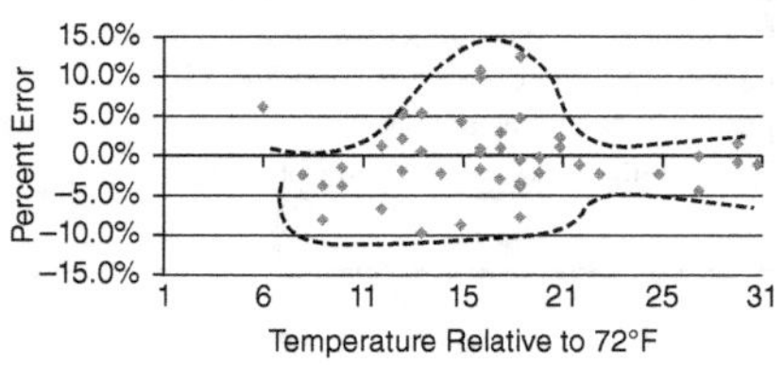

Step 4: Temperature
The model is a lot more accurate for high or low temperatures than it is for moderate temperatures. Most of the model's errors are in the range between 13°F and 20°F above the comfortable temperature. There isn't an obvious solution, but it is something to examine later.

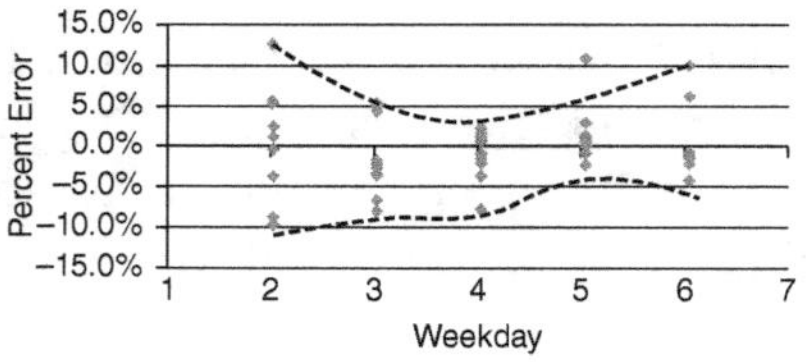

Step 5: Day of the Week
The largest errors are concentrated on Mondays. Although the model isn't perfectly accurate for all of the other weekdays, they don't have as wide a distribution of errors as Monday.

Figure 4.1.12 Error analysis

Finally, it's possible that some weekdays behave differently than other weekdays. For example, if workers tended to leave work a bit early on Friday, that might affect the demand for power on that day. Whether this happens at 2 p.m. is in doubt, but it's something that might be worth checking.

4.2

The Generation Stack

30-Second Summary

Purpose

This chapter discusses how power prices are determined. Although this chapter is mostly nontechnical, a general knowledge of the electrical market is helpful. An introduction to electrical markets can be found in Chapter 2.2—Electricity.

Summary

In deregulated markets where electricity trading is permitted, prices are set by daily auctions. Each power producer is allowed to submit bids and the lowest bidders are selected to supply electricity to the power grid. All active providers receive the same price for their power. The price that everyone receives is the price submitted by the highest active bidder.

Key Topics

- The physical capabilities of power plants, particularly the cost of their fuel, determine how they participate in the daily auctions.
- Small changes in the supply or demand of electricity can have a big effect on prices.
- Each market has a slightly different process for dispatching their generation stack.

In deregulated areas, the coordinating Independent System Operator/Regional Transmission Operator (ISO/RTO) for the area holds daily auctions to determine the price of power. These are competitive auctions where power plants bid against one another for the right to produce power. The physical capabilities of each generator are a major factor in their bidding strategies. Consequently, the primary way to estimate power prices is to examine power providers ordered by their cost of production. This ordering is called a *generation stack*. For example, if there are four power plants on a power grid with 450 megawatts per hour (MWh) of total capacity, a generation stack ordered from highest cost (on top) to lowest cost (on the bottom) might look like Figure 4.2.1.

Sample Generation Stack			
	Capacity (MW/h)	**Break-Even Cost**	
Diesel Peaking	50	150	Highest Cost
Natural Gas	100	85	
Coal	200	50	
Hydroelectric	100	10	Lowest Cost

Figure 4.2.1 A generation stack

Dispatch capacity, often just called *capacity,* indicates how much power each power plant can produce. The *break-even cost* indicates the minimum price the power plant can accept for its power and still make a profit. For fuel-dependent power plants, like the natural-gas-fired generator, this cost will be heavily influenced by fuel costs.

This ordering can help predict the prices produced by the day-ahead and real-time auctions. In most cases, power plants will place bids above their own cost of generation (their break-even cost), and below the costs of the next type of unit in the stack (Figure 4.2.2). For example, the coal generator will probably place bids somewhere between \$50 and \$85. The price of power (on the left axis) can be predicted by looking at the predicted consumer demand (on the bottom axis).

The Mechanics of Day-Ahead and Real-Time Auctions

In most deregulated regions, there are two auctions that determine the *clearing price* of power. The first is a *day-ahead* auction; the second a *real-time* auction. The day-ahead auction uses predictions of the upcoming day's load to schedule power plants the day before power is needed.

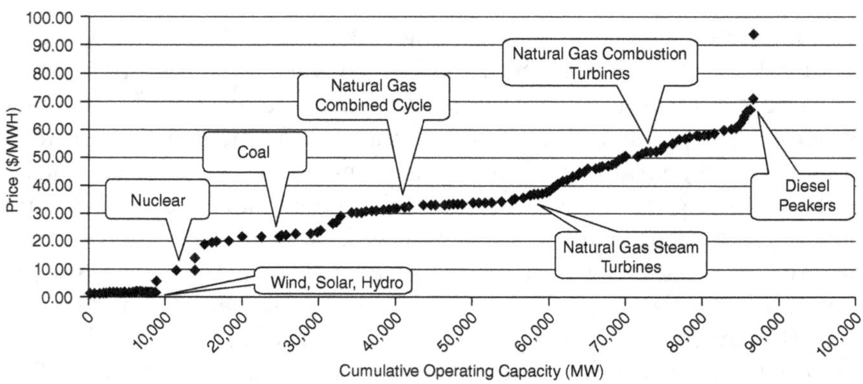

Figure 4.2.2 Visual representation of a generation stack

This auction schedules power producers to be active for an entire hour. If the demand fluctuates throughout the hour, or if the load forecasts are incorrect, an adjustment will be needed to balance production with demand. Adjustments are made in the real-time auction.

In both auctions, generators [also called *load serving entities* (LSEs)] participate by submitting offer curves (their generation levels associated with prices they are willing to accept) and their technical constraints (startup costs, minimum up time, and so on). After collecting offers from generators, the ISO selects the winning generators that minimize the cost to the market. For example, a coal power plant with a cost basis of $50 might want 100 MWh of capacity always operating during the period. So, it places its first bid at $0 for its first 100 MWh. Then, it will start placing bids for greater amounts of power at progressively higher prices. The last bid is placed just under the $85 break-even cost of the next generation unit in the stack (Figure 4.2.3).

When creating a bid, a generator needs to decide whether to attempt to sell all of its power in the day-ahead market or to reserve some capacity to sell into the real-time market. There are potentially greater profits in the real-time market, but the risk of being inactive is also higher. In both cases, bidding strategies are dictated by the physical characteristics of power plants. The most important characteristics are how quickly a power plant can come online and its efficiency at converting fuel into electricity. If a generator is not selected to operate in the day-ahead market, it is still eligible to participate in the real-time market.

Not every generator is capable of participating in the real-time market. The real-time auction requires that generators be capable of starting quickly and having their fuel supplies lined up. Inefficient power providers often have this capability. However, if a low-cost provider fails to sell their power in the day-ahead market, they often won't be able to participate in the real-time market either. Most of the daily generation requirement is auctioned off in the day-ahead market—the *real-time* auction is used for balancing short-term fluctuations and unexpected demand.

Bid Schedule 200 MWh Coal Plant	
Capacity (MW/h)	**Price**
100	$0
101	$51
150	$75
200	$83

Figure 4.2.3 Bid schedule

Generation costs determine how most power providers participate in the daily auctions. Low cost providers want to lock in profits. They will have already lined up their fuel supplies and are probably hedging their price exposure in anticipation of being activated. If they don't sell power in the day-ahead auction, they may be locked out of the real-time market by operating constraints. In comparison, higher price providers may benefit from waiting until the real-time auction if they can't lock in sufficiently high prices early.

The Dispatch Stack

In deregulated markets, LSEs are placed into *economic dispatch order* based on the results of the day-ahead and real-time auctions held by each TSO. The lowest bidding LSEs are activated first, followed by higher bidders. The order that power plants are turned on is called the *dispatch stack*. This is a last on, first off ordering that is similar to a stack of plates (Figure 4.2.4). The unit at the top of the stack (the marginal unit) is the last unit to be activated and the first to be deactivated. The top of the stack is a very important location. The provider on the top of the dispatch stack sets the *clearing price* of power for a region. This provider is often called the *marginal* provider.

In most cases, the dispatch stack will be ordered similarly to the generation stack. The cheaper a power plant can generate power, the more it has to lose if it doesn't get activated. Once the price of power rises substantially over a provider's cost of production, the power provider will risk losing a large profit if it isn't active. As a result, each power plant will usually actively bid only on a small portion of the generation stack—the part after it becomes profitable, but before it

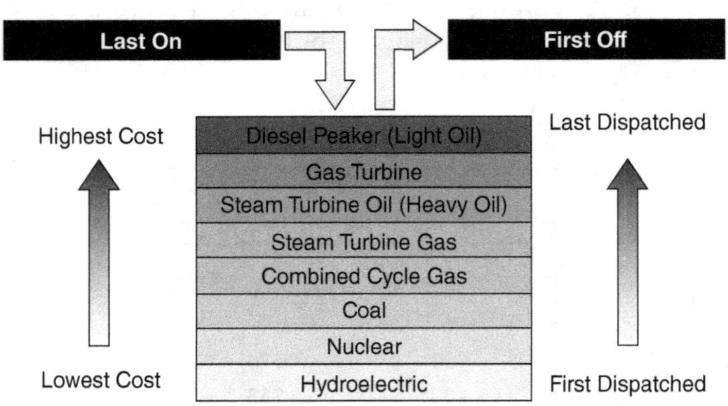

Figure 4.2.4 The dispatch stack

has too much money on the table. After that, they become *price takers,* allowing more aggressive bidders to set the clearing price of power.

Higher cost providers have a different problem—other power plants will know the break-even prices of the providers above them on the stack and bid just under that price. This behavior exists because everyone gets paid the same price for power—there isn't an economic penalty for bidding just under a competitor if someone else sets a higher clearing price.

As a result, power plants with similar capabilities tend to cluster their bids around the same price points. Only a few power plants at any time actively set the price of power. Consequently, the couple of power plants *on the margin* have a disproportionate effect on the price of power. Because similar units cluster their bids, it is usually possible to determine a profile of the marginal producers.

Baseload, Mid-Merit, and Peaking Suppliers

It is common to describe each of the load providers within a generation stack as a baseload, mid-merit, or peaking unit. These terms broadly describe the behavior of power plants.

Baseload plants are located at the bottom of the generation stack. These power plants are active all year and sell power in the day-ahead auctions. They produce power cheaply, are expensive to shut down, and run continuously even when demand is at its lowest level. Hydro, nuclear, and coal plants all fall into this category. Hydro plants don't have any fuel costs and may not be able to shut down without flooding nearby communities. Nuclear plants require the use of control rods to slow down their nuclear reactions. Without being cooled, a nuclear reaction will keep going at maximum capacity. It costs money to shut down a nuclear reactor. Coal plants are easier to shut down but can be expensive to restart if allowed to cool down completely. Coal plants are more costly than other baseload producers, but they have a huge cost advantage over other fossil fuel producers. Coal is by far the cheapest of the fossil fuels per Btu of energy. Almost all baseline plants run full time—they are rarely on the margin, and offer power at low costs in order to avoid going offline.

Peaking generation on the other extreme, provides short-term electricity during periods of peak demand (typically summer afternoons). These generators are at the very top of the generation stack. These plants need to start up quickly and be cheap to maintain. They don't need to be cheap to operate—conserving fuel is an afterthought when power can be sold at sufficiently high prices. Many of these power plants are essentially jet engines. Fuel is pumped in and ignited; there are a minimum of moving parts and a lot of wasted heat energy. Many of these plants only operate a couple hundred hours a year. In order to recover costs, these plants will charge very high prices. These plants will operate almost exclusively in the real-time auction market except when day-ahead prices are extremely high.

Mid-merit plants are somewhere between the two extremes. In some cases, these plants are older, less-efficient baseload plants that are no longer cost effective enough to run full time. In other cases, these are highly efficient natural gas plants that are easier to cycle than the baseload generators. These generators are commonly on the margin, and show a lot of variability in their bidding strategies. Baseload generators are always going to bid low—they need to operate full time. Peaking generators are always going to bid high—they are extremely expensive to operate. Mid-merit generators are going to bid in both day-ahead and real-time markets, and will usually set the price of power.

Active Versus Passive Bidding Strategies

There is a fair amount of gamesmanship in choosing how to bid in power auctions. Generators want to get the highest possible price for their product. However, since there is a single price for power in a region, it isn't important to be the top bidder. As long as a power plant is operating, it is getting the same price as the highest bidder. There is no downside to bidding a zero price if someone else sets the price at a higher level. In contrast, active bidding is risky—power plants that actively try to control the price of electricity run the risk of being inactive and not getting paid.

The basic decision on whether to actively participate in the bidding process, and risk being inactive, often comes down to how much money that a power plant stands to lose if it isn't activated. A power plant's profit is the spread between the price of power and the power plant's cost of production. If a power plant has a very low cost of production, it will give up substantially more profit by being inactive than a plant with a higher cost of production.

For example, it might be possible for a power plant to increase the price of power by $1 if it is willing to bid aggressively into the day-ahead market. However, if aggressive bidders stand a 10 percent chance of being inactive, the decision is complicated for providers that are already highly profitable. If the price of power is around $100, it wouldn't be worthwhile for a plant with a cost basis of zero to give up

$10 (a 10 percent chance of being inactive and giving up $100) for a chance to make an extra $0.90 (making an extra dollar 90 percent of the time).

At the other extreme, a power plant with a very expensive cost of production would have a different reaction to the same decision. With a $95 cost of production, a power plant benefits substantially from aggressive bidding. In this case, the power plant would only give up $.50 (giving up a $5 profit, 10 percent of the time) for an extra $0.90 (an extra dollar 90 percent of the time).

Optimal Bidding Strategies

Most generators split their bid into several smaller bids. It is not uncommon for some of these bids to be offered at or below the generator's cost of production. Since most generators are steam turbines that cost money to bring online, unaggressive bids ensure that the generator can avoid unnecessary stoppages. A power plant will often submit bids at higher prices in an attempt to maximize profits. Generally, the placement of the higher bids will depend on who else is bidding at that point.

For example, if a generator can profitably sell power at $50 and the next plant in the generation stack becomes profitable at $60, the first generator is likely to split their bid into two pieces—a piece below $50 to minimize the risk of being completely inactive, and the rest of their bid just under the $60 mark. Generally, this second bid will be as high as possible without tempting the next generator in the stack to undercut that price.

Bidding in this manner requires an in-depth knowledge of all the power plants around a certain point in the generation stack. In most cases, this is specialized knowledge learned through trial and error. Power generators usually have a detailed understanding of the generation stack around their own production costs. However, they won't understand other parts of the stack with the same detail. As a result, most power plants only bid aggressively on the portion of the generation stack near their own costs of production.

Because of the need to prevent unnecessary shutdowns and restarts, most optimal bidding strategies do not simply react to prices. Optimal bidding incorporates predictions of likely future decisions into the current decision. In many cases, it is worthwhile for a steam turbine to take a loss in some periods to avoid startup costs in a later period. These simulations are often based on a *Game Theory* analysis.

Game Theory

Game Theory is a branch of mathematics that is used in economics to analyze behavioral patterns. It focuses on how participants (*players*) make optimal decisions in complex situations (*games*). Since each participant's decisions can affect the other participants, these situations are often competitive; for example, two people bidding against one another in an auction. There are a number of other common Game Theory terms. The benefit (or loss) that a player receives from playing the game is called their *utility*. The goal of every player is to maximize their *utility*. If the utility maximizing decisions converge into a stable pattern, this is called a *Nash Equilibrium*.

Game Theory is often criticized for taking an overly harsh approach to competitive situations. The typical optimal strategy is to look out for oneself at the expense of other players. Intuitively, many people find this unacceptable and discard the approach altogether. The problem is often not in the Game Theory approach, but rather how games are defined. If a complex situation is incorrectly defined, the choice of *optimal behavior* will also be incorrect.

For example, an economist is out with a potential client on a business trip. He takes the client to a restaurant, and faces a decision at the end of the meal—should he tip the wait staff? The economist and his client received excellent service, but the economist doesn't believe he will return to the same town again. As a result, he decides not to tip—he has already gotten his good service, and he decides to save money as well. Unfortunately, his understanding of the game was incorrect. The only players were not the economist and the wait staff. The potential client also witnessed the event. This client might easily conclude that the economist does not value other people's contributions and would be a bad business partner.

Day-ahead and real-time power options are designed so that the optimal bidding strategy is for generators to bid their own cost of production. In general, this is what happens in the real world.

Variable Generation

It is common for the generation stack to change throughout the day. In particular, many renewable power providers can't supply a steady supply of power throughout the day. Solar power is a good example—it depends on sunlight. Sunlight is most abundant during the middle of the day. As a result, the generating capacity of a solar plant will be higher in the afternoon than in the early morning or late evening. The generation stack will change to account for this variable supply. Hydro power, wind generators, and imports and exports from other power grids are all examples of variable supplies of power.

In many cases, variable power providers can't turn off their power supplies or guarantee delivery. For example, once power is scheduled to be imported from another power grid, it can't be easily cancelled. Solar, wind, and hydro generators also can't shut down on short notice. They also can't guarantee that they will be able to deliver their power either. As a result, these power suppliers will be price takers—they will bid zero cost for their power and get paid the clearing price set by other market participants.

The production profile for a variable generator can change over time. Sometimes these changes are seasonally predictable, and other times they are random. It is usually possible to predict the variable supply of electricity a day ahead of time, but longer-term predictions become less accurate. For example, hydro power is very dependent upon seasonal rainfall that can occur anywhere within the space of a month or two. A day ahead of time, this water flow on the rivers will be well known. Likewise, solar power plants receive more sunlight in summer months but are also affected by cloudy conditions and precipitation. The most important impact is that even over small periods like a week or two, there can be substantial changes to variable production (Figure 4.2.5).

Even small changes to the generation stack can have a major effect on prices because the top of the generation stack is getting displaced. During August 2005, power prices in PJM were around $80. A 4,000-megawatt (MWh) change in power might change the power prices by $10 or more as shown in Figure 4.2.6. The graph shows part of the PJM generation stack containing the marginal generators during August 2005 and the effect that an additional 4,000 MWh of power would have on prices.

Variable generation is a major reason why periods in the same day with identical consumer demand can see a wide range of prices. This makes it difficult to back into a generation stack by looking at daily loads and prices published by ISO/RTOs.

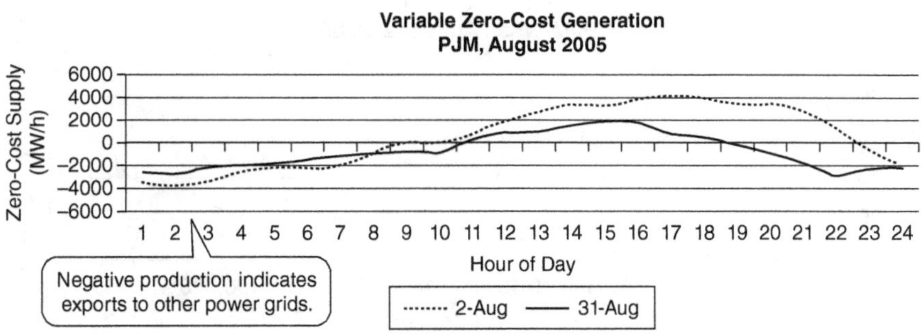

Figure 4.2.5 The variable generation in PJM on two different days in August 2005

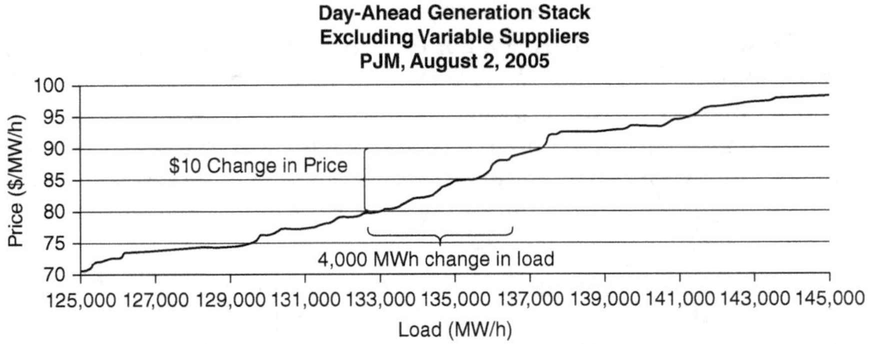

Figure 4.2.6 Small changes in supply can have a big impact on the price of power

Estimating Break-Even Costs Using Heat Rates

No one, except for the ISO/RTO coordinating the daily auctions, knows the exact makeup of the generation stack until the data are released several years later. Auction bids are not made public, nor do load producers publish their break-even costs. To predict power prices, it is necessary to look at historical prices and estimate the generation stack from other pieces of information (Figure 4.2.7). For example, normalizing power prices by dividing them by fuel prices to create a heat rate graph is a common way to estimate changing power prices.

For fuel-dependent load providers, the cost of fuel and the conversion efficiency of their power plant combine to determine where they become cost effective. Natural gas prices are particularly important in determining the price of power because marginal producers commonly use that fuel. The natural gas/power relationship is so pervasive that it has its own terminology. The ratio of power prices to natural gas prices is called an *implied market heat rate*.

An implied market heat rate is easy to calculate—it is the average price of power divided by the average price of fuel in a specific

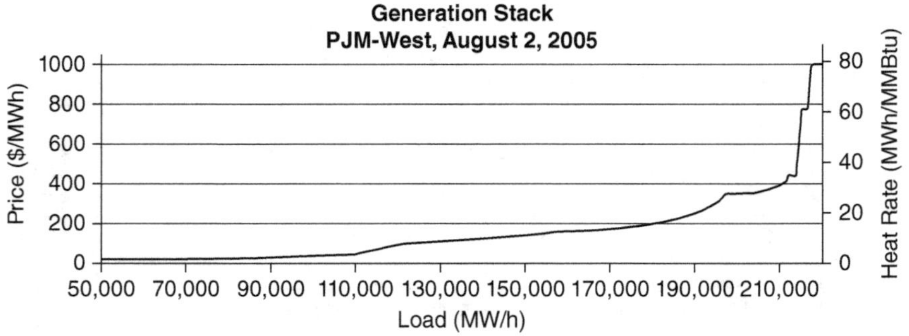

Figure 4.2.7 Generation stack

geographic area. Because fuel needs to be paid for and scheduled for delivery ahead of time, the price of fuel within a particular day is constant. A generation stack can be described by either prices or heat rates as shown below. The heat rates are calculated by dividing the prices by \$12.70 (the price of natural gas on that day).

When fuel prices rise, the break-even cost of power providers using that fuel will also rise. As a result, the generation stack for those producers will change. For example, in August 2005, the price of natural gas rose from \$8.02 to \$12.70. This coincided with a large move in the price of power (Figure 4.2.8). Power prices rose significantly for parts of the generation stack.

The implied market heat rate can identify how much of a change in electricity prices is due to a change in natural gas prices. If implied heat rates don't change, the ratio between power and gas prices remains constant. A constant ratio means that the fuel prices fully account for the change in electricity prices. In August 2005, on the portion of the generation stack where natural gas plants are profitable, there was very little change in market heat rates between the two days (Figure 4.2.9). In Figure 4.2.9, the part of the generation stack where natural gas is the marginal fuel is highlighted.

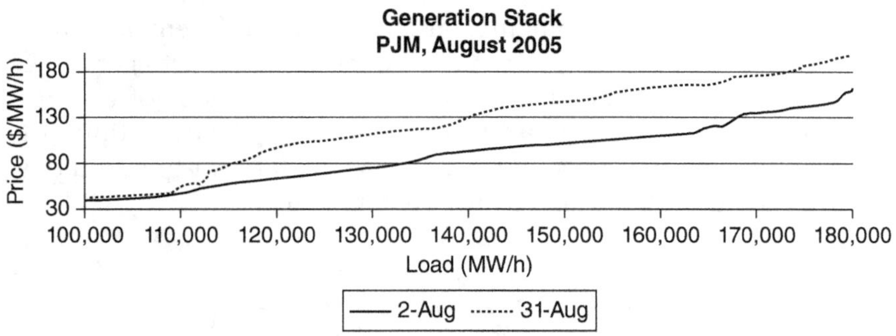

Figure 4.2.8 Generation stack shift

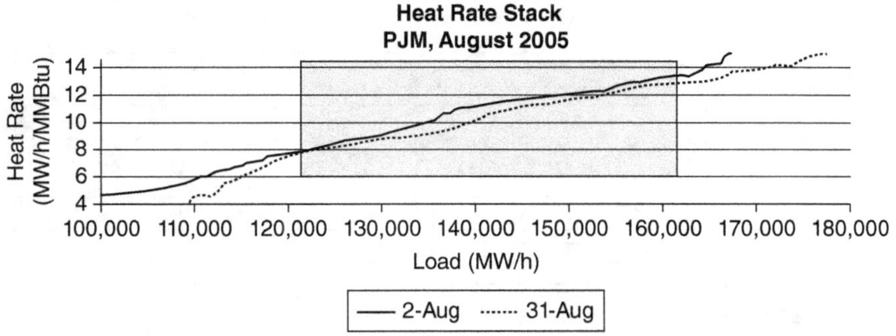

Figure 4.2.9 Heat rate stack

Day-Ahead and Real-Time Auctions

Although there are two separate auctions setting the price of power, the generation stack and the bidding strategies of power producers are nearly identical for both. Most of the generation capacity is locked in during the day-ahead market with a small amount of balancing required from the real-time market. Although there are fewer participants in the real-time auction, similar bidding dynamics lead to similar generation stacks. A comparison of real-time and day-ahead prices for two days can be seen in Figure 4.2.10. The auction prices are close together most of the time. Occasionally, prices in the real-time market are higher.

The inability of many power plants to react quickly to changes in load is the reason for two auctions. Typically, the day-ahead market activates power plants in half-hour or hour-long increments. The load at the start of the period determines the number of power plants that get activated. However, if demand rises before another set of power plants is activated (either a half hour or hour later), that demand will need to be met by the real-time market (Figure 4.2.11). The relationship between changes in hourly demand and the short-term change in prices can be seen in Figure 4.2.11.

In most cases, marginal power suppliers tend to use the same strategy for participating in both auctions. The highly efficient generators at the bottom of the generation stack are the most likely to get locked out of the real-time market. However, except for periods of very low demand, the bottom of the generation stack will be continuously active, and won't be on the margin. As a result, the real-time and day-ahead generation stacks are usually very similar.

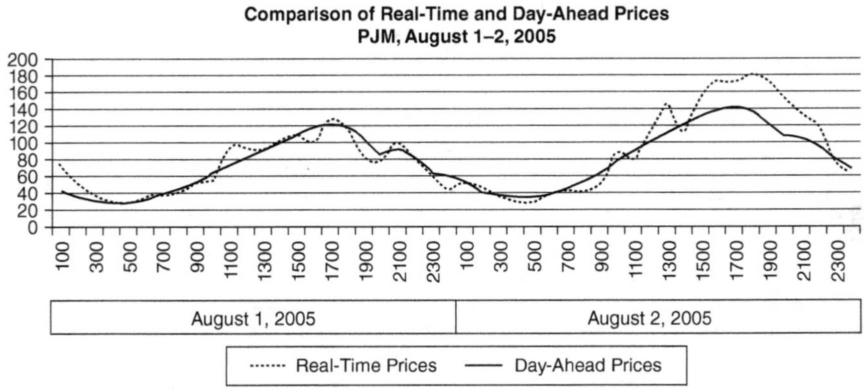

Figure 4.2.10 Day-ahead and real-time prices

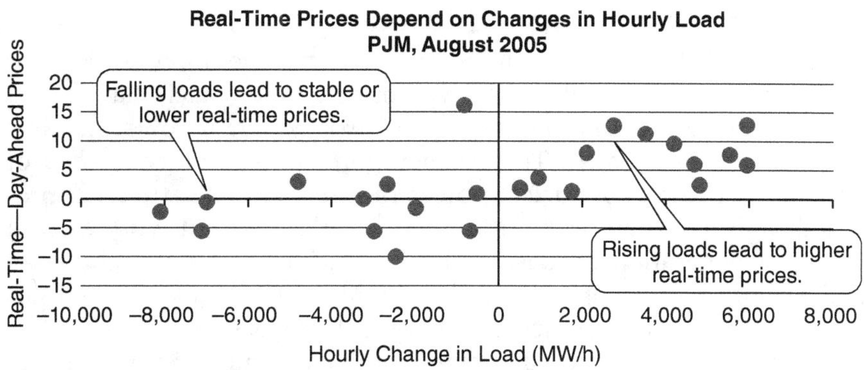

Figure 4.2.11 Changes in hourly loads

Efficient Versus Economic Dispatch

One of the problems facing economically dispatched markets (markets where generators are activated based on price) is how to deal with pollution. For example, coal-powered plants produce a lot of pollution. However, they are economically competitive because their fuel is extremely cheap in comparison to other fossil fuels. In an economically dispatched market, when environmentally friendly power is brought on line, it usually won't displace the coal generators. Instead, the marginal generators further up the generation stack will be replaced. Most commonly, these will be less polluting combined cycle natural gas plants.

For the same amount of pollution, natural gas produces much more energy than coal. However, due to the higher cost of fuel, natural gas generators will be deactivated before the coal generators. Politically, this creates a problem. When *green power* (environmentally friendly generation) is brought on line, it removes the more expensive fuels like natural gas from the generation stack. Environmental advocates would prefer to see an *efficient dispatch* of power—activating power plants based on minimal SO_2 and CO_2 emissions rather than on an economic basis.

To make efficient dispatch work in a deregulated market, the most common approach is to make coal power more expensive by charging for CO_2 and SO_2 emissions. Making coal production more expensive can raise costs for consumers, but these costs can be refunded by reducing other consumer expenses. Many markets are adopting the use of *emissions credits* for this purpose. Essentially, emissions credits are a tax upon highly polluting power plants so that an economic dispatch system also satisfies environmental efficiency requirements.

Problems with Marginal Pricing

Marginal pricing works well for the certain generation stacks. For example, it worked well for the type of generation stack that existed in the mid-1990s—the type of stack that existed when power markets were first being created. These generation stacks were composed of cheap baseload coal or nuclear power. More expensive natural gas provided high marginal prices. Marginal pricing does not work as well when the generation stack is flat. By 2015, 20 years of new technology and an influx of cheaper natural gas that resulted from natural gas fracking had created a much flatter generation stack.

In power grids where all generators have similar marginal costs, the marginal pricing mechanism makes it difficult to make a profit. For example, if the marginal unit on a power grid is a 10 MMBtu/MWh heat rate unit, and gas prices are $10/MMBtu, then power prices would be approximately $100/MWh. If gas prices fall to $4/MMBtu, then marginal power prices fall to $40/MWh. For a baseload coal unit that might have a variable cost of $35/MWh, the profit drops from $65 dollars (the difference between $100/MWh and $35/MWh) to $5/MWh (the difference between $40/MWh and $35/MWh).

An extreme version of a flat generation stack will commonly occur when all market participants choose similar technology. In other words, when a power grid with only one technology uses marginal pricing, everyone's marginal cost would be the same and no one would make a profit. Not making a profit is problematic because constructing new generation typically requires large initial investments that need to be recovered during operations. Anyone lending money to a developer will want to ensure that there is a steady stream of profits that can repay the cost of construction.

4.3

TOLLING AGREEMENTS

30-Second Summary

Purpose

A *tolling agreement* is a contract to rent a power plant from its owners. These agreements give the renter the ability to convert one physical commodity (fuel) into a different commodity (electricity). This chapter discusses how to determine the economic value of a power plant.

Summary

Owning (or renting) a power plant gives a trader the option of converting fuel into power. If power prices are sufficiently high, a power plant can burn fuel to produce electricity at a profit. Otherwise, the trader will usually leave the power plant inactive. This is very similar to the behavior of financial option contracts. As a result, the value of a power plant is often approximated as a portfolio of those contracts.

Key Topics

- Tolling agreements are commonly modeled as a portfolio of option contracts. This is called a *real options* model.
- Power plants run for years. Because electricity can't be stored, electricity in one part of the year is a different commodity than electricity at other parts of the year. From a risk management perspective, there are a large number of different underlying products being traded.
- The correlation between fuel and power prices is the single largest factor in determining the value of a tolling agreement.
- Tolling agreements are commonly modeled using spread options, like Kirk's approximation modification to the Black Scholes genre option formulas, or through Monte Carlo simulations. Examples of these formulas can be found in other chapters.

With deregulation, sweeping changes were made to the ownership of power plants. Power plant operators became responsible for selling power in an open market in addition to maintaining their power plants. The safe business of operating a power plant—once thought of as an ultra-secure investment—was now a very risky business. To address this new reality, power plant operators began to specialize. Some focused on maintaining the physical hardware of power plants, and others focused on marketing the power.

The general mechanism for outsourcing trading responsibility is to rent the power plant to a *power marketer*, a company specializing in power trading, through a *tolling agreement*. These agreements can run for any length of time (often 20 or 30 years) and divide the job of running a power plant between the two parties. The owner gets paid a fee to maintain the power plant while the power marketer makes all of the economic decisions. The power marketer is responsible for supplying fuel to the plant and selling the resulting electricity into a competitive market. The power marketer takes on all of the economic risks and earns all the profits above the fixed maintenance fee.

Renting a power plant gives the power marketer the ability to convert fuel into electricity. In a financial sense, this is alchemy—a power plant provides the ability to turn a low-cost commodity into a more valuable commodity. Best of all, the conversion doesn't have to be made if it is not profitable. For example, if the spread between electricity prices and fuel prices is unprofitable, the power marketer can turn off the power plant.

This ability to not operate is very similar to the behavior of financial options. The owner of a financial option has a choice of taking an action or doing nothing. As a result, tolling agreements are commonly modeled as a series of financial options. Based on this concept, one way to value a tolling agreement is equal to the cost of replicating a power plant's physical capabilities with financial option contracts. Approximating real behavior with a financial option model for the purposes of valuation is called a *real options* approach to modeling.

Converting Fuel to Electricity

Physically, power plants operate by burning fuel to produce electricity. Some power plants are more efficient at producing electricity than others—they burn less fuel to produce the same amount of electricity. The conversion efficiency of this process is called the plant's *heat rate*. The higher a plant's heat rate, the more electricity it produces for the same amount of fuel (Figure 4.3.1).

$$\textit{Profit per Unit} = \underbrace{\textit{Price}_{\textit{Electricity}}}_{\text{Sales Price}} - \underbrace{\textit{HeatRate} * \textit{Price}_{\textit{Fuel}}}_{\text{Cost of Goods Sold}}$$

Figure 4.3.1 Profit per unit

Calculating the profit from this conversion is a standard net profit calculation—a power plant's profit is the sale price of its product minus its cost of materials and operating costs. In most cases, since fuel costs are much larger than other operating costs, the operating costs are ignored and the net profit of a power plant is approximated only by the conversion efficiency of the power plant. For a single unit of output, this estimate of net profit is called a *spark spread*.

The net-profit formula for using a spark spread approximation is shown in Figure 4.3.2. This is a fairly standard net-profit formula—the number of units can be multiplied by the per-unit profit to calculate the total profit. The terminology in this formula will be used throughout the remainder of this discussion.

Since spark spreads can be negative, the ability of the power plant to turn off means that its profit needs to be approximated by a *spark spread option* rather than a *spark spread.* A *spark spread option* is a spark spread whose owner has the option of taking a zero profit. Taking zero profit is similar to a power plant shutting down. When spark spreads are positive, the power plant's total profit is its per-unit profit (the spark spread) multiplied by the total units of electricity that the power plant can produce. When the spark spread is negative, the power plant has zero profit.

Using Standard Terminology	
$Profit = (Number\ of\ Units)\ (Profit\ per\ Unit)$	
Using Energy Terminology	
$Profit = Dispatch(Price_{Electricity} - HeatRate * Price_{Fuel})$	
Dispatch	The dispatch level is the amount of generation capacity currently online. For example, a power plant might be able to produce 100 MW of power an hour operating at full capacity. The typical units are megawatts per hour (*MW/h*).
$Price_{Electricity}$	The price of electricity. This is usually in units of dollars per megawatt hour $(\frac{Dollars}{MW/h})$.
Heat Rate	A generator's *heat rate* determines the efficiency at which fuel is converted into power. This is specific to each power plant and can depend on the dispatch level of the plant, seasonal temperatures, and operating history. The units of this factor will be the heat energy of fuel required to produce one unit of electricity – most commonly, either $\frac{Btu}{KWh}$ or $\frac{MMBtu}{MW/h}$.
$Price_{Fuel}$	The price of fuel. Fuel prices are either quoted by volume (barrels or millions of cubic feet) or by heat energy (Btus). Prices are quoted in currency per unit, like $\frac{Dollars}{MMBtu}$.

Figure 4.3.2 Spark spread

As a general rule, any time spark spreads are positive, the owner will take the profit. Any time spark spreads are unprofitable, the owner will try to opt for zero payment by shutting down the power plant. Occasionally real life will interfere. For example, the owner might not be able to shut off the power plant for regulatory reasons. Alternately, the power plant operator might not want to let the power plant cool down too much and would consider it worthwhile to operate at a loss for a couple of hours to avoid the costs associated with restarting a couple of hours later.

Breaking Up the Model

Because the power marketer isn't going to make just one decision on the power plant, a large number of options are required to approximate the physical behavior of a power plant. Most commonly, a power plant will make operating decisions on an hourly, daily, or monthly basis. Typically a model of a tolling agreement will create an option for each operating decision. Each *leg* of the trade represents a set of decisions occurring around the same point in time. For example, a tolling agreement might be broken up into monthly pieces where a single on/off decision will be made for the month (Figure 4.3.3).

Even though a model of a power plant should be based on how the power plant actually operates, there are differences between estimating future decisions and making decisions for the current day. Detailed information, like hourly prices, is not available for future periods. As a result, there is little advantage to using very small time frames if the prices have to be estimated from longer time periods. Choosing longer periods for estimating decisions can simplify a model. Most models have an optimal point of complexity. At that point, being more complex doesn't make the model more accurate, it only makes it slower to calculate and harder to test.

The primary factor in choosing an appropriate number of legs is the availability of market data and the physical capabilities of the power plant. If the only available prices come from the forward market, which trades monthly contracts, there isn't much benefit in choosing a daily model or hourly model. However, if some type of daily price is available from a simulation, a daily model might be better.

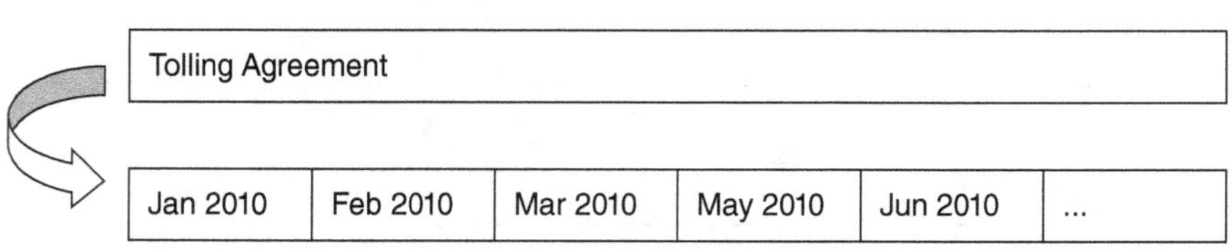

Figure 4.3.3 Breaking a tolling agreement into monthly options

The physical capabilities of the power plant being modeled also have an effect. For example, a gas turbine might benefit from a high-frequency model since it can start and stop quickly. However, a steam turbine, which takes a while to get operating at top efficiency, will want to operate for an extended period. In that case, a modeler might use a longer time frame to model a steam turbine.

Underlying Instruments

The description of a spark spread model might make it seem like there are only two underlying products—power and fuel. However, this is misleading. Each leg of a tolling agreement requires electricity and fuel prices at the right *time* and *location*. Unless storage is easy, energy products are not the same commodity at different points in the year. For example, August electricity is a fundamentally different product than May electricity. It is impossible to buy some electricity in May and hold it until August.

This has a big effect on risk management—any measure that tries to aggregate risk between multiple legs has to account for fundamentally different underlying exposures. Given the extended length of many tolling agreements, there can be several hundred separate commodities being traded over the lifetime of the contract.

Even within a single leg, there is often a need for separate underlying instruments. For example, if a tolling agreement is broken in monthly legs that correspond to the forward markets, it has to be based upon the products traded in that local forward market. Commonly traded contracts in the forward market are for peak power (5×16 power), off-peak power (7×8 power), or weekend power (2×16 power). As a result, it is common for each leg of a tolling agreement to depend on a variety of different instruments (Figure 4.3.4). Combined with the time of year effect, the different daily products can rapidly add up to huge numbers of uncorrelated exposures.

The impact of this on risk management is substantial. Because legs don't share underlying instruments, it is impossible to simply add up the exposures to get a meaningful number. For example, it is wrong to ask: "What's the exposure of this power plant to the price of electricity?" because there is no single price of electricity. It is dangerous to assume that all electricity prices will move together when prices have historically been uncorrelated.

Physical Model of a Power Plant

A physical description of the power plant is also required to build a tolling model. For example, a physical description might be: a natural gas

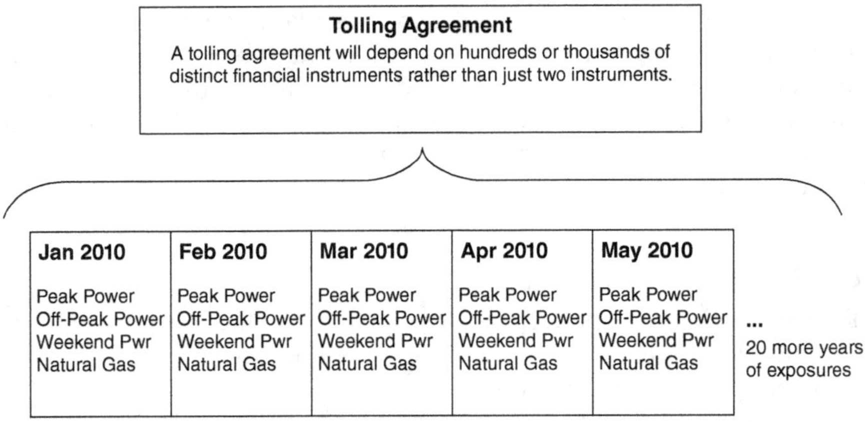

Figure 4.3.4 Multiple exposures per tolling agreement

combined cycle power plant with four turbines: two combined cycle steam turbines, and two gas turbines.

In this power plant, the steam turbines are large and efficient. However, they are expensive to maintain and can't respond quickly to changing power requirements. The power plant also has two peaking generators (the gas turbines). These two gas turbines are much smaller and less efficient than the combined cycle turbines. They are used to provide heat for starting up the combined cycle steam turbines, but otherwise operate as separate units. When operating separately, since they are fairly inefficient, the gas turbines are mostly utilized during periods of peak demand.

As an approximation, the combined cycle turbines have two operating modes—normal dispatch or maximum dispatch. Maximum dispatch mode is less efficient at converting fuel into electricity, but produces more power. The operational parameters of this power plant are summarized in the chart in Figure 4.3.5. This chart shows

Operating Capabilities of the Power Plant

	Output Dispatch Capability (MW/h)	Input Fuel Requirements (MMBtu)	Implied Heat Rate
CC Turbine Max	225	1,800	8
Normal	150	1,125	7.5
CC Turbine Max	225	1,800	8
Normal	150	1,125	7.5
Peaking 1 Max	45	540	12
Peaking 2 Max	45	540	12

Figure 4.3.5 Operating capabilities

the capabilities of each turbine installed in the power plant. Lower heat rates are more efficient and shown in units of MMBtu per MWh.

Both the efficiency of the plant and its total output determine its profitability. The total profitability of a power plant depends on its per-unit profit (the spark spread) and the quantity of electricity that it can produce (the dispatch rate). These two factors need to be balanced against one another. Higher levels of production are less efficient—they require more fuel per megawatt of power. As a result, the per-unit profit decreases as more power is produced.

Optimal Operating Mode

Running a power plant economically requires an optimization. Sometimes it is more profitable to produce a greater amount of electricity. This happens when the decreased profit per megawatt is overcome by the additional sales. At other times, it is more important to be extremely fuel efficient. Lower heat rates indicate a better utilization of fuel per amount of energy produced.

Most power plants are not simply on/off switches. Their value depends upon them being able to operate in the most profitable manner. Power plants typically have a variety of modes in which they can operate. Valuing a tolling agreement requires figuring out the best operating mode for each leg.

To simplify the process of determining the best way to operate the power plant, it is common to combine operating decisions for several turbines into an *operating scenario*. For example, it is possible that all of the units will be off, that only the most efficient units are operating, or that all of the units will be operating (Figure 4.3.6). The assumption behind these scenarios is that the less efficient turbines will never be activated before the efficient ones. The following scenarios were calculated by summing up the capabilities of generators described in the previous chart.

Power Plant Operating Scenarios

Scenario	Dispatch Capability (MW/h)	Input Fuel Requirements (MMBtu)	Implied Heat Rate
All Inactive	0	0	0
Efficient	300	2,250	7.5
CC Max	450	3,600	8
CC Max + Peaking	540	4,680	8.67

Figure 4.3.6 Operating scenarios

Operating Scenarios and Day/Night Power

Coming back to a point made earlier, there is often not a single price for power. There are usually several types of power prices that need to be analyzed in conjunction—for example, daytime and nighttime power. These periods will alternate, and it may not be possible to cycle the generator between periods. The value for each operating scenario will need to account for the profits in both periods.

Sometimes, turbines will need to operate at night if they are going to be active during the day. For example, steam turbines might find it impossible to completely turn off and then restart a short time later. Because of the cost associated with a restart, steam turbines might need to continue operating in a reduced capacity at night.

This creates a problem since prices on nights and weekends are generally much lower than during the day. A power plant might need to take a loss during nighttime hours to be profitable during the day. The value of each scenario needs to group profit and losses together when a single decision determines both values.

The operating scenario chart is expanded in Figure 4.3.7 to account for nighttime hours. It shows the required linkage between the day and night scenarios. For example, in the CC Max scenario, the combined cycle generators operate at maximum capacity during the day, but go to their most efficient operating mode at night to minimize the operating losses. In addition, a new scenario was added, Peaking Only. This new scenario addresses the possibility that especially low nighttime prices make the steam turbines unprofitable to operate at all during the day.

Correlation Between Electricity and Fuel Prices

A second set of problems comes from option pricing considerations. Regardless of which operating scenario is chosen, the value of the power plant will depend on assumptions about the future relationship between electricity and fuel prices. Fuel is being combusted to convert it into

Power Plant Operating Scenarios

Scenario	Dispatch Capability (MW/h)		Fuel Requirements (MMBtu)		Heat Rate	
	Day	Night	Day	Night	Day	Night
All Inactive	0	0	0	0	0.00	0.00
Efficient	300	300	2,250	2,250	7.50	7.50
CC Max	450	300	3,600	2,250	8.00	7.50
CC Max + Peaking	540	300	4,680	2,250	8.67	7.50
Peaking Only	90	300	1,080	0	12.00	0.00

Figure 4.3.7 Additional operating scenarios

electricity. Wide spreads are good—cheaper fuel and more expensive electricity means higher profits. However, the future of this relationship isn't known at the time of valuation and requires a number of assumptions to be made. For example, because no one is very good at predicting future prices, most models are going to assume each asset follows a *random walk*. However, because power prices are affected by fuel prices, this means that the spark spread is going to depend on the combined behavior of two random (but correlated) walks.

Since the power plant can be turned off to limit exposure, extreme moves in the spread are a good thing. Either the power plant makes a windfall profit or it gets turned off. From a profit perspective, high volatility in the electricity/fuel relationship is good. To a large extent, the value of a tolling agreement depends on the expected correlation between power and fuel prices. Highly correlated power and fuel prices mean less volatility and lower profits. Small changes to the correlation between these prices can have a major impact on the value of a tolling agreement.

Valuation and Volatility

Some of the value of a tolling agreement is known immediately. At a minimum, it is worth its *intrinsic value*—its value if all of the operating decisions were made immediately. This can be done by arranging firm agreements to buy fuel and sell electricity through the forward market. However, there is a second component to an option's value. Uncertainty benefits the owner of an option. The downside risk of owning an option is capped. In the case of a power plant, the power plant can be turned off. A 50/50 chance of making extra money is a great investment when losing doesn't involve spending more money.

The *valuation date* of an option is the day that its value is calculated. The *expiration date* of the option is the day that the power plant actually converts fuel into electricity. Up until the expiration date, it is possible to change the operating decisions for the power plant. After that date, it is no longer possible to change the decision. *Exercising the option* means making a permanent decision on how to operate the power plant. Usually, it is preferable to delay making a final decision on how to operate the power plant for as long as possible.

The payoff of a spark spread option is based on the spread between power and gas prices. Today's prediction of those prices is the *forward spread*. The spread at the time of expiration probably won't be identical to the spread that is being predicted today. However, it is likely to be distributed around the forward spread (Figure 4.3.8). Mathematically,

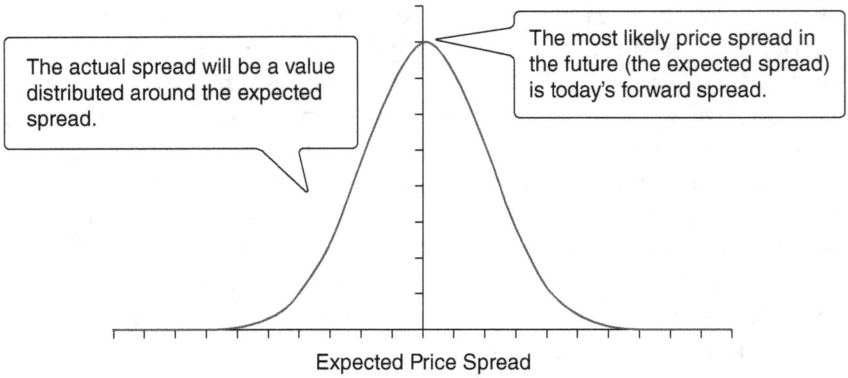

Figure 4.3.8 Expected price spread

the likely range of spreads is described by a statistical distribution centered on the forward spread.

Some of the possible spreads will be at points where it is profitable to produce electricity. Other spreads will be at points where it is unprofitable to operate the power plant. The efficiency of the power plant (its heat rate) determines which spreads are profitable and which spreads are unprofitable (Figure 4.3.9).

At expiration, the profit per megawatt is calculated by taking the average price of the profitable future spreads. Multiplying the number of megawatts (the dispatch rate) by the average profitable price calculates the expected profit from that scenario.

The width of the distribution is a key factor in determining the profit per megawatt. A spread option is more valuable when the range of possible spreads at expiration is high. The chance for an extremely positive payoff outweighs an increased chance of losing money.

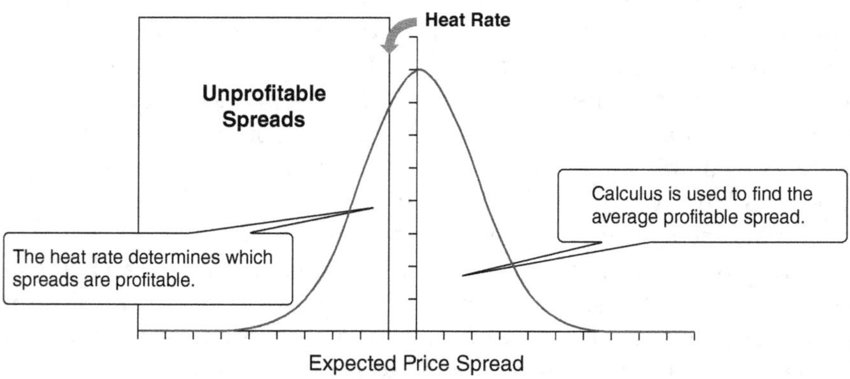

Figure 4.3.9 Heat rate spreads

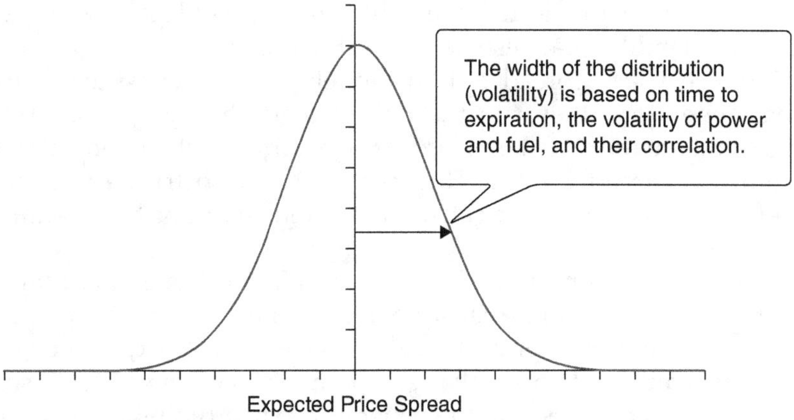

Figure 4.3.10 Volatility and correlation affect width of spread

This is due to the asymmetric nature of the payoffs—any loss is worth no worse than zero, but beneficial results are uncapped.

The width of the distribution depends on the time between valuation and expiration and the correlation between power and gas prices (Figure 4.3.10). If the prices of power and natural gas are highly correlated, the spread at expiration will be very close to the center of the bell curve. For example, if the prices are perfectly correlated, there won't be a bell curve at all because the relationship between prices will never change. Less correlated assets will have a wider distribution of possible spreads.

All options are highly affected by changes in volatility. In the case of spread options, the volatility of the spread depends on the correlation between power and gas prices. As a result, the value of a tolling agreement is incredibly sensitive to the predicted correlation between fuel and power prices. Even very small changes in this correlation can have a huge impact on the value of the power plant.

Dangers to Using Options

There are dangers to using options to approximate physical behavior—a spread option model can ignore important physical aspects of generation like the time it takes to turn on (*ramp up* or *cycle*) and variable operating costs. For example, a generator might take longer and use more fuel to start operating in the winter than during the summer. Options also assume power plant decisions can be made instantaneously. No matter how quickly a power plant can be cycled, it is going to be slower than instantaneous decisions implied by a *spark spread model*. Other real-life issues—like the effect of local laws regarding grid reliability—can also be difficult to quantify.

Because spark spread option models are less constrained than actual generators, they run the risk of overestimating profitability. This overestimation can be as high as 20 to 30 percent if overoptimistic assumptions aren't caught. These errors can also trickle into other systems, like value-at-risk calculations, and may not be recognized for years.

Another criticism of spark spread option models is that they are "reactive." They assume that a generator simply turns on or off in response to the current price. In reality, the optimal schedule for a generator must anticipate price changes, perhaps incurring a loss in some periods in order to position the generator to capture higher expected profits later on. Again, there is no one single rule for handling this issue. The relative importance of this problem is different for each generator and how the operating scenarios are selected.

4.4

WHEELING POWER

30-Second Summary

Purpose

Wheeling is a general term meaning the long-distance transmission of electricity, i.e., transporting electricity *as if it were on wheels*. Differences in regional prices provide the economic motivation for these trades. Wheeling trades are a good example of how a deregulated market can cost-effectively allocate energy resources.

Summary

Wheeling is the act of transporting power from one location to another. Usually wheeling occurs over power lines owned by a third party. Because adjoining regions often set their power prices differently, transmission trades are often very profitable. The driving force behind different prices might be different marginal fuels, weather patterns, or consumption in the two regions.

Wheeling trades must be made in the physical market. When a power line connects two regions, the owner of the power line can buy electricity at one end of a power line and transport it to the other end. At least one part of the trade, buying low-cost power and transferring it for delivery in another area, has to be made in the physical spot market. This makes wheeling trades different from pure financial transactions. With financial contracts, it is impossible to use a financial contract from one market to meet an obligation in another.

One way to think of a wheeling trade is as an option. After paying an up-front rental cost, the trader has the option of transporting power from one region to another. The trade will be a good investment if the (uncertain) profits from the power line are more valuable than its construction or rental cost. Financially the rental agreement will be modeled as a series of spread options—one option every time the trader could make the decision to transfer power. To determine if the trade makes sense economically, the value of these options can then be compared to the cost of renting a power line.

Key Topics

- The motivation behind wheeling trades is that adjoining power markets often have different prices caused by differences in marginal fuels, weather patterns, or consumer demands.
- The cost to rent a power line is usually proportional to the cost of building and maintaining the power line rather than its economic value.

Wheeling is the act of physically transporting electricity from one location to another. Wheeling trades require a physical transfer of electricity over power lines rented from a third party. Because of the way the electricity markets set their prices, adjoining markets can have very different prices of electricity. This is particularly true if the generation stacks of the two areas are different. Most regions set power prices based on the cost of operating their most recently activated generator. There can be a big price difference between regions when one region has most recently activated a natural-gas-fired generator and the other a coal-fired generator.

The purpose of *wheeling* is to get low-cost power into high price areas. There is a trade-off between the long-distance transportation of power and local generation. A substantial amount of power can be lost in transmission. Additionally, widespread power grids have many more points of failure than compact power grids. However, sometimes long-distance transportation is necessary. Many types of power generators have restrictions on where they can be located. For example, a natural gas cogeneration plant needs to be located adjacent to a large user of the steam. Nuclear power plants are often located far away from the communities they serve. Hydroelectric plants need to be located on a river at a dam. As a result, certain electrical generation choices necessitate the long-distance transmission of power.

A chart of average prices demonstrates the variability of electrical prices around the United States (Figure 4.4.1). Compared to low-priced regions, high-priced regions pay twice as much for their power *on the average*. During peak demand periods, the disparity may be even greater.

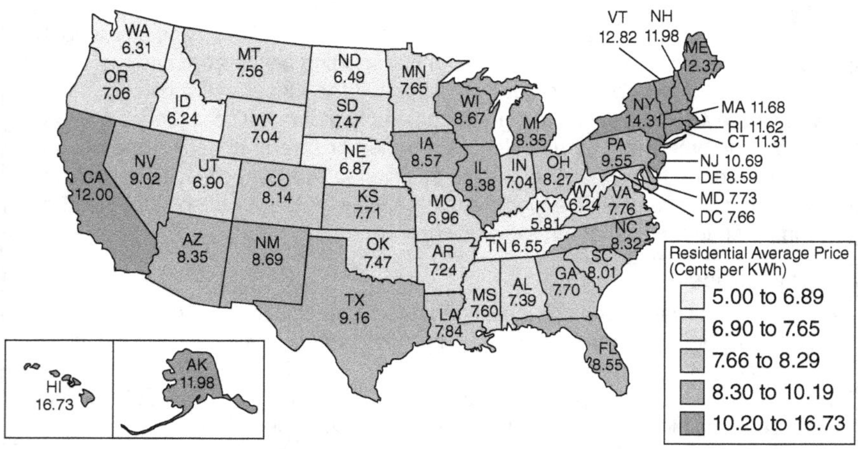

Figure 4.4.1 Average residential power prices (*Source:* U.S. Energy Information Administration)

In a deregulated power market, trading helps determine when it is economically worthwhile to build transmission lines. These lines connect areas of low-cost generation to high-priced consuming regions. Private investments—wheeling trades—pay for the construction of power lines, and those investors make profits from their investment. Eventually, as enough transmission capacity between the low-cost areas and high-priced areas is built, prices will converge. In this way, free market trading determines the right level of investment.

Examples of Wheeling Trades

- A power company builds a transmission line to connect the upper Midwest (where coal is the marginal fuel) to the southern United States (where natural gas is the marginal fuel). To a large extent, this trade is a bet on natural gas prices being much more volatile than coal prices.
- A power company examines a wheeling trade to import hydroelectric power from the Niagara Falls region into the New York City metro area. Since there is limited transmission capability between these two regions, this would involve bidding on a scarce resource.
- A cost analysis is done to study whether it is more cost efficient to build a nuclear power plant a long way from a population center or whether it is better to construct smaller natural-gas-fired generators close to population centers.
- A hedge fund invests in a photovoltaic (PV) solar installation in New Mexico and builds a long-distance high voltage DC power line to get the power to the East Coast.

In a physical sense, a wheeling trade involves building a power line to connect two separate areas. Most of the time, the cost of the trade is proportional to the cost of building the power line. Once the power line is constructed, its owner has the option of transporting some amount of power (the amount that the power line can physically handle) between the two regions. Since power lines are not free to build, there is a strong economic incentive for investors to build power lines that will have the biggest economic impact at the lowest cost.

For valuation purposes, wheeling trades can be modeled as financial options. After paying an up-front cost to rent the line, a trader has the option of transporting power over that line. The actual benefit is unknown at the time power line is rented. The up-front cost is similar to an option *premium*. The variable costs associated with transportation (line losses and any variable expenses) are similar to a *strike price*. The potential profit depends on the price difference between the two regions.

When the profit is greater than the transmission costs, it is profitable to transmit power over the transmission line.

From a trading perspective, wheeling deals are interesting because they allow traders to buy an option for the physical construction cost of a power line rather than on the financial value of the option. This is a key aspect of trading physical products. Option premiums can be extremely expensive. If the construction costs are affordable, physical investments provide an alternate way to get the same financial exposures at a much lower cost.

In most cases, the cost to rent a transmission line is proportional to the cost of building and maintaining the power line. If there is only one power line operator in a region, the rental price will probably be subject to government regulations for nondiscriminatory pricing. The logic is that if a lot of people want to rent power lines, there shouldn't be a competitive auction over a limited resource. Instead, the power line operator should be forced to build more power lines and charge back that cost to the investor groups.

Modeling Electrical Flows

Within a power grid, wheeling is closely associated with the problems of line congestion and predicting how power will flow across the grid. Electricity flows across the path of least electrical resistance. That resistance changes throughout the day depending on how much power each part of the power grid is consuming. Since each transmission line can only carry a limited amount of power, ensuring that the grid can handle imported power is a complicated job.

For example, in a power grid with three points (A, B, and C) it might be necessary to move imported power from location A to meet consumer demand at location B. It would be best if that power moves directly between those two points. However, if the line AB has a lot of load on it, power can also flow from A to C, and then from C to B. The power grid operator cannot control the exact path that the electricity follows. It also needs to make sure that too much power isn't transferred over any one line and causes a meltdown. As a result, the power grid operator needs to ensure there is sufficient transmission capacity available on every power line that might potentially handle the imported load. If that transmission capacity isn't available, power might not be able to reach point B. That means that the power grid would need to activate a fast-starting peaking generator close to point B to meet the shortfall.

One of the primary motivations for wheeling trades is to get low-cost power into high-demand areas. Usually, imported power displaces generation capacity that was already serving the high-demand area.

Importing power means decommissioning a local generation unit. However, if the low-cost imported power can't reach the necessary location, it isn't possible to restart a decommissioned power plant on short notice. The region will have to rely on an even more expensive high-cost peaking unit. A couple of days of using peaking units can eliminate any positive economic benefit from using imported power.

Long-Distance AC Transmission

The most common way of transmitting power across long distances is to use overhead high voltage, alternating current electrical lines. When power is transmitted across a power line, some of the power gets converted into heat. The amount of energy lost to heat is proportional to the square of the current. The primary way to reduce transmission losses is to decrease the current on a power line. The primary way to decrease the current is to increase the voltage.

Voltage and current combine to determine how much power a transmission line carries. Transformers can be used to modify the current and voltage of AC power lines, converting high current power into high voltage power. Transformers only work on AC power lines, which is why AC transmission is more common than DC transmission.

Transformers use magnetic induction to alter the current and voltage on a line while keeping the total power constant. The scientific principle behind a transformer is that magnetic fields create electrical currents and vice versa. It is possible to use an electrical current to create a magnetic field, and then use that magnetic field to create another electrical current at a different voltage. Transformers are typically composed of two coils of conductive wire wrapped around a shared core. Starting and stopping the current on one wire will induce a current on the other coil.

Transformers

An *iron core transformer* is a simple type of transformer. It consists of an iron frame connected to two electrical wires. The core of the transformer provides a path for magnetic flux. The *primary winding* is the electrical wire connected to an AC power source. The *secondary winding* is the wire connected to the electrical load. The primary winding creates a magnetic flux that induces an electrical current on the secondary winding. The relative voltage on each side of the transformer depends on how many times the wire on that side is wrapped around the core of the transformer (Figure 4.4.2).

(*Continued*)

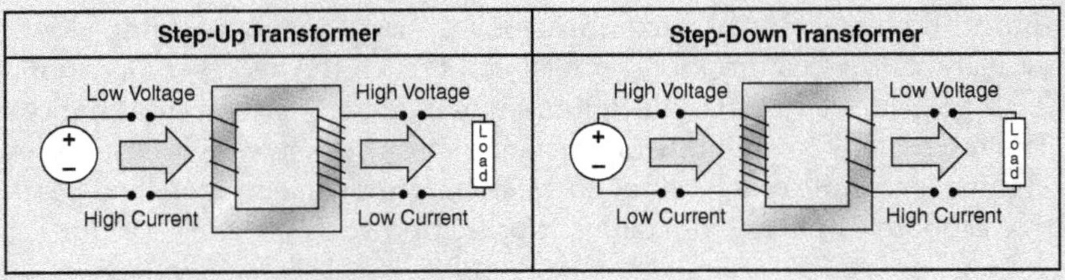

Figure 4.4.2 Electrical transformers

Long-Distance DC Transmission

An alternative to AC power transmission is high voltage direct current (HVDC) power lines. HVDC power lines have been used successfully around the world to transfer power over extremely long distances. Typically, these power lines are lower cost than AC power lines and lose less power in the transmission process. These lines are also commonly used to transfer power between unsynchronized AC power grids or through long distances underwater.

On the downside, DC power has to be converted into AC power at the endpoint. No one uses high voltage DC power in a residential setting. It is extremely dangerous, and the voltage can't be stepped up or down using a transformer. A normal DC to AC conversion can result in a 5 to 10 percent loss in power. These conversion losses have to be weighed against reduced transmission losses. As a result, HVDC is usually only used for extremely long-distance transmission where AC transmission losses are much larger than conversion losses.

Another disadvantage of a DC transmission is that multiple endpoints are problematic. Whenever any energy is removed from a DC transmission line, the voltage on the entire line will drop. Because DC voltage can't be increased by transformers, a DC power line with more than one endpoint won't have a constant voltage across the line. As a result, it can be very difficult to build an interconnected grid of HVDC power lines. Because of this, HVDC power lines are primarily long-distance, point-to-point connections.

For example, if HVDC power lines are built to connect a major solar installation in the Desert Southwest to two points on the East Coast of the United States, as in Figure 4.4.3, it would be very difficult to reroute any of that power from one point to another. If the rerouting were to be done on the East Coast, it would be necessary to convert the DC power to AC power and transmit it using the AC transmission grid. It would only be possible to reroute the DC power from the point of origin in the Desert Southwest. However, building direct

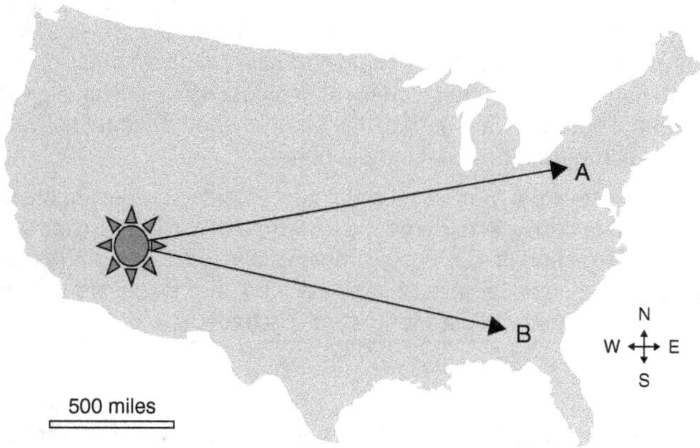

Figure 4.4.3 Point-to-point HVDC transmission

transmission lines to connect every generation station to every user is an operational nightmare. If there were thousands of generation locations, it would be impossible to control the power grid from any centralized location.

Trading Example—Wheeling Trade

A power company examines a wheeling trade to transfer power from the upper Midwest (where coal is the marginal fuel) to the southern United States (where natural gas is the marginal fuel). To a large extent, this trade is a bet on natural gas prices being much more volatile than coal prices.

1. **The Opportunity.** Low-ash, low-sulfur coal from Wyoming provides the midwestern United States with an abundant supply of low-cost fuel for electricity generation. The marginal fuel for the area is coal, and power prices do not see large fluctuations. In the southern United States, most power plants burn natural gas. The price of natural gas is much more volatile than coal. As a result, a transmission line between the Midwest and southern United States is a way to benefit from the different volatilities.
2. **The Intuition.** Renting a transmission line is like buying an option on natural gas. It will benefit from high volatility. Even if the average cost of power is the same in both regions, the natural-gas-fired areas will see much greater swings in prices and there will be periods where it is profitable to export electricity from the Midwest to the Gulf Coast.
3. **The Strategy.** A large number of trades will need to be made in the spot market to take advantage of the higher volatility. Seasonal trades are possible in the futures market. For example, hot summer weather begins earlier and lasts longer in the southern United States. It is possible to import power from the Midwest during periods when the Midwest is cool and the southern United States is experiencing hot weather.

(Continued)

4. **The Risks.** Renting a power line is a lot like buying an option—the biggest risk is in overpaying for the right to transmit power. Since this transmission line is long volatility, it may be possible to sell natural gas options or lock in seasonal trades using futures. There will be a substantial amount of operational risk due to the necessity of scheduling physical transactions.
5. **Executing the Trade.** A long-term rental agreement is a direct contract between two parties. Additionally, every time the power needs to be transferred, it will be necessary to schedule deliveries, transmission, and sale of the power. This requires a trading desk capable of handling all of the necessary paperwork. There is a high degree of operation risk in this trade.

Spread Trades Compared to Wheeling Trades

The key to a wheeling trade is the ability to transmit power between two regions. If electrical transmission isn't available, it is impossible to buy power in one market and resell it in another. Instead, all purchases must be sold back into the same market where the power was originally purchased.

Location spread trades are a financial speculation on the relative prices between two areas without having transmission available. These trades are a financial version of a wheeling trade. However, spread trades don't involve the physical transportation of power. As a result, they don't benefit from the ability to build a transmission line to obtain an option-like exposure at the cost of constructing a power line. Traders will often examine both physical and financial trades to identify the lowest cost transaction.

In many ways, location spread trades are much easier than wheeling trades. With a location spread, it is not necessary to arrange for physical purchases or sales of power. Everything can be done financially and settled in cash. Of course, the primary benefit of the wheeling trade is lost too. With a wheeling trade it is possible to buy power in one location and deliver that power to a different location.

Spread Trades Versus Wheeling Trades

A price spread is the difference in price between two regions. For example, if the price in New York is $100 and the price in California is $120, the New York/California price spread is –$20. Spreads are a way of combining two prices into a single number. Wheeling is an actual transfer of power from one region to another.

Location spread trades are financial trades made in the futures or forward market. They can be done financially with no physical trading capability. The trader takes a long position in one region and a short position in another. Typically, the trades are liquidated before physical delivery is required. Because transmission isn't available, it is impossible to take power from one area and use it to settle an obligation in another area. These trades make money when the actual relationship between two areas turns out to be different than the relationship that the market expected at the time of the initial trade.

Wheeling trades involve the physical transmission of power between two regions. These trades require money up front to rent a power line. The trades also require the trader to make physical trades. The benefit of a wheeling trade is that power purchased in one area can be delivered to meet an obligation in another area.

Trading Example—Location Spread Trade

The market is expecting that the snow will melt at its normal time in early April. A trader thinks that this consensus is wrong and that the snow will melt early this year.

1. **The Opportunity.** U.S. government meteorologists predict that warm water temperatures in the Pacific will bring an early warm front to the Pacific Northwest leading to an early thaw.
2. **The Intuition.** Normally, power prices in the Pacific Northwest reach their low in April when snow in the nearby Cascade mountain range melts. During that time, the rivers in the region swell to capacity and the local dams need to open fully to avoid major flooding. This causes the hydro plants to run at full capacity 24 hours a day regardless of consumer demand. The hydroelectric plants can't be turned off nor their power generation reduced because this would flood nearby communities.
3. **The Strategy.** The trader decides to make this trade as a locational spread between California (NP-15) and Pacific NW prices (MID-C) for March. He wants to benefit from higher California prices (long NP-15 price) and lower MID-C prices (short MID-C) than are expected by the market.
4. **The Risks.** A major risk in the position is that natural gas prices will decline. Natural gas is the marginal fuel for the California generation stack. As a result, the price of power in the California market is determined by natural gas prices. If those prices drop, the price of electricity in California will also drop. Another risk is the assumption that a spread trade is appropriate here. An early warm front and cheap power from the Columbia River is more likely to cause a decline in California power prices than an increase. The long position in California power doesn't make sense. An outright position in MID-C power might be less risky than this locational spread.
5. **Executing the Trade.** The trader would enter the trade using March futures (buying NP-15 peak power contracts and selling MID-C peak power contracts). When he wanted to get out of the position, he would have to make the opposite trades. Unlike a wheeling deal, these power trades can't be settled by transmission—it is necessary to close out the position by trading.
6. **The Results.** If the futures prices have changed by the time the trade is liquidated, the trader will make money. However, he can't hold on to the position until the physical delivery date. This trade has to be liquidated prior to the expiration of the futures contracts.

4.5

Solar Power

30-Second Summary

Purpose

The chapter introduces solar power. The amount of power that is generated by a solar installation depends on the amount of available sunlight. A solar panel will produce more power on a sunny day than on a cloudy day. From an investment perspective, solar power is more expensive than fossil-fuel-based electrical generation. As a result, investments in solar technology are heavily influenced by government programs to encourage renewable energy.

Summary

Photovoltaic (PV) power converts solar power into electricity. PV power is produced by solar panels exposed to sunlight. The type of equipment and the intensity of the sunlight directly affect the amount of power that is produced by a solar panel. Correctly estimating the amount of power that will be produced by a solar installation is critical to its successful adoption. If estimates are too conservative, solar power will be deemed uneconomical and bypassed for other technologies. If estimates are too high, there will be a power shortfall and the economic goals of an installation won't be met.

Thermal solar power uses sunlight to produce heat. In many cases, this heat can be used to produce electricity by powering steam turbines or to replace electricity that would have been used to produce heat. There are many types of thermal solar installations. They can be anything from small-scale systems to heat outdoor pools to electrical generation facilities. A big advantage of solar power is that heat is relatively easy to store, and this allows these facilities to operate around the clock. Although they can only store heat during the day, they can use the stored heat any time.

Solar radiation varies throughout the year—it is affected by weather, the changing location of the sun, and the amount of daylight. The angle of the solar panel, its efficiency of handling direct and diffuse light, and surrounding environment all affect how much power is collected. To analyze solar installations, historical averages of solar radiation are used. These averages are collected by regional or national governments, and provided for the purpose of estimating solar installations.

(Continued)

Key Topics

- Solar power depends on sunlight. More sunlight equals more power.
- Most commonly, when people talk about solar power, they are discussing PV power. This type of solar power uses solar panels to turn sunlight directly into electricity.
- Another type of solar power is *thermal solar* power. This type of solar power stores the heat of the sun to do useful work. Heating, air conditioning, and electrical generation can all be driven by thermal solar installations.

Solar power utilizes energy from the sun to produce electricity or heat. Electricity is most commonly produced by exposing large sheets of specialized semiconductors known as "solar panels" to sunlight. In other cases, mirrors are used to concentrate the heat from a large area onto a single point. This allows the concentrated heat to be used for a variety of purposes like creating steam to drive generators and powering air conditioners.

Solar panels produce electricity directly. Sunlight causes electrons to flow out of the semiconductor panels and into wires connected to a circuit. This creates DC power that can be converted into AC power if necessary. When electricity is generated in this way, it is called photovoltaic (PV) power.

Solar power can also be used to generate heat. This heat can be used to heat homes, warm swimming pools, or generate steam to power an electrical turbine. When solar energy is used to create heat, this is called thermal solar power. Both PV solar power and thermal solar power can be used to generate electricity. However, where PV power uses solar cells, thermal solar power will use stored heat to drive a steam turbine.

For any type of solar power generation, the amount of sunlight available in an area has a big effect on the efficiency of a solar collector. Dry climates at high altitude located close to the equator are generally the best areas to locate solar power units. The reason for this is that sunlight has to pass through the Earth's atmosphere. The less atmosphere that light has to pass through, the more energy will be available for use in a solar collector (Figure 4.5.1).

The amount of particulate matter suspended in the air also has a large effect on how much sunlight hits the ground. Water vapor, clouds, and dust particles all reduce the output of solar power installations. The combined effects of direct sunlight and particulate matter make certain areas more favorable for solar power than others. For example, in the United States, the Desert Southwest is favorably situated to get a lot of solar power. The region around the Great Lakes receives

Sun Directly Overhead	Sun at an Angle
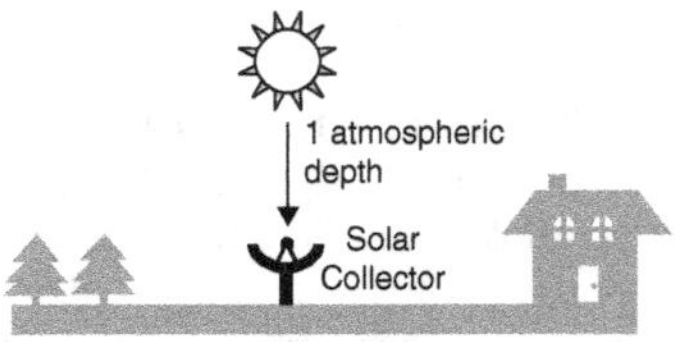	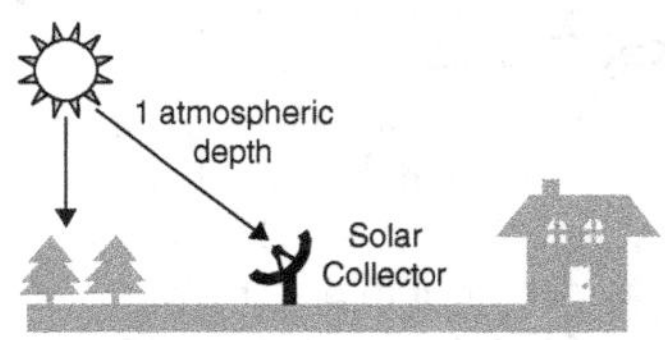
If the sun is straight overhead, it will pass through one atmospheric depth.	When the sun is directly over some other part of the globe, it will have to travel a longer distance. The long side of a right triangle, the hypotenuse, is longer than the length of either side.

Figure 4.5.1 Direction of the sun

much less sunlight. Likewise, in Europe, areas around the Mediterranean Ocean get a lot of sunlight, while Northern Europe receives comparatively little.

Concentrated Solar Power

Finally, it's possible to increase the amount of sunlight that hits a solar panel by collecting it over a large area and focusing it on a specific point. The total effect is a lot like using a magnifying glass on an ant hill during the summer. Sunlight from a wide area is redirected to shine on a very small area. There is trade-off with these systems—sometimes it is better to use a solar collector, in other cases it is easier to use more solar panels. For example, if there is a 10-by-10-foot plot available for a solar collector, it might be better to put in four 5-by-5-foot solar panels and fill the entire space with solar panels. Alternately, it might be better to put in a 10-by-10-foot concentrator and use only a single solar panel.

Particularly with concentrating collectors, but to a lesser extent with all solar installations, it is possible to increase the amount of sunlight hitting a solar collector by facing it toward the sun. In the Northern Hemisphere, this means mounting the unit facing south at a slight upward angle. This can also be improved by placing the solar collector on a motorized base that allows it to track the sun as it moves through the sky. Motorized bases increase the amount of energy that is produced. However, they also increase installation and maintenance costs.

The decision on how to configure a solar installation will depend on the efficiency of the solar panel and the maximum energy that it can absorb. Solar systems are rated by their efficiency at turning sunlight into useful energy. Most solar collectors can only absorb certain wavelengths of light, and much of the light is reflected or absorbed before it can be used. The percentage of the solar energy converted into useful energy is called the conversion efficiency of the solar unit. Conversion efficiency is a measure of energy produced to energy absorbed. Both the availability of solar energy and conversion efficiency of the unit contribute to the output of the unit.

How Solar Concentration Works

It is possible to concentrate sunlight on a specific point. The key to focusing energy is being able to change the direction of the sunlight without changing anything else. By sending a lot of sunlight at a very small area, a very high concentration of energy can be obtained. One common method of concentrating power is to use a parabolic mirror (Figure 4.5.2). This mirror takes sunlight spread out of a large area and reflects it to a precisely calibrated spot.

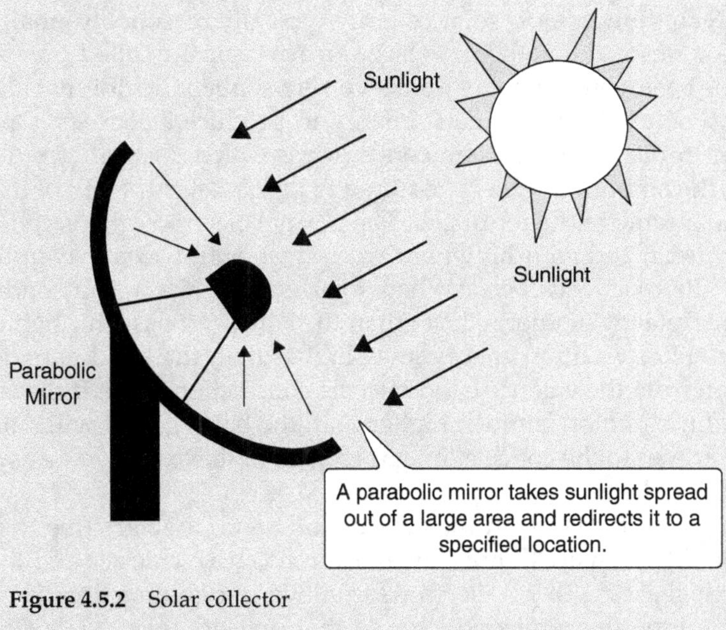

Figure 4.5.2 Solar collector

Sometimes it is a good idea to concentrate power, and sometimes it is not. First of all, a large mirror takes up a lot of space. It also has to be highly calibrated. If the sun changes its location, the focal point of the mirror will change unless the mirror changes its facing too. Moving the mirror requires adding a motor and moving parts to a solar array. That will mean higher maintenance costs. Also, mirrors are fairly vulnerable to damage. If a mirror gets scratched, or covered with dust, its efficiency will drop dramatically.

(Continued)

From an economic perspective, the relative cost of more solar panels has to be compared to the cost of adding mirrors and electric motors to a smaller solar panel. There usually isn't a space savings with a collector, it mostly allows the collection apparatus to be more compact and operate at higher energy or temperature.

Photovoltaic Power

When solar power is discussed, most commonly it refers to PV power. This type of power is named because of the effect that sunlight has on certain semiconductors. Shining electromagnetic energy like sunlight over a semiconductor will knock some of the electrons away from their nuclei. This effect, called the *PV effect*, creates an electromagnetic field around the semiconductor. That field can then be converted into electrical current by connecting the two sides of the semiconductor to a circuit. Even though most solar cells are typically reasonably small, they can be connected together into large arrays typically called *solar panels*.

The basic component of a solar cell is a semiconductor that absorbs some type of electromagnetic energy to produce electricity. One important property of this semiconductor is called its *band gap*. A band gap is the amount of energy required to kick an electron out of its orbit around a semiconductor nuclei. The normal electron orbit is called the *valence band*, and an orbit where an electron is free to move around is called the *conduction band*. When solar energy hits a semiconductor, photons at a lower energy level than the band gap pass through unabsorbed. Photons at an energy level higher than the band gap kick an electron from the valence band into the conduction band. If the energy level of the photon is much higher than the band gap, it will still kick an electron into the conduction gap, but all of the excess energy will be turned into heat.

Once electrons are in the conduction band, they are free to move around. Electrons will move away from negative charges and toward positive charges. To get electrons to move in one direction, it is possible to dope the semiconductor so that one side of it has a positive charge and the other side has a negative charge. A *p-type* semiconductor is doped with atoms that are missing electrons to give it a positive charge. An *n-type* semiconductor is doped with atoms that contain excess electrons. A wafer made by sandwiching an n-type and p-type semiconductor will move electrons in a consistent direction. As solar energy hits the n-type semiconductor, an electron is kicked into the conduction band. Once in the conduction band, the electron will move away from the negatively charged side of the semiconductor and move

A Simple Solar cell

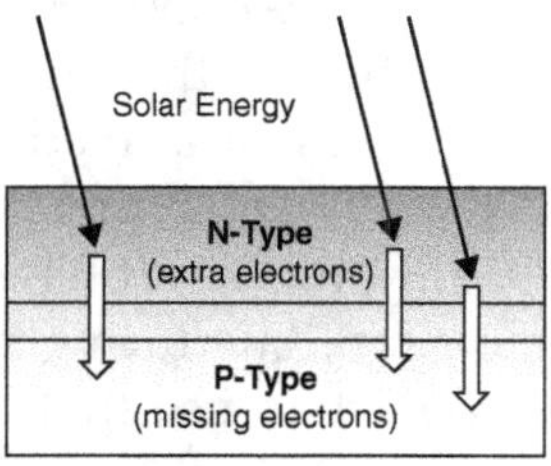

Solar cells operate by allowing sunlight to knock electrons into a conduction band. If the material is doped so that there are positive and negative sides, the electrons will be repelled from the negatively charged area and attracted to the positive side. This creates a current that can be used to power electrical devices. Eventually all of the electrons will be used up, but that can be fixed by connecting the solar cell into a circuit.

Figure 4.5.3 A simple solar cell

toward the positively charged side. This effect creates an electrical current between the n-type and p-type sides (Figure 4.5.3).

The efficiency of a simple solar cell isn't particularly high because a lot of solar energy is wasted. One way to reduce the amount of wasted energy is to have several layers of semiconductors. The first layer might be a material with a very high band gap, the next one with a lower band gap, and then the final material the lowest band gap. In this way, less energy is lost to heat, and more energy will be turned into electricity.

Solar Panel System Size

Solar panel sizes can be described in either alternating current (AC) or DC voltages. Solar panels produce DC power in response to sunlight. To be placed onto a power grid, this must be converted into AC power using another piece of equipment called an *inverter*. There is a maximum amount of power that can be converted into AC power. Using a larger inverter increases the system's output, but increases the cost of the solar installation. Typical losses from all sources, including DC to AC conversion and other system losses, will generally cause about a 25 percent loss in power. For example, if a unit produces 1 kilowatt (KW) of DC power then only about 0.75 KW of AC power will reach the power grid.

Thermal Solar Power

The other way to produce solar energy is to create heat. When sunlight hits almost anything, some of that energy will be absorbed by the object and turned into heat. By concentrating that heat, it is possible to achieve very high temperatures. The heat from thermal solar power is usually used to heat up water or another liquid that is stored in an insulated container until it is ready to be used.

For example, a high-temperature solar facility might use solar power to raise salt to a temperature of approximately 500°F. At that point, salt melts and turns into a liquid. As a liquid, the salt can be transferred into a heavily insulated container until it is ready to be used. This provides a big advantage over PV power—although heat can only be produced at certain times of the day, it doesn't have to be used right away. A thermal solar plant can use sunlight during the day to build up a store of superheated liquids, and then use that heat to produce electricity at night.

Of course, it might not be worthwhile to produce electricity with that heat. Heat can be used to drive a variety of other activities that may be more valuable than producing electricity. Air conditioning, heating, cooking, sterilization, and dehydration systems can all be built using a heat source. The primary way of producing electricity from heat is through a steam turbine. Steam turbines aren't particularly efficient when they operate at 500°F. They get much more efficient when they operate at higher temperatures. For examples, a steam turbine operating at 500°F might only turn 40 percent of its heat energy into electricity. A steam turbine operating at 1000°F might be 60 percent efficient. As a result, concentrated heat is more valuable—it is better to have a liquid at 1000°F than it is to have twice as much liquid at 500°F.

To get high temperatures, the key components of a thermal solar system are the solar power concentrator and the heat storage unit. These components directly impact the cost and complexity of thermal solar systems. The primary way to achieve high temperatures is to focus the energy from a large area onto a small point. Since the sun moves through the day, unless a thermal solar system can readjust its focus, the location where solar energy is being concentrated will also change. As a result, thermal solar systems commonly rely upon some type of tracking system to keep the energy headed to the right spot.

Solar Production Volume

The amount of solar power produced by a solar farm depends on both the type of solar installation and the location of the installation. Dry, arid climates (like a desert) close to the equator will produce the most power. As the distance from the equator increases, sunlight has to pass through additional layers of atmosphere. This reduces the amount of energy contained in sunlight and decreases solar production. For example, a solar farm located in the Desert Southwest of the United States, like Arizona, would produce more power than a solar farm located in the northeastern United States like New Jersey.

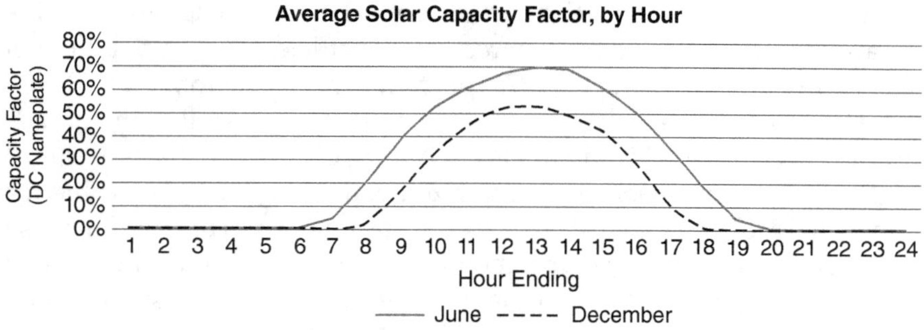

Figure 4.5.4 Average solar capacity factor, by hour

The output of generation units is often described using a *capacity factor*. The capacity factor is the amount of generation placed onto the power grid relative to the stated size of the unit. For example, a 100-KW solar installation will have a 70 percent capacity factor if it puts 70 KW of AC power onto the power grid. For example, a 70 percent capacity factor would be typical of a solar unit whose size is described relative to its DC size at the middle of the day (Figure 4.5.4).

Over the course of a year, a solar generation facility might have an average annual capacity factor between 10 and 20 percent when the unit is described in DC nameplate terms. This will vary by location and technology. However, given system losses and the fact that it is night approximately half the time, anything above a 35 percent capacity factor would be very unusual (Figure 4.5.5).

Technology often has a big impact on generation as well. For example, a fixed-panel solar array will typically have a 13 to 20 percent capacity factor. A solar panel with a fixed tilt that tracks the sun east and west (one-axis tracking) will be 25 to 30 percent more efficient than a fixed panel and typically have a 17 to 25 percent capacity factor.

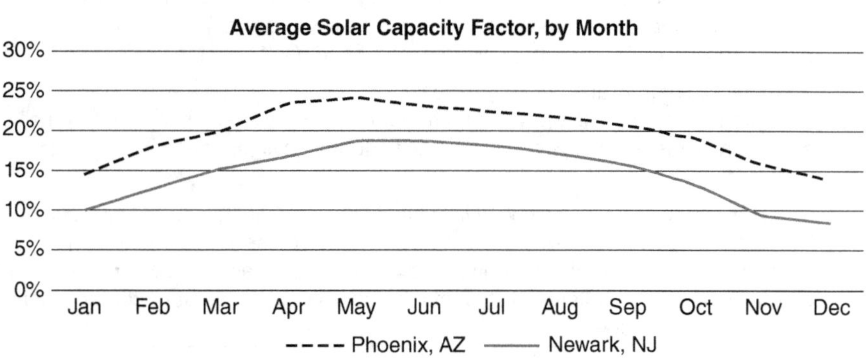

Figure 4.5.5 Average solar capacity factor, by month

A solar panel that tracks the sun on both the east-west axis and tilts up and down will be 30 to 40 percent more efficient than a fixed panel solar array and have an 18 to 27.5 percent capacity factor.

There is a trade-off between the cost of a solar installation and additional production. Fixed panels have very few moving parts and limited maintenance. By adding motorized components, it is possible for panels to track the sun as it moves through the sky. This will increase the effectiveness of the solar panel. However, motorized units will be more expensive to install and maintain relative to fixed installations.

Trading Example—German Solar Power

Although it doesn't receive a lot of sunlight, Germany is a world leader in installed PV solar power units. This is a simplified example of how a government subsidy can spur installation of solar power.

1. **The Opportunity.** As a general rule, solar power is more expensive than fossil-fuel-based power. To encourage consumers to use solar power, the German government adopted a policy of feed-in tariffs that paid homeowners higher than retail prices for any electricity that they fed into the power grid from residentially installed solar systems. This law was made in conjunction with net-metering policies that allowed households to both draw electricity from the power grid and place it back on. At the end of the month, the above-market cost paid for solar power was split evenly between all customers and added as a surcharge to utility bills.
2. **The Intuition.** This is as easy as a trade gets. Consumers who install solar power on their houses get a rebate on their electricity. Everyone else pays a higher cost. In this case, the rebate is significant—the power grid paid approximately triple the retail price of power. If power costs $30 per MW/H, and you can get paid $90 per MW/H placed onto the grid, almost any solar installation is economical.
3. **The Strategy.** When homeowners are getting paid triple for any excess capacity that they put on the grid, it pays them to install as much excess capacity as possible. Until you produce more energy than you use, solar power is only worth the avoided cost of buying electricity from the grid. However, after that point, the value of the electricity triples. The best strategy is to load up each house with as much solar capacity as can fit and conserve as much power as possible. That maximizes the net amount of power that can head back onto the power grid.
4. **The Risks.** There is an economy of scale involved in this trade—the real payoff is placing energy onto the power grid rather than just mitigating home use. Once a homeowner is a net exporter of electricity during daylight hours, it won't take long for the investment to pay off.
5. **The Results.** Germany, even with its limited sunlight, has the largest installed base of solar power generation in the world. Utility costs went up slightly for anyone who didn't install solar power. However, the increase in power prices was fairly minor, and a large portion of Germany's peak power requirements can be met from solar power.

4.6

Wind Power

30-Second Summary

Purpose

This chapter introduces the major concepts of wind-powered electrical generation.

Summary

The wind is a natural source of renewable energy. It has been used for thousands of years as a pollution-free way to power windmills and sailboats. Since the 1970s, specialized windmills, called *wind turbines*, have been built to harness the wind as a source of electrical power. These windmills are typically grouped into *wind farms* and located in areas exposed to sustained high winds.

Wind is inherently unpredictable. Fast gusts contain far more energy than slow steady breezes. As a result, the wind supplies irregular bursts of power. Occasionally, wind energy will provide a lot of energy. Power grids that plan on using wind-based electrical generation need to develop some way to minimize that unpredictability.

Key Topics

- The biggest issue with wind power is that it is variable. It is extremely difficult to predict when and how much power will be available. Usually gaps in supply have to be met by inefficient fossil fuel plants that are easy to cycle into the generation stack. Commonly these are natural gas turbines or diesel peaking units.
- Other large complaints about wind power are danger to migratory flying animals (birds and bats) and aesthetic concerns (where wind farms blot out the horizon).
- In some cases, electricity storage techniques can be used to time-shift the electricity production to a period of higher consumer demand.
- Maintenance on wind farms is more complicated than most other technologies. It is necessary to send repair teams to remote areas and have them climb tall towers carrying tools.

Wind power has been used for centuries to provide mechanical energy. Both windmills and sailing ships are examples of early uses for wind power. Since the 1970s, specialized windmills, called *wind turbines*, have been built to harness the wind as a source of electrical power. Wind turbines use rotating blades pushed by the wind to drive a generator. These turbines operate much like any other electrical turbine. Rotational energy (provided by the wind) spins an electromagnet to produce electricity. When a large number of wind turbines are located together, they are called a *wind farm*.

Wind

Wind is produced by an uneven heating of the Earth's surface. The equator receives considerably more sunlight than the poles, and sunlight is unevenly absorbed around the globe. Dark colors absorb more energy than light colors. Combined with the day/night cycles on Earth, there is a constant steam of expanding and cooling gas moving around the planet. This is a chaotic process where small changes in initial conditions can lead to substantially different atmospheric conditions later on.

There are three basic measures of whether a site is a good candidate for a wind farm. First, wind has to consistently blow across the area. Second, the wind has to blow at high enough speeds to generate a substantial amount of energy. Third, there has to be enough land available to place a major installation. As a general rule, coastlines and flat plains provide the easiest locations to install wind farms. Mountains or uneven terrain are much less attractive locations because of the limited space to place a wind farm and unpredictable wind conditions.

Governments have studied wind patterns for many years for aviation purposes. In the United States, wind research is often conducted by the National Renewable Energy Laboratory (NREL). This U.S. government agency is the primary source for renewable power data in the United States (Figure 4.6.1). Dark colors indicate areas with a lot of potential wind power, and light areas indicate less potential wind power.

Wind Energy

Wind is an inherently streaky type of energy supply. The amount of energy in wind increases with the cube of the wind speed. When the speed of wind doubles, it will contain eight times the energy as it did before. This means that very windy days will provide a disproportionately large amount of the wind energy available in an area (Figure 4.6.2).

From a trading perspective, the practical implication of this is that it's hard to predict the value of wind energy. The energy is going to be

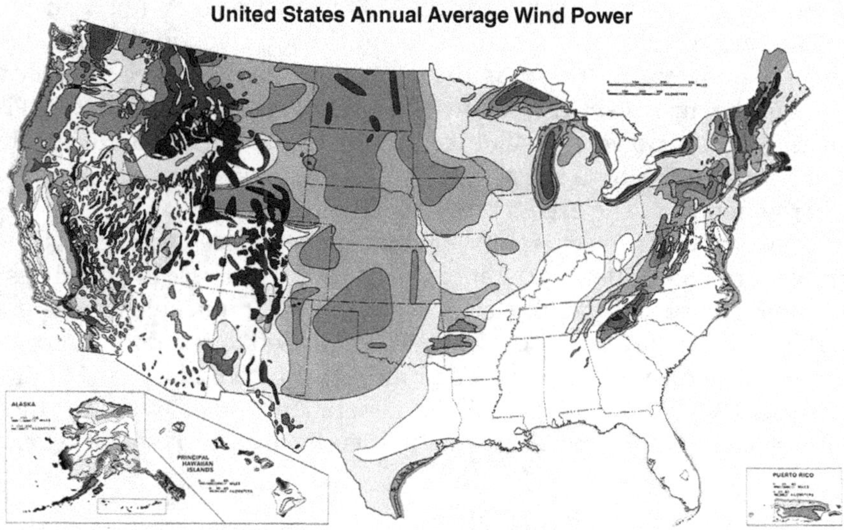

Classes of Wind Power Density

Wind Power Class	10 m (33 ft) Wind Power Density (W/m 2)	10 m (33 ft) Speed (b) m/s (mph)	50 m (164 ft) Wind Power Density (W/m 2)	50 m (164 ft) Speed (b) m/s (mph)
1	100	4.4 (9.8)	200	5.6 (12.5)
2	150	5.1 (11.5)	300	6.4 (14.3)
3	200	5.6 12.5)	400	7.0 15.7)
4	250	6.0 (13.4)	500	7.5 (16.8)
5	300	6.4 (14.3)	600	8.0 (17.9)
6	400	7.0 (15.7)	800	8.8 (19.7)
7	1000	9.4 (21.1)	2000	11.9 (26.6)

Figure 4.6.1 Average annual wind power
(*Source:* U.S. National Renewable Energy Laboratory)

Distribution of Wind Speeds

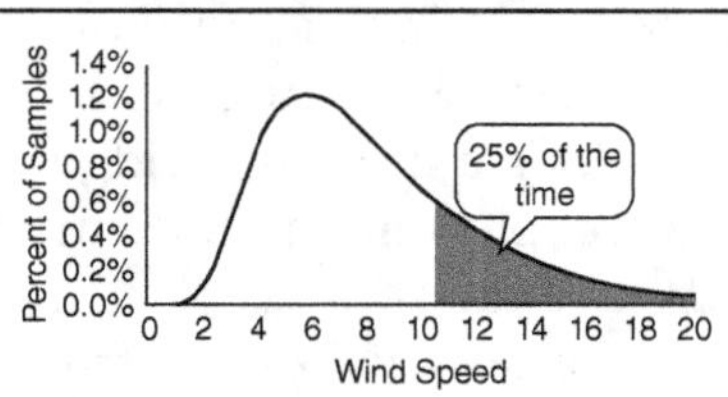

The distribution of wind speeds might be approximated by a lognormal distribution. An example of a lognormal distribution is shown above with the top 25 percent of the distribution shaded.

Percent of Total Energy Production

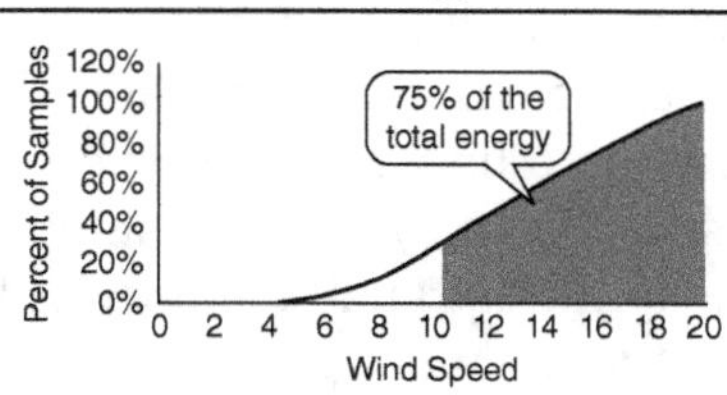

Most wind energy comes from high wind speeds. Since the energy in wind is proportional to the cube of the wind speed, relatively rare high wind gusts will provide a disproportionately large amount of energy. In this example, approximately 75 percent of the total energy produced comes from the samples in the shaded area on the right.

Figure 4.6.2 Wind energy

produced in relatively random spurts that may or may not coincide with a period when people actually want to use power. In addition, because the power production is so intermittent, it will still be necessary to fill in the missing energy with some other type of fuel. If that fuel is nuclear or coal power, those units can't be turned on or off quickly. In that case, even if the wind starts up, it is impossible to shut off those other generators. The excess power will be wasted.

Quickly cycling generators are also poor choices to address the problem of intermittent generation. These units are typically much less efficient than other types of electrical generation. If quickly cycling generators like gas turbines or diesel peakers are used to cover for intermittent generation, a wind farm is committing a region to the use of highly inefficient, highly polluting fossil fuel generation units. This pretty much eliminates any of the environmentally friendly aspects of wind power.

Installation and Maintenance

Wind turbines can be expensive to install and maintain due to the constant stress that the wind places on their large number of moving parts. When exposed to high winds for prolonged periods, a substantial amount of torque is placed on the frame of the wind turbine. This can cause the superstructure of the wind turbine to break down and deform over time. This is especially a problem when there are a number of wind turbines in close proximity. When a wind turbine is alone, the air flow around its fan blades is fairly predictable. However, when there are a large number together, the turbulence from the blades of the upwind units can cause chaotic air flow over the downwind units. This puts unpredictable stresses on the superstructure of wind turbines and can lead to equipment failure.

This makes it difficult to constrain the size of wind farms. The obvious way around the problem of having units upwind of one another is spread them out in a long line. Of course, having wind turbines strung out along a line 20, 30, or even 100 miles along a mountain ridge or a coastline is an eyesore. Aesthetically, few people want an unremitting view of industrial machinery as far as the eye can see.

Locating wind generation in remote areas also makes construction and maintenance more difficult. Building and maintaining wind farms is complicated by the need to bring specialized technicians, vehicles, and tools into a remote area. For example, changing the oil on a turbine requires driving a vehicle capable of carrying large amounts of oil to a remote area. It may also be necessary to truck in a portable elevator or rely on mechanics physically capable of carrying the necessary tools up a ladder to the top of a 20-story tower.

Typical Wind Production

The output of wind units is often described using a capacity factor. To calculate a capacity factor, the actual wind production is divided by the unit's nameplate capacity (i.e., a 100-megawatt [MW] wind farm) for each hour. For example, if a 100-MW unit were to operate all year at 100 percent capacity, it might theoretically produce 876,000 MW per hour of power (365 days × 24 hours/day × 100 MW per hour). If the unit only produced half that amount, it would be said to have a 50 percent capacity factor. As a rule of thumb, a typical wind turbine unit located in an advantageous location will often have an annual capacity factor around 35 percent. Particularly good wind locations (e.g., an offshore unit in a windy area) might have capacity factors as high as 40 percent.

One factor in wind production is the season. In the United States, wind will typically blow the least during summer months and most during the winter. However, the exact timing of the wind will vary by location (Figure 4.6.3). Average monthly capacity factors during winter months commonly are between 40 and 50 percent. Average monthly capacity factors for the summer might be much lower—perhaps 20 percent.

Another factor in wind production is the time of day. Wind speeds are typically highest overnight and lowest during the middle of the day (Figure 4.6.4).

Finally, the output of wind generation is heavily dependent upon location. Even locations very close to one another may experience very different wind conditions. For example, there is a big difference in the wind at the top of a hill compared to the wind behind the shelter of the hill. Another problem is that when one wind turbine is downwind of another, the downwind facility will experience chaotic wind flow due to the disruption in wind caused by the upwind facility. This typically

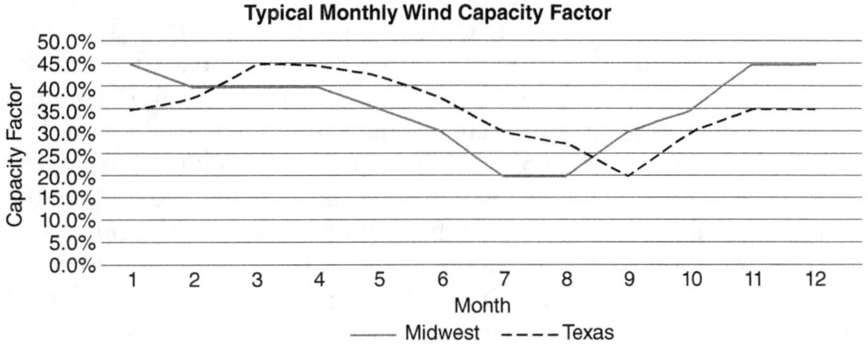

Figure 4.6.3 Typical monthly wind capacity factors

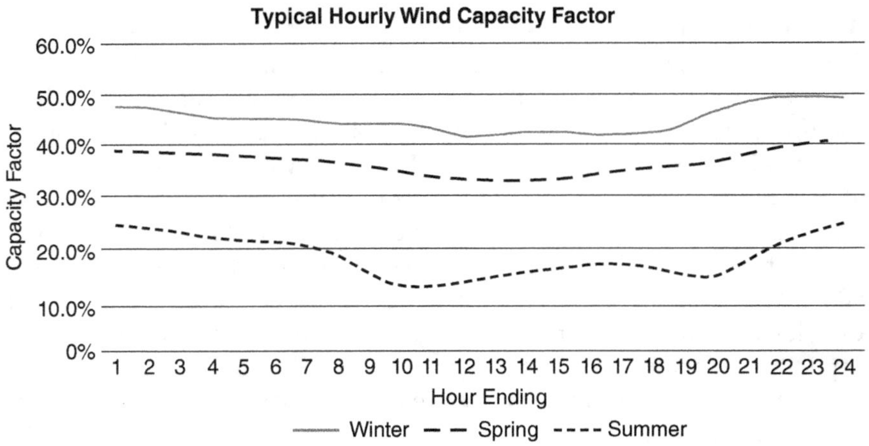

Figure 4.6.4 Typical hourly wind capacity factor

necessitates that wind farms be spread out in lines or organized to minimize disruption from nearby units.

Criticisms of Wind Power

The two most common reasons for consumer opposition to wind farms are the danger they present to migratory birds and aesthetic considerations. Wind turbines are often placed on major migration corridors due to the steady sustained winds in those areas. As birds fly past the wind turbines, they can be hit by the spinning blades and killed. Environmental groups are concerned that if wind power becomes common, the wild bird population will be decimated. Other protests are caused because people think that wind farms are ugly and don't want them located nearby.

Transmission is another constraint on wind power. Wind power is often limited by the availability of long-distance power lines. Long-distance power lines to remote locations require a substantial amount of money to build and maintain. They can be overloaded when the wind starts blowing. This overload risk occurs because all of the wind turbines will often start producing at the same time. Similar to a traffic jam during rush hour, congestion can make it difficult for all of the generation to get power to consumers. A related issue occurs when the wind stops blowing. Then, all of the wind turbines may stop producing power simultaneously. This requires backup generation to come on- and off-line very quickly. If the fast-start generation is not located near the wind units (unlike wind farms, these generators are typically not located in remote areas), this can prove challenging for the power grid to balance flows throughout its network.

4.7

Nuclear Power

30-Second Summary

Purpose

This chapter introduces nuclear power.

Summary

Nuclear power plants, like coal-fired power plants, operate by producing superheated steam to drive electrical turbines. Like coal plants, nuclear plants benefit by operating at extremely high temperatures. The higher the temperature that these plants can operate at, the more efficient they become. A low temperature plant might only return 25 percent of its heat energy as electricity. A larger, hotter plant might return 50 to 60 percent of its heat energy as electricity.

The primary difference between nuclear and coal plants is the way that they generate heat. Nuclear power plants generate heat through nuclear fission. Nuclear fission breaks protons and neutrons free from the nucleus of the nuclear fuel. This isn't a combustion process, so no carbon dioxide (CO_2) is produced. However, nuclear power produces a different type of pollution—radioactive waste.

When concentrated, uranium, the fuel used in most nuclear reactors, is highly toxic. The fuel can also be very difficult to obtain. Although there is a lot of uranium in the Earth's crust, it is seldom found in large deposits. There are a limited number of areas where sufficient quantities can be found to make its extraction economically feasible. Another worry is that the refining process is often identical to the process needed to make fuel for nuclear weapons. As a result, fears of nuclear weapon proliferation are closely linked to the construction of nuclear reactors.

Key Topics

- Nuclear power doesn't release CO_2 emissions, but it does cause other environmental problems.
- The primary fuel for nuclear power, uranium, has to be mined and purified before it is used.
- Nuclear fuel is not particularly common. Techniques to refine nuclear fuel are often government secrets.
- Nuclear plants, like coal plants, have an economy of scale. They need to be built large and no one wants one built in his or her backyard. As a result, nuclear plants are usually built far from consumer regions. That distance places a lot of strain on the electrical grid.

Nuclear power plants use steam turbines to generate electricity. This technology is identical to the technology used to generate electricity in large coal-fired power plants. Both heat water until it becomes pressurized steam. That steam is used to power a spinning turbine. Because of this, like coal plants, nuclear power plants produce more electricity per unit of fuel when they can operate at high temperatures. Also, they are most efficient when they operate full time without letting the water cool down overnight.

The primary difference between the two types of power plants is the fuel that they consume. Coal power plants produce heat through combustion. Combustion (burning) creates CO_2 and releases any particulate matter trapped in the coal. In contrast, nuclear power plants produce heat through nuclear fission. Nuclear fission involves splitting large atoms (like uranium) into two separate atoms.

Nuclear Fission

Nuclear fission is a natural process that occurs every day. It occurs when the nucleus of an atom splits into smaller particles. Certain elements, like uranium and plutonium, are naturally radioactive. In these elements, the nucleus is unstable enough that it splits spontaneously. This is called *spontaneous fission* or *radioactive decay*. Humans can speed up this process so that it happens very quickly rather than over a long period of time. When fission is sped up, it is called *induced fission*.

It is easiest to induce fission in an element that is already breaking down. That is why induced fission utilizes elements that are already radioactive like uranium and plutonium. When fission occurs, an alpha particle consisting of two protons and two neutrons breaks off from the nucleus of an atom. This also causes a pair of electrons to spin off from the nucleus (*beta particles*) and a release of electromagnetic energy (*gamma radiation*).

Almost any atomic nucleus can be broken apart by fission if enough energy is used. However, some atomic nuclei are especially susceptible to fission and require much less energy to break apart than others. These substances are the key to creating a *nuclear chain reaction*. In a chain reaction, the amount of energy released by fission will be sufficient to cause another nearby nucleus to split apart as well. If the nearby nuclei are stable, the first fission won't be enough to break another nucleus apart.

The difference between radiation, a nuclear reactor, and a nuclear bomb is the speed of the fission reaction. Nuclear radiation is a slow breakdown of atomic nuclei. There isn't enough energy being released to create a chain reaction. A nuclear reactor involves a faster reaction, where the energy being released from fission triggers additional nuclear reactions at a measured rate. A nuclear bomb explodes every atom in the fuel extremely quickly in a fast chain reaction.

The Nuclear Cycle

The life cycle of nuclear material is typically called the *nuclear cycle*. The first stages in the process are exploration and mining. These stages remove rocks containing nuclear fuel from the ground which are brought to a processing plant. At the processing plant, uranium is separated from other rocks and milled by grinding it up into a powder-like material called *yellowcake*. Uranium is then converted into a gas by combining it with fluoride to form uranium hexafluoride (UF_6). Then, uranium is ready to be enriched. The enrichment process brings fuel to a desired ratio of fissionable material (Uranium-235) to nonfissionable uranium (Uranium-238). The most common way to separate the uranium is to spin the uranium hexafluoride gas in a centrifuge. The heavier Uranium-238 will move to the outside of the centrifuge allowing the Uranium-235 to be collected from the inside.

For a sustained nuclear reaction, there has to be a sufficient quantity of fissionable material in a fuel. Most uranium that is found in nature is not the right type to sustain a nuclear reaction. *Nuclear enrichment* is the process of getting the right amount of fissionable material into nuclear fuel. One type of uranium, an isotope called Uranium-235, is very easy to fission. An atom of U-235 produces more energy when the nucleus splits apart than is required to break the nucleus. Other types of uranium are not as easy to break apart. As a result, getting the right amount of U-235 into nuclear fuel is the key to nuclear fission.

Isotopes and Atomic Mass Numbers

Substances that have different numbers of neutrons but the same number of protons are said to be isotopes of one another. Chemically, they behave identically. However, the stability of their nuclei is different due to the different atomic weights. In common usage, the term *isotope* refers to an atom with a specific number of neutrons in the nucleus. Isotopes are indicated by a number after the chemical symbol. For example U-238 and U-235 are both isotopes of uranium.

The number after the chemical symbol is the *atomic mass number*. The atomic mass number of an atom is the combined number of protons and neutrons present in the nucleus. These particles weigh about the same, but only protons have an electrical charge.

(*Continued*)

The atomic number of an element is the number of protons in its nucleus. That number is never explicitly stated on a chemical formula. However, it can be looked up on a periodic table. For example, helium is defined as any atom that contains exactly two protons. Therefore, the atomic number for any type of helium is two. An alpha particle, He-4, will have two protons and two neutrons. The number of neutrons can be found by subtracting the atomic number of the element from the atomic mass number.

When uranium or any other nuclear fuel is removed from the ground, it won't have the proper amount of fissionable material present. It is important that there is neither too much nor too little Uranium-235 in nuclear fuel. Otherwise, either a reaction won't happen or it will happen too fast. Processing raw uranium until it has the proper consistency is one of the most important steps in nuclear power. For example, a nuclear power plant might want its fuel to contain about 4 percent Uranium-235 for a moderate reaction. In comparison, a nuclear weapon might require 90 percent purity or higher.

After it is separated, the uranium is then converted back into a solid form (uranium dioxide, UO_2) in a fabrication plant and shaped into its final form. A nuclear power plant will partially control the speed of the nuclear reaction by the shape of the fuel. A nuclear weapon might want the fuel shaped into a ball to maximize the speed of a chain reaction. A nuclear power plant might want the fuel shaped into a flat sheet. That way, a lot of the energy will escape from the top and the bottom of the sheet. This will reduce the speed of the nuclear chain reaction. The speed of the fission process is fine-tuned by the use of graphite control rods. These rods can be used to slow down reactions. When they are inserted into the reactor chamber, graphite rods soak up radiation before it triggers fission in another atom.

After the nuclear fuel is used, it must be removed from the reactor. At this point, the fuel, control rods, and water used to cool the reaction and power the steam turbines are all radioactive. Those materials will be undergoing nuclear fission as well. However, this rate will be much slower than the rate at which the nuclear reactor was operating. The fuel may be reprocessed to remove any remaining Uranium-235 that is still unused. After that, it will be necessary to get rid of the wastes.

There are two choices with any toxic waste. The waste can either be diluted or concentrated. If diluted, a low level of toxic waste will be spread out over a wide area. If concentrated, the waste can become concentrated into something unbelievably toxic. Most areas have regulations to limit release of any toxic substances into the biosphere, so diluting the toxic waste is not a viable solution. As a result, the nuclear waste gets concentrated and placed in a storage facility that is hopefully far away from anywhere it can do any harm.

Thorium Cycle

Uranium-235 isn't the only fissionable fuel that is available. It is possible to create nuclear reactions with other materials. Generally, these other fuels are more expensive, but they commonly produce less radioactive waste and are more difficult to make into weapons. Thorium-232 is an example of a uranium alternative. Thorium is approximately three times as common as uranium, and nearly all of the thorium that is mined could be used as a nuclear fuel. Although it is not fissionable itself, it can be converted into another isotope of Uranium, Uranium-233, by bombarding it with atomic particles. This process produces much less radioactive waste than the uranium cycle and Uranium-233 is harder to use for nuclear weapons than Uranium-235.

Problems with Nuclear Power

From an engineering standpoint, nuclear power plants present many of the same challenges as coal plants. Both types of plants need to be built in an extremely large scale and placed far away from consumers. Adopting nuclear power as a primary power source means making a substantial commitment to a certain type of power grid—one that involves long-distance transmission of power. This type of power grid is inherently less reliable than a power grid where generation capacity is located close to consumers.

Compared to coal, nuclear power also doesn't address the problem of importing fuel from other countries. Uranium has to be mined from somewhere. This makes the nuclear power industry just as fuel dependent as any fossil-fuel-fired power plant. For example, North America has some uranium reserves, but these are much less extensive than its vast coal reserves. Other areas, like Europe, have to import nearly all of their nuclear fuel. As a result, nuclear power is not necessarily the best approach for a country to be energy independent.

Another problem is the concern of nuclear weapon proliferation. The enrichment process used to create nuclear fuel is nearly identical to the process used to create nuclear weapons. Ensuring there is a ready supply of nuclear fuel to supply civilian use without making it available for military use is a problem that challenges public policy.

From a pollution standpoint, the good thing about nuclear power is that it doesn't produce CO_2, sulfur dioxide, or nitrogen oxide pollution. However, none of those types of pollution are likely to kill people outright. Fossil fuel pollution might cause climate change, kill off wildlife, and destroy the environment, but it doesn't present the immediate health threat of nuclear waste. Nuclear waste is deadly when concentrated. Storing concentrated nuclear waste is very problematic because of how dangerous it is.

4.8

Electricity Storage

30-Second Summary

Purpose

This chapter looks at techniques that are used to store electricity. None of these technologies are currently efficient enough to store huge quantities of electricity, but they often make interesting investments. With the rapid improvement of battery technology due to the proliferation of portable electronics, electricity storage may become possible in the near future.

Summary

Electricity can be stored by converting it into another form of energy, like kinetic energy or heat. Then, that energy can be used to generate electricity. Even though efficiency of these conversions is usually low, there are cases where it becomes economically worthwhile. For example, any time electricity can be obtained for very low cost, even inefficient storage systems are economical if they are inexpensive to build. There are a large number of ways to store energy. Some of the examples of energy storage are batteries, pressurized gas, kinetic energy, and gravity.

Key Topics

- Storing electricity is not easy, and there are no widespread ways of doing it economically.
- Storing electricity usually means converting it into some other type of storable energy and then converting it back to electricity when it is time to use it.

Better energy storage is the Holy Grail of electrical markets. If it were possible to buy electricity in the spot markets and resell it at a later point, the electrical market would behave a lot differently than it does today. Currently, electricity prices oscillate over time. Prices are often highest sometime during the day and lower at night and on weekends. If it were possible to store energy, then it would be possible to buy electricity during low use periods and resell it when prices were high (Figure 4.8.1). Every night power is cheap. Every day it is more expensive. Buying

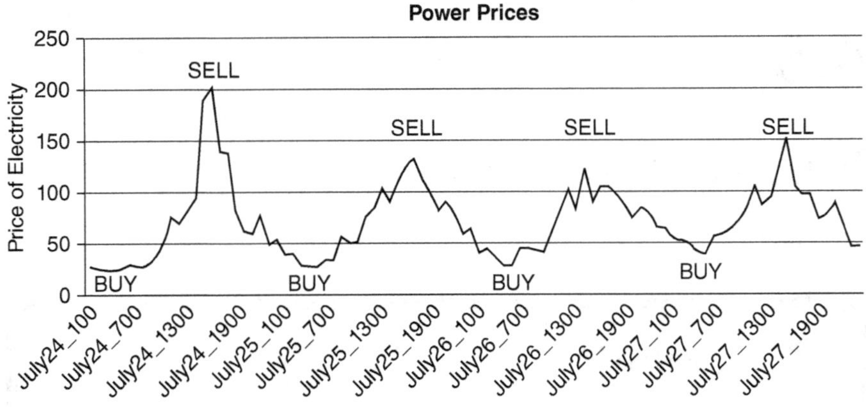

Figure 4.8.1 Regular daily variations in hourly electrical prices

power during the night and selling it back the next day would be an easy way to make money—if it were possible to store that power.

This sounds like a great idea, but in practice, electrical storage usually is not efficient enough for this type of trading. For example, a storage facility might have 25 percent efficiency. That means that 25 percent of the electricity placed into the facility can be returned after storage. If peak power prices were consistently four times off-peak prices, the system would break even on gross profit—and not even begin to pay the installation and ongoing maintenance costs of the storage system.

However, there are a number of cases where electrical storage does make sense. For example, large nuclear power plants and coal plants don't like to reduce their operations overnight. They are much more efficient when they run at high temperatures around the clock. If they reduce their output at night, they will have to use a substantial amount of fuel to increase the heat of their system in the morning. In those cases, it is more costly for these plants to reduce their output at night than it is for them to give away free power for several hours. For them, electrical power is free—if they don't use it, and they can't sell it, they have to throw it away.

Valuing any electrical storage solution can be fairly complicated. The core of the valuation will depend on how the storage is expected to operate. For example, a system that buys power overnight and then resells it during the following day would be a lot different than a storage facility that gets its power for free and plans on holding on to it for several months.

Batteries

One way to store electricity is through the use of a battery. Although there are a wide variety of battery technologies, conceptually these batteries might be very similar to those found in mobile phones or laptop computers. These are probably most desirable when linked to solar or wind generation. However, even without being attached to a low cost generation, batteries would provide short-term capabilities (ancillary services) that can help the power grid balance short-term variances in voltage.

Historically, battery storage has been extremely expensive. However, the popularity of mobile telephones, tablet computers, and laptops has steadily reduced the price of batteries to the point where it is possible to consider large-scale use of batteries on the electrical grid. Furthermore, as battery storage becomes more common, this is likely to increase economies of scale and lead to further price declines.

Electric Cars and the Power Grid

Electric cars are another mechanism that might bring large-scale battery storage to the power grid.

Electric cars use batteries and an electric motor instead of a standard internal combustion engine. This substantially reduces the number of moving parts. Should batteries become sufficiently cheap—something that looks very possible—fewer moving parts will make electric cars easier to construct and maintain compared to traditional cars. Also, there is a strong possibility that electric cars will have better performance characteristics—electric engines can produce more torque immediately, which gives electric cars excellent acceleration. In other words, electric cars might not be adopted for their perceived environmental benefits but because they are desirable to consumers.

When connected for charging, electric cars can feed energy back to the power grid. However, this is a relatively minor impact compared to what might happen when batteries need replacement. Batteries for many devices get replaced when they can no longer hold more than 80 percent of their maximum charge. These batteries might not be useful for cars, but they could have years of useful life remaining if they were connected to the power grid.

Compressed Air

A second way to store electricity is to use it to run an air compressor. The air compressor is run at night or on weekends when power prices are low to force air into a storage vessel. Then, when power is required, air is let out of the storage container (Figure 4.8.2). If the air pressure is high enough, it could be used to run a turbine to produce electricity. It also might be worthwhile to use the compressed air directly—pneumatic air tools are commonly used in a wide variety of industrial

Compressed Air—Storing Power	Compressed Air—Retrieving Power
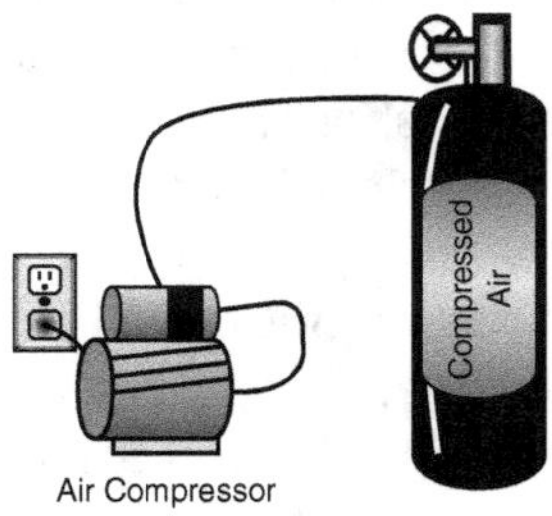	
Electricity is used to run a compressor. The compressor is used to load gas into a pressurized container. A small-scale unit might use a pressurized metal container, while a large unit might store air in an underground cavern.	When the compressed air is released from the storage container, it could be used to drive a turbine, power pneumatic tools, or operate an HVAC (heating, ventilation, and air conditioning) system.

Figure 4.8.2 Compressed air storage

jobs. Alternately, since compressed gas is hot and cools rapidly when it expands, it wouldn't be difficult to create a heating, ventilation, and air conditioning (HVAC) system using compressed air.

Flywheels

Another way to store energy is in a flywheel. A flywheel is a mechanical way of storing energy in a fast-spinning cylinder. A flywheel is a big, heavy wheel that spins extremely fast. The wheel is sped up to store energy, and slowed down to pull energy out of the system (Figure 4.8.3). The key part of the flywheel design is a way to eliminate friction on the spinning wheel.

Flywheel—Storing Power	Flywheel—Retrieving Power
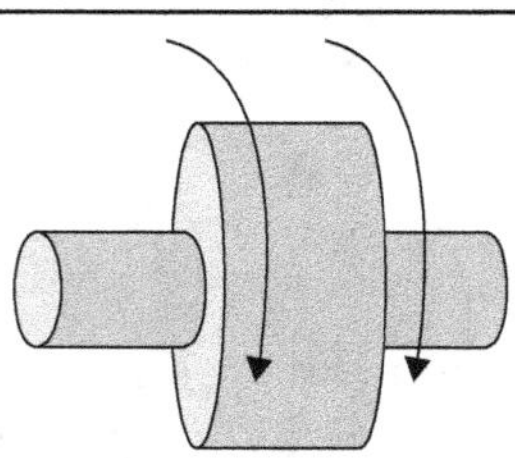	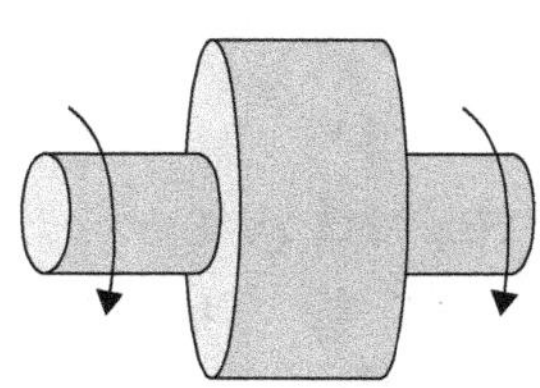
A flywheel stores kinetic energy in a rapidly spinning heavy disc. Energy is stored in the disc by increasing its rotational speed.	Power is removed from a flywheel by using the spinning motion of the flywheel to drive a turbine or other type of motor.

Figure 4.8.3 Flywheel storage

One advantage of a flywheel is that it can be relatively compact. Another advantage is that getting energy out of a spinning cylinder is relatively straightforward. The wheel can be connected to an electromagnet to create alternating current (AC) power. Or, the flywheel can be connected to a shaft to provide mechanical energy to drive a vehicle.

On the downside, a fast spinning wheel contains a lot of energy. A flywheel can do a lot of damage if an axle breaks. A single flywheel is also going to act like a gyroscope if it is mounted in a vehicle. This will make the vehicle much harder to turn. The gyroscopic effect can be avoided by running two flywheels side by side in opposite directions, but that exposes any shared axle to a lot of torque. However, these problems can all be addressed by engineering solutions.

Pumped Hydropower

A third way of storing power is to pump water high into an elevated storage facility. The basic concept is that water in an elevated location can drive a hydroelectric turbine. Water stored at the bottom of the facility can be pumped into the elevated reservoir during the storage phase. Then, it can be released to get the power back (Figure 4.8.4). This is similar to how a hydroelectric facility operates. Normally hydropower plants are powered by water flowing through a river. However, it would be possible to create a closed system that pumps water below a dam back to the top. With sufficiently large reservoirs at the top and the bottom of the facility, it is possible to store a large quantity of energy for an extended period.

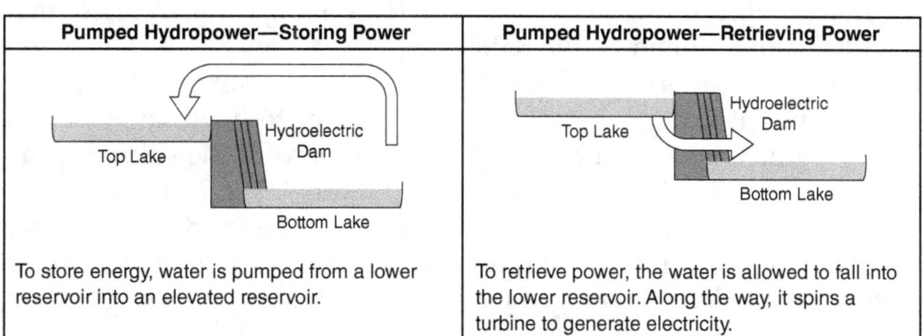

Figure 4.8.4 Pumped hydropower

Trading Example—Compressed Air

The owner of a chemical company needs to keep a large warehouse at a constant temperature. This is one of the major costs of doing business, and he is looking at alternatives to paying peak electrical prices.

1. **The Opportunity.** When a chemical company is building a new warehouse, one of the HVAC systems it is considering has the ability to run on compressed air. The air doesn't have to be compressed at run time. It is possible to compress the air overnight. Since the company buys its power wholesale, it can arrange a contract with its power supplier to buy off-peak rather than peak power.
2. **The Intuition.** Because most of the electricity used by the system can be purchased overnight, the price of operating this system is much cheaper than running the compressor during the day.
3. **The Strategy.** If peak power prices rise after the system is installed, it will become a better investment. In a similar manner, the company is obligating itself to buy off-peak power. The cheaper the price of that power, the better the investment becomes. Installing this system is equivalent to a long peak power, short off-peak power spread position. Subsequently arranging to buy off-peak power from a supplier will cancel the off-peak exposure of the unit, and leave the owner with just a long exposure to peak power. If peak prices rise, the system will become more valuable. If prices fall, it will have been a less beneficial investment.
4. **The Risks.** This is a piece of physical hardware and not just a financial investment. However, from a financial perspective, installing an energy storage system allows the chemical company to time shift its energy purchases.

Expected Profitability

Electricity storage can be valued several ways. For example, if the owner of the system is going to buy power overnight every night, there is not really a daily operating decision since the decision will always occur. Because of this, it might be possible to value this investment as a purchase of futures. This will require forecasting forward prices into the future, but limited mathematics.

Another way to estimate the value of an investment is to examine the typical relationship of overnight power to daytime power. In many regions, overnight power is about 50 percent the price of peak power, but this ratio varies by month (Figure 4.8.5). In the summer, power prices tend to spike in the afternoon due to the demand for air conditioning on hot days. Nighttime prices tend to be more stable. As a result, a smaller percentage of summer energy is used at night. This relationship could be used as the basis of a model to estimate peak prices based on marginal fuels, and then estimate off-peak prices from those estimates.

The complication to either approach is that adding electricity storage to a region can change expectations about future prices. If a

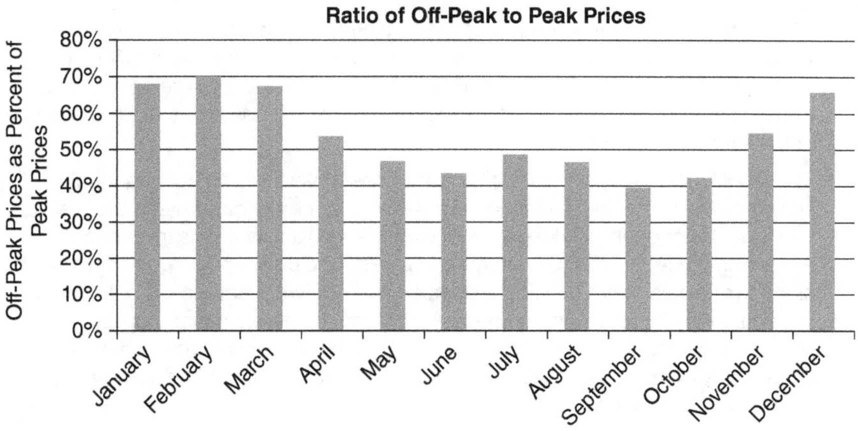

Figure 4.8.5 A typical off-peak to peak price ratio

sufficient amount of storage was available, there would be no intraday swings in power prices. The reason would be that storage units would be able to supply power during periods of peak demand. This would displace the peaking generators that created the high prices and made building the storage profitable. As a result, some care is needed to avoid over-optimistic assumptions of future profits.

Trading Example—Pumped Hydropower

Polluted coal ponds in upstate New York are located by large hydropower plants. During the spring snowmelt, these hydroplants run around the clock at maximum capacity. For a period of several weeks, the price of power plummets dramatically. By the summer, these hydroplants sell power into the high-cost New York City market. Using the polluted coal ponds to store the low-cost electricity generated during the snowmelt for sale later in the year seems like a possible investment.

1. **The Opportunity.** Pumped hydropower storage is a way to buy power during the spring and hold it until it can be sold into the high-priced August peak power market. Upstate New York is filled with toxic coal ponds. These are large lakes left over from a time when coal mining was less environmentally friendly. These lakes are conveniently located near mountain ranges, providing easy access to both a supply of water and vertical cliffs that can be used for building dams. The coal mining company is willing to offer this land for free to anyone willing to assume full responsibility for the toxic mess that was created.
2. **The Intuition.** Along with the spring/summer trade, there will probably be reasonably frequent opportunities for buying power when it is temporarily cheap and selling it when prices spike. For example, if a heat wave is coming, power prices can be expected to rise with a fairly high degree of certainty. Because most people can't store power, a pumped hydropower plant is one of the few market participants that might take advantage of this trade.

(Continued)

3. **Strategy.** The general strategy is to identify periods when prices are unusually high or low and either buy or sell power during those periods. Normally this is relatively easy since electricity prices are cyclical. Unless the reservoirs are at capacity, owning a pumped hydropower plant makes it possible to both buy and sell electricity on short notice.
4. **The Risks.** The cyclical nature of power prices makes buying, storing, and selling power a low-risk investment. However, that nearly guaranteed profit still might not be enough to take on the environmental liability of this investment. Assuming the legal liability for someone else's toxic cleanup is a potential nightmare. Additionally, building a pumped hydropower plant means building physical property and hiring an operational team to maintain that property. Maintenance costs are probably going to be high because polluted water is often highly corrosive. Overall, this is a complex trade with a lot of liability and operational complexity.
5. **Executing the Trade.** Once the facility is built, this is a physical trade that will involve arranging the purchase and sale of actual power. As a result, there is also a lot of paperwork involved. There will need to be a second team of people that coordinates the purchase and sale of power for this facility every day.
6. **The Results.** Taking on the responsibility for toxic cleanup is a huge risk. That risk alone will be enough to scare off nearly all of the potential investors. The physical complexity of the job is a second deal killer. Building a dam to pump water up and down a mountain isn't simple under any circumstances. That complexity, combined with the need to run highly acidic water, makes this a complex trade even if there were no liability concerns. Most investors will pass on this investment.

4.9

LEVELIZED COST OF ENTRY

30-Second Summary

Purpose

This chapter describes techniques to forecast an equilibrium price for electricity based on the break-even cost of building new generation called *levelized cost of entry* (LCOE).

Summary

To forecast prices over a very long horizon, it is often useful to examine the price at which developers will willingly build new generation in the future. If prices rise above that point, new generation will be built and push prices lower. As a result, it is possible to estimate an upper bound for power prices that might exist over a long horizon. This can be done by dividing the cost of building the unit by its expected generation volume adjusted by the time value of money. This value is called the LCOE. This can be expanded by incorporating the fixed and variable costs of running a unit (fuel, maintenance, operations overhead). This approach is commonly used to estimate prices in both capacity markets and *power purchase agreements* (PPAs).

Key Topics

- LCOE is a way to estimate the level of prices necessary to sustain a power grid indefinitely.
- LCOE calculations are mathematically similar to the annuity calculations taught in many MBA and finance classes.

LCOE is an analysis used to predict equilibrium prices where prices will incentivize new generation. This is often referred to as *fundamental analysis*. When forecasting prices of a very long time horizon, examining the price where new generation will be built allows the use of a supply and demand argument to establish an upper bound on power prices. If prices rise above that point, new generation will be built and push prices lower. In periods of continuously rising consumer demand for electricity, newly constructed generation will need to be constructed and this will set power prices.

Mathematically, LCOE is calculated by dividing the cost of building a new unit over its expected life span. Then, that value is divided by the unit's expected generation volume to find a price per unit of output. This can be expanded by incorporating the fixed and variable costs of running a unit (fuel, maintenance, operations overhead) and other real-life factors.

Common Uses for LCOE Analysis

There are a number of applications for LCOE analysis. These include:

- Negotiating prices for PPAs.
- Developing fundamental forecasts.
- Estimating prices for capacity markets.
- Estimating future prices in renewable energy certificate (REC) markets.

In addition, LCOE is a convenient way to compare the overall competiveness of different generating technologies. It represents the cost of building and operating a generating plant over a typical life span and duty cycle. Key inputs into this type of model include an estimate of the cost needed to construct new units, called the *cost of new entry* (or CONE). This cost is spread across the expected life of the facility using a *discounted cash flow* (DCF) analysis to calculate the amount of daily revenue (in units of \$/MW-Day).

Mathematically, the analysis is very similar to the calculation of an annuity (a fixed income product often used as an example in finance or MBA classes). A simplified version of the calculation is shown in Figure 4.9.1. First, it is necessary to determine the return that will incentivize a builder to construct a generation unit. This can be done by calculating the *weighted average cost of capital* (called WACC but abbreviated as r in this example) for a typical developer (Figure 4.9.1).

Next, the *capital recovery factor* (CRF) needs to be calculated (Figure 4.9.2). The CRF calculates the percent of the initial investment that needs to be earned back each year to achieve the WACC calculated in the prior step.

Finally, the LCOE (per megawatt-hour of production) is calculated by incorporating fixed and variable costs. Operating expenses, maintenance, and cost to purchase fuel all increase the amount of money required each year. Additional sources of revenue, like power sales, can be subtracted from the equation to find the unmet money necessary to build a new unit (Figure 4.9.3).

Weighted Average Cost of Capital (WACC)	
	$r = (\text{Debt\%})\ (1 - \text{taxrate})\ (r_{debt}) + (1 - \textit{Debt\%})\ (\textit{ROE})$
Where	
Tax Rate	**The corporate tax rate.** In the United States, this is typically around 35 percent.
Debt%	**The percent of debt financing.** Developments can be financed with either equity or debt financing. Higher amounts of debt will decrease net earnings and lower the company's tax bill. This is called a *tax shield* and can increase the return for equity owners. Many developers and utilities are 50 to 60 percent debt financed, but this does vary over time.
r_{debt}	**Debt rate.** For many developers, this is often similar to the rate paid by BAA-rated corporate bonds. Interest rates can be obtained from industry sources like the Federal Reserve H-15 report.
ROE	**Required return on equity.** For U.S. corporations, this is typically about 6 percent over risk-free rates like LIBOR or Treasuries.

Figure 4.9.1 Weighted average cost of capital

Capital Recovery Factor (CRF)	
	$CRF = \dfrac{r(1+r)^n}{(1+r)^n - 1}$
Where	
r	**Weighted Average Cost of Capital.** This is the interest rate used for discounting future cash flows.
n	**Economic Life of Facility.** The expected economic life span of the facility being constructed. Typically, this is 25 to 30 years.

Figure 4.9.2 Capital recovery factor

It is important to note that actual investments in new generation are affected by the specific technological and regional characteristics of a project; LCOE is simply a convenient approximation of those factors. For example, the existing generation units in a region, taxes, availability of transmission, and local regulations can all affect the economics of specific projects.

Government agencies will also use LCOE-style methodologies for regulatory purposes. This can provide many of the numbers needed to do an analysis. For example, the U.S. Energy Information Agency will publish construction and maintenance costs for units as part of its Annual Energy Outlook (Figure 4.9.4).

Levelized Cost of Entry (LCOE)	
$LCOE = \frac{(CONE)(CRF) + Fixed\ O\&M}{8760 \times Capacity\ Factor}$ + (Fuel Price) (Heat Rate) + (Variable O&M) – (Power Price)	
Where	
CONE	**Cost of New Entry.** The cost to construct a new facility.
CRF	**Capital Recovery Factor.** In the United States, this is typically around 35%.
Fixed O&M (FOM)	**Fixed Operating and Maintenance Costs.** These are fixed maintenance costs associated with maintaining a facility. This is different for each type of technology. This information can typically be obtained from industry sources like the U.S. Energy Information Agency.
Variable O&M (VOM)	**Variable Operating and Maintenance Costs.** Variable expenses are expenses occurred that are proportional to production. Like FOM, estimates of these costs can typically be obtained from industry sources like the U.S. Energy Information Agency.
8760	The number of hours in a typical year (365 days * 24 hours = 8760)
Capacity Factor	**Capacity Factor.** The capacity factor describes the percent of time that the unit will be operational. There are specific discussions in this book on how to estimate how often renewable (wind/solar) or thermal (natural gas, oil, coal, or nuclear) will operate.
Power Price	**Power Price.** The power price is the price that could be obtained by selling an output of the plant like power, steam, or renewable energy certificates into the open market. These prices are typically obtained from brokers or exchanges like ICE or NYMEX.
Heat Rate	**Heat Rate.** The heat rate describes the efficiency of the generator at converting fuel into energy.
Fuel Price	**Fuel Price.** The price that would need to be paid to obtain fuel for the unit. These prices are typically obtained from brokers or exchanges like ICE or NYMEX.

Figure 4.9.3 Levelized cost of entry

Estimated Levelized Cost of Electricity (LCOE) for New Generation Resources, 2020

U.S. Average Levelized Costs (2013 $/MW/h) for Plants Entering Service in 2020[1]

Plant type	Capacity factor (%)	Levelized capital cost	Fixed O&M	Variable O&M (including fuel)	Transmission investment	Total system LCOE	Subsidy[2]	Total LCOE including subsidy
Dispatchable Technologies								
Conventional Coal	85	60.4	4.2	29.4	1.2	95.1		
Advanced Coal	85	76.9	6.9	30.7	1.2	115.7		
Advanced Coal with CCS	85	97.3	9.8	36.1	1.2	144.4		
Natural Gas-Fired								
Conventional Combined Cycle	87	14.4	1.7	57.8	1.2	75.2		
Advanced Combined Cycle	87	15.9	2.0	53.6	1.2	72.6		
Advanced CC with CCS	87	30.1	4.2	64.7	1.2	100.2		
Conventional Combustion Turbine	30	40.7	2.8	94.6	3.5	141.5		
Advanced Combustion Turbine	30	27.8	2.7	79.6	3.5	113.5		
Advanced Nuclear	90	70.1	11.8	12.2	1.1	95.2		
Geothermal	92	34.1	12.3	0.0	1.4	47.8	−3.4	44.4
Biomass	83	47.1	14.5	37.6	1.2	100.5		
Non-Dispatchable Technologies								
Wind	36	57.7	12.8	0.0	3.1	73.6		
Wind - Offshore	38	168.6	22.5	0.0	5.8	196.9		
Solar PV[3]	25	109.8	11.4	0.0	4.1	125.3	−11.0	114.3
Solar Thermal	20	191.6	42.1	0.0	6.0	239.7	−19.2	220.6
Hydroelectric[4]	54	70.7	3.9	7.0	2.0	83.5		

[1]Costs for the advanced nuclear technology reflect an online date of 2022.

[2]The subsidy component is based on targeted tax credits such as the production or investment tax credit available for some technologies. It only reflects subsidies available in 2020, which include a permanent 10% investment tax credit for geothermal and solar technologies. EIA models tax credit expiration as follows: new solar thermal and PV plants are eligible to receive a 30% investment tax credit on capital expenditures if placed in service before the end of 2016, and 10% thereafter. New wind, geothermal, biomass, hydroelectric, and landfill gas plants are eligible to receive either: (1) a $23.0/MWh ($11.0/MWh for technologies other than wind, geothermal, and closed-loop biomass) inflation-adjusted production tax credit over the plant's first ten years of service or (2) a 30% investment tax credit, if they are under construction before the end of 2013. Up to 6 GW of new nuclear plants are eligible to receive an $18/MWh production tax credit if in service by 2020: nuclear plants shown in this table have an in-service date of 2022.

[3]Costs are expressed in terms of net AC power available to the grid for the installed capacity.

Figure 4.9.4 U.S. average levelized costs

4.10

Secondary Electricity Markets

30-Second Summary

Purpose

This chapter discusses several markets that have grown to help cover parts of the electricity market.

Summary

There are a variety of markets that have developed around the edges of the electrical market. Three of these markets—*ancillary services*, *capacity markets*, and *power purchase agreements* (PPAs)—help power grids reliably deliver power to consumers. Another market, *financial transmission rights* (FTRs) helps traders manage congestion risk. Finally, *renewable energy certificates* (REC) markets are a market to trade renewable attributes of electricity generation.

- **Ancillary Services.** Ancillary services markets allow a power grid to pay generators to stay partially unused so that the generator can increase or decrease production to match changing consumer demand.
- **Capacity Markets.** Capacity markets help power grids ensure that they have an ability to meet the consumer demand for electricity several years into the future. Capacity markets pay money to generators to incentivize new construction and ensure that generators don't close down too many underutilized generation units.
- **Power Purchase Agreements (PPAs).** In regulated markets, the regulated utility can ensure that it obtains a sufficient supply of renewable power by signing PPAs with third-party generators.
- **Financial Transmission Rights (FTRs).** FTRs are a hedge for congestion costs. They give market participants the ability to offset the cost of transmitting power over the power grid. In most cases, they can result in both positive and negative outcomes to the owner.
- **Renewable Energy Certificates (RECs).** RECs allow the owners of renewable generation to sell renewable credits. These are often purchased by load-serving entities to meet their obligations to acquire certain amounts of renewable energy.

Key Topics

- *Capacity markets*, *ancillary services*, and *PPAs* are all tools used by power grids to obtain sufficient generation capacity to meet uncertain consumer demand.

(Continued)

- FTRs allow electricity market participants a way to hedge congestion on the power grid.
- *RECs* provide a second source of income to renewable generation like wind and solar producers.

Several secondary markets have sprung up around the electricity market. Some these markets (*ancillary services, capacity markets,* and *PPAs)* are all ways to help power grids reliably deliver power to consumers. Another market, the FTR market, has developed to help traders manage congestion risk. Finally, the REC market provides a way for power grids to incentivize construction of renewable energy in a deregulated electrical market.

These markets have all developed due to the complexity of delivering electricity to consumers. For example, one major issue with the electrical market is the uncertain nature of consumer demand for power. The demand for power during a summer heat wave or winter cold snap can be double or triple the demand for power at other times of the year. If enough generation units have been built to meet peak demand during an extreme event, many of them will lay idle for several years in a row. Someone needs to pay for these units to be built and maintained. One way to compensate the owners of these underutilized facilities is to allow power prices to skyrocket during peak demand. This allows these units to earn enough money during their brief period of operation to be profitable. However, this also tends to be unpopular with consumers who are hit with unusually high electricity bills. As a result, markets have developed other mechanisms to compensate generators for meeting uncertain consumer demand through the ancillary services, capacity, and PPA markets.

Two other markets created by many power grids are transmission markets (typically called FTR markets) and renewable energy markets. FTRs allow traders and other market participants a way to manage the risk of delivering to a specific point on a power grid. RECs provide an additional source of income to owners of renewable energy systems. REC markets also provide a way to track renewable contributions once power has been placed onto the power grid. This allows owners of renewable generation to sell the renewable attributes of their power to consumers.

Ancillary Services Markets

For a power grid to run properly, generation units must constantly modify their output to match changing consumer demand or variable generation from wind and solar units. For areas with a regulated utility, the utility will take on this responsibility. However, in deregulated markets, ancillary services markets compensate generators for their contributions to the power grid above and beyond selling electricity.

Failure to match generation to consumer demand can lead to power lines melting (blackouts) or voltage falling too low (brownouts). Because the power grid can't control when consumers turn on or off a light switch or run a load of laundry, the power grid relies on generators to change how much power they produce. Often, this requires generators to rapidly ramp their output up or down. Since not all generators have the ability to increase or decrease production quickly, power grids will often pay additional fees to the ones that can respond.

Not all generation units can participate in an ancillary services markets. There are several types of ancillary services, each requiring a minimum level of performance. The four most common types of ancillary services are *regulation up, regulation down, spinning reserve,* and *nonspinning reserve.*

Regulation energy is used to maintain the frequency on a power grid at 60 hertz. Resources providing regulation services must usually be able to respond to automatic control signals that will increase or decrease the generator's production depending upon the need. Note that the performance requirements for each class of service will vary by power grid.

- **Regulation Up (Reg Up).** The generator needs to be able to respond to control signals to increase production. Units must typically be able to respond to signals in about a minute.
- **Regulation Down (Reg Down).** The generator needs to be able to respond to control signals to decrease production. Units must typically be able to respond in about a minute.

Reserve generation is used to replenish the regulation pool. Reserve units will be activated to take over for the regulation resources. This will free up the regulation units so that they can continue to provide balancing services. *Spinning reserve* is standby capacity from generation units already connected or synchronized to the grid. *Nonspinning reserve* is capacity that can be synchronized to the grid and ramped to a specified load within a couple of minutes.

- **Spinning (Synchronized) Reserve.** Spinning reserve is a type of ancillary service where the generator is operating but not feeding power into the power grid. A typical startup time for synchronized reserve units is to produce power within 10 minutes of activation.

- **Nonspinning Reserve.** Nonspinning reserve is a type of ancillary service where the generation unit can quickly come on line (perhaps in 30 minutes to an hour).

Frequency Response

On an alternating current (AC) power grid, the *system frequency* (the number of oscillations per second) depends on the power grid maintaining the proper balance between generation and consumption (Figure 4.10.1). When the frequency gets too low, the power grid will need to increase production (or reduce consumption). When the frequency gets too high, generators need to decrease production (or increase consumption). Because of this relationship, ancillary services are often discussed in the context of maintaining the system frequency.

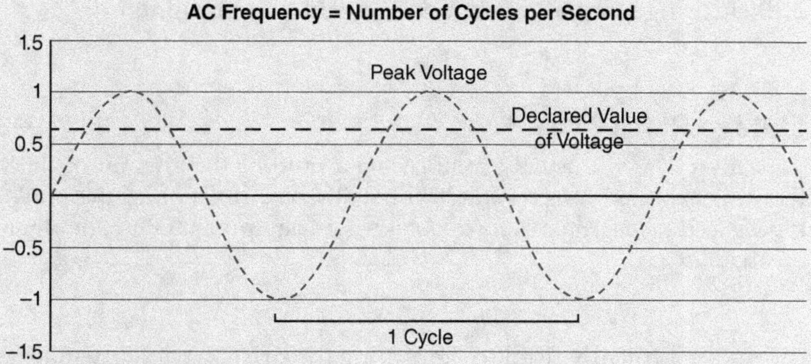

Figure 4.10.1 AC frequency

Capacity Markets

Capacity markets help ensure that power grids will have sufficient resources to meet the future demand for electricity. A typical capacity market will hold an annual auction several years in advance of the operating period for which the power grid wants to ensure sufficient generation. Winning participants in the auction will commit themselves to stay operational through that period in exchange for payment (called a *capacity payment*).

Capacity markets serve as a stable revenue stream for resources that help meet peak demand but don't run often the rest of the year. In addition to helping to maintain existing resources, a second goal for capacity markets is to help support the development of new resources.

For example, capacity markets might incentivize investment in battery technology or efforts to reduce consumer load on demand.

Each power grid can have its own approach to ensuring sufficient resources for its customer base. As a result, there isn't a single capacity market design, and some regions have no capacity market at all. Even so, for the regions that have capacity markets, many follow similar procedures.

- **Capacity.** Many power grids pay capacity payments based on the average amount of power that the unit could produce if it was fully active.
- **Capacity Performance.** Some capacity markets have special categories in capacity auctions for units that can guarantee their ability to produce power (usually by having their own fuel supply) or that can generate reliable power during periods of peak demand (like during summer afternoons or cold winter nights).

Outage Rates

Capacity rates will usually compensate a unit for the amount of time that it is expected to run. This will usually be a function of the unit's typical *forced outage rate*. A force outage is an equipment failure or other breakdown.

Auctions are typically used to determine the price in capacity markets. In these auctions, most power generation units are required to bid in their full generation capacity unless they plan to close down their generation units. The power grid will set an amount of generation capacity that it thinks it will be needed to meet consumer demand. Payment to generators will be based on whether the power grid has met its goal (whereupon no one gets paid) or there is a shortfall (where people will get paid because the power grid wants to incentivize new construction).

Capacity auctions of this type of auction tend to work well when there is consistently increasing consumer demand. However, capacity auctions often do not provide sufficient revenue to maintain existing units when demand is stable or falling. The reason is that incentivizing new construction is only part of the problem faced by power grids. The other problem is the need to compensate standby generation that will only operate intermittently—some units might only run once every 5 or 10 years.

Commonly Observed Design Flaws in Capacity Markets

One flaw with most capacity markets is that they were designed with the belief that consumer demand will be constantly increasing. However, with continued improvements in building insulation, energy-efficient appliances, lighting, and energy-efficient computers, consumer demand doesn't necessarily grow every year. For example, between 2005 and 2015, retail sales of electricity barely grew in the United States (Figure 4.10.2).

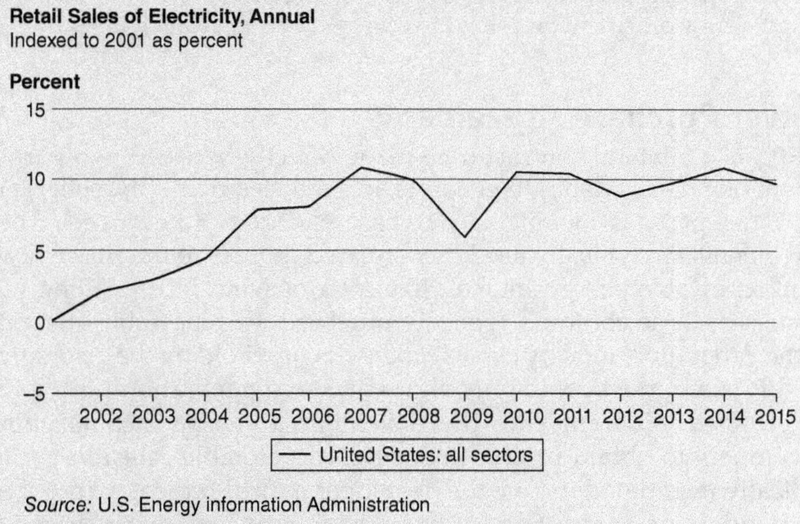

Figure 4.10.2 U.S. retail consumer demand for electricity

Another flaw in capacity markets is the assumption that newly constructed generation units will always be more efficient than previously constructed generation units. When building continuously more efficient generation, new units will displace older, less efficient units forcing the older units to serve as backup generation. The operating income earned by the new units would cover the cost of building the new unit, while capacity markets will cover the maintenance costs of the older units. However, when new units use the same technology or less efficient technology as existing units, new units may not displace existing units in the generation stack. As a result, the new units may not get access to the operating income that they need to pay for their construction.

In many cases, it is beneficial to add less efficient generation. For example, if a power grid primarily composed of wind and solar generation wants to build a natural gas turbine to provide reliability, the gas turbine would not displace the wind and solar units. The gas unit would only run infrequently and would need to be completely paid for by capacity payments.

Combined with the fact that capacity markets primarily compensate generation owners when new construction is completed, this makes

(Continued)

paying to construct new units difficult. For example, in an environment with flat demand growth, the power grid might need an additional generation unit, like a gas turbine, constructed only every couple of years. In a year that construction is needed, the capacity market would show a shortage and existing generation owners would get paid a capacity payment. However, once a developer builds the gas turbine, the power grid would no longer have a reliability shortfall and capacity payments would cease. The result is that the capacity market might not provide developers sufficiently consistent cash flows to construct new generation units.

Power Purchase Agreements

A PPA is a bilateral contract (one made directly between two parties) where one party wishes to generate and sell electricity (the seller) and the other party is looking to purchase electricity (the buyer). These agreements are typically used by regulated utilities to purchase power from renewable energy sources, like solar or wind farms. Along with electricity, these contracts typically purchase the renewable attributes of the generation and any capacity benefits provided by the generation.

PPAs are most commonly signed when a generation unit is first constructed. Guaranteeing the developer a steady income allows developers to obtain project financing at preferable rates. Prices are typically negotiated to give the developer a fixed return on its investment, allowing any savings to be passed on to consumers served by the utility. There is commonly a fixed price for power negotiated. This price is commonly determined using a levelized cost of new entry (LCOE) approach.

Financial Transmission Rights

FTRs are a hedge for congestion costs. They give market participants the ability to offset the cost of transmitting power over the power grid. FTRs are defined by their endpoints. When defining endpoints, the direction of transmission is important. The endpoints are called the *source* and *sink*. The starting point is called the *source*, and the ending point is called the *sink*. Energy is said to flow from the low-cost to the high-cost location. When the FTR flows energy in the same direction as the congested flow, it benefits the owner of the FTR. The FTR serves as a liability, or charge, to the holder when the FTR flows energy in the opposite direction as the congested flow.

FTRs are commonly acquired in auctions. Typically, the power grid coordinating the FTRs will hold an auction one to three years before the flow date associated with the FTR. Smaller monthly auctions will commonly allow market participants to post FTRs for sale or to purchase FTRs that were unpurchased in previous auctions.

From a trading perspective, many FTRs are extremely difficult to value because they are not limited to major points on the transmission grid. FTRs between two major hubs can be valued with a spread option model. However, many FTRs are not between major locations. For example, a power line running from a substation to an abandoned factory will still have locational marginal prices (LMPs) created at both the substation and the bus-bar. However, without power regularly being transferred over the power line, the price assigned to those locations might largely be a random number determined by flows in adjoining areas.

Because of this difficulty, many participants in the FTR market will mark-to-market their FTRs against the last reported auction price rather than using independent models. This provides a visible, independent source for data.

Renewable Energy Certificates

RECs are the most common way to trade renewable electricity. RECs allow their owners to claim that they have purchased renewable energy. They typically have value because regulators require certain market participants to purchase them or be faced with a penalty (sometimes called an *alternative compliance payment*). In other cases, there is a voluntary REC market, which allows consumers or businesses to claim that they are using renewable energy, usually for advertising purposes. REC markets primarily coexist with deregulated power markets. In regulated markets, the monopoly utility will typically meet its renewable requirements through PPAs with renewable generators.

Common Terms

Some common terms related to renewable energy are *green energy* and *brown energy*. Green energy refers to energy produced from renewable sources like solar or wind generation. Brown energy refers to energy produced from conventional sources, typically fossil fuels or nuclear generation.

Green Energy. Energy produced from renewable sources.

Brown Energy. Energy produced from conventional fossil fuels.

In the United States, each REC represents proof that one megawatt-hour (MWH) of electricity was generated from an eligible renewable energy resource and fed into a power grid. After an REC is generated, it is traded and sold separately from electricity. RECs primarily exist as an electronic record. They are used because once electricity is placed on the power grid, it is impossible to differentiate renewable electricity from any other type of electricity.

RECs are largely created by government regulations. As a result, there are many different types of RECs—one for each type of regulation. For example, some RECs belong to a specific compliance program while others are voluntary. The name of the product, like a New Jersey solar renewable energy certificate (a NJ SREC), would indicate that this was a REC intended to meet solar energy requirements in New Jersey.

Environmental certificates and emissions allowance typically have no intrinsic value. They only have value because consumers want to purchase RECs. Consumers might wish to pay these costs directly through voluntary markets. Alternately, consumers can decide to indirectly purchase RECs by requiring that generators purchase them.

The dependence on regulation creates a great deal of uncertainty in the pricing of RECs. Typically, government regulations will specify a penalty payment if enough RECs are not purchased by a utility called an *alternate compliance payment.* When there is too little supply, prices quickly get bid up to the penalty price. As long as shortage conditions exist, prices will stay high. When there is too much supply, prices rapidly fall to zero. For example, if 10 million RECs have been created and utilities are only required to buy 2 million of them, the REC owners will bid prices close to zero to make a sale at any price.

Some features of RECs and similar environmental products are:

- They have no inherent value.
- Demand stems from a need to comply with regulations.
- Prices are very sensitive to supply and demand.
- They are only useful within a limited geographic area specific to the regulator.

In the United States, most RECs are the result of *renewable portfolio standards* that are adopted at the state level. Renewable portfolio standards, or RPSs, will typically define a certain amount of power that needs to come from renewable generation. They will also specify the conditions that generation facilities must meet to qualify as renewable power. Some common criteria used to define renewable power are location of the generator, technology for generation, and a generation date. For example, Ohio might establish a requirement that 10 percent of all consumer power be met from renewable power. It might further specify that at least half of that power needs to be from solar photovoltaic generation. It might also further require that half of that required generation—for both solar and nonsolar—come from facilities within the state. This will lead to four traded products: Ohio in-state solar REC, Ohio in-state nonsolar REC, Ohio out-of-state solar REC, and Ohio out-of-state nonsolar REC.

To produce RECs, generators need to register their production with a *registry*. When a renewable power is generated, a record of that generation is placed into the registry. The registry can cross-check with the power grid to audit that the generator has actually placed the correct quantity of power onto the power grid. When RECs are traded, transfer of ownership is accomplished by changing the owner of record electronically.

REC products are also quoted in terms of the year in which the REC was generated. This date, called a *vintage*, determines the window of time that an REC can be used to meet compliance requirements set out in the RPS. For example, an RPS may specify that RECs have to be used within three years of the date that they were generated.

Common Terms

Brown Energy. Brown energy is electricity produced from conventional generation like fossil fuels or nuclear power. In many areas, hydropower is considered brown power.

Green Energy. Green energy is electricity produced from renewable sources. The primary sources of green power are solar and wind generation. Other green energy sources are tidal and geothermal generation.

Registry. A registry is an organization that keeps track of RECs by cross-checking the production of generators that create them with the power grid and keeps track of the owner of the REC.

Renewable Energy Certificate (REC). An REC is a tradable contract that can be delivered to a regulator to meet RPS requirements.

Renewable Portfolio Standard (RPS). An RPS is a regulation that requires generators in the region to purchase some amount of power from renewable sources. In the United States, this is typically done at a state level.

Solar REC (SREC). A renewable energy certificate generated by a solar generator. These are created when the RPS specifies that power be generated from solar generation units.

Vintage. Vintage describes the year in which an REC was created. This is important to RPS markets where the REC has to be used within a certain number of years after creation.

Voluntary REC Market. An REC market that allows REC buyers to claim that they have purchased power from renewable sources.

5.1

NATURAL GAS TRANSPORTATION

30-Second Summary

Purpose

This chapter examines trading opportunities associated with the use of pipelines to transport natural gas.

Summary

Pipelines are for-profit companies that transport natural gas. Pipelines are an economical way to transport large amounts of gas over long distances. It is very difficult to transport natural gas without using a pipeline. Moving natural gas by truck or railroad is difficult because of the need to use high-pressure metal storage containers. Alternatively, it is possible to freeze natural gas until it becomes a liquid at –260°F and transport it in an insulated container. However, the complications of delivering supercold liquids and heating them up at the delivery point makes that approach impractical on a small scale.

Key Topics

- Gas pipelines can't shut down. They must operate continuously. For traders that have access to storage facilities, this can be a source of profits.
- Pipeline operators are private companies that make a profit by guaranteeing delivery of natural gas. Gas transportation is not cheap, and the financial side of the pipeline business is similar to offering insurance. The various service levels offered by pipelines are often similar to insurance contracts.
- A large portion of natural gas trades involve transferring natural gas from the buyer to the seller. Even in the financial trades, which are settled in cash with no transfer of the commodity, the cost of transporting physical gas will determine the settlement price of the contract.

Because of cost considerations, natural gas is typically transported by pipeline. Natural gas needs to be kept in airtight containers to prevent it from dispersing. If gas is transported in a container, the weight of the container affects transportation costs. Pipelines eliminate the problem of moving heavy containers, and, as a result, have become the most common method of transporting natural gas.

Once they are built, pipelines are cost-effective. They have relatively few moving parts and can operate around the clock. This has effectively eliminated interest in building alternative distribution networks. The downside is that natural gas transportation is generally restricted to areas connected by pipelines. These pipelines form an interconnected network that allows natural gas to flow from production areas to consumption areas. However, when an area is not connected into the pipeline network, it is very difficult to get gas in or out. When natural gas can't be placed onto a pipeline network, it is said to be "stranded."

Natural gas pipelines also have substantial operating constraints. The largest constraint is that they need to operate continuously. Unless there is continuous movement of gas over a pipeline, it won't work. Pipelines must maintain areas of high and low pressure to keep gas moving. If the pressure in the pipeline fully equalizes, the gas will stop flowing and it can take a very long time to get moving again.

As their name would suggest, pipelines are long pipes that use compressors to move gas from one end of the pipe to the other. A compressor (like a fan) at the start of the pipe creates a high pressure area, and a compressor at the end of the pipe pulls gas out of the pipeline by suction (a low pressure area). Gas is drawn through the pipe by the pressure differential between the high pressure injection point and the low pressure suction point.

Pipeline Terminology

Pipelines are often separated into categories based on how far they transport gas. *Transportation* pipelines involve the long-distance transportation of natural gas. *Distribution* pipelines are concerned with delivering gas to end-users. Of the two, distribution pipelines tend to be much more complex. With a distribution pipeline, gas is delivered to a large number of consumers. This creates a complex branching structure. In contrast, a long-distance transportation pipeline might only have one or two branches. The complexity of local delivery pipelines is expensive. It often costs as much to deliver gas the last mile from a *citygate* to a consumer as it costs to move the gas across the country.

Special terms are given to the locations where pipelines connect with one another. The intersection of two or more long-distance pipelines is called a *hub*. The connection between transportation pipelines and a distribution pipeline is called a *citygate*. Both hubs and citygates are common delivery locations for natural gas contracts. Consumers of natural gas are often called the *burner tip*.

Adding gas to a pipeline is called *injection*. Removing gas from a pipeline is called *withdrawal*. Pipelines typically have a variety of locations where gas can be injected or withdrawn from the system. An injection point is called a *receipt point* since it is where the pipeline receives the gas. A point where gas is removed is called a *delivery point*. The names are based on the pipeline's obligation, rather than the obligations of the purchaser of the transportation contract.

Common Terms

Burner Tip. A term referring to a consumer of natural gas.

Citygate. A citygate is an interconnection between a transportation pipeline and a distribution pipeline.

Delivery Point. A delivery point is a location where natural gas is removed from a pipeline (where the pipeline delivers the gas).

Distribution Pipeline. A natural gas pipeline primarily concerned with distributing gas to consumers.

Hub. A hub is an interconnection between two transmission pipelines. Storage facilities are commonly located at hubs.

Receipt Point. A receipt point is a location where gas is placed into the pipeline (where the pipeline receives the gas).

Transportation Pipeline. A natural gas pipeline primarily concerned with long-distance transportation.

Pipeline Operations

There are many different types of pipelines (Figure 5.1.1). Some pipelines connect wells to refineries. Others are transcontinental in nature, moving the gas from producing regions to consuming regions. Still other pipelines are used to deliver gas to consumers. All pipelines work in a similar manner—gas moves along a pipe from an area of high pressure to an area of low pressure. By manipulating the pressure in different areas of the pipe (through compressors), pipeline companies can control the flow of gas through their networks.

It is important that a pipeline maintains the proper ratio of pressures throughout its length. If the pressure at the discharge end of the pipe were to be higher than the pressure at the well head, gas would flow back into the well. In practical terms, this means that if a pipeline is to remain operational, gas must be continually injected at one side and removed at the other. If gas isn't added continuously at the injection point (to create a high pressure zone) and removed at the consumer end (to create a low pressure zone), gas won't flow in the proper

Pipelines and Trading

The trading of natural gas can occur on a number of different levels. There are transportation markets on national, regional, and intraregional levels.

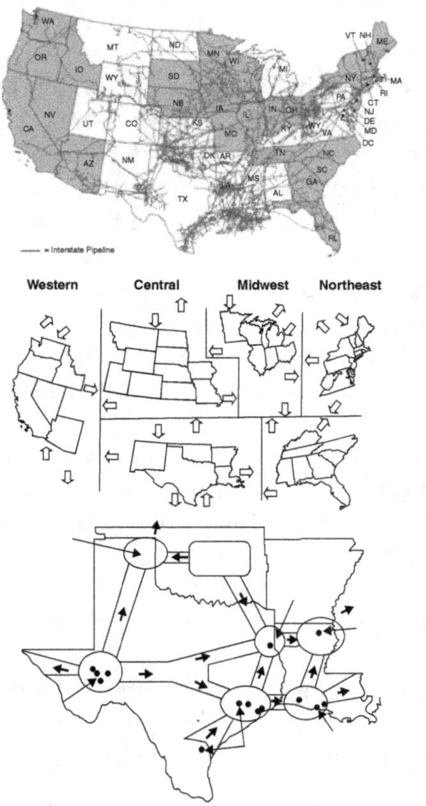

Nationally

The prices anywhere in an interconnected pipeline network are related to the prices everywhere else on the network. Even though a pipeline network is composed of both consuming regions (shaded gray) and producing regions (white), the ability to transport gas between areas means that prices are correlated most of the time.

Between Regions

Regional supply and demand can have a localized effect on prices. There is a limited amount of transportation capacity between regions. The amount of capacity relative to consumer demand determines how far regional prices swing away from the national average.

Within a Region

Knowledge of natural gas pipelines is also the key to understanding prices within a region. The prices at each hub will depend on the nature of the areas that are connected to the hub by a pipeline. For example, even though hubs in East and West Texas are connected and geographically close, their relative prices are determined by different dynamics of the East and West Coast markets.

Figure 5.1.1 Pipeline networks
(*Source:* Maps courtesy of U.S. Energy Information Agency)

direction, and the pipeline won't operate. This is a very important concept—for a pipeline to operate, neither injections nor removals can stop because they are uneconomical. Because of the time required to restart pipelines, it might be necessary to run a pipeline even if no consumers are using gas and there isn't any storage available.

Compressor Stations

Compressor stations form the heart of the pipeline network. Similar to how a heart pumps blood throughout a human body, compressor stations push natural gas through the pipeline network. When liquid or gas is compressed, it moves toward an area of lower pressure. By controlling the location of high and low pressure areas, compressor stations are used to control the flow of gas through pipelines. The simplest way to think of a compressor is a household fan. On one side of the fan, gas is being pulled in and a low pressure zone exists. On the other side of the fan, air is being pushed out to create a high pressure zone.

One key issue with compression is that it will increase the temperature of the gas being compressed. Cold gas is denser than hot gas. If the pipeline is operated at a constant pressure, a greater quantity of gas can be transported if the gas is kept cool. As a result, most compressing stations include several cooling stages as part of the compression process. Cooler gas also causes less corrosion. Natural gas is never perfectly pure methane. It almost always contains trace amounts of other gases. Some of these trace gases can be highly corrosive and cause mechanical breakdowns if they are allowed to accumulate. As a result, compression stations also provide scrubbing systems to remove trace impurities.

A modern compression station will usually contain several compressor units running in parallel (Figure 5.1.2). Gas enters the station through a suction header, and then moves through the scrubber system. The scrubber system removes particulate matter and most liquids from the gas. Then the gas goes through a series of compression and cooling stages before being discharged into the next segment of the pipeline.

Compression stations are located along the entire length of a pipeline. These compression stations divide the pipeline into small segments. Gas moves between pipeline segments by traveling from the

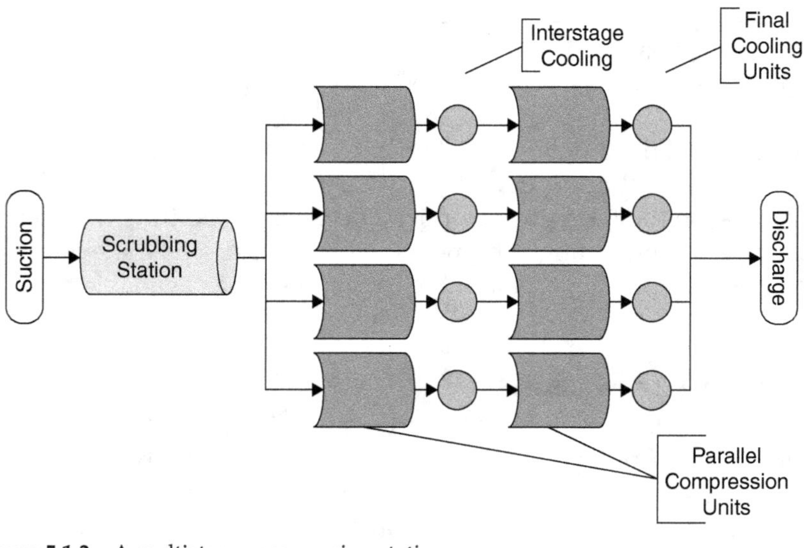

Figure 5.1.2 A multistage compression station

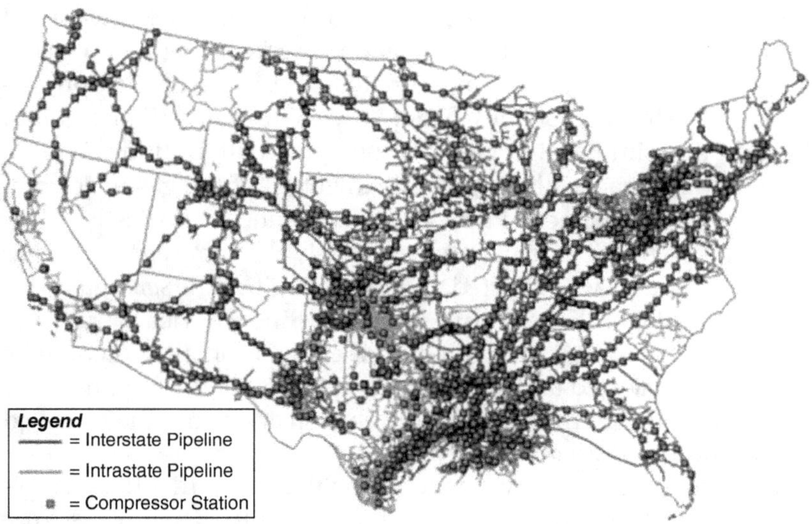

Figure 5.1.3 Interstate pipelines and compressor stations
(*Source:* Map courtesy of U.S. Energy Information Administration)

high pressure discharge point of one station to the low pressure suction point of the next station. Chaining these sections together allows a steady flow of gas through the pipeline. It is very important that all of the stations on a pipeline work together or else the pipeline will stop operating. Most compressor stations are fully automated and coordination between stations is handled by a computer at a central location. On most pipelines, compression stations are located approximately every 50 miles (Figure 5.1.3).

Transportation Contracts

When arranging transportation on a pipeline, there are two major levels of service—*firm* service and *interruptible* service. Firm service is offered with a guaranteed availability except when prevented by act of *force majeure*.[1] *Firm* service is highly reliable but also relatively expensive compared to interruptible service. Interruptible service is offered on a "best efforts" basis and is relatively cheap. However, it can be interrupted for any reason and may not be available at all. There are a number of valid reasons why interruptible service might be disrupted. The most

[1] ***Force majeure*** is French for "greater force." This is a common clause in contracts that frees both parties from liability in cases of wars, natural disasters, and other extraordinary events. Typically these events are outside the control of either party, which would prevent one or both of the parties from fulfilling their obligations under the terms of the contract.

common reason is to balance the flow of gas on a pipeline. Because of the nature of gas, its movement can never be precisely controlled—it always moves from areas of high pressure to low pressure. Even optimizing a relatively simple pipeline can get very complicated (Figure 5.1.4).

Even in this simple case, gas is being spread all around the pipeline. It would be practically impossible to get all of the gas injected at Point 2 out of the pipeline at Point 3. If the pipeline were mostly full of gas, it would be possible to get approximately the same *amount* of gas out of the pipeline as was injected, but it wouldn't be the *same* gas. This has some advantages. For example, if the pipeline was nearly full, and the amount of gas being transported was relatively small, gas could be simultaneously injected and removed from the pipeline. It would take some time for the pipeline to reach equilibrium again, but the so-called "transportation" would occur very quickly.

The rate at which gas flows depends on the pressure difference between areas. High pressure gas moves more quickly than low pressure gas. In the previous example, injecting gas into a nearly empty pipeline and injecting gas into a nearly full pipeline give two very different operational results. Starting empty, since the gas will spread throughout the entire pipeline, it would probably be impossible to fully remove the full quantity of the gas from the pipeline at Location 3.

Pipeline operators have a vested interest in keeping the pipeline as full as possible. While they can't keep the pipeline at maximum

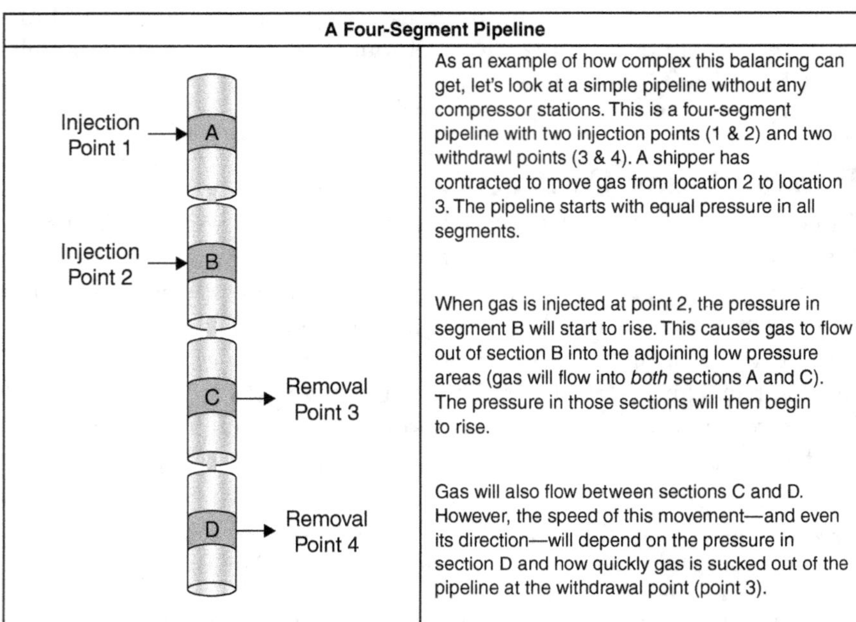

Figure 5.1.4 A four-segment pipeline

capacity since it would be impossible to inject additional gas, neither can pipelines be operated at very low pressure.

The *firm* shipper pays a large premium (a *reservation charge*) in order to guarantee that enough capacity is available at all times for its use. However, the shipper doesn't actually have to put its gas into the pipeline—perhaps it is a warmer than expected winter, and residential demand is much lower than expected. The pipeline operator still needs gas in the pipeline—the pressure in the pipeline can't be allowed to drop too far—so it will offer much lower cost interruptible service to other clients. When the firm shipper wants to make a delivery, the interruptible clients will get shut off.

There are valid business reasons for using either type of contract. It is important that a public service company provide gas heat to residences without interruption. A power plant or industrial facility might also want to guarantee its supply of gas as well. On the other hand, a gas storage facility might opt to use interruptible service for buying gas. A storage facility wants to buy gas cheaply (during periods of low demand) and sell high (during periods of high demand). There is no need to pay a high premium to buy during periods of minimal usage—minimal usage indicates that interruptible service contracts are operating.

For regulated pipelines in the United States (this covers pretty much every pipeline that is available for public use), the fee structure

Common Terms

Annual Cost Adjustment (ACA) Charges. The ACA charge is a small charge that adjusts transportation costs for inflation.

Commodity Charge. A commodity charge is the variable cost for transportation. This charge is usually quoted per unit of gas to be transported.

Delivery Adder. A delivery adder is a fixed price adjustment used to determine the price at the delivery point relative to a price of a nearby benchmark.

Fuel Usage. Fuel usage describes the amount of natural gas lost in transportation. This lost gas is commonly used as payment in kind to provide power to the compressors responsible for moving the gas.

Gas Research Institute (GRI) Charges. For U.S. pipelines, the GRI charge is a small fixed charge used to fund a nonprofit industry group, the Gas Research Institute.

Postage Stamp. A postage stamp is the cost to transport gas on a pipeline with a single rate zone.

Receipt Adder. A receipt adder is a fixed price adjustment used to determine the price at the receipt point relative to a price of a nearby benchmark.

(*Continued*)

Reservation Charge. The reservation charge is a fixed monthly charge paid to the pipeline to reserve transportation capacity.

Tariff. Pipeline rates are commonly public documents. These documents, called tariffs, describe the charges used to transport gas over the pipeline. Tariffs can usually be found on the pipeline or the regulator's website. For example, in the United States, pipeline tariffs can be found on the eFERC site.

Volume. The quantity of natural gas that can be transported.

Zones. Different areas on a pipeline are commonly divided up into zones.

charged by the pipeline will be listed in a public document, called a *tariff*, which can be obtained from either the pipeline company or the regulating agency (Figure 5.1.5).

Transportation Contracts Between Buyers and Sellers

As opposed to transportation contracts with pipelines, there are three common levels of contracts between buyers and sellers of gas—*short term interruptible contracts, baseload contracts,* and *firm contracts*. These use similar terminology to the transportation contracts, but mean slightly different things.

Short term interruptible contracts are short-term contracts between buyers and sellers utilizing interruptible service. Usually these are only for a couple of days or the balance of a month. If the seller has supply, and the buyer wants it, and there is available transportation, then the trade gets made. If any of those things does not happen, there is no obligation on anyone's part.

Baseload contracts are another type of interruptible contract between buyers and sellers. They are generally made with the understanding that both parties will make a "best effort" to meet the terms of the contract every day. They may or may not use firm pipeline transportation, or they might use a combination of firm and interruptible transportation. These contracts are based on trust that each side will hold up its end of the deal.

Firm contracts between buyers and sellers are binding agreements obligating both parties to the transportation—the seller is obligated to deliver, and the buyer is obligated to receive gas. There is legal recourse if either side fails on its side of the agreement. In these cases, the pipeline also needs to be obligated to reserve delivery capacity—these types of contracts will almost always utilize firm transportation contracts.

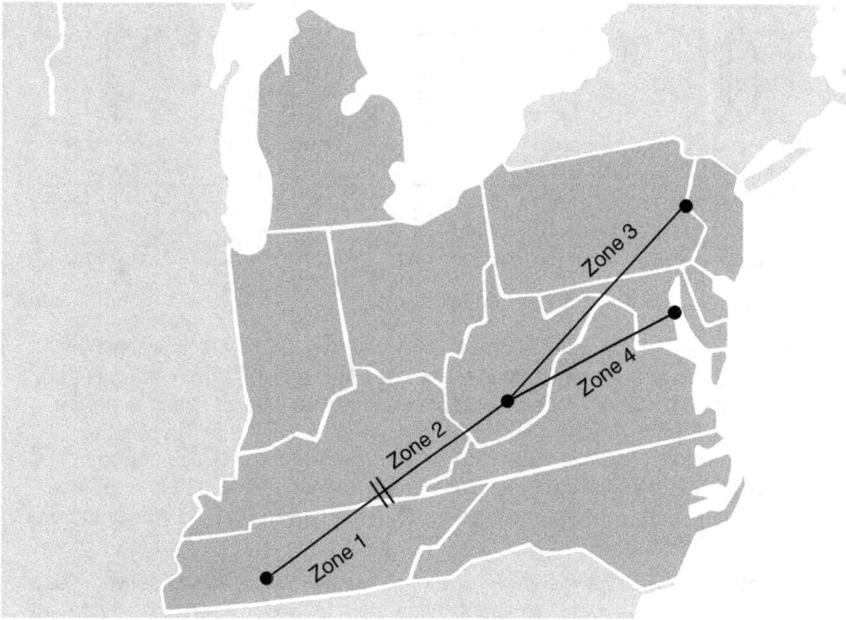

From Zone	To Zone	Reservation Charge ($/MMBtu)	Commodity Charge ($/MMBtu)	Fuel % Winter	Fuel % Summer
1	2	$0.13	$0.0150	0.21%	0.24%
1	3	$0.27	$0.0350	0.21%	0.24%
1	4	$0.22	$0.0250	0.21%	0.24%
2	3	$0.14	$0.0200	0.21%	0.24%
2	4	$0.09	$0.0250	0.21%	0.24%

Notes:
All changes are per MMBtu per day.

Figure 5.1.5 Pipeline map and tariff schedule

Trading Example—Pipelines as Insurance Providers

A pipeline offers capacity on its pipeline at two levels of service—guaranteed service and nonguaranteed service. The pipeline wants to offer as much guaranteed service as possible to earn a higher margin. It is considering whether to buy backup compressors along the pipeline.

1. **The Opportunity.** A pipeline consists of five compressor stations located in a row. Each compressor is active 85 percent of the time and has a scheduled maintenance of one week a year. The pipeline can continue to operate unless adjacent compressing stations are down simultaneously. However, every compressor that is offline the pipeline loses 20 percent of its capacity. A graphic of the pipeline is shown in Figure 5.1.6.

(Continued)

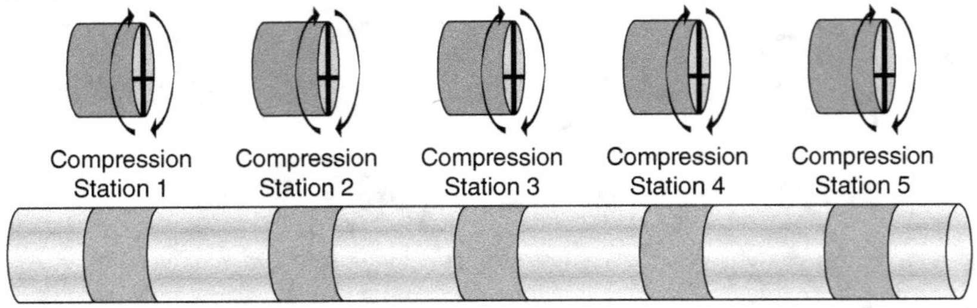

Figure 5.1.6 A pipeline with five compressors

A large portion of the pipeline's profit comes from guaranteed contracts. The pipeline offers annual contracts to deliver gas at two levels, firm contracts and interruptible contracts. The pipeline faces a steep penalty for failing to deliver on a firm contract. For each MMBtu of *firm* transportation that the pipeline successfully delivers, it receives $1. For each undelivered MMBtu of firm transportation, the pipeline must pay $12.50. For each MMBtu of *interruptible* transportation, the pipeline receives $0.15. If the pipeline fails to deliver the gas, it costs no money.

2. **The Intuition.** The pipeline is losing a lot of money when it fails to deliver on a firm contract. For the past five years, it has been unable to operate on 8 percent of the days. It is only able to operate at full capacity 42.5 percent of the time (Figure 5.1.7). The pipeline has offered 60 percent of its capacity in firm contracts. Although it has delivered 91.7 percent of its firm contract successfully, the penalty for nondelivery of the remainder has eaten up all of those profits.

Capacity	Days
0%	8.00%
20%	0.00%
40%	0.30%
60%	8.60%
80%	40.60%
100%	42.50%

Figure 5.1.7 Operating availability

3. **The Strategy.** The pipeline operator plans to increase its profits by improving the reliability of the pipeline. It plans to add a second compressor to each compression station. Even though the second compressor will be idle most of the time, by increasing the reliability of the pipeline, more firm capacity can be sold, cutting down on penalties for nondelivery of firm contracts.

4. **The Results.** The pipeline goes from making 15 cents on 40 percent of its capacity, to making $1 on 80 percent of its capacity. The pipeline starts making 100 times the profit it made previously. Even with doubled maintenance costs, this is a tremendous improvement in profitability.

Trading Example—Short Term Interruptible Trades

A chemical processor can produce methanol from either agricultural waste or natural gas. When natural gas is expensive, the manufacturer will use the discarded stalks and leaves of corn plants (corn stover). When natural gas is cheap, the manufacturer will use natural gas.

1. **The Opportunity.** One way to think about the natural gas markets is as an auction. The people willing to pay the highest amount for natural gas at that moment win the available supply. Everyone else has to wait for a later time to buy natural gas. Around the country, each area has a different amount of supply arriving at any given point and a different pool of people demanding fuel. The natural gas marketer would like to buy natural gas at a bargain price whenever there is no one else interested in using it.
2. **The Intuition.** The chemical processor would like to buy natural gas when it is cheap. However, the processor finds natural gas uneconomical to use as a feedstock when prices are high. For this type of strategy, it doesn't make sense to reserve firm transportation on a pipeline. If the chemical processor is only going to buy natural gas when prices are low, this coincides with the times when the demand for pipeline transportation is also low.
3. **The Strategy.** The chemical processor agrees to buy natural gas from a natural gas processor using a swing contract. This contract is a nonbinding contract to purchase gas on an as-available basis using nonguaranteed transportation. In other words, the chemical processor agrees to buy gas when no one else wants it.
4. **The Risks.** The chemical processor has little risk in this trade. It is getting a product at low cost when almost no one else is buying natural gas. The chemical processor can then convert that gas into a more valuable product, methanol.
5. **The Results.** Arranging for gas to be purchased with swing contracts and interruptible transportation is the lowest cost way to purchase physical gas. The main downside is that the supply of gas isn't guaranteed and during periods of high demand, almost no supply will be available. The chemical processor will have to rely on its other feedstock, corn stover, in those periods.

5.2

Natural Gas Storage

30-Second Summary

Purpose

This chapter discusses the storage of natural gas and trades related to natural gas storage.

Summary

Because it is a gas, and gases disperse into the atmosphere, it is necessary to store natural gas in a sealed, pressurized location. A huge volume of space is required to contain an economically significant amount of natural gas. For example, to store the natural gas equivalent of the energy contained in a single gallon of gasoline, 900 gallons of natural gas storage are required at standard atmospheric pressure. This space requirement can be reduced by pressurizing the natural gas. However, even highly pressurized natural gas takes up a lot of space and requires a gigantic storage facility. As a result, the most common locations for storing natural gas are naturally occurring underground reservoirs because of their vast storage capacity.

The owners of storage facilities make a profit by buying gas when it is cheap, storing it, and selling it when it is expensive. The value of a natural gas storage facility is based on the value of buying and holding natural gas. Pipelines need to operate continuously—they can't turn off. As a result, storage facilities play a critical role purchasing gas when consumer demand is low and supplying gas when consumer demand exceeds the pipeline's capabilities.

Key Topics

- Gas pipelines have minimum operating levels and can't completely shut down. Storage is needed to take in the excess natural gas that can't be immediately used.
- Natural gas storage facilities are usually located underground in large rock formations. The physical capabilities of every facility are different and depend on the geology of each area.
- The economic value of a storage facility is difficult to calculate. It requires a path-dependent option calculation. As a result, approximations of a facility's economic value, like intrinsic value, are commonly used.

Natural gas is constantly moving through pipelines. To avoid wasting gas, it must be used, stored, or sent somewhere else when it arrives. Pipelines can't stop delivering gas. They must send a constant supply of gas from producing regions to consuming regions. Although the rate of flow can be adjusted somewhat, it is important that it never be stopped or interrupted completely.

Because the demand for natural gas is highly cyclical, and pipelines need to operate continuously, it is seldom possible to precisely match the supply of gas coming out of a pipeline with the amount demanded from each consuming region. Storage facilities are necessary to take in surplus during periods of oversupply, and deliver gas in shortages. Storage facilities stockpile gas during periods of low demand (buying cheap) for use in higher demand periods (selling high). Common trading opportunities are nights versus days, weekends versus weekdays, or shoulder months versus peak demand months.

Fortunately, natural gas is chemically stable. It can be safely stored in underground facilities for extended periods. It is nontoxic, so leaks don't hurt the environment, and it has already survived millions of years in storage. While it might evaporate, it isn't going to spoil or poison the environment. Natural gas storage provides a crucial margin of safety for short-term regional fluctuations in demand.

The most common type of storage facilities are *depleted gas reservoirs*. These are underground caverns that once contained natural gas. It is possible to reuse gas reservoirs after they have been depleted by pumping gas back in. Other types of facilities are *salt caverns* and *aquifers*. The main difference between facilities is the cost of construction, the quantity of gas that they can store, and how quickly they can inject and remove gas from storage.

It is common for gas to be stored in several storage facilities before it is finally delivered to the customer (Figure 5.2.1). The first set of storage facilities are typically in producing regions like the U.S. Gulf Coast near refineries and major pipeline hubs. The second set of storage facilities are near consumer regions at the far end of the pipeline.

All storage facilities work in a similar fashion—a facility with a large volume suitable for storing natural gas is found and connected to a gas pipeline. To maximize the amount of gas that can be stored in a limited amount of space, the storage facility will usually keep the gas at higher pressure than a pipeline. As a result, gas will need to be compressed to get it into the storage facility. This compression is done by applying suction to a pipeline (similar to attaching a vacuum cleaner to it). As long as the suction is stronger than the pressure in the storage area, the gas will flow into the storage area and not back into

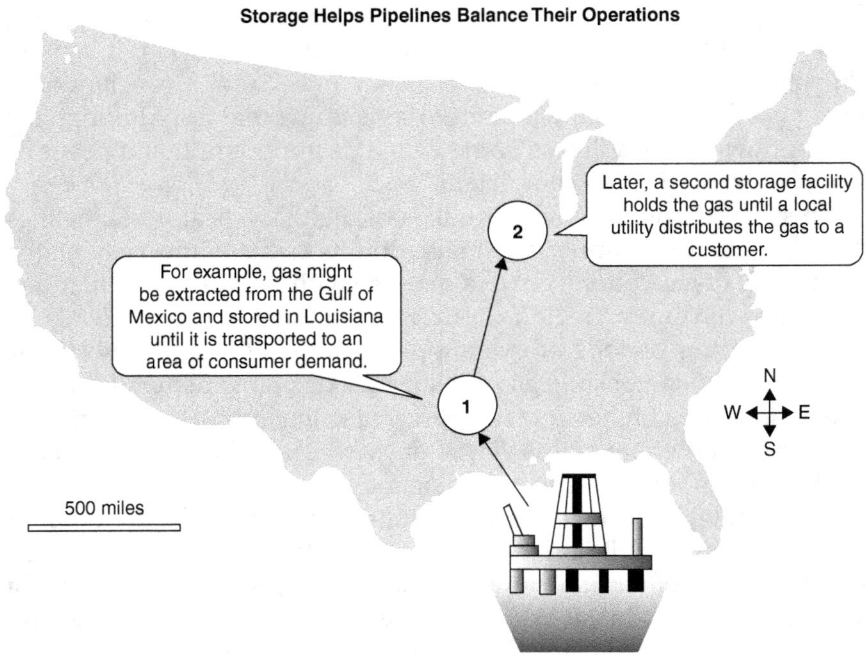

Figure 5.2.1 Benefits of storage

the pipeline. When the suction is turned off, the connection between the storage facility and pipeline will need to be closed.

The speed at which gas can be inserted or extracted from storage depends on the relative pressure of a storage facility and the pipeline. When the storage facility is nearly full, gas can easily be removed from storage. It is possible to open up the pipeline connection and have the gas flow into the pipeline. However, as the pressure decreases, it takes progressively longer to get the gas out of storage.

As a result, the extractable gas is generally divided into two pieces—*base gas* (or *cushion gas*) and *working gas*. The *base gas* is used to create sufficient pressure to get the *working gas* out of the storage facility in a reasonable amount of time. Base gas is rarely removed during normal operation. Operators of a storage facility have to trade off having a large volume of working gas that can only be removed slowly or a smaller volume of working gas that can be removed quickly. During periods of peak demand, some of the base gas can be removed from the facility and delivered as working gas. However, over the long run, since removing the gas cushion slows down the speed at which gas can be removed (because removing gas lowers the pressure of the storage facility), keeping a fixed cushion of gas is required to meet performance targets.

Inserting and Removing Gas from a Storage Facility

Gas normally flows from high pressure areas to low pressure areas. To move gas in reverse, it is necessary to use compression to artificially create a high pressure. This is similar to how a vacuum cleaner operates. A fan spins, creating suction on one side (the intake side) and a high pressure on the other side. If the high pressure is above the storage pressure, gas can be pulled out of a low pressure pipeline and placed into a high pressure storage container (Figure 5.2.2). A compressor is typically used to pull natural gas out of the pipeline and place it into the storage facility.

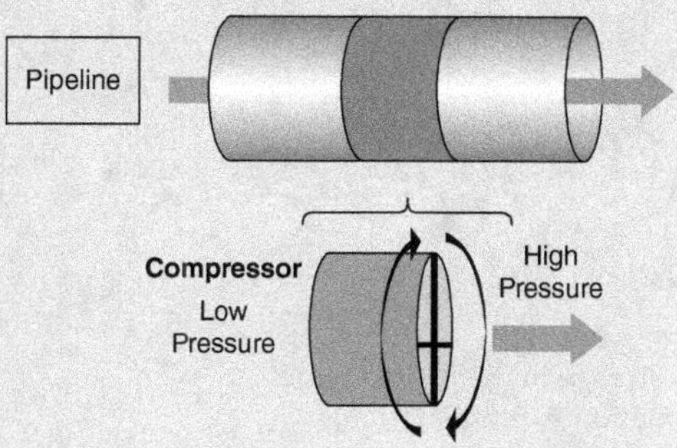

Figure 5.2.2 Compression

As gas builds up in the storage facility, it will start to push back against the compressor (Figure 5.2.3). To keep the same rate of insertion, more compression will need to be used. At some point, the maximum safe pressure for the storage facility will be reached and insertions will need to stop.

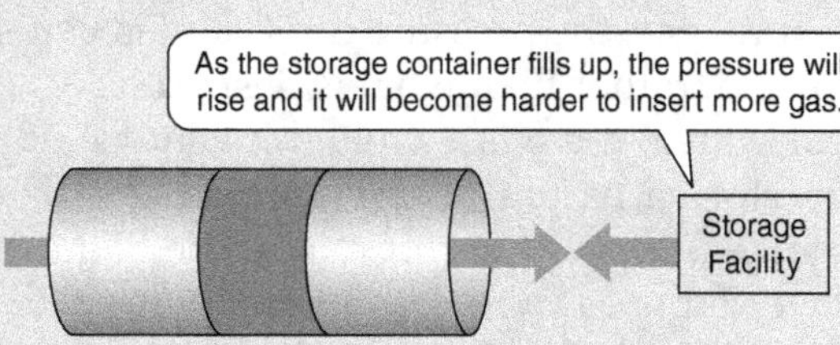

Figure 5.2.3 A nearly full storage facility

Removing gas out of the storage facility works in the opposite manner. A compressor is used to create suction to pull gas out of storage and push it into the pipeline. However, there are limits to how quickly this can occur. Once a perfect vacuum is achieved, the high/low pressure differential between storage and pipeline doesn't get any larger. Since the speed of gas movement depends on that differential, the pressure of the storage facility is the limiting factor on the speed of the removal.

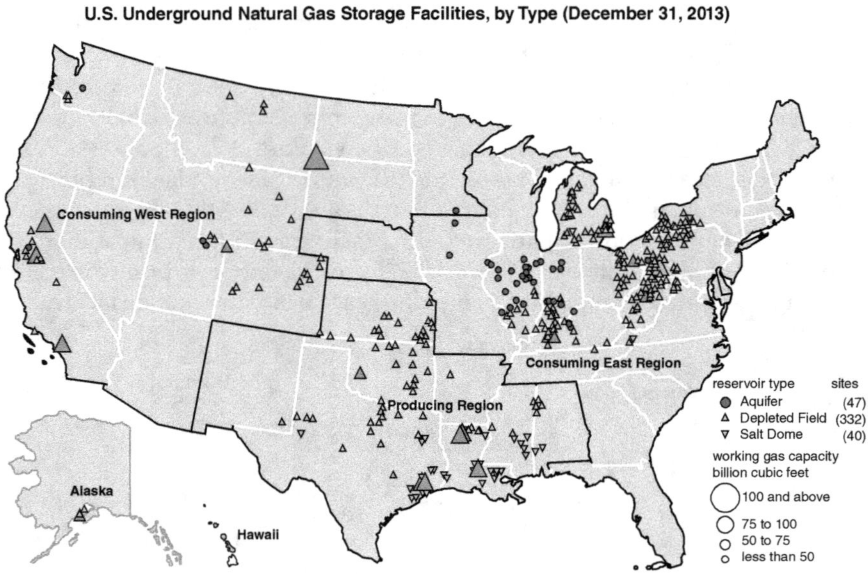

Figure 5.2.4 Natural gas storage in the United States
(*Source:* U.S. Energy Information Administration)

This last major physical constraint on a storage facility is its maximum pressure. Higher pressure means that you can store more gas in a given volume and that you can get the gas out more quickly. However, higher pressure can also cause structural problems—more stress on the facility—and a greater possibility of gas escaping into the environment. Since there are a fairly limited number of locations suitable for the storage of natural gas, the pressure constraint is usually a function of what can be found, rather than what is desired.

For a particular area, there is a limited inventory of possible locations suitable for storing natural gas (Figure 5.2.4). The cheapest and most reliable storage is *depleted gas reservoirs*. The highest performance facilities are converted *salt caverns*. In an area where neither of those two is available, *aquifers* can be used. Aquifers are permeable layers of underground rock often containing ground water. Methane is nontoxic and present in the air we breathe every day. It doesn't present the health threat that other fuels might create if they start leaking into the environment. From a performance perspective, salt caverns are far superior to the other options—they can stand up to significantly higher pressures.

Geology

A storage facility is a large underground area where gas can dissolve, surrounded by an impermeable area that prevents the gas from escaping (Figure 5.2.5). Overall, natural gas storage facilities are similar

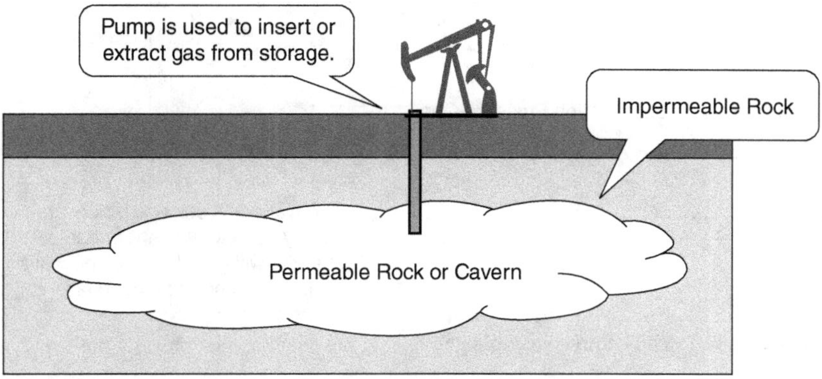

Figure 5.2.5 Inserting gas into a storage facility

to other types of pressurized containers and identical to wells where natural gas is found in nature.

Natural gas storage facilities are often located underground. They aren't usually excavated with pressurized metal walls. Instead, they are commonly constructed in areas where naturally existing porous rock is surrounded by a layer of impermeable rock. There are several advantages to reusing existing geological formations. All of this rock makes the facilities fairly sturdy. Equally important is the low cost of reusing existing rock formations. Finding an appropriate existing reservoir is one of the largest jobs in building a new natural gas storage facility.

Natural gas storage shares terminology with natural gas extraction. *Porosity* is a measure of empty space in a rock. Even though many rocks look solid, they often contain microscopic openings where gas can dissolve. These openings are called *pores*. If the pores in a rock are connected together, the rock is said to be *permeable*. Having connected pores allows the gas trapped in the rock to flow in and out of the storage facility quickly. The greater the size of the pores, and the more they are interconnected, the faster the gas can enter or leave the facility.

A storage facility requires a porous, permeable pocket of rock to be surrounded by a layer of impermeable rock. Since gas rises, it is especially important for the layer of rock directly above the storage volume to be impermeable. In every gas storage facility, some gas becomes permanently embedded into the walls. This is called *physically unrecoverable gas*. Even when the facility closes, it is impossible to recover this gas (Figure 5.2.6).

The greater the pressure in the storage volume, the more gas gets pushed into the walls. If enough pressure is added, gas will eventually reach a more permeable area and start to escape from the storage facility. This level is different for each facility. It is determined by the specific geology of the rocks that form the storage facility.

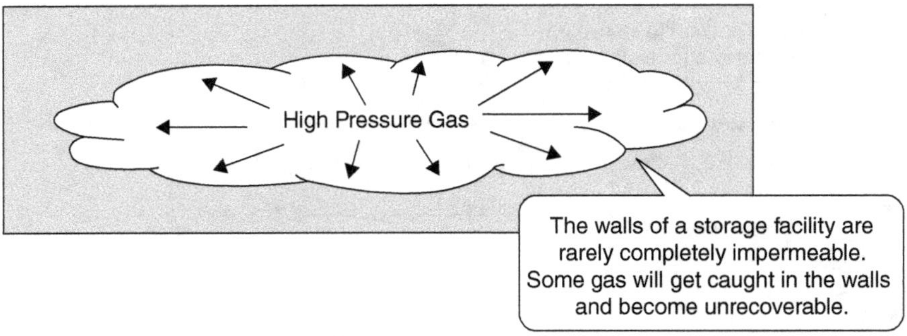

Figure 5.2.6 Physically unrecoverable gas

Depleted Gas Reservoirs

Once a natural gas reservoir has been emptied, it can be refilled. This is a very easy way of creating a storage facility. While not all reservoirs are suitable for refilling, if one exists in the right area, is close to pipelines in a consuming region, and has the right geological properties, this can be a very fast, reliable, and cost-effective way of getting a storage facility operational.

The physical characteristics of depleted gas reservoirs are usually well known since they already had wells on them. The maximum pressure and geological stability of the area would have been under continuous observation for years. Additionally, since natural gas has been stored in the reservoir for millions of years, there are few concerns about the geological impact of using the facility.

Another advantage of depleted reservoirs is that many still have the equipment that was originally used to remove the gas. Since this equipment can be reused, this allows for substantially lower startup costs than buying all of the equipment again.

Finally, storage facilities and reservoirs tend to have similar constraints on unrecoverable gas. Because unrecoverable gas can't be removed from a reservoir, it will still exist in the storage volume. As a result, a depleted reservoir won't require additional gas to be injected to form an unrecoverable gas barrier. When natural gas was exceptionally cheap in the early 1980s, pumping in unrecoverable natural gas was not a huge economic concern. However, because natural gas prices have risen substantially, unrecoverable gas is now an important economic consideration.

Overall, depleted gas reservoirs are quick and cost-effective to bring into service. Historically, depleted natural gas reservoirs have been the most abundant form of natural gas storage. Given the cost effectiveness of reusing an existing gas reservoir, alternative storage facilities must either provide better functionality or have a location advantage compared to a depleted gas reservoir. Depleted gas reservoirs need to reserve about 50 percent of their total capacity as a gas "cushion." Salt caverns, which only need to reserve about 33 percent, provide better performance characteristics. Aquifers, which often need to reserve about 80 percent of their capacity, are the least desirable type of storage facility.

Salt Caverns

Underground salt caverns offer excellent properties for natural gas storage. They are more expensive to develop than depleted gas reservoirs but have much better performance characteristics. These caverns allow very little gas to leak out, have extremely strong walls, and are generally resistant to damage. Essentially, they are high pressure storage vessels. They can operate at higher pressures than the other types of storage facilities, allowing gas to be cycled in and out of the facility more often. This is a huge benefit for customers who require erratic supplies of natural gas.

These storage facilities are constructed by removing salt from deposits and reusing the remaining cavern for gas storage. The best type of salt deposit to use for a storage facility is a "salt dome." Salt domes can be several miles across and over a mile high. Typically, salt domes are formed when a marine basin evaporates and is covered with sediment. The salt, being lighter than the surrounding sediment, will tend to move upward forming a dome.

Salt domes are typically excavated by injecting water into the rock formation and dissolving the salt deposit. This leaves a large empty cavern suitable for storing natural gas. The usual method for doing this is to drill down into the formation and cycle enough clean water through the salt deposit to fully dissolve the softer materials. After all the salt is dissolved, the remaining walls are extremely strong—they are the rock layers that proved impenetrable to the rising salt formation.

In areas where it is not possible to find well-formed domes, it may be possible to form storage facilities out of salt beds. Salt beds are much shallower, thinner formations usually a couple hundred feet in height. Because of their wide, thin construction, salt bed caverns are much more prone to collapse than caverns formed from salt domes. Compared to salt domes, salt beds also contain a higher quantity of insoluble rock. This slows down the speed at which gas can flow inside the facility. In general, salt beds tend to be more expensive to excavate and maintain than salt domes.

Because salt caverns store natural gas at high pressure, they require more specialized equipment than other types of storage facilities. Salt caverns are often pressurized to double the level of a standard gas pipeline. As a result, the pipes and fittings used to extract the gas from the facility often need to be much heavier grade than standard pipeline equipment. In addition, since the temperature of gas increases with pressure, gas being discharged from a salt cavern can be extremely hot. All of the pipes, fittings, and valves need to be rated for very high temperature gases, and resistant to the greater corrosion that comes with higher temperatures.

From an economic perspective, salt caverns are much more profitable than the other types of natural gas storage. The ability to insert and remove gas quickly allows salt caverns to benefit from short-term shortages in the natural gas supply. Combined with a fast-starting gas turbine electrical generator, they can provide a good way to benefit from short-term spikes in electricity prices.

Aquifers

Aquifers are the least desirable and most expensive type of natural gas storage. Aquifer storage facilities are water reservoirs modified to store natural gas. They are only built if they have a large geographical advantage—they are in the right place when nothing else is available. Most of the gas in aquifer storage facilities is unrecoverable. Aquifers have the lowest percentage of working gas to total volume of any storage facility, and the slowest injection/withdrawal cycle of any storage type.

Since there is no gas present when a facility is built, a large volume of gas must be placed into a facility. Compared to other storage types, there is also less leeway to remove the gas cushion before impairing the ability of the facility to operate. All existing aquifer facilities were built when natural gas was relatively inexpensive, and it would be difficult to economically make the initial investment in unrecoverable gas today.

The U.S. government has placed restrictions on building new facilities in areas where the water is usable for human consumption or irrigation. This policy, combined with the limited economic viability of aquifers, has made it unlikely that substantial future development in aquifer storage will occur.

Common Terms

Cycling. The number of times that a storage facility can be emptied and refilled within a calendar year. For example, many storage facilities are a single-cycle facility. It takes so long for them to fill up that they cannot sell gas in both the summer and the winter. If they sold gas in the summer, they wouldn't have enough time to fill up again prior to the winter season.

Deliverability. The ability to pull gas out of a storage facility for sale. The deliverability of a facility depends on the amount of gas in the facility. When the facility is nearly full, the deliverability will be at its highest.

Gas Storage Capacity. The storage capacity of a facility is typically broken into two pieces—base gas and working gas. Base gas is not normally removed from the facility. The working gas is the gas that is added and removed during the injection and delivery cycle.

Injection Capacity. The speed at which gas can be placed back into a facility. The more gas that is in the facility, the longer it takes to inject additional gas. Injection capability is just the opposite of *deliverability*—it is lowest when the facility is nearly full.

Trading Example—Natural Gas Storage

A high-performance natural gas storage facility in the New Jersey area has just been constructed. The storage capacity in the facility is being auctioned off to the highest bidder.

1. **The Opportunity.** There is a limited amount of natural gas storage facilities anywhere on the East Coast. Because of this, natural gas prices see more cyclical variations than other parts of the country. Capacity in the storage facility is being sold at auction, so it is necessary to develop an appropriate bid.
2. **The Intuition.** A natural gas storage facility will allow a trader to buy during periods of low demand, hold the gas, and resell it during periods of high demand.
3. **The Strategy.** The valuation of the strategy will examine a number of trades limited by the physical characteristics of the storage facility. The best combination of trades will determine the value of the bid.
   - *Seasonal Trade*. The largest amount of gas will be purchased during the spring and fall months when natural gas is normally inexpensive. It will be resold in the summer and winter when prices are higher. Many storage facilities can only empty and refill once a year—they can't meet both the summer and winter demand. However, in this case, the facility is a high-performance facility that can be emptied and refilled twice in a single year.
   - *Weekday/Weekend.* The trader is also considering buying gas on weekends and reselling it during weekdays. This will affect the seasonal trade by slowing down the speed at which gas is injected and removed from the facility. Instead of seven days of insertion or removal of gas, there will only be three net days of insertion or delivery for the seasonal trade. On the two weekend days, gas will be placed into the facility so that it can be sold on a weekday.

   An optimization of trading will be required to determine which combination of trades is expected to be the most profitable. For example, the operational limits of the facility might make it impossible to do both the weekday/weekend trade and the seasonal trade throughout the year.

(*Continued*)

4. **The Risks.** Since this is a competitive bidding process, there is a risk of doing the analysis wrong and bidding too high. If that happens, the trader will probably end up winning the auction and overpaying. This is an asymmetric risk, because if the bid was much too low, someone else would always win the auction. Traders use a term from economics, the "winner's curse," to describe this possibility.

   Another risk of the trade is a change in seasonal dynamics. For example, in the mid-1980s there were very few natural-gas-fired power plants. As a result, there was relatively little demand for natural gas during the summer. Natural gas was almost exclusively used during the winter by homeowners. Twenty-five years of building natural-gas-fired power plants has changed that dynamic. Natural gas is now a major fuel used for electrical generation. As a result, summer natural gas prices have skyrocketed.
5. **Executing the Trade.** Owning a physical storage facility means hiring an operations team to coordinate the physical delivery and sale of natural gas. This is no longer a financial deal—it is a 20-year commitment to keep a staff in place to service this contract. Even if a lot of the trading is arranged ahead of time in the futures market, there will be a substantial amount of daily housekeeping that is required.
6. **The Results.** One side benefit of owning a storage facility wasn't mentioned yet. In addition to being a potential profit opportunity, a storage facility gives a natural gas trader the ability to deliver and receive natural gas. This might make it possible for the trader to enter into other trading opportunities. For example, the trader might decide to sell other traders insurance that their natural gas deliveries would occur. He would make an up-front premium for the insurance, and if he had to cover deliveries in the event of a shortfall, he wouldn't have to resort to buying the gas on the (probably skyrocketing) spot market.

Natural Gas Storage Reports

The U.S. government agency responsible for producing natural gas statistics is the Energy Information Agency. It publishes a weekly report that indicates the amount of natural gas currently being stored. There are two main parts to this report. The first part is a table indicating the amount of natural gas stored in each region. The second part is a graph that shows the total amount of natural gas currently in storage relative to the past five years (Figure 5.2.7).

Working gas in underground storage, Lower 48 states Summary text CSV JSN

	Stocks billion cubic feet (Bcf)				Historical Comparisons: Year ago (05/20/15)		Historical Comparisons: 5-year average (2011-15)	
Region	**05/20/16**	**05/13/16**	**net change**	**implied flow**	**Bcf**	**% change**	**Bcf**	**% change**
East	511	490	21	21	395	29.4	433	18.0
Midwest	629	606	23	23	387	62.5	435	44.6
Mountain	171	166	5	5	128	33.6	121	41.3
Pacific	298	293	5	5	304	−2.0	252	18.3
South Central	1,216	1,199	17	17	856	42.1	814	49.4
Salt	372	371	1	1	258	44.2	216	72.2
Nonsalt	844	828	16	16	598	41.1	599	40.9
Total	**2,825**	**2,754**	**71**	**71**	**2,069**	**36.5**	**2,056**	**37.4**

Summary

Working gas in storage was 2,825 Bcf as of Friday, May 20, 2016, according to EIA estimates. This represents a net increase of 71 Bcf from the previous week. Stocks were 756 Bcf higher than last year at this time and 769 Bcf above the five-year average of 2,056 Bcf. At 2,825 Bcf, total working gas is above the five-year historical range.

Working gas in underground storage compared with the 5-year maximum and minimum

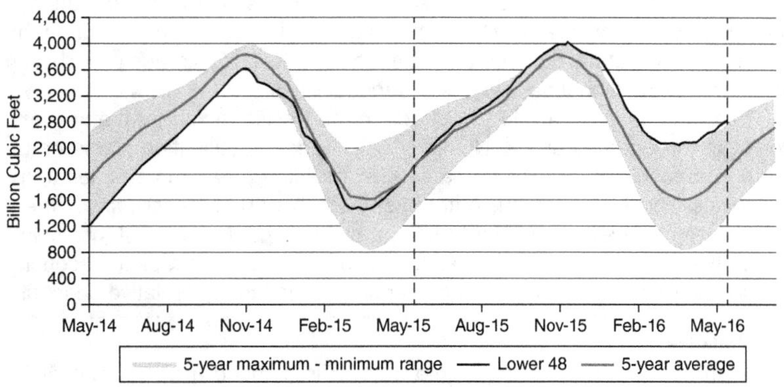

Source: U.S. Energy Information Administration

Note: The shaded area indicates the range between the historical minimum and maximum values for the weekly series from 2011 through 2015. The dashed vertical lines indicate current and year-ago weekly periods.

Figure 5.2.7 EIA natural gas storage report
(*Source*: U.S. Energy Information Agency)

5.3

LIQUEFIED NATURAL GAS

30-Second Summary

Purpose

This chapter introduces liquefied natural gas (LNG).

Summary

LNG facilities convert methane from a gas into a liquid that takes up much less volume. Allowing natural gas to take up less volume makes it economical to transport overseas with transport ships. As a result, LNG technology is closely associated with a global market for natural gas. Although there are few trading opportunities specifically related to LNG, it is having a big effect on the structure of the natural gas market. On a small scale, LNG storage provides an alternative to traditional natural gas storage facilities.

There has been an active LNG trade in the Pacific region for many years. However, the opening up of LNG liquefaction and regasification plants in the North American and European markets is providing greater international opportunities. This increased customer base has allowed aggressive investment into research, development, and LNG production that have substantially improved the efficiency of this technology. As a result, LNG is rapidly becoming a major factor in natural gas trading after several decades of relative obscurity.

Key Topics

- Being able to turn methane into a liquid is creating a global market for natural gas (methane) to replace the isolated regional markets that have historically defined the natural gas market.
- As liquefaction and gasification technologies become more energy efficient, LNG becomes more efficient and more economical too.

Natural gas can be converted into a liquid at standard atmospheric pressures by lowering its temperature to –260°F. This reduces the volume of natural gas to 1/610th of its gaseous volume. Being more compact allows liquid natural gas to be stored or transported when regular storage facilities and pipelines are not available. Although small-scale transportation is still not cost-effective, cargo ships can transfer enough fuel at a low enough cost that LNG is becoming an economical alternative to domestic production of hard to extract natural gas.

In the early 2000s, the driving force behind LNG was the expectation that the U.S. and European markets would soon require natural gas imports. The United States and Europe consume a large portion of the world's natural gas but were believed to contain only a small percent of the world's proven natural gas reserves. Sooner or later, the thinking was that it would become cheaper for those regions to import natural gas from other parts of the world than to extract gas from domestic reserves. By 2015, the expansion of natural gas fracking in the United States led to a sudden influx of cheap natural gas. This has led to LNG terminals that were once expected to be regasification terminals being converted into liquefaction units to export gas.

Natural gas producers benefit from being able to transport their natural gas overseas. Historically, the only real markets for LNG were the Asian markets of Japan, South Korea, and Taiwan. Unless natural gas could be shipped to those markets, a natural gas well without a pipeline connecting it to a major consuming region was stranded. The natural gas couldn't be sold. Even if the gas could be liquefied, there were only a few markets that could accept delivery of the liquefied gas. However, opening the North American and European markets to LNG changes that dynamic. Shipments can enter the North American and European markets from almost anywhere and feed into their transcontinental pipeline systems.

For natural gas producers, the LNG market allows them to monetize their investment. They can build an LNG liquefaction terminal and then sign long-term agreements to sell their product overseas. Instead of sitting on a natural gas field that might or might not ever be worth something in the future, producers can build a pipeline to the nearest LNG terminal and ship their product as a liquid into a major consumer market. This gets low cost producers access to the best consumer markets and provides them with money to search for new supplies.

There are three main steps in the LNG process—*liquefaction, transportation,* and *regasification.*

- **Liquefaction and Exporting.** Liquefaction plants are located near regions where natural gas is produced. Short-range pipelines transfer the gas from wells to the liquefaction plant. The liquefaction plant cools the natural gas down to –260°F, and then loads it into storage containers for transfer to specially designed tanker ships.

  Bringing natural gas to –260°F is an extremely energy-intensive process. A considerable amount of energy is consumed during the liquefaction and subsequent reheating processes. From a climate perspective, the CO_2 emissions resulting from this processing have to be included in the greenhouse gas emissions of LNG as a fuel source.

- **Transportation.** LNG tankers have to be specifically designed to handle extremely cold liquids and keep them insulated. Even then, some of the liquid methane will convert back into a gas. A small percentage of the natural gas will be lost in transportation for this reason. Faster journeys and cryogenic systems to refreeze the boiled-off gas can reduce these losses.
- **Regasification and Importing.** Once LNG is transported, it must usually be turned back into a gas before it is delivered to customers. This is typically done at a regasification plant. This plant transfers the LNG from the tanker ships and stores it in specially designed containers that can keep the LNG at low temperature until it is ready to be warmed up. After it is warmed up, the LNG can be placed into a pipeline for delivery to customers.

Concerns

The safety of LNG storage and regasification facilities is the source of major controversy. It is one of the primary reasons for the limited number of LNG terminals worldwide and a continuing reason why politicians block new facilities. LNG facilities contain a tremendous amount of fuel in a confined space. The concern is that these facilities could cause catastrophic damage in the event of a disaster.

Proponents of LNG claim a strong safety record. Like all natural gas, LNG is primarily composed of methane. Methane is an odorless, nontoxic gas that we breathe every day. It won't poison the environment or kill wildlife in the event of a spill. Unless it is in a contained environment, LNG is also not explosive. Although it can burn, it doesn't transition rapidly enough from liquid phase to gas phase to form the overpressure necessary to create an explosion. In the event of a leak, like normal natural gas, LNG only combusts when it exists at the right ratio of methane to air.

Peak Shaving Units

As the technology for liquefying and regasification gets less expensive, LNG may become attractive alternative to more traditional methods of storing natural gas. By turning it into a liquid, the amount of storage space required by a storage facility is dramatically reduced. This allows natural gas to be stored in areas that don't have the proper geological formations required for traditional storage facilities. From an investment perspective, these facilities are valued similarly to normal storage facilities.

Trading Example—Peak Shaving Unit

Small-scale LNG storage facilities can provide a way to buy natural gas at periods of low demand for use during heavy demand periods.

1. **The Opportunity.** A company owns natural gas peaking generators and is looking to lock in a fuel supply. They are considering investing in a small-scale LNG-based storage facility. To reduce the amount of energy consumed by liquefaction and reheating, this facility is partially powered by a thermal solar facility. The solar installation heats rock salt around 600° F, liquefies it, and then stores it in an insulated container so that the melted salt can be used to convert LNG into gas when needed.
2. **The Intuition.** This is a combination of two technologies—a thermal solar installation and a small-scale LNG facility. Both facilities need insulated storage. Liquefying and heating natural gas requires a tremendous amount of energy. However, most of those energy requirements can be met by the thermal solar installation. The size of the solar facility determines how much heating and cooling can be done.
3. **The Strategy.** This facility will operate similar to any other storage facility. However, instead of being located in an underground rock formation, the natural gas will be stored in insulated containers. Since this does not require a lot of room, it is easier to locate this facility close to an electrical consuming region that often experiences congestion. The combination of being able to buy fuel at low cost, use solar power to handle the ongoing energy requirements, and then resell the electricity at the highest possible price makes this an interesting investment.
4. **Valuation.** This valuation incorporates elements of several other types of models. The ability to sell power makes this installation look a lot like a tolling agreement. However, the LNG storage allows a time shifting of the natural gas purchase from low cost to high cost periods.

6.1

Mark-to-Market Accounting

30-Second Summary

Purpose

This chapter describes the concepts behind mark-to-market and fair value accounting.

Summary

Mark-to-market is a type of fair-value accounting that applies to financial investments. It is the most common valuation standard used for energy transactions. Accounting policies around mark-to-market define what is meant by a trading price. As a result, mark-to-market affects anything that uses prices as an input (like risk management and financial reporting). The primary alternative to mark-to-market accounting, *historical cost accounting*, applies to physical assets like buildings and equipment. With a few exceptions, this type of accounting values assets at their acquisition cost and this value does not change over time.

Key Topics

- Mark-to-market is the standard accounting applied to energy trading.
- Mark-to-market depends on trading markets for prices. This doesn't always coincide with the reality of energy markets since many markets are illiquid or intermittent.
- Accounting recognizes that not all prices are equally visible and has developed a *fair value hierarchy* for companies to report illiquid or heavily modeled prices to shareholders.

Mark-to-market is a type of fair-value accounting that applies to financial investments—anything that is considered a derivative needs to use this standard. As a result, mark-to-market is the most common valuation standard used for energy transactions. This has a cascade effect on many areas since accounting policies around mark-to-market define what is meant by a trading price. Consequently, this standard affects anything that uses prices as an input (like risk management and financial reporting). Sometimes this creates unexpected consequences.

The primary alternatives to mark-to-market accounting are *hedge accounting* and *historical cost accounting*. *Historical cost accounting* applies to physical assets like buildings and equipment. Hedge accounting applies to derivatives that are used to hedge physical assets. Hedging is discussed in its own chapter.

Mark-to-market is not always easy to implement for energy transactions. One reason it is difficult is a lack of potential trading partners. Sometimes there is no counterparty willing to transact a particular commodity at a specific location. In other cases, a contract might not be easily assignable to another party. For example, a power purchase agreement (PPA) might obligate a utility to purchase power and various nontradable items like capacity and ancillary services from a specific electrical generation unit. If this contract specifies the generation facility, it might not be possible to sell the contract to anyone else without selling them the physical unit at the same time. This might result in a gray area where accountants would need to determine which accounting rules might apply to a particular investment.

Even so, there is a big advantage to using mark-to-market accounting—it is fairly intuitive for most assets. If an asset is purchased for $100 and the same asset starts selling for $120, under mark-to-market accounting, it will show a $20 profit. The alternative, *historical cost*, keeps assets marked to their purchase price until they are actually sold. Historical cost accounting can be misleading in the cases of long-dated assets because the value of those assets isn't regularly updated. Typically, there is little choice about which type of accounting can be applied—accounting rules will specify the type of accounting that must be used.

- **Mark-to-Market Accounting.** Mark-to-market accounting uses recent prices quoted in the financial markets to determine the value of investments. Any contract that can be traded (futures, swaps, options) will typically be subject to mark-to-market accounting.
- **Historical Cost Accounting.** Historical cost accounting uses the purchase price of assets to determine the value of investments. This is most commonly used for physical investments (buildings, equipment) that can't easily be traded.

How to Manipulate Mark-to-Market Accounting to Manage Earnings!

Mark-to-market accounting is only safe to use in liquid markets where there is enough trading to guarantee rational prices. For illiquid assets, it is sometimes necessary to supplement mark-to-market prices with models.

(*Continued*)

Having a second check on pricing not only limits the risk of transacting at illogical prices, but it also limits the ability of traders to play accounting games to smooth out earnings.

Consider two traders at rival firms that recently had large losses on their energy trading desks. If those losses are reported to the risk committee of their respective firms, they will be forced to curtail some of their trading and will get smaller performance-based bonuses. To avoid this, they each agree to buy a small amount of an illiquid asset held by the other at a high price. They don't need to transact with each other at all.

By making a trade at the high price, the other trader will be able to mark a profit on the illiquid asset. The actual size of the trade used to set prices can be very small. If the traders are smart enough to make small trades in a large number of illiquid assets, particularly ones they don't own themselves, this manipulation can be very difficult to catch. This type of abuse can be eliminated if the trades are compared to a modeled price in addition to a market price.

Fair Value

Fair value accounting, which includes mark-to-market, is used to value many tradable assets. The general premise behind this approach is that trading is possible—that cash can be paid or received to transfer the item being valued to another person. If cash would be received to transfer the item to someone else, that item is called an *asset*. If cash has to be paid, the item is called a *liability*. The act of transferring either an asset or a liability for cash is called *liquidation*. For instruments that get traded regularly, the mark-to-market price is usually the last reported trade price.

Common Terms

Mark. The term *mark* means "to record for accounting purposes."

Market. A market is a mechanism, like an exchange or brokerage, that allows market participants to convert assets or liabilities into cash.

Asset. An asset is a financial instrument where a third party would pay money to take ownership of the item.

Liability. A liability is a financial instrument that would require paying someone to take ownership of the item.

Liquidation. Liquidation is the act of converting an asset or a liability into cash.

Liquidity. Liquidity describes the ease of converting an asset or liability into cash. A *liquid* instrument can be converted to cash quickly and at low cost. An *illiquid* instrument will be difficult to convert into cash quickly and/or will involve a high cost.

Fair Value. The fair value of an item is the amount of money required to liquidate an asset or liability under current market conditions. Value is an amount of cash. This can be found by multiplying a quantity of an asset by the price per unit.

There is often a symmetric relationship between the value of assets and liabilities. For example, if one person has an asset (perhaps owning title to a undelivered barrel of oil) there might be an equal and opposite liability (like someone's obligation to deliver that barrel of oil). In common usage, the price of the asset, as in "the price of a barrel of oil," is used to describe the price of both the asset and liability. In other words, there is typically a single price used to value both assets and liabilities. When a single price is used, this is often an approximation. For example, if valued for trading, an actual transaction might need to incorporate bid/ask spreads, transaction costs, and (if payment isn't in cash) the credit quality of the participants.

Relationship with Risk Management

Many risk management policies will trigger events, like forcing a trader to liquidate, as a result of prices reaching a certain level. Mark-to-market accounting is closely related to risk management because it determines the primary input into that process—the prices. The exact mechanism for risk management triggers can vary between market participants. For example, this can be done directly (a stop-loss if prices fall below a specific amount) or indirectly (a risk limit based on volatility, where a large price change will increase volatility).

Mark-to-market does address one specific type of risk. One of the primary drivers behind the adoption of mark-to-market was to prevent accounting fraud. It does this by forcing everyone in the market to use visible, recently updated prices. Most commonly, these prices are obtained from brokers, exchanges, or similar data providers that are independent of the group using the data. This reduces the need for traders to mark their own books and prevents them from adjusting prices to smooth out earnings.

On the downside, reducing one type of risk (accounting fraud) has created a new set of risks (exposure to bad prices) that has to be managed. Some of the problems associated with mark-to-market accounting are an increased likelihood of market panics, a temporary disappearance of liquidity, and bank failures. The underlying reason for these problems is that only a fraction of the total assets that exist in tradable form are bought or sold on any given day. As a result, a small number of transactions will determine the value of an entire industry. Additionally, since risk management limits margin, and capital requirements for banks all incorporate prices as their primary input, problems can cascade very quickly. This can turn a small issue into a major crisis.

Another problem with mark-to-market is that prices are not necessarily rational. Financial analysis makes a lot of assumptions about markets. For example, some common financial assumptions are that the time value of money links current and future prices, that markets are efficient, and so on. However, when everyone's prices are based on a very small volume of trades, those assumptions can fail. Traders can agree to transact at any price that they want.

For example, on a Friday before a long holiday weekend, a trader might be finishing up a large transaction before going on vacation. Due to some news event, concerns are raised that there is too much supply of the product being traded by the trader and prices start to decline. Selling into a falling market, the trader runs out of buyers who are willing to buy enough of the asset. Not wanting to deal with trading while on vacation, and with only minutes left to finish the transaction before the end of the day, the trader agrees to sell the final 1,000 contracts at a substantially lower price than the earlier trades. Because this happens right at the end of the day, this is highly likely to be the last trade that gets reported. As a result, everyone who owns the asset will have to mark a substantial loss on their balance sheets.

Even though selling at the last minute was perhaps an irrational decision since it did not maximize the firm's profit, the trader's decision to finish up before leaving on vacation wasn't indication of a distressed market. The market was operating normally and the transaction occurred between two willing market participants in the normal course of business. However, because of mark-to-market accounting, the trader's final transaction price will be used for everyone in the market.

If the impact was limited only to the transacting firm, this would not be a big deal. However, since everyone in the market is affected by this price, there is the potential for systemic problems that could cross multiple industries. For example, a bank might be required by its regulator to maintain a minimum level of liquid assets to be able to provide depositors ready access to their money. If one of their assets were to lose value, they would need to sell other assets to obtain more cash. This could cause a *market contagion* where prices in other markets are driven down.

Alternately, a large loss in value of an asset might trigger a margin call for other traders holding that asset as collateral. Those traders would then be required to obtain additional money, or sell assets, over a holiday weekend when doing so will be difficult. This can spiral out of control, when additional assets start being sold to cover losses, creating a sell-off crossing several markets. Ultimately, this can snowball into a market crash.

Key Concept

Risk managers need to be alert to the potential impact of mark-to-market accounting. On one hand, it prevents many fraud risks by creating a barrier between financial reporting and trading. On the other hand, mark-to-market increases the probability of systemic problems like forced liquidations and market crashes. Additionally, because of the barriers between trading and price reporting, it can also lead to critical business decisions being made without input from the people most in tune with the market—the traders.

Fair Value Accounting

Businesses often are required to use mark-to-market accounting due to accounting regulations. For example, in the United States, the U.S. Financial Accounting Standards Board (FASB) defines fair value as part of its accounting standards codification 820 (ASC 820). Internationally, the International Accounting Standards Board (IASB) defines fair value as part of the International Financial Reporting Standards topic 13 (IFRS 13). The definitions in the two standards are similar and define fair value on the basis of a price to liquidate a transaction under typical market conditions, called an *exit price*. Both standards also incorporate a way to describe the precision of the fair value estimate through the use of a *fair value hierarchy,* which ranks the accuracy of a fair price.

In some cases, there are multiple ways to liquidate an asset or liability. If a single market exists where a majority of trading occurs, a *primary market,* prices from that market should be used to calculate the exit price. Otherwise, accounting standards typically specify that companies should use an approach that maximizes the value of an asset. This is called the *highest and best use* or *most advantageous market* for an investment. Although these are distinct concepts, it should be noted that the primary market is very commonly the most advantageous market.

Common Terms

The definitions between ASC 820 and IFRS 13 are largely interchangeable. Some common terms used in calculating fair value:

Exit Price. The price that would be received to sell an asset or paid to transfer a liability in an orderly transaction between market participants at the measurement date.

(Continued)

Fair Value. The quantity of cash that would be received to sell an asset or paid to transfer a liability in an orderly transaction between market participants at the measurement date. This is typically found by multiplying the exit price by a quantity. In the case of a single asset or liability, this term is interchangeable with the term *exit price*.

Market Participant. Two traders who are independent of one another are defined as *market participants* if both are knowledgeable of current prices and other relevant market information, have an ability to enter into a transaction, and are willing (not forced) to enter into a transaction.

Orderly Market. An orderly market is one where market participants have a sufficient amount of time allocated to make a transaction.

Active Market. An active market is one in which transactions occur with sufficient frequency and volume to provide pricing information on an ongoing basis.

Principal Market. The principal market is the financial market with the greatest volume and level of activity for the asset or liability.

Highest and Best Use. The highest and best use of a nonfinancial asset (e.g., an oil well, natural gas pipeline, or wind farm) is the use that would maximize the value of the asset or the group of assets and liabilities (e.g., a business) within which the asset would be used. The highest and best use of an asset must be legal, physically possible, and financially feasible.

Most Advantageous Market. The market that, in the absence of a principal market, maximizes the amount that would be received to sell the asset or minimizes the amount that would be paid to transfer the liability, after taking into account transaction costs and transport costs. This is similar to "highest and best use" except that it applies to financial products and does not allow consideration of the related business.

If a primary market exists for an asset or liability, prices from that market should be used to mark the asset or liability to market. Otherwise, traders should try to identify the highest and best use or most advantageous market.

It should be noted the exit price is based on the definition of an orderly market rather than an active market. As a result, it may be necessary to mark-to-market assets and liabilities where pricing data are not regularly available.

Additionally, the terms *orderly* and *active* typically relate to the market in a particular asset or liability (like a natural gas futures contract) rather than a trading venue (like a commodities exchange). A commodities exchange will have markets in a variety of different commodities, some of which will be active markets and some inactive.

Prices published by the primary market must typically be considered for fair value with a few exceptions. The primary exception is when transactions were not orderly. There are two types of disorderly prices—*distressed* transactions and *forced* sales. In a distressed transaction, the company is in or near bankruptcy, experiencing a severe cash shortage, or having assets repossessed by creditors. In a forced sale, the trader is being required to sell to meet legal or regulatory requirements. A company's internal policies, like forcing traders to liquidate when risk limits are exceeded, or a trader rushing to finish a large number of transactions before a long weekend, are not considered disorderly transactions.

It is also important to note that the market as a whole will never be considered distressed. In other words, as long as the market is open and some market participants could be transacting, then the published prices have to be used. Accounting guidance has specifically stated that even when the market is crashing, it is not acceptable to calculate the value of the asset based on a hold-to-maturity approach (by discounting expected future cash flows) or use assumptions based on normal market conditions.

> *Even if there has been a significant decrease in the volume and level of activity for the asset or liability and regardless of the valuation technique(s) used, the objective of a fair value measurement remains the same. The FASB defines fair value as the price that would be received to sell an asset or paid to transfer a liability in an orderly transaction (that is, not a forced liquidation or distressed sale) between market participants at the measurement date under current market conditions.*
>
> (*Source:* FASB ASC 820-10-35-51D)

Disorderly Transactions

Market data produced through trading markets should generally be used except in cases of distressed or forced transactions. Some indications of disorderly transactions:

1. **Insufficient Marketing Time.** A transaction may be disorderly if it was exposed to the market for an inadequate period of time prior to transacting. An adequate period of time is generally defined as the customary period provided to similar trades under current market conditions.
2. **Single Buyer.** A transaction may be considered disorderly if the seller marketed the asset only to a single market participant even if a customary marketing period was used. Transactions where multiple buyers saw the trade, but only one was interested, are not disorderly.

(*Continued*)

3. **Distressed Sale.** A distressed sale occurs when the seller is in or near bankruptcy, is experiencing severe cash shortage, or is having assets repossessed by creditors.
4. **Forced Sale.** A forced sale occurs when the seller is required to sell assets to meet legal or regulatory requirements. A forced sale can also occur when the company has entered into a supervisory agreement with regulators. Forced sales do not occur when the trader's internal policies require a sale.
5. **Erroneous Price/Outlier Price.** An outlier price occurs when the transaction price is an obvious outlier compared to other recent transactions in the same (or similar) securities. For example, this might occur if a decimal point was misplaced when the trade was reported. An abnormally high or low price that results from normal market activities is not considered an outlier.

Fair Value Hierarchy

Because exit prices are based on the definition of an orderly market rather than an active market, it is often necessary to mark-to-market assets and liabilities even if pricing data are not regularly available. Accounting guidance recognizes that pricing is less certain for these assets and liabilities. As a result, accounting guidance requires companies to report the size of illiquid investments to shareholders.

To standardize reporting of illiquid investments, a significant element in both ASC 820 and IFRS 13 is the use of a three-level fair value hierarchy. This hierarchy differentiates the types of inputs, like prices, that are used to value investments. Inputs are separated into three categories ranging from highly liquid level 1 inputs to extremely illiquid level 3 inputs (Figure 6.1.1). Level 1 fair value inputs are highly

Type of Input	Description
Level 1 Input *All market participants exactly agree on a value for the input.*	Level 1 fair value inputs are highly observable and every market participant can agree on the exact price. Typically, these prices are published by a principal market.
Level 2 Input *A tight range of estimates exists for the value of an input.*	Level 2 fair value inputs are observable with a tight range of values. Market participants won't all agree on an exact price for a level 2 input, but prices will be in a tight range. For example, if trading is conducted through brokers rather than a principal market, it is common for each broker to be quoting a slightly different price.
Level 3 Input *The input is unobservable and a wide range of estimates exist.*	Level 3 fair value inputs are unobservable. Different market participants might develop a wide range of values for these inputs. These inputs are typically heavily modeled or based on illiquid markets where data is unavailable.

Figure 6.1.1 Fair value inputs

observable inputs—typically prices directly from an exchange. Level 2 inputs are more subjective and often result from fragmented markets where trading is spread out between multiple venues. Level 3 inputs are unobservable and associated with markets with limited liquidity.

Assets and liabilities are described as level 1, level 2, or level 3 securities depending on the market data used during their valuation. Level 1 securities are based exclusively on level 1 inputs. In a similar manner, level 2 securities can use a combination of level 1 and level 2 inputs. Finally, level 3 securities incorporate at least one level 3 input (Figure 6.1.2).

For example, the price of natural gas at Henry Hub is the benchmark natural gas price in the United States. It is the delivery point for U.S. natural gas futures. Prices at this location would be considered level 1 inputs, and natural gas futures settling at Henry Hub would be considered level 1 securities. Natural gas prices in Texas are priced as a spread to Henry Hub prices, typically within a couple of cents of the Henry Hub price. This spread is primarily quoted by brokers and is a level 2 input. Natural gas swaps settling in Texas would be level 2 securities since they incorporate both a level 1 input and a level 2 input. These swaps are considered level 2 inputs even if the basis spread happens to be zero at the valuation date—to be considered level 1 securities, all of the data have to come directly from the primary market.

The determination on how to level a particular security needs to be made by the management of each firm. This designation depends on the market data the firm has access to and can change over time.

Level	Description
Level 1 *The exit price was directly observed on the principal market.*	Level 1 securities have an exit price (fair value) published by the principal market. There can be no modifications or adjustments to this price regardless of significance. Additionally, the data must be current (e.g., published on the valuation date).
Level 2 *There is no principal market or the valuation involves use of widely accepted, non-proprietary models.*	Level 2 securities can include both level 1 and 2 data or involve the use of widely accepted, non-proprietary models (like Black Scholes option models). This is the most common classification for energy trades or investments.
Level 3 *The valuation involves the use of non-observable inputs or proprietary models.*	Level 3 securities involve the use of proprietary data or models. Commonly, these securities are infrequently or intermittently traded. Different market participants may assign substantially different value to these investments.

Figure 6.1.2 Fair value levels

6.2

VALUE AT RISK

30-Second Summary

Purpose

This chapter is an overview of an important part of risk management—how to create a meaningful, high-level summary of trading risk without going into a lot of detail. *Value at risk* (VAR) is a very popular statistic used to summarize risk across a variety of instruments.

Summary

VAR is a risk management statistic that describes the size of an investment. Knowing the size of investments allows risk managers to set limits on the size of positions that traders can amass. To describe the size of investments, VAR examines likely daily (or weekly) profit and loss (P&L) on an investment. While risk management practices vary widely, size is one of the most important components of risk, and almost all risk management is at least partially based around a VAR methodology.

Like all measures of size, VAR does not do a particularly good job describing what will happen under extreme market conditions (like a stock market crash or a natural disaster). Although mathematics can try to extrapolate previously observed large losses, estimating what happens under extremes is largely guesswork.

Mathematically, VAR summarizes the risk of a portfolio by predicting the size of P&L movement that will occur with some frequency. For example, it is possible to calculate an estimate of the largest daily change in value that will occur approximately once a month.

Key Topics

- VAR is a measure of size. It attempts to describe "the big picture" rather than an analysis tailored to any specific investment.
- VAR is based on mark-to-market accounting prices.
- By design, a summary report like VAR obscures or ignores individual trades. Even though this supersummarized measure of risk doesn't include those risks, they still exist.
- VAR analysis is almost always done in conjunction with more detailed examinations of risk like *stress testing* or a *worst-case scenario* analysis.

VAR is a risk management statistic that describes the size of an investment. It was originally developed to combine different types of investments into a single measure of size. For example, describing the combined size of a $15 million stock investment and 15,000 crude oil futures is difficult. The cost to enter the transaction is not a good measure of size—the stock investment required $15 million in cash, and the crude oil investment didn't require any money down except for a refundable margin deposit. It isn't immediately clear which of the two investments is larger and more risky unless some analysis is performed.[1]

VAR addresses this by describing the combination of investments by something that they have in common—daily changes in value. Daily changes in value are also known as earnings or P&L. While risk management practices vary widely, size is one of the most important components of risk, and almost all risk management is at least partially based around a VAR methodology.

VAR is a "big picture" summary of the combined trading risk of an organization. It is a way of taking a lot of trades and understanding how they interact. This involves breaking down trades into a simple common denominator that is general enough to describe almost any type of trade. However, because it is a summary, VAR can ignore or obscure details that may be important to managing a trading operation. Risk management involves paying attention to both the big picture and to details. As a result, VAR is only part of the story. However, it is an important part of the story, since size is the headline of almost every risk report.

Because of its simplicity, VAR is the primary tool used to describe trading. Its popularity is largely based on the fact that the result of a VAR analysis is a single number, so it is easy to read the results every day. VAR analysis is almost always done in conjunction with other types of more detailed analysis.

There are two parts commonly associated with a VAR analysis—mark-to-market accounting (discussed in Chapter 6.1) and an analysis of P&L volatility. Typically, the term *risk of a portfolio* is synonymous with its P&L volatility.

A High-Level Summary

The purpose of VAR is to give a simple description of risk. For example, a VAR report might be "once a month the trading desk can be

---

[1] Since each crude oil future is for 1000 barrels, 15 thousand crude oil futures is 15 million barrels of crude oil. If oil prices are approximately $50 per barrel, then the trader is exposed to price movements on $750 million of crude oil. In this case, the crude oil investment is 50 times larger than the $15 million stock investment.

expected to lose at least one million dollars over a one-day period." This description is both meaningful and short enough to be conveyed to a large audience. As a single number, it is simple enough to use in daily reports and easy to examine for trends. For example, if the VAR had decreased by $20 million in the past week, this would represent a significant change in the risk of a portfolio.

There are four parts to a VAR description:

1. The first part of VAR is the description of the *frequency* at which some event will occur. Since there are approximately 20 trading days in a month, the frequency of a *once a month* daily move is 1 day out of 20. Translating that to percentages, a 1-in-20 chance means an event that occurs 5 percent of the time. More commonly, this is described as exceeding the 95th percentile of samples. A value that exceeds 99 percent of samples would occur about two and a half times a year.
2. The second part of VAR is a description of the *time horizon* of the expected move. In this example, the change in P&L is measured over a one-day period. Another possible time horizon might be a weekly move in P&L.
3. The third part of the description is the *sidedness* of the move. In the example, the measure is looking at the size of losses, so it is a one-sided VAR. If the report were describing the possible size of profits or losses, then it would be a two-sided VAR.
4. Finally, the last part of VAR is a description of the magnitude of the move. The magnitude of the expected move in the example was up or down by a million dollars.

Because it is so simple, a VAR report does not include a lot of details. For example, it doesn't give any information about what will happen if the price of oil doubles or the stock market crashes. It also doesn't give any information about how bad things could get in the event of a natural disaster or financial crisis. VAR is not a worst-case event either—VAR gives the minimum threshold for a move that can be expected with some frequency. In the example, a daily profit or loss of *at least* a million dollars was expected once a month. However, the report does not give a lot of insight into whether the move is likely to be a $1 million, $2 million, or $10 million.

Calculating VAR

Standard definitions of risk are based on the concept that prices can be assigned to assets through mark-to-market accounting and that those price changes lead to either profits or losses. Given that assumption, it

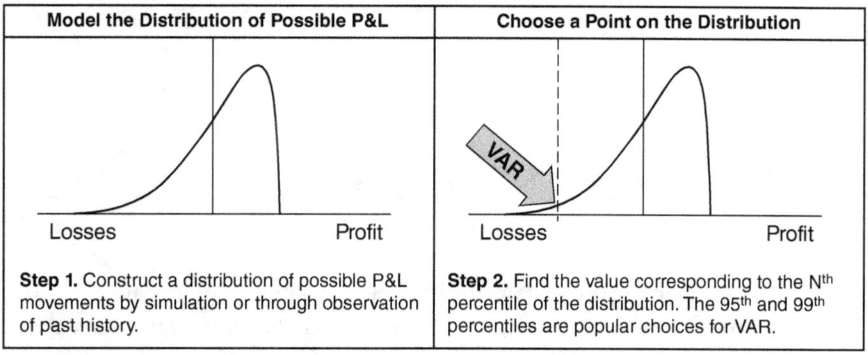

Figure 6.2.1 Constructing VAR

is possible to define the *risk* of a portfolio as the expected volatility of its profits and losses. In this way, P&L provides a common denominator for almost any type of investment.

VAR summarizes the risk of a portfolio by predicting the size of P&L movements that will occur with a specific frequency. It will use a single number to describe either a distribution or a bunch of distributions added together. For example, since there are approximately 20 days in a month, a P&L movement at the least as big as the one at the 95 percent frequency can be expected to occur, on average, at least once a month. As a result, a 95 percent level might be chosen to describe the entire distribution. As shown in Figure 6.2.1, there are two main steps to calculating a VAR number.

Not everyone uses the same frequency for VAR—some people prefer points that are more likely to be accurate and can be checked commonly while others prefer numbers that are more representative of a worst-case scenario. However, by picking a single point, VAR produces a simpler estimate of risk than having to use an entire distribution of predicted results.

VAR gives up accuracy for simplicity. In many cases, different assets can have the same VAR (Figure 6.2.2).

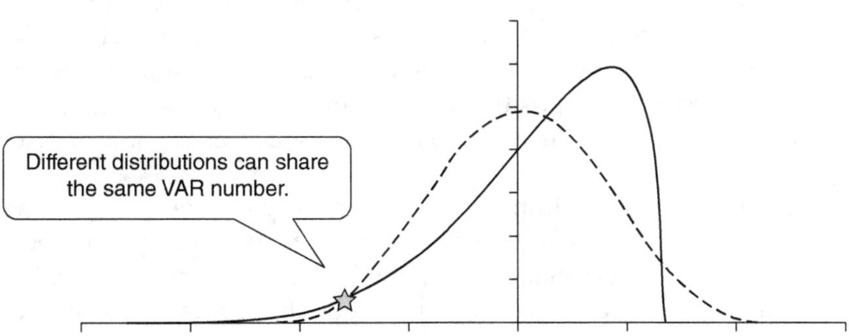

Figure 6.2.2 VAR for two assets

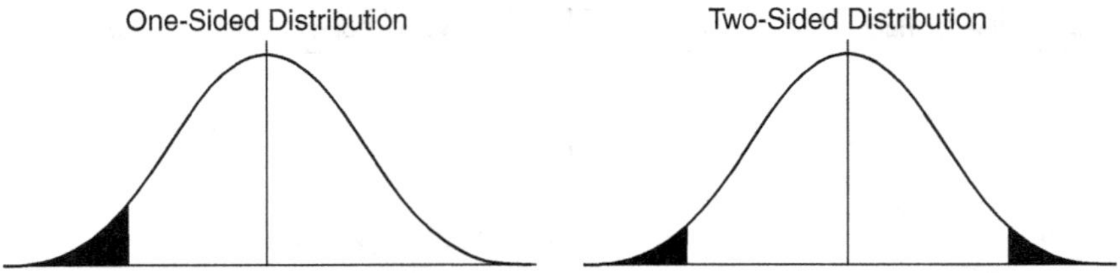

Figure 6.2.3 One-sided and two-sided VAR distributions

The methodology for calculating the percentile also can vary between firms. Some risk managers prefer to examine only losses; others prefer to look at the volatility of both profits and losses (Figure 6.2.3). If only losses are examined, the VAR is called a *one-sided VAR*. If both profits and losses are examined, it is called a *two-sided VAR*. A two-sided VAR will force an asset to have the single VAR regardless of whether it is long or short; it is largely a measure of volatility. One-sided VAR is more commonly used than two-sided VAR because risk managers often want to use VAR to calculate worst-case scenarios or potential losses in stress events.

Portfolio VAR

On a portfolio level, when multiple assets are combined, VAR becomes more complicated. This is due to the need to incorporate *diversification*. Diversification means that when two equal sized assets are combined, the combination of the two assets is less risky than either asset alone. This is because the assets may not move together and some of the extreme moves may partially cancel out. For example, when one is losing a lot of money, the other might be doing nothing or gaining money.

The amount of diversification gained by combining multiple assets depends on the relationship between the assets. At one extreme, if two assets are perfectly correlated, perhaps two identical crude oil contracts, then there is no diversification benefit. The risk of the combination will be twice as large as the risk of a single contract. At the other extreme, perfect negative correlation, the assets might be identical but with the opposite positions. For example, an agreement to buy a barrel of crude oil will offset the risk of an agreement to sell a barrel of crude oil.

Mathematically, combining the VAR of multiple assets can be done in two ways—*observed/simulated VAR* or *parametric VAR*. With observed/simulated VAR, the risk manager will construct a portfolio and value it over past data or some simulation of possible future price movements. The distribution of possible earnings can be directly sampled

Variance of Correlated Assets

$$\sigma^2_{Portfolio} = \sigma^2_A + \sigma^2_B + 2\rho\sigma_A\sigma_B$$

Where

$\sigma_{Portfolio}$	**Volatility of Portfolio.** The volatility of the combined P&L from two investments.
σ_A	**Volatility of investment A.** The volatility of an investment's P&L approximated as a normal distribution.
σ_B	**Volatility of investment B.** The volatility of an investment's P&L approximated as a normal distribution.
ρ	**Correlation between Investments.** This is typically calculated based on an analysis of historical relationships.

Figure 6.2.4 Variance of correlated assets

to identify VAR. With parametric VAR, each asset can be modeled as a well-known statistical distribution (like a normal distribution) and combined.

Parametric VAR is often based on the assumptions that assets have normally distributed returns. This makes it easy to find the risk of an entire portfolio because normal distributions are only based on two parameters (mean and standard deviation). One of those, the average return, can generally be approximated as zero for financial assets.

From a terminology perspective, volatility is typically abbreviated by the lowercase Greek letter sigma (σ). It is a synonym for the standard deviation of a portfolio. Variance is the square of the volatility. It is a synonym for mean square error and typically is abbreviated as sigma squared (σ^2). The variance of a portfolio can be calculated as the sum of the component variances plus a correlation adjustment (Figure 6.2.4).

Weaknesses of VAR

Because VAR is a single number, it has some limitations—it abstracts away the fundamental behavior of a portfolio. Typically, P&L is not normally distributed—there isn't an equal chance of making and losing money. Many energy assets—particularly the ones that can be modeled by options—have asymmetrical payoffs.

For example, a peaking power plant is going to lay idle for most of the year—it will lose money regularly whenever it is inactive. In all but the summer months, small operational charges will accumulate daily. A couple times a year—usually hot summer afternoons—the power plant will have the opportunity to make large windfall profits as it is pressed into duty (Figure 6.2.5). This is an example of a portfolio that benefits from volatility.

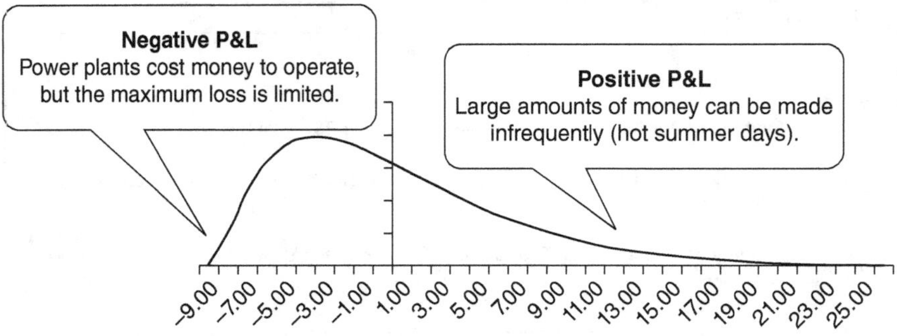

Figure 6.2.5 Asymmetric P&L

Stress Testing

It is often necessary to augment VAR with additional tests called *stress tests*. VAR is an approximation. It is a trade-off between simplicity and insightfulness. Being simple means that it is straightforward to implement and can be regularly examined by business leaders. However, VAR is not going to handle all types of portfolios well. Sometimes additional analysis will be required. There are so many possible special cases that no general model will be able to address them all. This doesn't make VAR worthless, just limited. It is useful precisely because it is a simple measure. Some common types of stress testing are to identify what might happen under certain scenarios. For example, it would be possible to track and report expected losses in a financial crisis or a natural disaster alongside VAR on a daily basis.

6.3

Counterparty Credit Risk

30-Second Summary

Purpose

This chapter introduces counterparty credit risk.

Summary

A large number of energy trades are contractual agreements made between two trading partners. Both partners depend on the other partner to meet their contractual obligations. *Counterparty credit risk* is the term used to describe the magnitude and likelihood of danger. This risk is commonly separated into two pieces. The first piece is being able to describe the magnitude of the risk (the *credit exposure*) and second is the likelihood of default (the *credit quality*).

Key Topics

- *Credit exposure* is the magnitude of a company's contractual obligations with a trading partner.
- *Credit quality* is the likelihood that a company will default on its obligations.
- Having credit limits that are too strict will hamper a firm's ability to do business. However, limits that are too loose will expose a trading company to the risk of bankruptcy.

In addition to various types of price and model risks, energy traders are commonly exposed to the danger that their trading partners will be unable to fulfill their obligations. The energy market is full of agreements made directly between two counterparties. Assessing the ability of a trading partner to meet their contractual obligations is crucial to trading energy products.

There are two parts to examining credit risk—establishing the magnitude of the potential loss (the *credit exposure*) and the likelihood of a loss will occur (the *credit quality*). Getting this information correct is important to running an energy trading business. Firms will often have hard limits on how much exposure they can have to a single counterparty. If exposure estimates are too high, business will be hurt because trading will have to be curtailed. However, if the estimates are too low, there is a risk of catastrophic losses due to a trading partner not fulfilling its obligations.

Some common terms related to credit risk are:

- **Obligor.** A person who is obligated to do something required by law.
- **Default.** A failure to do something required by law—like paying off a debt.
- **Counterparty.** From the perspective of one participant, the counterparty is the other participant involved in a contract or transaction.

Credit Exposure

Credit exposure identifies how much money could be lost in the event of a default. At its simplest, calculating credit exposure assumes a complete loss on every contract. The size of the complete loss is called the *exposure at default* (*EAD*). This places an upper bound on the potential loss, but also tends to overestimate the severity of the loss because some of the lost money may be recovered through bankruptcy proceedings. The percentage of money recovered during bankruptcy is called the *recovery rate*. The percentage of money that is not recovered during bankruptcy is called the *loss given default* (LGD).

Common Terms

Exposure at Default (EAD). The EAD is the amount of money that could be lost if a counterparty defaults on its obligations and goes into a bankruptcy situation.

Recovery Rate. The recovery rate describes the percentage of money lost due to credit exposure that might eventually be recovered through the bankruptcy process. On average, about 40 percent of unsecured debt is repaid.

Loss Given Default (LGD). The LGD is one minus the recovery rate. This is the amount of exposure that will be lost if the counterparty goes into bankruptcy. On average, about 60 percent of unsecured debt is lost.

In a bankruptcy, there is a priority order that determines which creditors get paid first. This can have a large effect on credit exposure. Unfortunately, most trading obligations are unsecured debts and fairly low on the priority list. The first creditors to get paid are employees

Bankruptcy Priority

1. Unpaid Wages
2. Unpaid Taxes
3. Secured Debt (collateralized bonds)
4. General Obligations & Unsecured Debt
5. Preferred Stock
6. Common Stock

Most trading credit risk is considered unsecured debt. It has a fairly low priority in a bankruptcy.

Figure 6.3.1 Bankruptcy priority

who are owed wages. Next, the company must pay any unpaid taxes. After that, the senior debt holders (typically the bondholders) get paid. After that, the trading partners (unsecured debt holders) are paid. The company's stockholders have the lowest priority when it comes to getting repaid in a bankruptcy (Figure 6.3.1).

Credit Quality

Credit quality is the other aspect of modeling credit risk. It attempts to describe the probability that a firm will default on its payments. This usually needs to be a forward-looking measure since energy contracts commonly last several years. There are a number of ratings agencies that provide credit ratings. These ratings can be augmented by in-house research focusing on a couple of key counterparties. There can be several layers to this analysis—a trading partner's credit risk will depend on the credit quality of its own clients. Also, a company is less likely to default if its large trades have moved in its favor, and it is more likely to default if trades have moved against it.

A good example of a cascading credit crisis was the bankruptcy of Enron. Enron was the single largest energy trader in the world. Enron was almost everyone's largest trading partner. As a result, even companies that didn't trade directly with Enron were exposed to its bankruptcy. When Enron went bankrupt, its assets were frozen. It stopped meeting its financial obligations. As a result, firms that traded with Enron had problems meeting their obligations, and so on. When Enron went bankrupt, the credit quality of many energy trading firms dropped at the same time.

Credit quality is often described by the term *probability of default* (PD). PD indicates the likelihood that the obligor will be unable to make scheduled repayments or similar obligations. When an obligor is unable to pay its debts, the obligor is said to be in default of the debt. Typically, this will lead to bankruptcy or similar proceedings where the creditors will seek partial repayment.

There are a number of ways to estimate probabilities of default. For something like a credit card portfolio, there will be enough defaults that direct observation is possible or a company, like Fair Isaac, may publish credit ratings (i.e., a person's FICO score). However, trading portfolios typically have low default probabilities, making it difficult to directly observe default rates. An alternate way to estimate default probabilities is to use credit ratings. A second alternative for large counterparties, like international investment banks, is to look at the credit default swap (CDS) market. The CDS approach can only be used for counterparties who have traded CDS products. This limits the CDS approach to very large counterparties like oil majors and large banks.

Common Terms

Probability of Default (PD). The probability that a default will occur on or before some date in the future. For example, there might be a PD estimated for the expiration date of the company's bonds or for a fixed time frame like sometime in the next month.

Protecting Against Credit Risk

The most obvious way of avoiding credit risk is to *know your trading partner*. Before trading with someone, most energy trading firms will want to know something about that person or company. For example: What is their line of business? How many assets do they have? What is their business model?

A second way of limiting exposure is to limit the amount of credit that can be extended to a trading partner. Combining payments and receipts is a common way of limiting exposure. In this way, only the net exposure needs to be watched. Another way to limit credit exposure is to have a *credit limit*. A credit limit prevents additional trading when the net exposure to a trading partner gets too large.

A third way to limit credit exposure is to use collateral. *Collateral* is an asset that is used to guarantee performance of a financial obligation. Typically, collateral is held in trust until the financial obligation is resolved. The collateral remains the property of the person or company guaranteeing performance. It might be in the form of bonds, stocks, or other investments.

If a company doesn't have the assets necessary for collateral, and is a fairly high credit risk, it might be required to buy insurance in the form of CDS. There is a trading market specific to CDSs where it is possible for a high-risk company to pay a low-risk company a fee to guarantee the payment of its obligations. This doesn't eliminate credit risk completely, but it does mean a company with a good credit rating is backing the exposure.

A fourth way of limiting counterparty credit risk is to incorporate *contractual terms* that mitigate the effect of credit risk. Two of the most common contractual terms used to limit credit risk are cross-default clauses and master netting agreements. A cross-default clause is a contractual clause that prevents a trader from selectively defaulting on an obligation. If a borrower defaults on any obligation, all of its obligations are considered to be in default. A master netting agreement forces a bankruptcy court to combine the exposures from various trades and treat the offsetting exposures as a single exposure. Without this netting, a bankruptcy court will invalidate only the monies owed by the bankrupt party.

Ring Fencing and Structural Subordination

In the energy market, a major complication to knowing one's trading partner is complex organizational structures. Many energy companies are actually conglomerates that are composed of multiple subsidiaries. The reason that many companies are conglomerates is that regulatory agencies (like public utility commissions) typically require that the companies that they regulate are protected from unregulated business.

Common Terms

Parent Company. A parent company is a company that owns a controlling interest in the stock of another company.

Holding Company. A holding company is a special type of parent company whose primary business is holding equity positions in its subsidiaries.

Subsidiary. A subsidiary is a company whose voting stock is controlled (i.e., at least 50 percent owned) by another company.

Affiliate. Companies will have an affiliate relationship when one company owns a substantial, but not majority, interest of the voting stock in the other company or if the companies are both subsidiaries of the same parent.

Corporate structure affects investors because affiliates (subsidiaries of the same parent company) may or may not be liable for obligations made by other subsidiaries of the parent company.

In some cases, a holding company and all of its subsidiaries will cross-guarantee the debt and obligations throughout the entities. In these cases, there is no difference created by doing business and lending to one entity over another. This is the best situation from a credit risk perspective.

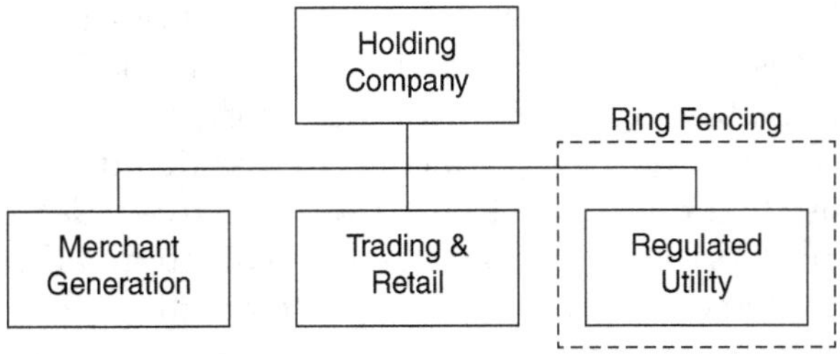

Figure 6.3.2 Ring fencing

Another common structure is *ring fencing*. Ring fencing is an economic strategy that legally separates a regulated utility from its unregulated parent or holding company. Effectively, this makes the parent company a shareholder in the subsidiary rather than an owner. This is problematic because the parent company can't directly access cash or assets located in the regulated utility. For example, they can't sell off an unused generation plant to raise money for another business (Figure 6.3.2).

When a subsidiary is ring fenced, the parent is entitled to dividends from the ring-fenced company and can sell off its ownership stake. However, the parent company often can't increase the dividend for the regulated utility (this would usually require approval from the utility's regulator) or liquidate the assets of the subsidiary to pay its own debts.

A second common organizational structure is *structural subordination*. This occurs when a conglomerate does business on several organizational levels (Figure 6.3.3). In the event that the company goes bankrupt, each subsidiary will pay its own creditors first. Only after that is done will money go to the parent company. This gives anyone with credit risk to the parent level a very low priority to get repaid using the assets owned by a subsidiary.

Dangers of Limiting Credit Exposure

If credit controls are too strict, it is impossible to conduct an ongoing trading business. A trading firm wants to enter contracts that result

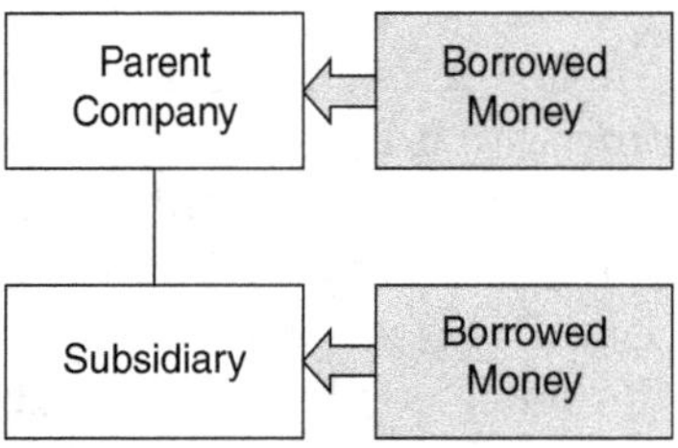

Figure 6.3.3 Structural subordination

in other people owing it money. That is the purpose of the trading company's existence. From that regard, it is both impossible and undesirable to completely eliminate credit risk. Companies trade with other companies that want to do business with them. As a result, strict credit limits mean missed trading opportunities and damaged relationships. On the other hand, credit limits are essential to keep from being pulled into bankruptcy when another firm goes bankrupt or refuses to meet its obligation. Credit limits involve a balancing act between having no limits (and doing lots of business) and having limits (and possibly losing some profit).

Credit Risk, Valuation, and Financial Reporting

Accounting guidance specifies that credit adjustments need to be incorporated into financial reporting. The process for financial reporting is a bit different than risk management because both assets and liabilities need to be adjusted for reporting purposes.

- **Credit Value Adjustment (CVA).** An adjustment in the value of an asset owed to the reporting company reflecting the potential effect of counterparty default. This will lower the value of assets a company is owed by its counterparties.
- **Debit Value Adjustment (DVA).** An adjustment to a liability, similar to CVA, reflecting the reporting company's own potential for default. This will lower the value of liabilities that a company owes its counterparties.

Financial Accounting Standards Board (FASB) Accounting Standards Convergence Topic 820 (ASC 820) is the accounting guidance that describes the relationship between fair value and credit adjustments. The credit guidance is discussed in Subtopic 10, Section 55, Paragraph 8:

> *55-8. A fair value measurement should include a risk premium reflecting the amount market participants would demand because of the risk (uncertainty) in the cash flows. Otherwise, the measurement would not faithfully represent fair value. In some cases, determining the appropriate risk premium might be difficult. However, the degree of difficulty alone is not a sufficient basis on which to exclude a risk adjustment. (FASB, 2009)*

Both CVA and DVA are based on the concept of value as the liquidation cost of an investment. Liquidation cost is the amount of money that must be paid or received to transfer an asset or liability to another market participant. With a DVA adjustment, there is the possibility

Expected Loss	
	$EL = (PD)(LGD)(EAD)$
EL	**Expected Loss.** The expected amount of money that will be lost due to credit.
PD	**Probability of Default.** The probability that a counterparty goes into default at some point in the future.
LGD	**Loss Given Default.** The percent of money lost in event of a default. Commonly, this is around 60 percent.
EAD	**Exposure at Default.** Exposure at default is the amount of money that could be lost if a counterparty defaults on its obligations and goes into a bankruptcy situation.

Figure 6.3.4 Expected loss calculation

that if a company might be going into bankruptcy, a creditor might accept less than full value for monies that it might be owed in exchange for getting that money before bankruptcy proceedings.

To calculate CVA or DVA, it is necessary to calculate the expected loss of an investment. This can be found by multiplying the exposure at each payment date by the PD on that date multiplied by the percent of money lost if a default occurs (Figure 6.3.4).

6.4

Model Risk

30-Second Summary

Purpose

This chapter introduces the concept of model risk—the risk that a valuation or risk management model isn't doing its job properly.

Summary

Energy trading is full of models—risk models, pricing models, and asset valuation models to name a few. These models are a simplification of real life. Because of this, ensuring that models work correctly is a major component of managing risk. It is fairly common for models to break at some point. When this happens, the problem needs to be quickly identified and solved.

Key Topics

- Bad assumptions, parameter estimates, or market data can lead to financial disaster.
- The primary ways to reduce model risk are setting position limits, taking reserves against potential losses, and reviewing models regularly.

A risk commonly faced by energy traders is *model risk*—the risk that either the methodology or assumptions used to value assets becomes invalid. Poor assumptions and incorrectly designed models cause risk management problems in every financial market. However, the complexity of energy models and their extended lifetimes, make these problems especially common in the energy markets.

The primary regulatory guidance around model risk comes from the U.S. Federal Reserve in its SR 11-7 guidance to banks. This guidance is generally appropriate to all types of models, including those used in the energy market:

> *The term model refers to a quantitative method, system, or approach that applies statistical, economic, financial, or mathematical theories, techniques, and assumptions to process input data into quantitative*

estimates. A model consists of three components: an information input component, which delivers assumptions and data to the model; a processing component, which transforms inputs into estimates; and a reporting component, which translates the estimates into useful business information. Models meeting this definition might be used for analyzing business strategies, informing business decisions, identifying and measuring risks, valuing exposures, instruments or positions, conducting stress testing, assessing adequacy of capital, managing client assets, measuring compliance with internal limits, maintaining the formal control apparatus of the bank, or meeting financial or regulatory reporting requirements and issuing public disclosures. The definition of model also covers quantitative approaches whose inputs are partially or wholly qualitative or based on expert judgment, provided that the output is quantitative in nature.

Source: U.S. Federal Reserve, SR 11-7 attachment

All models are less complicated versions of reality. There is always a risk that something vital is left out of a model, or something unnecessary is incorporated. There is a trade-off between model risk and model complexity. Very simple models may not include enough factors to accurately describe reality. On the other hand, simple models are easy for people to understand. It is possible to address model risk by having a lot of people looking for problems. Complex models include more factors, but they are harder to understand. It is often unclear when a complex model stops working, and it is unrealistic to assume that people can verify a model that they don't understand.

The Federal Reserve identifies two main causes of model risk—poorly built models and models being used incorrectly. In addition, there are several more practical problems that are commonly observed in the energy markets—bad assumptions, bad market data, and difficulty estimating model parameters.

Model risk occurs primarily for two reasons:

- *The model may have fundamental errors and may produce inaccurate outputs when viewed against the design objective and intended business uses. The mathematical calculation and quantification exercise underlying any model generally involves application of theory, choice of sample design and numerical routines, selection of inputs and estimation, and implementation in information systems. Errors can occur at any point from design through implementation. In addition, shortcuts, simplifications, or approximations used to manage complicated problems could compromise the integrity and reliability of outputs from those calculations. Finally, the quality of model outputs depends on the quality of input data and assumptions, and errors in inputs or incorrect assumptions will lead to inaccurate outputs.*

- *The model may be used incorrectly or inappropriately. Even a fundamentally sound model producing accurate outputs consistent with the design objective of the model may exhibit high model risk if it is misapplied or misused. Models by their nature are simplifications of reality, and real-world events may prove those simplifications inappropriate. This is even more of a concern if a model is used outside the environment for which it was designed. Banks may do this intentionally as they apply existing models to new products or markets, or inadvertently as market conditions or customer behavior changes. Decision makers need to understand the limitations of a model to avoid using it in ways that are not consistent with the original intent. Limitations come in part from weaknesses in the model due to its various shortcomings, approximations, and uncertainties. Limitations are also a consequence of assumptions underlying a model that may restrict the scope to a limited set of specific circumstances and situations.*

Source: U.S. Federal Reserve, SR 11-7 attachment

Model Documentation

Ensuring adequate model documentation is the first step toward managing modeling risk. This requires both organizing model information and requiring accountability from people using and developing models. For example, keeping a record of all of the models in an organization is a good start to this process. Ensuring that each model meets a minimum documentation standard and has someone assigned to keep the model updated are other essential steps. Another beneficial step is to have someone in a leadership position at the firm review each model. Accountability and a defined approval process is important (Figure 6.4.1). For example, there is a world of difference between "We use the model because a college intern that we hired over the summer five years ago said it was OK" and "A senior member of the firm, in consultation with the quantitative staff, approved the use of the model after the model was compared to three separate alternatives."

Some good practices to limit model risk are:

- Ensure that the firm keeps a record of all models used in the firm and that this list is updated whenever models are put into use (or retired).
- Assign each model a unique ID so that there is no confusion about which model is which when a model breaks or needs to be maintained.

- Require each model to achieve a minimum level of documentation and be approved by an appropriate party before being used.
- Assign a model owner to be responsible for maintaining the model and making sure the model is still in use at the end of each year.

Using Models Appropriately

One of the keys to ensuring that models are used appropriately is to have a plain English description of the model. This ensures that everyone who interacts with the model, from professional mathematicians, to traders, to software professionals and company leaders, understands the purpose of the model.

Models are typically composed of three parts—inputs, outputs, and a processing component that converts inputs to outputs. Examining each of these pieces will often indicate potential trouble areas. For example, a model might have initially relied on a data vendor to ensure that the input data were free of errors. If a cheaper data vendor was hired as a replacement, it would be necessary to ensure that similar checks on the data were being performed (perhaps the lack of checking is why the data are less expensive!).

Important information required to understand if a model is appropriately used is whether there were any restrictions placed on the model by the model developers. Other important information includes

Question	Guidance
Does the firm have a model inventory?	SR1107a, p. 20 - "Banks should maintain a comprehensive set of information for models implemented for use, under development for implementation, or recently retired."
Does the documentation contain a unique model ID that can be used to uniquely identify this model in the firm's model inventory?	SR1107a, p. 20 - "Banks should maintain a comprehensive set of information for models implemented for use, under development for implementation, or recently retired."
Does a model risk management policy exist at the firm?	SR1107a, p. 17 - "Consistent with good business practices and existing supervisory expectations, banks should formalize model risk management activities with policies and the procedures to implement them."
Does the model risk management policy establish a minimum level of documentation that must be met by each model?	SR1107a, p. 21 - "Documentation takes time and effort, and model developers and users who know the models well may not appreciate its value. Banks should therefore provide incentives to produce effective and complete model documentation."

Figure 6.4.1 Documentation questions

the theoretical foundation of the model, assumptions made by developers, and whether the people who have reviewed and developed the model were authorized and qualified to make that decision (Figure 6.4.2).

Question	Guidance
Does the model documentation describe why the model exists (the purpose of the model) and where the model is to be used (the scope)?	SR1107a, p. 5 - "An effective development process begins with a clear statement of purpose to ensure that model development is aligned with its intended use."
Does the model documentation describe the theoretical foundation of the model?	SR1107a, p. 6 - "The design, theory, and logic underlying the model should be well documented and generally supported by published research and sound industry practice."
Does the model documentation list the model's key assumptions and any limitations?	SR1107a, p. 21 - "Documentation of model development and validation should be sufficiently detailed so that parties unfamiliar with a model can understand how the model operates, its limitations, and its key assumptions."
Does the model documentation describe which policies apply to the model (and how to find the policies)?	SR1107a, p. 17 - "Consistent with good business practices and existing supervisory expectations, banks should formalize model risk management activities with policies and the procedures to implement them."
Does the model documentation describe the model approval process, in particular the current status of the model (in development / in validation / approved) and an approval timeline (names and dates associated with each approval)?	SR1107a, p. 18 - "The model owner should also ensure that models in use have undergone appropriate validation and approval processes..."
Does the documentation list all of the inputs used in the model? For regression models, this should contain a list of all factors considered for inclusion as well as those chosen.	SR1107a, p. 6 - "The data and other information used to develop a model are of critical importance; there should be rigorous assessment of data quality and relevance, and appropriate documentation."
Does the documentation have a section that describes all of the inputs needed to run the model?	SR1107a, p. 3 - "A model consists of three components: an information input component, which delivers assumptions and data to the model; a processing component, which transforms inputs into estimates; and a reporting component."
Does the documentation have a section that describes data processing (e.g., how the inputs are converted into outputs)?	SR1107a, p. 3 - "A model consists of three components: an information input component, which delivers assumptions and data to the model; a processing component, which transforms inputs into estimates; and a reporting component."
Does documentation describe the process for assessing the expert judgment used in the model (or state that the model does not rely on expert judgment)?	SR1107a, p. 14 - "When a model itself relies on expert judgment, quantitative outcomes analysis helps to evaluate the quality of that judgment. Outcomes analysis should be conducted on an ongoing basis to test whether the model continues to perform in line with design objectives and business uses."
Does the documentation have a section that describes outputs? In particular, does this section describe the units and range of outputs as well as any error codes?	SR1107a, p. 3 - "A model consists of three components: an information input component, which delivers assumptions and data to the model; a processing component, which transforms inputs into estimates; and a reporting component."

Figure 6.4.2 Model appropriateness questions

Testing the Model

It is often easier to watch a model for potential problems than it is to design a foolproof model. Observation is almost always easier than prevention. Having people pay attention to what is happening to a model means that problems can be found quickly. Most problems start to occur months or years before there is a financial loss. This makes observation a viable solution to most problems. People who depend on the model need to ensure that problems get reported and examined in a timely manner.

However, it is also possible to catch a lot of potential problems by testing models (Figure 6.4.3). *Backtesting* is the process of testing a model against as much historical data as possible. A related concept is *stress testing*. Stress testing simulates extreme conditions and unusual combinations of events. This is a way to catch combinations of events that might not have happened historically. *Benchmarking* involves comparing a model to alternative models and intuition. *Stability testing* ensures that small changes in model inputs give small changes to outputs.

- **Backtesting.** Backtesting involves testing a model to ensure that it works over some historical period.
- **Stress Testing.** Stress testing involves understanding how models work under unusual market conditions like a financial crisis, the bankruptcy of a major market participant, an unusually cold winter or hot summer, or a natural disaster.
- **Benchmarking.** Benchmarking involves comparing a model to alternative approaches or alternative models. For example, if an option model is being benchmarked, it might be compared to alternative option formulas, trader intuition, or historically observed payouts for similar options.
- **Stability Testing.** Models convert inputs into outputs. Generally, models produce progressively more severe outputs when progressively more severe inputs are used in the model. This is a good property for a model since this allows the use of inputs that have never been previously observed. Models that are unstable or chaotic (models that produce large, unpredictable changes in outputs given small changes in inputs) are much more difficult to manage.

Maintaining Models

Many modeling problems are caused by the failure to maintain models over time. Some of these issues are caused by changes to model assumptions while others are due to errors introduced as the model is updated. Models are a simplification of real life. They are based on

Question	Guidance
Does the model documentation describe alternative modeling approaches or state that the modeling approach is a commonly observed or de facto standard in the industry?	SR1107a, p. 6 - "Comparison with alternative theories and approaches is a fundamental component of a sound modeling process."
Does the documentation demonstrate that progressively more extreme inputs lead to progressively more extreme outputs? If not, does the model documentation describe how the results of the model might be extrapolated to situations that have never been observed?	SR1107a, p. 8 - "Therefore, banks should justify and substantiate claims that model outputs are conservative with a definition and measurement of that conservatism that is communicated to model users. In some cases, sensitivity analysis and other types of stress testing can be used to demonstrate that a model is indeed conservative."
Does the documentation describe the expected relationship between input and output? For example, does the model output (like the loss that is expected in a trading book) increase linearly or exponentially with changes in inputs?	SR1107a, p. 11 - "Where appropriate to the particular model, banks should employ sensitivity analysis in model development and validation to check the impact of small changes in inputs and parameter values on model outputs to make sure they fall within an expected range. Unexpectedly large changes in outputs in response to small changes in inputs can indicate an unstable model. Varying several inputs simultaneously as part of sensitivity analysis can provide evidence of unexpected interactions, particularly if the interactions are complex and not intuitively clear." SR1107a, p. 8 - "Therefore, banks should justify and substantiate claims that model outputs are conservative with a definition and measurement of that conservatism that is communicated to model users. In some cases, sensitivity analysis and other types of stress testing can be used to demonstrate that a model is indeed conservative."
Does the documentation describe the precision of the model outputs?	SR1107a, p. 8 - "Because they are by definition imperfect representations of reality, all models have some degree of uncertainty or inaccuracy. These can sometimes be quantified, for example, by an assessment of the potential impact of factors that are unobservable or not fully incorporated into the model, or by the confidence interval around a statistical model's point estimate. Indeed, using a range of outputs, rather than a single point estimate, can be a useful way to signal model uncertainty and avoid spurious precision."
Does the documentation compare model outputs to benchmarks like alternative models, business intuition, or support it with other data?	SR1107a, p. 13 - "Benchmarking is the comparison of a given model's inputs and outputs to estimates from alternative internal or external data or models. It can be incorporated in model development as well as in ongoing monitoring."
Have all numerical approximations, like Taylor Series Expansions or Delta/Gamma approximations for options, been tested under stress conditions?	SR1107a, p. 3 – "Errors can occur at any point from design through implementation. In addition, shortcuts, simplifications, or approximations used to manage complicated problems could compromise the integrity and reliability of outputs from those calculations."
Does the model contain backtesting or similar type of outcomes analysis? Was the model tested under historical stress conditions like a recent financial crisis or natural disaster?	SR1107a, p. 13 - "The third core element of the validation process is outcomes analysis, a comparison of model outputs to corresponding actual outcomes." SR1107a, p. 14 - "Backtesting is one form of outcomes analysis; specifically, it involves the comparison of actual outcomes with model forecasts during a sample time period not used in model development and at an observation frequency that matches the forecast horizon or performance window of the model."

Figure 6.4.3 Model testing questions

an analysis of typical behavior that may or may not be predictive of the future. Real life has exceptions to almost every rule, and it is not always clear where those exceptions are likely to occur. The most dangerous part of a model is getting basic assumptions about how the market operates wrong. If those assumptions are wrong, every conclusion made afterward is probably invalid too.

Models and the viability of the models' assumptions change over time. If a model lasts 20 years, a lot of things can change. Investments like power plants, pipelines, and natural gas wells all have an extremely long life span. Even when a pricing model is sufficient to describe the investment initially, there is no guarantee that things won't change. Assumptions made years earlier can be invalidated by regulatory changes, population shifts, and technological changes. Exacerbating this problem is the problem of employee turnover—commonly, the original developers of the models have moved to another job or retired before problems develop.

An example of a reality changing underneath a model is daylight savings time. When the energy savings from shifting the clock an hour was first calculated in the mid-1970s, air conditioners were still relatively uncommon. The 1975 study showed that energy use was cut slightly if the clock was shifted in the summer to have more sunlight in the evening. Thirty years later, Indiana finally switched over to daylight savings. Compared to the period before the switch, adopting daylight savings time caused a noticeable increase in that state's power consumption. The widespread adoption of air conditioning in the intervening years was thought to be the culprit since air conditioning, rather than lighting, was now the major use of electricity in the region.

Models often exist for a long period of time. Typically, when models are first created, the team that creates the model understands the details and knows where all of the documents supporting the model are located. Over time, those team members often get promoted, leave the firm, or pass on the work to new team members. Those new team members weren't part of the initial discussions and often will not know where to find calculations or supporting data unless that information is stored in the documentation (Figure 6.4.4).

There are several procedures that model developers can use to reduce maintenance problems:

- **Model ID.** Models need a name or other unique identifier. A modeling group might deal with hundreds of different models, and being able to uniquely identify models is the key to ensuring that they are all documented and the source code for the model can be found.
- **Model Owner.** Models need to have someone responsible for their maintenance. Otherwise, they can get lost or outdated.

Question	Guidance
Does the model contain a change log?	SR1107a, p. 12 - "... tests employed as part of model development should be included in ongoing monitoring and be conducted on a regular basis to incorporate additional information as it becomes available."
Does the documentation describe the main point of contact for questions about the model (e.g., a model "owner")?	SR1107a, p. 16 - "The role of model owner involves ultimate accountability for model use and performance within the framework set by bank policies and procedures. Model owners should be responsible for ensuring that models are properly developed, implemented, and used. The model owner should also ensure that models in use have undergone appropriate validation and approval processes, promptly identify new or changed models, and provide all necessary information for validation activities."
Does the documentation list model interactions and/or dependencies with other models (or explicitly state that no interactions exist)?	SR1107a, p. 4 - "Banks should consider risk from individual models and in the aggregate. Aggregate model risk is affected by interaction and dependencies among models; reliance on common assumptions, data, or methodologies; and any other factors that could adversely affect several models and their outputs at the same time."
Does the documentation describe which party is responsible for assessing aggregate model risk?	SR1107a, p. 4 - "While each line of business may maintain its own inventory, a specific party should also be charged with maintaining a firm-wide inventory of all models, which should assist a bank in evaluating its model risk in the aggregate."
Does the documentation include sufficiently detailed mathematical formulas that an experienced developer could use to replicate the model?	SR1107a, p. 6 - "The model methodologies and processing components that implement the theory, including the mathematical specification and the numerical techniques and approximations, should be explained in detail with particular attention to the merits and limitations."
Does the documentation have a section that describes data processing (e.g., how inputs are converted into outputs)?	SR1107a, p. 3 - "A model consists of three components: an information input component, which delivers assumptions and data to the model; a processing component, which transforms inputs into estimates; and a reporting component."
Did the documentation contain a test case that could be used by validators and developers changing the model to verify that the model is working as originally intended?	SR1107a, p. 12 - "Process verification checks that all model components are functioning as designed ... Computer code implementing the model should be subject to rigorous quality and change control procedures to ensure that the code is correct."

Figure 6.4.4 Model maintenance questions

- **Change Log.** Models will typically get updated many times over their lives. Every time a model is updated, it is necessary to document what changed and the reason for the change. That way, future model owners can understand why things have been done in a certain way.
- **Source Code Control.** Storing old versions of the model (version control) also ensures that if an update accidently introduces an error to a model, it is possible to go back to the previously working version of the model.

- **Test Case.** A test case is a known set of inputs and outputs that can be used to test that a model is still working as originally intended. If the model is tested against a known scenario every time it is updated, the likelihood of errors being introduced is minimized.
- **Interactions List.** Models often interact with one another. For example, the inputs to a model may be the outputs of a different model. As a result, changing a model may result in unintended changes in related models. The only way to prevent this from happening is to keep track of which models might be affected by changes and may need to be updated. This list must also be updated to keep it current.

Bad Market Data

Another issue that commonly comes up in energy trading models is that many physical trading points aren't very liquid. It is possible to trade at places that don't usually have prices. Of course, the price at the time of trading is known. However, any future prices will depend on other people trading at the same location. If no one trades there regularly, it might be a while before another price exists. As a result, illiquid trading locations often need to be approximated by prices at a nearby liquid benchmark. Sometimes, this is a good assumption. At other times, the expected relationship between a benchmark and an illiquid location breaks down.

The problem of limited data is related to the problem of how to estimate parameters. For example, a spread option will depend on an estimate of the correlation between two assets. If there are no readily available prices, the correlation can't be readily determined. As a result, it is fairly common for a couple of model parameters to be chosen (fairly arbitrarily) when a model is created. If any of those parameters turns out to be poorly chosen, the model might change dramatically (Figure 6.4.5).

Model Overlays and Reserves

If a model can't be trusted—and no model can be completely trusted—it makes sense to limit the total amount of money lost due to a single problem. This can be done by limiting the total amount of risk that can be taken on by a specific type of trading. This enforced diversification is called a *position limit*. Essentially, it is a mandate that a trading desk not place all of its eggs in the same basket.

A second way of limiting risk is to delay recognizing profits from a valuation model. If a model is hemorrhaging money, a lot of attention will get focused on it. Because of the attention, any modeling problems are likely to be found quickly. A more dangerous situation is a model

Question	Guidance
Does the documentation have a section that describes all of the inputs needed to run the model?	SR1107a, p. 3 - "A model consists of three components: an information input component, which delivers assumptions and data to the model; a processing component, which transforms inputs into estimates; and a reporting component."
Does the documentation detail the range of permissible values associated with each input. For example, what is the maximum and minimum value that has been tested to work?	SR1107a, p. 21 - "Documentation of model development and validation should be sufficiently detailed so that parties unfamiliar with a model can understand how the model operates, its limitations, and its key assumptions." SR1107a, p. 4 - "... the quality of model outputs depends on the quality of input data and assumptions, and errors in inputs or incorrect assumptions will lead to inaccurate results." SR1107a, p. 13 - "If models only work well for certain ranges of inputs values, market conditions, or other factors, they should be monitored to identify situations where these constraints are approached or exceeded."
Does the documentation describe the source of the data? This should be sufficiently detailed that a reader could obtain a copy of the input data using only the description provided.	SR1107a, p. 6 - "The data and other information used to develop a model are of critical importance; there should be rigorous assessment of data quality and relevance, and appropriate documentation."
Does the documentation describe whether any inputs are proxied by more available data? If so, have the proxies been tested to ensure that they are reasonable over time and have the same volatility as the input being replaced?	SR1107a, p. 6 - "If data proxies are used, they should be carefully identified, justified, and documented."
Does the model contain one-time adjustments or similar data overrides? If so, and the overrides substantially alter model performance, does the documentation justify the use of overrides through use of benchmarking or alternative models?	SR1107a, p. 14 - "Banks should evaluate the reasons for overrides and track and analyze override performance. If the rate of overrides is high, or if the override process consistently improves model performance, it is often a sign that the underlying model needs revision or redevelopment."

Figure 6.4.5 Model input questions

that shows a steady stream of profits. That model has a much higher probability of being ignored. To limit those problems, it is possible to set aside some of those profits to cover the possibility of future losses. This is called taking a *modeling reserve.*

Common Terms

Modeling Reserve. A modeling reserve is an amount of profit that is not recognized as earnings until after a model has been operating for some period of time.

Model Overlay. A model overlay is an adjustment made to a model from an external source. For example, the management of a firm might decide that it wants a more conservative estimate of worst-case losses and double the value produced by the firm's risk management team.

6.5

HEDGING

30-Second Summary

Purpose

This chapter introduces the concept of *hedging*—trading to financially protect investments from future market movements.

Summary

Trades intended to offset the risk of other investments are called *hedges*. In the energy markets, hedging is commonly used to lock in profits from a physical asset (like an oil well or wind farm) by entering contracts to sell the expected production of those facilities using futures or forwards. Hedging can also be used to reduce the risk in trading portfolio during periods when trading will be difficult. For example, a trader might hedge prior to taking a long holiday weekend or when awaiting a government announcement that might shake up the market.

Hedging often presents specific accounting issues since it often involves both tradable and nontradable investments. A hedged item, like the expected production of an oil well, is typically valued differently than a financial derivative like a future or swap. For example, a derivative is typically subject to mark-to-market accounting but a physical asset, like an oil well, is subject to different accounting rules. As a result, a hedged item may not be valued the same way as the hedge. Hedge accounting addresses this issue by allowing the hedger to avoid marking-to-market the hedged item as long as it passes certain hedging tests.

Key Topics

- When used appropriately, hedging reduces uncertainty and locks in profits and losses. In other words, it removes the possibility of both future gains and losses.
- There is substantial academic debate as to the value of hedging.
- Hedging can be very expensive—it can have both up-front costs and hidden opportunity costs.
- There are special accounting rules that apply to hedges. These rules are generally very beneficial but require that certain tests, called *hedge effectiveness tests*, be performed.

A *hedge* is a type of trading position that is intended to lock in profits or losses associated with another investment. The contract associated with a hedge is called a *hedging instrument*, and the other investment (the one being *hedged*) is called the *hedged item*.

Hedging transfers risk from one trader to another. Traders often use hedging to protect against risks when liquidating their trading position would be undesirable, difficult, or impossible. For example, the bondholders who lent to a wind farm might require that the owners of the wind farm lock in future income by hedging as a requirement for their money. This would guarantee that the wind farm could meet its bond payment obligations. Since the wind farm will generate power that it would need to sell, the sale price could be locked in by selling forward contracts. On the downside, locking in prices would prevent the wind farm owner from benefitting if prices rose in the future.

Although it is often hidden, there is a cost associated with hedging. Many producers would like to fix a price for their products. This would allow them to finance projects with other people's money (e.g., bondholders), since production and locked-in prices would present a very safe cash flow. The issue is that there are only a limited number of counterparties who would have an incentive to arrange purchases. This can lead to forward prices that are not necessarily unbiased estimates of future prices. Long-term energy is often a buyers' market, and the buyers like to buy cheap.

Hedging also presents a substantial number of risk management issues. Although a hedge is equal in size (and risk) to the original investment, it generally receives much less scrutiny. This can create its own set of risks. Whereas a company might have hundreds of people review a major investment to ensure that it is worthwhile, it might rely on a single employee right out of graduate school to figure out a hedge for that investment. This hedge would be equally large (but directionally opposite) to the investment that everyone else thought was a good idea and might get only cursory review from senior managers.

Hedging also presents specific accounting issues. Hedging is often used to lock-in profits on nontradable investments with tradable investments. The hedged item (like power that a power plant might produce in the future) may not be valued the same way as the hedge (like futures). Hedge accounting rules allow the hedger to avoid marking-to-market the hedged item as long as it passes certain hedging tests.

Modigliani-Miller Proposition on Hedging

Academic theorists, like Franco Modigliani and Merton Miller, have spent a substantial amount of effort to determine how much value would be created for shareholders when companies hedge their investments. Unfortunately, one of the key insights from their work is that hedging often does not make the firm more valuable to investors; it only serves to enrich investment banks and distract business leaders.

The theory behind this result comes from the proposition that the total risk-adjusted present value of cash flows to investors in a frictionless market is the same regardless of whether a company takes on a hedging program. For example, an individual investor who desires less risky cash flows can purchase shares in a company that doesn't hedge and enter into their own hedges. As a result, investors have relatively little to gain (and therefore no incentive to pay more for) the shares of a company engaged in hedging.

The key to the Modigliani-Miller Proposition on Hedging is the assumption that markets are frictionless. Markets are, of course, not completely frictionless. Ease of borrowing money; bankruptcy expenses; transaction costs; and conflicting interests among shareholders, creditors, and company managers all are possible sources of market friction.

Comparing the cost of market friction to the cost of hedging is one possible way to quantify the benefits of hedging. For example, the cost of a hedge can be compared to the possible benefits that might result from avoiding bankruptcy. Otherwise, the primary benefit of a hedge is to improve the firm's ability to manage its assets and investment strategy. For example, a subsidiary might benefit from hedging by avoiding the friction associated with micromanagement if it undertakes a hedging program.

Modigliani and Miller

Academically, the Modigliani-Miller Proposition on Hedging states that hedging does not increase the value of a firm unless it helps that firm avoid some type of market friction. The largest takeaway is that hedging often doesn't add value to a firm except in certain circumstances. The most common situation where hedging makes sense is to avoid bankruptcy. For example, reducing the possibility of bankruptcy makes it much easier to borrow money from lenders.

Types of Hedges

Almost any type of financial instrument, from futures to exotic options, can be used to construct a hedge. However, the two most common types of hedges are based on either futures or costless collars. The primary reason for this is that these trades can be entered for free or with only a limited amount of money needed for a margin account. Some hedging strategies are commonly implemented with a couple of trading types:

- **Future.** A variety of futures, forwards, and commodity swaps can be used for hedging purposes. These instruments are typically very liquid and are available at low cost. These lock in both profits and losses for the hedger.
- **Costless Collar.** A costless collar is a combination of a short call option (that caps prices) and a long put option (that provides a floor on prices). This allows the company to be exposed to price movements between those two levels. Since one option is a long position, and the other short, the strike prices can be adjusted so that the collar requires no money up front.
- **Option Strategies.** Single options can also be used to hedge. However, the price needed to purchase single options is often prohibitively high, making this an unpopular choice for hedging.

"Costless" Doesn't Mean Free!

Even if a hedge costs no money to enter, that doesn't mean that it is free. Hedging often has hidden costs. This is particularly true if there are more buyers than sellers or vice versa. In the energy market, there are many energy companies that want to lock in prices of future production. For example, if a wind farm can lock in a price for future production, it can get much better financing than if it didn't. Locked-in prices also mean largely guaranteed cash flows for investors. However, there are fewer long-term buyers—consumers like homeowners don't want to be locked into a 25-year contract for power. As a result, energy companies often need to transact with a counterparty that wants to trade for profit. For an energy company, because many hedges don't involve an immediate cash payment, hedging typically involves giving something of value away for no compensation.

For example, a bank has been approached to provide hedges to energy companies. The bank doesn't have any need to purchase energy products long term. It would need to take on a risky position and hold it for some time. Given the lack of buyers, it would probably need to hold the position for the life of the contract—possibly 10 or 20 years. Banks have to set aside a portion of their capital for these types of positions, and shareholders would want the bank to earn a sufficient return on that capital to make the trade worthwhile. This means that the bank needs to build in some way to make a profit. For example, if the hedge were transacted using futures, the bank would need to negotiate a price lower than the expected future price in the market so that it could sell the power in the future at a profit.

(*Continued*)

Of course, if the bank wanted to make additional profit, it might substitute in a more complicated transaction where profits could be hidden in less obvious ways. For example, a bank might recommend that its clients use costless collars for hedging. Costless collars have some advantages over futures, like giving the hedger exposure to moderate price moves while getting protection from extreme events. However, the bank might also be able to arrange the collar so that it is worth quite a bit of money, and then acquire the combination of options for free. The hedging company thinks it is getting a great deal—a risk management hedge for free. However, in reality, it is signing option contracts for which it has given the counterparty substantial compensation.

Minimum Variance Hedge Ratio

Ideally, when a hedge is transacted, it is best if the hedged item and the hedge are identical in every way. However, that is not always possible in practice—typically the financial instruments used for hedging are limited to major benchmark commodities. In that case, it is often necessary to identify the best possible hedge. Identifying a good hedge starts with identifying a financial instrument that is highly correlated with the hedged item. Then, it is necessary to determine the proper size of the hedge.

Getting the size of the hedge correct is important. When the hedge is too small, it will leave residual risk. In that case, it is possible to further reduce the size of the risk by increasing the size of the hedge. However, if a hedge is too large, hedging can actually increase risk to the portfolio.

Since the goal of hedging is to minimize either changes in value or cash flows, it is necessary to properly size the hedge to the hedged asset. The combination of hedge and hedged item that produces the smallest expected risk is called the *minimum variance hedge ratio*. The minimum variance hedge ratio is determined by three factors—the volatility of the hedge, the volatility of the hedging item, and the correlation between the two. This minimum variance occurs when the volatility of the hedge and hedge item (in dollar terms) match one another, scaled by the correlation between the two (Figure 6.5.1).

Hedge Accounting

Mark-to-market accounting can create problems when hedging. Mark-to-market accounting requires financial instruments, like the futures or costless collars that might be used for hedging, to be revalued on

Minimum Variance Hedge Ratio	
The first step to hedging is converting everything into a single type of unit, like the value of the commodity in some currency (U.S. dollars, Euros, or similar currency). This substantially simplifies the work involved in calculating an appropriate hedge ratio.	
$$h = \rho \frac{\sigma_a}{\sigma_b}$$	
Where	
h	**Minimum Variance Hedge Ratio.** The ratio (in currency units) that best minimizes the risk associated with a portfolio composed of the initial investment (asset a) and the hedge (asset b).
ρ	**Correlation.** The correlation between the investment and the hedge.
σ_a	**Volatility of Initial Investment.** This is the volatility of initial investment (the "hedged item").
σ_b	**Volatility of the Hedge.** This is the volatility of the hedge.

Figure 6.5.1 Minimum variance hedge ratio

a daily basis. However, nonfinancial investments like ownership of a wind farm or oil well are not valued on a daily basis. The mismatch between the two reporting frequencies can create misleading swings on financial statements that can obscure the true value of a company.

Accounting rules address this problem by allowing the combined value of the asset and hedge to be reported. This prevents the mark-to-market valuation of just the hedge from flowing into financial statements. Instead, the combined value of the asset and the hedge is reported. In effect, daily mark-to-market reporting is suspended for the hedge.

A hedge needs to be proven effective before hedge accounting can be used. A hedge is proven effective by developing a testing plan prior to entering a hedge. The testing plan needs to describe the objective of the hedge, the frequency at which tests will be performed, and an objective standard for determining if the hedge is highly effective. Analysis justifying that the hedge will be effective (usually over a historical period) also needs to be performed. The initial testing and the documentation are called *prospective testing*.

Most hedges are tested by the use of a statistical technique called *regression testing*. Although there is no accounting requirement for specific types of tests that must be performed, there are commonly accepted standards for most types of regression testing. Additionally, if the hedger has multiple hedges, all of the hedges must use the same methodology to test effectiveness. This type of testing is called *retrospective testing*. These tests are usually performed whenever financial statements are published. Most commonly, this is four times a year at quarterly reporting dates.

Common Terms

Some common terms related to hedge accounting are:

Hedge Accounting. Hedge accounting is an accounting methodology used to reduce the volatility caused by daily mark-to-market of the hedge (which is typically a derivative and subject to mark-to-market accounting) in cases where the hedged item is subject to a different type of accounting.

Hedge Designation Memo. A memo used to describe a hedging relationship that is seeking to obtain hedge accounting treatment. This document describes the rationale and detailed descriptions of the hedge and the methodology used to perform the prospective and retrospective tests.

Mark-to-Market Accounting. An accounting methodology that determines the fair value of an asset or liability based on current market prices. This accounting is commonly applied to derivatives and other financial instruments.

Prospective Testing. A prospective test is documentation and testing used in hedge accounting to support the premise that the hedge and hedged item are likely to be closely related in the future.

Retrospective Testing. A retrospective test is used in hedge accounting to verify that the hedge has been effective over some period of time (typically since inception).

Hedge Effectiveness Tests

The most commonly observed method for performing retrospective tests is through the use of a statistical test called *linear regression*. Although they may not always be enabled by default, modern spreadsheets and statistical software typically have linear regression testing tools built into them. As the name suggests, linear regression examines the linear relationships between two series.

In simple language, the goal of this mathematical analysis is to assess if the change in the value of one series is equal and opposite to the change in the value of another series. For example, if the hedged item gains $1, the hedge should ideally lose $1. Statistical regression is commonly used to assess whether this is happening with some degree of confidence. A common way to visualize the relationship between two data series is to use a scatter diagram. In a scatter diagram, the horizontal axis (X axis) represents values from one data series and the vertical axis (Y axis) represents values from the second data series. Then, a line is fit to the data to describe the relationship (Figure 6.5.2).

To be an effective hedge, if the value of the hedged item changes in price by $1, the value of the hedge should also change in price by $1.

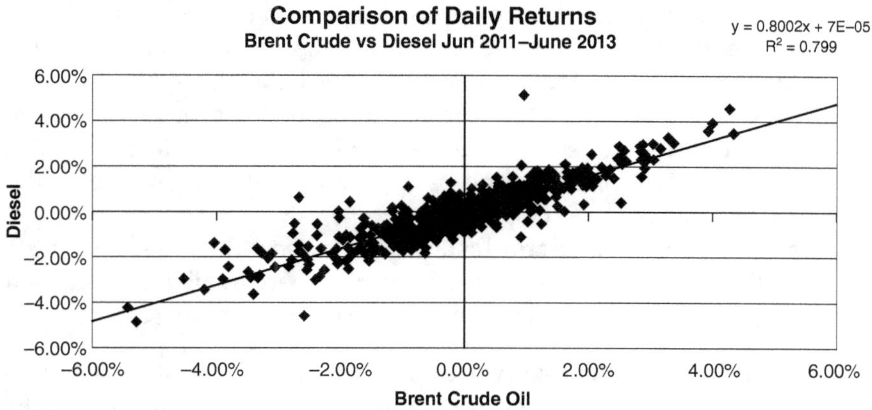

Figure 6.5.2 Regression analysis

As a result, hedge effectiveness tests typically examine day-to-day changes in the value of the hedge and the hedged item rather than the value of the two items. As long as the hedge and hedged item have similar changes in value, the hedge is effective. For example, if the hedge is twice as volatile as the hedged item, the size of the hedge should be approximately half the size of the hedged item so that the changes in value are similar.

In practice, the need to compare changes in value means there is an additional step prior to running a regression analysis on assets with mismatched volatilities. This can be done by calculating changes in value, or perhaps percent changes in value, prior to running the regression analysis.

After linear regression analysis is complete, a number of summary statistics will be produced. These statistics are commonly used to evaluate the effectiveness of the hedge. The two most important tests involve testing the slope and correlation coefficient (usually squared and abbreviated as R^2). Other common tests include checking whether enough observations were available to conduct a valid test, and checking that the slope and R^2 tests are sufficiently stable to trust the results.

For example, a prospective test for a hedge might define five tests to determine a highly effective hedge. These tests could be defined as:

- **Test 1 (Slope).** The slope of the regression line should be between –0.80 and –1.25. This test ensures that changes in the hedge and hedged item largely offset one another. In other words, if the value of the investment goes up $1.00, then the value of the hedge should drop between $0.80 and $1.25.
- **Test 2 (R-Squared).** An R^2 test indicates how well the paired observations match the line of best fit. A commonly used threshold for an R^2 test is to ensure that R^2 is greater than 0.80.

- **Test 3 (Slope Significance).** This is a secondary test that assesses whether the slope test is mathematically significant. Commonly, this is done by checking that the p-value[1] of the t-statistic is less than 0.05.
- **Test 4 (Significance F Test).** This is a secondary test, similar to the slope significance test, that assesses whether the R^2 test is significant.[2] This is typically done by checking that the p-value of the F-statistic is less than 0.05.
- **Test 5 (Number of Samples).** This is a secondary test that tests whether a sufficient number of samples were available to make a valid test. For most situations, this means 30 or more samples.

Generally, statistical software or a spreadsheet will be used to calculate these statistics. Assuming the inputs are entered correctly, the software will perform the necessary tests and the user will have to identify the test results in the output (Figure 6.5.3).

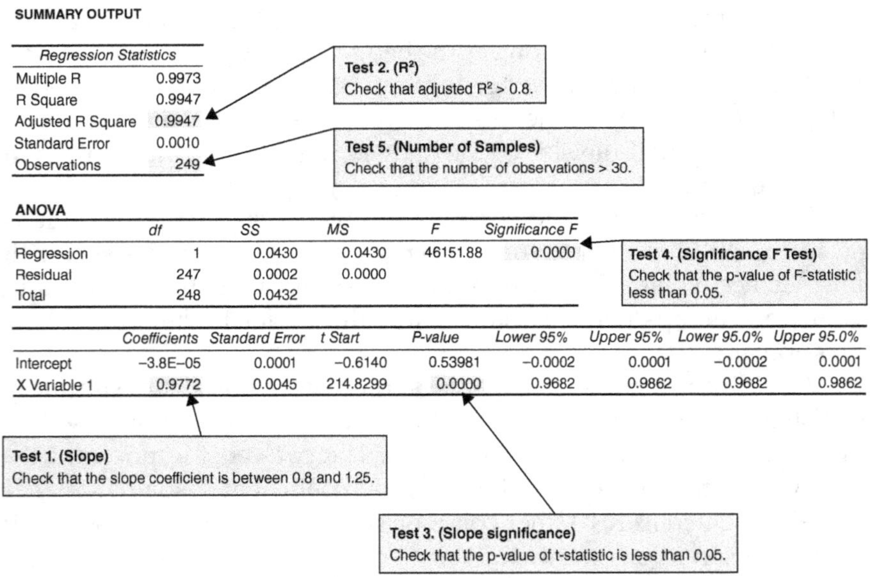

Figure 6.5.3 Common statistical tests for hedging

---

[1] A p-value is a "probability value" produced by statistical tests. This is typically the name given to the output of a statistical test that is used to determine if a test passes or fails by comparing it to some threshold value (like 0.05).

[2] Statistical tests are typically calculated as an estimate plus or minus an error. The term "significant" indicates a comparison of the estimate to the size of the error band. In practical terms, this might mean that an estimated value of $1 million +/− $50,000 is considered significant because the error range is small in comparison to the estimate. However, an estimated value of $1 million +/− $10 million would be considered not significant (and fail the test being applied) because the error band is much larger than the estimated value.

6.6

WEATHER DERIVATIVES

30-Second Summary

Purpose

This chapter introduces a type of financial instrument based on published weather data like average daily temperature and rainfall called *weather derivatives*.

Summary

Weather derivatives are financial products whose payoff is tied to weather conditions. These derivatives are used by utilities to protect against volumetric risk. *Volumetric risk* is the risk that consumers served by a utility will use more of an energy product when prices are high and use less when prices are low. This will force the utility to purchase more supply at high prices and dump excess supply at low prices.

Key Topics

- Weather derivatives have payoffs linked to some type of weather data (like average temperature or rainfall).
- There are many types of weather derivatives including swaps and options.
- Weather typically behaves differently than prices. Valuing weather derivatives requires examining historical weather data to quantify what an expected or typical temperature might be in some area.

Weather derivatives are financial products whose payoff is tied to weather conditions. These derivatives are usually bilaterally negotiated between market participants who want protection from or exposure to weather events. The most common weather derivatives are based on temperature. However, derivatives can also be constructed on average rainfall, snowfall, hurricanes, or similar weather data. Typical users of weather derivatives include utilities and insurance companies.

Weather presents an unusual set of risks to energy companies because it affects both volume and prices. This makes it difficult to hedge using typical financial products. For example, an uncharacteristically

Weather Derivative	Insurance
• More common events • Less extreme events • Payoffs are typically triggered based on a formula on a weather index like average daily temperature recorded at a major airport.	• Less common events • More extreme events • Payoffs are typically triggered by damage to a physical asset like flooding or a tornado.

Figure 6.6.1 Differences between weather derivatives and insurance

cold winter might lead to natural gas companies depleting their stored natural gas because more heating is required. At the same time, natural gas prices can spike due to utilities competing to acquire dwindling reserves of fuel for their customers at progressively higher prices.

Weather derivatives are similar to insurance but there are differences (Figure 6.6.1). First, weather derivatives tend to deal with events that happen with a reasonably high degree of probability. Second, weather derivatives tend to deal with less extreme events than insurance. For example, insurance might be purchased to protect against flood or hurricane damage (involving a very large loss that might only happen once every 100 years). Weather derivatives might be purchased to protect an airline from lost business if rainfall is 10 percent more than average (a smaller loss, but one that might happen several times over a 10-year period).

Weather derivatives can be found in both swap and option forms. With a weather swap, both parties to the contract are at risk and entering the contract won't cost either any money. With a weather derivative option, the buyer will pay a premium to the seller and only the seller will be at risk. This premium will typically be quite large—often about 20 percent of the maximum payout. It is fairly common for these derivatives to cap the maximum profit or loss associated with the derivative.

Heating and Cooling Degree Days

The most common weather derivatives are *heating degree day* (HDD) or *cooling degree day* (CDD) contracts. Heating degree days occur when temperatures are cold (when heating is required). CDDs occur during hot weather (when air conditioning is required). The payoff of these contracts is based on the accumulated difference in daily temperatures relative to some baseline over some period of time. Commonly observed baselines are 18°C (in Europe) or 65°F (in the United States). For example, an average daily temperature of 85°F would contribute 20 CDD

Day	Average Temp	HDD	CDD
		=Max(Baseline – Average Temp, 0)	=Max(Average Temp – Baseline, 0)
Sunday	35°F	30	0
Monday	30°F	35	0
Tuesday	32°F	33	0
Wednesday	45°F	20	0
Thursday	65°F	0	0
Friday	75°F	0	10
Saturday	64°F	1	0
Total		**119**	**10**

Figure 6.6.2 HDD and CDD calculations

(since 85 minus 65 is 20). The HDDs or CDDs are then accumulated over some period of time to compare to a strike price.

- HDD = Max(Baseline – Average Temperature, 0).
- CDD = Max(Average Temperature – Baseline, 0).

For example, a weather derivative might pay $1,000 for every HDD in excess of 100 HDD for the first week of January 2016. The first step to determining the payoff would be to calculate the number of heating degree days in the week. First, it is necessary to find the average temperature reported each day. The official source for the weather data, the location, and the baseline temperature for the HDD calculation will all be found in the contract. Then, an HDD is created for each degree that the daily temperature is cooler than the baseline temperature. Finally, the weekly HDD can be found by summing the daily HDD (Figure 6.6.2).

Weather Contracts

Like most other derivatives that are traded under master netting agreements, there will typically be a trade confirmation that defines all of the terms of the transaction (Figure 6.6.3).

Common Terms

There are common parts to a weather derivative contract:

Buyer. For an option transaction, the person paying the premium. For a swap, the two parties might not be described as buyer and seller. If that is the case, the contract will describe the responsibilities of each party.

(Continued)

Effective Date. The date that the payoff calculations start.

HDD Reference Level. The temperature that is used as a baseline for the HDD calculation.

Maximum Transaction Payment Amount. The maximum amount of money that in this example the seller would need to pay the buyer. This limits the total amount of money at stake if there is a really unusual event. In this example, since this contract is an option, the buyer never pays the seller anything but the premium. Not all contracts work that way. For example, a weather derivative swap might have limits for both the buyer and seller.

Notional Amount. A quantity of money that will be multiplied by some factor defined in the contract. The payoff formula will typically be listed in the contract at some point. For example, it might look something like, Payoff = (Notional Amount) * Max(Strike – Accumulated HDD, 0).

Payment of the Premium. Instructions regarding how the premium gets paid.

Premium. A quantity of money that the buyer pays the seller to convince the seller to enter into a transaction. In a weather derivative swap, this is often zero.

Premium Payment Date. The date that the premium needs to be paid.

Reference Weather Station. Weather derivatives are based on the actual observations of weather at one or more weather stations. If there is more than one weather station, the contract will state how the calculation will work. For example, this might be a weighted average temperature observed at three specific stations.

Seller. For an option transaction, the party that receives the premium. For a swap, the two parties might not be described as buyer and seller. If that is the case, the contract will describe the responsibilities of each party.

Strike. A quantity of HDD that will be compared to the accumulated HDD observed over some period of time to determine the payoff of the transaction.

Termination Date. The date when the payoff calculations end.

Trade Date. The date that the buyer and seller agreed to the transaction.

Transaction Type. Most contracts will provide a high-level description of the trade. This is mostly for the reader's benefit as the contract will typically spell out all of the trade details in the body of the contract.

Weather Index Unit. The weather index unit describes the underlying commodity upon which the derivative is based.

Dear Sirs,

The purpose of this communication (this "Confirmation") is to confirm the terms and conditions of the Weather Index Derivative Transaction entered into between Bravo Zulu Trading Company Limited ("Party A") and BigTime Re ("Party B") on the Trade Date specified below (the "Transaction").

This Confirmation, which includes the Weather Index Appendix set out in the Commodity Definitions (as defined below), constitutes a "Confirmation" as referred to in, and supplements, forms part of, and is subject to, the ISDA 2002 Master Agreement, dated as of June 14, 2013, as amended and supplemented from time to time (the "Agreement"), between Party A and Party B. All provisions contained in the Agreement shall govern this Confirmation except as expressly modified below.

The definitions and provisions contained In the 2005 ISDA Commodity Definitions, including, without limitation, Sub-Annex C thereto (the "Commodity Definitions"), as published by the international Swaps and Derivatives Association, Inc., are incorporated into this Confirmation. In the event of any Inconsistency between the Commodity Definitions and this Confirmation, this Confirmation will govern for purposes of this Transaction.

The terms of the Transaction to which this Confirmation relates are as follows:

Transaction Type	HDD Put Option
Trade Date	June 1, 2016
Buyer	Party A
Seller	Party B
Weather Index Unit	Heating Degree Days (HDD)
Reference Weather Station	Newark Airport, Newark NJ
Effective Date	Jan 1, 2016
Termination Date	Jan 31, 2016
Notional Amount	$5000 per Weather Index Unit
HDD Reference Level	65°F
Strike	1,000 HDD
Maximum Transaction Payment Amount	$1,000,000
Premium	$150,000
Premium Payment Date	The tenth business day after Party B delivers an invoice to Party A
Payment of the Premium	The Buyer shall pay the seller the premium on the Premium Payment Date.

.... *Additional trading details ...*

Figure 6.6.3 Example weather derivative confirmation

Temperature Modeling

Prior to expiration, the expected payoff of a weather derivative is typically based on observing historical data. This is different than how forward prices are created for most other financial products. For example, most forward commodity prices are developed through trading markets (for nonstorable energy products) or buying the product today and storing it (for stocks, bonds, and storable commodities).

One problem with using historical data is that weather data appear to trend over time. The data do not consistently revert to an expected temperature. This makes it very difficult to describe an "expected temperature" that might occur in the following year (Figure 6.6.4).

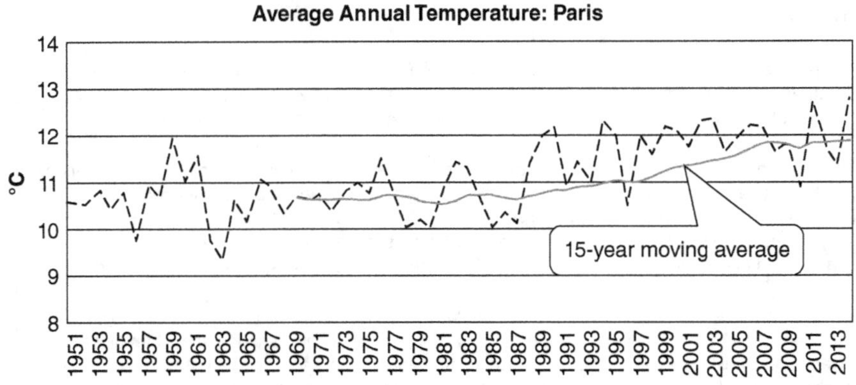

Figure 6.6.4 Average annual temperature: Paris

Because there is no typical or average temperature that can be observed historically, this means that anyone trading or valuing weather derivatives needs to make assumptions. Two of the most important decisions are whether to trend adjust or truncate the data set.

- **Trend Adjustment.** One important modeling decision is whether the data be trend adjusted. If it is trend adjusted, a second important decision is when to start the adjustment calculation. In the Paris example, starting the trend adjustment in 1958 (a very warm year) will give a different result than starting the trend adjustment in 1963 (a very cold year).
- **Data Truncation.** Another modeling decision is choosing the length of the data set that should be used to model temperatures. Based on visual inspection, there appear to be multi-year periods of relatively stable temperatures followed by trending data. This raises the possibility that older data may not be as predictive as more recent data.

AFTERWORD

In the preface to this book, I stated that *there is no substitute for understanding what is actually going on.* This axiom can be applied to almost anything in life. However, as a truism, it is especially applicable to trading, risk management, and energy policy. This is the philosophical core of the book and a key factor to successfully investing in any market. The reason for this focus is that details are a rich source of trading opportunities. Details are not obstacles to the investment process; rather, they allow traders to pick and choose their investment opportunities.

The more complex an issue, the more opportunities exist for trading. Traders don't have to be smarter than everyone else all the time because *they don't have to be invested in the market all the time.* Traders can wait for a good opportunity before investing. Understanding details allow traders to invest only when they have a better than average chance of making money.

However, even when details are perceived as good things, they can still be intimidating. When I first approached the energy market, the sheer number of details made it difficult to understand how the market fit together. In this book, I've tried to subtly introduce two ways of dealing with this problem. I started the book with a high-level overview that mapped out where things would go, and then I delved into the details. In each chapter, I typically took the opposite approach—I started with a couple of specific details, and then I slowly increased their complexity.

Another major theme in this book is applying quantitative modeling to energy trading. Because there is so much going on in the energy market, the core of quantitative modeling involves eliminating and ignoring some information to concentrate on other information. This is a fairly risky process, and when models fail, it is usually due to bad initial assumptions or bad input data. The only way to prevent these types of errors is to have a large group of people paying attention to details. Obviously, the source of any data and assumptions should be noted in a model. However, the importance of understanding the real world that is being approximated by the model can't be emphasized enough. There is no substitute for having everyone understand what a model is trying to accomplish.

I hope that this book sparks an interest in energy policy and an appreciation for the infrastructure that makes modern life possible. I know it did for me. Starting with the basics of the market and working upward from there made me rethink things that I used to take for granted.

I enjoyed writing this book, and I hope that you enjoyed reading it.

Davis W. Edwards

INDEX

Note: An *f* follows page numbers referencing figures; an *n* follows footnotes.

B

C

N

Q

R

W

About the Author

Davis W. Edwards is a senior manager of Deloitte & Touche's National Securities Pricing Center. He is a well-known author and speaker on the topic of risk management, modeling, and trading. Prior to joining Deloitte, he worked as director of credit risk at Macquarie Bank and as senior managing director on the proprietary trading desk at Bear Stearns. Davis Edwards directs the Global Association of Risk Professional (GARP)'s chapter in Houston, Texas. He is also an expert-level programmer with extensive artificial intelligence experience and a certified Project Management Professional (PMP). Davis has degrees in electrical engineering and history from Stevens Institute of Technology and a Master of Finance from Tulane University.

www.ingramcontent.com/pod-product-compliance
Lightning Source LLC
LaVergne TN
LVHW052213200926
848481LV00001B/99

* 9 7 8 1 2 6 5 9 1 5 8 7 2 *